The United States and Latin America

Fredrick B. Pike

THE UNITED STATES AND LATIN AMERICA

MYTHS AND STEREOTYPES OF CIVILIZATION AND NATURE

UNIVERSITY OF TEXAS PRESS, AUSTIN

∞ The paper used in this publication meets the minimum requirements of American National Standard for Information Sciences—Permanence of Paper for Printed Library Materials, ANSI Z39.48-1984.

Library of Congress Cataloging-in-Publication Data

Pike, Fredrick B.
    The United States and Latin America : myths and stereotypes of civilization and nature / by Fredrick B. Pike. — 1st ed.
        p.   cm.
    Includes bibliographical references and index.
    ISBN 0-292-78523-2 (cloth : alk. paper). — ISBN 0-292-78524-0 (pbk. : alk. paper)
        1. Latin America—Relations—United States. 2. United States—Relations—Latin America. 3. Latin America—Civilization—Public opinion. 4. Latin America—Foreign public opinion, American. 5. Public opinion—United States. I. Title.
    F1418.P555   1992
    303.48'27308—dc20   91-42454
                                                        CIP

For Helene and Tom Stritch;
and for my children, Paulita, June, and Fred

Contents

Illustrations

Preface

Lest you the reader become lost, especially in the overgrown thickets of the first chapter, let me provide a few hints as to the overall direction in which I want to lead you. Let me suggest how it is that ambivalent myths and stereotypes of civilization and nature seem to lie at the heart of American attitudes toward Latin Americans and, for that matter, toward all those people we once called primitives but in recent years have accorded the more euphemious title of Third Worlders.

We, meaning most Americans most of the time, like to see ourselves as prime exemplars of all that it means to be civilized. Always up to date and scientific, we successfully pursue linear progress, measured most readily by material accomplishments but always accompanied by moral, spiritual, and cultural advancement. In contrast, Latin Americans, as we are wont to see them, remain static; they are trapped in a primitive state of nature, the victims of rather than the masters of nature. Attainment of full human potential always eludes them, for that potential is realizable only in proportion to the degree to which people manage to conquer nature, both within and without. From the conviction that we embody civilization while they remain mired in a state of nature derive the American stereotypes that through the years have, justifiably, infuriated Latin Americans.

Initially in North America the stereotypes by which "civilized" people judged "people of nature" arose out of the attitudes of British settlers toward Indians and imported African slaves. Later these attitudes, embodied in various stereotypes, were transferred to Latin Americans. At about the same time the stereotypes were attached to newly arriving immigrants, especially to Orientals, the Irish, and central, southern, and eastern Europeans. Because the child has always been a prime example of a state-of-nature being, civilized Americans referred to natural persons, whether Indians, blacks, Latin Americans, or unassimilated immigrants, or the indigent in general, as childlike. Traditionally, moreover, American males tended to regard themselves as the exclusive movers and shapers of civilization. Women, they assumed, remained enslaved by their nature, incapable of attaining the heights of civilization. In consequence, the American patriarchy customarily referred to benighted, state-of-nature people not only as childish but also as effeminate.

Americans, though, are a complex people. Along with those who glorify civilization and claim a virtual national monopoly over it stand others who from earliest colonial times have questioned the values of the prevailing civilization and lamented its costs and distortions. These questioners of characteristic national values tend to extol what is natural, primitive, and instinctual. In the unspoiled and the undeveloped they find the repository of virtue and the potential for a better humanity that will issue out of the return to origins. From the time of the first British settlements in the New World, the bards of the natural, the champions of the raw rather than the cooked, have constituted a counterculture or an adversary culture: they have challenged the assumptions of the "establishment," whose representative figures uncritically hail the onward march of civilization as it pulverizes and transforms the natural. Much of the time, counterculture voices are barely audible. Periodically, though, perhaps even cyclically, these voices begin to reverberate in such volume as to threaten to drown out the spokespersons of traditional values. When this occurs, nature has its day in America, and the public begins to pay some heed to the rights of the environment, of Indians and blacks, of immigrants and Latin Americans, of the impecunious in general, and of women and children. So long as this moment endures, the ostensible exemplars of the natural bask in stereotypes that have suddenly turned flattering and even adulatory. Because counterculturalists invariably sentimentalize and romanticize the objects of their affection, those objects pay a price. They cannot possibly live up to the romanticized stereotypes, and so it is not long before the pejorative stereotypes customarily attached to them come back into vogue, often with an intensified virulence.

Shifting perceptions of the encounter between civilization and nature shape not only American stereotypes but also myths: those emotionally charged beliefs that give meaning and even transcendence to personal and national existence; those beliefs that arise out of inward or intuitive powers, that may or may not be true but are never verifiable by the outward world's scientific, empirical measurements. Americans drawn to establishment, mainstream values venerate myths that impute moral virtue to civilization's total victory over nature. But counterculturalists find the highest value in situations that permit the natural to remain unconquered by the civilized. These opposing viewpoints have produced an underlying duality in national mythology. And this duality carries over into our perceptions of and attitudes toward Latin Americans.

Most of the time in our approach to Latin Americans, we Americans have aspired to domination—whether in order to "uplift" them or to exploit them. But every now and then we have sought renewal by turning to the "simple" virtues of those "childlike" people, those "emotional, passionate, uninhibited people of nature"—the Latin Americans. Rather than disdaining them for their stereotyped inability to wax prosperous by dominating and destroying their natural environment, we have perceived in them—at least until relatively recent times—a virtue that springs from their continuing proximity to redeeming, virgin land and to a primordial id.

There is also a middle-ground position for Americans disposed to think and to dream about the encounter of civilization and nature. In one of its many guises, the frontier myth derived from a vision of the perfect fusion of civilization and nature. This fusion, ostensibly, would strengthen and perpetuate American exceptionalism. When America's national frontier disappeared (or, just as important, was thought to disappear), the old vision persisted, but took on hemispheric dimensions. In its expanded form the vision or myth posited a synthesis of the civilized, Anglo North with the natural, Latin South.

What impels Americans toward synthesis is their nagging two-minded approach to the rival claims of civilization and nature. Perhaps no one has revealed this reaction more fully than Mark Twain, and this is one of the traits that makes him the quintessential American writer. *Huckleberry Finn* strikes most readers as a plea in behalf of the state of nature. But, in *Roughing It,* Twain delivers himself mainly of harsh evaluations of the frontier state of nature and the deleterious effects it has on people who in more refined settings might comport themselves in reasonably civilized manner. What is more, Twain shows ambivalence in dealing with pristine nature. He can extol the idyllic delights afforded by camping on the shores of Lake Tahoe while elsewhere stressing the horrors that the unimproved, natural habitat can inflict on humans and on itself. Moreover, like the majority of his countrymen, Twain is of two minds about human exemplars of what purportedly are the highest refinements of civilization, regarding them often but not always as shams. And he is just as undecided in evaluating such primitives as Indians, dismissing them sometimes as little better than animals while at other times contrasting them with civilized beings to the disadvantage of the latter. Had Twain been closely acquainted with Latin Americans, he would, I feel certain, have been of two minds about them, thereby reflecting once more the typical split-mindedness of his fellow Americans.

Throughout this book I refer to those of us who live in and are citizens of the United States as Americans. I know that Latin Americans insist they have just as much right as we in the United States to term themselves Americans. By their own choice, however, they seldom avail themselves of this right. Lester D. Langley, a preeminent diplomatic historian of the hemisphere, points out that Latin Americans invariably refer to themselves by the name of their native countries: they are Argentines or Bolivians or Peruvians or Haitians or Brazilians or Mexicans. Very seldom do they, first and foremost, name themselves Americans.[1] Latin Americans have alternatives to calling themselves Americans, alternatives for which, by their own choice, they generally opt. We in the United States really have no suitable alternative.

One personal feeling that has resulted from writing this book is antipathy for politicians and business leaders and intellectuals and ministers and indeed persons in all walks of life who piously invoke the word "civilized" to encompass American actions and mainstream attitudes and who assume that all persons who oppose those actions and attitudes are somehow beyond the pale of civilization. "Civilization" has almost displaced patriotism as the last refuge of scoundrels. Pascal once observed that people never do evil so completely and cheerfully as when they do it from religious conviction. Maybe he's right, much of the time anyway; but those who act in the name of civilization give Pascal's scoundrels a good run for the money. Still, cynicism should not blind one to the fact that—as a blessedly inconsistent Pascal himself recognized—people sometimes perform beneficently, honorably, and even heroically in the name of religious conviction. Occasionally they perform similarly—according to their lights, which is all one can ask of them—in the cause of civilization.

Simón Bolívar predicted the United States would afflict Latin America in the name of liberty. Actually, affliction has come just as often in the name of civilization, virtually impossible to define except as *our* way of life, real, imagined, and mythologized. Once in a while when Yankee affliction has been visited upon them in consequence of our missionary instincts to convert the wayward to civilization, Latin Americans have rather enjoyed the visitation and, arguably, even benefited from it—however much their intellectuals deem it a point of honor to voice irate indignation over the alleged affliction.

Owing in part to the often covertly welcomed "afflictions" from the north, Latin Americans by the end of the twentieth century have undergone a significant degree of Americanization. Meantime, as I argue in the final chapter, the United States has been in many ways Latin Americanized, transformed into a land whose citizens flaunt in abundance the very worst traits that stereotypes through the years imputed to Latin Americans. With role reversals the order of the day, the old myths and stereotypes that underlie hemispheric relations should have lost most of their credibility. But as the twentieth century entered its final decade, neither political rhetoric nor the opinions of the American Everyman—and woman—reflected awareness of the new realities. In all too many instances, politicians and average citizens continue to deal in woefully outdated clichés.

By way of acknowledgments, my primary debt is to my wife Helene who, as always, offered only additional encouragement in the face of the neglect and irritability that inevitably issue from my writing projects. My next largest debt is to Tom Stritch, friend and teaching companion for nearly forty years at Notre Dame. A good proportion of the ideas I've had during those years have been sparked by him, or, if not sparked then certainly enriched and polished as we tossed them around, often in heated disagreement. He has been my principal teacher about matters most deeply meaningful to me, such as art, music, and literature.

To the two persons who first started me thinking seriously about relations between the United States and Latin America, I am forever indebted. First, there is Carlos Eduardo Castañeda, an inspiring and lovable mentor throughout my graduate studies at the University of Texas, which because of my happy intellectual awakening at its Institute of Latin American Studies has always remained my favorite academic institution. In addition to his role as mentor, Don Carlos proved a true friend. Then there is my former wife Pachita Tennant de Pike, who hails from El Salvador. Pachita used to talk about her grandmother and grandfather when they were based in Washington, where he served as his country's diplomatic representative to the United States toward the end of the nineteenth century. Americans, they soon observed as they traveled about the country, seemed to puzzle over the fact that they, the two Salvadorans, acted, dressed, and spoke like civilized human beings. Somehow the Americans had assumed that Central Americans were barely out of the wigwam and still wore feathers in their hair. The couple from El Salvador in the diplomatic service upset these stereotypes. Since first hearing the story, and then listening to the grandmother herself elaborate on it, I've had some forty-five years to think about American stereotyping and how it has affected hemispheric relations. Some of the results of that thinking emerge in this book.

After those persons just cited, I am most indebted to the students in several undergraduate seminars who, prior to my retirement from the history faculty at the University of Notre Dame in 1988, carried out research projects that deepened my understanding of some of the topics I explore in this book. Students whose papers proved especially helpful to me in the years between 1985 and 1988 include Stephen Breaux, Giusette Cosme, Chris Edwards, Michael Feeley, Robert France, Glenn F. Kosse, Mary Lee Parker, Efraín Ramos, William Sammon, Timothy Shea, Patrick Timon, and most especially Neal Palmore, who became my primary consultant on rock-and-roll. These and many other students listened patiently and charitably to my first tentative exposition of some of the ideas that have found their way into this book; often they helped to refine and expand those ideas. In the late stages of writing I also incurred a debt to Rafael Tarragó, the endlessly resourceful librarian of the Notre Dame Latin American collection, for his help in clearing up several botched references. Later still, I was fortunate to have Bob Fullilove as copy editor, benefiting enormously not only from his sharp editorial eye but also from his substantive comments that led me to revise some interpretations.

My dear friend Thomas M. Davies, Jr., an eminent Latin Americanist who teaches history at San Diego State University, has suffered cruel and unusual punishment. Three times he has read manuscripts for subsequently published books of mine. Invariably, he has been favorably disposed in my behalf, while nevertheless leveling criticism that attests to his consummate skill as an editorial reader. In the present case, I sought to incorporate the bulk of Tom's suggestions. Readers owe him a debt of gratitude. But for him, these pages would have contained many more quotations and footnote references. Had I heeded all of Tom's suggestions, the book would have been undoubtedly better and surely shorter.

Professor Donald C. Hodges of Florida State University, whom I've not met but whose work I have long admired, served as the manuscript's first reader in the evaluation process that the University of Texas Press conducted. Had I examined so unrefined a manuscript, I likely would have counseled rejection. But he returned a verdict on the whole quite favorable, thereby helping to assure publication and garnering my eternal gratitude. In his reading, he caught numerous mistakes, thus compounding my indebtedness. In addition he objected to many of my sweeping generalizations, forcing me to rethink and revise some while omitting others altogether. A few of the challenged generalizations, however, strike me still as likely to be right more often than not, and I have retained them.

History that generalizes, the Mexican philosopher Antonio Cano once contended, is history that falsifies. To Cano's generalization I subscribe, most of the time. And yet, history that eschews the risk of occasional generalization is history that trivializes. It pretends to substitute cut-and-dried "reality" for the murky mystery of human existence that sometimes can only be fathomed, if at all, by the lucky guess and the inspired generalization. If my guesses and generalizations have been neither lucky nor inspired, may they at least challenge readers to apply their own judgment and intuition as they puzzle over situations of endless complexity and confusion. History is a process; generalizations, if only by their power to challenge and annoy, can help the process along.

Limping generalizations are one thing, but quite another matter are the flat-out errors that inevitably still lurk in these pages. No amount of rationalization can excuse them. The best of friends, the brightest of students, and the most knowledgeable of readers have not been able in every instance to save me from myself. For all the errors that mar this book, I alone am responsible.

Despite the shortcomings that haunt me, I claim a certain timeliness for my book as it goes to press in 1992. In this quincentennial anniversary year of Columbus's first voyage to the New World, the civilization-nature debate flares anew. Spearheading a new counterculture, multiculturalists issue denunciations of the Western civilization that Columbus helped introduce into the New World's natural paradise. There must be something to this viewpoint, originally propounded by some of Columbus's contemporaries, that responds to a basic human need. Otherwise it would not have periodically attracted new disciples during the past five hundred years. Inevitably, though, just as the pro-nature perspective recurrently waxes so does it wane; for it provides only one view of an endlessly complex reality. Those who argue the cause of civilization also respond to a basic human need.

In the pages that follow I write about the waxing and waning of the two sides to a civilization-nature debate. One of the Old World's oldest issues, it came to the New World with the arrival of Columbus. As waged for the past two hundred years or so from north of the border, this debate has often set the tone of United States–Latin American relations. Let us not forget, though, that from south of the border we Americans are often perceived as the natural barbarians who threaten civilized refinement.

The United States and Latin America

CHAPTER 1

Nature and Its Enigmatic Images in American Lore

Nature in One of Its Manifestations: An Evil to Be Conquered, Reformed, and Exploited

Americans, who to their own satisfaction embody the virtues of civilization, tend to look askance both at unimproved wilderness and at persons perceived to be living in a state of nature: a state wherein wildness, both in the environment and within the individual, has remained unconquered. Invariably, though, feelings of distaste for the natural are tempered by recognition of the potential that inheres in it and by visions of the moral improvement that will accrue to persons when they refine, uplift, enhance, and perfect what exists, as mere potency, in the state of nature. Moreover, visions of profit often animate those who set themselves the task of developing nature's potential. In their attitudes toward the natural, Americans reveal the essence of both their capitalist and their imperialist drives. Sometimes they point to the Bible in justifying these drives.

"Increase and multiply, replenish the earth and subdue it . . ." (Gen. 1:28). This the Bible commanded, and English settlers in the New World obeyed, thereby proving their virtue.[1] Not only from Genesis but also from Isaiah and Revelation American settlers received their orders. From these combined sources they deduced that "God's chosen people were commissioned to subdue and improve the New World's land in order to prepare the millennial New Earth."[2] Colonial literature vibrates with recognition of the imperial necessity to refine, correct, and repair the natural landscape, to exalt the valleys, lower the mountains, and make straight the crooked so as to bring on the millennium.[3] In the confusion and imperfection of uncorrected nature abided sin and even Satan himself. In "that wild, heathen Nature of the forest, never subjugated by human law, nor illuminated by higher truth," as Nathaniel Hawthorne put it in parodying

Puritan beliefs, resided the Black Man or the devil, with whom witches rendezvoused.[4]

In their perceived role as "agents in the regeneration process that turned the ungodly and useless into a beneficent civilization,"[5] early settlers felt revulsion for what later generations of Americans came to treasure as examples of nature at its most sublime. An observer of Niagara Falls in 1679 referred to it as a "horrible precipice," foaming and boiling in "the most hideous manner imaginable, making an outrageous noise," a "dismal roaring" that could be heard for fifteen leagues. Some seventeen years earlier, Michael Wigglesworth contended that outside the settled areas of New England, all was "a waste and howling wilderness, where none inhabited but hellish fiends, and brutish men that devils worshipped."[6]

Seeking to imitate their God (or at least paying lip service to that objective), many early American settlers devoted themselves to bringing order out of chaos.[7] To do so meant molding the environment and in turn not permitting themselves to be molded by it.[8] Upon this their very salvation depended. Thus, in a way, the struggle to master frontiers was intimately associated with the quest to escape perdition and save the soul from hell's fire. Little wonder that New Englanders welcomed winter as a subduer of the profligacy and excesses unleashed by the warm season. Winter tamed the "flaming signs of procreation" and facilitated greater self-control "than was possible during the ragings" of spring and summer.[9] The worst effect of frontiers, according to Timothy Dwight (1752–1817), "the Federalist Pope of Connecticut," was that they were "too nat'r'l" and, like spring and summer, gave "too much freedom to fallen human nature."[10] But winter tamed even the excesses of the frontier, and by putting the soul on ice, Puritans could guarantee its eternal life.

Many of their attitudes toward the natural America's early Anglo settlers brought with them from England. Their cultural baggage included the attitudes expressed by English Renaissance writers, for many of whom natural settings represented the fallen world. Antipastoralist sentiments mingled with the mechanism popularized by Francis Bacon who in *Novum Organum* (1620) asserted man's independence of and his right and even duty to establish total hegemony over nature. Behind Bacon's "comprehensive mechanistic explanation of nature and man" lay, according to one persuasive analysis, "the new will to power over nature and the desire to work upon her on the part of the rising bourgeoisie."[11] Later, in 1687, John Bunyan returned to Biblical sources of inspiration when, in *Pilgrim's Progress,* he "summarized the prevailing viewpoint of wilderness as the symbol of anarchy and evil to which the Christian was unalterably opposed."[12]

English settlers once in the New World developed their own rationales for mastering nature, rationales that drew both on Biblical and secular sources. Soon the Enlightenment added its input to the case against nature. For Enlightenment thinkers, the material progress enjoined by rationality demanded that nature be tamed. Obsessed by the imperative to tame and settle the "Great American Desert" to the west of the 100th meridian, Union veteran and onetime governor of territorial Colorado William Gilpin showed the influence both of Enlightenment and Puritan thinkers when extolling progress in an 1873 publication: "Progress," he declared, "is God."[13]

In 1900 William Ellsworth Smythe published his enormously influential *Conquest of Arid America*. In it Smythe combined Enlightenment approaches with American adaptations of Darwinism as he hailed war against nature as "unambiguously heroic." Such warfare rendered the continent habitable, improved it, and put it to the uses for which it was intended. Beyond any doubt, according to Smythe, the earth and its resources were destined for human domination.[14]

Justified by their favorite myths, Americans in "one frontier venture after another sought to extract the wealth held by nature, and the processes used were not gentle."[15] To all their other justifications, they added racist assumptions. At the turn of the twentieth century the prominent anthropologist W J McGee (he insisted that no periods be used after his initials), organizer of the anthropological displays at the St. Louis Louisiana Purchase Exposition of 1904, averred that it was the duty of white men, or Caucasians, in whom resided the virtues of the "strong man, to subjugate lower nature, to extirpate the bad and cultivate the good among living things, to delve into the earth below and cleave the air above in search of fresh resources . . . , to halter thin vapors and harness turbulent waters into servile subjection, and in all ways to enslave the world for the support of humanity and the increase of human intelligence."[16] Long before McGee wrote, indeed by the time Englishmen first reached the New World, "the story of . . . [American] progress and expansion . . . took the form of a fable of race war," pitting against each other the opposites of savagery and civilization, primitivism and progress, paganism and Christianity, black (or red or brown) and white skin color.[17]

Driven beings in their crusade against nature in its various manifestations, Americans even by the time of their Revolution had made striking progress in carrying out the perceived intentions of Providence. In *Sketches of Eighteenth-Century America,* J. Hector St. John de Crèvecoeur (1735–1813) wrote of the settlers of his adopted country: "I think, considering our age, the great toils we have undergone, the roughness of some parts of this country, and our original poverty, that we have done the most in the least time of any people on earth."[18] Already, America had become a land of stumps, and that was good. Here is how a historian put the matter in 1967: "The American measurement of progress 'has been to conquer the wilderness and convert it to economic use.' In other words, 'a stump was our symbol of progress.'"[19]

Since their earliest arrival in the New World, Americans tended to equate wilderness and Indians, seeing the latter as the personification of the former; and from this equation derived the race-war aspects of America's frontier expansion. One basic reason for the nature-Indian connection in American perceptions was the native's alleged preference to live in harmony with rather than in striving to master nature. In the purview of the new arrivals, virtue and its fruits of property ownership and economic aggrandizement all depended on continuing, systematic, concentrated exploitation of the land. And this approach to land, according to the quickly developed myth that totally ignored the farming triumphs of some Indians, the Native Americans steadfastly resisted. The failure of "savages" fully to exploit the natural resources of the land they claimed justified the actions of civilized men as they seized Indian property. Frontiersmen, therefore, cleared "the wilderness of primitive men in order that civilization might root and flourish."[20] Even as with the conquest of allegedly unoccupied virgin land, so also the conquest of the Indians had seemed to American settlers "not just a nationalist victory, but an achievement made in the name of humanity—the triumph of light over darkness, of good over evil, and of civilization over brutish nature."[21]

As the frontier advanced, many Americans took pride in the fact that wilderness and Indians vanished together. In the process, though, the armies of civilization sustained many casualties. It was not just that many soldiers of progress succumbed to the retaliatory blows struck by nature (storms, snake bites, and the like) and to the arrows, knives, and bullets of Indians. This was bad enough, but even worse was the degree to which the emissaries of a higher life committed cultural suicide by reverting to savagery and primitivism. Historian James Axtell in a 1981 publication pointed to materials suggesting that, prior to the Revolutionary War, some 15 percent of white Americans captured by Indians in New England opted for native life and often along with it the Roman Catholicism to which many of the region's Indians had been converted by French missionaries. No wonder Crèvecoeur could write, not long after the Revolution had triumphed, that "thousands of Europeans are Indians."[22] Obviously there was some basis to the question still being raised throughout much of the nineteenth century: "Will the virgin West encourage virtue and abundance, or a reversion to savagery?"[23]

This very question concerned James Fenimore Cooper (1789–1851) in his Leatherstocking Tales. He depicts, among others, Thomas Hutter in *The Deerslayer*, Billy Kirby in *The Pioneers*, and Ishmael Bush and his brood in *The Prairie* as examples of regression to a state of savagery worse in many respects than that of most Indians.[24] Two superb western novels of the mid–twentieth century follow in this tradition. In A. B. Guthrie, Jr.'s *Big Sky* (1952) and in Vardis Fisher's *Mountain Man* (1957) Boone Caudill and Sam Minard, respectively, suffer regression in settings of natural paradise. Larry McMurtry's Pulitzer prize–winning *Lonesome Dove* (1985), a later novel of the West that is almost as good as the Guthrie and Fisher books, also leaves the reader feeling that some of the characters rather than prevailing over nature in their prolonged exposure were permanently blighted by it. Countless thoughtful Americans have pondered the disturbing truth that, in spite of the happy endings of classical Puritan captivity tales, nature often triumphed over vulnerable humans.

Nevertheless, as the nineteenth century advanced American men, by and large, managed to ignore discomfiting facts and to pride themselves on their ability to overcome nature. Beyond this, they frequently took satisfaction in snuffing out the independence that many of their women had begun to take for granted during the colonial period.[25] Because women had, almost since time immemorial, been stereotyped by males as close to nature, much like the American Indian was stereotyped, masculine ascendancy received a psychological boost with the conquest of nature on the frontier. Along with the assertion of male ascendancy went an imperialist mentality; for invariably the objects of imperialism, the colonial "races," have been stereotyped not only as primitive but also as effeminate. Briefly, I will explore both of these points: women as exemplars of nature rather than civilization, and the assumed right of the masculine to dominate effeminate races.

What she terms the "pan-cultural second class status" of women, Sherry B. Ortner associates in part with the identification or symbolical association of women with nature. It is always civilization's project "to subsume and transcend nature," she writes. Hence, with women "considered part of nature," it followed that civilization "would find it 'natural' to subordinate, not to say oppress, them."[26]

Self-control, in the perception of males, was a masculine trait. Women, on the other hand, rather like nature itself, were uninhibited, unpredictable, chaotic. And, they were ruled by feelings rather than reason. Cooper has Natty Bumppo proclaim in one of the Leatherstocking Tales, "Woman was created for feelin's, and is pretty much ruled by feelin'."[27] Women were the pawns of their emotions, and in the latter part of the nineteenth century "medical science" discovered that women inclined naturally toward the hysterical state.[28] In myriad other ways, women manifested their inability to escape the restraints and weaknesses of nature, at least in the judgment of innumerable male observers. These latter found it altogether understandable that witches were far more likely to be female than male, precisely because witches were assumed to be lascivious creatures who freely indulged their passions and liked to cavort in the wild country beyond civilization's pale. Overcome by nature's beauty at Lake Tahoe, Mark Twain described the scenery as "always fascinating, bewitching, entrancing," and therefore as obviously feminine.[29]

The conflation of nature and woman has helped to perpetuate the widespread male conviction that woman is somehow outside the bounds of and antithetical to civilization. Men, as they tend to perceive the situation, are the creators of civilization and the architects of progress, whereas "women are the manifestations of nature. The implication is that men develop culture in order to understand and control the natural world, while women, being the embodiment of the forces of nature, must be brought under the civilizing control of men."[30] This quotation brings me to the second point mentioned above, that dealing with the alleged right of so-called masculine races to dominate those whom they have stereotyped as effeminate.

At some point in history, male thinkers decided "that the ovum is passive and the sperm adventurous,"[31] and that these respective traits must characterize females and males in general. From here, male logic jumped to the conclusion that the adventurous enjoy natural rights to dominate the passive. Martin Green, a penetrating observer of some of Western culture's irrationalities, hits the mark when he concludes that the lust for adventure is often antifeminist. The classical literature of adventure and imperialism has assigned only peripheral and ancillary roles to women. "Women are the objects of lust and piety, seizure and rescue, but they are not subjects who themselves act. They are prizes, measures of success, rewards and responsibilities for men. In matters of emotion, they are apparently subjective centers, but their own passions usually make them more passive—they faint, fail, or freeze in a crisis. The effective emotions, those which are embodied in action, are those they inspire in men."[32] Herman Melville approached the same conclusion when in *Moby-Dick* he referred to the "mere negative" trait of "submission and endurance."[33]

A good deal of male-authored American frontier literature, and of nineteenth-century British literature justifying imperialism, rests squarely on assumptions of the unquestionable superiority of civilization and its total rights not only over nature but also over such slaves of nature as women, Indians, and also blacks. Out of these attitudes flowed the sex- as well as race-war aspect of frontier penetration by Caucasians, whether in the American West or in the expanding British Empire. Writing on the "colored races," abolitionist editor and writer Lydia Maria Child had this to say: "The comparison between women and the colored races is striking. Both are characterized by affection more than by intellect; both have a strong development of the religious sentiment; both are exceedingly adhesive in their attachments; both, comparatively speaking, have a tendency to submission."[34] Child intended to flatter the colored races, but most white Anglo Saxon men—on either side of the Atlantic—would have taken her words as a concession of the Negro's, as well as the woman's, inferiority. They would have interpreted similarly the appraisal of Robert E. Park, one of the founding fathers of American sociology at the turn of the twentieth century, when he referred to the Negro as, "so to speak, the lady among the races."[35]

Certainly few American men would have doubted that Henry Rowe Schoolcraft, considered one of the leading authorities on his country's native races in the first half of the nineteenth century, wrote pejoratively of Indians when he referred to their "luxurious effeminacy," the product of mores allegedly adverse to personal enterprise.[36] Given the view, moreover, that a majority of Americans shared in assessing their neighbors to the south, made up largely of colored and native "races," the Child, Park, and Schoolcraft statements would have seemed accurate appraisals of Latin Americans.

Alexander Kinmont, a Scottish intellectual who emigrated to America in 1823 where he helped popularize the mystical faith of Swedenborgianism, directly ascribed to Latin Americans the traits that Child, Park, and Schoolcraft had imputed to blacks and Indians. In one of his highly influential Cincinnati lectures of 1837–1838, Kinmont posited a psychological connection between Latin Americans and Negroes. Both, he maintained, were stronger on feeling than reason, in part because their religions valued feminine mysticism rather than manly rationality and intellectual probing. Both possessed a strong measure of licentiousness, in contrast to the northern European stock primarily responsible for peopling America. Contrary to the prevailing attitudes of his time, Kinmont praised the effeminate qualities of Latin Americans and Negroes: ". . . those who are now pre-eminent only for the softness of a sensual effeminacy may become remarkable for the loveliness and delicacy of their nature and appropriate virtues."[37] His praise flew in the face of American conventional wisdom, whose spokes*men* through the years have consistently expressed anxiety lest they and their fellow citizens lose the keen edge of their virile qualities.

In contemplating women, American male writers—much as males in general since the very origins of literature—alternately and sometimes simultaneously stressed their attributes as pure, ethereal spirits somehow above the worldly, materialistic life and as hot, passionate vixens wallowing in creatureliness and sensuality. In one of his poems the great English satirist Jonathan Swift (1667–1745) pokes fun at masculine indecisiveness in appraising the nature of woman. He tells about a young man who idealizes his beloved Caelia, imagining her as an ethereal being who operates altogether above the realm of physicality. Subsequently, the youth is dismayed and well-nigh loses his wits upon discovering that Caelia shits.[38]

In contemplating the stereotyped qualities of Latin America's allegedly altogether natural women, American males as often as not have felt at least a furtive admiration for their supposedly wanton physicality, together with a desire to take advantage of the Latin woman's passionate nature. Perhaps these attitudes arose out of the fact that the first Americans to encounter Latin Americans often were rough-and-ready frontiersmen advancing into territory claimed and occupied by Spain and later by Mexico. Wherever the imperialist process unfolds, daring colonists expect to be rewarded by readily available sex proferred by inferior creatures who ostensibly welcome seduction and subjection. Such attitudes, which developed in the American South as white males eyed their black colonials, appeared anew on the western frontier as settlers claimed Indian and Hispanic concubines. Both in the South and in the West, racist and sexist beliefs coincided to the point of being indistinguishable. Moreover, the civilized, white wives of settlers sensed sexual rivals in dusky female inhabitants of frontier areas and heaped opprobrious stereotypes of racial inferiority on them.[39]

A quality that New Mexican writer Harvey Fergusson attributed to the Mexican woman Magdalena in his 1954 novel *The Conquest of Don Pedro* coincided with one that probably a majority of Americans already by the mid–nineteenth century imputed to most Latinas: "Magdalena . . . trusted completely in her own feelings, [and] never made the mistake of trying to think. It is often a mistake to think and also painful, but a man has to think and conquer his feelings by thought."[40] But the quality that many Americans, male and female, found most noteworthy in the Latin American woman was her alleged sensuality. Whether attracted or repelled by it, Americans cast the Latina in the role of primitive sensualist.

Again I turn to *The Conquest of Don Pedro*, something of a masterpiece in its genre. Here is how Fergusson describes Lupe, a New Mexican woman of Mexican origins: "Lupe came of a class and race of women for whom sex had been their whole profession and relation to life for centuries, and they had made an art of it and of every phase of it, from the first faint smile of flirtation to the final spasm. . . . She was truly an artist of love. . . . She was supremely discreet, cunning as a coyote and happily free of guilt."[41]

Many eminent American writers including, it has been alleged, Hawthorne succumbed to the "racial folklore of the Anglo-Saxon people, which tends to depict tainted women . . . as . . . Mediterranean, or Jewish."[42] This tendency seeped down to the level of popular literature. Authors of the potboilers liked to cast Latin Americans, especially Mexicans, in the role of the sultry temptress. This stereotype still had life in 1932 when Dolores del Rio returned to the screen after a two-year absence in *Girl of Rio*. She played, as the film blurb put it, "a fiery daughter of her romantic Mexico—where blood runs hot and flashing eyes beckon to bold adventurers."[43]

A darker side of the Mexican woman's sexuality emerges in another Harvey Fergusson novel as mountain man Rube Thatcher warns a young friend about the dangers of taking a Mexican girl too seriously. "I ain't lived in these mountains since the Rio Grande was a spring branch for nothin'. I seen many a good man marry Mexican and I ain't seen one yit that wasn't sorry. Them women breeds like prairie dogs an' just as careless. They look good when they're young but after they've calved a time or two they swell up like a cow in a truck patch. . . . They do nothin' but holler like a guinea keet. . . . And all their kids is just as Mexican as they are."[44]

Despite the prevalence of attitudes expressed by Fergusson's mountain man, many American men who settled in the Southwest, or who visited points south of the border, married Latinas. Perhaps they were lured in part by stereotypes of Latin women as docile and submissive—an image not necessarily compatible with that of the Latina as spitfire, but then stereotyping is notorious for its inconsistency. For a Yankee man to marry a Latin woman did not upset imperialist concepts about races meant to dominate and races destined for dependence. However, for an American woman to marry a Latin man did upset the natural balance. It meant that the woman of a race destined for dominance would be dependent (in line with sexist assumptions) on the man of a race naturally destined for submission.

Additional stereotypes and preconceptions beyond those already considered probably figured in the readiness of many American men to take Hispanic women as their brides. The brides they chose were often comparatively fair-skinned representatives of little islands of virtue and civility surrounded by fancied seas of dark-skinned animality. In taking their brides, American men assumed the protective, chivalrous role that moved

many a southern aristocratic male to find his very raison d'être in protect-
ing virtuous flowers of white femininity against the lustful designs of a
surrounding mass of dark savages.[45]

More often, though, American males seem to have attached the imagery of sensuousness rather than purity to the Latina. In a way, this is understandable considering the circumstances of the most frequent contact
between Anglos and Hispanics. When the encounter took place on the
frontier, it was generally the rougher sort of Anglo male who encountered
the rougher sort of Hispanic female—though not always, for Kit Carson
represents only one among many adventurers in the West who found Hispanic wives of gentility. Contact also occurred as Americans ventured
south of the border. Many a Yankee adventurer was likely to find himself in
dives, in saloons, in brothels. Thus he inclined to jump to conclusions
about the general availability of dusky señoritas.

A stock figure in many depictions of America's nineteenth-century
western frontier has been the prostitute. The overwhelming majority of
those who took up the calling were, according to Anne M. Butler, American Indians, Orientals, blacks, and Mexicans. These women, together with
the minority of lower-class Anglo prostitutes, came from what Butler describes as "the background of pre-industrial cultural experience."[46] Thus
they seemed the products of nature rather than of civilization, with whatever connotations one wished to attach to those circumstances. For rough-
hewn frontiersmen often in flight from urban refinement and constraints,
women in the natural state could be preferable to those immersed in the
artifices and greed of civilization. The refrain of a popular nineteenth-
century cowboy ballad, "The Trail to Mexico," conveys this preference.

> I'm going to Mexico,
> Where the longhorn steers and cactus grow,
> Where the girls are good day after day
> And do not live just for your pay.[47]

What would the West be without its great icon, the good-hearted
whore? (See illustration 1.) Yet good-heartedness depended very much on
the eye of the beholder. Apparently the rougher elements of American society who turned up their noses at civilization and its restrictions perceived
this virtue in the women of easy availability. Defenders of civilization's
moral order, however, detected little that was good-hearted in the frontier
whore; and they delighted in moral crusades to cleanse the West of its all
too natural vice of prostitution. In the West, this vice had assumed at least
in part a Mexican identity. So, attempts to eradicate the vice assumed anti-
Hispanic overtones.

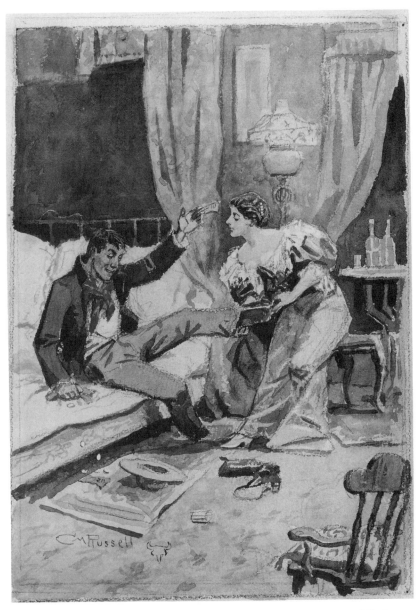

1. Charles M. Russell. *Just a Little Pleasure*. Ca. 1898. Watercolor, 13⅜ × 10⅜″. Courtesy Amon Carter Museum, Fort Worth, Texas.

Russell, the preeminent artist of America's disappearing frontier, shows the good-hearted whore as more refined than her client. But that was not the prevailing opinion among members of "respectable" society, especially when the prostitute sprang from an "inferior" race.

While some watchdogs of morality sought to stamp out prostitution, other typically enterprising Americans sought to profit from it by becoming the proprietors of dance halls, saloons, and out-and-out brothels. Thereby as nature (the whore) was rendered subordinate to the representative of civilization (her Anglo customer), another representative of civilization (the entrepreneur) profited from that subordination. Prostitution in the West thus became a typical example of the way in which capitalism "sought to extract the wealth held by nature" by processes that generally "were not gentle."[48]

The entrepreneur could salve his conscience because the whores who sprang from lesser races than Caucasian Americans could be considered virtually bereft of human rights—just as could their Anglo sisters because of their low social status. Mexican whores and Mexican women in general (and, by extension, most Latin American women, given the historical tendency of Americans to judge all Latin America by what they think they know of Mexico) were less than fully human because, to begin with, they lacked modesty. As one early Taos fur trader alleged, there was "much romance to a superficial observer in having a Mexican wife," but "the only attractions are of the baser sort. . . . We look in vain for the true woman's attraction—modesty."[49] Throughout the nineteenth century the Western world clung to the conviction that modesty was equivalent to culture and civilization. Indeed, "Christianity's introduction of the feeling of shame or modesty was viewed . . . as the major indicator of the move away from the primitive to the civilized."[50] Only among savages could women go naked or partially disrobed in front of men without blushing. Those who lacked modesty, allegedly, had the moral development only of infants.[51]

In the following chapter I deal at greater length with Anglo perceptions of the immodesty of Latin American women. For the moment, I refer only to Charles J. Deblois, captain's mate aboard the USS *Macedonia,* which plied the waters off the Chilean coast in 1819. New England–born Deblois expressed shock at the immodesty even of upper-class Chilean women: "I should like them very much if they kept their Boosoms [*sic*] covered," he wrote. "I believe it is the custom here to go uncovered, the most respectable of the female class goes this way." In his opinion, the custom was "not only indecent but unladylike."[52]

The degree to which Latin Americans have come to accept, however grudgingly, the fact that they are regarded as, by nature, subject to the desires of Yankee imperialists (who extend even to the Latin male the view they have of the natural subordination of Latin women) is revealed by a story that John Bartlow Martin relates. In a 1966 book in which he chronicles his adventures as U.S. ambassador to the Dominican Republic during

John F. Kennedy's presidency, Martin refers to a prominent Dominican who regretted U.S. imperialism in his country but deemed it inevitable. "He likened our behavior to that of a man left alone in a room with a woman—even if she were ugly, he'd have intercourse with her."[53] As this man saw the situation, Dominicans would be screwed regardless of whether the act involved a free-will offering on their part, or a money transaction, or for that matter, rape. The Dominican's view of U.S. imperialism derives from a long history in which Latin Americans, regardless of gender, were stereotyped as feminine and destined by nature to satisfy Yankee lust.

Along with the whore, good-hearted or not, stands the schoolmarm as one of the stock figures of the American West. Just as the whores stood for nature that would be exploited and ultimately, if right-thinking reformers had their way, eliminated, so the schoolmarm stood for the forces of civilization that would accomplish the "domestication of the wilderness."[54] Women schoolteachers on the frontier came generally from the genteel elements of white American society, and their success in introducing refinements where barbarism had previously reigned impressed many upholders of civilized standards, among them the Argentine Domingo Faustino Sarmiento who served as his country's minister in Washington (1865–1868) and then as its president (1868–1874). The author of a study of the life of a provincial *caudillo* (political boss) that bore the title *The Life of Facundo* and the subtitle *Civilization and Barbarism,* Sarmiento perceived in the Argentine interior a barbarism and state of nature even more degraded than that on the U.S. frontier. He thrilled over the success of the teachers who tamed the American West and prevailed on his friends the Horace Manns to send New England schoolmarms to help eradicate barbarism in provincial Argentina. Responding enthusiastically, the Manns mustered some sixty-five American women teachers for service in Argentina. There they extended the civilizing mission of their sisterhood from the wilds of the American West to the backwaters of the Latin South.[55] So, Latin America provided Yankees with whores, while the United States sent women teachers to Latin America. What greater symbolical proof could there be that Latin America represented lowly nature while the United States embodied uplifting civilization?

The Mythology of Regeneration in Nature

Influenced by an inner compulsion to dominate wild nature, American males have resorted to rationales of gender and race to sanction a related urge to master purportedly close-to-nature primitives: people who obviously belong to the human species but whose distinctive ways of being render them some sort of Other. Stereotypes of the Other arise out of complex psychological factors and are never simple or free from ambiguity.[56] Indeed, what stands out as remarkable about stereotyping is its dichotomies and its mingling of opposites. It is not really surprising, then, that even as they responded to an urge to dominate what they construed as natural, Americans have simultaneously longed to immerse themselves in the natural so as to be reborn. Psychiatrists might associate this with the return-to-the-womb instinct.

The conflation of women and nature could lead not only to the denigration but also to the exaltation of both. At the core of what has been termed a uniquely American "pastoral impulse" lay a "yearning to know and respond to the landscape as feminine." Because the American continent was seen "as the birthplace of a new culture" with enhanced human capabilities, then it must also be, "in fact as well as in metaphor, a womb of regeneration and a provider of sustenance."[57] Even while insisting on absolute domination over women, American men—like many European culture giants including Goethe, Beethoven, Wagner, and Mahler—have tended simultaneously to pine for rebirth through an idealized eternal feminine. In many instances, moreover, American men have attributed their vaunted uniqueness to the most abundant supply among all civilized nations of an untapped natural wilderness that, of course, they feminized. However, in the typical fantasies of mythically inclined American males, nature could redeem only those men who after having surrendered to her then directed their born-again energies toward her ultimate pacification and conquest. In this process American manhood fulfilled its calling and assured the onward march of civilization. This, at least, is the conclusion I reach in this section. It rests on what may be termed the "hard" facet of regeneration mythology. Before treating this hard aspect, though, I turn to a fuller consideration of the "soft" side of regeneration myth: the need to surrender to the ineffable wonders of nature in order to be reborn, without incurring any subsequent obligations to crusade with renewed energy to advance civilization by obliterating nature.

Historian Frederick Jackson Turner as much as any American deserves recognition as the prophet of the frontier myth. Writing in 1893 of Americans and their recurrent return to nature through frontier settlement, Turner stated: "This perennial rebirth, this fluidity of American life, this expansion westward with its new opportunities, its continuous touch with the simplicity of primitive society, furnish the forces dominating American character."[58] Here in the frontier "was a magic fountain of youth, in which America continually bathed and was rejuvenated."[59]

Well before Turner developed his frontier thesis, the validity of which historians have debated through the years, Jedediah Smith, one of the greatest of the mountain men and one of the few literary ones, expressed some of its central tenets: "Having been so long absent from the business of trapping and so much perplexed and harassed by the folly of men in power, I returned again to the woods, the rivers and the prairie, the Camp and the Game with a feeling somewhat like that of a prisoner escaping from his dungeon and his chains."[60] Like Smith, many an American optimist in the nineteenth century took the view that "even if the overlanders [who made their way west in covered-wagon trains] were not the finest men when they started, they certainly would be when their trek was finished, thanks to the healing powers of western nature."[61]

Wallace Stegner, one of the outstanding twentieth-century writers on the American West, observes: "For an American, insofar as he is new and different at all, is a civilized man who has renewed himself in the wild."[62] Paul Horgan, justly celebrated for his writing that focuses principally on the Southwest, insists that America seems "to be . . . the land of mankind's second chance";[63] and a well-known environmentalist maintained midway in the twentieth century: "We Americans are the people we are largely because we have had the influence of the wilderness in our lives."[64] All of the quoted authors would agree that America's history as a frontier nation has been the story of a continuing series of rites of passage or liminal moments in which we slough off determinants that have heretofore shaped us and thereby open ourselves to the possibility of emerging into enhanced identities. Even the Puritans believed that "the step *back* into the time of sacred beginnings [in nature] provided the resources for a step *forward* into fuller vision and practice."[65]

The cowboy, perhaps America's greatest mythic personage, has the aura—at least in some of his many manifestations—of perpetual youth, for he constantly undergoes renewal. Bulah Kirkland, the daughter of a Texas cowboy, once observed: "I believe I could walk along the streets of any town or city and pick out the real cowboy, not by his clothes especially, but because one can nearly always notice that he has a very open countenance and almost innocent eyes and mouth. He is not innocent of course; but living in the open, next to nature, the cleaner life is stamped on his face. His vices leave no scars or few, because old mother nature has him with her most of the time."[66]

Long before Kirkland offered her commentary on the unscathed, perpetually young cowboy, Helen Hunt Jackson had pronounced on nature's ability to keep persons forever youthful. In *Ramona,* her ever-popular tearjerker published in 1884, Jackson declared: "Whom the gods love, dwell with nature; if they are ever lured away, return to her before they are old. Then, however long they live before they die, they die young. Whom the gods love, live young—forever."[67]

A similar moral emerges from *Two Years before the Mast* (1840). At one point in his classic narrative Richard Henry Dana relates his encounter in San Francisco with a Congregational deacon he had previously known in New England. How the man had changed! "Gone was the downcast eye, the bated breath, the solemn, non-natural voice, the watchful gait," all of which had suggested that the deacon felt responsible for the "balance of the moral universe." Now, in San Francisco, "he had put off the New England deacon and become a human being." The West had transformed the New Englander, for "nature triumphs over the old forms of culture, in this man as in the nation at large."[68]

Dana had himself undergone transformation during his two-year voyage, which constituted his own rite of passage. Indeed, in America's rebirth mythology sea voyages serve quite as well as frontier experiences to bring about the born-again experience, as any reader of Melville will attest. In some ways, the ocean is even more appropriate as an agent of regeneration, since its water can be seen as an extension of the baptismal font that in Christian mythology confers rebirth. Cooper, deeply concerned in his Leatherstocking Tales with themes of regeneration, quite appropriately used land and sea wilderness interchangeably. The prairie he describes in the book of that title, with its billowing grass that resembles waves, seems almost as inseparable visually from the sea as it is metaphorically. For other writers, frontier rivers serve as well as oceans and prairies to create the new American Adam. Mark Twain demonstrates this with his tales set on the Mississippi, and so does English visionary poet and artist William Blake (1757–1827) when he records his vision of what another American river can accomplish:

> Tho' born on the cheating banks of Thames,
> Tho' his waters bathed my infant limbs,
> The Ohio shall wash his stains from me:
> I was born a slave, but I go to be free.[69]

Ralph Waldo Emerson and many of the nineteenth-century Transcendentalists, as well as their spiritual heirs through the years, looked to nature as "the ultimate restorer and purifier of a humanity corrupted by civilization."[70] "To the body and mind that have been cramped" by civilization's "noxious work," Emerson wrote, "nature is medicinal and restores their tone. The tradesman, the attorney comes out of the din and craft of the street, and sees the sky and the woods, and is a man again. In their eternal calm, he finds himself." [71] Emerson's friend Henry David Thoreau, of course, felt similarly. In its pattern of movement from "corrupt city" to "raw wilderness" and then "back toward the city," Thoreau's *Walden, or Life in the Woods* (1854), according to one of its most perceptive commentators, stands as a "prologue to American literature." [72]

When he retreated to a Wyoming cattle ranch in 1885, prior to writing his classic novel *The Virginian* (published in 1902), Owen Wister wrote: "The ancient earth was indeed my mother and I have found her again after being lost among houses, customs, and restraints." [73] Also in 1885, Wister declared, "I'm beginning to be able to feel I'm something of an animal and not a stinking brain alone." [74] Theodore Roosevelt, who believed that America's outstanding leaders had been men "of stalwart frame and sound bodily health," many of them sprung from the frontier and accustomed to hunting in their youth, shared the faith of his good friend Wister in the revitalizing forces of wilderness. Time spent in the wilderness, pitting oneself "against the wild forces of nature," cultivated "that vigorous manliness for the lack of which in a nation, as in an individual, the possession of no other qualities can possibly atone." [75] Very much like Thoreau, Roosevelt appeared to believe that if the Indian was indeed doomed, then at least "the reborn white savage . . . could incorporate his virtues, metaphysically eating him as the Indian warrior ate the heart of his enemy." [76]

Wister and Roosevelt are important in this instance, it seems to me, not primarily because they exemplify the American faith in regeneration in nature. Instead, their significance lies in the fact that as well as any other two Americans among the countless who have shared their outlook, Wister and Roosevelt stressed the importance of the *return* from wilderness over the original entry into it. This brings me to the already-alluded-to "hard" facet of regeneration mythology. The hard facet concerns not the heedless wallowing in the joys and freedoms of nature but rather the way in which energies revitalized in the barbaric existence are subsequently turned to the conquest of nature so as to advance the cause of civilization. When regeneration assumes its hard demeanor, it takes up the myth of the eternal return; it enjoins the reborn to return to civilization and to apply newly awakened animalistic, competitive, "masculine" powers to things that really matter. After undergoing regeneration on the frontier, Owen Wister's Virginian went east to practice a form of robust capitalism that guaranteed worldly success. [77] After being restored in the wilds first of the Dakota Badlands and later of Africa and Brazil, Theodore Roosevelt returned to wage political battles with renewed intensity. [78]

Cooper's Natty Bumppo has been described "as a symbol of purification through regression."[79] Natty remained in a state of regression, choosing not to return to civilization where he could have exerted his powers that had been strengthened in the wilds. By and large, though, Americans seem to prefer the men, or the women protagonists of many captivity tales, who come back from the wilds, as Daniel Boone did, often, and as Mary Rowlandson did, helping thereby to strengthen the citadel of civilization and the values on which it rests.[80] Along with Boone and Puritan captivity-tale archetype Rowlandson, Americans admire a Richard Henry Dana type. At the end of the voyages that he described in *Two Years before the Mast,* Dana was back in Boston, where an old acquaintance did not recognize him, with his "long hair and face burnt as dark as an Indian's." According to Martin Green, "no nineteenth-century writer or reader could be quite at ease as an American until he had passed through being an Indian."[81] The real-life and the legendary Davy Crockett also illustrate this point: that Americans of epic proportions *passed through* the Indian stage and then returned to civilization better able to serve the cause of progress.

In the case of Wister's Virginian and in the real-life case of Roosevelt, the successful urban man of affairs passed through the stage of being not an Indian but rather a cowboy. The rejuvenated cowboy might, as with Roosevelt, turn to politics. More often, as in the case of the Virginian, he would turn to capitalist enterprise, and parlay a small nest egg into a cattle ranch, a mercantile emporium, or even a bank. A variant of this mythology still endures and may help to account for the popularity among eastern tycoons of western artist Rory Wagner's canvases. In the 1980s Wagner built a thriving career painting cowboys with faces that suggest hard-driving, even ruthless, acquisitive instincts.[82] By contemplating these paintings that hang on the walls of their expensively appointed homes and offices, businessmen who have never experienced an actual frontier link themselves to its mythic, energizing qualities. They see themselves as spiritual heirs of the cowboy whose relentless and often amoral ambition was shaped by an initial descent into and a remorselessly waged conflict with nature.

The mountain man shared in much of the mythology associated with the protean cowboy. Not just his plunge into but also his return from nature has guaranteed the mountain man a place among archetypal American heroes. The mountain man can be seen as an "expectant capitalist," imbued with motives of upward mobility, who ventured westward precisely in order to take the first step up the ladder of material success. The wilderness experience gave the expectant capitalist his start, after which he could return to an urban setting, very possibly one of the young western towns, to hasten his climb up the success ladder, abetted by the sharpening of his survival and competitive instincts that had taken place in the wilderness.[83]

The more myth-fulfilling expectations they placed in the nature plunge, and the return from it, the more Americans worried about the eventual disappearance of wilderness.[84] Concern about causing the wilderness to disappear in consequence of their success in pacifying and civilizing it gnawed at Americans as they engaged in relentless continental expansion. A proud and self-satisfied frontier people, Americans even in the nineteenth century were simultaneously a haunted people, neurotically driven always to find new frontiers. (See illustration 2.)

When nineteenth-century Americans grew most concerned about the ultimate consequences to character- and fortune-building of the frontier's diminution, they turned to Latin territorial possessions as the source of real estate that would prolong spiritual and economic regeneration. In acquiring the Louisiana Territory in 1803, they turned to the French. Had it not been for the freakish circumstances that saw France acquire Louisiana from Spain at the beginning of the century, they would have turned in this instance to the Spaniards, from whose descendants they would later acquire most of their dream-and-myth-prolonging new territories. Thomas Jefferson anticipated this development when he wrote in 1801: "However our present interests may restrain us within our own limits, it is impossible not to look forward to distant times when our rapid multiplication will expand itself beyond those limits, and cover the whole northern, if not the whole southern continent, with a people speaking the same language, governed in similar forms, and by similar laws."[85]

Even if they did not clearly articulate their hope, Americans turned instinctively to the Latin countries to their south as the repositories of wilderness necessary to prolong exceptionalism. In a way, the Monroe Doctrine of 1823 arose out of this instinctual perception. The doctrine proclaimed as one of its cardinal tenets that Old World powers must abandon hope of future expansion into Latin America. By means of this increasingly venerated principle, Americans safeguarded for their own use what many regarded as a virtual extension of their own frontier.

Already in the 1850s, that remarkable filibuster from Tennessee, William Walker, felt that the time had come for the United States to begin to occupy more of the Latin area predestined for its use. When he invaded Nicaragua and established himself as its president, Walker of course was animated in part by the desire to enlarge America's slaveholding territory. Beyond this, though, he clearly saw Nicaragua as an extension of the less and less boundless West, an extension that promised rewards of mythic as well as economic dimensions. To Walker and his men, Nicaragua seemed a "vision of enchantment,"[86] even if the people currently inhabiting it left as much to be desired as had American Indians. In Nicaragua Walker also beheld a land that promised strong Americans the chance to remain

2. George Inness. *The Lackawanna Valley.* 1855. Oil on canvas, 33⅞ × 50¼″. National Gallery of Art, Washington. Gift of Mrs. Huttleston Rogers.

The machine has entered wilderness and created a garden: for the moment, civilization and nature coexist in ideal harmony. But the moment cannot endure, for soon civilization will swamp nature. Hoping to recreate the magic garden, Americans were driven to seek new frontiers.

strong, by claiming land that would enable them to become, as the invader from the north put it, "fixed to the soil." [87] In line with the Antaeus myth, which seems to have cast a spell over many Americans, Walker sensed that prodigious strength came from intimate contact with the earth—who, of course, happened to be Antaeus's mother.

Happily for Nicaraguans, Walker was ahead of his time. His expansionist schemes, buttressed by visions of civilized men being reanimated as they established mastery over primitives, came to naught. But the idea of a boundless West that could prolong itself by turning southward continued to fascinate Americans, among them the artists George Catlin and Frederic Edwin Church. In different ways, both men saw Latin America as an American frontier in reserve.

When Catlin (1796–1872) grew heartsick over the disappearance of North America's wild man, the Indian, he turned to South America and happily acquainted himself with that area's vast stock of aborigines who could still live in nature because nature seemed infinite and relatively unthreatened. Latin America thus might become in a way the great national park, the vast preserve of nature and close-to-nature people, that Catlin had tried but failed to have Congress set apart within the confines of the United States. Thereby, Latin America could serve as the area where Americans, even if they did not establish ownership claims, could endlessly renew themselves.[88]

By the time he turned forty, Frederic Edwin Church (1826–1900) had begun to worry about the looming demise of America's source of distinctive virtue and innocence. Church's close friend and fellow artist Martin Johnson Heade painted Florida as an uncontaminated paradise that might restore Americans to pristine innocence.[89] But Church looked farther southward; he buoyed his spirits by turning to the discovery of scenes of sublime, restorative nature in Latin America. Like so many Americans who followed him in time, Church somehow assumed that the vast tracts of virgin land to the south were providentially set aside to help sustain the uniqueness of Americans by providing psychological and spiritual wholeness—a point to which I return in this chapter's final section.

Artists and men of letters might worry about psychological and spiritual aspects of renewal, but more numerous were those Americans concerned with economic renewal. To these latter, Latin America promised a frontier in which they could continue to fulfill the mountain-man variety of expectant capitalist dreams. There, in the wild and chaotic lands to the south, they could acquire the raw skills, the vitality, and also the initial capital holdings, that would enable them someday to return to civilization as thriving entrepreneurs. Or, they might choose to remain in the Latin wilderness, converting its savage wastes to civilization and, like their pioneer forebears, beseeching Washington for military protection when surrounding "savages" threatened their economic and personal security.

In the southern frontier, of course, some Americans would regress, even as their counterparts in the western wilderness did. Sometimes civilization's emissaries in lands to the south would succumb to the lure of nature and go native. And sometimes Americans who sought wilderness opportunities in the southern frontier would simultaneously provide both inspiring examples and cautionary tales. Such a person was Henry Meiggs who in the latter part of the nineteenth century brought railroad civilization to Chile and Peru while at the same time undergoing moral regression in the southern heart of darkness, where he unleashed his sexuality, broke up marriages, and acquired virtual harems—if the gossip is to be credited.[90] But has not part of the appeal of imperialism, whether territorial or just economic, always resided in its promise that civilized man, even as he spreads his civilization, could replenish and also freely indulge his savage, "masculine" energies? Imperialism thrives as much on images of regression as of progress, and both images beckoned North Americans southward as their own frontier receded.

The Myth of Nature as Beneficent Goddess

John Muir (1838–1914) had been on his way to the Amazonian wilderness, hoping there to appease his yen for immersion in nature, when a serious bout with malaria sidetracked him. Upon his recovery Muir, recognizing that the United States still possessed its own sources of virtually limitless stretches of unsullied nature, headed to California rather than Brazil. Arriving in San Francisco in 1868, he asked directions to any place that was wild. Only in such a place, he believed, could "he purge himself of the 'sediments of society' and become 'a new creature.'"[91]

In 1903 Muir camped out for three nights in his beloved Yosemite, accompanied only by the president of the United States, Theodore Roosevelt. The two men had much in common as they fulfilled one of America's "most persistent dreams: creative truancy in the wild heart of the New World."[92] They also had vast differences, as Roosevelt discovered when Muir admonished him about his addiction to hunting. The most fundamental difference between the two men, though, was this: Roosevelt was obsessed by the need to return from nature, refreshed and reanimated, to struggle for the advance of civilization. His was the establishment view on the blessings of nature that has generally prevailed in America. Muir, and with him the majority of those who through the years have asserted counterculture (or adversary-culture) values, accepted a no-strings-attached commitment to nature, one that did not entail an obligation to return.

Roosevelt, remember, honored the hard aspect of nature mythology, with its assumption that the value of wilderness experience lay in its ability to toughen men so they could struggle in behalf of civilization with renewed intensity. Nature to him was a goddess to be employed in the service of the god of civilization. Muir honored an altogether different aspect of nature mythology. For him, nature promised not rebirth but rather preservation of the virtues with which humans originally had been born. There was no need to be twice-born; rather, humans had to retain the innocence with which they had first entered life. In this quest, nature was their greatest ally.

Both Roosevelt's and Muir's approaches grow out of traditions extending back to the very origins of America, although neither man, happily, took on the extremes of the school from which he descended. In the Puritan elders one finds attitudes that resonate in the Rough Rider's nature philosophy. And Thomas Morton (d. 1646 or 1647, author of *New Canaan* [1637]) as much as anyone deserves to be designated the father of the American school that sees good in pristine nature and regards what civilization has wrought with suspicion—at best. Morton scandalized the upholders of Puritan propriety by retreating to nature and accepting Indians, the children of nature, as equals. Bedecking themselves in flowers as they celebrated whatever it struck their fancy to celebrate, Morton and his followers may be seen as America's first flower children. They initiated the counterculture tradition.[93]

Washington Irving, perhaps the first author whom Europeans accepted as offering hope for America's cultural coming of age, also worshiped the goddess nature—but only part of the time, so he cannot be accepted as a full-fledged counterculturalist. In *The Adventures of Captain Bonneville* (1837), Irving fairly rhapsodized on the wilderness as a good in itself. Indeed, according to a perceptive commentator, Irving found it difficult "to do justice to the exulting feelings of the worthy captain, at finding himself . . . fairly launched on the broad prairies, with his face to the boundless West. The tamest inhabitants of cities, the veriest spoiled child of civilization, feels his heart dilate and his pulse beat high, on finding himself on horseback in the glorious wilderness."[94] Irving complained of the American tendency to send youth abroad "to grow luxurious and effeminate in Europe." He recommended instead a tour on the prairies as most likely to produce American men in whom there might flower the innate virtues of simplicity. Henry Wadsworth Longfellow (1807–1882) sometimes expressed sentiments similar to Irving's. "There is," he once wrote, "nothing which so frees us from the turbulent ambitions and bustle of the world, nothing which so fills the mind with great and glowing conceptions and at the same time so warms the heart with love and tenderness, as a frequent and close communion with natural scenery."[95]

As with so many other aspects of Americana, Walt Whitman (1819–1892) has written perhaps more effectively than anyone else on the need to retain innate virtue by living close to nature. Whitman, who elsewhere advised, "Fear grace, elegance, civilization, delicateese," holds up to readers his own example in the poem "Rise O Days from Your Fathomless Deeps":

> The cities I loved so well I abandon'd and left, I sped to the certainties
> suitable to me,
> Hungering, hungering, hungering for primal energies and Nature's
> dauntlessness,
> I refresh'd myself with it only, I could relish it only. . . .

And, in "Song of the Open Road," one encounters this typical example of the Whitman credo:

> Now I see the secret of the making of the best persons
> Is to grow in the open air and to eat and sleep with the earth. . . .
>
> The earth is rude, silent, incomprehensible at first, Nature is rude and
>   incomprehensible at first,
> Be not discouraged, keep on, there are divine things well envelop'd,
> I swear to you there are divine things more beautiful than words can tell.[96]

In a similar vein artist Thomas Moran, who often trudged about Latin America in search of sublime vistas and who in the early 1870s helped persuade Congress to establish America's first national park at Yellowstone, stressed his preference for "the natural scene before it was reduced or marred by the hand of man."[97] Invariably, critics of what is wrought in the name of progress have "compared invidiously the contrived and intricate workings of civilization to the artlessness and simplicity of the natural state."[98]

Writing in the mid-1960s, a renowned student of these matters concluded: "Glorification of all things primitive, the culture-less as a characteristic of the true, the complete, the only and original bliss: that is one of the fundamentals of our Western civilization."[99] Especially in America, glorification of the natural has provided strong and persistent counterpoint to the main melody that accompanies hosannas in praise of civilization. Harking all the way back to the first European settlers, many of whom expected to find in America a natural paradise, the counterpoint again and again becomes audible, threatening at times even to drown out the main melodic line. From some of the early settlers down through their counterculturalist descendants to the present day, Americans have felt the pinch of civilization, hoped to abandon "the cares of adult life" and return "to the primal warmth or womb or breast in a feminine landscape." These Americans have responded to the "paradisiacal" vision of New World frontiers as blessed areas where people might live in carefree plenitude.[100]

Midway in the first half of the nineteenth century Thoreau, feeling jacketed by convention in the settled East, concluded he must go westward, for "westward, I go free."[101] By the late decades of the century many Americans, fearing that too much of their own West had been settled and subjected to civilization's restraints, decided that by going southward, among the Latin peoples whom establishment culture had always derided for living heedlessly in a state of nature, they stood the best chance of attaining a paradisiacal life-style. Indeed, as early as 1820 Moses Austin, as he prepared to lead Anglo settlers into Hispanic Texas, felt the lure of the temporal paradise in which the Latin Other lived. Here are his words: "The notion of new and more beautiful woods and streams, of a milder climate, deer, fish, fowl, game, and all those delightful images of enjoyment, that so readily associate with the idea of the wild and boundless license of new regions; all that restless hope of finding in a new country, and in new views and combinations of things, something that we crave but have not,—I am ready to believe, from my own experience, and from what I have seen in the case of others, that this influence of imagination has no inconsiderable agency in producing emigration." [102]

Invariably the new lands that beckoned Americans grown restless in civilization were inhabited lands. In the establishment view—the view of "respectable" Americans not grown excessively discontented with civilization—the inhabitants of unconquered wilderness domains were savages or barbarians. However, for disaffected counterculturalists, those living beyond the reach of civilization were fortunate beings who had escaped spiritual disfigurement "by the imposition of social restraints" and the artifices of civilization. [103] Most counterculturalists have had little doubt as to the cardinal sin of civilization. Like Karl Marx, they perceive it as the aggrandizing spirit: the greed for individual gain that underlies the whole capitalist ethic. Ostensibly, men and women living in the natural state suffer no taint from this blight. Inspired by this conviction, American novelists, with William Faulkner's *Go Down, Moses* providing one of the most conspicuous examples, have fashioned some of their nation's finest literature.

Most people, it has been observed, "estranged from their own society tend to drift to the idealization of others—,or, rather, they cannot idealize others without a previous alienation from their own." [104] This has been true from Thomas Morton up to present-day Americans who glorify Indians. In Indians they have found the children of nature "who drew directly from nature virtues which raise doubts as to the value of civilization." [105] Once the "vanishing race" had indeed virtually vanished (with Indian population shrinking to around 250,000 by the latter part of the nineteenth century), critics of American civilization often looked to Latin Americans as repositories of primitive virtues: virtues protected by the natural paradises they occupied, free as yet from massive invasion by capitalist exploiters. Ultimately, to leap far ahead for a moment, invasions did occur and nature to the south came under siege. But, when Fidel Castro came to power in Cuba at the end of the 1950s, American counterculturalists thrilled to his and Ernesto "Che" Guevara's purported attempt to lead people back from the distortions of capitalist civilization to a natural state of being unsullied by materialism and individual greed. "Utopia for many intellectuals," writes historian James H. Billington, "had simply returned to a tropical island in the New World—which is where the intellectuals of early modern Europe had always imagined it might be."[106]

Back in the second half of the nineteenth century, American males had wondered where the utopia might be that would provide escape from the vexations of civilization. This was the period when what historian Ann Douglas refers to as the feminization of American culture came into full swing,[107] when women reformers of every conceivable type, often allied with clergymen, set out to remove all the rough edges from society. Up to now, women have been considered mainly as symbols of nature. But stereotypes generally exist in pairs of opposites, and women—proper women at least—have also been perceived as agents of civilization who jeopardize the freedom of males to lead unrefined lives. In some ways, this is how frontier ruffians saw the schoolmarm.

In consequence of a perceived feminization of American culture, many men felt pressured to abandon free-and-easy, natural life-styles. Even fashions for males began to encourage corseting, the ultimate assault on the natural. In their enthusiasm to spread a new morality of refinement and control,[108] women drove men to fantasize about, and sometimes actually to escape to, sanctuaries where the right to lead uninhibited and unexamined lives was never questioned.

Perhaps escapism inspired Edgar Allan Poe's *Narrative of Arthur Gordon Pym* (1838). Pym, modeled in many ways on Poe himself, felt he must escape a mother who became hysterical at the mere mention of his going to sea. Undoubtedly the great western artist Frederic Remington (1861–1909), "with his celebrated fear of women," associated his beloved West with escape from a domineering mother. Later in life, he experienced a "compulsive desire to make long trips to distant environments unaccompanied by his wife." On these trips, Remington eluded the feminine, "enfeebling influences of luxury and modern life"[109] and managed to live naturally, as a man. Mark Twain's sympathy, however inconsistent, with Huck Finn's desire to strike out for the territory unquestionably had something to do with the "utter domination" that his wife exercised over him.[110] Surely Twain had himself in mind when he has Huck complain of how Miss Watson and the Widow Douglas want to "sivilize" him.

In their respective eras Nathaniel Hawthorne (d. 1864) and Henry James (d. 1916) grumbled about female scribblers and reformers but nevertheless put up with what they regarded as feminine conventions. But others, among them Poe, Remington, Twain, and also Melville, rebelled and either wrote in a way to glorify masculinity with all its rough edges or else actually took to the frontier or to the sea to immerse themselves in the rough delights of primitive existence. In doing so, they stood on its head the captivity tale's morality that equated virtue with the flight from nature, back to civilization. In one of his guises, the mythic cowboy also stood the captivity tale's morality on its head. In many stories, the cowboy acts out the masculine desire to escape an enervating civilization and the female enforcers of its restraints. Uneasy and tongue-tied in the presence of the lady, but at home with the whore, the cowboy exemplifies—at least in some of his manifestations—the "adolescent revolt against femininity and feminine standards."[111]

The masculine spirit that finds natural circumstances most congenial exemplifies an archetype by no means confined to American culture. In fact, this archetype clearly inspires the song "La Natura" by Mozart's eighteenth-century contemporary Vicente Martín y Soler. In the lyrics, a peasant contrasts his natural approach to love with the refinements and blandishments of the aristocracy. Lords and ladies court and woo with surface dignity, with ceremony, and also with artifice. They pine and sigh as they contemplate doing what peasants do with instinctual directness. Peasants, the lyrics suggest, savor pleasures of the flesh more fully, more honestly, more spontaneously. They don't dillydally. They go right to the point, because they follow the school of nature.

From the very inception of English settlement in America, male Caucasian newcomers acted as a fair number of colonial invaders always act. They abandoned themselves to the school of nature. And they found Indian maidens who provided love according to that school. In the latter part of the nineteenth century, though, Indians were either vanishing (as we have seen) or at war with Caucasian Americans, and their women were no longer readily available to satisfy male fantasies about guilt-free, uninhibited liaisons.[112] Increasingly, those fantasies focused on women of the Southwest, of Mexico and Central America and the Caribbean islands. Here lay the source of hot-blooded sex as counseled by the school of nature.

For John Muir and many another exalted figure who flew in the face of conventional wisdom, unrestrained sexuality seems not to have figured among the ways in which the natural approach demonstrated its superiority to the customs of civilization. However, for many others who chafed at social restraints, uncurbed sexuality seemed what the return to nature was all about. For them, the Latin American woman, as the Indian squaw before her (in imagery that goes back to Pocahontas[113]), became a choice object of carnal fantasies. She retained this status until the sexual revolution that accompanied America's most ballyhooed counterculture rendered her superfluous in the 1960s. That was when American women began to act out the roles that male fantasies had once assigned to the dark-eyed and erotic Other.

Nature Within, Nature Without, and Phenomena of Projection

Among Americans Thoreau illustrates, as well as anyone, the universal tendency to equate nature "out there" with inward nature. In much of his writing on nature, Thoreau concerned himself only superficially with the external natural world. "Following Emerson's dictum that 'the whole of nature is a metaphor of the human mind,' Thoreau turned to it repeatedly as a figurative tool. Wilderness symbolized the unexplored qualities and untapped capacities of every individual. The burden of his message was to penetrate the 'wilderness . . . in our brains and bowels, the primitive vigor of Nature in us.'"[114] For Thoreau, and countless others before and since him, "the landscape lies fair within." Thus discovery and conquest of frontier wilderness came to mean also self-discovery and self-conquest, and the desire (voiced by Huck Finn) to strike out for the territory became tantamount to yearning for adventures of inward immigration. English novelist, critic, and self-professed seer D. H. Lawrence, when contemplating the glories of a Mexican landscape shortly before 1920, felt himself "pierced . . . with insight into his own nature."[115] Thoreau and those numerous Americans referred to above similarly recognized that the glories and the terrors of the unsubdued landscape helped to explain and were in turn explained by the wonderful and frightening elements of the unsubdued psyche.

Ever since the Puritans, Americans in large numbers have approached wilderness with a compulsion to reform and improve it so as to render it more useful to humans. Surely this compulsion bears an intimate relationship to an equally obsessive desire among America's guardians of the moral order, from the Puritans onward, to wage war against mankind's base nature.[116] Elizabeth Temple in Cooper's *Pioneers* observes: "It is our duty to struggle with our natural feelings."[117] Allan Bloom expresses the same conviction in his *Closing of the American Mind,* which became a best-seller in 1988. "Civilization," he writes, "or, to say the same thing, education, is the taming or domestication of the soul's raw passions."[118]

Americans have by no means been unique in finding in the "boundless West" a metaphor for the unconscious, characterized by the qualities that Sigmund Freud imputed to the id. Johann von Goethe (1749–1832), to cite just one Old World witness, suggested close ties between outer and inner realms of disorder and chaos; and, like many Americans, he perceived that a large share of the energies of civilization "must be directed at defeating wilderness in nature and controlling it in human nature."[119] When in his best-known masterpiece he has Faust embark on the project to reform nature by draining the Zuider Zee, Goethe makes it perfectly clear that his protagonist's compulsion "to tame the wild power of the sea parallels his own inner struggle for self-control."[120]

Goethe's perception harks back to the intellectual traditions of alchemy. Psychiatrist Carl G. Jung (1875–1961) has made a convincing case that alchemists engaged principally in the quest for inward treasure. They believed, though, that concomitant to this search, and indispensable to its successful outcome, was the outer-world endeavor to discover how to convert dross to gold.[121] Americans have been alchemists, as Jung perceived these latter. They have recognized a clear connection between domesticating what was wild and reckless inside of them and taming their country's boundless wilderness.

Psychiatrist Erik Erikson has written extensively about the quest for identity, and about the uses people make of positive and negative identities. The positive identity, as he explains in a 1974 book, is the ideal persona, the sort of being who embodies all the virtues that the identity-seeker would like to incorporate into his or her own persona. But all kinds of unconscious, aggressive instincts, some related to the sex drive, wage battle against attainment of the ideal identity. Seeking to overcome rebellious inward forces, the struggling human tends to project those forces onto persons in the outer world. Such persons come to represent, to incarnate, the negative identity.[122] By fostering hatred of the outer-world embodiment of inner demons, seekers of ideal identities strengthen their hatred of the natural passions and instincts that impede attainment of personality goals. Perhaps imperialists respond to a hope, either conscious or subliminal, that conquest of primitive Others who personify the negative identity will facilitate the quest to master worrisome inner forces. In short, they may perceive that overcoming the inner heart of darkness requires conquest over what is seen in the outer world—in part because of projection—as a heart of darkness.

All racial and sexual stereotypes result from projection, according to Sander L. Gilman, a close student of these matters. He believes that in the late nineteenth and early twentieth centuries, American males of the "respectable" classes projected undesirable traits onto women, blacks, and Jews, prime examples of traditionally repressed people who were beginning to assert themselves as they struggled toward equality.[123] By projecting onto social upstarts all of the wild and natural appetites that constantly threatened to overwhelm psychic control mechanisms, defenders of society's status quo could justify the perpetuation of repressiveness and in turn bolster the repression of psychic upstarts.

Before women, blacks, and Jewish immigrants (along with such other "undesirable" immigrants as Orientals and the Irish) had begun to cause concern, staunch defenders of American morality and civilization had projected their inner demons onto Indians. Transcendentalist teacher and writer Bronson Alcott gave mid-nineteenth-century expression to a widely shared conviction when he wrote: "I say that he [the Indian] goes along with the woods and the beasts, who retreat before and are superseded by man, and the planting of orchards and gardens. . . . Man's victory over nature and himself is to overcome the brute beast in him." [124] Indeed, much of American identity was forged through the long series of Indian wars that fostered Indian stereotypes embodying all the traits of the negative identity. And, from a point early in the nineteenth century and extending up to the present time, Americans often projected onto stereotyped Latin Americans all that they feared or disliked in themselves.

Happily, the story of the formation of "national character" in America is not nearly so simple as the above material might suggest. Americans (perhaps even more than many other nationalities) have perceived the unconscious not only as a frightening repository of psychic trash, but also as a treasure trove; they have perceived the unconscious not just as Freud's id, but as the sanctuary in males of the Jungian anima (feminine principle) and in women of the animus (male principle), the great interior opposite, or Other, that *must* be accepted and assimilated into the personality in order to attain wholeness. For Jung, psychological wholeness depends on frequent journeys of interior immigration, in consequence of which elements that lurk in the unconscious—collective and personal—are reintegrated into a personality that, as a result of this ongoing process, is constantly reborn.

Given their frontier experience that encouraged metaphors of rebirth in nature, and given their often-remarked tendency to put the best face on things, Americans have responded warmly to the optimistic view of nature within. In evaluating the unconscious, they have tended to be Jungians, even when calling themselves Freudians. To a remarkable extent a nation of wholeness-seekers, Americans have pursued the synthesis of positive and negative identities, male and female principles, adult and childlike characteristics, superego and id, ego consciousness and the unconscious, discipline and dissipation. Historian Michael Kammen contends that "compromise is the quintessential American way." [125] Just as accurately, Americans could be described as a people characterized by the quest for synthesis or fusion of opposites—including the opposites of nature and civilization.

Worlds Within, Worlds Without, and Myths of Reconciling Opposites

For every American who has indulged "the metaphysics of Indian hating,"[126] another has sought, like Thomas Jefferson, to combine "the Indian's high level of instinctual gratification with those refinements of civilization based on performance—work—hence a degree of repression."[127] And for every puritanical American intent upon repressing the natural, another has sought to renew connections to the spontaneous, natural self, without renouncing membership in society. For Frederick Jackson Turner, the very word *frontier* served as a "basic metaphor" for reconciling opposites "through interpenetration and transcendence."[128]

Recall, now, that the American frontier was peopled not just by Indians but also by Latin Americans. And as Americans mused on combining wilderness and urban life, nature and civilization, they also thought about becoming new people by synthesizing their self-perceived penchant for discipline, control, and domination with what they imagined to be the Indians' *and* the Latins' spontaneity, childishness, uninhibited exuberance, improvidence, and unrestrained sexuality. They followed in the footsteps of Philip Freneau (1752–1832), "the poet of the American Revolution," who remained obsessed by the need to reconcile his faith in civilized America with his admiration for the "noble savage."[129] Only through reconciliation of this sort could Freneau and generations of Americans after him envision attainment of wholeness and transcendence.

Perhaps because their civilization from the very outset established itself in a huge sea of wilderness, and perhaps because they have been historically compelled to confront the "primitive" Other in such large numbers (Indians, blacks, immigrants, Latin Americans), Americans have seemed singularly preoccupied with creating a whole out of opposites. Maybe this preoccupation helps explain their love affair with psychiatrists and psychologists: the people who claim the power to end alienation and provide psychic wholeness. And psychic wholeness, remember, is simply one side of a coin whose reverse is outer-world wholeness. Outer-world alienation ends when people who personify civilization's superego merge with the wild, chaotic frontier or absorb the energies of a natural and unrestrained people who personify the id. Just possibly the hopes some Americans place in psychology bear a relationship to the expectations that, throughout their history, they have attached to religious revivalism. Often after initially succumbing to outbursts of wild emotionalism, the reborn person gains a new degree of order and control, the whole process mediated by the religious counterparts of secular psychiatrists and psychologists.

According to psychiatrist Robert May, the typical or archetypal male fantasy is one of great adventure that ends in catastrophe—a fantasy captured by the Icarus myth. Women, on the other hand, are said to fantasize about suffering, trials, and tribulations, followed by contentment and happiness. Feminine fantasies are epitomized by the Persephone myth.[130] Americans, it seems to me, have fancied that in their exceptionalism they could pursue both fantasies, that they could combine the male, civilizing, capitalist spirit (with its resignation to inevitable falls, to recurring cycles of depression) with the feminine spirit of resigned suffering that results ultimately in a bonanza rather than a crash. Americans, in short, did not have to choose between opposing alternatives. They could live as Emerson advised: rejecting either-or approaches and recognizing that "there is just one thing, this old double."[131] Americans could become, in a way, a nation of hermaphrodites. With ample justification poet Archibald MacLeish wrote in 1929: "It is a strange thing—to be an American."[132]

It is a strange *and* wonderful thing to be an American, to be a hermaphrodite. And Simone de Beauvoir in the 1960s captured the wonders of the vision of combining opposites—this vision that has a universal but also a peculiarly American appeal.

> Man seeks in woman the Other as Nature and as his fellow being. But we know the ambivalent feelings Nature inspires in man. He exploits her, but she crushes him, he is born of her and dies in her; and she is the source of his being and the realm that he subjugates to his will; Nature is a vein of gross material in which the soul is imprisoned, and she is the supreme reality; she is contingence and Idea, the finite and the whole; she is what opposes the Spirit, and the Spirit itself. Now ally, now enemy, she appears as the dark whence life wells up, and this life itself, as the ever-yonder toward which life tends.[133]

No small thing is the male vision not just of subjugating but symbiotically fusing with the elusive Other, ever changing in her characteristics according to the perspective from which she is perceived.

De Beauvoir's compatriot Honoré de Balzac described Cooper's Natty Bumppo as "a magnificent moral hermaphrodite, torn between the savage and the civilized worlds," and somehow fusing elements of both.[134] Many American artists have been similarly torn and similarly determined to bridge opposite poles. One such artist was Thomas Cole (1801–1848). Although English-born, Cole became consummately American in outlook as he fathered the Hudson River school of landscape painting; and in many of his most celebrated canvases he "idealized a combination of the wild and the civilized." [135] (For artist Asher B. Durand's depiction of Thomas Cole in the midst of his beloved nature, see illustration 3.) Some thirty years before Cole arrived in America, native-born artist Charles Wilson Peale in 1785 established the country's first natural history museum of any consequence. Located in Philadelphia, the museum stood as a temple for the wedding of opposites. In it Peale exhibited his paintings, symbols of civilization's art and artifice, together with such products of the natural world as mastodon bones he had excavated, Indian peace pipes (one of them presented to the museum by Meriwether Lewis), taxidermic trophies, among them buffalo, as well as live animals, including for a time two grizzly bear cubs donated by Zebulon Pike. [136] Peale hoped visitors to the museum would admire his art even as they entered into what he termed "the great school of nature." [137]

Men of the pen as well as the brush celebrated the harmonious reconciliation of opposites. Despite the popular misunderstanding that has falsified his image, Thoreau hailed not virgin nature or the untamed Indian, but rather their symbiotic union with civilization. Wildness and refinement Thoreau saw as "equally beneficent influences that Americans would do well to blend." [138] Thus he called on his countrymen to combine "the hardness, the physical vitality, of the frontiersman with the reflections of a civilized man." Thereby Americans could claim "the innocence of each without the vices of either." [139]

When Hawthorne, in his short story "The Maypole of Merry Mount" (1836), deals with Thomas Morton and his back-to-nature flower children, who in the 1620s were imprisoned by John Endicott and his fellow defenders of Puritan propriety, he sympathizes with neither side. Hawthorne sees some of the Merry Mount revelers as "transformed to brutes, . . . midway between man and beast," abandoned to the "flow of tipsy jollity." On the other hand, he scorns the Puritans as "most dismal wretches," grim, self-righteous, and vindictive. [140] Hawthorne's hopes for the future lie with the young couple whose marriage the Merry Mounters were celebrating at the moment the Puritans intervened to arrest and flog the alleged servants of the devil. Revitalized but not yet corrupted by their fling with nature, the young couple could be tempered by the salutary aspect of Puritan discipline without being dehumanized by it, or so Hawthorne seems to suggest. They could unite opposites that had warred in the past so as to create a new American. In what may be his best-known work, *The Scarlet Letter* (1850), Hawthorne sounds a similar theme. Here, according to one critic, the writer suggests "we are all mixed bloods, and rather than attempt to

3. Asher B. Durand. *Kindred Spirits*. 1849. Oil on canvas, 46 × 36″. Collection of The New York Public Library Astor, Lenox and Tilden Foundations.

William Cullen Bryant (on the left) and Thomas Cole retreat into nature, seeking inspiration for their respective arts: poetry and painting. They envisioned an American civilization rooted in reverence for nature.

negate one or the other side of our dual heritage, we ought to learn like Hester Prynne . . . to live between these extremities of the self, between the red man's wilderness and the white man's Boston." [141]

Whitman conveys a similar message in suggesting that America's uniqueness lay in the promise that it could attain outdoor, indoor harmony. One such moment of fusion he experienced on hearing the Seventeenth Regimental Band play Italian music in Dakota. Nature, "sovereign of this gnarl'd realm," listened "well-pleas'd" to the delicate tones of civilization. For Whitman, the great promise of America lay in its unique potential to fuse "man and art with Nature." [142]

Utopian hopes resting on the fusion of opposites appear also in decidedly more modest examples of nineteenth-century literature. Take the case, for example, of Edward L. Wheeler's *Deadwood Dick on Deck* (published at the end of the 1870s and one of the most popular of all dime novels). Minnie, the saloon keeper in the town of Whoop-Up, rejects her dandified suitor from Washington, D.C.: "Do you suppose I'd give up this glorious life here for the sake of indulging myself in . . . social miseries . . . ? No! a thousand times, no! I know all the delights you picture, but they don't tempt me. In Washington, you have well-clothed gold-enamored dummies, here, in the mines, though of times rudely dressed, you find men." Washington, she concludes, is a "refined hell," while Whoop-Up "is a rough paradise." [143] In this passage, Minnie does not praise nature in its most isolated wildness. What appeals to her is the early moment of fusion, when miners, responsive to capitalism's inducements, first begin to penetrate Mother Nature and to extract her treasures. The miners are figures of cultural androgyny, in whom wildness as well as the drives and ambitions of civilization mingle together in harmonious equality. Here is the great creative moment, central to American mythology, that witnesses the birth of the New Adam.

However much they would come in the twentieth century to hate communism, Americans from an early point in their cultural development embraced the dialectical process that lies at the heart of Marxian analysis. They assumed that a thesis could interact with its antithesis to produce a synthesis. Inspired by this assumption, they have insisted, according to one historian, that the good life embody both civilization and savagery. [144] Myths reconcile contradictions in real-life situations; and Americans have chosen as one of their favorites a myth that rests on the esoteric, gnostic, Heraclitean, Hegelian, and coincidentally, Marxist vision of opposites combining to produce wholeness.

Ever insistent upon combining opposites in the quest of fashioning a new and unique American civilization was landscape architect Frederick Law Olmsted. Well before fashioning his New York masterpiece, Central Park, Olmsted had created his first "bourgeois utopia" near Chicago in 1868. Describing the philosophy that inspired this project, Olmsted wrote: "I never lose an opportunity [to urge] the ruralizing of all our urban population and the urbanizing of our rustic population." [145] For Olmsted, suburbia represented the true bourgeois utopia; for suburbia combined the savage vitality of the rural setting with the civilizing arts of the city. Little wonder that suburbia has become "the defining metaphor of modern American life, the symbol of our social-moral dreams and frustrations."[146]

As of 1980, more than 40 percent of America's population lived in sub-urbs—more than in cities *or* in rural areas. Thus suburbia helped Americans to avoid either-or decisions and to choose simultaneously both one pole of a dichotomy and its opposite; they opted, in short, for Emerson's "old double." As much as any single phenomenon, suburbia has enabled Americans to live as many of their nation's great writers advised: rooted in the natural and shaped by civilization's artifice.[147] Moreover, suburbia al-lowed Americans to combine the opposites of individualism and collec-tivism: they could live in individual homes while sharing one vast, collec-tive lawn.

The singular love affair that Americans have carried on with the auto-mobile also springs in some measure from their obsession with melding opposites. The automobile allowed urbanized Americans periodically to renew themselves in natural settings and thus to remain a people uniquely urban *and* rural.[148] The automobile also facilitated the return to nature by providing a place where cramped urbanites could release their passions in illicit sexual encounters. Even before the automobile, the Pullman sleeping car, according to lore, rivaled the ocean liner as the best place for "making it" with some acquaintance. Like the automobile, the train seemed to promise a miraculous coupling of opposites. Just possibly, moreover, Americans' romance with the Pullman car sprang, in part, from the fact that from its windows they could view in immediate juxtaposition such marvels of modern enterprise as bridges and deep cuts, viaducts, roadbeds, and signals, along with scenes of unsullied natural splendor. What is more, "every intersection of railroad and way represented a crossing of two kinds of space, one metropolitan and futurist in character, one essentially rural and traditional."[149] Railroad rights-of-way also symbolized the meeting of the right side and the wrong side of the tracks.

In the formative stages of what might be seen as a form of civil religion, Americans well-nigh venerated the figure who combined the gifts of In-dian savagery and Caucasian restraint, of nature's heedlessness and civiliza-tion's calculation. Such a figure was Daniel Boone, who alternately could be seen as the person who returned to nature and lived as an Indian and as the archetypal capitalist who conquered wilderness so that land companies could bring development and garner profits.[150] (See illustration 4.) At least one historian has perceived an attempt by Parson Mason Weems to trans-fer the Boone mantle to George Washington. While Weems stressed that our first president was a successful man of affairs, he also portrayed Wash-

4. George Caleb Bingham. *Daniel Boone Escorting Settlers Through the Cumberland Gap*. 1851. Oil on canvas, 36½ × 50¼″. Washington University Gallery of Art, St. Louis, Missouri.

As depicted here, Boone wears the expression of the land developer. Intent on conquering nature, he proceeds westward for profit, not for the rebirth-in-nature experience. Other Americans prefer a romanticized Boone, seeking escape from money-grubbing civilization.

ington in his hagiographic biography of 1800 as an explorer, hunter, warrior, and adopted Indian.[151]

Sam Houston seemed better fitted even than Washington for admission into civil religion's pantheon by dint of his combining of opposites. The first president of the Republic of Texas had lived with the Cherokee as a young man, demonstrating that the qualities of the red and the white man could harmoniously coalesce. But the most likely candidate for special exaltation by America's civil religion is Andrew Jackson. By background, Jackson could be seen as a "roaring, rollicking, game-cocking, horse-racing, card-playing, mischievous fellow."[152] Here was an uninhibited, close-to-nature man who shared the stereotyped qualities of the Indians and of the Latin Americans he successfully fought. Yet as president, Jackson learned to combine the ruthless energies and the rash determination of the natural man with the purpose and self-discipline of the natural aristocrat. Jackson himself saw as his special mission the combining of opposites. Early in his second term (1833) he announced his intention to preserve and exalt American civilization by restoring "to our institutions their primitive simplicity and purity," thereby "banishing those extraneous corrupting influences" that threatened to bring monopoly and hereditary, or unnatural, aristocracy.[153]

Just as the virtuous politician must channel primitive and simple drives toward attainment of lofty goals, so also the virtuous capitalist must devote savage energies to the pursuit of personal gain and, ostensibly, national progress: pursuits that could not succeed without primordial energies, but pursuits that simultaneously imposed restraint, control, and focus on instinctual drives. For the American businessman, then, even as for the politician, success lay in the marriage of opposites, in reconciling what seemed irreconcilable. Probably the contempt that Jackson felt for Latin Americans—a contempt shared by the majority of those Americans who fancied themselves self-made men—sprang partially from the perception that the savage Latin masses had not advanced to the stage at which men concerned themselves with economic gain and national progress. Meanwhile the Latin elites, heirs of privilege rendered effete by artificial refinement, seemed to eschew the uninhibited, manly pursuit of gain and relied instead on status and connections, graft, manipulation, and above all else, guile, so often characterized as a feminine trait. Thus the shortcomings of Latins originated in their attempt to keep wildness and refinement in separate spheres. For Jackson and his partisans, the United States faced the threat of what amounted to Latin Americanization. Spearheading that threat were America's sheltered, hereditary elites who saw in the Bank of the United States the means to perpetuate special privilege and artificial advantage. Jackson's successful war on the bank had overtones of a crusade against Latin American cultural flaws, as typically stereotyped by Americans.

In the very year that they celebrated their first centennial, Americans acquired a new semideity for their pantheon, this time a martyr. Just as much as Jackson, Gen. George Armstrong Custer combined opposites. A laid-back student at West Point who obeyed the whims of the moment and as nearly as possible eschewed self-restraint and discipline, Custer placed at the bottom of his graduating class. He did manage to produce a paper while at West Point that dealt primarily with Indians.[154] Many historians have concluded that the pro-Indian attitudes Custer expressed in his paper were insincere at worst, patronizing at best. Maybe not, though; maybe

Custer, in his own perennial skirmishes with the restraints demanded by civilization, felt drawn to the image of the Indian as the uninhibited child of nature. While he learned to be a stern disciplinarian of others, and even occasionally of himself, Custer nevertheless continued to manifest the uninhibited traits of the adolescent or the Indian—the two had much in common, so far as most nineteenth-century Americans were concerned. Throughout the late years of his career Custer continued to be known as the "Boy General"; and his initial successes as an Indian fighter sprang in part from his ability, even as with Boone, Washington, and Jackson, to employ something of the Indian's approach to warfare. Custer, like his illustrious predecessors, can be seen as combining the professionalism and genteel sensibilities of the military aristocrat with the hunter-warrior's affinity for wildness.

The very appointments in the frontier house where he lived for a time after the Civil War attest to Custer's personal penchant for mingling opposites. The rough house included a library where, as a friend observed, "Ruskin lay beside a revolver . . . where delicate lace curtains were held in place by antlers." Custer, according to the same friend, illustrated "in himself the anomaly of a hunter and literateur; an associate of savages and a patron of the arts." Finally, with his famous long hair, with cheeks ruddy as if rouged,[155] and with his undisguised impulsiveness, emotionalism, and petulance, Custer can be seen not only as Indian-like but also—in line with conventional stereotypes—as womanlike. He emerges, in short, as the paradigm of fused opposites, the hermaphrodite.

Unlike Latin Americans who have sometimes hailed actual race mixture as a means of producing a "cosmic race" that will subsume opposites, North Americans have generally insisted on cultural rather than biological mixing. Biological miscegenation they associated with inevitable retrogression, with debasement rather than invigoration of the civilized person's gifts. If American exceptionalism depended on an ongoing cultural fusion of civilized and natural beings, what happened when the supply of primitive Others dried up? Biological inbreeding might have led to products in which opposites came permanently together. But, when acceptable mixture was limited to the blending of cultures, then each new generation of civilized persons had to have available to it a vast reservoir of primitives with whom to interact. Without that reservoir, were Americans doomed to suffer the defects of unmitigated, unalloyed civilization?

Seeking to salvage old dreams, Americans toward the end of the nineteenth century began to wonder if they could not turn southward to compensate for the imminent demise of their own western frontier, with its natural supply of native primitives. Perhaps the resources to the south, of wilderness and primitives, were adequate to sustain the dreams through future generations.

Latin America Assumes Its Place in America's Fusion-of-Opposites Mythology

Even before envisioning the southward turn as the means to provide for ongoing national renewal, some American prophets had proclaimed that salvation lay in westward expansion beyond the American West. Whitman, for example, grew obsessed with passage-to-India mythology. Gazing toward India and the Orient, he thrilled to the prospect that Americans would "re-occupy for Western tenancy the oldest though ever-fresh fields, and reap from them the savage and sane nourishment indispensable to a hardy nation, and the absence of which, threatening to become worse and worse, is the most serious lack and defect to-day of our New World." [156]

For many Americans, the Orient was too far distant and too exotic. Easier to consummate, and just as promising as to issue, was the hemispheric, North-South marriage. It was to this prospect that, among a fair sprinkling of other American visionaries, artist Frederic Edwin Church (already mentioned in connection with his regeneration-in-nature faith) responded. Church's mystical leanings led him to construct, beginning in 1870, a palatial home he called Olana. The name may have been a corruption of an Arab word meaning "our place on high." Olana stood some 125 miles up the Hudson from New York City. [157] In its architecture, appointments, furnishings, and artwork, Church intended his home to symbolize the center of the world and to suggest the divine harmony that issues from the merging of opposites at a sacred center. Olana conveyed Church's vision of hemispheric redemption that would result from adding a North-South dimension to the East-West conjunction that Americans had experienced in their frontier, and that they would continue to realize as they penetrated the Orient in pursuit of the passage-to-India ideal. [158]

Some Americans looked on the Civil War as a great religious rite from which Americans would emerge reenergized, reborn through violence and bloodshed. In some ways wars and frontiers have always been interchangeable in American mythology (as Theodore Roosevelt demonstrated in his twin passions for wilderness and martial experience). However, Church found nothing in the War between the States to appeal to his mythical longing for national renewal. To him the war suggested that Americans might be ordinary mortals after all. In quest of images of hope meaningful to him, Church traveled far to the south, capturing on huge

5. Frederic Edwin Church. *Rainy Season in the Tropics*. 1866. Oil on canvas, 56 ¼ × 84 ¼". The Fine Arts Museums of San Francisco, Mildred Anna Williams Collection.

canvases some of the lush, sublime wilderness landscapes of Latin America, peopled if at all by only a few Indians here and there. (See illustrations 5 and 6.) Latin American wilderness and its primitive peoples (not the effete and overly refined aristocracy that had so disgusted Andrew Jackson) provided the new antithesis that American civilization required. The American hope of escaping the corruption and divisions of the Old World was still valid, Church seemed to tell viewers of his paintings; but it had to be reformulated so as to overflow continental confines and take on hemispheric proportions.[159] Church turned his artist's gaze northward as well. He delighted and excelled in painting icebergs. For him the arctic cold would fuse in the hemispheric synthesis with the Latin tropics. Americans were the fortunate beneficiaries of both sources of natural potency.

Like Church, William James, destined to become one of his country's greatest philosophers and one of its most interesting seekers after the extrasensory experiences that promised wholeness, found redeeming repositories of raw nature in Latin America as his country's Civil War came to an end. Traveling to Brazil in 1865 on a specimen-collecting expedition headed by naturalist Louis Agassiz, James waxed rhapsodic over the natu-

6. Frederic Edwin Church. *Cotopaxi*. 1862. Oil on canvas, 48 × 85″. The Detroit Institute of Arts, Founders Society Purchase with funds from Mr. and Mrs. Richard A. Manoogian, Robert H. Tannahill Foundation Fund, Gibbs-Williams Fund, Dexter M. Ferry, Jr. Fund, Merrill Fund and Beatrice W. Rogers Fund.

As pessimism gripped Church over his own country's descent into civil war, his fancy turned to the south. Southward, in the Latin regions, lay new sources of the pristine that could cleanse an errant civilization of its transgressions.

ral scene. The breathtaking brilliance of the Brazilian landscape, James wrote, "makes you admire the old gal Nature. . . . [H]ere she strikes such massive and stunning blows as to overwhelm the coarsest apprehension." Indeed, Brazil impressed James as the "original seat of the Garden of Eden." And Brazil had people to match its landscapes. In a letter home, James enthused not only over the lush mountains but also over the picturesque "Africans" in the streets. In the back country, the "savage inarticulate cries" of the people fit in appropriately with "the primordial incandescence of the landscape."[160] Like many an American painter of this era, James sensed that God had withdrawn from the Catskills and other national shrines that had once suggested divine immanence; in consequence, one "had to travel to further and more inaccessible places to hear His voice at all."[161] At about the time that James found traces of the Almighty's presence in Brazil, nature poet William Cullen Bryant (see illustration 3) discovered them in Mexico, with all its "panoramic glories" of a "new, natural world."[162]

By the latter part of the nineteenth century, even Americans who lacked Church's, James's, and Bryant's opportunities for personal observation came to accept that to their south lay gigantic preserves of sublime nature together with people of a piece with their primordial setting. As stereotypes concerning the precivilized estate of Latin Americans had originally developed, they were intended overwhelmingly as pejorative images, designed to document the inferiority of Latins, and this is the subject that primarily concerns me in the following chapter. However, by the late nineteenth century a smattering of Americans, among them some of the figures of highest cultural attainment, sensed that something had gone wrong with their civilization and that it required renewal. To them, the Latin American stereotyped as a primitive being became a figure fraught with hope. Thanks to the primitive, passionate, emotional, intuitive, heedless, childlike, effeminate Latin American, the civilized, restrained, rational, calculating, mature, masculine Yankee had some fair promise of being able to forge a hermaphrodite hemisphere. In the next century, this pattern more or less repeated itself. At least on two occasions (in the 1930s and the 1960s), American counterculturalists would turn southward (among other directions) in quest of the beneficent Other who would make Americans complete and revitalize their exceptionalism.

To the vast majority of late nineteenth-century Americans faced with the diminution of continental wilderness, only material considerations made Latin America begin to appear important. The area mattered because it held an abundance of virgin land and untapped resources, as well as a plenitude of people more like black than red natural men in that they could be disciplined into a subservient labor force. The virulence of the negative stereotypes that this breed of Americans applied to south-of-the-border people led them into the metaphysics not of Indian but of Latin American hating. The two forms of hating—or, at the very least, of disdaining—were, as this study will make increasingly clear, closely related.

CHAPTER 2

Wild People in Wild Lands: Early American Views of Latin Americans

Stereotyping the Other:
An Overview of Nature-and-Civilization Images

Since ancient times, groups or "races" arriving at some sense of identity or "peoplehood" have turned to nature-and-civilization imagery as the basis for stereotyping. To those beyond the pale of their own peoplehood, they have attached pejorative stereotypes. Often for the Western world's Christian people, the Jew became the reviled Other who somehow could not measure up to the standards required by civilization.[1] In the nineteenth century when unabashed anti-Semitism thrived among North Americans, Gentile native sons and daughters categorized newly arriving Jewish male immigrants as sneaky and conniving, resembling such denizens of the wild as weasels and foxes—the predators of wilderness or jungle rather than the noble and courageous killers. According to the stereotypes of American nativism, Jewish women were lascivious creatures of unbridled sexuality. In different ways, then, both Jewish men and women were dismissed as unredeemed creatures of nature.

The time finally came when Jews had the chance to avenge the decades and centuries in which they had suffered rejection as despicable Others. In the second half of the twentieth century, the Jews of Israel took to depicting Arab adversaries as "primitive and tribal," as brutal and bloodthirsty and less-than-human predators, as people who "don't respect reason," as emotional creatures easily incited and manipulated by monstrous leaders, as wily and cunning in battle but basically cowardly and not truly manly, as undisciplined, illogical, unable to distinguish between fact and fantasy, as threatening machos lusting after pure and refined Jewish women. On one hand, according to Jewish stereotypes, the Arab might benefit from contact with Israeli "civilization"; on the other, the Arab might be hopelessly refractory to civilization and therefore basically undeserving of full-scale human rights. In consequence, agents of progress could kill the Arab with impunity.[2]

Jewish stereotypes of Arabs resemble those that Americans attached to Negroes and also to the Indians and Latins who at one time ringed their borders and held the land that emissaries of civilization coveted, ostensibly because they alone understood how to improve that land and thereby fulfill the moral injunctions of the true religion. Indeed, Jewish stereotypes of the Arab bear striking similarity to those that virtually all colonialists have attached to colonials.

In approaching American stereotypes of the Latin American, what I wish to stress is their lack of originality. Human evil, it has been suggested, exhibits the traits of ordinariness, commonness, and banality; it is seldom unique and larger than life in its dimensions. With stereotypes, it is the same. Rather than reflecting original responses to unique situations, they have become part and parcel of day-in, day-out, humdrum existence; they are the ordinary creations of human nature at its most typical. With almost boring regularity they rest upon the distinction between what in the eyes of the would-be exploiters of other humans is the civilization of the former and the unmitigated naturalness (meaning savagery or barbarism) of the latter. Just as stereotypes become normal, routine, and taken for granted, so does the terrorism perpetrated in their name. Soon the terrorists become capable of remembering only those incidents that reinforce the stereotypes that in turn justify terrorism, and utterly incapable of heeding other instances that challenge the stereotypes and cast doubt on the moral acceptability of terrorism.

Stereotyping is by no means the exclusive habit of stronger groups that assert themselves in one way or another over weaker ones. Invariably, the weaker elements in asymmetrical relationships devise sweeping stereotypes with which to defame the stronger, not unlike the way some present-day Arabs distortedly depict the Jew. Similarly, in their generalized criticism of Americans during much of the past century and a half, Latin Americans have seemed blind to the fact that "differences in a population are often greater than the differences between populations."[3] By their stereotyping, Latin Americans have also confirmed that "the most prevalent form of racism in the world in recent decades has been anti-Americanism."[4]

Most especially, large numbers of Latin Americans, along with Africans set upon disparaging various nationalities of white imperialists, like to contrast their own spirituality and concern with "higher values" to the alleged cloddishness and calculating, cold-hearted materialism of the Caucasian Other. Throughout history, in fact, the tendency of underlings to contrast their spirituality with the base creatureliness of aggressors is just as much a constant as the imperialist's resort to contrasting his civilization to the colonial's primitivism. Someday, I trust, a comprehensive study will set forth the various facets of Latin American stereotyping of the North American. When it appears, the study will, I am confident, show that Latins have been just as bigoted, extreme, irrational, and self-serving in impugning the character of the gringo as North Americans have been in their collective character assassination of the generalized greaser. Undoubtedly it will also confirm that, as Mexico's grand old man of letters and Nobel laureate Octavio Paz has suggested, Latin Americans have been as divided in their assessments of norteamericanos as Yankees have been in their appraisals of the Latins with whom they share the hemisphere. According to Paz, his countrymen and their fellow Latin Americans feel an "unambivalent fascination" about the United States, "the enemy of our identity and the unavowed model of what we [want] to be."[5] It is ambivalence on both sides of the Rio Grande that has saved stereotyping in the Americas from sinking to the levels it has reached elsewhere.

Latin American elites frequently have sought to define themselves and to strengthen their own sense of identity and peoplehood by contrasting themselves to the negative identity imputed, most of the time, to North Americans. Before Yankee-baiting became the preferred method for establishing identity, Latin elites bolstered self-awareness by reviling the inhabitants of sister republics along their borders, with whom they frequently engaged in armed hostilities. Furthermore, elites nourished a racism that contributed to white and whitish upper-class cohesiveness by disparaging the dark-skinned masses (Indian, black, mestizo, and mulatto) that comprised a majority of the population in almost all republics. In justifying their own power status, Latin elites tended to use the same sort of civilization-barbarism stereotyping whereby North Americans contrasted themselves to allegedly inferior peoples. All the while Latin America's privileged sectors expected that North Americans would go along with local Latin customs that dictated perpetuation of a gulf between the *gente decente* (decent people) and the dusky masses.

Disappointed in expectations of acceptance as equals by North Americans, frustrated because all too often they were lumped together with the unwashed herd by insensitive gringos, Latin America's gente decente responded with anti-American stereotyping. Often the intensity of their anti-Americanism bore a direct relationship to the strength of their disdain for their own lower classes with whom, they felt, gringos tended to lump them. Needless to say the gente decente's anti-Americanism soared to new heights when, during the course of the twentieth century, various Americans (many of them the champions of blacks and Indians in their own country) began to side with the downtrodden elements of Latin society as they protested against ongoing exploitation.

Nineteenth-Century American Stereotyping of the Latin Other

Prior to the mid-nineteenth-century gold rush, early Anglo settlers in California, and even short-term visitors, distinguished between the cultured, gracious, hospitable ranch owners and the rabble. The prosperous *Californios* (original Hispanic occupants) they referred to as Spanish, and the ragged, dirty masses they designated Mexicans. [6] That this division had long-lasting consequences is suggested by what passed for a joke still in circulation in the 1990s. Question: When does a Mexican become a Spaniard? Answer: When he marries your daughter.

The Anglo ability to distinguish between worthies and unworthies, which initially delighted upper-sector Californios, fell victim to the huge influx of fortune-hunting immigrants arriving on the scene just as the second half of the nineteenth century began. Rough, tumultuous hordes of Anglo gold-seekers arrived in the region, and so did scruffy hordes of Latin American adventurers from as far away as Chile and Argentina. Before long the first group branded all those in the second (together with Orientals afflicted by gold fever) as wild and depraved. Next, the Anglos extended their pejorative evaluations to the old-line, property-owning Californios. All the more did these persons of substance cease to be Spanish and become Mexican when Anglos embarked upon wholesale procedures to strip them of their old political powers along with their property. To justify such stripping, racist stereotyping proved highly useful.

Lumping all Latin Americans together and tarring them with the same brush was not confined to America's roughneck elements. With notable exceptions, influential men of affairs and letters shared in the tendency to see all Latin Americans as little removed from barbarism. In his most widely read novel (*The Yemassee*, published in 1839) William Gilmore Simms, "the greatest story-teller the Old South produced,"[7] pontificated that when a higher race encountered a lower, the great danger was that the higher would sink to the level of the lower.[8] Southerners, and Americans in general, contrasting themselves to ordinary mortals, assumed that when *they* met inferior races they did not sink. But, when it came to Latin Americans, the civilized elites had clearly begun their descent into the surrounding morass of barbarism.

In his 1858 account of travels in Mexico, an American writer captured the prevailing mood of his countrymen when he criticized the upper classes for having succumbed to the "passionate and emotional" and "lighthearted" approach to life that also characterized the masses.[9] Nor did the social polish of Latin upper classes fool William Gilpin toward the end of the century. An enormously influential soldier, politician, visionary writer, and prophet par excellence of the Anglo American's mission to uplift the world, Gilpin had Latin America partially in mind when in 1890 he disparaged societies that had "grown to be polished and enervated without emerging from semi-savage barbarism."[10]

Emerson encapsulated the prevailing national wisdom of his age—and subsequent ages as well—when he declared: "All great men come out of the middle classes."[11] Already in the age of Emerson Americans had begun to conclude that the trouble with Latin America lay in the absence of a middle class. The area to their south seemed populated by profligate elites and a vast herd of rambunctious wastrels. Unlike their counterparts in Europe, members of an emergent U.S. middle class did not have to struggle against an established aristocracy or fret over the risks posed by a large marginalized class.[12] But, they shared the antiaristocratic bias and also the suspiciousness of shiftless lower classes that characterized Europe's rising bourgeoisie. This bias and suspiciousness inevitably poisoned their attitudes toward the sort of people who, in their imagination at least, populated Latin America.

Above all, American middle-class men esteemed the so-called manly qualities, as opposed to feminine weakness and emotionalism and childish fecklessness and fantasizing. Qualities that Americans admired, they consistently failed to find among Latin Americans. The appraisals that led a mid-twentieth-century U.S. diplomat to dismiss Dominicans already flourished at least a century earlier in the attitudes of Americans toward Latin Americans in general. "The longer you worked with Dominicans, the more you . . . disliked the weakness of the men, and, searching for explanations, you noticed how pampered are the infant males in Dominican families, how undisciplined the schoolboy males, how feckless the teenage males, and how vain and proud and sometimes absurd the adult males. They were not men, many of them, only spoiled brats grown up."[13] Even some Latin Americans have concurred in the gringo diplomat's appraisal and have applied it more broadly than just to Dominicans. I remember an ambitious, upwardly mobile Venezuelan student whom I knew in the mid-1960s. He assured me that the pampered permissiveness in which upper-class male children were raised in his country turned them into weak, self-indulgent, effeminate *animalitos* (little animals).[14]

About the time of the American Revolution, Patrick Henry, "with wonder in his voice," proclaimed to an audience: "We are in a state of nature."[15] If Americans had started in a state of nature, already in the early nineteenth century they had begun to take inordinate pride in overcoming and defying nature. Even their democracy, which had become the object of their smug satisfaction, seemed to attest to their ability to triumph over nature; for many Americans, among them Edgar Allan Poe, recognized that democracy, being a "system nowhere observable in nature,"[16] emerged only out of the ability to transcend nature. Latin Americans, in contrast, seemed incapable of progressing toward democracy or anything else worthwhile precisely because they simply could not get the upper hand over nature—either within or without.

An observer in California in 1848, shortly before it became a part of the United States, saw only an indolent Hispanic and Indian people. In California, he averred, "Nature [was] doing everything, man [was] doing nothing." One year later another American commented on the widespread conviction among his countrymen that Californios grew "as the trees, with the form and character that Nature gives them." About a decade later, a U.S. traveler to Brazil noted that there "nature has done everything, . . . but as yet man has done next to nothing."[17] So, while Americans had started in but shortly emerged out of a state of nature, Latin Americans remained in the original state.

The first Latin Americans that significant numbers of Americans encountered resided in territory that ultimately became a part of the United States—among them the already-mentioned Californios. Historian Francis Parkman when engaged in research for his classic study *The Oregon Trail* (1849) encountered a group of Mexicans from New Mexico on the banks of the Missouri River. Here is how he describes the scene: "On the muddy shore stood some thirty or forty dark, slavish-looking Spaniards, gazing stupidly out from beneath their broad hats." Crossing the river, he encountered a boat in which "the rowers, swarthy, ignoble Mexicans, turned their brutish faces upwards to look, as I reached the bank." A while later, Parkman came upon some "squalid Mexicans, with their broad hats, and their vile faces overgrown with hair." About the time Parkman encountered the Hispanic occupants of New Mexico, who obviously impressed him as animal-like, fur trapper Rufus Sage visited Taos. Here is his impression of its Mexican residents: "There are no people on the whole continent of America, whether civilized or uncivilized, with one or two exceptions, more miserable in condition or despicable in morals than the mongrel race inhabiting New Mexico." Another trapper found the Mexicans in his part of the country "depraved, indolent, untrustworthy, dishonest, cowardly, servile, ignorant, superstitious, and dirty"—among other undesirable traits. An American army officer on duty in the Texas–New Mexico region believed that the Indians he encountered were actually superior to the Mexicans. These latter, allegedly, "were content if they could satisfy their animal wants."[18]

The French-born Jean-Baptiste Lamy, appointed first as bishop (1853) and later as archbishop (1875) of Santa Fe (on whose life Willa Cather based her enduringly popular novel *Death Comes for the Archbishop* [1927]), inclined sympathetically toward his Mexican-origin wards, in a paternalistic and condescending way. Toward the end of his life, though, even he revealed certain prejudices common among native-born Americans. "Our Mexican population," he wrote, "has quite a sad future. Very few of them will be able to follow modern progress. They cannot be compared to the Americans in the way of intellectual liveliness, ordinary skills, and industry. . . . The morals, manners, and customs of our unfortunate people are quite different from those of Americans." He concluded that men of progressive spirit would have trouble understanding the spirit of "our Mexican population," for it "is almost too primitive."[19]

A traveler from Connecticut who journeyed through Texas in the mid-1850s concluded that his countrymen would find it difficult "to harmoniously associate with the bigoted, childish, and passionate Mexicans" who comprised a good part of the state's populace.[20] Reporting on the California scene in the early years after the gold rush, an editorial writer for the *National Intelligencer* assured his readers that the Hispanic portion of the inhabitants "are a thieving, cowardly, dancing, lewd people, and generally indolent and faithless." Another witness to life in California at this time commented on the coarseness and lasciviousness of the Mexicans as well as their "degraded tone of manners." A generation or so later, even the tolerant, Californian Josiah Royce (1855–1916), who gained renown as a Harvard professor of philosophy, described his native state's Spanish Americans as "an essentially amoral and childlike people" who could scarcely be held morally accountable for their actions.[21]

When Americans began to arrive in some number in Mexico during the latter part of the nineteenth century, many felt compelled to scale the heights of Popocatépetl. "Climbing and trekking became a kind of mania among them. Hardly would a party return with stories of its climb up Popo, before another individual reported the exploits of his party's climb." Scaling Popo became for Americans a way to manifest their concern for physical fitness, a concern that rested on the values of self-control and of the muscular Christianity by then deeply embedded in Anglo American culture. At the same time, the American mania for conquering Popocatépetl served as a reproach to Mexicans, who showed absolutely no interest in this pastime because they had no cult of muscular Christianity and evidenced scant concern for physical fitness as an end in itself.[22] People without interest in disciplining their own bodies so as to be able to assert human mastery over nature lacked, so far as the American climbers were concerned, the basic prerequisites of civilization.

The relatively few Americans who journeyed farther south than Mexico in the nineteenth century often found little more to praise than their compatriots who had encountered the Latins of Mexico or the American Southwest. To many of the women who accompanied the Forty-Niners as they made their way to California across Panama's isthmus, Panamanians were swarthy-visaged, often half-naked racial mongrels, as repulsive in their features as in their actions. When in the proximity of the natives' stench, women had to hold their noses and keep cologne handy. According to one lady traveler, "the natives were so impetuous and excitable that it was almost impossible to do anything with them." Their customary "tempestuousness was further aggravated by their tendency to drink, gamble, and fight," another lady averred. These judgments were rendered in 1849 and 1850. A few years later, in 1856, some other women made the Panama crossing and to their enormous relief discovered that safety was now assured "by a sizeable contingent of U.S. Marines. Like the U.S. Cavalry stationed throughout the American West, these Marines guarded the intrusive immigrants from the . . . native people."[23] Thus were Panamanians equated with the "savage" Indian tribes of North America whose animality could be kept in check only through Uncle Sam's organized military might.

Those Americans who ventured still farther south generally recorded impressions of the natives no more flattering than those of travelers in Mexico or Central America. U.S. naval officers charged with defending their country's neutral rights during the Latin American struggle for independence from Spain and Portugal (1810–1824) often sailed as far south as Chile and Peru. What impressed them most was the pervasive lawlessness, the disregard for personal property rights, the venality of public officials, and the evasion of financial obligations by virtually all the natives. Naval officers also expressed disgust for the pagan superstitions that allegedly characterized the local practice of religion. Latins could also strike the American observer as intellectually underdeveloped. Typically, a U.S. minister resident to the Republic of Ecuador commented on the beauty of upper-class women, who seemed largely free from the taint of race mixture. But, even among these females, the minister complained, "faces very generally lack the expression which intellectuality alone can give."[24]

What Americans thought of Latin American men could be even more unflattering, as some of the material already presented indicates. What lay at the heart of the trouble with Latin American males as perceived by the gringo? Perhaps F. Scott Fitzgerald without intending to hints at an answer in his marvelous 1920 short story, "The Ice Palace." Fitzgerald deals directly here with some of the cultural differences that led to a virtually unbridgeable gulf between North and South within the United States. In some ways, though, his probing of attitudes is just as applicable to the chasm between Americans and Latin Americans. At one point in the story Harry, the northerner, shocks the southerner Sally Carroll, to whom he is at the time affianced, when he says: "I'm sorry, dear . . . , but you know what I think of them [southern men]. They're sort of—sort of degenerates. . . . They've lived so long down there with all the colored people that they've gotten lazy and shiftless." [25]

Up to now I have used the scattergun approach in pointing to evidence of North American disdain for the Latin American, owing to the latter's alleged stagnation in a state of nature. Next (and there will be some overlapping here), I focus on some of the specific traits that purportedly attested to the Latin American's incompatibility with civilization.

Sex and Alcohol, and Latin American Primitivism

For Victorian-age Americans, middle-class respectability came increasingly to be associated with control over the sexuality that aristocrats and riffraff alike ostensibly indulged all too freely. Sublimation of sexual desire emerged as the hallmark of bourgeois civilization, whereas sexual abandon became the sure indication of atavism.[26] In his 1906 book *The Future in America*, English writer H. G. Wells cast his eyes overseas and found many qualities to admire in Americans. They had, he opined, shaped "an intensely moral land" by curbing all lusts save one, the lust of acquisition.[27] In an era of industrial revolution and some of the most dramatic conquests over nature and its resources in all the annals of history, it seemed fitting, at least to self-admiring Americans, that by their very lust for acquisition they could tame all other lusts.

Control over the libido was by no means a new quest for Americans when they enlisted in its cause in the nineteenth century. Some truth inheres in the popular image of seventeenth-century Puritan attitudes toward sexuality. For example, Puritans did indeed arrest, fine, and even whip married couples whose first child had arrived too soon. If anything, though, concern with mastering sexual excesses had sharpened by the mid–nineteenth century as the remnants of Calvinist fatalism gave way to entrepreneurial faith in the self-made man whose self-control would yield treasure in this life and the next. Just as Americans became obsessive about improving the body so as to guarantee physical health, so they turned relentlessly to self-discipline as a means to economic and spiritual well-being. For many of them, at least to judge by their words, sexual self-control seemed the source of every other form of self-control.

Among men's and women's reform societies appearing early in the nineteenth century were those dedicated to seeking "social regeneration through sexual purification." The women's societies might seem especially hostile "to the licentious and predatory male,"[28] but men could sometimes be as zealous as women reformers in seeking to banish licentious conduct. Indeed, manliness came to be associated with sexual self-control. Theodore Roosevelt was by no means unusual in priding himself on an abundance of both virtues. Honoring manliness in himself and others, Roosevelt also exulted in his sexual continence. "Thank Heaven, I am at least perfectly pure," Roosevelt confided to his diary in 1878 when at the age of twenty he speculated on a future wife. "Two years later, by then engaged, he again 'thanked Heaven' and rejoiced that he could tell his fiancée 'everything I have ever done.'"[29]

For the businessmen intent upon building America's economic foundations, thrift seemed a cardinal virtue; and thrift meant establishing strict control over spending—both dollars and sperm. Economic and sexual self-control, ostensibly, went hand in hand. Roosevelt, with the patrician's contempt for the businessman, saw national strength and grandeur in far more than economic criteria. Just as much as with the businessman, though, Roosevelt's goals—including the military strength and the requisite power to discipline and uplift pauper classes and nations—demanded the kind of manliness and virility equated with stoic self-control, cold showers, and the stiff upper lip. Very possibly the more Americans proved incapable of living by the standards of continence, the more they reviled the Others who did not pay even lip service to the ideal and overtly indulged in "loose" life-styles.

Nineteenth-century defenders of American middle-class respectability assumed that excess spending of male sperm was bad both for the nation's economy and its morality. Beyond that, excessive sexual activity whether channeled into intercourse or masturbation resulted in race degeneracy, a gradual sinking into weakness, effeminacy, and—ultimately—barbarism. The antisex crusader Anthony Comstock (1844–1915) staunchly opposed birth control because it would encourage lust, which he saw as the basis of most evils that beset society. "Lust defiles the body, debauches the imagination, corrupts the mind, deadens the will, destroys the memory, sears the conscience, hardens the heart, and damns the soul." Impure and libidinous acts and even thoughts "unnerve the arm, and steal away the elastic step"; they "create rakes and libertines in society—skeletons in many a household. The family is polluted, home desecrated, and each generation born into the world is more and more cursed by the inherited weakness, the harvest of this seed-sowing."

John Harvey Kellogg (1852–1943), who eventually founded the food company that bears his name, agreed on all counts with Comstock, as did Sylvester Graham (1794–1851), whose name would be attached to a highly popular cracker. Both Kellogg and Graham sought to devise foods and diets for Americans that would curb the sexual appetite. According to Kellogg, "the reproductive act is the most exhausting of all vital acts. Its effect upon the undeveloped person is to retard growth, weaken the constitution, and dwarf the intellect."[30] To Kellogg's litany of sexuality's evils, Graham added this wisdom: "It were better for you not to exceed in the [annual] frequency of your [sexual] indulgences the number of months in the year; and you cannot exceed the number of weeks in the year, without impairing your constitutional powers, shortening your lives, and increasing your liability to disease and suffering; if indeed, you do not thereby actually induce disease of the worst and most painful kind; and at the same time transmit to your offspring an impaired constitution, with strong and unhappy predispositions." Graham concluded that by abusing the sex organs through overindulgence of "instinctive appetites," man became "a living volcano of unclean propensities and passions. . . . [H]e sinks himself in degeneracy, below the brutes."[31]

As they concerned themselves with stamping out sexual excesses among the male members of respectable, middle-class society,[32] Americans also worried about the sexuality of women. Frequently both women and men bandied about notions of the moral superiority of women. Invariably, the morally superior woman was a Madonna rather than an Eve, one who took no pleasure in the sexual act and accepted it only as a duty that must be stoically fulfilled in order to speed the propagation of society's better elements. Sometimes male obstetricians even intervened surgically to guarantee woman's indifference to sex by assaulting the clitoris. And, in fortifying both men and women psychologically against temptations of the flesh, conjuring up the unwholesome, sensuous Other proved helpful, or at least so it was assumed.

Nineteenth-century European imperialists divided humanity "into an Occident and an Orient, the latter being the sphere" of illicit sex and "fleshly delights."[33] Europeans also divided the world into North and South spheres. Far to the south lay Africans, oversexed and not fully human; less far southward resided the Spaniards, Portuguese, and Italians, worthier than Africans but vitiated by their propensity for "unmanly" conduct.[34] Americans tended to place the libidinous Other either in the West (Indians, Latin Americans, and the debauched elements of white society) or in the South. Within their own country, the South was home not only to the mythically lustful black but to sexually uninhibited white upperclass males as well as profligate white trash. Especially as the tide of abolitionist fervor rose, northerners eroticized the entire South,[35] picturing it as one "great brothel."[36] Southern males, whether black, white upper-class, or white lower-class, afforded proof that "man reduced to a pure state of nature is not a Noble Savage but a neolithic satyr." Early in the twentieth century novelist Upton Sinclair, an antisouthern southerner and a sexual prude, still chose to depict the plantation of the slavery era, and even later, as a "house of shame, where black, half-naked girls, most of them harlots at heart, competed for sexual favors from the master (or anyone else readily available) and generally became pregnant by the time they reached age fifteen."[37] In far less prudish manner, Mississippi's consummately great novelist William Faulkner developed this theme in such books as his 1936 classic *Absalom, Absalom!*

For many American northerners, the South lay also south of the border. The Other who occupied this South belonged both to morally dissolute classes (aristocracy and dependent peons) and to an inferior race. Both class and race shaped the Latin southerner as a lustful creature whose lifestyle challenged the accepted values of decent classes and races. As with Upton Sinclair's South, the Latin American South was dotted with plantation houses of shame where seminaked, dark-skinned sluts pranced about and competed for the honor of satisfying the master classes' animalistic urges. Corruption of this sort served to justify Americans in their imperialist designs on Latin America, just as Europeans found moral sanction for imperialism in the Dark Continent by envisioning Africans as creatures of unmitigated savagery and licentiousness,[38] the two qualities being inseparable.

After spending some time in Latin America in the early 1890s, an American writer remarked that the Anglo Saxon "is a monogamous animal, while at any given moment the Latin's horizon is apt to be occupied by a petticoat or a succession of petticoats."[39] In this instance, the writer dealt light-heartedly with character blemishes that had provoked stuffy self-righteousness from earlier observers of Latin American sexual mores. Here are the words that the author of an 1838 romance put in the mouth of a Texan addressing a Mexican army captain: "In point of chastity, . . . the most important and influential qualification of Northern nations, we are infinitely superior to you—Lust is, with us, hateful and shameful; for you, it is a matter of indifference. *This* is the chief curse of the South; the leprosy which unnerves both body and mind. It is what caused the Roman empire to sink. . . . The Southern races must be renewed and the United States are the *officina gentium* for the new Continent."[40]

Josiah Gregg (1806–1850), a nine-year resident in Mexico and author of the classic account of the early Santa Fe trade, sympathized with certain aspects of the culture he discovered south of the border; but he professed outrage at the pervasive licentiousness. For Mexicans, he charged, "the institution of marriage changes the legal rights of the parties, but it scarcely affects their moral obligations. It is looked upon as a convenient cloak for irregularities." In his 1857 book *El Gringo,* W. W. H. Davis registered full accord with Gregg. Among Mexicans, he averred, marriage served "as a cloak to hide numerous irregularities" engaged in by both partners. While married men "support a wife and mistress at the same time," Davis added, "too frequently the wife also has her male friend." In Davis's estimation, three-quarters of the married population among Mexicans went in for adultery.[41]

In trying to account for alleged lack of sexual restraint among Latin Americans, Americans sometimes drew on their knowledge of Indian culture. The "fact" that Indians conducted themselves like "brute beasts," flaunted the ties and obligations of marriage, and gave free rein to sexual appetites originated, according to some Caucasian Americans, in aboriginal child-rearing practices, especially the custom of "allowing the wild freedom and nudity of children." This custom not only gave rise to sexual abandon as children matured but also induced generalized social disorder and undermined respect for all restraint.[42] In general, Americans took the nudity of Indians as sure proof that they were barbaric, and the pawns of their passions.[43] A similar line of reasoning consigned Latin Americans to barbarism.

In a book he published in 1838, a Yankee traveler to Colombia registered shock over the fact that children, especially of the abundant poor classes, ran about naked. Susan Shelby Magoffin traveled the Santa Fe Trail in the 1840s and also spent some time in northern Mexico. An intelligent and tolerant observer, she responded positively to many aspects of Mexican culture, observing at one point: "What a polite people these Mexicans are, altho' they are looked upon as a half barbarous set by the generality of [American] people." Nevertheless, she found it "repulsive to see the children running about perfectly naked." Nor could she calmly accept the state of nudity or near nudity in which women casually allowed themselves to be seen. She found it "truly shocking to my modesty" to encounter such sights while in the company of gentlemen and noted: "I am constrained to keep my veil drawn tightly over my face all the time to protect my blushes."[44] Set against the prevailing standards of her time, Magoffin's comments are significant. As noted in the preceding chapter, nineteenth-century values in America equated modesty with culture, civilization, and Christianity. Those who lacked modesty, allegedly, had attained the moral development only of children.

Certain men, of course, especially those of "low social station," might respond with frank fascination to the Latina's casualness toward nudity. At the outset of the Mexican War in 1846 when Gen. Zachary Taylor's army arrived on the Rio Grande, the soldiers realized at once "that the Mexican women were different. Standing on the river bank in early morning or evening, they gaped as the young women of Matamoros came down to the river, disrobed without hesitation or embarrassment, and plunged into the stream." Later on during the war one soldier observed of Mexican women: "Nearly all of them have well-developed, magnificent figures . . . [and] dress with as little clothing as you can well fancy." A "sharp-eyed Indianan" noted of the Mexican women: "Their bosoms were not compressed in stays . . . but heaved freely under the healthful influence of the genial sun and balmy air of the sunny south."[45] Here were attractions indeed, but probably many an American soldier assured himself he would not want to marry one of these natural and uninhibited women, especially given the often-remarked tendency of Mexican and Latin women in general to surrender to obesity well before middle age—a reminder of the unpleasant consequences that befell women who let themselves go.

Some American male observers of Latin women liked nothing of what they saw. Gilbert Haven, an American preacher who spent a winter in Mexico in the 1850s, found the women, especially of the lower classes, ugly, their physical features reflecting their debauched morals. One explanation as to why most women remained single was the fee the clergy charged to administer the wedding rites. The underlying explanation, though, according to Haven, was that debauchery and fornication resided "in their blood. There was no seeming sense of shame . . . , no modesty."[46]

An American geologist visiting Cuba and Puerto Rico in 1898 noted that the women had little regard for marriage, and this accounted for the fact that 40 percent of all births were illegitimate.[47] He did not blame the situation so much on the basic immorality of the Caribbean women as on the worthlessness of the men: what right-thinking woman would accept marriage to one of them? Still the notion that debauchery and fornication lived in the blood of Latin American women persisted. Indeed, the image of Latin America as one extended brothel seemed deeply engraved in the minds of many Americans. In the 1850s an American official wrote that standards of female chastity were deplorably low among the Mexican populace of New Mexico, where "the virtuous are far outnumbered by the vicious. Prostitution is carried out to a fearful extent; and it is quite common for parents to sell their daughters for money to gratify the lust of the purchaser." Both in New Mexico and Mexico, American soldiers seemed to believe that the majority of women were "primarily prostitutes."[48]

Early in the twentieth century women members of some forty interdenominational missionary societies felt a special need to convert Latin American women to Protestantism so as to rescue them from the prevailingly low standards of morality that led so many to take to prostitution. And, when the white-slave panic "reached its unaccountably hysterical peak in . . . 1913," the common assumption was that an American girl who disappeared (injected by the needle of some white-slave trafficker) "would wake up, helpless, in the brothels of Rio or Constantinople."[49] Thus were Latin Americans and Turks lumped together as the worst offenders against sexual purity.

While some stereotypes may have remained constant, others have changed. No longer prevalent is the nineteenth-century conviction that smoking indicated a woman's uninhibited sexuality and probably her ready availability. Many a nineteenth-century American who traveled south of the border registered amazement not only at female immodesty but at the fact that women of all classes smoked—publicly and unabashedly. In appraising women, American males tended to agree with John Harvey Kellogg's assessment that smokers were likely to be addicted to sexual practices "still more filthy." A Yankee visitor to Colombia in the 1830s took female smoking as a sure indication of lack of willpower: if addicted to nicotine, it followed they were addicted to depravity in general. A woman visitor to Chile in the 1860s recorded her disgust not only with female but also male use of tobacco. The fact that Chilean men smoked provided a tip-off as to their "loose . . . notions of morality."[50]

Even in the 1920s, Americans still tended to associate female smoking with illicit boudoir encounters. The *New York Times* editorialized in 1925 that whenever "the average sort of chap first saw a woman smoke he knew very well what he felt about her." As late as the 1930s and 1940s, although female smoking had by then become far more acceptable, American tobacco industry advertising specialized in images of sexy females, often in low-cut, provocative attire with a phallic-symbol cigarette either in the mouth or caressingly fondled by long and elegant fingers.[51]

American males were not unique in being, until comparatively recent times, titillated by cigarette- or cigar-smoking women. The "dirty postcards" of the early twentieth century that French males liked to collect in their North African colonies featured obviously available women, bare-breasted and invariably with a cigarette in hand or mouth.[52] Just as the prostitutes of Rio and Constantinople seemed linked in the public fancy, so were the Latin American and North African women, products respectively of popish and Islamic depravity.

Together with uninhibited sexuality and free indulgence in nicotine, excessive use of spices and condiments, of caffeine and chocolate struck many nineteenth-century North Americans as indicators of moral depravity bordering on barbarism.[53] The "stimulant," though, that produced by far the worst effects on character and that undermined all of civilization's restraints when used to excess was alcohol. By what Americans believed to be pervasive alcohol addiction, Latin Americans dulled their intellectual capacity, loosened restraints on passions and instincts, and dropped out of the march toward progress. Americans themselves when their Republic was young had succumbed to alcohol addiction at an uncommonly high rate. Unlike Latin Americans, however, Americans liked to believe that they, or at least the decent elements among them, had overcome an addiction that consigned its sufferers to a state of nature.

Between the Revolution through which they gained independence and approximately the first quarter of the nineteenth century, American per capita consumption of alcohol registered an all-time high, as W. R. Rorabaugh documents in his book *The Alcoholic Republic*. Since then, consumption per capita has never come close to matching the early, heroic proportions of alcoholic intake. Helping to curb alcohol consumption was the rise of middle-class values of respectability. Increasingly, abstemiousness in drinking habits emerged as the recognized prerequisite for the "self-command, prudence and fortitude, and a strict control of the passions and appetites . . . [required] to maintain the empire of reason over sense."[54] Freedom itself demanded the constant exercise of self-control through which humans liberated themselves from animalistic impulses. Out of self-denial issued independence, both from sin and from economic want.

By 1831, Rorabaugh has discovered, "the American Temperance Society reported more than 2,200 local organizations with more than 170,000 members; in 1834, 7,000 groups with 1,250,000 members."[55] Together with men's and especially women's reform societies, Protestant ministers spearheaded the temperance movement, persuaded that salvation, and with it economic success, came only to those who withstood the temptations of demon rum. In the combined secular-religious campaign against alcohol abuse, Americans could draw cautionary tales from the experience of Native Americans. By their inability to withstand the temptations of alcohol, these children of nature blighted whatever potential they might once have had to advance to the civilized state. Chingachgook, Cooper's once noble red man of the Leatherstocking Tales, came in his besotted old age to embody for Americans of the respectable classes a frightening symbol of decadence.

Increasingly satisfied that ability to curb the intake of spirits evidenced not only religious but also social and even racial superiority, Americans grew increasingly censorious as they became acquainted with Latin American drinking habits—real and imagined; and remember that for most Americans initial contacts with Latin Americans got under way just as the zeal for temperance asserted itself in the northern republic. Americans who observed Mexicans in Texas, New Mexico, and California in the first half of the nineteenth century invariably commented on their addiction to drink—an addiction that men and women allegedly shared equally.[56] Among the many Americans complaining about drunkenness as they crossed the border into Mexico itself was artist Thomas Moran. The natives delighted in filling themselves with pulque, and the more they drank, he complained, the more they voiced anti-American sentiments—sentiments that they emphasized by vulgar gestures. The same minister resident in Ecuador quoted earlier as he complained about the lack of intellectuality in the expression of upper-class women, attributed to alcoholism the "ugly, stupid, simpering look" that distinguished the country's Indian women. With utmost distaste, he observed that "the ruling passion of Indian women and men for drink" led them to "bacchanalian orgies." An American traveler who made it all the way to isolated Paraguay toward the end of the nineteenth century commented on the lack of ambition that characterized its inhabitants. It did not occur to them to improve their circumstances, for with a bit of food, ample liquor, and "some cigars to smoke all day," they had all they wanted of life. An earlier traveler had scorned Bolivians, in part because of their drinking habits and addiction to coca-leaf chewing, but he had found the Chileans more to his liking. Perhaps because of the prevalence of white blood among them, he surmised, they seemed relatively free from alcohol addiction.[57]

Few Americans traveled to Latin America, or even to the Hispanic Southwest. For impressions of their Latin neighbors, most Americans relied largely on travel accounts published by their more adventurous or wealthier compatriots. From these accounts they gleaned the impression that Latin Americans were largely Indian in racial composition and overwhelmingly in thrall to alcoholic spirits—even as North America's "savages." What is more, they learned from censorious travelers that the Catholic church, instead of fighting demon rum, as did North America's

Protestant denominations, actually encouraged alcohol consumption as a means of honoring innumerable saints on their feast days—a point I return to toward the end of this chapter. The expression "Rum, Romanism, and Rebellion," coined by a Protestant clergyman during the political campaign of 1884, cast aspersions on the character of Irish Americans. But long before the Irish issue entered U.S. politics, many Americans had concluded that the true lair of rum and Romanism (or pulque and popishness) lay in South America, and that these two devilish forces contributed to another curse—chronic rebellion. The unholy trinity's power pretty much proved that Latin Americans were refractory to civilization.

Anger and Passion, Rebelliousness and Anarchy: More Symptoms of Latin American Primitiveness

Along with temperance both in sexual and drinking habits, Americans by the early nineteenth century had decided that middle-class respectability required strict control over anger. From the "relative unconcern with anger per se" that often typified the colonial period, Americans developed an "increasing insistence that emotion be demoted and reproved." In this mood, they embarked on a "long and complicated war against anger." They accepted the need to avoid falling under "the tyrannical sway of . . . animal propensity," lest they weaken the underlying principles of civilized life. Increasingly those who took charge of establishing the morality suitable to democratic, enterprising people condemned emotional outbursts as the badge of the child and of inferior classes. Uncontrolled temper evidenced not only "grossness of mind," but might even suggest diabolical influences. Beyond all of this, temper tantrums, together with such displays of emotion as frequent weeping and boisterous outbursts of joy, earned contempt as the habits of primitive, medieval, premodern societies.[58]

Every age, it seems, requires its "wild men" whose evil example must be abjured by the righteous, and onto whom the virtuous may project their troubling and sinful inclinations. "Medieval, like ancient Roman, thinkers conceived barbarians and wild men to be enslaved to nature, . . . unable to control their passions," to be chaotic and "incapable of self-discipline, and of sustained labor; to be passionate, bewildered, and hostile to 'normal' humanity." Even from Biblical times, what is more, "the notion of the Wild Man was associated with the idea of wilderness—the desert, forest, jungle, and mountains"—in short, with frontier regions such as Americans tamed in their own continental confines and such as they might eventually have to tame in Latin America, their frontier for the future. Increasingly as the nineteenth century advanced, and in spite of the countervailing tendencies of Romanticism and transcendentalism, "primitive man," more mythical than real, came to be seen "as an example of arrested humanity, as that part of the species which had failed to raise itself above dependency upon nature, as atavism, as that from which civilized man, thanks to science, industry, Christianity, and racial excellence, had finally (and definitively) raised himself."[59]

While exceptions certainly existed, most Americans who expressed themselves on the matter found the "wild man" to their south repellent in many ways. In a moment when his patience had been tried especially hard by the Mexicans from whom he sought recognition of his newly established colony in Texas, Stephen F. Austin observed, "To be candid the majority of the people of the whole [Mexican] nation as far as I have seen them want nothing but tails to be more brutes than Apes." Another observer of Mexicans in the first half of the nineteenth century found them "childish and passionate."[60] A traveler in Central America noted that a Guatemalan strongman probably could not fulfill his good intentions to benefit his people because, like those he ruled, he was "the slave of violent passions."[61] Even a twentieth-century poet sympathetic to Hispanic culture traded on stereotypes of passion, temper, and cruelty. Consider these four lines from Witter Bynner's 1930 poem "Volcano":

> how eyes that were laughing
> can go suddenly hot with lava, like Garifo's—
> Who had to leave Chapala for a while
> Because there was too much fire in his knife.[62]

Volatile and quarrelsome were the words most used by American naturalists, embarked on specimen-gathering expeditions to Latin America in the nineteenth and early twentieth centuries, to describe the people they encountered. These words found their way into the accounts even of Americans who considered the Latins rather nice in most ways.[63] A century or so later, Senator Jesse Helms (R., N.C.) gave voice to the common wisdom that still prevailed in the 1980s when he observed, with obvious distaste, "All Latins are volatile people."[64]

In the two great heroes who emerged respectively out of their own independence struggle and that waged by Latin Americans, nineteenth-century Americans had already found mythic-proportioned exemplars of incompatible ways of life. One hero symbolized dignity, modesty, perfect gentlemanliness, serenity, grandeur, gravity, loftiness, and also "a strong passion controlled by deliberate reason."[65] This hero, of course, was

WASHINGTON'S FAREWELL TO THE OFFICERS OF HIS ARMY.

At the old Tavern, corner Broad and Pearl Sts. New York, Dec. 4th 1783.

Entering the Room where they were awaiting him, Washington said,"With a heart full of love and gratitude I now take leave of you." Knox turned and grasped his hand, and while tears flowed from the eyes of both, the Commander-in-chief kissed him; this he did to each of his Officers. The scene was one of great tenderness. Weston's Life of Washington

7. Nathaniel Currier. *Washington Taking Leave of the Officers of His Army at Francis's Tavern, Broad Street, New York, Dec. 4th, 1783.* 1848. Lithograph. The Harry T. Peters Collection, Museum of the City of New York.

Announcing his withdrawal from public life, Washington toasts his officers. When the Currier and Ives firm reissued the lithograph in 1876 the temperance movement had gained momentum and in deference to it all signs of alcoholic spirits were removed.

George Washington, whose acquired control over temper, conceded to be at one time his worst personality flaw, moralists saw as his greatest personal triumph. Commendable also was the fact that Washington, like Cincinnatus, sought to discard power after his military triumphs (see illustration 7); but the will of the people joined to his own sense of duty forced him back into public service. Soon he proved as adept at nation building as he had been at waging revolution. Moreover, even while serving the nation he kept an attentive managerial eye on his own affairs, leaving behind a tidily organized, well-administered estate. This was George Washington, hero par excellence for Americans. And then there was Simón Bolívar

(1783–1830), the mercurial revolutionary who helped free his continent. Once the fighting ended, he avidly, passionately sought virtually unchecked political power. But he proved as woefully inept in nation building as in husbanding his personal resources. Remember, I am dealing only with American perceptions of truth, not necessarily the truth itself.

Parson Weems, as noted in the first chapter, depicted the young, Indian-fighting Washington as Indian-like himself.[66] Subsequently, however, Washington had matured and outgrown his Indian or wild-man state—or at least he contrived to wed primitivism's vitality to civilization's controls. In contrast, Bolívar, as observed from the north, retained the qualities of the Indian and Negroid culture that Americans assumed surrounded and molded him: he remained capricious, irresponsible, jealous, proud, and lustful. Qualities such as these demonstrated not only by Bolívar but also by most generals of the Latin American independence movement doomed all subsequent efforts at confederation. Like the Indians, and like African potentates, even the most heroic of the Latin leaders exhibited a passion for self-aggrandizement that undermined the quest for continental unity. Thus they were fated to preside over the disunited states of Latin America.

Hot-blooded and often unable to control his temper, Bolívar also proved incapable of curbing his sexuality; he was, according to overwhelming evidence, a notorious womanizer. Eventually, admirers destroyed stacks of amatory letters exchanged between Bolívar and his mistresses and would-be mistresses. Americans could take pride that Washington's admirers never had to salvage their hero's reputation by destroying evidence of improprieties.

According to one perhaps apocryphal story, toward the conclusion of the Guayaquil (Ecuador) banquet that ended his historic 1823 meeting with José de San Martín, the liberator of La Plata and Chile, Bolívar leapt onto a table and began to break china and crystal underfoot, exclaiming that this was how he would crush the remaining Spanish strongholds in Peru. Imagine the staid, contained Washington engaging in such antics!

Frederick the Great, it has been said, sought—even if not with total success—to make war the pursuit of reason rather than passion. A case could be made that Washington, given to careful analysis and planning, waged war with reason. Bolívar, who sometimes had intuitive flashes of genius when it came to strategic planning, often lacked the patience to attend to tactical details. In many ways, he seemed indeed to make war a matter of passion.

Incapable of subjecting his own passions to control even as he fought for independence, Bolívar in the course of the struggle liberated outward symbols of passion and primitivism: he freed the slaves of Latin America—before the African Americans were ready for freedom, according to many Americans—and established a close alliance with the tumultuous blacks and mulattoes of Haiti (already by the early nineteenth century a frightful object lesson to most Americans of the consequences attendant upon liberating the wild man). Washington had the sense, according to the prevailing judgment at least of preabolitionist Americans, to retain his slaves under benevolent control at Mount Vernon. And, unlike Bolívar, Washington did not entertain utopian dreams about the speedy incorporation of Indians into the political and social mainstream.

Unable to maintain control over others any better than he had managed to establish self-control, Bolívar ultimately succumbed to the ceaseless plotting of other Latin hotheads and went into a brief, poverty-stricken retirement before dying in 1830 at age forty-seven of tuberculosis or consumption—the disease already associated in America's popular lore with licentiousness, with lack of restraint and overspending, not only of money but of sexual energy. In contrast, Washington died in ripe and serene old age. In further contrast to Bolívar, who toward the end had abandoned his early liberalism and sought to establish close ties between politics and—as Americans saw it—superstition-ridden and authoritarian Catholicism, Washington never deviated from his Enlightenment faith in separation of church and state. Furthermore, Bolívar, guided by "womanly" intuition and "childish" fantasizing, produced unworkable constitutions that lasted a few years at best. Washington, responsive to rationality and the lessons of experience, helped father a constitution that endured through the ages. And Washington, who could recognize virtue and sagacity in others, did not, like Bolívar, insist upon single-handedly creating his nation's first constitution. Vanity figured among the vices that Washington, unlike Bolívar, managed to check.

A glance at the portraits of Bolívar and Washington might seem, at least to some observers from north of the border, to substantiate the stereotypes by which Americans judged not only Bolívar and Washington but Latin Americans in general and themselves. Bolívar's dark and brooding eyes are of the type that invite use of the adjective *passionate,* and perhaps also *visionary.* His full-lipped mouth almost compels use of the adjective *sensuous.* Worst of all, in light of white Americans' prevailing racism, some of Bolívar's portraits hint at a tinge, however slight, of African blood. That issue aside, portraits of Bolívar suggest, at least to me, tension, precariously focused nervous energy, barely controlled passions, a tenuous, fragile layer of restraint fixed atop a volcano. Washington in the best-known portraits exudes a serene quality of total control, of equanimity, of resolve and determination balanced by prudence. Washington's placid, carved-in-rock-like visage on a dollar bill invites trust in the currency. While I bow to few persons in my admiration for Bolívar, I concede that his visage, suggesting volatility and impetuousness, affixed to a coin or bill would not inspire confidence in the currency's soundness.

Finally, one cannot conceive a historical novel that depicts Washington as a failed revolutionary, striving in his dying months to reliberate an America that, following independence, had plunged into an abyss of hopeless disorder. Yet this is precisely the way in which Colombian author Gabriel García Márquez depicts Bolívar, the archetypal utopian who never comes close to fulfilling basically unrealistic dreams, in his debunking but nonetheless empathetic novel *The General in His Labyrinth* (1989).

Contrasts between the two great leaders seem to apply also to the way in which the two hemispheric revolutions unfolded. The struggle against Britain produced only one notorious traitor, while the Latin freedom fighters sometimes seemed as bent upon betraying and combating one another as upon fighting Spaniards. Francisco de Miranda, the Venezuelan-born precursor of the independence movement who for a time instructed his compatriot Bolívar on how to wage it, himself fell victim to betrayal, in which his protégé may have played a role. Of his inconstant companions in the struggle against Spain, Miranda disgustedly observed, "Riots, tumults, that's all these people know." As the fierce Spanish American wars for independence dragged on (in contrast to the relative calm in which Brazil won its freedom from Portugal), internecine struggle, assassinations, and guerrilla warfare among the insurgents persisted unabated, spilling over into the postindependence era as officers continued to nourish the grievances against fellow officers that originated during the struggle against Spain.

Whether standing in the Puritan or deistic traditions, Americans saw their own independence movement as the vehicle of Providence (in the case of Puritans) or the laws of history (in the case of deists). To them, the Revolution seemed a "mighty turning forward, both regenerative and organic, confirming the prophecies of Scripture as well as the laws of nature and history." Their Revolution stood in stark contrast to the Old World upheavals that amounted only to rebellions: the destructive, negative paroxysms of a people slipping into decay. Americans, as true revolutionaries, "were agents of the predetermined course of progress."[67]

A bit of Puritanism and also a bit of Deism tinged the thinking of New England's Daniel Webster when he contrasted the American and French revolutions, finding order and control in the first and frightening chaos in the second. When "the great wheel of political revolution began to move in America," according to Webster, its "motion was guarded, regular, and safe." However, when the great wheel started anew in France in 1789, its motion took on "an irregular and violent impulse . . . spreading conflagration and terror around."[68]

Americans transferred appraisals originally shaped by impressions of the Old World to the southern portions of the New World as they assessed the latest turning of "the great wheel of political revolution." Satisfied that rebellions to the south had little in common with their own Revolution, they saw them instead as the ineradicable mark of Old World contamination. Still, there was a difference between Latin Old and New Worlds. Rebellions in the former suggested the decay of once flowering civilizations; but Latin upheavals in the New World issued from a people who had never risen very far toward the levels of civilization.

Emerson pretty well summed up American majority attitudes on the Latin American independence movement. Not all revolutions lead to progress, he explained. Those made "in the interest of feudalism" always ended in "barbarism."[69] In contrast, Emerson saw the American Revolution as a new act in the ongoing drama of progress. Virginia-born, Kentucky-bred statesman Henry Clay and a few other articulate Americans might find similarities in the New World revolutions, north and south;[70] but Emerson and with him surely a substantial majority of Americans saw no reason to compare the anarchic violence of the Latin American fight for self-rule with what they deemed the principled and orderly sobriety of their own Revolution.

About the nicest thing that could be said about a people who parlayed their rebellion against Spain into conditions of permanent disorder was that they were "unpredictable."[71] In addition to being unpredictable, according to the author of several turn-of-the-century textbook histories of the southern republics, Latin Americans were "creatures of impulse, moved by sentiment and easily stirred to love or hate." In short, he concluded, Latin Americans "are people of sudden changes."[72] It could scarcely occasion surprise, then, that the Latins produced a political history marked by that badge of nature—sudden change. How starkly this contrasted to the predictability and consistency that Americans increasingly found at the core of their civilization and its steady, ongoing progress—once they got the Civil War out of the way and established once and for all among themselves the predominance of capitalist civilization over lower modes of existence.

Even before the struggle for independence got under way against Spain and Portugal, that dark branch of the Latin American family, the Haitians, had initiated a cataclysmic upheaval against French colonialism. Haiti's slave revolt, with "its destructiveness, . . . and its lasting imagery of mindless violence deeply affected those who shaped American policy toward the hemisphere."[73] The subsequent rebellions against Spain and Portugal waged generally by men at least a shade or two lighter in skin color than Haitians—and therefore rather more pleasing to Americans—may have been somewhat less violence-prone and bloodthirsty than the great Negro uprising; but only in degree, not in kind, did they differ from the Haitian cataclysm. Furthermore, the lighter-skinned Latin Americans seemed just as incapable as Haiti's Negroes and mulattoes of subjecting chaos to order once they ousted European colonialists.

Mexicans, "a wild, wandering race, half Indian, half Spanish,"[74] turned their country, after 1828, into one where peace broke out only once in a while and seldom endured more than a moment. Viewing the sweep of Mexican history since independence, a U.S. Supreme Court justice in the late 1890s wrote: "Revolutions and counter-revolutions, empires and republics, followed each other with great rapidity and in bewildering confusion . . . in a country where revolution seems to have been in the natural order of things."[75] About the same time, another distinguished American referred contemptuously to Mexican attempts "to initiate our republican system." As carried out by Mexicans, these attempts produced only a burlesque of American accomplishments that provided "food for satires."[76]

Observing the scene farther to the south in the 1830s, a U.S. chargé d'affaires in Guatemala City noted the area "was constantly in a revolutionary state, . . . involved in civil strife and the paths to the coast infested with banditti." He likewise branded Nicaragua a country in which "civil strife, and intestine commotions" had become endemic. From El Salvador at about the same time came word that "the roads were infested with ladrones [robbers], and travelling was considered unsafe in any quarter." From the U.S. chargé d'affaires at Lima, Peru, came this information in 1835: "We are still almost in a state of siege from the operations of the armed bands who rob and plunder almost daily, on the great thoroughfare between this city and its port-town, Callao, and, amongst others, some of our countrymen have been attacked and wounded." Early the next year he wrote that Lima and Callao had fallen into utter anarchy, with "every species of vexation being practiced. . . . [T]he roads, even the immediate vicinity, and up to the very gates of the city, . . . are infested with banditti . . . who rob and plunder indiscriminately, all they meet." On Venezuelans, an American traveler reported: "The value of stability in government is something they cannot be made to understand. It is not in their power to see it, and the desire for change and revolution is in the blood."[77] From Buenos Aires, an American traveler reported in 1832:

> I sleep with four loaded pistols and one musket in my room, as well as a sword. . . . [I]t is best amongst these wild people to rely somewhat on my

own aim. . . . I wish our romantic and mad headed, imaginative politicians whose sympathies were so strongly excited in favor of our *Republican* brethren in S. America could reside in this city which is perhaps the best one week, and if they were not cured of their madness, they must be fatally diseased. . . . There is here neither law or liberty—no sense of national honor or national justice or national dignity—a kind of schoolboy government with all the mischief and none of the ingenuity of school-boys . . ., a burlesque of everything that is connected with national greatness or national dignity.[78]

On another occasion the same observer wrote, "The peoples and government were no better than barbarians."[79]

In Latin America, Americans confronted conditions that Herman Melville once described as "a permanent *Riotocracy*."[80] Whether one consults American travel accounts, diplomatic correspondence, or novels the descriptions and appraisals seem the same. Here is one sample, fairly representative I believe, gleaned from an American novel, Robert Montgomery Bird's *Calvar*, published in 1834. In the novel, Bird has one of his characters, a Mexican priest, confide to an American visitor: "The barbaric romance which loiters about the brains even of European nations, is the pith and medulla of a Mexican head. The poetry of bloodshed, the sentiment of renown—the first and last passion, and the true test, of the savage state— are not yet removed from us. We are not yet civilized up to the point of seeing that reason reprobates, human happiness denounces, and God abhors, the splendour of contention. Your own people—the happiest and most favoured of modern days—are . . . not so backward."[81] Here is another sample from American fiction. In his first book, the collection of short stories titled *Cabbages and Kings* (1904), William Sidney Porter, better known by his O. Henry pseudonym, intended the mythical republic of Anchurria not only to represent Honduras, where not very happily he had spent some time, but also to serve as a microcosm of Latin America. Of the republic (whose inhabitants one character in the book refers to as "simple-minded children of nature"), the novelist writes: "Everything's rotten. From the executive down to the coffee pickers, they're plotting to down each other and skin their friends."[82]

So far as most Americans were concerned, Latin Americans were as hopelessly inept and chaotic in their economic practices as in their politics. But, before taking up Yankee stereotypes of Latin economic shortcomings, I want to remind readers that Latin Americans also have their stereotypes— of us. In the 1970s, Culiacán, in northwestern Mexico, acquired a bad reputation because of the frequent disputes and shoot-outs among rival gangs that competed for profits derived from sating the appetite for heroin and marijuana of those paragons of self-control, the gringos. As Culiacán grew wilder, the Mexican press began to call it "Little Chicago."[83]

Economic Failure and Latin American Primitiveness

"Democracy looks with suspicious, ill-satisfied eyes upon the very poor, the ignorant, and on those out of business," Walt Whitman wrote. "She asks for men and women with occupations, well-off, owners of houses and acres, and with cash in the bank."[84] Here is an attitude that goes back a long way in American history, to a point even before democracy had appeared. Upon first encountering Indians in the New World, the English ancestors of the American people could not forgive them their poverty. How could they be so poor in the midst of a land so rich?[85]

In the nineteenth century, Americans asked the same question about Latin Americans. Like Baron Alexander von Humboldt, they saw Latin Americans as "beggars on golden stools." Golden stools served as a metaphor for the richly endowed lands the Latins occupied, and whose potential they had proved utterly incapable of transforming into cash in the bank. The great nineteenth-century historian William H. Prescott defended "American seizure of Mexican territory in 1848 on the grounds that 'beggarly Mexico' lacks the human energy to make the land productive, while the descendants of the Puritans have proven their capacity to make the wilderness a garden."[86] Prescott voiced the common wisdom of his generation. Indeed, from the 1820s onward American frontiersmen had decided that "'greasers' were a lazy, indolent breed who had no right to the rich lands they occupied."[87] It took only a glance to convince the Americans that laziness largely explained the failure of the Latin Other to improve nature's bequest.

"Give them but *tortillas, frijoles,* and *chili colorado* to supply their animal wants for the day," stated a contemptuous American observer in the early nineteenth century, "and seven-tenths of the Mexicans are satisfied."[88] At midcentury John Woodhouse Audubon, passing through Mexico on his way to the California gold fields, conceded his "hatred for everything Mexican" but singled out for particular censure the "indolence . . . [that] reigns supreme" throughout the land. Toward the end of the century, artist Frederic Remington observed disgustedly that Mexicans passed through life in a long siesta. "A man of the North," he added, "who has a local reputation as a lazy man should see a Mexican . . . loaf, in order to comprehend that he could never achieve distinction in the land where poco tiempo [in a little while] means forever."[89]

One might well fill a long book with quotations from nineteenth- and early twentieth-century American travelers and diplomats disgusted by the laziness that seemed an ingrained way of life south of the border. Here follows what I judge to be a representative sampling. From a traveler in Mexico and Central America: "It [dictatorship] is a form of government not entirely unfitted to a people in the bulk utterly indifferent as to who or what rules them so [long as] they are left to loaf in their hammocks in peace." [90] From a diplomat who served in the same region: "The bland climate [predisposes them toward] . . . an indulgent, easy and voluptuous life. . . . [T]he temperatures are so genial [that] men are naturally indolent. . . . [T]he eternal summer [proves] fatal to enterprise and industry." [91] From an observer of Mexico in the 1880s we learn that only the children show energy, spark, and vivacity; unhappily, these children "will grow up and become Mexicans!" [92] In Panama, Colombia, and Venezuela travelers garnered these impressions: "These people love to dance, but they hate to work." [93] The natives lack "the energy and ambition to improve their miserable state. . . . When a matter cannot be conveniently attended to today, it is put off till tomorrow; and when tomorrow comes, it may be again postponed indefinitely." [94] A traveler to Brazil disparaged the swarms of beggars, contrasting "the thrift and enterprise of Americans with [the] . . . laziness" of nearly all Brazilians, regardless of class. They "lack industry, energy, and perseverance." Indeed, they exhibit "contempt for labor." [95]

Laziness alone did not account for the poverty and backwardness that dismayed American observers. Travelers and merchants from the north commented upon Latin irresponsibility. "They make fair promises, but very seldom conform with them." [96] Arriving in Veracruz in 1908, an American registered shock when informed by a lady acquaintance that "here, Sir, there are no fixed rules." Without fixed rules, the traveler reflected, no people could progress. Although he tended personally rather to like Mexicans, the American could understand why most of his fellow citizens detested the country and found it virtually impossible to say "a kind word about anything in it." [97]

Early in the twentieth century an American who considered himself an authority on his country's Indians reiterated a belief that two hundred years of repetition had seared into the national consciousness. The Indians' penchant to think only of today and its immediate necessities testified to their savagery. In contrast, civilized men looked to the future; [98] and this is what fitted them for life in modern times. Americans detected the Indians' mark of savagery on Latin Americans. A Brazilian laborer, according to an American traveler, as a general rule "spends all that he earns. The habit of savings seems to be entirely unknown." Mexicans were no better, according to an American businessman writing in 1887: "The lives of most of them seem to be occupied in obtaining food and amusement for the passing hour, without either hope or desire to a better future."[99]

Unconcerned with progress, Latin Americans, like all primitives, abhorred change in the basic patterns of life; and so in agriculture and other modes of production they had scarcely improved upon the "mechanical arts" that prevailed "among the aborigines."[100] Ill disposed toward innovations, other than the superficial changes that accompanied political revolutions, preferring things "as they are, not . . . as they should be,"[101] Mexicans, according to an American diplomat's mid-nineteenth-century assessment, "are content to live and die like the beasts of the field." Colombians and Venezuelans fared no better in the appraisal of an American who had grown discouraged about prospects of commerce with them. They had "few wants above such as are incident to mere animal existence."[102]

Like the beasts of the field, Latin Americans also lived in utter disregard of civilized man's concept of time. Again and again, American observers commented on this failing of their neighbors. Typical of his countrymen, a U.S. diplomat complained that Latin Americans "squander time without ever reflecting that it is the capital of industrious men."[103] If they thought of time at all, they thought of it as a cyclical occurrence—the rising and setting of the sun, the eternal changing of the seasons—rather than as a linear determinant that measured the advance from one point to another. In this, too, they reminded Americans of Indians or Africans, or any other group of "primitives," capable of seeing time only in terms of endless repetition rather than as a measure of progress. At best, Latin Americans resembled medieval peasants in an age before clocks became widely used.[104] In sharp contrast, Americans prided themselves on observing a system of time that was "freakish . . . [and] unnatural" (i.e., not based on cycles of natural time).[105] Living by this man-made system of time, they manifested their control over nature. Theirs was the system, purportedly, of civilized peoples, and it distinguished them from primitives who blindly accepted time as laid down for them by nature, totally oblivious to the human capacity to control and make use of it.

People who believe that wealth is conferred through fate, through good luck, in short through factors that they deem as uncontrollable as natural phenomena, could hardly be expected to use time in the efficient and rational manner of civilized, calculating capitalists. For many early Anglo settlers in America, the addiction of Indians to gambling, along with their inability to challenge and surmount natural, cyclical time, attested to their barbarism. With the spread of middle-class values in the nineteenth century, "respectable" Americans grew less and less tolerant of gambling. Increasingly, too, they showed the "peculiarly Protestant aversion to gambling, which relates to the notion that a person should only possess what has been gained by hard work and also to the sense that life should be viewed as a predictable, orderly experience." [106] Inevitably, disdain for Indian gambling by extension encompassed Latin Americans. Observing Mexicans around Santa Fe in 1822, Thomas James denounced their reliance on what he titled not Dame Fortune but "the Demon of chance." The inveterate gambling instinct among Mexicans, he concluded, had caused "the loss of what little reason nature had originally made theirs." [107]

A U.S. attorney general in New Mexico Territory following the Mexican War charged that among the Hispanic populace gambling was "almost universal, and considered a gentlemanly and respectable calling. . . . This vice seems to be a national amusement among the Mexican race." Even children of ten years of age or less played cards for pennies "with as much apparent interest as professional gamblers." A Yankee trader in California about the time it passed under U.S. control also commented on the small children who wagered "the buttons of their clothes until they had none left to hold their shirts together." The average adult Californio, he added, "would bet on anything." Edward Thornton Tayloe, who served as unpaid secretary to Joel R. Poinsett, the first U.S. minister to Mexico in the 1820s, wrote, "Gambling is . . . the general vice of this nation." He made no attempt to hide his disapproval as he detailed numerous scenes of reckless wagering. In this conduct he found all the proof he needed of the Mexican's economic irresponsibility. In Yucatán, an American adventurer in the early 1840s found that "the degrading habit of gambling is general among all classes of society. . . . All moral responsibility seemed to disappear before its irresistible fascination." In Bogotá, Colombia, according to an American eyewitness in the 1830s, people of all classes and colors, from white to black, "were compulsive gamblers." As for Peruvians and Ecuadorans, a roving American reported in the 1860s that they would rather gamble and "spend their time repeating traditions of treasures buried by the Incas" than contemplate honest work. [108]

Many of British America's earliest settlers had proved notoriously lazy, assuming that in their New World haven they could eschew hard labor. [109] From this early stage of childhood innocence, however, Americans prided themselves on having matured into adulthood, with its accompanying work ethic. Later, in the first stages of frontier penetration, Americans had again shown aversion to sustained, systematic work; and frontiersmen had developed keen appetites for gambling, boozing, womanizing, fighting, and all-around rowdiness. But Americans found it easy to excuse this stage in their national development. The early days of frontier settlement consti-tuted, after all, a renewal of childhood and youth in which self-control could hardly be expected. With the arrival of successive waves of settlers, the West attained maturity; and westerners increasingly took to the ways of civilization, with its restraints and demands, its planning and responsi-bilities. If in some areas Americans persisted in the irresponsibility of childhood, they were—allegedly—the baser social elements or the newly arrived Chinese and Irish, and later the Italian and southeast European, immigrants. Maybe even the later-arriving immigrants would someday mature. Meantime, for most "self-respecting" Americans, they remained objects of disdain. So did Latin Americans, about whose ability to advance quickly into civilized adulthood many Americans remained dubious.

Capitalist civilization clearly required the ability to defer gratifications; it demanded the honing of a "modern personality" that emphasized im-pulse control.[110] As Max Weber (1881–1961) contended, and as American middle classes seemed to intuit long before the German thinker developed his celebrated thesis of the "Protestant Ethic," the most urgent task facing the emergent capitalist was "destruction of spontaneous, impulsive enjoy-ment."[111] Already by the mid–nineteenth century Americans seemed also to intuit, in advance of Sigmund Freud, concepts of sublimation that posited the need to control the explosive outbursts of the libido and chan-nel its energy into capital-producing enterprise. In short, "right-thinking" Americans had grasped the truth that they must eschew passion and pur-sue their economic interests.[112] In doing so, they must steadfastly avoid the example of the childishly impulsive Latin American commoner and also of the idle and profligate aristocrat.

As epidemics of economic malaise raged throughout most of Latin America in the nineteenth century, Americans grew ever more convinced as to the inferiority of their neighbors in the sphere that really mattered: material development. Mexicans, the Latin people closest to them and most widely observed by Americans, provided seemingly overwhelming symptoms of economic inferiority. Mexico's per capita income fell from 166 pesos at the beginning of the century to 56 pesos in 1845. Meantime, U.S. per capita income more than doubled. In consequence, Mexicans who had earned 70 percent of U.S. per-capita income in 1800 were reduced to 14 percent in 1845. Even more significant, Mexican output that had equaled 51 percent of U.S. gross national product in 1800 declined to 8 per-cent in 1845.[113] Nineteenth-century Americans could not have been aware of these precise statistics. Nevertheless, they could sense readily enough that something was dreadfully wrong with Mexico, both politically and economically, as it fell ever further behind "in the great race of improve-ment" that morally healthy people delighted in running.[114]

Not just in Mexico but wherever observed, Latin Americans seemed economically to be falling behind Americans. Many Latin Americans themselves observed this phenomenon with distress, among them Chilean historian Diego Encina. In his 1912 book *Nuestra inferioridad económica* (Our economic inferiority), Encina concluded that his compatriots and their neighbors might need to undergo moral renovation before they could anticipate material progress. Moreover, a whole generation of turn-of-the-century Latin American innovators and reformers, calling themselves positivists, concurred in Encina's conclusion. Here is only a hint of the countless instances in which Latin Americans themselves bore witness at least to the partial validity of Yankee stereotypes.

Religious "Primitivism" and Latin American "Retardation"

A Forty-Niner headed for California recorded, as the very first entry in his diary, that he was on his way in order to eradicate "the detested sin of being poor."[115] A substantial majority of his countrymen right up to the present time have continued to associate sinfulness and poverty. Their own prosperity, "however slight," Americans regard as "the reward of virtue, while the other's poverty, however great, [represents] the penalty of vice."[116] In the case of the Latin American Other, they assumed that poverty and underdevelopment arose out of the vices inculcated by a false and primitive religion.

George Bancroft, who perhaps above all other nineteenth-century American historians celebrated his country's progress and saw in it the hand of a God well pleased with His chosen people, praised the spirit of Puritan Protantism, "from the first, industrious and enterprising and frugal." From this spirit, he concluded, "affluence followed of course."[117] Though decidedly less devout in a conventional sense than Bancroft, Bostonian Ralph Waldo Emerson, at least in some of his moments, was no less certain that worldly success rewarded the virtuous and the wise. "Open the doors of opportunity to talent and virtue," he intoned, "and they will do themselves justice, and property will not be in bad hands. In a free and just commonwealth, property rushes from the idle and imbecile to the industrious, brave and persevering."[118] Yet another New Englander, Daniel Webster, wondered if the "wars, plagues and famines" so often visited upon Latin Americans might not be construed as God's punishment for their savage and immoral ways. In this he reflected a conviction still widespread in eighteenth- and nineteenth-century Europe as well as America that God employed natural disasters to castigate people unpleasing to Him.[119]

Accustomed to fighting Catholic Spain and France, nurtured on depictions of Rome as the "whore of Babylon" and the pope as anti-Christ, suspicious of Jesuits and other priests and Roman Catholics in general, purportedly plotting to subject them to papal tyranny, English settlers arrived in the New World with a deeply ingrained detestation of Roman Catholicism; and if they could attribute the perceived moral flaws of whatever foes they encountered anywhere in the world to the latter's Catholic faith, they jumped at the chance to do so. As they engaged in savage imperial warfare in the New World with French and Spanish Catholics and their hordes of Indian converts, English settlers only sharpened their hatred of everything associated with Roman Catholicism. For them, their struggle against Catholics in the New World took on the aura of a holy war—an attitude that their Catholic adversaries fully reciprocated. A good number of New Englanders, moreover, saw in the revolution against British rule in 1776 a new holy war; for in their eyes the Church of England had succumbed to popish ways.[120]

Catholic Spain, playing the game of opportunistic international politics, sided with the Americans in their Revolution, hoping thereby to assure humiliation of her perennial foe, Great Britain. Subsequently, though, Spain did all in her power to keep the newly independent America contained within the smallest possible territory. Soon, then, American Protestants took up anew the imperial struggle against Roman Catholics and their nominally converted savage allies, the Indians. Once more, Americans saw themselves as waging the struggle of good against evil. Then, as the nineteenth century advanced, they perceived new threats from the forces of evil as Irish Catholics, driven out of their homeland by the Great Famine of 1845–1849, arrived in such numbers as to strike fear into native sons and daughters that the Protestant religion was in jeopardy.[121]

According to Ray Allen Billington, one of the most distinguished historians of his country's anti-Catholic bigotry, "The average Protestant American of the 1850s had been trained from birth to hate Catholicism; his juvenile literature and school books had breathed a spirit of intolerance. . . . [H]is religious and even his secular newspapers had warned him of the dangers of Popery." From early childhood on, Americans were shaped "to believe that 'to be a Catholic, was to be a false, cruel and bloody wretch,' and that Popery included everything that was vicious and vile."[122] Tumults and crime in their country, Americans attributed largely to Catholic immigrants whose immorality and animalistic ways sprang partially at least from their false religion. It was not difficult, then, for them to ascertain the source of Latin American shortcomings. Both among Latin Americans and immigrants from popish lands, Catholicism emerged as the overarching source of corruption and decadence in governments,[123] and of turbulence and lack of self-control in individuals.[124]

Prevailingly convinced that "feminine values sanctioned irresponsible emotionalism and dependent passivity,"[125] American men—and often women as well—found repugnant the prominent role that Catholicism assigned to the Virgin Mary. Catholicism's Virgin smacked too much of the emotional and the tearful, while Protestantism's Christ stood for the male logos, the rational principle.[126] Known among many of her Latin devotees as "the lawyer of sinners," the Virgin represented not only feminine emotionalism and irrationality but also softhearted indulgence. As a special pleader for sinners, the Virgin inspired confidence in them that they could "beat the rap."

Not only the Virgin but also countless saints, the Latins apparently assumed, to the total disgust of their northern neighbors, intervened in their behalf to arrange the bending of rules, natural and divine. Cults of saints, like the cult of Mary, "thrive in societies where petition and boon are commonplace and power lies in a single person's gift."[127] In this respect the Latin religious approach, based upon assumptions of the ordinary individual's powerlessness and need for a supernatural coterie of boon-granters, led to a dependence-prone temporal society whose members lacked a spirit of self-reliance. In such a setting, at least as viewed by Americans, neither political freedom nor economic liberty could flourish. Both fell victim to social systems that reflected and emerged from a religion that encouraged "feminine" dependence while spurning "manly" self-reliance.

At least some Americans must have realized that Hispanic Catholicism also included a masculine strain exemplified by the great warrior Santiago, or Saint James. The widespread Spanish medieval conception of Santiago as a brother of Christ, and perhaps just as important if not more important than Christ himself, found its way to the New World. Santiago, however, represented the values not of the democrat or the capitalist but rather of the person who established domination over others by military might aided and abetted, purportedly, by God's direct and miraculous intervention in the temporal order—a person whose economic success proceeded from plundering the losers in ostensibly religious wars. Thus even the manly element of Latin Catholicism, in the eyes of American Protestants, seemed counterproductive both to democracy and to ongoing, self-sustaining, and orderly economic progress.

A religion perceived as manly only in a limited, predatory sense, but basically feminine and incorporating even the alleged worship of a goddess, struck American Protestants as little removed from primitive paganism. Such a religion could satisfy only a people who, like the American Indians, had not yet become logical,[128] who clung to a ritualism that appealed exclusively to the senses and accepted a worldview resting on animism. Priding themselves on having caused Indian gods to disappear, Anglo Americans condemned their Latin neighbors for their readiness to accept Indian deities only slightly disguised as saints, thereby in effect perpetuating pagan polytheism. When an American writer in the 1920s discovered that Mexicans kept idols behind altars, her countrymen and women were scarcely surprised. For over a century they had understood that Catholicism "was not Christianity, but an idolatrous religion."[129]

For American Protestants, the religion of Latins in both the Old and New Worlds incorporated at best an element of genuine Christian revelation grafted onto the pagan rites and superstitions of a peasantry still immersed in nature, still venerating natural forces rather than committed, as the true God commanded, to subduing the earth and all of nature. Rather than from heaven, the religion of pagan Indians and papist Latins grew out of the soil. So at least it seemed to American Protestants who prided themselves on their liberation from dark and chthonic forces.

Had American Protestants known about some of the theological teachings emanating from the mid-sixteenth-century Council of Trent, they might have found confirmation for their prejudices. At Trent, Catholic theologians embraced "an incarnational theology that stressed divine immanence" in the human, earthbound situation. Thus, they gave their imprimatur to a theology that stood in "marked contrast to the keystone of all classical Protestant teaching, the notion of the transcendence of God." In fact, "Trent tried to walk a line between the spiritualism of its sectarian opponents and an age-old paganism which deified the powers of nature."[130]

Seldom has the conflation of the divine and the natural that shocks American Protestant sensitivities when they view Latin American culture been so tellingly highlighted as by Mexican writer Carlos Fuentes. In one of his many remarkable novels he draws attention to the custom of ladies not only in Mexico but also in many Latin American countries of wearing long lace nightgowns with the Sacred Heart of Jesus embroidered in front of their genitalia, or as Fuentes puts it, "in front of their cunts." Fuentes seems to glorify—as well he might—in a religious approach that does not seek, as in the northern republic, to liberate the redeemer from the flesh.[131]

Max Weber and British historian Keith Thomas agree that the desacralization of the natural world and the elimination of magic from it preceded and helped facilitate the rise of modern technology whose precise purpose was the no-holds-barred conquest of nature.[132] Nineteenth-century American Protestants may have anticipated these findings as they drew a connection between religious practices and lack of material progress in Latin America. Be that as it may, there is no question that Americans already in that century perceived as decided impediments to progress Iberian Catholicism's fatalism and its insistence that life on earth was a time of tribulations and useful only as a process that gradually stripped away temporal wants and prepared one for supernatural rewards. What is more, Iberian Catholicism, with its message that poverty is the estate richest in the means of eternal salvation, actually taught that nothing succeeded, supernaturally, so much as temporal failure. Americans sometimes suspected that this message was concocted by elites, in a society that lacked middle sectors and bourgeois values, to keep underlings resignedly in their ascribed places. Whether inspired by genuine religious convictions or the lust for worldly power, the message obviously contradicted the success drive that so many Americans believed their religion commanded.

Helping further to blunt the success drive among Latins, so their northern neighbors concluded, was the power of the priesthood. For one thing, the priestly custom of conferring absolution after hearing confession only exacerbated the immorality encouraged by reliance on the Virgin and saints as lawyers who would help sinners "beat the rap." A priest-ridden people fell naturally into the assumption that all they had to do was, as one disdainful American observer charged, "follow the forms, go to confession, go to Mass, pay the priest, and all their sins are erased and they can start all over again. They can drink, gamble, run after women, curse all they like."[133] To some Americans, of course, the moral slackness allegedly encouraged by Catholicism was not without its appeal. One detects good-humored tolerance, even approval, when an American novelist in 1989 traded on stereotypes of the immorality of Catholic culture. He put these words in the mouth of the novel's protagonist as he surveys mid-nineteenth-century Santa Fe, New Mexico: "There was bars and cat houses and card parlors enough for everybody because it's a Catholic town. Any place run by Catholics is generally more tolerant of people's vices than the Protestants."[134]

Even had the Latin American clergy led exemplary lives, nineteenth-century Americans undoubtedly would have found, or invented, grounds for condemning them and excoriating their servility to the Vatican, which one Yankee writer referred to "as a great big lady of pleasure, patched and painted and drunk and dressed in scarlet."[135] In truth, Americans during approximately the first two-thirds of the nineteenth century had considerable grounds for criticizing the Latin American clergy, though their images of the Vatican owed more to Renaissance than to modern pontiffs. During the first generation or two after independence, Latin America's priesthood sank to what may well have been its all-time nadir in the New World.[136]

Many Americans had their first opportunity to observe a presumably priest-ridden people in New Mexico, beginning in the 1820s when trade along the Santa Fe Trail began to intensify. That trader par excellence Josiah Gregg noted that New Mexico's inhabitants had been "bred to look upon priests as infallible and holy examples of piety and virtue." Thus the "excesses of the flock" seemed scarcely surprising "when a large portion of the pastors, the padres themselves, are foremost in most of the vices of the country."[137] Gregg described the clergy as "first at the fandango [uninhibited dances where drinking and gambling, at the very least, abounded]— first at the gambling table—first at the cock-pit—first at bacchanalian orgies—and by no means last in the contraction of those 'liaisons' which are so emphatically prohibited by their vows."[138] Critical appraisals of New Mexico's Catholic clergy rested not just on Protestant prejudice. When the American Catholic bishops convened their 1849 synod in Baltimore, they placed credence in the accounts of American army officers and political officials according to which vices of every sort—ranging from drinking and gambling to womanizing—prevailed among the clergy. The bishops concluded New Mexico must be regarded as a mission territory, awaiting establishment of a valid religious structure.[139] Reflecting American impressions formed in the preceding century, Willa Cather in *Death Comes for the Archbishop* has a local Hispanic priest justify a sexually active clergy on the grounds that they are only acting in accordance with nature.[140]

Americans rushed to read the lurid novels of the 1830s and 1840s according to which priests in both the Old and the New Worlds had virtually unlimited access to nunneries, where they sated their carnal appetites. "Their unbridled lust," according to one writer, "stalks forth in broad daylight; and deeds of iniquity are daily committed by them, which are enough to make the savages of the wilderness blush." That fictionalized accounts of such immorality were credited, "perhaps by a majority of the evangelical Protestants in America," owed not a little to reports by American eyewitnesses not only of their own Hispanic Southwest but also of Latin America proper. Undoubtedly these reports played their part in encouraging credence in Rosamund Culbertson's 1836 potboiler *Rosamund; or, a Narrative of the Captivity and Sufferings of an American Female under the Popish Priests in the Island of Cuba, with a Full Disclosure of their Manners and Customs, Written by Herself.* "In this vulgar little volume," as Ray Allen Billington describes it, an update of colonial-period captivity tales that lauded virtuous whites while denigrating depraved Indians, Culbertson included detail after detail of clerical debauchery.[141]

While certainly not so lurid, bona fide accounts by American travelers and diplomats provided ample material to convince a Protestant home audience of the debasement of the keepers of the Latin American conscience.

From Peru, Francis H. Gregory in 1834 described a "priest-ridden" society in which clergymen headed many families, their moral laxitude permeating all society. Four years later an American published his impressions of Bogotá, reporting that the clergy lived openly with their concubines. After spending some time in Brazil in the 1860s, a Protestant clergyman charged, "There is no class of men in the whole Empire whose lives and practices are so corrupt as those of the priesthood." Many years later John Reed in his *Insurgent Mexico* (a book published in 1914 that became something of a classic) recounted the following: "We drank *sotol* and *aguamiel,* while the *cura* [priest] made away with a whole bottle of looted anisette. Exhilarated by this, His Reverence descanted upon the virtues of the confessional, especially where young girls were concerned. He also made us understand that he possessed certain feudal rights over new brides. 'The girls, here,' he said, 'are very passionate.'" When the priest left the room, one of Reed's Mexican companions "hissed, shaking so that he could hardly speak: 'I know the dirty————! And my sister . . . !'" [142]

Even a generally worthier breed of priests in colonial times had, in the American appraisal, contributed to the moral and economic failures of their societies through the widespread charitable institutions that the Catholic church maintained. Charity, according to nineteenth-century middle-class assumptions, not only undermined economic drive but also produced a citizenry deficient in virtue. These assumptions lived on into the next century and found expression even in the words of the great architect of the New Deal, whom many conservatives accused of encouraging dependence on government handouts. In his annual message to Congress of January 4, 1935, President Franklin D. Roosevelt maintained: "The lessons of history, confirmed by the evidence immediately before me, show conclusively that continued dependence upon relief induces a spiritual and moral disintegration fundamentally destructive to the natural fiber." To dole out relief, he averred, is to administer a "narcotic, a subtle destroyer of the human spirit." "It is a violation," he added, "of the traditions of America." [143]

Equally inimical to America's traditions that fostered the enterprising spirit was the Iberian clergy's custom of forcing the faithful to finance a never-ending series of religious festivals (fiestas) commemorating the feast days of a veritable legion of saints. In the second half of the twentieth century, a fair number of American scholars, among them historians, anthropologists, and sociologists, discovered the degree to which the fiesta system impeded economic development by constantly channeling the accumulated capital of villagers throughout colonial nineteenth- and even twentieth-century Latin America into economically nonproductive religious celebrations. Nineteenth-century American travelers were well ahead of their country's scholars in discovering, and lamenting, the consequences of the fiesta system. In fact, even more than the sexual license of the Latin clergy, they criticized the priestly mania for draining parishioners of their meager income. This the priests accomplished by charging to administer the sacraments but above all by extracting money to finance festivals that, most Americans believed, contributed not to religious zeal but to drunkenness and debauchery. If the typical Latin American did not lose his money at the gambling table, he surrendered it to the priest. The result, according to an American who traveled in Mexico during the 1880s, was that money had little value for the natives, for they were reconciled to its quick loss.[144]

From El Salvador, Ephraim George Squier reported in the 1850s that, left to themselves, the Indian populace might well have accumulated a little capital as well as some property. Instead, because of conniving priests the Indians spent their money on "the festivals of the saints, which are rather eating and drinking bouts than sacred feasts." About a decade later John Lloyd Stephens noted that priests enhanced their income and at the same time stimulated religious fanaticism by keeping the masses amused with "fetes and Church ceremonies." Well before Squier and Stephens made their observations, a U.S. naval officer had witnessed the celebration of Easter in Valparaíso, Chile. The spectacle led him to conclude that Chileans could achieve neither economic development nor political liberty, for they were held by their clergy in pagan superstitions that drained them economically and induced "ignorance, prejudice and bigotory [sic]."[145]

U.S. travelers, scientists, and diplomats in the second half of the nineteenth century continued to publish similarly bleak accounts, from which their fellow citizens gleaned most of their impressions of Latin America. From Brazil came these reports: "Festivals and processions constitute the chief amusement of the masses—are their principal sports and pastimes, during which the saints themselves come out of their sanctuaries." "Unhappily, a great deal of their [Brazilians'] liberality . . . is expended upon Church fiestas, street processions, saint's days, and the like, more calculated to feed superstition than to stimulate pure religious sentiment." "Among the influences unfavorable to progress is the character of the clergy. . . . As long as they believe that the mind can be fed with tawdry street processions . . . and as long as the people accept this kind of instruction, they will be debased and enfeebled by it." An American with fairly extensive experience in Colombia and Venezuela censured not only the steady flow of feast days but the manner in which the natives celebrated every sabbath. On the "Lord's Day," he lamented, one witnessed more squandering of money and "more drinking and general dissipation amongst the lower classes . . . than on any other [day]." The great New Orleans–born pianist and composer Louis Moreau Gottschalk had partially in mind the priestly manipulation of the fiesta system when he wrote, in his reminiscences of a Latin American recital tour of the late 1860s, "The clergy have shown themselves to be what they always have been here— rapacious, cowardly, corrupt, hideous, egotistic."[146]

During the period from the 1830s to the 1890s Americans in increasing numbers chased after "respectability" and turned their backs on "rowdy entertainment"—including boxing—that encouraged "dissipation [and] raucous abandon," and other manifestations of baser instincts deemed inimical to "decency, civilization and republican virtues."[147] Precisely at this time, they learned about religious practices in Latin America that, allegedly, encouraged just such debauchery, thus banishing all possibility of moral and economic progress. No wonder Latin American republics, like "every Roman Catholic nation in the history of the world," according to a *Harper's* magazine correspondent reporting from Madrid in the 1860s, always went "from bad to worse."[148]

John Adams in one of his letters to Thomas Jefferson had concluded that basically it was the religion of the American Indians that had spawned their "invincible aversion to civilization."[149] For a later generation of Americans, religion explained rejection by Latin Americans of all paths leading to modern civilization. Summing up the conviction of many of his countrymen, Thomas Ewback, who traveled south of the border in the 1850s, wrote: "I believe Romanism, as it exists in . . . South America generally, to be a barrier to progress, compared to which other obstacles are small."[150]

In the seventeenth century Puritan divines, among them John Eliot and Cotton Mather, entertained the modest hope to "Protestantize" not only the Indians of the New World but the Latin Americans as well. Inspired by millennialist expectations of hemispheric dimensions, realization of which would "be attended by pardonable material gains," Eliot translated the Bible into Indian tongues and Mather took up the study of Spanish as he dreamed of spreading the one true faith throughout the southern, Latin sections of the hemisphere.[151] In the early nineteenth century, hopes originating with the first Puritans lived on. Presbyterian and Congregationalist ministers agreed—whether wittingly or not—with Thomas L. McKenney, appointed superintendent of Indian trade in 1816, that conversion of primitives to Protestantism must precede all expectations of transforming them into economically productive humans fit for membership in modern societies.[152] In the mind of the ministers, and of Americans in general, primitives included not only Indians but also Latin Americans. John Quincy Adams (principal architect of the Monroe Doctrine) and Henry Clay (champion of an American System of economic integration intended eventually to expand to hemispheric dimensions) figured among those Americans who, in effect, applied to Latin Americans McKenney's line of reasoning vis-à-vis Indians. Adams and Clay insisted, with only partial success, that commercial treaties signed with the newly independent republics to the south include guarantees of religious liberty so as to permit proselytizing by Protestant missionaries.[153]

In his splendid study *The American Jeremiad* (1978), Sacvan Bercovitch, an authority on religious history and comparative literature, points to a belief common among ministers in colonial America that it was rare, but not inherently impossible, for "religion and profit [to] jump together." After independence, more and more ministers and Americans in general came to the understanding that their country was a "rare place," one where "the wheel of fortune and the wheel of grace revolved in harmony."[154] Perhaps under their tutelage, Americans thought, Latin Americans could learn to spin both wheels.

For all their optimism and self-confidence, America's religious leaders since Puritan times also entertained dark visions of impending moral and material ruin. Perhaps, though, they preached the jeremiad not because they really believed in impending doom but rather to exhort their congregations to the sort of self-improvement and moral cleansing that would perpetuate the processes of worldly success,[155] thereby both earning and demonstrating God's continuing approbation. Whatever the intention of those who preached the gloom of the jeremiad, Americans did in fact seem uniquely adept at avoiding prolonged catastrophe. Economic depressions might be perceived as "moral judgments" from on high;[156] but economic setbacks always righted themselves and triggered new periods of greater progress and wealth. Americans must be doing something right—something morally right! On the other hand, the jeremiad's admonitions seemed applicable to nineteenth-century Latin America, an area in retrogression, buffeted by disaster, both natural and man-made, after disaster. Providing proof that "every Roman Catholic nation in the history of the world has always gone from bad to worse," Latin Americans obviously were doing something wrong.

Not all Americans of the past century, however, chose to believe in the success myth. Some persisted in jeremiad-tinged views of their country and its citizens, fretted over what they perceived as the substitution of Mammon for God, and wondered if success by American standards might actually be failure. Their country's civilization, they feared, suffered a serious malaise. Latin Americans, they suspected, might be blessed rather than cursed because of their divergence from the values of U.S. civilization. Perhaps the Latins lived not in a howling wilderness but in a benign and virtuous state of nature, one that enabled them to live by *being* fully themselves rather than constantly obsessed with *becoming,* economically, something more. In any event, nineteenth-century American questioners of conventional national wisdom wanted nothing to do with a God that visited natural catastrophes on humans who had not contrived to become prosperous.

CHAPTER 3

Latin Americans and Indians: Ambiguous Perceptions of an Alleged Connection

Latin Americans: Potential Saviors of an Unfulfilled Civilization?

Americans in the midst of Latin Americans have often felt as James Russell Lowell did when surrounded by Spaniards. Serving as U.S. minister to Spain (1877–1880), Lowell confessed to profound ambivalence. "There is something oriental in my nature which sympathizes with the 'let her slide' temper of the hidalgos," Lowell wrote in an 1878 letter. At the same time, he complained that the causes for Spain's backwardness lay in "something in the character of the people." He could criticize "Dr. Mañana" even while recognizing the need for treatment from him.[1]

Dismissing Hispanics in one breath as "lazy and lustful, reckless and turbulent," an early historian of the California mining camps praised them in the next breath for their "freedom from care."[2] Another Anglo observer of California midway in the nineteenth century found the Hispanics indolent; but he warmed to their innocent, happy spirit. "Close to nature," yet innocent rather than depraved because of this, they were childlike, generous, rich in the social graces, lavish in hospitality, and uncorrupted by avarice. For better or for worse, and the observer seemed to puzzle over which word applied, Californios did not understand the meaning of profit.[3]

Venturing into Mexico in the 1880s, two American women travelers responded to the local scene much like some Anglos had responded earlier to Hispanic life-styles in California. They complained about unbathed and indolent natives but also recognized compensating virtues: "ignorant of care, untroubled by longing, untortured by ambition, their lot may have more of blessings than we can imagine."[4] A hundred years later, Americans still remained both dubious about and yet enchanted by what struck them as the Latin American's refusal to be "molded by modern industrialism."[5] Many modern-day observers of the Latin Other could sympathize with the governor of California who described life in his jurisdiction in the early 1840s in these terms: "It is the gayest, the happiest, the most careless in the world. But how long will it last? Curse the Americans! They are coming."[6]

In the text he wrote for his 1986 *South American Journey*, an eight-part television documentary, Jack Pizzey referred to the Latin American ambience as "lawless, violent, volatile, and delightful." Americans could respond to Pizzey's juxtaposition of contradictory characteristics; for surely many of us in our fantasy worlds find at least fleeting delight in what customary norms admonish us to shun. If we are supposed to be law-abiding, self-contained, and calm, most of us will try, outwardly, to be so, while at the same time enjoying and admiring persons who "let it all hang out" and thereby embody our negative identities. American novelist Edward Bellamy hit the nail pretty squarely toward the end of the nineteenth century when he observed: "There is only a very narrow margin between a morbid aversion for a thing and a morbid attraction to it. One is always in danger of passing from one extreme to the other. A man's feelings, you know, are subject to the law of the see-saw."[7] Among Americans, Latin Americans have activated the seesaw principle just as surely as Orientals did for nineteenth-century Europeans. "Oriental life," observes the author of an early twentieth-century account of life in Madras, had "an irresistible fascination for some [European] natures; the glamour, the relief from convention . . . the lure of attractive and voluptuous women, idleness, ease, luxury, *drugs!*"[8]

"Great is wickedness," wrote Walt Whitman. "I find I often admire it just as much as I admire goodness. Do you call that a paradox? It certainly is a paradox."[9] Whitman seemed to anticipate what Carl Jung has seen as the need for all individuals to be reconciled with their shadows so that they might attain wholeness. The shadow signifies for Jung what the negative identity implies for Erik Erikson—and something of what the id means to Freud. Americans, predominantly, have associated the shadow, the negative identity, and the id with nature, and therefore with wickedness. So, they have remained dubious, much of the time, about coming to terms with the shadow; they have tried to keep bottled up an inner spring of vitality. Sometimes, though, they have sought to incorporate into their lives the drive, energy, ebullience, and vitality, the pranksterism and worse, of the shadow, the negative identity, the id. The resulting benefit they anticipate is the same one promised by so many of the world's great myths: the end of alienation and the attainment of wholeness. Thus the Other,

usually dismissed as the embodiment of wickedness, can be seen as the savior, the redeemer of humans who in their civilized lives are incomplete and
unfulfilled.

The sort of double mystique—both repelling and luring—that Americans tend to associate with Latin Americans emanated at an earlier time
from the Indian. Most commonly, Caucasian Americans dismissed the Indians as dirty savages; yet white men and women captured by natives often
decided, as previously noted, to live permanently with their captors, drawn
to Indian life because it offered "the most perfect freedom, the ease of
living, [and] the absence of those cares and corroding solicitudes" that so
often beset civilized existence.[10] Ever since Thomas Morton first observed
them in the early seventeenth century, Indians had caused many a white
man and woman to puzzle over this riddle: "If Indians lived richly by
wanting little, then might it not be possible that Europeans lived poorly
by wanting much?"[11]

Because Indian culture seemed to have something they lacked, something they needed to complete their human potential, even some early European settlers had begun to worry about the disappearance of the natives
and their way of life from the North American scene. This worry lived on
through the decades, surfacing consistently among counterculture movements. Feeling somehow incomplete in the midst of American civilization,
the counterculturalist wants Indians to remain themselves not necessarily
for their own sake but for the psychic well-being of the alienated Caucasian American. "We don't want the Indians to change," it has been said,
"because we have them comfortably in the back of our minds like a kind of
Shangri-La, something we can turn to even if we work ourselves to death
in New York."[12] Similarly, some Americans have wanted Latins to remain
themselves not for their own sakes but in order to provide a remedy to the
emotional emptiness of the Americans' own lives. If some Americans compensate for an absence of the natural by hunting or fishing or even attending rodeos,[13] others have found it psychologically reassuring to let their
thoughts wander southward where natural men and women still flourish
and, ostensibly, remain steadfast in their resistance to modernity.

However much Americans employed words that admonished Latin
Americans to transform themselves and abandon ostensibly primitive
ways, they simultaneously communicated in, as it were, a body language
that cajoled the Latins to remain the same. Just as artist George Catlin
hoped to establish a museum of his Indian paintings that would reconnect
his overly civilized countrymen to their primitive selves, so Americans despite all their development plans and modernization schemes have wanted
Latin Americans to remain a living museum of premodern life-styles. No

wonder the Latins, even as American Indians, puzzled over just what it was that Anglo Americans expected of them.

Not surprisingly, American attitudes toward Latin Americans have revealed striking similarity to, and in fact to some considerable degree originated in, attitudes inspired by the original New World children of nature, the Indians. Just as Americans disaffected by the lacunae and the hobbles of their own civilization developed stereotypes of the good Latin American, so some of the original American counterculturalists—beginning with Thomas Morton—had stereotyped the Indian as something of a redeemer who could reconnect them to the life-enhancing rhythms of nature.

Stereotypes of the Good Indian

"The philosopher," according to a late eighteenth-century American writer, "weary of the vices of refined life, thinks to find perfect virtue in the simplicity of the unimproved state."[14] If so, Americans through the decades can boast of having produced an impressive number of philosophers, among them novelists who have delighted in glorifying the Indian as a symbol of the "unimproved state." William Faulkner is one of the most distinguished of the novelists to have worked this theme, finding in the aged hunter of Indian ancestry the symbol of a wilderness being developed into oblivion, to humanity's everlasting loss. Dozens of hack novelists as well as a good number of filmmakers, distinguished and otherwise, have also depicted the red man as America's collective hero, stressing his noble but doomed struggle to maintain his "moral and legal rights against the ruthless whites."[15] In fact, "had the Indians never existed, perhaps white writers would have had to invent them, as a utopian antithesis to everything they disliked or found alienating about their own world." In myths concocted by white thinkers, Indians have been offered "cosmic compensation for five centuries of anguish and insult."[16]

Like Bartolomé de Las Casas, the great "Apostle of the Indians" in sixteenth-century Spanish America, Roger Williams a century later in New England did not doubt the superiority of Christianity over Indian religious beliefs. But, like Las Casas, Williams, after observing Indians in "their natural piety," came to wonder if the natives "were not potentially better Christians than those who so arrogantly wore that mantle."[17] A century after Williams, some Englishmen in New England concluded that greater generosity and charity prevailed among Indian "*barbarians,* than amongst thousands that call themselves *Christian.*"[18] Other Englishmen reached similar conclusions from a southern vantage point. Robert Beverly, in his *History and Present State of Virginia* (1705), pronounced the Indians "gentle, loving, generous, faithful." He praised the natives' "fabulous freedom from care," the result of the richly endowed environment in which they lived that permitted them to feed themselves through the labor of only a few summer days, the rest of the time "being wholly spent in the Pursuit of their Pleasures."[19] Their propensity for sharing, Beverly believed, contributed to the ability of Indians to lead pure, natural lives uninfected by civilization's avarice. Well before Rousseau, then, America had its philosophers who praised Indians for not having invented the "frightful words thine and mine."[20]

The same tendencies that led American leftists in the twentieth century to praise every Latin American political movement that smacked of Marxism or socialism of any variety already operated among some colonial observers of the American Indian. To them, the Indians' virtue lay not only in their "worshipful reverence for nature, acceptance of the body and the sensual appetites." It lay also in the alleged inclination of Indians to accept as natural the "subjugation of the individual for the good of the group."[21]

Admiration for Indian communalism began with Thomas Morton in the 1620s—and perhaps even earlier, with some of the first English settlers in Virginia who shared in establishing Pocahontas mythology.[22] Many observers subsequent to Morton attributed American Indian communalism to a commendable lack of greed and avarice. Quaker botanist William Bartram in the late eighteenth century praised the Seminoles he wandered amongst in Florida for their "freedom from want or desires."[23] Early in the following century writer Washington Irving and artist George Catlin drew attention to the "natural liberty" of the red man, resting ultimately, so they believed, on his freedom from acquisitiveness.[24] Cooper could also enter into this approach. In one of his Leatherstocking Tales he has Natty Bumppo declare that Indians escaped the vanity and greed of civilized men because they allowed themselves to be overwhelmed and sated by the glories of nature. Living "in a house with the clouds for its roof, where he can at any moment look both at the heavens and the earth," the Indian remained impervious to civilized man's acquisitiveness.[25] This admiring spirit found its way also into the short story by William Dean Howells (1837–1920) titled "Mrs. Johnson." About the part-Negress, part-Indian protagonist that he created in this story, Howells wrote: "We were conscious of something warmer in this old soul than in ourselves, and something wilder, and we chose to think it the tropics and the untracked forest. She had scarcely any being apart from her affection; she had no morality, but was good because she neither hated nor envied; and she might have been a saint far more easily than far more civilized people."[26]

One wonders how much Marx and Engels may have been influenced in their praise of primitive communism by the noble-savage legends emanating from America. However that may be, admiration for the red man's primitive communism remained unabated among America's counterculturalists on through the 1980s. In that decade, sounding a theme that had reached crescendo volume in the 1960s, an American disillusioned by the prevailing spirit that his compatriots displayed during the Ronald Reagan presidency praised Indians in these terms: "If there is one evil which [they regard as] greater . . . than all others, it is selfishness. When someone owns something which can benefit others and does not share it, it is a great wrong."[27]

Even in their most romantic assessment of the Indian, however, Americans generally did not go so far as to succumb to a mythology that saw redemption in total immersion in the virtues of the natural life. Instead, they pursued the dialectical myth that promised temporal salvation in the synthesis of opposites. Even at times when the cult of the Indian peaked, most American enthusiasts of the noble savage dreamed of forging a cultural blend of white and red, Christian and heathen, cultivated and wild. Moreover, Americans sympathetically inclined toward Indians in one moment might in the next moment react in revulsion. They vacillated between "deploring and adoring" Indians.[28] In this they resembled a good number of whites in the antebellum South who looked on Negroes sometimes as children to be loved, and sometimes as beasts to be hated.

In his deeply probing novel *Anthills of the Savannah* (1987) Nigerian writer Chinua Achebe cautions readers to suspect "those who see no blot of villainy in the beloved oppressed nor grant the faintest glimmer of humanity to the hated oppressor."[29] Such single-minded beings, Achebe opines, are party-liners and ideologues. Rather than party-lining ideologues, Americans in assessing Indians have as often as not been confused, for they have entertained more than one idea about the nature of their country's aborigines. A particularly striking example of confusion is provided by the so-called Humphreys card decks first produced in 1819 and named after James Humphreys, a Philadelphia playing-card manufacturer. In the Humphreys deck, famous Indians substituted for the figures (kings, queens, and the like) on traditional card decks. Some Indians, as depicted by Humphreys, were knavish, others noble, some deceitful, others innocent, some ferocious and fearsome, others kindly and admirable.[30]

Like nineteenth-century card decks, twentieth-century movies have reflected the national ambivalence toward Indians that has often prevented Americans from being single-minded bigots. In the Arthur Penn–directed *Little Big Man* (1971), Indian-fighting U.S. soldiers come across as brutes who gleefully slaughter peaceable natives and take particular delight in shooting down helpless women and children. The movie exemplifies one important genre of American cinema. Just as important is the opposite genre exemplified by the John Ford–directed *Fort Apache* (1947), starring John Wayne as the typically courageous, jocular, and essentially decent sort of army trooper who conquers cruel, threatening savages and thereby opens the American West to civilization.[31]

True to life in its projection of American ambivalence, the radio drama series "Fort Laramie," whose popularity peaked in 1956, alternately depicted Indians as vicious creatures deserving all the rough treatment they received at the hands of U.S. soldiers and settlers and as the hapless victims of a rapacious bunch of land-hungry whites who goaded peaceful beings into becoming violent defenders of their rights. "Fort Laramie" spoke to the fact that Americans have difficulty making up their minds about the true nature of Indians, that they have been of two minds in evaluating the conquest of their West. Americans have been similarly confused about how to appraise all the other "primitives" they have confronted in their long history, from Latin Americans to Filipinos to Vietnamese. In consequence, they are often of two minds when assessing their imperialist experiences.

In judging American penetration into Indian domains or into Latin America, whether through military occupation or the spread of cultural influence and economic hegemony, one school of thought is represented by those who have been described as "externalists." Externalists stand in the "black legend" approach in their evaluation of imperialism. According to this approach, Latin Americans lived in a tranquil natural estate (just as America's aborigines allegedly did) until black-hearted outsiders from the north (or, in the case of Indians, from the east) intruded into their idyllic existence, upset its balanced and harmonious ways, introduced the flaws of civilization, foremost among which was capitalist greed, and before long transformed settings of serenity into contentious cockpits of greed and exploitation. Here is the perennial myth of how civilized men soiled the character of the wilderness dweller, casting once proud and noble people into moral and material misery. Externalist perceptions underlie the 1955 movie *The Man from Laramie*. When his brother is killed by Indians, the movie's hero (played by James Stewart) wreaks vengeance not upon Indians but upon the white men who had sold arms to the natives. Similarly, many Americans disgusted by the abuses perpetrated by the Latin American military direct their outrage against those North Americans, public and private, who have sold arms to, and in general nourished and encouraged the military—thereby, allegedly, creating monsters of cruelty and inequity and setting them loose to prey in an ambience once pure and undefiled.

In contrast to externalists, "internalists" respond to legends of the blackness not of colonialists but of colonials.[32] They like to imagine the objects of American imperialism, whether Indians or Latin Americans, as having lived in a vicious Hobbesian state of nature before their exposure to Anglo American civilization. The subsequent difficulties that beset colonials, occasioned by their failures to learn how to achieve a civilized state of grace, are attributed to pervasive flaws of nature or culture, or both. Because they cannot or will not abandon old ways, they remain mired in inferiority of their own making.

Depending on their mood of the moment, many if not most Americans are, I suspect, alternately (or even simultaneously) externalists and internalists. Sometimes, though, a great many become single-minded bigots. In certain historical moments, numerous Americans find virtue only in cultures and peoples that are outstandingly different—the more different the better; and they blame their own countrymen for having introduced all the vices afflicting cultures that once, prior to penetration, were pure and innocent. The United States lived through such a moment in the 1960s. During that decade, and well into the following one, most books and treatises on Indians portrayed them as "uniformly ingenious and innocent," while the white invaders emerged as "greedy, brutal, and faithless."[33] Similar bias pervaded contemporary books dealing with U.S.–Latin American relations, and resurfaced in Kevin Costner's 1990 movie *Dances with Wolves.*

On the other hand, Americans periodically swell with pride in their civilization and find it well-nigh impossible to detect virtue in anyone identified as alien or Other. As internalists, they see all flaws among Others as homegrown, as inherent. This spirit pervaded the 1980s, just as it did the era of Manifest Destiny (1820s–1840s) as expansionist Americans unleashed a massive assault against both Indians and Latin Americans. Justification for expansion came in part from the negative stereotypes of Indians and Latin Americans, bound together in their joint role as obstacles to Manifest Destiny. If Indians could not aspire to higher status than members of, as Supreme Court chief justice John Marshall phrased it early in the nineteenth century, "domestic dependent nations," so Latin Americans, in Yankee eyes, would have to settle for the status of residents of foreign dependent nations.

The Bad Indian and the Merging of Indian and Latin American Stereotypes

In an appraisal as applicable to attitudes toward Latin Americans as toward Indians, D. H. Lawrence wrote: "It is almost impossible for the White people to approach the Indian without either sentimentality or dislike."[34] Until the Indian menace virtually disappeared in the 1880s, most nineteenth-century Americans—especially those who had direct contact with Indians in their country's West—found the only virtue of the Indian to be his reminder to civilized persons of what they could but must not allow themselves to become. They agreed with their eighteenth-century countrymen who concluded that red skin was not just an accidental condition resulting from long exposure to the sun and from rubbing the skin with berries and herbs—as many seventeenth-century settlers had imagined—but a permanent, innate condition attesting to a dark and debased nature.[35]

By and large, the more Americans came into proximity with Indians the more they disliked them, a situation that is understandable enough considering that most of these Americans coveted land that Indians regarded as theirs, and that the latter defended what they thought belonged to them with all the resources and cunning at their disposal. Even a writer given to occasional noble-savage musings concluded that "the Indian, like a fire, was best admired from a distance."[36]

Most Americans who trekked westward assumed they had a mission to cleanse "the wilderness of primitive men in order that civilization might root and flourish."[37] To many overlanders, Indians were no more than "a troublesome and dangerous species of wild beasts." According to a western newspaper editorialist demanding extermination, Indians—without distinction—were as depraved "a set of . . . dirty, lousy, . . . thieving, lying, sneaking, murdering, graceless, faithless, gut-eating skunks as the Lord ever permitted to infect the earth." All white persons, except Indian agents and a few traders, prayed for their "final extermination."[38] Some westerners acquainted with Indians might content themselves with relatively mild condemnations, limiting themselves to observations that Indians were addicted to such venial sins as impulsiveness and recklessness, laziness and cheating; some might even manage to distinguish among different tribes of Indians and even among individual natives, finding some utterly despicable and others well-nigh human. But only a few could rise above a general dislike of "those unfortunate children of Nature," as President John Quincy Adams described them in his final message to Congress in December 1828.[39]

Had those nineteenth-century Americans who disliked or detested or execrated Indians been able to foresee the cult of the noble red man that flourished in the 1960s, they would have been outraged and ready to agree with a critic of that cult who in 1969 dismissed the Indian as "an incorrigibly murderous bum who today raids the conscience and pocketbook of the nation with scandalous impunity and success."[40] Lewis Cass, governor of Michigan Territory (1813–1831), anticipated this critic when he attacked the weak-minded credulousness of East Coast romantics who recognized as religion the foolish superstitions of Indians and mistook their inveterate laziness for "pious resignation," their "astonishing improvidence" for hospitality.[41]

When it came to specifics, nineteenth-century Americans reviled Indians largely on the same grounds their compatriots chose for deriding Latin Americans. Thus, Indians demonstrated their baseness by their unbridled sexuality and their characteristically "impermanent marital relationships." Typical of many observers, a Presbyterian missionary complained that the loose sexual ways of Indians began with their failure to exercise control over their children, a custom that reflected their disinclination to control themselves, the result being the polygamy of some Indians and the "casual promiscuity" of others.[42] Moreover, if Indian men distinguished themselves as much by laziness as by unbridled eroticism, Indian women, forced into habits of work by domineering men, gained notoriety for their promiscuity and also for the rapid aging process that soon transformed alluring temptresses into repulsive hags.[43] Artist Frederic Remington seems to have been especially taken with the promiscuity imagery. Something of a misogynist who once observed he did not understand women and could not paint them, Remington nevertheless completed some paintings "never yet seen in public, in which the thought of American Indian women inspired in him a certain sneaky indecency."[44] The sexual immorality of Indian women also impressed Mary Eastman, the wife of nineteenth-century military officer and artist Seth Eastman. She attributed this particular aspect of the Indian's pervasive moral failure to the native's chronic inability to achieve "the greatest victory" of which a person is capable: "the conquering of one's self."[45]

Further proof of the Indians' incompatibility with civilization derived from their lack of economic drive. In searching for the cause of this malaise, Americans in the late twentieth century could be just as divided as their forebears had been when trying to explain why Latin Americans remained beggars on golden stools. *Wall Street Journal* reporter Bill Richards in 1984 authored a provocative piece on the Crow reservation in Montana. Although set atop fabulously rich coal resources, the reservation was home to some of the poorest, most wretched and diseased of all Americans. Where did the fault lie? Were Yankee wheeler-dealers, through a long history of defrauding gullible and guileless Indians, responsible? Or, did graft, corruption, and indolence among the Crows themselves account for the reservation's underdevelopment?[46] Just as twentieth-century externalists and internalists debated the reasons for economic failure in Latin America, so also did they dispute the causes of poverty among Native Americans. In the nineteenth century, however, Americans did not much debate the cause of Indian backwardness. They debated little because the overwhelming majority came naturally to the internalist position, satisfied that the causes of Indian economic retardation lay within the natives themselves.

Gambling, so it was said, attracted Indians just as much as sustained labor repelled them.[47] Massive anecdotal material pointing to the Indian's intractable laziness found its way into American lore. For example: when asked by the white blacksmith to whom he had brought a wagon wheel for repair to assist in the task, the Cheyenne named Two Moon haughtily exclaimed, "Jeesy Chrise! Me big Chief! Me no work!"[48] From chief on down to lowliest tribal member, Indian men, according to Anglo observers, refused absolutely to engage in productive labor. Though indefatigable as hunters and athletes, they shunned all tasks that might remotely seem unpleasant and therefore require self-discipline, assigning such tasks to their women—just as Latin American elites assigned onerous functions to their peons.

Immersed in tribal communalism, Indians also lacked a sense of private property. Thus they had not learned how to be "intelligently selfish,"[49] without which trait humans could not progress. For the natives, the road to prestige lay in dispensing rather than accumulating wealth,[50] and so they jumped at any opportunity to squander resources on lavish rites of entertainment. Furthermore, "habits of sloth" led Indians "utterly to despise the value of time."[51] By numerous natural traits, therefore, the Indian seemed refractory to capitalism. Set resolutely against overcoming his natural traits, the Indian seemed just as averse to conquering the natural environment—a conquest that lay at the very heart of capitalist success. When admonished in 1877 by government agents to, in effect, become a capitalist farmer, Smohalla, leader of the Columbia Basin Indian tribes, replied, in what became one of the most frequently quoted statements ever made by an American Indian: "You ask me to plough the ground; shall I take a knife and tear my mother's bosom? Then when I die she will not take me to her bosom to rest. You ask me to dig for stones; shall I dig under her skin for her bones? Then when I die I cannot enter her body to be born again. You ask me to cut grass and make hay and sell it and be rich like white men; but how dare I cut off my mother's hair?"[52]

Senator Henry Teller of Colorado concluded in 1881 that religious conviction led to the Indian's inability to understand the concept of individual property ownership and the imperative for developing natural resources.[53]

Just as much as with the Latin American, then, Indian economic inferiority ultimately could be traced to the influence of purportedly false religious beliefs. Especially for Indians, but to only a slightly lesser degree for Latin American Catholics, religion encouraged humans not to dominate nature but to become one with it.

If Americans suspected pagan influences and animism in Roman Catholicism, they knew they had encountered the real thing in the "superstitions" of Indians. From the very outset they were repelled but often at the same time guiltily fascinated by a people who "made everything in Nature alive and responsive to man,"[54] and who believed they could perform prodigies not through self-effort exercised in the sentient world but rather by tapping into the power (medicine, or manitou) of creatures and forces of nature. Just as Roman Catholics to the south had their Virgin and saints—who also repelled but sometimes fascinated North Americans—so the Indians had legions of spirit helpers through whose aid they could, purportedly, upset rational laws of probability and cause and effect. Just as Catholics had priestly mediators, so Indians (some of them at least) had their shamans. Obviously, thought most Americans, if there were anything to Indian beliefs, the natives would not continue as beggars on golden stools. Practical-minded Americans found it virtually inconceivable that Indians might seek in their religion the means not to improve but rather to remain integrally within nature, in which they found rewards surpassing all understanding.

In the tendency of some Indians to regard the dreamworld as more important than the outer world of sentient reality, in their reverence for spiritual forces of nature that could impart ecstatic experiences of wholeness of such all-consuming intensity as to cause people to lose interest in the phenomena available to the senses, more than a few Americans thought they detected the influence of the Orient.[55] This confirmed the belief that the original Indians were wanderers from the East (some of them perhaps Jews), the region par excellence of mystical concepts that practical men deemed not only foolish but also inimical to progress. Through a gradual trek southward, some of the Indians introduced their Oriental religious concepts into Central and South America, where Spanish conquistadores and their heirs made the mistake, according to American Protestants, of incorporating the concepts into their Catholic faith. Moreover, Spanish Christianity itself, the religion of the conquistadores, even before the conquest had already been vitiated by an Oriental influence introduced by Islam during the centuries it held sway over much of the Iberian Peninsula. To some American Protestants it seemed that Iberian Catholicism had been further vitiated by Jewish mysticism during the years when Iberian

Christians had been so misguided as to live almost tolerantly and harmoniously with both Jews and Muslims. Whatever the roots or connections, real or imagined, some Americans detected in the Latin Catholicism to their south an affinity to the religious beliefs of their own aborigines, with their tendency to seek exalted states of mystical enlightenment and their acceptance of the enchantment of "the universe by spirits and phantoms" that determined "the course of the world and its salvation."[56]

An American did not have to be a zealous Protestant to abhor Indian or, for that matter, Latin American religious beliefs and cosmology. The rational spirit of the Enlightenment provided grounds enough. Thomas Jefferson, who professed that Roman Catholicism blocked Latin American progress,[57] believed that Indians were similarly impeded by the "Platonism" that underlay their religious precepts. To speak of "immaterial existences," Jefferson stated in an 1814 letter to John Adams, "is to talk of nothings." Indian faith, therefore, in the ability to reach what lay beyond or behind the corporeal world was nonsense or worse. Six years later, again writing to Adams, Jefferson contended that "when once we quit the basis of sensation, all is in the wind."[58] Adams agreed, just as he agreed with Jefferson's pessimistic appraisals of Latin America's immediate prospects. The main deficiency in the Indian's faith, according to Adams as he echoed Jefferson, was its considerable tinge of Platonism. And Platonism struck Adams as perhaps more absurd and unintelligible than Judaism. How to account for those common elements of Platonism and Oriental and Indian cosmology that reduced physical reality to the realm of the inconsequential? It all began, Adams suggested, with Plato's travels in India and Egypt and his borrowing from their philosophers.[59] Thus did two of America's leading men of reason join with most branches of Protestantism in dismissing contemptuously the mysticism that underlay much of Indian religions and that, whether in similar or distinct guises, supposedly influenced Latin Catholicism.

Americans who placed their trust in reason or who worshiped God in what they deemed a practical and realistic manner had only disdain for Indian beliefs. According to a distinguished novelist with a keen respect for historical accuracy, few things more astonished mountain men and trappers "or brought from them more vigorous expression of contempt, than the redman's fanatical devotion to a mysterious and intricate system of ceremonial magic. The Indian's world was so overrun by . . . spirits and . . . powers that there were times when he was immobilized." No activity of any kind, however much its immediate undertaking was dictated by practical, material considerations, could be approached "without . . . first going through . . . interminable childish rituals."[60]

In much the same way as they responded to Indian ceremonial dances, pipe smoking, drumbeating, and chanting, nineteenth-century Americans reacted—as I have already stressed—to Latin America's alleged combination of Catholic ritual and pagan rites. Religiously, culturally, and often racially as well, because of the large Indian element in the Latin American populace and because of widespread race mixture, Americans found little to distinguish the New World's aborigines from its Latin inhabitants. Sharing virtually identical flaws, Indians and Latinos left themselves unimproved, in a state of nature. And, in consequence of their moral, cultural, and possibly racial debasement, they also left the land they claimed in an unimproved state of nature, thereby virtually inviting civilized men to seize and improve it.

Swept forward by the tide of Manifest Destiny, Anglo Americans lumped Mexicans together with Indians as people who lacked valid claim to full-fledged human rights. Mexicans, and by extension the rest of Latin Americans (all of whom Americans tended to lump together as they had often lumped Indians together), had only those rights that men like Lewis Cass saw fit to extend to Indians: "The Indians," Cass stated, "are entitled to the employment of all the rights which do not interfere with the obvious designs of Providence, and with the just claims of others." [61] In the age of Jackson, the ideas of Lewis Cass reflected his countrymen's prevailing opinion not only toward Indians but toward Latin Americans as well.

An American traveler in California during the early 1840s dwelt on the Indian characteristics of the Hispanic lower classes. Wherever he observed them he saw "the dull suspicious countenance, the small twinkling piercing eyes, the laxness and filth of a free brute, using freedom as a mere means of animal enjoyment . . . dancing and vomiting as occasion and inclination appear to require." [62] Another Anglo resident in California reported in 1845 that the area's Mexican inhabitants seemed "scarcely a visible grade, in the scale of intelligence, above the barbarous tribes by whom they are surrounded." He disparaged the Mexican soldiers dispatched to California in the early 1840s as "mere Indians." "With these wild, shirtless, . . . heartless creatures, headed by a few timid, soulless, brainless officers, . . . these semi-barbarians intend to hold this delightful region, as against the civilized world." [63] Not only in California but in New Mexico and Arizona as well, American observers both before and after the war with Mexico (1846–1848) could find few grounds to distinguish between Hispanics and Indians. Both groups appeared "similar in racial background, language and religion." [64] According to the 1835 observations of a U.S. Army officer in New Mexico, the settlers of Hispanic background "are the meanest looking race of people I ever saw, [and] don't appear more civilized than our Indians generally. Dirty, filthy looking creatures."[65]

Overcoming the setback at the Alamo (March 1836), Texans in effect won their independence from Mexico by their victory at the Battle of San Jacinto in April 1836. In the years immediately following establishment of the Lone Star Republic, Texans remained in constant readiness to defend themselves against Mexican reconquest and at the same time sought to exterminate the Indians in their region or at least to drive them onto reservations outside Texas territory. The Texas Rangers came into existence essentially to fight Indians, defend the border against Mexican incursion, and discipline Mexicans who had stayed on in Texas after the region ceased to be a part of Mexico.[66] In their disinclination to distinguish between an Indian and a Mexican, the Rangers reflected prevailing attitudes among Anglo settlers in general. The settlers agreed that, as an American soldier in the war against Mexico would shortly put the matter, "like the . . . Indian, the Mexican is doomed to retire before the more enterprising, energetic Anglo Americans. The fertile plains north of the Rio Grande will soon know him no more."[67]

Anglo Americans who crossed the border and viewed Mexico either before the war or, as soldiers, during it had little doubt that Mexicans and Indians were pretty much one and the same. A Negroid element across the border added still another dimension to alleged Mexican inferiority. According to one Texan, "We feel toward the Mexicans just like toward the nigger, but not so much."[68] To Native Americans and to the large Hispanic population incorporated into the United States in consequence of the Mexican War, Anglos soon applied the term *greaser*. In Anglo perceptions, greasers were part Negro, part Indian, filthy and greasy in appearance.[69]

With the signing and ratification of the Treaty of Guadalupe Hidalgo (1848) that ended the war with Mexico, Americans had virtually completed the mission they began after defeating England in the struggle for independence: wresting much of a continent from Spanish-speaking Catholics who, like Indians, vainly pitted themselves against the tide of civilization. When James Polk triumphed in the 1844 presidential election, U.S. national territory stood at approximately 1,788,000 square miles. Three weeks before Polk's presidential inauguration in March 1845, the Lone Star Republic of Texas was annexed to the United States, helping to precipitate the war with Mexico. Less than four years later, with Senate confirmation of the Guadalupe Hidalgo treaty, U.S. territory registered very close to 3 million square miles. In their country's phenomenal expansion, Americans saw the hand of God rewarding them for their proved success in taming wilderness and its barbaric inhabitants.

On the newly acquired lands lived perhaps as many as 75,000 Hispanics: in round figures, some 7,500 in California, 1,000 or so in Arizona, about 60,000 in New Mexico, and perhaps 5,000 in Texas. In addition, some 250,000 Indians fell under U.S. sovereignty as a result of the war, about 72,000 of them in California and the remainder scattered through the rest of the territory that had once belonged to Mexico.[70] Thus the United States faced not only the settlement of a new territorial frontier but the pacification of a "racial frontier" as well.[71] In dealing with nature as encountered on the racial frontier, Americans often proved as thoughtless and brutal as in confronting the physical environment. In fact, the real tragedy emerging from the racism revealed by the stereotypes that underlay Manifest Destiny occurred *after* the war that Manifest Destiny helped bring about.[72]

Thoreau had opposed the Mexican War because he understood that the attitude Americans had already developed in their dealings with Negroes and Indians meant that any of the less-than-fully-white people incorporated into the United States as a result of the conflict would be treated as less than fully human.[73] Thoreau's fears proved well founded—just as had the earlier fears that drove Thomas L. McKenney, the first head of the Bureau of Indian Affairs (1824–1839), to support President Andrew Jackson's Indian removal policy. Only by removal, McKenney reluctantly concluded, could natives escape victimization by the white citizens who surrounded them in the already-settled parts of the country.[74]

The first person lynched in California after the Mexican War was a Mexican. According to a respected historian of the Bear Flag State, "vast research would be required to arrive at an estimate of the number of Mexican lynchings between 1849 and 1880. In the mining camps, every crime or reported crime was promptly blamed on some Mexican and lynching was the accepted penalty for crimes in which Mexicans were involved."[75] In Texas, a literary society actually debated the topic "Is it wicked to lynch Mexicans on Sunday?"[76] While people of culture debated, the majority of Texans "easily convinced themselves . . . that the Texas Rangers knew best how to whip Mexicans and exterminate Indians, and their impatience with the clumsy methods and humanitarian policy of the United States Army was colossal."[77] Outside of Texas, Anglo methods of dealing with Hispanics and Indians may have been, by some slight degree at least, less violent. The methods, though, proved more than adequate to deprive the Other of economic, political, and full-fledged legal rights. On the racial frontier, the triumph of the American over the "Spanish-Mexican-Indian" was widely hailed at the time as "the triumph of virile and intellectual qualities over effeminate and brutal ones." Later generations applauded the triumph as part of the "process of evolution in which superior races arise and replace the inferior," while the industrial-technological stage triumphs over hunting-and-gathering cultures and over "feudalism and primitive capitalism."[78]

In a way, Mark Twain's *A Connecticut Yankee in King Arthur's Court* (1889) reads as a parody of America's conquest of its territorial and racial frontiers acquired by the annexation of Texas and the war with Mexico. The primitives whom the Connecticut Yankee Hank encounters in sixth-century England are "white Indians." They are overgrown children; they are dominated by the dead hand of tradition and Roman Catholic superstitions that induce them to think primarily of the next world. Unconcerned with progress in their caste-ridden society, elites devote themselves to cruel, infantile pursuits of chivalry, freely indulge their sexual and all other passions, and perfect various methods for exploiting serfs and underlings in general. Twain, even though no consistent lover himself of Others, employs dark and biting satire as he describes Hank's efforts to uplift savages literally by destroying them in a bloodbath of monumental proportions. Many Americans, though, saw no reason for humor, satire, or moral regret as they contemplated their actions on the racial frontier in the years when Manifest Destiny flourished. And in some ways Manifest Destiny—the desire to spread civilization into new lands of unspecified extent occupied by subhuman races who very well might perish in the endeavor to civilize them—has always been a part of the American mind-set.

Indians, Latin Americans, and Massacres

As American imperialism expanded to include visions of incorporating lands that belonged not just to Indians but also to Latins, the two ethnic elements grew ever more indistinguishable in Anglo perceptions. The savagery of both groups was proved by the demoniacal ferocity with which they resisted the white man's advance, beginning with the March 22, 1662, Indian massacre at Jamestown. On that occasion Indians killed some 347 English settlers, men, women, and children. Massacres of whites punctuated the entire process through which Americans took possession of a steadily advancing frontier. Once they occurred, the massacres were never forgotten, in contrast to white massacres of Indians which were seldom remembered—at least not until the counterculture's halcyon days in the 1960s.

Particularly vivid in the minds of Americans for decades after the event was the massacre at Fort William Henry on Lake George. James Fenimore

Cooper built one of his most popular novels, *The Last of the Mohicans* (1826), around this event. Following the fort's surrender to French forces under Gen. Louis de Montcalm in 1757, during one of the imperial wars that pitted the Protestant English against the Catholic French and their nominally Catholic Indian allies, the latter carried out a massacre of the English, while the French allegedly looked on indifferently. Estimates as to the number of English victims ranged from five hundred to fifteen hundred. Meanwhile, as they engaged in warfare in the Southeast against Spanish papists and their Indian cohorts, Englishmen considered themselves besieged by Satan's minions, in constant danger of devilish conspiracies that if not circumvented would lead inevitably to massacres of innocent white men, women, and children. One narrowly averted massacre in South Carolina lies at the heart of the anti-Indian, antipapist novel *The Yemassee* that William Gilmore Simms published in 1835—just about the time Anglos in Texas faced Mexican-inflicted massacres that were not averted.

Americans forgot neither the massacre that accompanied Mexican capture of the Alamo in March 1836 nor the one that occurred the following month at Goliad after Texas troops had surrendered to Mexicans. Walt Whitman helped perpetuate the Goliad massacre in America's collective memory. Here are some of the stanzas from his notable poem "Song of Myself."[79]

> I tell not the fall of Alamo . . . . not one escaped to tell the fall of Alamo,
> The hundred and fifty are dumb yet at Alamo.
> Hear now the tale of a jetblack sunrise,
> Hear of the murder in cold blood of four hundred and
>   twelve young men.

Whitman then tells of how nine hundred Texans, outnumbered nine times, their ammunition exhausted, their commanding colonel wounded, surrendered to the Mexicans.

> They treated for an honorable capitulation, received writing and seal,
>   gave up their arms, and marched back prisoners of war.
> They were the glory of the race of rangers,
> Matchless with a horse, a rifle, a song, a supper or a courtship,
> Large, turbulent, brave, handsome, generous, proud and affectionate,
> Bearded, sunburnt, dressed in the free costume of hunters,
> Not a single one over thirty years of age.

The second Sunday morning they were brought out in squads and
    massacred . . . . It was a beautiful early summer,
The work commenced about five o'clock and was over by eight.
None obeyed the command to kneel,
Some made a mad and helpless rush . . . . some stood stark and straight,
A few fell at once, shot in the temple or heart . . . . the living and dead
    lay together,
The maimed and mangled dug in the dirt . . . . the new-comers saw them
    there;

          . . .

At eleven o'clock the burning of the bodies;
And that is the tale of the murder of four hundred and twelve young men,
And that was a jetblack sunrise.

Americans suffered other massacres in the next few years and decades at
the hands of "savages." In 1847 Cayuse Indians killed missionaries Marcus
and Narcissa Whitman in Oregon Territory along with a dozen other
American settlers. The press attributed the massacre not only to Indian
savages but, falsely, to Catholic missionaries and their alleged prime instrument, a mestizo called "Canada Joe."[80] The year before this, as the war
with Mexico began, Mexicans and Indians and half-breeds joined in New
Mexico to massacre some of the Anglo Americans to whom the area had
been officially surrendered by its Mexican officials. Soon the American
press had other provocations, as Americans made their way into Mexican
territory, to write about both Mexicans and Indians whose nature led
them to acts of savage butchery. Like the Indians, Mexicans were said "to
kill the wounded, torture prisoners, and mutilate the dead." Against a
background of frontier mythology, the Mexican War was made to appear a
"grand-scale Indian war," with the cause of civilization depending on an
American victory.[81]

Civilization in due course triumphed in Mexico but remained under
challenge by savagery in its own heartland. Thus in 1862—skipping over
other massacres, whether perpetrated against whites by Mexicans and Indians in the Southwest or by whites against "savages" in various parts of
the land—occurred the Santee Sioux uprising in Minnesota. It resulted in
the deaths of some seven hundred whites, including housewives and little
girls who were in some instances tortured before being killed. In 1876 came
the "massacre" of Gen. George Armstrong Custer and his Seventh Cavalry
regulars. Clearly Americans lived in a period when brave men and innocent women and children faced death at the hands of savages, and among
the latter Mexicans (as representatives of the entire Latin American "race")
were not distinguishable from Indians.

The Civilized and the Wild, and Myths of Death and Regeneration

In facing death at the hands of savages, and then in overcoming that threat and in turn meting out death to the denizens of the wild, Anglo Americans in the nineteenth century acted out the myths that had begun to energize their forebears not long after their arrival in the New World. According to one school of thought, Americans—or, rather, their English ancestors in the New World—believed from early in the colonial period that they had "solved the ills that had always destroyed republics in the past." Discarding old cyclical views of the inevitable rise and decline of civilized, republican virtue, Americans began to glimpse the possibility of perpetuating the life of that virtue. America's "huge reservoir of land would . . . insure its progress virtually in perpetuity. Unlike the nations of the past, Americans would never grow old" and vice-ridden. In the millennialist mind-set into which many of them fell, Americans beginning even in the colonial period "projected utopian fantasies onto the New World." As distinguished intellectual historian J. G. A. Pocock sees the situation, belief in the escape from history promised them by their boundless natural resources constituted the "metahistorical structure within which Americans have understood their relationship to the past and to the future down to the present day." [82]

Toward the end of the twentieth century, to judge at least from a vast body of science fiction, Americans transferred their frontier hopes to space. Yet even this last frontier began to go the way of earlier land frontiers. A congressional report issued in October 1990 pointed out that space was already cluttered by debris left from old rockets and other human-made objects. If the cluttering continues at its present pace, the report stated, shuttle activity and other spaceflights could become too risky to undertake within the next twenty to thirty years.

So, Americans have remained ever frustrated in their frontier expectations. (See illustration 8.) Somehow the redeeming wilderness, together with its exotic and nonwhite occupants, always disappeared (the former through heedless waste and improvements that contributed equally to its destruction, the latter through extermination or acculturation) before their cleansing, renewing, re-creating tasks had been completed. But the myth lived on, impelling Americans to press on in search of new wilderness and new exotics so as to stave off the aging, corrupting process. Here is how Ernest Hemingway expressed the matter in the 1935 nonfiction book he titled *Green Hills of Africa*:

> The earth gets tired of being exploited. A country wears out quickly. . . . Our people went to America because that was the place to go then. It had been a

8. Thomas Hart Benton. *Boom Town*. 1927–1928. Oil on canvas, 45 × 54″. Memorial Art Gallery of the University of Rochester, Marion Stratton Gould Fund.

Even as the new town begins to boom, it already shows signs of ruin. This phenomenon, repeatedly endlessly in American frontier settlement, drove seekers of utopia, and profit, ever farther westward and, eventually, southward as well, into Latin America.

> good country and we made a bloody mess of it and I would go, now, somewhere else as we had always had the right to go somewhere else and as we had always gone. You could always come back. Let others come to America who did not know that they had come too late. Our people had seen it at its best and fought for it when it was worth fighting for. Now I would go somewhere else. We always went in the old days and there were still good places to go.[83]

In the past, Americans had moved out into an ever-expanding western frontier, or into the southern reaches of unsullied nature that Florida and other wilderness areas afforded up to the late nineteenth century. No matter that this frontier and wilderness had belonged to Indians and to Latin Americans. We would renew ourselves in their land and in them, even though the process—which Richard Slotkin describes as "Regeneration through Violence" in his superb 1973 book of that title—would in many ways destroy the land and its wild inhabitants. When the continental West and South no longer afforded untapped Indian or Latin lands, we would turn farther west, to the Philippines for example, whose natives our conquering armies at the turn of the twentieth century referred to as Indians and "Niggers." Or, in fulfilling our Manifest Destiny, we would turn to the south that lay beneath our own continent, justifying our actions by applying to Latin Americans there the same stereotypes by which we had come to rationalize our conduct toward Indians and African Americans. Late in the twentieth century the myth of regeneration through violence took on a new guise. Insisting on the right to arm themselves to the teeth, Americans justified themselves by imagining scenes in which they killed threatening, dark-skinned savages who inhabited the wilderness of inner-city ghettos.

Latin Resentment of American Prejudices

Since colonial times, Latin American society in general has been a "pig-mentocracy,"[84] with the dark-skinned masses of Indians, Africans, and mixed-bloods constituting the base of a social pyramid. The higher one looked on the pyramid, the lighter the skin color was likely to be. Society, however, remained to some extent open, providing opportunities for the exceptional person of color—assuming the color was not too dark—to rise. When the truly exceptional person of the lower, subordinate sectors advanced upward and underwent "whitening" in the eyes of the beholder, he or she could anticipate some degree of acceptance by society, precisely because his or her rise was exceptional and did not pose the threat of the rise of underlings en masse. What resulted from this process was the co-optation by elite sectors of the natural leadership element among underlings. Generally, the recently risen persons identified with the higher status into which they climbed and turned their backs on the lower status from which they had emerged, often in fact proving less tolerant than long-established elites of the multitudes below. However, long-established as well as new elites converged in the conviction that dark skin color was, in general, associated with stupidity and evil. From colonial times onward, in fact, Indians were labeled *gente sin razón* (people without reason), while mestizos and Africans fell into the category of *mala raza* (bad race): although possessing reason, they allegedly inclined to exercise it in twisted, perverse manner.

Latin America's leading, whitish classes, while accepting it as natural that they should disdain and dominate those of darker skin, reacted with outrage upon discovering that in the United States they themselves might be taken for less than white and discriminated against accordingly. Criminals from Europe, a prominent nineteenth-century Ecuadoran intellectual and statesman declared, could gain acceptance in the United States if they presented a white skin, whereas the most respectable Latin Americans suffered endless affronts if their skin showed the slightest color. In Venezuela, Peru, and Ecuador, he added, persons of dark skin could aspire to gaining acceptance by respectable, white society; and by dint of application they could fulfill their aspirations. However, in the United States, the sine qua non for acceptance as a human being was a white skin.[85]

An eminent Peruvian man of letters and affairs traveled to the United States in the early 1940s, when the Good Neighbor policy was in full bloom. He quickly discovered that among the Yankees anyone with even the slightest portion of African blood was judged a Negro. From the American viewpoint, all of the mixed-bloods of Andean America who had even a minuscule admixture of African blood "are Negroes, and only Negroes." The same was true in regard to Indians, the traveler complained. "Who is an Indian in the United States? Anyone with even a drop of Indian blood." In the United States, he added, "persons who for us would be white (if they had economic position) are . . . Indians." Stressing the obvious, the Peruvian (himself a man of white skin) concluded, "From our point of view . . . , racial attitudes in the United States have built a bad road for achieving permanent solidarity between the two parts of America."[86]

Latin Americans first became generally aware of the "bad road" not long after their independence as the United States took to a policy of Manifest Destiny directed not just against Indians but also against Latins—specifically against Mexicans. Mexican diplomatic representatives in the United States "were shocked at the rabid anti-Mexican attitudes and at the manner in which Mexicans were lumped together with Indians and blacks as an inferior race."[87] Of the great masses of their Indian populace, privileged Mexicans thought no more highly than did Americans. In the 1830s, for example, the Mexican government paid bounties in its northern provinces for Indian scalps.[88] At this time a prominent Mexican observed: "The contempt with which the Indian is viewed in Mexico is very marked. There are educated people in Mexico who consider themselves polluted by the mere fact of having to think of the Indian."[89] Obviously, Mexicans of this persuasion reacted with outrage to the inability of Americans to distinguish between Mexicans and Indians and to recognize the different grades of virtue within the pigmentocracy.

Mexican general Manuel Mier y Terán, writing in 1828, complained bitterly that Americans judged his countrymen by the "most ignorant" Negro and Indian riffraff they encountered in the borderlands. Mier y Terán noted that he and worthy Mexicans held these border elements in the same disdain that Yankees accorded them. He could not forgive Americans for judging all Mexicans by the country's social trash. American insensitivity had helped kindle what the general described as "smouldering fires" that endangered friendly relations with his country.[90] Like Mier y Terán, Mexican elites in general prided themselves on sufficient discernment to bar from access into the ranks of the gente decente the unsavory elements by which gringos judged all Mexicans. And they bitterly resented gringo inability to recognize their discernment in deciding which few exceptional representatives of the barbarian hordes to admit to the ranks of civilization.

Also infuriating to Mexicans were those condescending Yankees who however much they disparaged Mexicans in their present state piously expressed faith in the possibility of uplifting them—just as other Americans sometimes pronounced on the possibility of uplifting Indians and persuaded themselves that at least the "better elements" among the aborigines relished the opportunity for uplift.[91] Americans bent on uplift afforded examples of an enduring national type that novelist John Updike referred to in *Rabbit Redux* (1971) as the "good-hearted imperialist racist."[92]

Some American soldiers who participated in the war against Mexico believed that by the power of their example they had helped prepare the southern country to enter the modern age. Under the prod of American occupation, old customs and traditions were disappearing, according to one soldier. Mexicans "could not resist the go-ahead-ism of the victorious North Americans."[93] An American businessman who had followed the war from a safe distance saw it as the beginning of Mexico's regeneration; for the war afforded Americans the chance to "innoculate Mexico with the commercial spirit."[94] In his novel *Jack Tier,* written during the hostilities, James Fenimore Cooper suggested that the war would break the hold of feudalism in Mexico and breach the walls that had enclosed it in bigotry and superstition. As the light of reason began to enter, Mexicans themselves would rejoice over what had at first glance seemed a disaster.[95] Moreover, even Americans who opposed the war sometimes justified their position on the condescending grounds of uplift. Noble ideas, they reasoned, inspiring deeds "to raise up fallen races," could flourish better in peace than in the circumstances of war.[96]

As the war ended, Mexico's gente decente perceived no need among themselves for uplift under the surveillance of a people who, judging from some invading soldiers and also from uncouth and sadistic border settlers, impressed them as northern barbarians and "half savages," creatures who professed false religions and delighted in perpetrating atrocities.[97] As for the gente sin razón and the malas razas comprising the bulk of the population, these were people who lay, by and large, beyond the possibility of uplift, in the eyes of many of Mexico's gente decente. Any misguided Yankee endeavor to elevate them would result only in social turmoil and general backsliding.

Prior to the war, some members of the Mexican upper classes, dismayed by the general loosening of the ties of civilization that they perceived in the immediate postindependence period, had themselves hoped for an expansion of U.S. influence in their land, persuaded it might contribute to a sorely needed process of reform. In outlook, they resembled the "friendlies" among Indian tribes who often welcomed Uncle Sam's helping hand. And who is to say, with certainty, that the friendlies—both Indian and Latin American—did not include high-minded individuals sincerely concerned with the interests of their own people and honestly convinced that collaboration with get-ahead outsiders was the policy most likely to improve their conditions? In any event, by the end of the war with the United States, Mexico's gente decente included few friendlies, although the type would begin to reappear within a decade in the face of mounting internal problems. Farther south, Latin American intellectuals and political leaders continued throughout the nineteenth and early twentieth centuries to include many friendlies. But, as U.S. imperialism entered a more assertive phase at the turn of the century, their position grew increasingly vulnerable to attack by local figures, some of them sincere patriots and others theatrical breast-beaters out to serve personal ambitions.

A quarter century after the Mexican War when artist Thomas Moran ventured south of the border, he generally responded unfavorably, as previously indicated, to the people, finding them—like American Indians—no better than "dirty savages."[98] At least his particular brand of ethnocentrism did not lead him to offend these "savages" by harping on the need of Americans to provide models of regeneration and uplift. It was his own uplift and regeneration that concerned Moran as he set eyes on the land of Mexico.

Moran fell in love with and felt renewed by the splendors of the natural setting, particularly by the majestic mountains. Many Americans who first set eyes on Mexico as invaders in the 1840s also fell under the spell of its scenery. Some actually used the words "Garden of Eden" as they sought to express their wonder at the country's miraculous beauty;[99] for this, after all, was an age in which Americans remained close to their Bibles but not abashed, in their frequent millennialist moments, to give unorthodox interpretations to biblical myths. The Mexican people might not be much in American eyes—might not, in fact, be any better than American Indians—but the natural terrain afforded a virtuous and masculine race an opportunity to enter once again into an energizing relationship with virgin nature, and to be reborn.

Frontier Mythology and the Poisoning of Hemispheric Relations

Some Americans gazing on Mexico's Edenic setting must surely have felt the compulsion that their forebears had experienced when first contemplating an Eden of their own, whether in New England or the southern colonies: the compulsion "to take dominion by reforming" its pristine, virgin qualities.[100] This, after all, was how Americans treated their frontier. The fact that Mexicans and Latin Americans in general had not dealt similarly with their frontiers, leaving them instead undeveloped, unreformed, and unpeopled, attested to their backwardness. Indeed, divergent responses to frontier opportunities, north and south of the border, formed the basis for a good deal of the stereotyping by which Americans denigrated Latin Americans.

In a 1990 review essay, literary critic Robert M. Adams referred to an unconquered Latin American frontier that inevitably has left an enduring mark on the people, for better and for worse. "A vast heartland of jungle lies at the center of South America, and outlying patches of it can be found not only in Lima and Bogotá but at the core of the region's most artful imaginative achievements. What's more, the savagery is not something to be excised or deplored; it is a vital element of the culture, a birthmark of ugly authenticity with which writers will be wrestling for generations to come."[101]

The unconquered frontier may inspire some of the finest of Latin America's literary accomplishments. But relatively few Americans appreciate this fact. For most of them, the unmastered frontier has stood as the badge of the area's inferiority, a proof of the lingering, unpardonable backwardness and savagery of the people. Finally in the late twentieth century as Latin Americans began to move ruthlessly against the huge surviving areas of wilderness in their midst, Americans still found them wanting in the higher gifts of civilization. By that time environmental issues had risen to the fore; and many Americans regarded the Latin's unbridled, heedless tapping of wilderness resources as an atavistic throwback to an earlier time, a throwback that civilized beings could not condone. Thus the frontier and all that it conjures up in American values and expectations remained a source of discord in hemispheric relations. The following chapter traces the origins of this discord.

CHAPTER 4

Our Frontier and Theirs: American Perceptions of Latin American Backwardness

Iberian and Anglo Approaches to New World Frontiers: Underlying Differences?

According to an interpretation that enjoys broad support among Latin America's Catholic conservative intellectuals, the Iberian conquest of the New World was a principled, ethical effort, carefully controlled by altar and throne, aimed at bringing religious enlightenment to pagan Indians and guiding them gently into new life-styles, temporal and spiritual. Intellectuals of this persuasion see the conquest as shaped by a profound juridic conscience. Moreover, they maintain that control from above, inspired by Catholic principles of social justice and charity, continued to inform the entire colonial period. Seen in this light, the Iberian experience in conquering and ruling the New World stands in stark contrast to the allegedly lawless way in which Americans gradually conquered their frontier, obeying principles no higher than the rule of force and personal greed.

Americans have tended to take pride in what Latin American thinkers condemn as the anarchism of their frontier expansion. They like to believe that they conquered their part of the New World in the manner appropriate to free and independent human beings, and in ways that strengthened the seeds of individualism brought from England. From their point of view, the Latin American frontier experience derived out of the original sin of statism. The state, for example, claimed ownership of subsoil wealth, insisted upon licensing all persons who mined this wealth, and collected taxes generally pegged at about one-tenth of the value of the precious metals or jewels extracted from the earth. Thereby did Iberian governing institutions stifle the enterprising spirit and, at the same time, guarantee that settlement would proceed in a timid, half-hearted manner that left the environment unsubdued and underutilized.

In the centralizing regime of the Latin American colonial period, in which church and state, religion and politics combined to suppress individual initiative, Americans have tended to find the root of much of what they consider wrong with the southern portions of the New World. Always having to reckon with control from above, upper-sector citizens sought to improve their lot not through enterprise focused by relentless self-control but rather through striking deals with the wielders of centralized authority. They advanced not by extracting wealth from nature but by extracting concessions from government. They sought what a twentieth-century Spanish intellectual has called the "money of power": money, that is, derived from special arrangements with the wielders of political power.[1] In consequence, upper-sector Latin Americans remained in some ways almost as dependent, as childlike and "effeminate," as the masses of peons at the bottom of society. These latter depended abjectly upon a class of overlords who in turn depended upon ingratiating themselves with the interlocking bureaucracy of churchmen and political officeholders who ostensibly carried out the wishes of the Crown. This is why success for elites derived from extracting fortunes out of the system, not out of nature.

In a provocative study published in 1961, Mexican historian-philosopher Edmundo O'Gorman contends that Iberian settlers of the New World adapted the new environment to the political, social, economic, and religious models that had obtained in the Old World. Latin America, he maintains, "was never a frontier land in the sense of dynamic transformation that has been given to the term by American historians ever since Frederick Jackson Turner; it was rather the passive object of transplanting and grafting." Unlike "their English brothers in the northern part of America," Iberians abjured adaptation to the circumstances of the New World. Instead, they remained mired in traditionalism and therefore failed to develop the progressive traits that spring from adaptation. Depending on the favoritism of centralized institutions for their worldly success, they "never engaged in any widespread and tenacious effort to transform forests and deserts into cultivable areas; they confined their settlement to regions that seemed to be naturally destined by Providence for man's benefit." Moreover, the Iberians retained the medieval religious concepts of a "God-given world," regarding as impious any concerted endeavor "to dramatically transform their environment." Thus when Jesuit priest José de Acosta at the end of the sixteenth century suggested the possibility of opening a canal in Panama to join the two oceans, he quickly abandoned the idea. Why? Because of the "fear of Heaven's punishment for 'wanting to correct the work which God, so wisely and providentially, ordered in the making of the Universe.'"[2] If God wanted human beings to prosper materially in the world that he had made, he would reward them, providentially, not for their conscious efforts to achieve wealth by transforming nature but rather for their loyal, selfless, unquestioning service to him and their dependence on him for their temporal succor. Similarly, civil authorities on earth serving the cause of a theocratically united church and state would reward certain worthies not in accordance with their pursuit of wealth so much as in accordance with their political loyalty and subservience.

In their approach to the riches of nature and to their God, according once more to O'Gorman, Spaniards and Portuguese stood in stark contrast to their northern neighbors. These latter regarded the New World not as a "forbidding reality made by God" and not to be tampered with by mere mortals; instead, they saw it as "a vast inexhaustible quarry out of which man may carve out his world, depending not on divine permission, but solely on his own initiative, daring and technical ability."[3]

The Iberians' approach to the New World reflected and grew out of the social system they brought with them from the Old World. That system, based on what political scientists and sociologists designate *ascription,* demanded that, with only occasional exceptions, people accept the status decreed by birth. Birth, that most natural of all phenomena, determined all; one did not struggle against what was natural. In Iberian society at the moment of conquest, the values of ascription were solidly entrenched, and the circumstances of birth pretty much determined a person's life chances. Even the old means to upward mobility through demonstrated military prowess in fighting Islam had come to an end as Christian Spain, in 1492, completed its triumph over its Moorish adversaries. Opportunities for spectacular upward social mobility did accompany the conquest of indigenous civilizations in the New World, as we shall see later in this chapter. Within a century, though, such opportunities had become relatively rare. More than ever, ascription, with all its attendant social values, had come to prevail in the Iberian Old and New worlds.

When the English embarked in the early sixteenth century on their New World settlement, already they had taken the first steps toward an achievement-oriented society; and, both in Britain and the colonies, these steps grew longer and became less faltering as time passed. In the achievement-directed society, one struggles against what is ordained by the circumstances of birth, seeking to upset what is given, what is natural. The very fact that Iberians and Anglos at the moment they began New World settlement responded, in relative or comparative terms, to ascription on one hand and achievement on the other ordained that Iberians would accept nature as it was found while Anglos struggled to alter it. Already the die was cast that ordained vastly different approaches to New World frontiers—or so conventional American stereotypers have seen the situation, their interpretations often backed by Latin American thinkers.

Although not specifically employing the terms ascription and achievement, O'Gorman did attribute to the unbreakable chains of the Old World's culture the failure of Iberians, as compared to Englishmen, to transform and develop their part of the New World. With this assessment Americans through the years have tended to agree. On the other hand, Latin American thinkers, departing from O'Gorman, have often preferred to blame temporal failures not so much on Iberian influences as on the allegedly static psyche of the Indian populations that so vastly outnumbered the conquerors and colonial settlers. A Peruvian writer summarized widespread attitudes throughout most of Latin America when he asserted in 1888 that Indians suffered the permanent curse of static natures that made it impossible for them to undergo adaptation. Through the years, the Indians had preserved unaltered "their limited horizons of desires, their same enervated nature" that had typified them even in preconquest days. "The same dim light that barely illuminates the understanding of their ancestors today paralyzes the intellectual ability of this singular race."[4]

With this conclusion many Americans agreed, thanking their God for having spared them the Latin curse of an overwhelming population of benighted aborigines. From both the Iberian and Indian components of their racial formation, Latin Americans had acquired traits that rendered them, in the eyes of their observers to the north, the pawns rather than the masters of nature. In consequence of their dual racial-cultural heritage, Latin Americans had proved unable to deal with frontier opportunities in a way that would have brought them the fruits of a modern and progressive civilization. The point to stress is the degree to which American stereotypes of Latin Americans are reinforced by—and perhaps sometimes even originate in—Latin American stereotypes of themselves.

In his enormously provocative book *The Great Frontier* (1952), historian Walter Prescott Webb speculates that the New World, from the dawn of the sixteenth century, served as a great frontier to virtually all of the Old World. Its vast resources, made available after 1492, dramatically changed the ratio of Old World population to available metallic riches, to the wealth-producing potential of virgin land, and to additional natural resources of virtually every conceivable type. The changing ratio between population and wealth (actual and potential) undermined the centralized institutions of government that had emerged to allocate and apportion the Old World's limited economic resources. The apparently unlimited wealth of the New World lay behind the loosening of the Old World's political institutions and ushered in the age of laissez-faire enterprise.

Webb's thesis seems to make some sense when applied to the English Old and New worlds. But it makes little sense in the Iberian world, whether Old or New. In neither Iberian realm did America's vast potential wealth lead to a dramatic undermining of old institutions and the advent of political and economic liberalism. Nineteenth-century Americans, it seems to me, by and large recognized this fact, or at least vaguely intuited it. Their virtuous progress and the Latin Americans' benighted backwardness attested, in their minds, to the inability of the Latins to modify their old assumptions about nature's limited good even when nature suddenly made itself available in unlimited bounty.[5] Sitting atop their golden stools, Latin Americans stubbornly retained a traditional, premodern mentality and remained comparatively indifferent to the opportunities the frontier offered men and women to make themselves anew by mastering nature, both within and without.

Frontier Experiences and Pejorative Comparisons: The United States and Latin America

Pious national myths to the contrary notwithstanding, government had a great deal to do with establishing the character of frontier settlement in America. In the classic example of Washington's largesse to "private" enterprise, the federal government bestowed huge amounts of land upon railroad builders avidly pursuing profits by opening the West to settlement. In the West, moreover, vast tracts of national territory remained public range lands in the domain of the national government. In 1897, in order to encourage a growing cattle industry, Congress ruled that western ranchers could henceforth lease public range lands, for a pittance. Here was a form of government subsidized private enterprise, of privatized socialism, of the privatization of social property. Whatever one wishes to call the hybrid, it attests to a larger role for government in the settlement of the West than frontier mythology acknowledges. And the handling of public range lands is only one example of government intervention in behalf of "private" western capitalists, an intervention that was far more extensive at the state and local level of government than at the national. But Americans like to forget this aspect of their history and to overlay it with myths of uninhibited free enterprise as the great motor of westward expansion and development. In this as in countless other instances, the myths rather than the reality have tended to shape American self-images. And in this section (as, indeed, in most of the chapter), it is more often the myths than the reality of frontier development, whether in America or Latin America, that concern me. But the myths, as tends to be the case with these pesky acts of faith in general, have some basis in fact some of the time.

Here is one myth (partially, but no more than that, rooted in reality) that has commanded widespread reverence among Americans for well-nigh two centuries. In the United States, the frontier generated sustained and dramatic increments in national productivity largely because the government in Washington refrained from establishing controls over its resources, either before or after private citizens laid claim to them.[6] In contrast (and here comes another myth, rooted only partially in reality), government in Latin America, whether in the colonial or republican periods, largely succeeded in its consistent endeavor to manage and control frontier resources. Americans moved westward as free and independent agents, unfettered in their quest of self-gain. Latins appropriated frontier resources only after reaching an accommodation with a central government—an accommodation often rendered expensive by the need for bribery of one sort or another. The Latin system restricted the spirit of enterprise, ostensibly in the interests of the common good as defined by Scholastic or Thomistic philosophy. Restrictions may or may not have served their professed moral purpose. Definitely, though, they dimmed prospects for sustained and dramatic increments in economic productivity.

Already by the time they began to settle America, English men and women had developed, according to some historians at least, a family system that placed relatively few barriers in the way of true love and individual ambition; they had also developed notions about unfettered private property.[7] Enormously important in removing the restrictions that premodern customs had imposed on private ambition and property was the spread of the enclosure system: a system that, beginning in the thirteenth century, unleashed an assault on communal lands by encouraging erection of fences, ditches, and other barriers that demarcated individual holdings. Facilitating the breakdown of the manorial system, in which aristocrats had been restricted by various social and economic obligations to serfs and free tenants, the enclosure system rose to a peak during the late seventeenth century. Imported to the New World, its principles from the very outset of settlement lent impetus to fee-simple land ownership that fostered the spirit of economic individualism. Not until the nineteenth century did Spain and Portugal experience comparable onslaughts against the manorial and communal traditions of land ownership. And not until the nineteenth century did the rise of liberalism in the newly independent Latin American republics result in a challenge to traditional barriers to laissez-faire economics by triggering a crusade for untrammeled rights of individual property ownership. Even late in the twentieth century, how-

ever, the liberal assault against economic traditionalism in much of Latin
America had made less headway than it had already achieved in seventeenth-century England and English America.

Shaped by precedents imported from the Old World, Iberian frontier
expansion proceeded initially through huge land grants from the Crown.
"The *latifundio* [i.e., the large estate or hacienda], not the homestead, became the typical rural institution." Prevailingly undercapitalized, it was
worked "by a virtually enserfed, debt-ridden peon labor force."[8] Still, the
hacendado (large-estate owner) incurred, in line with Iberian traditions,
numerous social and economic obligations, designed to render peons relatively content and, above all, quiescent. The result was a static setting that
suppressed the capitalist spirit and frustrated innovations both among hacendados and serfs. Such, at least, was the judgment that Americans beginning in the nineteenth century generally rendered on the large estate. The
judgment may have rested on oversimplified generalizations; but not until
the second half of the twentieth century have historians and social scientists, employing the most sophisticated research methodology, begun to
modify hoary American stereotypes of the large estate.

Departing occasionally from the hacienda pattern of private ownership
and collective labor, the Crown issued communal grants to groups of persons, most of them relatively destitute, "who desired jointly to form a new
settlement." The New Mexico territory, for example, before it fell into
American hands, counted some sixty of these land grants, with most property held in common.[9] According to Americans who observed such communities, whether in New Mexico or across the border in Mexico or even
farther south in Latin America, they bred life-styles of economic subsistence, passivity, and fatalism.[10] American observers may not have been altogether mistaken in these assessments, for the communities in question
did not arise out of any struggle to maximize individual gain. Instead, they
were inspired by visions of cooperative enterprise and the sharing of gains
and losses. Secure in their sense of place and self-contained isolation,
settlers "lived intimately with the land."[11]

Given prevailing cultural values, the typical American by the mid–
nineteenth century felt increasing revulsion toward initiative-stifling collectivism, equating it with primitivism.[12] Thus the typical American deplored the collectivism of the Latin American estates that formed halfway
points between urban civilization and a wild frontier. It mattered not to
the American whether the detested collectivism permeated entire communal entities (as in New Mexico) or prevailed only among peons on the
large, privately owned estate, the hacienda. Hacendados (and also *ranche-*
ros who presided over smaller estates, or *ranchos*) may have been incipient

capitalists, seeking to maximize private gain as they marketed estate produce to the outside world; but they stifled the rise of grass-roots capitalism by maintaining collectivized, fatalistic laborers in dependence on their largesse. Unlike the American frontier that provided emancipation from inequality,[13] and egged the emancipated being on toward the unrelenting conquest of nature as the means to sustain economic independence, the Latin American hinterland with its large private estates fostered the subordination and dependence of a collectivist labor force. Steadfastly, the hacendado sought to stamp out all incentives for private gain that might erode the servility of serfs. He rendered capitalism impossible by depriving it of a foundation.[14] In the very process he incurred burdens of social spending that worsened the estate's chronic undercapitalization.

In stark contrast to what has been sketched above (remember that the sketch reflects both reality and flawed stereotypes), the Anglo frontier expanded through land sales engineered by private companies, augmented at later times by the principle of squatter's rights. Relatively free from government regulations, land became the basis of speculation aimed at maximizing profits for those private entities, companies, and individuals that dealt in it. As a commodity, land provided the basis for a system of individual profit seeking, unfettered by social-economic obligations to a serf class. With good reason, Arthur P. Whitaker, one of the most distinguished historians ever to consider some of the points here under discussion, notes: "The importance of the land speculator in the history of westward expansion in the United States . . . can hardly be exaggerated."[15] In comparison to North America, one looks almost in vain for the counterpart of the land speculator in the expansion of the Latin American frontier during the colonial and early republican periods. Comparatively, then, one looks nearly in vain for "the increase in land values and rising return on speculative investment [that] provided capital for further investment and expansion,"[16] and thereby helped spark the birth of American capitalism. Spain and, after their independence, certain Latin American republics occasionally offered food, clothing, livestock, and money "in order to lure people toward the frontier; yet these subsidies were often ineffective." In America, on the other hand, land hunger and the prospects of real-estate speculation became self-generating forces "that coursed through . . . history without artificial stimulation," moving people generation after generation "out onto the trails."[17]

With the mining frontiers in Anglo and Latin America, the stories stand in similarly stark contrast. Thus when California offered Anglos their first significant mining frontier in the mid-1800s, precedents originating in England dictated that this frontier would be exploited through private enterprise. In contrast, traditions of medieval Spain (according to which subsoil wealth inhered inalienably in the Crown, to be employed partially at least in serving the common good) ordained that mining would become a government-supervised enterprise, hedged about by all sorts of restrictions that impeded individual enterprise. Therefore, to some considerable degree, time-serving bureaucrats provided stimulus, such as it was, for the expansion of both the agricultural and the mining frontiers in Latin America. The bureaucrats did not come close to matching the impetus that untrammeled, spontaneous, private enterprise brought to the expansion of these frontiers in America.

As with so many topics that concern frontiers, historian Ray Allen Billington best sums up conventional wisdom: spearheaded by "cocksure pioneers," American frontier expansion "emphasized the role of the individual in the subjugation of nature," always providing him "free rein to exploit the new land for his own benefit. The frontier philosophy of Spain, on the other hand, subordinated the individual to the state."[18] Billington regarded the American approach as a testament to national virtue, but a new generation of frontier historians in the 1980s had their doubts. Both Billington and his critics agree, though, that, for better or worse, the American frontier experience lent impetus to individualism (though sometimes, as the critics stress, to the paradox of government-assisted individualism), to a passion for private gain, and to total indifference to the environmental consequences of the quest for economic aggrandizement.

The hunter provides one of the great symbols of the conquest of nature that attracted Americans to frontier expansion. And, to a degree to which one finds no parallel in Latin American lore, Americans elevated hunting to epic, even mythic, proportions. In one instance at least, the hunting myth focused on a communal experience. In Ohio, five hundred men and boys gathered in 1818 to clear their area of "pests." "They marched forward into the forests blasting away" and within a few hours killed three hundred deer, twenty-one bears, seventeen wolves, and "uncounted numbers of foxes and other small game." Generally, hunting lore developed around the solitary killer. A Pennsylvania-born hunter gained widespread fame for having killed two thousand buffalo in his mainly pre-1850 career. In the second half of the century this same hunter, William F. ("Buffalo Bill") Cody, shot buffalo, for five dollars a month, for the Kansas and Pacific Railroad. In the year and a half he worked for the company, he dropped an estimated 4,280 of the animals. In a contest to see "who could kill more buffalo in a single day he bested one Billy Comstock, sixty-nine to forty-six." The year was 1872. Within the next two years, an estimated 3,158,730 of the animals were killed "by the white hide hunters."[19] Hide hunters! There was an economic motive to much of the killing, for buffalo-skin blankets and coats had become popular in the East. The two hundred thousand hides shipped out of Montana, Wyoming, and the western portions of Dakota Territory in 1882 found eager purchasers back East.[20] Often, though, the animals were simply left where the hunter's bullet had felled them, perhaps only the tongue being salvaged as a delicacy to be served up by nearby or even distant restaurants. The "sportsmen" who in the two decades after the Civil War hired space on railroad cars from the roofs of which they shot buffalo were generally not interested in deriving commercial profit from the slaughter. Some were motivated by the patriotic desire to rob Indians of their means of sustenance, thereby driving the natives into oblivion so that civilization might redeem their lands. More times than not, though, what lay behind American fascination with killing buffalo was the commercial use to which that killing could be put. The same motivation inspired hunters in late nineteenth-century Florida to threaten alligators as well as plumed birds with extinction. From this extinction came huge profits from the sale of hides and feathers.

One of the great archetypal characters in twentieth-century western fiction is Sam Chance, created by Texan Benjamin Capps in his 1965 eponymous novel. A stunning chapter in that novel, titled "The Slaughter," describes Sam Chance's participation, inspired by expectations of dramatic profit, in the killing of hundreds of buffalo within a few days' time. By the end of the shooting spree, "the carcasses were scattered in groups everywhere, black against the gray grass and the new light-green grass. . . . The air was heavy with the smell of rotten meat, the stench increasing now with warm weather setting in."[21] In this saga of the plains in which buffalo serve as the equivalent of Melville's whale Moby-Dick, the advance of capitalism demands ruins—the ruins of nature. To progressive Americans, such ruins seemed as sacred as churches, shrines, and religious fiestas were to unprogressive, benighted Latin Americans.

Only with Brazil's late twentieth-century assault on Amazonian forests do figures of the Sam Chance type begin, with some regularity, to take their place in Latin America's frontier lore—and here is a symptom of the Americanization of Latin America referred to in the Preface. Now that Americans can no longer freely play the game themselves, now that they have been frightened by the consequences of their excesses into acquiring environmental consciousness, they piously condemn Latin pioneers who seek to mold themselves in the epic proportions of northern models.

In colonial and even in nineteenth-century Latin America, if one ventured out into the frontier, he or she most likely would encounter a mission (see illustration 9), perhaps accompanied by a *presidio* (fort or gar-

9. Edward Everett. *Mission of San José near San Antonio de Béxar.* 1847. Pen and ink and watercolor on paper, 7⅝ × 9⅜″. Courtesy Amon Carter Museum, Fort Worth, Texas.

Everett painted this famous Texas mission as the American war with Mexico was under way. In American eyes, the Spanish mission as a frontier institution was suspect: it sought not to inculcate but to snuff out the spirit of worldly success.

rison). The venturer into the American frontier would have looked in vain for missions but would have come upon forts, often privately owned and managed. Altogether unlike presidios, the American forts served private commercial as much as public-defense purposes. (See illustration 10.) Devoted to trade, one facet of which was to supply overlanders with necessary goods, the forts were "vestiges of the cutthroat national and international competition which had characterized the quest for beaver pelts." With a little inquiry, the venturer would have learned that "most of the canny entrepreneurs who anticipated the profit potential in catering to the many needs of overland travelers [at the trading forts] were formerly mountaineers,"[22] men who had completed the transformation from adventurer to entrepreneur.[23] Absent along with trading forts from the Latin Ameri-

10. Alfred Jacob Miller. *Fort Laramie or Sublette's Fort Near the Nebraska or Platte River.* Ca. 1851. Watercolor on paper, gouache, graphite, ink, 6½ × 9½". Joslyn Art Museum, Omaha, Nebraska.

Miller depicts the tenuous moment when civilization confronts Indian "savagery" at a trading fort. Emissaries of civilization hoped to enrich themselves and perhaps at the same time to uplift savages by awakening in them the mercantile spirit.

can frontier was another staple of the American West: the Jewish trader. His presence symbolized free competition among religions as well as economic competition, two constants of American civilization missing from the south-of-the-border scene.[24]

As Spaniards and Portuguese advanced into the frontier, they encountered sedentary Indians who were valued primarily for their potential as agricultural laborers. Thus Iberians could scrupulously refrain from digging into the soil with their own hands, from going *mano a mano* (hand to hand) with nature in the struggle to wrench from it the last ounce of profit. When intermediaries are utilized in the contest with nature, the refined classes who supervise the process can take little direct, personal pride in whatever victories may be won. And this guarantees that the victories will generally be less than spectacular. Nor will the labor force feel inspired to all-out effort, for laborers will derive at best only limited personal gain from their efforts. Furthermore, social harmony on the large estate, always stressed by an interventionist church and state bureaucracy, demanded restraints on the degree to which underlings were prodded into the tasks of taming nature. Prevailingly, masters controlled their serfs through some measure of appeasement. Under these circumstances a culture emerged that tended to equate virtue more with restraint and paternalism than with the all-out exploitation of labor and, through that labor, of nature. To American observers, such a culture smacked of primitivism. Thus nature remained unconquered, and to Americans this proved Latin America's backwardness.

Early nineteenth-century American travelers expressed amazement over the degree to which Latin American frontiers lay unclaimed. An American southerner who explored part of the Brazilian Amazon in the 1840s reacted in typical manner. The Amazonian frontier, he concluded, could never be settled by "an imbecile and indolent people." This task demanded "a go ahead race that has energy and enterprise equal to subdue the forest and develop and bring forth the vast resources that lay hidden there." [25] Many contemporary American travelers in Latin America agreed that the untapped frontier attested to a debased people, willing to live in an indolent standoff with nature because they lacked the moral stamina to conquer it. In picturing Latin America as a frontier of unlimited opportunities awaiting only the intervention of a worthy people, Americans reflected the prejudices of Englishman Alfred Wallace, sometimes credited as a co-discoverer, along with Charles Darwin, of evolution. In a book describing his travels on and along the Amazon, Wallace wrote:

> When I consider the excessively small amount of labour required in this country, to convert virgin forest into green meadows and fertile plantations, I almost long to come over with half-a-dozen friends disposed to work, and enjoy the country; and show the inhabitants how soon an earthly paradise might be created, which they had never conceived capable of existing. . . . I fearlessly assert that here the primeval forest can be converted into rich pasture and meadow land, into cultivated fields, gardens, and orchards containing every variety of produce, with half the labour, and what is more in half the time that would be required at home. [26]

Behind Wallace's optimistic and chauvinistic fantasizing lay assumptions broadly shared by Americans of his era: the trouble with Latin Americans was their lack of drive, best exemplified by their utter failure as frontiersmen. And to some degree, so many Americans believed, the lack of drive derived in part from Latin American religious beliefs.

Latin Americans simply were not drawn to the frontier by the religious symbolism of rebirth that inspired many Americans. In their Catholicism, Latins believed that one spiritual birth supplied by baptism directly following physical birth covered all needs. The born-again experience that many American Protestants sought, and that many underwent at frontier revival meetings and through rurally centered awakenings,[27] did not figure in Latin American religion. To Latins, religion on the frontier meant the mission, established by the religious orders to convert Indians. For the gente decente, though, the focal point of religion had nothing to do with the frontier. Instead, it was found in the cities, with their clusters of churches, convents, and monasteries, with their constant flow of processions and endless repetition of ceremonial rites.

John Steuart Curry's splendid painting *Baptism in Kansas* (1928) depicts an adult baptism taking place against a rural background in which the fields stretch out forever, having recently been redeemed from wilderness by a windmill that appears in the middle ground. (See illustration II.) There is no similar painting in the history of Latin American art—though one might appear any day, now that more and more Protestant missionaries are penetrating the region. The absence of the sort of rebirth depicted by Curry's painting reinforces Edmundo O'Gorman's thesis that Latin Americans in responding to their New World environment resolved not to depart from established custom and tradition. In contrast, Americans encountering their frontier embraced concepts of change and rebirth, including religious rebirth, or the born-again experience. For Americans, moreover, in total contrast to Latin Americans, new and virgin land encouraged the proliferation of new religions.

To be born again meant to reenter the realm of childhood innocence in which human nature began. And what could better give rise to this experience than immersion in an endless expanse of primordial nature? By being born again in Edenic nature, Americans set themselves on the path to the millennium: returning to origins so as then to advance to new perfection.[28] Latin Americans would have none of this. Outside of mystics, generally distrusted by the hierarchy of church and state for their free-thinking (or free-feeling) individualism, Latin Americans seemed willing to rely on traditional, institutionalized methods of salvation. They saw no need to become new humans by learning simultaneously how to dominate the sinful inclinations of inward nature and the wild domains of outer nature. If many Latins did indeed suspect that the divine might inhere in sacralized nature, they believed that divinity could more readily and more reliably be found through priest-administered rituals, the more lavish and sumptuous the better, performed in urban churches.

The American's return to nature on the frontiers as a source of a born-again experience can be viewed as a dialectical process. The civilized per-

11. John Steuart Curry. *Baptism in Kansas*. 1928. Oil on canvas, 40 × 50″. Collection of Whitney Museum of American Art. Gift of Gertrude Vanderbilt Whitney.

The Christian born-again experience in frontier and rural America, a prominent feature in the nation's religious and cultural life, has been conspicuously lacking, until recent times, in Latin America.

son arrives in America. He or she represents the thesis. Then the civilized person plunges into nature, embodying the antithesis. Ultimately, out of this process emerges the re-made human, the synthesis in which opposites fuse. From the American perspective, Latin Americans remained only half alive, because of their failure to undergo comparable experiences. Latins did not know how to use their encounter with the primitive to complete, to fulfill, and periodically to revitalize civilization.

Latin Americans did not follow the course that Walt Whitman recommended as he rendered homage to the great American myth:

> The cities I loved so well I abandon'd and left, I sped to the
>   certainties suitable to me,
> Hungering, hungering, hungering, for the primal energies and
>   Nature's dauntlessness,
> I refreshed myself with it only, I could relish it only.[29]

A distinct and yet somewhat related sentiment is captured in these words by America's great twentieth-century poet Robert Frost: "The land was ours, before we were the land's."[30] Americans, having conquered the wilderness, then surrendered to and assimilated its primordial vitalities. Thus they were reborn in a way that Latins, given their initial failure to make the land truly theirs, never could be reborn.

American frontier mythology corresponded in some ways to that developed by English settlers in Australia and New Zealand. At least as depicted by Anthony Trollope in his 1873 novel *Australia and New Zealand*, Englishmen believed the struggle to tame and master virgin soil would rehabilitate the convicts exiled by the British judicial system to penal colonies in the Pacific. Responding to the opportunity to master wilderness land, Britain's fallen men would undergo spiritual rebirth. At the same time, the penal system would permit them to stake out ownership claims on the land they had tamed. Thus they would acquire the sense of property that Trollope took "to be the core of social morals." In their frontier mythology, Americans, too, believed their compatriots gained not only the rebirth experience in wilderness regions but along with it the sense of property and the social morals that property inculcated. Denied rebirth, denied property and concomitant social morals by their frontier experience, Latin Americans by and large remained bereft of civilization's highest virtues.[31] Such, at least, was the conclusion to which their frontier myths drove Americans.

Gospel, Glory, and Gold, and Iberian Frontiers

From at least the time of William H. Prescott, who produced classic, widely read histories of the conquests of Mexico and Peru (in 1843 and 1847, respectively), to beyond the time of Archibald MacLeish, whose epic poem *Conquistador* (1932) acquainted a new generation of general readers with the dramatic feats of Cortés and his followers in New Spain, Americans evinced fascination—whether arising out of approval or revulsion or a mixture of both—with Iberian conquest in the New World. Often, they have puzzled over why Iberians failed to follow up on the original heroic *entradas* (entries) of conquistadores into endless expanses of pristine nature. What went wrong? In North America, once the original entry had been made by explorers, such as George Rogers Clark, Daniel Boone, Zebulon Pike, and Meriwether Lewis and William Clark, wave after wave of settlers flocked to the newly entered areas to redeem them from their wilderness estate and in turn to be redeemed by wilderness. How to account for the lack of subsequent waves in Latin America? Why were there no settlers, for example, to follow up on the sixteenth-century entradas of Coronado and de Soto into areas that much later became a part of U.S. territory? Following a series of initial entradas farther to the south, leading to establishment of three hundred or so cities and towns by 1600, why did Iberians permit the frontier that lay between these urban communities to remain "hollow"?[32] Why were frontiers once discovered quickly abandoned rather than consolidated? Did America's pioneer historian of Latin America, William R. Shepherd, perhaps put his finger on part of the explanation when, early in the twentieth century, he suggested that the original conquistadores had been inspired in their epic deeds by Gospel, glory, and gold? By the time Shepherd wrote, Americans had long since developed stereotypes that derogated the particular way in which Iberians seemed to perceive, honor, and pursue this trinity.

For Iberians in the New World, Gospel seemed to mean not the deepening of the conquerors' own religious lives but merely the introduction to Indians of Catholicism's most superficial rudiments. In the conquistador's concept of holy war, as perceived by Americans, the purposes of God were accomplished once Indian settlements had been opened up by the original entrada for the coming of the missionaries. Convinced he was already saved (baptism, after all, along with the ministrations of Virgin, saints, and priests attended to that), the conquistador thought only about bringing the Gospel to the nonsaved. In contrast, when the Anglo American carried out holy war, the objective was not so much the conversion of Indians as the perfecting of the Anglo's religious estate. This objective Anglo Americans pursued by engaging in the unrelenting struggle with the wilds of nature, whether external or internal. God's people had constantly to measure themselves against a wilderness environment and simultaneously to pit themselves against "the howling chaos in the depths of the mind."[33]

Invariably, self-salvation inspired more prolonged, systematic, and chronic effort than the quest to bring salvation to others. Moreover, in the quest for self-salvation the seeker fortified that veritable fountain of all other virtues: individualism—really another word for independence. As Prescott put the matter in the nineteenth century: "What a contrast did these children of southern Europe present to the Anglo-Saxon races who scattered themselves along the great northern division of the western hemisphere!" For the Anglo Saxons the impetus to action was not "the . . . specious pretext of proselytism, but independence—independence religious and political."[34]

As to glory, Iberians pursued it with an aristocratic set of values that Americans disdained. Iberians craved a glory equated with the recognition that others accorded them, a glory that was especially enhanced by recognition and distinction conferred by the Crown. Heroic entry into the American frontier provided one of the few means remaining to Iberians who were not to the manor born to catch the Crown's attention and gain the supreme gift of noble status. In the Iberian Peninsula, commoners had often risen to the ranks of at least the lesser nobility by means of their service to the medieval church and state in cleansing the native soil of its Islamic occupiers. But this means of upward mobility came to an end with the completion of the *Reconquista* in 1492, when the last Islamic outpost of Granada surrendered to the "Catholic Monarchs," Ferdinand and Isabella. Henceforth, glory, recognition, and noble status could best be attained through a spectacular deed of exploration and conquest in the New World. Once glory had been won, the fortunate Iberian trusted to continuing royal favors to enhance still further his stature. He did not think of sustained struggle with newly explored terrain as the means to assure ongoing success. In stark contrast, the American who entered virgin nature sought independence rather than recognition from governmental and religious establishments, and the economic basis for sustained independence demanded ongoing struggle with the land.

Gold, in its comprehensive sense, signified not just the precious metal but wealth in general. The intrepid conquistador, as seen by many an American at least, hoped to acquire gold by plundering the accumulated treasure of those he conquered. He clung to what was in a way a "cargo-cult" mentality:[35] if he did what the gods (the Trinity, the Virgin, the saints) desired, then, providentially, miraculously, wealth in abundance would come to him. The cargo-cult tradition had been firmly established for hundreds of years in the course of the Iberian Peninsula's middle ages. As soldiers of the Crown and Church crusaded against Islam in the Christian version of a *jihad*, or holy war, they gained the providential rewards of the accumulated wealth of their far more economically able and energetic Islamic foes. Whatever Islamic wealth escaped plunder fell to the Christian tax gatherer—or, until 1492, the Jewish tax gatherer employed by Christian kings. Furthermore, as Iberians expanded the Christian frontier at the expense of Islam, they came into possession of flourishing towns and cities: they did not have to establish cities in the wilderness. Instead, they could sit back and enjoy, thanks to God's miraculous intervention on their behalf, the wealth and treasure created and accumulated by others.

In true cargo-cult fashion, Spaniards after 1492 awaited the treasure shipped back from "the Indies." In the marvelous seventeenth-century flamenco song "Por la Vela" ("By Sail") a despondent man expresses the hope that from overseas will come, providentially, the treasure that will enable him to lavish gifts upon his beloved, to stem her tears and end her suffering. Then, at last, he will be happy. For Spaniards in general questing after what gold could provide, deliverance came miraculously, by sail.

In many ways, conquistadores in the New World repeated the history of the *reconquistadores* in the Old. The conquistadores came upon splendid cities established by advanced, sedentary Indian civilizations. They skimmed off the accumulated wealth of those cities and impressed Indian laborers into service to refine the cities and give them a Christian facade, while at the same time devising means to exploit the labor of Indian farmers and also to extract tribute from the natives. Gold, or wealth, thus derived from settled areas where Indian culture had flourished, not from the sparsely settled or uninhabited frontier. Not only gold but glory as well derived from areas already settled by sedentary Indians, for glory arose in part out of the number of beings of whose dependence the aristocrat could boast. Finally, gold and glory, in the form of concessions and perhaps even titles of nobility extracted from the Crown, arrived from overseas, "por la vela." The cargo-cult mentality thus flourished in the Iberian New World as well as in the Old.

Noting that the first settlers had come to Brazil a century before their Anglo counterparts began their permanent occupation of the New World, Theodore Roosevelt in 1914 puzzled over the fact that the greatest of the "last frontiers" lay not in North America but rather in Brazil. In Brazil, he conjectured, frontier settlement had progressed slowly because "Portuguese colonial government . . . was almost as bad as Spanish."[36] Roosevelt, of course, objected to a government symbiotically joined to an established church, and one set upon the pursuit of Gospel, glory, and gold in such a way as to diminish individual initiative. Moreover, to judge from most of his pre-1914 publications, Roosevelt agreed with such outstanding nineteenth-century American historians as Prescott, Francis Parkman, and George Bancroft when they ascribed "effeminate" ways to Frenchmen, Spaniards, and Portuguese, and also to Negroes and Native Americans.[37] Such people, ostensibly, could not hope to rival the sustained efforts of the honest, energetic, and masculine Anglo Americans in taming frontiers.

True, less-than-masculine Latins might be able to rouse themselves to perform one-time-only prodigies. Thus the early conquistadores could claim distinction in any company; and seventeenth-century Brazilian *bandeirantes* or frontier explorer-prospectors undertook awesome treks into the wilderness in quest of gold and Indian slaves.[38] But conquistadores and bandeirantes impressed most Americans who had heard of them as rootless plunderers who neither wanted nor knew how to establish permanent settlements. They lacked, purportedly, the capacity for the sustained, disciplined efforts on which civilization depended.

Waves of Frontier Settlement in America, and the Missing Waves in Latin America

Americans, according to James Fenimore Cooper, recognized that the first type of Caucasian settler to occupy their wilderness was "inadequate for the kind of life for which he clears the way"; for the first settler is, "to a significant degree, a savage."[39] Even before Cooper, Hector St. John Crèvecoeur had dismissed first-wave frontiersmen as "no better than carnivorous animals" who comprised the "most hideous parts" of American society. Hope for a better future lay in the passing of the first-wave frontiersmen into the deeper woods, yielding the places on which they had been squatters to respectable people of disciplined industriousness.[40] However, so far as most Americans who first ventured into the Southwest could see, the semihuman Hispanics who had penetrated the area might never have been followed by humans of a decent sort had not Americans come providentially to claim the old Hispanic frontier for themselves. The rest of Latin America's "hollow" frontier, too far removed to receive an immediate civilizing impetus from Yankees, appeared doomed to remain in the hands of primitives, while that part of the population that could claim a veneer of civilization, however warped and rotten, chose the static existence of their unprogressive towns and haciendas. Such, at least, were the stereotypes by means of which Americans judged Latins and found them altogether wanting as tamers of New World frontiers.

The history of the Great Plains provides one of the most dramatic examples of American success in unleashing successive waves of frontier conquest, and the story contrasts dramatically with one of Hispanic failure. Spaniards had entered the Great Plains in their southern and western reaches, but they had never managed to do "more than nibble around the margins" of the area.[41] Indeed, by the end of the Spanish regime in 1821 the Plains Indians had fairly well routed the Iberians and exercised greater control over the area than in the late eighteenth century. Upon acquiring independence, Mexico assumed sovereignty over a large part of plains territory, but Mexicans nibbled even less successfully around the margins than Spaniards had.

In stark contrast to Latin failure, Americans in the short span between the 1860s and late 1880s conquered the Great Plains and began to transform their potential into economic gain. Cattle herding provided the opening wedge of conquest: here was "a natural occupation which used the land in its natural state and altered it hardly at all." But Americans were not the type to leave nature unaltered. Along with cattle the industrial revolution began to penetrate the Great Plains and to alter the region forever. The mass-produced six-shooter, along with newly refined repeating rifles, helped cowboys and troopers subdue the Indians.[42] Along the margins of the plains appeared packing plants, connected to the cattle-raising areas by railroad lines. These developments, combined with the introduction of barbed wire in 1874, facilitated the raising of blooded cattle, transformed the meat industry, and increasingly altered the natural state of the plains. Meanwhile windmills began to dot the area, facilitating not only the cattle industry but the advent of farming. Rain might not follow the plough, as some optimists had predicted it would; but thanks to the windmill water actually preceded the plough, making possible a farming frontier, even in areas once assumed to comprise part of the so-called Great American Desert. Conquest of this desert rested not on the natural phenomenon of rain but rather upon the technological innovativeness of Americans. Few events provided greater nourishment to American hubris than taming the great desert. No wonder John Steuart Curry in his *Baptism in Kansas* gave as much prominence to a windmill as to the person being baptized. Thanks to the windmill, the plains themselves had been born anew.

In due course new waves of plains settlers, abetted by the Federal Homestead Law of 1864, proceeded toward the all-out conquest of nature, this process more and more facilitated by the ongoing industrial revolution. New industry provided "the machinery for drilling wells," manufactured "practical windmills," and produced "the big machines so well adapted to the level land and the firm soil of the Great Plains and so necessary to the extensive method of dry farming." Without the products of modern technology, the Great Plains would have remained the "almost purely grazing country" that vast stretches of the northern Mexican frontier did in fact remain[43]—the fact helping to reinforce American notions of Mexican inferiority. Because of technological ingenuity applied to virgin land through successive waves of frontier settlers, Americans demonstrated that human industry could "mend rude nature's works"—as a writer had boasted already in the late eighteenth century.[44] And the process went on not only in the plains and the western frontier in general but in Florida as well. There, developers and entrepreneurs utilizing the latest technological breakthroughs in railroad construction and earth-moving equipment replaced the first wave of "Cracker" homesteaders who had come to the area once it was cleansed, in bloody battles, of its Seminole occupiers.

Since the early days of the Massachusetts Bay Colony, Puritans had disdained Indians because of their alleged inability to cultivate the earth "as God had commanded."[45] In the latter part of the nineteenth century their descendants directed that disdain increasingly toward Latin Americans. True, spectacular progress in cultivating the Argentine pampas had commenced. But it seemed to depend, at least in the jaundiced view of most North Americans, largely upon English technology and railroad-building know-how, as well as upon the massive immigration of industrious, ambitious Italian laborers less debased than Argentina's native stock. In the latter part of the nineteenth century Mexico began finally to get the upper hand over some of its natural resources. Success, though, as observed from north of the border, resulted from Yankee investment and, in its wake, the transfer of technology. Americans liked to believe that only because of civilizing influences introduced from abroad did some areas of Latin America witness at last an effective follow-up to the daring entradas of colonial times.

Where among Latin Americans, Yankees wondered, were the counterparts of, to choose just one example, Charles Stillman? Arriving as an impecunious young man in the Brownsville area at the mouth of the Rio Grande in the 1830s, Stillman undertook a number of business ventures, built up his capital, and eventually became a partner in river navigation with Richard King, future founder of the colossal King Ranch. Stillman's philosophy was, whether in peacetime or in war, to use what he made to make still more.[46] He personified the late-wave settlers who played a key role in delivering the coup de grace to nature's primacy on the frontier. He and dozens, even hundreds, of men like him rode the edge of the industrial revolution as it rippled across frontiers. They succeeded because they understood that the American nation "is pushing out. New opportunities are sure to arise, bigger opportunities than ever existed in the fur trade. Transport, merchandising, agriculture, lumbering, fisheries, land!"[47] The possibilities seemed limitless. But only a people with an abundance of Charles Stillmans could realize those possibilities. And men of this sort the Latin race in the New World seemed singularly to lack. Above all, where among the Latin Americans were the railroad builders? Had Englishmen not served that function in Argentina, or had Americans like Henry Meiggs and George Earl Church not made their way to Chile and Peru, and to Bolivia, respectively, Latin Americans might well have remained without that consummate tamer of wilderness, the railroad—or so Americans believed.

Never mind the demographic and geographical factors that militated against rapid railroad construction south of the border. So far as Americans were concerned, the late appearance of the railroads derived exclusively from lack of Latin technological and entrepreneurial skills and from absence of single-minded concern with progress. Meanwhile, without railroads, Latins continued to lack that indispensable badge of civilization, a sense of time. Only with the coming of the railroad to rural communities did those Americans just beginning to fill in national frontiers learn to center their lives around the coming and going of trains and acquire the habit of attending to watches. According to a song, "Folks around these parts get the time of day, / From the Atchison, Topeka, and the Santa Fe."[48] In Latin America, where the equivalents of the Atchison, Topeka, and the Santa Fe arrived late and owed their founding, allegedly, only to Yankee or English impetus and genius, people remained innocent of the civilizing influence of linear time. Trapped in cycles of natural time, they failed to understand that time was money.

Not long after the end of the Civil War, Gen. William Sherman described the railroad as the essential agent "in the great battle of civilization with barbarism."[49] Some years earlier Emerson had depicted "railroad iron" as a magician's wand, endowed with the power to awaken "the sleeping energies of land and water."[50] But the railroad was not a gentle civilizer or awakener of sleeping nature. It was an aggressive intruder that would, so one of its champions maintained, provide the U.S. military with the mobility needed either to awaken Indians to civilization or to exterminate them.[51] (See illustration 12.)

In other ways as well, masculine railroad iron proved an aggressive conqueror of nature. William H. Hall in rhapsodizing over the iron horse's civilizing mission to an 1847 railroad convention assembled in Chicago saw in the locomotive "a virile masculine force." Hall extolled this force, plucking out the forests and tearing up hills and flinging them aside, as it made its way "into the body of the continent" with the step of a "bridegroom [going] to his chamber." Historian Ronald T. Takaki seems to detect in Hall's words more the description of a rapist than a bridegroom. In any event, "with its locomotive ejecting the pure white jet," writes Takaki, the railroad "was penetrating . . . 'virgin land.'"[52] Americans have suspected that only serious deficiencies of virility could account for the Latin American's unwillingness to leave virgin land unviolated. Surely a people who failed to penetrate and leave their mark on the frontier lacked manliness:

ACROSS THE CONTINENT.
"WESTWARD THE COURSE OF EMPIRE TAKES ITS WAY."

12. Fanny Palmer and James M. Ives. *Across the Continent: Westward the Course of Empire Takes Its Way*. 1848. Lithograph. The Harry T. Peters Collection, Museum of the City of New York.

Widely distributed by the famous Currier and Ives firm, this enormously popular lithograph depicts the railroad, together with telegraph lines, as beneficent forces spreading civilization into wilderness. Not all Americans have seen civilization's penetration as an unalloyed blessing.

unable to practice sublimation, they poured their sexual drive solely into dalliances with the opposite sex.

American experience proved that the railroad was necessary to transport new generations of frontiersmen and women, people who brought with them "the artifacts of a machine civilization: mining machinery, steel plows, harvesters, windmills, and all the rest." The frontiersman "had begun his battle against nature with only his hands and his brawn to aid him." But he "was to continue that battle with such efficient tools" that by 1890 "the continent had been conquered and all the Far West subjected to the elevating forces of civilization."[53] Man the conqueror, man the civilizer, was Anglo American man. In the great tasks of civilization, Latin American men had demonstrated their glaring inferiority. Comparative railroad mileage in the United States and in Latin America underlined this fact.

Cowboys and Vaqueros and Comparative Frontier Experiences

Romantic myths notwithstanding, American cowboys led the hard and exploited lives of any subculture or underclass.[54] Badly paid hired hands, they tried to form a union in the early 1880s,[55] only to sustain crushing defeat at the hands of the cattle barons who saw labor organizations as subversive of American values. Lashed by poverty, cowboys also led unnatural lives. Housed in barrackslike accommodations in all-male camps, their "bachelor experience" was occasionally relieved by ranch dances and by "blowouts in saloons and whorehouses."[56] Many were fugitives from the law, and not just American but Mexican law as well: for at least one-tenth of "American" cowboys were Hispanics, generally mestizos. Blacks and mulattoes comprised about a fifth.[57] Already by the turn of the twentieth century, though, many Americans had conveniently forgotten this racial mixture lest it tarnish an increasingly mythologized being.[58]

When possible, Americans—at least the romantics among them—also liked to forget that huge chunks of the West had been owned by East Coast and even European conglomerates, whose profits derived in part from ruthless exploitation of western laborers in general—not just cowboys. At the same time, the romantics liked to forget that in their country's development, race prejudice had facilitated and excused this exploitation. Practical-minded Americans, though, remembered these facts, and not apologetically. Therefore, they could never sympathize with Latin Americans incensed over alleged exploitation of native labor by "Yankee imperialists." After all, it was through mean and tough labor relations that civilized men had won the West and made it amount to something. So, despite the appeal to American romantics of the cleaned-up, whitened, knight-of-the-plains version, the cowboy from the outset served the needs, practical and mythological, of hard-headed American capitalists.

The cowboy is a puzzling icon, beset by ambiguity and contradictory elements. Extolled by many as unexcelled in mastering nature, the cowboy also acquired the reputation of being unable to put a rope on his own instinctual appetites. When not on the trail, he set himself to serious competitive drinking (one thinks of such cowboy songs as "The Boasting Drunk in Dodge" or "Rye Whiskey"), with periodic time-outs to patronize the local prostitutes. American counterculturalists might admire the cowboy's uninhibited indulgence of his appetites, and some of them

perhaps sympathized with the homosexuality that they suspected the prolonged "bachelor experience" must encourage; but defenders of established mores have had somehow to rationalize the unbuttoned ways of the
national hero.

Already in an earlier chapter we have seen that sometimes defenders of
conventional values rationalized the foibles of the cowboy by picturing his
life as a rite of passage. In this rite a youth tested his mettle, explored his
inward resources, and built up his physical endurance in preparation for
entry into the life of the capitalist entrepreneur. Upholders of conven-
tionality liked to point out that "many of the most wealthy and respected
citizens now living in the border states rode the range as cowboys before
settling down to quiet domesticity."[59] Hispanic and African American
cowboys did not make this transition. Their dark faces are absent from the
photographic galleries of cowboys turned capitalists. Racist Americans, of
course, did not permit dark-skinned Others to complete the rite of passage. In order to preserve the myth of their open and democratic system,
Americans found it convenient to purify the ranks of American cowboys
of the Others' presence. Moreover, the reputation of cowboys as Indian
fighters demanded that their ranks be whitened; for stereotyped Hispanics
and African Americans hardly measured up to such a manly calling.

Here is a passage from an 1891 novel that conveys the cowboy's reputation: "Who is to keep the Injuns in order?" asks a leading character. "Do
you think it is Uncle Sam's Troops? Why, the Red-skins just laugh at them.
It's the cow-boys."[60] In reality, the U.S. armed forces had to be pressed
into service to contain the Indian menace on the plains in the post–Civil
War era—just as they had earlier been required to suppress, among other
natives, the Seminoles. But Americans, with the obvious exception of military buffs, liked to ignore the fact that conquest of the plains depended on
the central government's regimented forces, including a good number of
Negro "Buffalo Soldiers," carefully segregated, of course, from white
troops and always commanded by white officers. Americans preferred to
believe that freewheeling, ruggedly individualistic cowboys opened the
plains and other frontiers to civilization. And they liked to contrast their
all-conquering cowboy to the "effete" Mexican vaquero, so often disdained because of his penchant for fancy clothes, silver bridles and spurs,
and silver-decorated saddles, chaps, and holsters. Such preening, effeminate dandies could hardly rise to the task of repressing barbarism. No
wonder when Americans first entered the plains area they found the
Apaches and Comanches on an unchecked rampage, haciendas and ranchos abandoned, their ineffectual vaquero defenders having fled or been
slaughtered by Indian savages. Unlike the advancing tide of American

civilization, which had never encountered a serious setback, Hispanic society allowed itself to be stalemated, "physically, culturally, and economically . . . by the Indian menace."[61] Ostensibly, this failure in Mexico derived from the area's inability to produce knights of the plains who excelled in the conquest of nature.[62]

What little Americans might know about Argentina's cowboy type, the gaucho, qualified him for no higher regard than that accorded vaqueros. To begin with, the gaucho, like the vaquero, was of mixed blood and vulnerable to the purportedly baneful influences of his Indian lineage. Like the Mexican vaquero or desperado (and like stereotyped African Americans) the gaucho preferred to fight with the primitive knife or lance rather than with modern man's technologically advanced weapons, such as the six-gun and repeating rifle. Although perceived as more self-reliant than the vaquero, more akin to a Bedouin than to a peon, the gaucho was an adventurer who failed to complete the transition to civilization. And, like Brazilian frontiersmen or bandeirantes, he seemed content merely to skim off from nature the most readily available cream. Unable to clear the Argentine plains of their nomadic Indians or to discipline the pampas into the ways of capitalist productivity, the gaucho (as Americans tended to view him) left these tasks, respectively, to the Argentine army and to the racially superior European immigrants who began to arrive in huge numbers in the latter part of the nineteenth century.[63]

Indians and Comparative American–Latin American Frontier Perspectives

Not only had Argentines until late in the century failed to subject their Indian frontiers to civilization, Latins in general had failed in this task. A Kentuckian boasted in 1828: "No longer the yell of the savage alarms us, / Industry, and Arts too, our country adorn."[64] Latin Americans, however, who had occupied their territory far longer than Kentuckians had theirs, could make no comparable boast. Americans jeered Latins for the inability after more than three hundred years to pacify their Indian frontiers. Americans found it shocking that supposedly civilized beings resigned themselves to living juxtaposed to and in tolerant symbiosis with primitivism. Often Americans ignored the altogether different circumstances that had led them, on one hand, to become killers of Indians while, on the other hand, steering Latins toward dependence on Indian labor that demanded preservation of the natives. Especially but by no means exclusively in their own South, Americans had tried to become masters rather than killers of Indians. They had sought to enslave the natives.[65] But, encountering aborigines who could not adapt to enforced servitude, they had settled for being killers rather than masters. Facing different sorts of natives, whom they encountered in huge numbers, Latins enjoyed greater success in, if not exactly enslaving, at least reducing Indians to forms of nonvoluntary labor. Somehow, Americans never forgave the Iberian conqueror and settler for succeeding where they had failed, and for adapting, sometimes profitably and pleasurably, to a socioeconomic system predicated upon the preservation of natives and even their preconquest patterns of culture.

Henry Lewis Morgan (1816–1881), "the most prominent nineteenth-century American anthropologist,"[66] popularized a theory that humans progressed through stages, from savagery to barbarism to civilization.[67] Obviously under the influence of Morgan's theories, the U.S. Bureau of Ethnology, in its first project in South America conducted in 1894, concluded that the area's huge aboriginal population lived "partly in the higher stage of savagery and [partly] the lower stage of barbarism."[68] The Bureau of Ethnology placed the U.S. Indian population in the same status. But Americans could comfort themselves with the realization that their Indians were a vanishing race, because of either acculturation or extermination. On the other hand, Latin America's Indian population (with "Indianness" determined by cultural characteristics as well as by race) had been on the rise since the eighteenth century. From this fact Americans were wont to conclude that, in contrast to Latin Americans, they were doing something right.

In the course of his 1913–1914 exploration of the last frontier in Brazil and some of its adjoining lands, Theodore Roosevelt sojourned briefly in Paraguay. There he encountered some evidently not very prepossessing Indians living on the outskirts of a town. The Indians, he noted, lived in the "usual squalid fashion" of those "who are hangers-on round the white man but have not yet adopted his ways."[69] In line with prevailing stereotypes, Americans of Roosevelt's time—and also those before and after that time—believed, by and large, that virtually all Latin American life was demeaned by Indian "hangers-on" who either would not or could not rise to the ways of white persons and who pulled these latter down to their own level.

Many Americans—including, I suspect, Roosevelt—saw Latin America's tragedy as one for which its conquerors and settlers could not be held altogether responsible. The tiny stream of Latin America's white race had simply been swallowed, inevitably, by a vast aboriginal ocean. In contrast, Americans had faced a relatively unoccupied frontier, a blessing for which they often thanked Providence. John Lloyd Stephens, one of America's most perceptive nineteenth-century travelers and diplomats, published his still valuable *Incidents of Travel in Central America, Chiapas, and Yucatan* in 1841. In the work he expressed sympathy for the good intentions of some Guatemalan leaders. Good intentions might go unfulfilled, however; for through no fault of their own, the leaders were "consorting with a wild animal which might at any moment turn and rend them in pieces."[70] The Guatemalan Indians, accounting for three-quarters of the population, constituted the "wild animal" to which Stephens referred. For other Americans contemplating the Latin American scene, Negroes and mulattoes represented the wild animal.

African Americans, Palenques, *and* Quilombos, *and Frontier Differences*

Iberian settlers throughout the colonial period had imported vastly larger numbers of African slaves than their English counterparts to the north. While the British in North America purchased between 750,000 and 1 million Africans to labor on their mainland and Caribbean island estates, far more blacks made the forced journey to Mexico and to Peru, and a great deal many more reached Brazil. In all, New World Iberians imported somewhere between 10 and 12 million African slaves. Of these, between 3.5 and 5 million went to Brazil. Even though relatively few Africans were imported into the region that comprised the future republics of Argentina, Paraguay, and Uruguay, nevertheless some estimates of the Negro portion of the Buenos Aires population as of 1700 ran to between 20 and 30 percent—after that the percentage declined as Africans underwent whitening through the race-mixture process that most North Americans frowned on. To many Americans, the large presence of the African in Ibero America was altogether damning. Instead of civilization dedicating itself to eradicating the natural, as in America, in Latin America ostensibly civilized Iberians persisted in introducing overwhelming new doses of the primitive into their gene pool, thereby dooming themselves and their countries to backwardness.

Once introduced into the New World's Iberian civilization, Africans contrived to set at naught many of its control mechanisms. A large number escaped into the vast frontier regions that lay beyond the control of Portuguese and Spanish settlers. In the unconquered frontier, runaway blacks (generally called maroons, a name deriving from the Spanish word *cimarrón,* first used to designate the domestic cattle that escaped to the hills of Hispaniola) congregated in communities called *quilombos* or *mocambos* by the Portuguese and *palenques* by Spaniards. The famous quilombo of Palmares in northeastern Brazil claimed some twenty thousand inhabitants before the Portuguese finally managed, after great effort, bloodshed, and expense, to suppress it in 1697. Elsewhere, though, out in the frontier that Iberians had proved unable to tame, mocambos and palenques continued to flourish throughout the colonial period and even into the nineteenth century, all the way from Rio de la Plata on up through Florida.

Some of the low opinions that occupants of the American Southeast originally formed of Hispanic civilization derived from the loathing, fear, and anger inspired in them by communities of runaway slaves established in Spanish Florida. There the escaped slaves often joined with another group of "savages" that Spain had been unable to tame, the various Indian tribes that eventually coalesced in the Seminoles. Thus, just across the dividing line from civilization, there appeared that abomination of nature, the black Indian. American desire to deal appropriately with this menace lay behind the raids that Georgia's founder James Oglethorpe led into Spanish Florida in the 1740s. The same desire sparked the raids that Andrew Jackson masterminded, beginning in 1816. The sort of pressure that Jackson applied induced Spaniards to agree in 1819 to cede East Florida to the United States, the official transfer taking place in 1821.[71]

Meanwhile Americans contemplated additional trouble spots, farther distant than Florida but nonetheless uncomfortably close to home. At the end of the eighteenth century, the large maroon community in Haiti lent its support to the general slave revolt that drove out the European occupiers and brought about the formation of an unstable, violence-prone black-and-mulatto republic. Haiti, becoming as it were one great palenque, provided an image of violent upheaval from below that terrified not only America's Iberian master class but also English and Dutch masters whose very survival depended on their ability to maintain control over the sable children of nature. In the view of some alarmist Americans, all Latin America was a potential Haiti, where the bush threatened to spread over the enclaves of civilization that remained tenuous after three centuries. If the bush started to spread in early nineteenth-century Latin America, if maroons and similar types took over, the precedent might produce ripples to the north, and even Americans could find themselves hard pressed to maintain the civilized order. As late as the 1930s Americans responded with rage and perhaps some fear to the support that their country's burgeoning Communist party gave to a plan that called for establishment of a black republic within the United States. This threat conjured up visions of the Latin American palenque and indicated the repugnant consequences that could proceed from Marx and Engel's deluded reverence for the allegedly instinctual communism of primitive peoples.

To some Americans, the all-too-successful struggle that maroons waged to escape civilization's controls took on religious significance. Upon returning to the bush, the blacks resorted to what hostile whites saw as devil worship, appropriating "their enemy's enemy."[72] Maroons thus strengthened American inclinations, going back to Puritan times, to associate the natural with the diabolical. Conceivably, the phenomenon of the "devil-worshiping" palenques that thrived in Latin America could have intensified North American religious prejudices: prejudices that rested on the conviction that Latin backwardness, manifested by an inability to overcome nature's challenge, derived ultimately from false religious beliefs. Logically enough, then, Satan thrived in the bush that surrounded Latin America's precarious beachheads of heresy-infested civilization.

Not only maroons threatened Latin America's precarious enclaves of civilization; in the eighteenth century a series of upheavals originating in tenuously pacified rural areas had threatened to overrun urban centers and destroy the pigmentocracy's social order. The most serious threat came from the 1780 Túpac Amaru II uprising in highland Peru that pitted Indians and a considerable number of mestizos against the urban-based, white, and whitish gente decente. For at least a century after this uprising, the suppression of which had proved a bloody and, for a while, touch-and-go affair, Peruvians lived in fear, indeed in terror, of another assault by savages. They are bound to have voiced their pervasive fears to American visitors and to have impressed upon them civilization's precariousness throughout the Andean region. Even in the early 1960s when living in this region I listened often enough as defenders of the established order told of the continuing menace of the surly, dark masses. Civilization's upholders, some of them at least, still felt besieged. Many Americans, I suppose, could sympathize with them, while at the same time suspecting that their inability to get the upper hand over nature, once and for all, attested to basic inferiority.

Throughout the nineteenth century, moreover, Venezuelan upper classes in Caracas and other cities feared the mestizo and mulatto *pardos* (browns) who lived free and untrammeled lives out on the plains or llanos, where only a few estates, or *estancias,* dotted the countryside. A similar breed of mixed-bloods roamed the Brazilian interior, or *sertão,* flouting the decrees of the bureaucracy in Rio de Janeiro or in provincial capitals. Moreover, in turn-of-the-twentieth-century Colombia vast sections of the national territory lay beyond the reach of authority—and some of them still do toward the end of the century. Much of the Cauca Valley, for example, was a veritable no-man's-land. The blacks residing there on inalienable communal lands that theoretically lay under the control of estate owners actually lived beyond the reach of national laws and of civilization's restraints. Here and elsewhere in Colombia, black and mulatto peasants "formed a new social class that stood outside society" and brought to its life-style the traditions of the *palenquero,* or slave outlaw. Living in jungle or bush alongside failing estates as the nineteenth century ended, the peasant outlaws arrogated more and more power unto themselves even as that of the estate owners and civil authorities declined and sometimes disappeared altogether.[73]

Comparative Frontiers: Our Racial Purity, Their Mestizaje

Race mixture, according to Harvard professor Louis Agassiz as he reported in 1868 on a trip through parts of Brazil, engendered a people both physically and morally degraded, "a mongrel crowd as repulsive as mongrel dogs."[74] In this conclusion, the professor was preceded by novelist James Fenimore Cooper. Through one of his characters in *The Prairie* (1827), Cooper advanced what probably were his own sentiments. The character insists that "the half-and-halfs" encountered on the frontier "are altogether more barbarous than the real savages."[75] Within half a century or so after publication of this early Cooper novel, the vile and treacherous mestizo became a stock character in western fiction, finding his way into Mark Twain's Tom Sawyer tales in the diabolical personage of "Injun" Joe.[76] It seems tragic that the former colonialists in Latin America, the Spaniards, and would-be future colonialists, the Americans, concurred in the conviction that mestizaje yielded a result far worse than the ingredients that went into it.

Even before the midway point in the nineteenth century, American writers who published their impressions of the western frontier had made it almost a truism that the crossing of two races produced a product that inherited the worst features of each[77]—even implying sometimes that these features interacted synergistically to compound the nefariousness of the product. Transcendentalist thinker and social reformer Margaret Fuller often exalted the Indian. Yet, in the early 1840s she registered her disdain of mixed-bloods, alleging "they lose what is best in either type, rather than enhance the value of each, by mingling. There are exceptions,—one or two such I know of,—but this . . . is the general rule."[78] Also in the 1840s, an Anglo American in California wrote: "The law of nature which curses the mulatto here with a constitution less robust than that of either race from which he springs, lays a similar penalty upon the mingling of the Indian and white races in California and Mexico."[79] In the same decade an American trapper dismissed half-breeds as "neither one thing nor the other." They were, he concluded, "a spurious breed," much like the ass that resulted from crossing the mule and the horse.[80] Writing at the end of the 1840s, historian Francis Parkman referred contemptuously to some mongrel types he encountered on the frontier and exulted that Anglo Americans were "thoroughbreds."[81] Later in the century a Protestant missionary in the West found the half bloods far more difficult to deal with than Indians. Invariably, he charged, the real troublemakers and those who most resisted missionary attempts to impose rectitude and moral order were the half-breeds.[82] Antimestizo prejudice found its way also into the western novels on which British writer Thomas Mayne Reid (1818–1882) built his reputation. One of the illustrations for his novel *The Death Shot* (published as a dime novel in New York, n.d.) shows a mestizo serving as a guide to a group of Indians planning to assault a wagon train of white overlanders.[83]

The passing of time did little to temper American prejudice toward the mestizo. An "authority" on matters of race rendered this judgment in 1923: "You cannot dodge the Mendelian laws. . . . Like begets like, but in a union of opposites we get throwbacks." Superior races, he insisted, must not "run the risk of mongrelizing the species."[84] Six years later a graduate student at the University of Arizona insisted in his master's thesis that the mestizo combined the worst features of Latins and Indians. Because of their race mixture, Latin Americans allegedly had less in common with Anglos than almost any other racial group.[85]

Some of the early Englishmen in Virginia, it is true, had taken Indian wives. Later settlers, though, both in Virginia and the Carolinas, had come to their racial senses and passed laws against miscegenation. Then, as the frontier advanced early in the nineteenth century, some mountain men entered into actual matrimony, not just casual sexual liaison, with Indian women. They accepted the fact, though, that to bring their wives back with them into "civilized society" was "out of the question."[86] Thus even America's wildest elements who comprised the first wave of early nineteenth-century frontier settlers had sufficient propriety to defer to society's judgment that there was something terribly wrong about union with the Other. By this time, Americans thought they had learned enough about Indians to understand the viciousness of their character and to comprehend that no good could come from miscegenation; by midcentury the "squaw man, the White who had settled down with an Indian woman, was a stock object of derision in the literature of the American West."[87] Furthermore, consensus had formed that when mestizaje did occur on the frontier, the whites who entered into it were the lowest and most debased specimens of the race.[88] A woman settler in the West counted it a "shame and disgrace to our country" that some early frontiersmen of a lowly sort had fathered mestizo broods. Another found it "perfectly astounding" that "a man who has ever seen civilized people can intermarry with the natives"; for yet another it was "the greatest absurdity . . . for a white man to live with black dirty squaws."[89] By the time these women wrote, early in the second half of the nineteenth century, the increasing presence of white "gentle tamers" on the frontier had helped to restore white men to a sense of propriety, inducing them to abandon their absurdities.

Because Americans, even in the Wild West that tempted civilized beings to revert to nature, had retained some sense of propriety, they had managed, according to Charles Francis Adams, Jr. (writing in 1889), to guarantee "the salvation of the race." Essential to that salvation, in Adams's view, had been the policy of Indian extermination. The only alternative might well have been for Americans to become "a nation of half-breeds,—miscegenates, to coin a word expressive of an idea."[90] Natty Bumppo had also warned Americans against this fate. Again and again in Cooper's fiction, he boasted of being a man "without a cross." His example prevailed, and the United States remained the Northern Star, contrasted with Latin America's Southern Cross.[91]

Visiting Mexico in 1883, artist Thomas Moran voiced typical gringo attitudes when, in spite of his admiration for the sublime scenery (as noted at the end of chapter 3), he complained about the bad-smelling Indians and "half breeds" who comprised much of the population. In general, he found them a "wretched lot, especially the half breeds, and all look in a most degraded condition."[92] Like most Americans who trekked south of the border, Moran responded in disdain to the overwhelming evidence of ongoing mestizaje. Moran and most of his fellow Americans took enormous pride in the fact that Anglo settlers in the New World had responded in ways dramatically different from Iberians in confronting racial frontiers.

Throughout most of its history, the Anglo American frontier had remained one of "exclusion." In contrast, as geographer Marvin Mikesell puts the matter, the Latin American frontier had been one of "inclusion."[93] Predicated upon exclusionist strategy, U.S. Indian policy throughout the nineteenth century generally "fixed limits beyond which the Indian should never come after he had once parted with . . . title [to his land] for a consideration of goods and trinkets. . . . The Indian was regarded as an encumbrance to be cleared off, like the trees and the wolves, before white men could live in the country."[94] In contrast, Latins in the New World, whether French, Portuguese, or Spanish, generally put a melting-pot policy into effect upon encountering aborigines. They poured in whatever they found, even though they might turn up their noses at and discriminate against—as a general rule, subject to many exceptions—what the pot ulti- mately yielded. Owing to the operation of the melting pot, the population of New Spain in 1800 (some twenty years before the area acquired inde- pendence as the Republic of Mexico) included an estimated 420,000 mes- tizos and 360,000 mulattoes, to go along with its approximately 700,000 whites (the number included many mixed-bloods able to pass) and—at a rough estimate—about 2.5 million Indians.

According to a viewpoint that came to prevail in nineteenth-century America, those Latin Europeans who migrated to the New World revealed an inherent flaw: a natural inclination toward miscegenation.[95] Typical of his countrymen, Ephraim George Squier accepted the fatal-flaw inter- pretation when he served as U.S. chargé d'affaires to Central America be- ginning in 1849. And he thanked Providence for having spared Teutonic races this flaw. "If the United States as compared with the Spanish Ameri- can republics has achieved immeasurable advance in all the elements of greatness, that result is eminently due to the rigid and inexorable refusal of the dominant Teutonic stock to debase its blood, impair its intellect, lower its moral standards, or peril its institutions by intermixture with the in- ferior and subordinate races of man. In obedience of Heaven, it has res- cued half a continent from savage beasts and still more savage men."[96] Squier urged upon Central Americans an immigration or colonization pol- icy that might, in effect, someday redeem them from the consequences of original inclusionary policies: "It is only by a judicious system of coloniza- tion, which shall ultimately secure the predominance of white blood, at the same time that it shall introduce intelligence, industry, and skill, that . . . [Central Americans] can hope to achieve peace, prosperity, and great- ness." Unless such a policy came to prevail throughout the area, Squier predicted the inferior, dark, Indian and mixed-blood population would continue gradually to overwhelm the white race and eventually cause its disappearance.[97]

About a decade after Squier served as U.S. chargé d'affaires to Central America, William Walker arrived as an unofficial emissary. In Nicaragua, as noted in the first chapter, he enthused over the Edenic qualities of the land and the opportunity it presented Americans to reroot themselves in na- ture. But he expressed nothing but contempt for the people who presently occupied that land. Installing himself by armed force as president of Nica- ragua, whose incorporation into the United States he devoutly desired, Walker pontificated on what had gone wrong with the people not only of Nicaragua but also of Ibero America as a whole. "Instead of maintaining the purity of the races as did the English in their settlements, the Spaniards had cursed their continental possessions with a mixed race." Describing mixed races as "the bane" especially of Central America, he attributed to them the disorder that had afflicted the area since independence.[98] Implying that Americans should extend to Central America the sort of war they had waged on their own frontier against Indians, Walker concluded: "The history of the world presents no such Utopian vision as that of an inferior race yielding meekly and peacefully to the controlling influence of a superior people. Whenever barbarism and civilization . . . meet face to face, the result must be war."[99] While most Americans demurred from extending civilization's war into Central America (early in the next century they would manage to overcome that restraint, whether in Central America or Cuba or the Philippines), overwhelmingly they joined with Walker in celebrating their exclusionary approach to frontier settlement. In consequence, they were not cursed, like the majority of Mexicans were cursed according to a Cincinnati phrenologist in the mid–nineteenth century, with skulls that reveal "very coarse organization, rather animal than intellectual."[100]

By no means was it only in Mexico and Central America that Iberians had demonstrated their inability to act properly when set loose in a racial frontier. An American visitor to the Argentine pampas in 1849 came upon swarms of mixed-blood inhabitants, whom he dismissed as no better than "savage Indians." Encountering fewer traces of Indian blood among Chileans, he managed to praise them for their relative orderliness.[101] However, another traveler in Chile, this one a woman, encountered all too many mestizos, "for the most part excessively ugly."[102] Two Americans who wandered over parts of Panama, Colombia, and Venezuela concluded: "The deterioration attending this commingling of Spanish and Indian races is painfully apparent. We observe a loss of intellectual force, a union of the worst qualities of both, of which there is no lack in either, and an elimination of . . . a broad and vigorous manhood."[103] These travelers rendered their judgment at the beginning of the 1870s. Toward the end of that decade an American who traveled in Brazil noted that not even a third of the population was "pure-blooded." In consequence, "the proportion of really good families, refined educated ones, is very much smaller than in the United States."[104] Many years later the distinguished, emotionally disturbed, and alcoholic poet Hart Crane visited Cuba. The Havana of 1926 impressed him as "a funny little metropolis," inhabited by "such trashy, bastard people—without any sense of direction or purpose."[105]

With some validity, Americans generally assumed mestizos to be a "bastard people." While original Iberian male settlers had frequently married Indians, later generations made every possible effort to find white brides, or brides who could at least more or less pass as white. But Iberian men married to whites by no means abandoned their sexual alliances with Indian women. Unlike the gentle tamers of the American West, upper-sector Latin American women tended to turn a blind eye to their husbands' peccadilloes. Increasingly, then, mestizos bore the opprobrium of illegitimacy. In Anglo eyes, the very presence of the burgeoning numbers of a spurious race attested to the inability of Latins to control their passions and to develop the social responsibility that distinguished civilized people.

Rather than the mestizo products of Spanish and Indian union, whom Crane actually came to admire in Mexico, the "trashy, bastard" Cubans about whom he complained were largely mulattoes. And to most Americans the degree to which Spaniards and Portuguese throughout the Americas had bred with blacks provided one more proof of Latin inferiority when measured against Teutonic standards. Already for several generations before Crane observed Cubans, it had been apparent to most Americans that "amalgamation between black and white . . . is the most abhorrent" of all.[106] The majority of Americans who expressed themselves in writing on the matter seemed to agree with Englishman Henry Dunn who traveled to Guatemala in 1829. Mulattoes, he concluded, unite to their "considerable degree of cunning . . . an energy to which the simple Indian is altogether a stranger." They were, in all, more menacing to civilization than Indians or mestizos.[107]

Renowned landscape architect Frederick Law Olmsted in 1857 recorded his contempt for Mexicans because of "their intimacy" with Negroes. Not long before Olmsted wrote, an Ohioan dismissed Mexicans as "a sad compound of Spanish, English, Indian, and Negro bloods." The result, he maintained, was a "slothful, indolent, ignorant race of beings." An American northerner traveling to La Plata and Brazil in 1856 complained that "mulattoes, quadroons, and demi-quadroons, and every other degree of tinted complexion and crisped hair, met, at every turn, indicate an almost unlimited extent of mixed blood. This cannot fail to be revolting . . . to a visitor from . . . our country."[108] Yet not all Americans could agree as to which was the more vile contributor to racial degeneration south of the border, the mulatto or the mestizo. Congressman Thaddeus Stevens, the Radical Reconstructionist who wanted to extend suffrage to Negroes (and who maintained a Negro mistress), found mulattoes acceptable. But he argued heatedly against enfranchising New Mexicans on the grounds that they constituted "a hybrid race of Spanish and Indian origin, ignorant, degraded, demoralized and priest-ridden."[109]

Unlike Stevens, most Americans by the early to mid–nineteenth century drew a line of demarcation "between every man who has a drop of African blood in his veins," on one hand and "nondebased" people on the other.[110]

Little wonder, then, that in the 1850s several prominent U.S. public figures endorsed a plan to subsidize the colonization of American Negroes, once liberated from slavery, in Central America. The "sable race," as one proponent of the plan put it, would remain "a blot on the fair prospect of our country." Apparently, though, an additional blot in Central America would not matter, for there the people already were debased beyond remedy. Just as the unoccupied West provided a dumping ground for undesirable Indians, so Central America, occupied by a semihuman populace, might furnish a dumping ground for blacks. Indeed, during the first two years of the Civil War, President Abraham Lincoln himself worked on plans to acquire tracts of land in Panama and Haiti on which American Negroes could be settled. Early in the Civil War at least, Lincoln looked on colonization as the means to overcome the great fear that gripped so many Americans as they contemplated black emancipation: the fear of future racial contamination through miscegenation with the African.[111]

In their response both to Indians and blacks, Iberians in the New World seemed to conform to the previously mentioned pattern that Edmundo O'Gorman attributes to them. Rather than adjusting to the conditions of a New World frontier, they tried to adapt the New World to the style of life they had become accustomed to in the Old World. Rather than learning themselves how to exploit America's vast virgin resources, and in the process developing the self-reliance and independence and democracy that Americans liked to imagine they acquired as a result of their frontier experience (whether these traits actually grew out of the frontier experience remains a contentious point among historians), Iberians mated with both Indians and Africans. Thereby, even as European diseases and cruelty wiped out an aboriginal populace, Iberians created new pools of dependent laborers so that whites, at the top of the pigmentocracy, could continue to cultivate the life-styles of the lord, the *patrón*, the master. While American observers disliked what they took for a feudalistic caste system, "with its hereditary rank and privileges," they nonetheless concluded it was certainly right and natural that mestizos and mulattoes, along with Indians, "should be fixed in the lower order of society."[112] Still, this arrangement did no more than keep a bad situation from getting worse, and it perpetuated the sexual and other abuses of power that had created the situation in the first place.

To justify the bondage in which they tried to keep the dark, mixed-blood masses, Latin American elites by and large subscribed to theories about the inferiority of "half-breeds" that differed only by degree from the views that prevailed in the United States. At least, though, as already noted, Latin Americans did provide possibilities for their mixed-blood underlings to escape the onus ordinarily attaching to them, to undergo whitening and thereby gain relative acceptance among the gente decente. Through the years, moreover, a few Latin American thinkers proclaimed race mixture a positive virtue, destined to produce the "cosmic race" that by harmoniously bringing together a multitude of different traits would rise to cultural heights unattainable by relatively unmixed races.[113] Occasionally Americans themselves, alienated by various features of the national culture as shaped by the values of sexual continence, white supremacy, and abhorrence of mixture, have embraced cosmic-race expectations and welcomed mestizaje as a blessing that heretofore they had denied themselves, out on their racial frontier.

Positive and Ambiguous Perceptions of Mestizaje *among Americans*

Americans concerned with wholeness, with overcoming alienation, often respond positively, as already noted, to androgyny imagery. In the androgynous being they find a symbol that transcends cultural stereotypes fashioned by the single-minded, either-or arbiters of national values.[114] Like the androgyne, the mestizo appeals to persons who seek to undermine rigid controls established by defenders of one-dimensional orthodoxy, who aspire to surmount fragmented, alienated consciousness so as to forge an inclusionary society—and psyche—of diversity based upon community with the Other. The mestizo, like the androgyne, encompasses and personifies many of the clichés through which American counterculturalists have challenged establishment norms. If most American writers extolled manly values in their fiction and lionized the entrepreneurial "man of force," at least a few hailed a masculine figure attenuated by the feminine principle.[115] Almost as much as the androgyne, the mestizo provides such a figure. The mestizo combines, to employ the customary stereotypes, the forceful "masculine" characteristics of civilization with the "feminine," bonding, communalist traits of premodern beings.

Alexis de Tocqueville upon visiting America praised half-breeds as "the natural link between civilization and barbarism."[116] Since de Tocqueville's miraculously fruitful visit to the New World in 1831, some American writers, flying in the face of traditional prejudice, relished half-breed imagery for its ability to imply completeness and redemption. In this they reflected the fascination that some of their fellow Americans have found in the Pocahontas–John Rolfe union as a symbol for the beginning of a new humanity.[117]

Even before de Tocqueville's homage to the mestizo, the future abolitionist Lydia Maria Child published (in 1824) her historical romance *Hobomok: A Tale of Early Times*. In it, she imputed positive traits to mestizaje and thus challenged the moralizing of the traditional captivity tale that attributed virtue solely to the civilized being who rejected union with barbarism.[118] About the time that Child raised the hackles of orthodox Americans with her views on mestizaje, Scottish-born reformer Fanny Wright (who first toured the United States between 1818 and 1820 and settled in New York City in 1829) caused scandal not only by championing equal rights for women but also by endorsing miscegenation. Another woman, Quaker Helen Hunt Jackson, sparked indignation among many Americans with her previously mentioned novel of 1884, *Ramona*. Sharply rebuking the prejudices that caused Americans to reject the possibility of a more complete humanity, Jackson exalted mestizaje. In *Ramona*, she provided Indians and mestizos with the vindication that Harriet Beecher Stowe offered African Americans in her *Uncle Tom's Cabin*.[119]

Not only among "offbeat" women writers did mestizos find champions. In the 1830s Albert Pike published short stories and "prose poems" that "prefigured the sensibility of those modern writers who have seen an interesting and aesthetically satisfying combination" in the union of European and Indian.[120] Edgar Allan Poe published his previously cited and probably semiautobiographical *Narrative of Arthur Gordon Pym of Nantucket* in 1838. A central character in this masterpiece is the half-breed Dirk Peters. In Peters, many critics have seen an archetypal mestizo savior, symbolizing the possibility for civilization to be reborn in the strength of savagery.[121] Subsequently, during an 1872 trip to Mexico, nature poet William Cullen Bryant praised mestizos, but not for the strength they derived from rootedness in savagery. Instead, Bryant praised the artistic and literary talents of Mexico's mestizos, implying, surely, that artistic intuition arises out of intimate ties to nature.[122]

Twentieth-century American writers who have exalted the mestizo, seeing in the union of the civilized with the natural the source of renewed vigor, expanded intuitive powers, or both, include Ernest Hemingway (with his character Dick Boulton in *In Our Time*), William Faulkner (with Boon Hogganbeck and Sam Fathers in *Go Down, Moses*), and perhaps Ken Kesey (with Broom Bronden in *One Flew Over the Cuckoo's Nest*). Moreover, Norman Mailer's celebrated essay "The White Negro" (1957) hails the cultural, if not necessarily the biological, crossbreed. For a while in the 1960s, as one literary critic notes, amalgamated black-and-whites overtook the Natty Bumppos and Davy Crocketts as preferred American icons: "The mulatto is the incarnation of youth. He is the top of the pops."[123]

American fiction writers, it has been suggested, often accept a "tight mental allegiance" to the morality of racial purity, even while with all their passion they long to embrace the Other and produce the hybrid.[124] They understand that the creative literary spark must combine the Apollonian restraint of the civilized being with the instinctual, Dionysian passion of the primitive. Americans in general, not just writers, are both repelled by and drawn to the imagery of the hybrid. Ordinarily they advertise the repulsion; occasionally they confess the attraction. For themselves, though, when attracted by the imagery of mestizaje Americans in general choose the "White Negro" model, opting for cultural, not racial, mixture. They deem it acceptable for the white person voluntarily to take on the ways of the primitive. Whites who symbolically (or actually) paint their faces black or red are all right. Indeed, the American minstrel-show tradition that flourished from the 1840s to the 1920s arose partly out of the blackface mystique; and Elvis Presley, the White Negro of the 1950s and 1960s, borrowed from and added to the mystique. But, to mix racially or biologically with the Other, that is something else again: something that often brings pause to the most avid American seekers of wholeness. Thus Americans, even while sympathizing with cultural mestizaje, are apt to wonder about those Iberian frontiersmen who had the courage to go all the way, to use unashamedly their genitals instead of their minds and psyches to create the hybrid—thereby acting ever naturally and deepening the differentiation between their frontier and ours.

CHAPTER 5

America in the Age of the New Imperialism

The Alleged End of the American Frontier

Dawn of April 12, 1889, found some fifty thousand land seekers assembled in Oklahoma Territory. At noon a cannon was fired, and simultaneously various cavalry signal-corps personnel, spread out over a miles-long line, sounded their bugles. Here were the signals the land seekers had awaited, and now they raced out to establish their claims on property recently "liberated" from Indian ownership.[1] "It was a day the participants would never forget, and by dusk, seven hours later, nearly every town lot in what became Norman, Oklahoma City, Guthrie, and Kingfisher had been staked."[2] In all, nearly two million acres had been claimed. A little less than three and a half years later, on September 16, 1893, about one hundred thousand persons participated in an even vaster land grab, managing in one day to stake out claims to some six million acres in the "Cherokee Strip" area of northwestern Oklahoma, just across the border from Kansas. In two fell swoops, civilization had rescued close to eight million acres from savages who, allegedly, knew no better than to keep the land in wilderness estate.

In the 1930s many descendants of the Oklahoma civilizers, victims of drought, of their own heedless farming methods, and perhaps of the exploitation of banking and railroad magnates, fled the horrors of the Dust Bowl to seek survival in California, where they were treated no better than immigrants from south of the border. But this is getting ahead of the story.

Edna Ferber in her fast-paced novel *Cimarron* (1929) creates in Yancey Cravat an unforgettable participant in the 1889 Oklahoma land grab. Cravat saw his land claim as a chance to start clean, right from scratch. Live and let live. Clean politics instead of the skullduggery all around; a new way of living and of thinking, because we've had a chance to see how rotten and narrow and bigoted the other way has been. Here everything's fresh. It's all to do, and we can do it. There's never been a chance like it in the world. We can make a model empire out of this Oklahoma country, with all the mistakes of the other pioneers to profit by. New England, and California, and the settlers of the Middle-West—it got away from them, and they fell into the rut.[3]

Substituting a few words, here is a description of the great American frontier myth that could have been written virtually any time between the 1620s and the 1880s. But not even the American frontier was vast enough to survive the steady assaults that settlers unleashed upon it beginning in the seventeenth century, and in 1890 the Bureau of the Census officially declared the end of the frontier—meaning that it was no longer possible to draw the traditional line separating settled from frontier territory, the latter occupied by only two to six persons per square mile. America had become, ostensibly, a settled, occupied country.

Even before the mid–nineteenth century, thoughtful Americans dreaded the material and spiritual consequences they connected with reaching the end of the frontier. In 1835, for example, artist Thomas Cole (depicted in illustration 3), concerned about a rising tide of mean-spirited materialism, urged protection of unspoiled oases along the Hudson River wherein Americans might benefit for generations to come from the cleansing, purifying influences of pristine nature.[4] In the 1840s, national anxiety "for the loss of nature" reached new heights. While abundance had originally encouraged "myths of inexhaustibility," by the second half of the century "eroded lands, flooded fields, stump-spotted forests, and ruined prairies . . . stood in silent judgement of those who had acted . . . irresponsibly."[5] In an elegiac mood in 1892 not long before his death, Francis Parkman wrote a revised preface to his midcentury classic *The Oregon Trail*. There could no longer be any doubt, he declared: "The Wild West is tamed, and its savage charms have withered."[6] Indeed, "the uncomfortable sense of bearing witness to a vanishing Eden runs like a leitmotif" through the writing of the entire nineteenth century, as Americans came increasingly to recognize "the waste and unnecessary destruction that had accompanied the westward movement."[7]

Given this background of apprehension, the Census Bureau announcement in 1890 concerning the end of the frontier seemed almost anticlimactic. And, like all great and enduring historical interpretations, the importance that Frederick Jackson Turner attached to the closing of the frontier in his 1893 address to the American Historical Association in Chicago reflected as much conventional wisdom as it did bold new perspectives. Already, the image of the frontier had "entered deeply into the American identity," and become a part of the nation's civil religion—a civil religion being defined as "any set of beliefs and rituals, related to the past and/or future of a people ('nation') which are understood in some transcendental fashion."[8] More than anything else, "scientific" historian Turner responded to the frontier as a vision of ongoing rebirth, as already suggested in the second section of my first chapter. And like countless Americans before him influenced by this great national myth, Turner wondered as to the consequences attendant upon the fact that with the frontier at an end, easy, automatic rebirth could no longer be taken for granted. Nor could America's ongoing revitalization of savage energies be taken for granted, unless moral equivalents of the frontier, such as imperialist wars, became a part of national policy—an idea that assumed paramount importance for, among others, Theodore Roosevelt.

Turner's vision of the frontier also contained eminently practical and rational elements. In his address he noted that for nearly three hundred years the dominant fact in American life had been expansion. With settlement of the Pacific Coast and occupation of the free lands, this movement seemed to have come to an end. But, Turner predicted, the energies of expansion would continue to operate. The demands for a vigorous foreign policy, for an interoceanic canal, for a revival of sea power, and for the extension of American influence to outlying islands as well as nearby and distant countries served notice that the expansionist thrust would still prevail. Turner concluded: "Movement has been the dominant fact, and unless this training has no effect upon a people, the American energy will continually demand a wider field for its exercise. But never again will such gifts of free land offer themselves."[9] The mythical elements of the frontier as a guarantor, through its gifts, of American exceptionalism might have become more tenuous and problematic, but the practical, wealth and power-conferring aspects of frontier conquest could be found in an assertive and expansionist foreign policy.

Two years after Turner's address, Frederic Remington produced one of his most haunting paintings, to which he gave the title *The Fall of the Cowboy.* (See illustration 13.) Two cowboys have halted before a fence that announces the end of the open range. One has dismounted from his horse to perform the highly symbolical act of closing a gate in the fence. "Closing? There's probably no reason why he shouldn't be opening it," writes an art critic. "But everything in Remington's capacious, still, elegiac canvas sug-

13. Frederic Remington. *The Fall of the Cowboy.* 1895. Oil on canvas, 25 × 35⅛".
Courtesy Amon Carter Museum, Fort Worth, Texas.

In their apprehension over the supposed end of the frontier, Americans in the 1890s
tended to assume the gate in Remington's allegorical painting was closing. This assumption helped spark the desire for imperialist expansion.

gests a closing, an end. If there are to be new beginnings, they'll have to be
dealt with somewhere else."[10]

In 1894, one year after Turner's address and a year before the Remington painting, Jacob Coxey led a tattered and hungry army of the unem-
ployed, comprised mainly of people from the western and midwestern
states, into Washington, D.C. The object of the "invasion," which was
soon dispersed by federal forces, was to persuade Congress and the Grover
Cleveland administration to create public works projects and to increase
the money supply so as to stimulate the national economy. In the old days
when depression had struck urbanized, "civilized" America, the economically discomfited could make their way, so the myth (often more important than the reality) had it, to the frontier where new opportunities
awaited them. With the frontier closed, however, well-fed and comfortable
Americans beheld the revolutionary spectacle of the down-and-out flock-
ing not to unoccupied lands but instead invading the nation's capital to
demand reforms that to establishment elites smacked of socialism. To

many Americans of the not-so-gay nineties, the most likely area in which the frontier experience could be repeated, so as to put off the day of psychological and economic reckoning, was Latin America. Here lay the area that for many Americans constituted "their" new frontier.

"All imperialism in history," British historian V. G. Kiernan asserts, "has been largely imitative; it has seldom or never grown spontaneously out of the needs or impulsions of a single state. Greece caught the contagion from Persia, Rome from Carthage, Islam from Byzantium, Holland and England from Spain and Portugal. European states themselves [in the second half of the nineteenth century] were . . . to a great extent rushing after one another in search of colonies because they saw their neighbors doing it." [11] In the late nineteenth century, America was the country whose example European statesmen began to chase after. America's virtually unparalleled economic expansion they attributed, at least in part, to the nation's vast frontier of virgin land and its pool of cheap labor deriving from massive immigration. Acting upon these resources, new technology produced a dramatic multiplier effect. Unquestionably, part of the impetus for the so-called new imperialism on which European nations embarked in the latter part of the nineteenth century derived from their attempt to imitate the successes of the United States by finding vast new land resources and matching pools of cheap labor.

Europeans also proved susceptible to the same sort of mythology that had appealed for over a century to the American imagination. Thus in the late nineteenth century Europeans often dreamed of a plunge into primitive settings inhabited by primitive beings in quest of the vitality needed to keep their civilization not only profitable but young and vibrant. German writer Karl May (1842–1912) attests to the interchangeability and imitativeness of imperialist mythology. May drew on the setting, imagery, and stereotypes of America's western frontier to write the enormously popular adventure tales that inflamed the imagination of late nineteenth-century Teutonic expansionists—and later of Adolf Hitler himself.[12]

Ironically, at the precise moment that Europe began to emulate the United States in the actions inspired and sanctified by its frontier reality and mythology, that country had run out of frontier lands. If Americans hoped to keep up with the economic and great-power-status gains as well as the mythological rewards that imperialism seemed to promise, then they must themselves begin to imitate Europeans and find new lands and new sources of cheap labor. In short, Americans must embark upon extracontinental imperialism. Here is how Henry Cabot Lodge put the matter: "The great nations are rapidly absorbing for their future expansion and their present defense all the waste places of the earth. It is a moment which makes for civilization and the advancement of the race. As one of the great nations of the world, the United States must not fall out of the line of march." [13]

In the 1989 novel *The Whales in Lake Tanganyika*, Swedish writer Lennart Hagerfors gives these words to Britain's journalist-explorer Henry Morton Stanley as he stands on the shores of Lake Tanganyika in 1871: "After the success of our expedition, European settlers would soon come streaming into Africa. The savannah would be plowed and sown with wheat and rye. The wild beasts would be shot or domesticated, railroads would be built across the continent, . . . and the forests would be cut down for buildings and fuel for the factories that would spring up by the railroads. The Negroes would be baptized and taught to work. On the navigable rivers, shining white British steamers would transport goods and people." [14] Change a few key words, and you have the attitudes of many Americans as they contemplated the opening of new frontiers beyond their continental confines. Rather than the Gospel, glory, and gold that had sparked yesterday's Iberian imperialists, conversion, competition, and commerce (not necessarily in that order) fired the imaginations of Europe's and America's new imperialists.

The American Quest for New Frontiers

According to a prescient student of the topic, imperialism is most apt to occur when conditions of anarchy in underdeveloped areas of the world potentially available as new frontiers intersect with "instability in the evolution of relations among the rival great powers." [15] As the inducements of imitation cast their spell and one great power after another embarked on the new imperialism, instability in their relations increased. In particular, U.S. statesmen concerned themselves over the rise of Germany and Japan. Security considerations dictated that the United States move to protect its flanks against these potential rivals. Several generations of nineteenth-century Americans had assumed that the most natural direction for expansion lay to the North, in Canada. But rapprochement with Britain toward the end of the century effectively closed off the possibilities of northward expansion. Americans now stood ready to turn southward, and they were in no mood to share their new frontier with Germany or Japan.

Two major ingredients fed into American desire to expand southward, though not necessarily to create a United States that extended from pole to pole, as historian John Fiske had envisioned the national destiny in 1885. [16] Both ingredients or components we have already glimpsed, but they require a moment's additional scrutiny. First, there is the "hard" component that lies behind the lure of expansion southward. Comprising the hard component are inseparably intertwined economic and security considerations. Present also is the desire of a "masculine" civilization to assert itself over untamed natural environments and primitive peoples just for the adventurous hell of it, just for the thrill of proving who's boss. In its "soft" manifestation, the lure of expansion derives from millennialist visions of rebirth in nature, of combining two half-worlds in wholeness—a theme sounded in the preceding chapter and also in those to come. I suspect a majority of expansionist Americans fell primarily under the influence of hard, power-inspired and materialistically driven impulses. They were the sort who would snap to attention when the Department of Commerce, as in one of its 1918 studies, harped on South America's enormous economic opportunities.[17] Often, though, soft, mythological-spiritual drives operated, subliminally at least, even in persons who believed themselves responsive almost exclusively to practical or economic-security determinants. These mythological-spiritual drives came into play when Americans read some of the early twentieth-century literature that referred to Latin America as an area still covered with primitive vegetation, still bathed by some of the waters of the great flood that had driven Noah onto his ark.[18] With American expansion southward, conscious or economic-security motivation gained reinforcement from drives buried deep in the psyche and best reached through myth. So it seems to me, though I can no more prove this conviction than doubters can disprove it.

At mid–nineteenth century diplomat Ephraim George Squier felt attracted to Central America not just for its future practical importance to the United States but also because of what he intuited as its mystical or cosmic significance. Given its location, Central America fulfilled "the ancient idea of the centre of the world. Not only does it connect the two grand divisions of the American continent, the northern and the southern hemispheres, but its ports open to Europe and Africa on the east, and to Polynesia, Asia, and Australia on the west."[19] By moving to establish their sway over this "centre of the world," Squier believed—and in this he anticipated the previously described vision of artist Frederic Edwin Church—that Americans would qualify themselves to harmonize opposites and bring an end to alienation for themselves and for much of the rest of the world. As the century advanced, some Americans in addition to Church seemed to feel that the time had come to proceed toward fulfilling the visions that Squier had glimpsed.

"Wonder, astonishment and sublime devotion fill and elevate the mind," wrote Charles Darwin upon beholding the splendor of Brazil's Amazon forests. And since the time of Darwin, Americans have felt the same wonder and astonishment as they contemplate the natural wonders of the Amazon and other oases of unspoiled nature in Latin America, even as they regret the gradual disappearance of many such sanctuaries of the pristine in the United States. Among these Americans has been Harvard University's father of sociobiology, Edward O. Wilson. To the sense of fulfillment one experiences upon contemplating nature in its purest splendor, Wilson has given the name *biophilia*. Biophilia, the experiencing of transcendence, Wilson believes is rooted in the human mind. It is triggered, he wrote in 1984, by experiencing what seems a return to origins.[20]

Biophilia was alive among Americans as the last century ended. As an American thinker put the matter in 1898: "We want the earth—not consciously as a formulated program, but instinctively, with a desire that is too deep for consciousness."[21] At the turn of the twentieth century, when Oriental religions gained one of their recurring vogues in America, when Theosophy and Swedenborgianism constituted strong spiritual and spiritualist influences, when William James concerned himself with the power of the extrarational and the parapsychological, and when Henri Bergson's "élan vital" principle (stressing the primacy of spiritual over material influences) gained enthusiastic followers, the country's thinkers and dreamers did not shy away from pursuits inspired by desires "too deep for consciousness."

As they prepared to enter a new century, many Americans longed for fresh sources of biophilia's "high." Fearful that not only frontier but pastoral realms were threatened in their own country, that America was losing its "virginity," they sought new retreats "from the bafflements of the modern age."[22] They sought something more precious than gold; and not a few suspected their particular version of the grail might be found to the south.

In stark contrast, America's "hard" expansionists looked greedily to the south as the area where fortunes could be made as civilization rode roughshod over all that was pristine. And these Americans relished the fact that much of Latin America was already occupied. People were at hand to help Americans in the task of taming nature, a process that under proper tutelage might direct the natives toward civilization at the same time that they enhanced the fortunes of those already civilized. America's original frontiers had lacked a large and docile labor force. The new frontier would not suffer this lack.

Soft and/or Hard Inducements to U.S. Penetration of the Latin American Frontier

Thomas Jefferson perceived, as he put it, "the advantages of a cordial fraternization among all the American nations, and the importance of their coalescing in an American system of policy, totally independent of, and unconnected with that of Europe." "I wish to see this coalition begun," he concluded.[23] Voicing these sentiments in 1820, Jefferson anticipated an idea much in vogue in the latter part of the nineteenth century: the idea of the unity of American-hemisphere nations based on their shared interests and convergence of values. In his early, and inconsistent, articulation of the "Western Hemisphere Idea,"[24] did Jefferson respond to soft or to hard sources of inspiration? The answer must be that he responded to both.

As a soft hemispherist Jefferson managed, at least for moments at a time, to overcome the negative feelings he had about Latin America's Roman Catholicism and other afflictions. In these moments he professed that, above all others, the people of the New World, North and South, were destined to attain the fullest measure of freedom, happiness, and virtue of which humanity was capable. Jefferson's mystical notion of hemispheric destiny, voiced as early as 1813,[25] rested on the assumption that the commercial spirit as exemplified in the Old World was basically alien to the American hemisphere, which must guard itself culturally and if necessary militarily against contamination by that alien spirit. Yet Jefferson recognized the importance of commercial interests, as shown by his conviction that the main purpose of the Lewis and Clark expedition (1804–1806) was to open new areas and awaken new peoples—the Indians—to commerce.[26] Jefferson's approach to both continental expansion and the spread of U.S. influence in Latin America thus arose out of mystical and practical or economic considerations. And, like Woodrow Wilson a hundred years later, Jefferson's desire to exclude Old World influences from the New responded both to the desire to safeguard the spiritual potential of America and to monopolize its commercial possibilities. Put into the terminology favored by Marxists, both Jefferson and Wilson believed that the unity of the New World's "superstructure" or ideological-cultural values demanded a cohesive "base" of economic ties and institutions. However, more often than not in the course of U.S. history, economic factors have undoubtedly claimed pride of place in determining hemispheric policy.

When Americans first began to move resolutely in the post–Civil War era to establish the hard or economic base of an American hemispheric system, they stood in the midst of the so-called Gilded Age in which private greed seemed to provide the main impetus to domestic and foreign policy. They saw landscapes in terms not of spiritual renewal but of commodities; and their desire to accomplish "material conquest" over areas to the south arose not from mysticism but from the hope of guaranteeing Americans another century of prosperity. Increasingly, this objective appeared to demand exclusion of European and Asiatic powers lest by the intrusion of their alien interests, especially into the circum-Caribbean region, they interfere with those "higher laws" that somehow reserved America's hemispheric resources for Americans. Undergoing a gilded age of their own, Latin Americans witnessed the rise of a new capitalist class that welcomed collaboration with "can-do" Yankee businessmen. Entertaining few if any mystical ideals about collaborating with North Americans so as to nourish human freedom and spiritual development, the Latin capitalists found inspiration in the profits likely to accrue from the conquest of nature in their native lands by Yankee mining and canal- and railroad-building projects.

Already by the turn of the century, U.S. capital had turned to Andean mining. In 1902, for example, the Cerro de Pasco Mining Company began its operations, staking out for its field of operations the rich copper, silver, lead, and gold deposits that lay at a height of some fourteen thousand feet in the Andean ranges to the northeast of Lima. Within a few years, the company had laid some eighty-three miles of railroad track to link its plant to the national line and had opened a refinery complex eight miles south of the town of Cerro de Pasco. The smelter for some years functioned improperly, owing in part to the low-grade fuel employed. Peruvians not sympathetic to the penetration of Yankee capital began to criticize the way in which the foreign concern polluted the atmosphere, allegedly ruining vegetation for miles around with the smoke of its ovens. Critics also charged that the mining company's penetration of the Peruvian frontier had created a replica of America's Wild West, where gambling, drunken fights, assassinations, and assaults on Indians abounded.[27] Evidently some Latin Americans believed they had a better record of dealing with frontier situations than Americans. In any event, initial attempts by Americans to tame the frontier to the south sparked considerable Latin complaint. Almost a century later, that complaint showed no signs of abating, even though the Latins who benefited from the advancing tide of civilization, capitalists as well as many workers, applauded the process.

Nowhere was civilization's advance more clearly discernible than in Cuba where, in the late nineteenth century, U.S. steelmakers had begun to extract iron ore. Steel, it has been said, "represented the triumph of American will, the conquest of nature by technology."[28] Perhaps in no industry up until that time did technology move so dramatically to "revolutionize the face of nature."[29] In Cuba, the steam-driven behemoths that extracted iron ore from the soil symbolized the advance guard of assault troops out to revolutionize nature.

Initiating their 1898 campaign against Spain in the Spanish-Cuban-American War (to use the designation that Cubans most properly insist upon giving the struggle), U.S. forces landed in the region of Siboney and

Daiquiri, precisely where the Pennsylvania Steel Company and some lesser Yankee firms had established their operations. Thus, in "freeing the Cuban people from the yoke of [Spain's] colonial oppression, the U.S. Army also liberated some valuable Yankee investments." This does not imply collusion between American steel interests and the U.S. government. The choice of landing spot derived from the fact that in bringing modern progress to Cuba, the American steelmakers had established conveniences coveted by invading armies, including docks, warehouses, and railroad facilities.[30]

Once U.S. hegemony replaced Spanish dominion over Cuba, American mining firms began to operate in a highly protected setting, for Cuban governments were "in the awkward position of incurring the official displeasure of Washington if attempts were made to impose taxes or other fees on American . . . interests."[31] Moreover, even when the U.S. government maintained, as it often did, a hands-off attitude toward the operation of American mining firms on the island, Cubans assumed that Washington stood squarely behind the gringos. After all, the Latin American frontier had been settled largely through official encouragement and control. Cubans, and other Latin Americans as well, could not understand that as North Americans penetrated the Latin frontier, they often did so basically on their own.

Even without consistent and official backing from Washington, U.S. steel interests possessed more than adequate power to transform Cuba's economy and its natural environment. Pennsylvania Steel, for example, introduced "steam-shovel mining . . . to help tame the recalcitrant mountains. Two steam shovels were shipped from the U.S. in 1901 and painstakingly dragged up . . . [Lola] hill [that rose above Daiquiri, some five miles from the coast] on mine tracks. Hand shovels were thrown aside as the big machines moved three tons of rock in their buckets. Five other steam shovels were placed on the hillside, along with dynamite and equipment houses."[32] Nature was no match for the technology that lent impetus to American industry as it moved into Cuban, Andean, and also Mexican mining and as it established banana plantations in Central America.

To provide middle-level workers to supervise unskilled Cuban hands, Pennsylvania Steel (which the giant Bethlehem Steel Company acquired in 1916) at first considered using some of the Negro workers it employed at the lowest levels of its refining facilities at Sparrows Point, just outside of Baltimore; ultimately, though, the company decided to import its middle-level workers from Spain. The Spanish workers were judged more docile than American blacks; and in almost all respects they were deemed superior to Cubans, with their alleged spendthrift habits and gambling instincts, quarrelsome ways, and penchant for carrying concealed weapons. More often than not, Cuba's gente decente shared the Yankee's pejorative estimation of the native working classes. While Spaniards supervised the Cubans (thereby seeming to deprive them of the recently won fruits of independence), U.S. workers and foremen arrived in Cuba to oversee both Spaniards and natives. The foremen received a four-week vacation every year in the United States. Thereby, they might better resist temptations to go native. Thereby, too, they could escape for a time the influence of "tropical light," thought by some to cause "severe biological distress to Caucasians." Indeed, an American expert on the topic averred that tropical light caused brains to shrink,[33] and not just Caucasian brains.

Although concerned by the threat to civilization stemming from excessive exposure to nature, Pennsylvania and (after 1916) Bethlehem Steel worried not one whit about the adverse effects on the natural environment produced by the waste products of civilization's technology. So, the Baltimore region and Chesapeake Bay suffered increasing pollution from the refuse that resulted from the refining of Cuban ore. Ironically, iron ore that economic imperialism ripped out of Cuban soil ultimately poisoned the environment of the imperialists.

Yet another symbol of manly civilization's triumph over effeminate nature emerged out of the building of the Panama Canal during the 1904–1914 decade. One of America's greatest engineering achievements, the canal clearly indicated civilized man's ability to correct nature's deficiencies. It demonstrated, too, in Americans' eyes, their superiority to those Latin Europeans—the French—who had tried and failed to correct nature's deficiencies in Panama. Furthermore, completion of the canal rested on the ability of science-proficient Americans to overcome the natural scourges, in this instance yellow fever and malaria. In still another way, the canal stood for civilization's ability to control the natural, for labor on the monumental project came mainly from blacks, most of them West Indians imported to Panama for the project, who toiled under the supervision of white Americans. Most appropriately, Michael L. Coniff titles his fine 1985 study of America's momentous achievement *Black Labor on a White Canal*.

This same theme pervades the painting to which Norwegian-born artist Jonas Lie (1880–1940) gave the title *The Conquerors (Culebra Cut), Panama Canal*. (Formerly on display in the Metropolitan Museum of Art, where I saw it in 1986, the painting was sold at auction at Christie's in 1990.) On his canvas, painted a year before the canal opened, Lie (who came to America as a youth) presents a view from high above the scene that he features. He looks down on huge earth-moving machinery spewing forth clouds of steam (just like the bridegroom-locomotive making its way into virgin territory, as referred to in the previous chapter). In the right foreground appear a few dark-skinned laborers, while just above them on the ascending terrain stand white foremen or bosses. Lie expresses virtually all there is to be said about the canal as a symbol of modern technology's triumph over nature and modern man's supremacy over primitives.[34]

Once completed, the canal, and the American Zone set aside along its course, formed a thin ribbon of civilization surrounded by threatening jungle, and thus exemplified the relationship that Americans believed they had to Latin Americans. Here is how novelist and travel writer Paul Theroux describes the scene as the train on which he rides across the Panamanian isthmus emerges from a tunnel: "Deeper and deeper the jungle began, tree jammed next to tree, vine creeping on vine, pathless and dark. It [the scene] bears no relation to the Canal; it is primitive jungle, teeming with birds. This is the margin of the [American] Zonian's world, where Panama resumes after the interrupting ribbon of the Zone. It does not matter that there are alligators and Indians there, because there are puppydogs and policemen here, and everything you need to ignore the jungle that does not stop until the Andes begins."[35]

Not only in Panama but in Chile and Peru, among other countries, Americans had built railroads in Latin America. In Cuba, shortly after the Spanish-Cuban-American War, they continued this tradition. American capital helped finance the building of the 360-mile railroad from Santa Cruz to Santiago. This line "opened up virgin lands of timber and attracted the venture capital of such noted Americans as E. H. Harriman, J. J. Hill, and Henry M. Flagler, the Rockefeller man who developed Miami and Key West through the Florida East Coast Railway."[36] Perhaps it is symbolically important that most of the railroad track laid in late nineteenth- and early twentieth-century Latin America (whether or not the construction firms were American) came from the United States. Underdeveloped, backward Latin America shipped the raw material, the iron, to the advanced United States, where it underwent transformation into track that was then shipped back to facilitate the advance of civilization into a primitive frontier.

Those Americans, including J. P. Morgan, who at the turn of the century dreamed of building a New York City to Buenos Aires Pan-American railway,[37] believed that the iron horse could be just as effective a money maker below the border as it had proved to be while facilitating conquest of the American West. As often proved the case with commercial penetration of frontier areas, an American was at hand to provide mythological meaning to what hard-headed, practical railroad builders hoped to accomplish through the Pan-American railway. That American was William Gilpin, a successful politician and highly decorated Union officer who has appeared in previous chapters. Once completed, a Pan-American railway, fed by tributary lines and steamship routes from all parts of the globe, would, according to Gilpin, place the United States at the center of the world—how that idea keeps recurring, even among "practical-minded" Americans! From mythology's sacred center, the United States could proceed to mediate and harmonize all the opposites in the world. In consequence, according to Gilpin, even the remotest nations would "be grouped and fused into one universal and harmonious system of fraternal relations."[38]

Even before moving south of the border, American railroad entrepreneurs encountered Latin workers as they brought the iron horse into the Southwest that had been wrested from Mexico in 1848—and also into Florida, redeemed from Spanish possession in 1821. The Southern Pacific, for example, relied upon the cheap labor of Hispanics already on hand, and imported additional hands as needed, as it wove Tucson and other settlements "into an iron web extending from the West to the East Coast," a web that transformed the Southwest "into an extractive colony of U.S. corporations."[39] Moreover, both in the Southwest and later in the Latin American countries where they established railroad communications, American railroad builders prided themselves on introducing wayward, dark- and yellow-skinned primitives to the disciplining mechanisms of civilization.

American manufacturers who established plants in the Southwest and later in Latin America also prided themselves on acting as emissaries of progress as they introduced principles of labor discipline and self-control and the sort of managerial planning associated at the turn of the century with Taylorism.[40] Americans operating south of the border also derived satisfaction from transforming jungles into plantations. According to one of them who wrote in celebration of this process: "The difference between the jungle and the dividend-paying plantation is one of organization, capital, administration, and toil. Add these to the jungle and you have the plantation."[41] Here was the symbolic mix that had fascinated Americans for over a century: the Other (Indian or Latin) provided nature, Americans contributed the accoutrements of civilization, and the result was a profit-maximizing synthesis. And, just in case anyone wanted to ease his conscience about the avid pursuit of maximum profits, he could descant on the uplift, the boost toward civilization, that Latin America's laboring classes received through their exposure to American enterprise and culture.

The Uplift of Colonials

As the likelihood of U.S. entry into Cuba's struggle for independence from Spain increased in May 1898, Dennis O'Connell, soon to become rector of the Catholic University of America, addressed a letter to John Ireland, archbishop of St. Paul and Minneapolis. In the course of his letter, O'Connell had this to say:

> For me, this is not simply a question of Cuba. If it were, it were no question or a poor question. Then let the "greasers" eat one another up and save the lives of our dear boys. But for me it is a question of much more moment—it is the question of two civilizations. It is the question of all that is old and vile and rotten and mean and cruel and false in Europe against all that is free and noble and open and true and humane in America. When Spain is swept off the seas much of the meanness and narrowness of old Europe goes with it to be replaced by the freedom and openness of America. This is God's way of developing the world, and all continental Europe feels the war is against itself, and that is why they are against us.

Then, near the end of his missive, O'Connell added, "Americanism . . . is the banner of God and humanity."[42] Here was one of the clearest expressions in the entire nineteenth century of the Western Hemisphere Idea, an idea articulated (as we have seen) at the beginning of the century by Thomas Jefferson, and an idea that would help impart to the Roman Catholic church in the United States an Americanist or hemispherist orientation that has ever since worried Rome.

Implicit in the Western Hemisphere Idea was the notion that the United States must assume the burdens of uplifting the Latin populace so that they could join in helping to fulfill the New World's unique destinies. However, many Americans turned away from the imperialist ambition to uplift stagnant peoples, whether in Latin America or in the Philippines and the Orient. Those who resisted taking on the burdens of uplift did so for, among others, two major reasons. Either they regarded the masses to the south or in the Orient as inherently incapable of responding to civilization's call; or, they feared that imperialist attitudes assumed in the quest to uplift distant Others would undermine respect for the principles of freedom and democracy among Americans themselves. "The serious question," according to a representative voice among this second school of anti-imperialists, "is what effect imperial policy will have upon ourselves."[43] He and those who stood with him understood that for every action there is a reaction. For every act of poisoning the social environment in a colony, the imperialist country suffers the poisoning of its own social environment.

Perhaps the most prestigious intellectual holding up the caution flag as he contemplated his country's entry into imperialist ventures of uplift was Yale University's William Graham Sumner, one of the fathers of American sociology. In his 1899 book *The Conquest of the United States by Spain,* Sumner cautioned that in the attempt to gain control over colonials to the extent ostensibly necessary to uplift them, Americans would undergo the same sort of cultural erosion, the same undermining of moral restraints and self-control that Spaniards had suffered in their New World imperialism. Rather than civilizing primitives, Sumner warned, in effect, that imperialism led to the primitivization of the civilized.

Although paying considerable attention to the anti-imperialists' warnings, by and large Americans simply rejected them. They simply were too confident of their abilities to mold nature—in this case, human nature. Just as a wide array of early twentieth-century American engineers expressed complete confidence about their ability to dominate and improve nature and to correct the various mistakes inherent in the physical environment,[44] and just as newly emerged psychiatrists boasted of their ability to correct flaws in the psyche, so Americans in the political realm and the social sciences succumbed to hubris as they contemplated the wonders of social engineering. Even in religious circles, increasing approval greeted the notion that mankind's ability to control both the environment and human nature was virtually without limits.

The early years of the new century witnessed the rise of a professional reformer-philanthropist class, often religiously affiliated, whose members firmly believed they could do good among the world's underlings and eagerly sought out people on whom they could exercise their transforming powers. Zealous reformers saw virtually "no limit to the possibilities for ameliorating and reforming the human condition" and looked forward to the day, not far distant, when even the insane would be cured.[45] Insanity, so it was widely believed both in America and Britain, resulted from the breakdown of control over passions. In a way, the insane were simply people who had reverted to primitivism; and they could be induced to take to the ways of civilization, to strengthen the will, and thereby be cured.[46] Furthermore, family experts increasingly took to advising parents on how to control anger in children, thereby easing and hastening their entry into adulthood. During the same early twentieth-century period, cartoonists in the popular press insisted more than ever on depicting Latin Americans as rowdy children.[47] By taking on roles of parental tutelage, Americans assumed they could advance Latin Americans' maturing processes.

Underlying part of the confidence in uplift was the peculiar way in which some Americans understood the social implications of Darwinism. As generally interpreted, social Darwinism taught that those who struggled most resolutely and most conscientiously ascended to the highest ranks among civilized beings, whereas those conditioned by their natures to live in noncompetitive balance and harmony with nature remained mired in inferiority. As applied in its social ramifications, however, Darwinism as seen by some Americans provided a non-Darwinian opening to ideas about possibilities for the prompt improvement of old habits. According to a leading student of the matter, until around 1920 American "Darwinists" largely ignored random natural selection and took instead to teleological, purposeful, progressive ideas based on neo-Lamarckian concepts of acquired characters. In consequence, Darwinism, as these American adherents saw it, taught that most individuals could improve themselves, once provided with proper stimuli.[48] Out of this mind-set came the faith, as expressed by John J. Ingalls in his 1898 book *America's War for Humanity,* that civilized beings could easily uplift barbarians. Sharing Ingalls's faith, many Americans saw no reason why the people of such far-off locales as Manila or Havana could not be civilized and taught, as a Protestant missionary expressed it, to transform their "pestholes" into veritable health resorts.[49] Even more than to the interests of the House of Morgan, *initial* U.S. imperialism in the Caribbean responded to "widespread beliefs that the Caribbean was a disorderly (and unclean) place that needed shaping up."[50] Indeed, Americans often trotted out economic justification as a rational excuse for an imperialism based on almost mystical dreams of elevating wayward human beings to states of relative perfection.

Just as Americans took the iron of Cuba and other Latin American countries and transformed it into steel, that glorious product emblematic of civilization, so they could take the raw material of Latin humanity and refine, mold, and burnish it. Typically, an American who oversaw the restructuring of education in Puerto Rico at the beginning of the twentieth century perceived the island's people as "passive and plastic."[51] Not only Latin America's natural resources but its people were "feminine" raw materials, waiting to be acted upon and shaped by an assertive "masculine" civilization. Even as Victor Frankenstein in Mary Shelley's masterful 1818 novel (*Frankenstein: Or the Modern Prometheus*) expected to mold from clay and straw a being altogether suitable to his purposes (and one who would prove gratefully dependent upon him), so Americans, Prometheus-like, would fashion creatures to their liking from Latin America's human clay. Thus, American visions of uplift found justification in the latest scientific theories of evolution and also in Promethean mythology and equally ancient myths that posited the mystical, transcendent consequences of Father Sky's union with Mother Earth.[52] When actions arise in part from myth-inspired convictions, arguments against them based on mere rationality make little headway. Perhaps this is one reason why through the years

Americans have turned a deaf ear to Latin Americans when they resort to logic and reason (in addition to passion and emotion) to insist that they do not wish to be "uplifted."

Sinclair Lewis knew that Americans, despite their contrary self-appraisals, often guided their lives by the most irrational expectations. In his 1920 novel *Main Street* he brings to life a scene in which Carol and Dr. Will Kennicott attend a movie in Gopher Prairie:

> The feature film portrayed a young Yankee who conquered a South American republic. He turned the natives from their barbarous habits of sinning and laughing to the vigorous sanity, the Pep and Punch and Go, of the North; he taught them to work in factories, to wear Klassey Kollege Klothes, and to shout, "Oh, you baby doll, watch me gather in the mazuma." He changed nature itself. A mountain which had borne nothing but lillies and cedars and loafing clouds was by his Hustle so inspired that it broke out in long wooden sheds, and piles of iron ore to be converted into steamers to carry iron ore to be converted into steamers to carry iron ore.[53]

Rather more prosaically but just as accurately diplomat Sumner Welles in the early 1920s described the American mania for uplift: "Unfortunately, the American people became so imbued with the role of the evangel, that there soon became apparent an earnest desire not only to reform the conditions of life and government of the peoples inhabiting the insular possessions of the United States, but likewise the conditions of life and government of the independent peoples inhabiting the sovereign Republics of the American hemisphere. All sense of proportion was lost."[54]

In U.S. endeavors of the late nineteenth century to uplift and Americanize the American Indian, one encounters another instance in which all sense of proportion was lost. Indeed, when anti-imperialists objected to U.S. expansion into the Caribbean and the Philippines on the grounds that such policies clashed with national traditions, the majority of Americans knew better. Indian policies had cast Americans in an imperialist tradition ever since the seventeenth century, and had prepared the way for the Latin American policies that heralded the rise of the United States to great-power status.

The Indian Background to Turn-of-the-Twentieth-Century U.S. Latin American Policy

In an 1803 letter to a friend, Thomas Jefferson expressed optimism about uplifting Indians. The means he advocated included instructing Indian men in farming methods and women in household arts. Then, in the spirit of mythology's prevailing vision of the fusion of opposites, Jefferson declared that for Indians the "ultimate point of rest and happiness" was to let our settlements and theirs meet and blend together, to intermix, and become one people." [55] In a way, the Western Hemisphere Idea that Jefferson developed later, and that posited the blending together of Americans and Latin Americans, grew out of his ideas on Anglo American–Indian relations. However, both Indian and future Latin American policy faced a common menace as Jefferson appraised the situation: the interference of Britain and Europe in the affairs of "unfortunate people" that would contaminate them with Old World vices and thus thwart American efforts aimed at their temporal redemption.

In the 1880s, as the Pan-American movement came into existence in part under the aegis of James G. Blaine (secretary of state and Republican presidential candidate, statesman and ward-heeling politician, visionary and opportunist), Americans moved more resolutely than ever before to try to banish the extrahemispheric influences that had once, allegedly, corrupted Indians and interfered with their assimilation. Jefferson and a succeeding generation of statesmen had hoped to eliminate intertribal warfare,[56] allegedly instigated by devious British and French interlopers, so as to permit the spread of civilization among the natives and facilitate the commerce that would serve this goal. Now, the Pan-Americanists, with Blaine in the lead, formulated plans for a Pax Americana that would stamp out the incessant inter–Latin American wars that impeded progress and commerce and thus interfered with the Americanization of Latin Americans. And, just as Secretary of the Interior Carl Schurz believed in 1881 that Indians could conceivably be "sufficiently civilized to support themselves, to maintain relations of good neighborship with the people surrounding them, and altogether cease being a disturbing element in society," [57] so Blaine and other Pan Americanists in the same decade entertained similar hopes for Latin Americans—hopes that could be realized, allegedly, only if non-American influences were eliminated from the Western Hemisphere.

The Indian precedent remained at work in 1905 when President Roosevelt proclaimed what came to be known as his corollary to the Monroe Doctrine. In effect, the corollary established that quarrelsome Caribbean countries would no longer be allowed to pursue internecine wars that interfered with their progress—and that invited European powers to fish in troubled waters in ways that might threaten U.S. security and economic interests. Inspired by an altogether similar spirit, a law of 1834 had granted the War Department authority, under the direction of the president, to use military force to end or prevent Indian wars that, in effect, interfered with processes of Americanization.

With the foreign menace long since eliminated on the Indian frontier, Americans prepared confidently in the post–Civil War era to complete their mission to uplift the natives. Because Anglo Americans would no longer suffer Indians in their midst to remain "half-civilized" wanderers and vagabonds, the only alternative most Americans could conceive was "education for civilized life."[58] In the widespread confidence about Indian "upliftability" one finds evidence of America's neo-Lamarckian interpretation of Darwinism, resting on belief in acquired characters. American Darwinism found embodiment in Thomas Jefferson Morgan, appointed commissioner of Indian affairs in 1889. One of "the most important commissioners in the nation's history," Morgan evidenced an "absolute and unswerving conviction" that the Indian must and could be "completely Americanized." Indeed, the whole concept of "expansion with honor"[59] that Americans developed as they completed settlement of their western frontier, a concept that President William McKinley would later apply to the Philippines as he envisioned Filipinos' "benevolent assimilation,"[60] rested on the assumption (or rationalization) that Indians could be detribalized and rendered fit for the full enjoyment of an American way of life. U.S. Army Lt. James Calhoun fully accepted this assumption when in 1874 he envisaged the transformation of Indians through education. In consequence of education, he averred, "hives of industry will take the place of dirty wigwams." Civilization would soon reign supreme "and throw heathen barbarianism into oblivion."[61]

For Senator Henry Dawes of Massachusetts, who designed the Indian reform legislation of 1887 that bore his name and that aimed at transforming Native Americans into fee-simple owners of their own plots of land, manliness was equated with the self-reliance of the individual property owner. Unless the Indian learned self-reliance by abandoning atavistic tribal or communal property ownership, Dawes proclaimed, "he will never be a man." Only the "creative power" of private capitalism, he added, "can put the elements of man into an Indian." Specifically, just how did civilized Americans teach Indians to become men? Well, according to Dawes, they had to teach the natives first to "stand alone, then to walk, then to dig, then to plant, then to hoe, then to gather, and then to *keep*. The last and the best agency of civilization is to teach a group of Indians to *keep*."[62]

Owing to communal property traditions, thought to encourage the sharing qualities that belonged properly only to women, Indians had failed, in the view of Henry Dawes, to develop the selfishness that lay at the heart of modern, progressive civilization. Until they acquired the trait of selfishness, which the Dawes Act intended to impart, Indians could climb no higher than the bottom rung of civilization. Senator Henry Teller of Colorado proved correct when he predicted that the ultimate consequence of the Dawes Act would be simply to "despoil Indians of their lands and to make them vagabonds on the face of the earth."[63] Surely, though, more than a few Americans were naively, ethnocentrically sincere when they sought to lead Indians into civilization by enhancing their competitive, individualistic manliness. In this instance, the sincerity may be more frightening than the hypocrisy.

When outlining his 1905 additions to the Monroe Doctrine, President Roosevelt undoubtedly was sincere in implying that once they had become sufficiently masculine, Latin Americans could expect to be treated as equals by Anglo Americans. Note the language he used in laying down his corollary's new rules of the game for Latin Americans who lived in the circum-Caribbean area. If they showed they could act with "reasonable efficiency" in maintaining order and paying their obligations, then they "need fear no interference from the United States." However, "chronic wrongdoing [i.e., childishness, savagery], or an *impotence* [i.e., lack of manliness] which results in a general loosening of the ties of civilized society" would force the United States, "however reluctantly," to assume "the exercise of an international police power."[64]

In addition to foreseeing establishment of hives of industry that would replace dirty wigwams, Lieutenant Calhoun, back in 1874, had envisioned establishment of "Christian temples" that would banish forever "places of heathen mythology."[65] Like the lieutenant, many Americans in the post–Civil War era assumed that freedom and individualism, whether in their economic or political manifestations, went hand in hand with the manly self-reliance of Protestant Christianity. Consequently, Protestant Christian mythology played an important role in shaping America's policy not only toward Indians but also, two or three decades later, toward Latin Americans.

Even in 1607, the handful of adventurers who came to establish Virginia seemed certain that mercantile profits and political aggrandizement went together with the "civilizing and Christianizing of the savage heathen." Indeed, economic, political, and religious aspects all merged in "that glorious plan" whereby a genuinely New World would be summoned into existence in Virginia.[66] President Ulysses S. Grant seemed to respond to the same glorious plan when in 1869 he began to entrust to American churches and missionary bodies the task of Americanizing Native Americans. In April of that year Congress authorized the president to name a board of commissioners consisting of "not more than ten persons, to be elected by him from men eminent for their intelligence and philanthropy, to serve without pecuniary compensation." Establishment of the Board of Indian Commissioners, as distinguished historian of Indian affairs Francis

Paul Prucha aptly observes, "set post–Civil War Indian policy ever more firmly in the pattern of American evangelical revivalism, for the men appointed to the board were Christian gentlemen who had been caught up in the awakening represented best by the Young Men's Christian Association."[67] Creation of the board manifested government's conscious intent to enlist religious groups and religiously minded men, and women, in the task of teaching Indians how to compete successfully in the quest for salvation and economic aggrandizement.

Before fifteen years had passed, most Protestant churches that had originally entered enthusiastically upon the mission of Indian uplift had grown disillusioned by the meager results. However, the Catholic church remained active in the civilizing mission. Soon it was garnering the lion's share of government subventions paid to churches engaged in Indian education. Protestants found this intolerable and moved to end the official affiliation between churches and state in the crusade for Indian assimilation.

Even if their churches no longer enjoyed government subsidies, individual Protestants remained active in the quest of Indian conversion and Americanization. In particular, Merrill E. Gates, who in a distinguished career served as the president first of Rutgers College and later of Amherst, played a conspicuous role in rallying important Protestants to take up, privately, the cause of Indian assimilation. Appointed to the Board of Indian Commissioners in 1884 (he later became its president and then served as its secretary), Gates had no doubt that when it came to assimilation, Protestantism and capitalism went, inseparably, together. Addressing an audience of like-minded Protestants, Gates insisted on the need to awaken material wants in the Indian. "In his dull savagery he must be touched by the wings of the divine angel of discontent. Then he begins to look forward, to reach out. The desire for property of his own may become an intense educating force." Once aflame with the desire for property, the Indian would discard the womanly and childish blanket in favor of the manly attire of trousers—"and trousers with a *pocket in them, and with a pocket that aches to be filled with dollars!*" The feminine and immature traits of sharing would become taboo in the assimilated Indian male: "The person who blindly gives away everything in the mere wish to be smiled upon—and without any consideration of the value of what he gives—is not fitting himself to be a helper of others, but is taking the first step toward becoming a . . . pauper."[68]

Wildly optimistic about prospects for uplifting the Indian through instruction grounded on Protestant principles, Gates declared in 1900: "We have learned that education and example, and, pre-eminently, the force of Christian life and Christian faith in the heart, can do in one generation most of that which evolution takes centuries to do."[69] And an optimism not unlike that of Gates seems to have infused President McKinley when, musing on Filipinos in 1898, he expressed confidence in the ease with which true Christianity could redeem those primitives. There was nothing left for the United States to do "but to take them all, and to educate the Philipinos [*sic*], and uplift and civilize and Christianize them, and by God's grace do the very best we could by them."[70]

As with Indians and Filipinos, so was it also with Latin Americans. In all instances, the moral uplift of true Christianity demanded the development of capitalist values. William Howard Taft, soon to become president of the United States, recognized the linkage when in 1906 he went to Cuba—the virtual colony of the United States since 1898—to address the opening exercises of the National University of Havana. "The right of property and the motive of accumulation," he averred as he virtually paraphrased Gates, lay at the heart "of all modern, successful civilization." Continuing, Taft exhorted his Cuban listeners to sharpen their interest in the acquisition of material wealth, thereby enhancing their virtue and with it "the mercantile spirit."[71] Addressing Cubans on economic progress, Taft in effect preached to them about acquiring godliness—Protestant godliness.

Having become accustomed to pitting themselves against Roman Catholics for control over Indian hearts and minds, American Protestants stood ready, in the years immediately preceding Taft's exhortation to Cubans, to compete with the Catholic church for control over Latin souls. Whether Indians or Latins were involved, Americans deemed manly capitalism and muscular Christianity the two sides of the coin of civilization destined to drive baser currencies out of circulation.

The war against Spain and the staking out of an empire in the Caribbean would provide the entry by means of which many Protestant leaders hoped to slay the Catholic dragon in one of its favorite lairs. In fact, Protestant clergymen encouraged the faithful to see among Latin peoples the same sort of opportunity that earlier generations of missionaries had found among Indians: the opportunity to destroy a prevailing culture and then to usher in regeneration through the Gospel of Jesus Christ. The Reverend James M. King in 1892 had praised the Almighty for not permitting the territory of the future United States to have been settled by people of Latin culture.[72] Now the time had come to correct Providence's temporary oversight and sweep away that culture's theological underpinnings from the Rio Grande to Cape Horn.

Some Americans, of course, recognizing the failure of past efforts to uplift Indians both in the religious and civil realms, opposed imperialism on the grounds that the intended colonials would respond to Yankee tutelage by coming to despise their mentors; and out of hatred for their purported benefactors, they would set themselves more resolutely than ever in their old ways. Such an opponent of American imperialism was the already mentioned Carl Schurz. As a onetime Republican secretary of the interior (1877–1881) who in this capacity had supervised the Bureau of Indian Affairs, Schurz had acquired firsthand experience as to the difficulties of uplifting recalcitrant primitives into "good neighborship"; and he regarded extension of these efforts to the Caribbean and Philippines as an endeavor foredoomed to failure. If American imperialists who surrounded a total U.S. Indian population of some 250,000 as of the late 1880s had made such scanty headway in "de-Indianizing" them,[73] how could they possibly expect to wean a huge mass of far-off Latins and Filipinos from their culture?

Americans who favored imperialism sometimes read a different meaning into past failures with those internal colonials, the Indians. Failure had arisen, they averred, out of the excessively mild and permissive approach of the Indian-service bureaucracy.[74] If Americans resorted to more heavy-handed methods, and doubled the hand into a formidable fist, then they could function successfully as masters of overseas alien hordes. Perhaps they could not uplift those hordes, but at least they could impose on them the requisite discipline to make them efficient laborers. Thus as the century ended, Americans often inclined either to reject imperialism or to become harder and harsher imperialists than they confessed to having been in the past. Ominously for their own future as well as for that of their overseas wards, Americans opted for the second alternative, although they toned down the implications by clinging to the rhetoric, and sometimes to the sincere motivation, of uplift.

In deciding on an imperialist course, Americans brought to their endeavors some of the lessons they had already acquired in dealing not only with such internal aliens as Indians but also with immigrants. Both in regard to Indians and immigrants, more and more citizens of the United States decided between 1900 and 1920 that "there was to be a new category of Americans—those who did not share in the dominant culture, but who served it and were expected to benefit from their peripheral attachment to 'civilization.'"[75]

Immigrants, Indians, and Latins: The American Quest to Control the Other

As the nineteenth century neared its end, American missionaries and also educators began to have doubts about their ability to uplift not only frontier Indians but certain lower-class elements who lived in the very heart of urban civilization. Protestant churchmen grew dubious about the possibility of taming the "turbulence and anarchy" that prevailed among the "lower orders" in many American cities.[76] Various Protestant women's groups in particular expressed doubt about the likelihood of introducing the "higher moral standards" of their own faith among the hordes of Catholic immigrants.[77] At the same time, some educators began to have second thoughts about the "great school legend," according to which the public schools were up to the task of Americanizing an increasing flow of immigrants from Europe and Asia,[78] of persuading them to exchange anarchist leanings for civilizing restraints.

The year 1876 proved critical in leading a good many Americans to reassess earlier assumptions. In that year redskin "savages" revealed how impervious to civilization they had remained, despite all the opportunities supposedly afforded them for uplift. They arose and martyred the blond-haired boy general George Armstrong Custer, that romantic emissary of civilization on the Indian frontier. Within a year a significant number of editorialists in the American press began to establish a connection between Indians who remained refractory to civilization and hordes of immigrant laborers who stoutly resisted Americanization and clung to their alien turbulence. Indians, as frontier savages, merged with immigrants, a motley array of internal, urban barbarians, to threaten the American way of life. According to a newspaper editorialist writing in 1877, alien strikers in America's industrial heartland had joined in an unofficial alliance with Indian insurrectionists to "make war on civilization itself." Numerous articles in popular journals as well as editorials in high-circulation newspapers repeated the message, as their authors juxtaposed references to Custer's Last Stand "with accounts of Negro disorder in the South, strikes and crime waves in the North."[79] Stern repression, most of the alarmed writers agreed, was the only answer.

The spirit of the Paris Commune of 1871, according to some American journalists, lay behind the labor violence of 1877. In that year, as Reconstruction ended and with it most of the optimistic expectations of the speedy assimilation of the African Other, a bloody coal strike erupted in Pennsylvania. It ended with the hanging of twenty Irish miners. In that same year a railroad strike approached the dimensions of an insurrection. Troops eventually occupied Baltimore; Pittsburgh; Martinsburg, West Virginia; and a dozen or so other towns as soldiers and police killed more than forty people. Newspapers in the affected locales described immigrant laborers "as though they constituted a separate racial group, like blacks or Indians, who were incapable of altering their inherently uncivilized and uncivilizable nature."[80] Even in Massachusetts Harvard University's president Charles W. Eliot began to drill Harvard riflemen "to defend properties of New Englanders against the eastward spread of rioting workers." Rather than having submitted to civilization, the Wild West, with new allies, was striking back against eastern refinement and order!

Throughout the East and Midwest, concerned community leaders "banded into a number of vigilante 'Law and Order' Leagues during the 1880s. By the end of that decade, massive armories brooded at the center of every American city—testimony to the official fears of domestic insurrection."[81] To many defenders of established values, it seemed the preparations had begun not a moment too soon, for in 1886 the rapidly growing Knights of Labor staged a May Day strike to support demands for the eight-hour day. On May 4 the Haymarket Square riot occurred in Chicago. A bomb thrown into the midst of policemen breaking up a workers' gathering killed seven officers and wounded sixty. Within a short time, fifty or more civilians also lay dead or wounded in the streets. The remainder of the 1880s, moreover, witnessed the sort of strikes, lockouts, boycotts, and disorders that later led Winston Churchill to describe American industrial relations as "the most violent in the Western world."[82] With only slight hyperbole, Ida M. Tarbell, destined to gain fame as the muckraking historian of Standard Oil, wrote: "The eighties dripped with blood."[83] One reason for the prevalence of blood and violence on the labor scene, coinciding not so accidentally with the rise of U.S. imperialism, was this: just as incipient imperialism, so also industrial relations had become the moral equivalent of Indian wars, pitting civilization against barbarism.

By the end of the century, all the states had established national guards, which accounted for state expenditures of close to three million dollars by 1896. With their officers drawn from the ranks of the middle and upper classes, guard units epitomized the endeavor not to uplift but simply to browbeat into submission the swelling ranks of internal colonials. At one time, Americans had coveted endlessly renewable supplies of immigrants who would, after revitalizing old-line society, disappear through acculturation or Americanization. Now it began to seem that many of the imported savages would, like the American Indians, refuse to disappear through assimilation. All that could be done with the two varieties of Others was to keep them subjected to civilization's ironhanded restraints.

The connection between Indians and immigrant agitators that journalists had begun to draw in the late 1870s, Frederic Remington still harped on in the 1880s. He wrote to a friend: "Jews, Injuns, Chinamen, Italians, Huns—the rubbish of the earth I hate—I've got some Winchesters and when the massacring begins, I can get my share of 'em, and what's more, I will."[84] It seems strange that Remington omitted the Irish from his hate list. Many of the Irish immigrants who began to pour into the United States in consequence of the Great Famine (1845–1849) had struck Americans as unimprovable social deviates and "rubbish." Many turned to crime, and soon prisons and asylums bulged with Irish occupants. According to historian Oscar Handlin, at least half of the inmates in the Boston House of Corrections were Irish. Even Irish women, it seemed, drank and brawled like the men, while their children "roamed the streets engaged in mischief and petty crimes." [85]

By their massive and heroic contributions to the North's military machine during the Civil War, the Irish began to improve their image. By the latter part of the century, as the Irish joined in the war effort against Spain and as their clergy joined with Archbishop John Ireland in cheering the war, Americans worried not so much about the Irish as about the "yellow peril" and the swarthy immigrants from southern and eastern Europe, sprung from "communistic and revolutionary races." [86] In particular, they worried about a new stranger in their land, "the vicious yet cowardly Sicilian with his ever-ready knife." Not just Sicilians but Italians in general soon acquired the same stereotypes that Americans had long since attached to Latin Americans. For Americans, Italians "bore the mark of Cain. They suggested the stiletto, the Mafia, the deed of impassioned violence." [87] Acquiring reputations akin to those of Mexicans in Texas, Italians were sometimes disciplined in accordance with traditions of the American Southwest. In New Orleans, law-and-order Americans lynched eleven Italians in 1891. The victims were suspected of involvement in the murder of a superintendent of police.

Certainly without condoning it, Theodore Dreiser expressed in his widely read novel of 1925, *An American Tragedy,* what had long ago become a gospel that associated success with godliness. Those who possessed sufficient self-discipline "to become inured to a narrow and abstemious life" and who as a result gained material success, deservedly comprised America's ruling class. As to those who lacked the self-control to take to "a narrow and abstemious life," why, "they should be kept right where they were!" [88]

As the twentieth century began, many of America's most successful businessmen, politicians, and journalists had consigned immigrants to the status that Indians were to occupy in a rationally organized society. Like Indians, the immigrants in their bulk could be incorporated only into society's bottom ranks. In this way, alien elements not up to becoming true Americans "could serve the dominant culture without qualifying for social and political equality." [89] Here was an imperialist mind-set that applied to internal colonials. It would be no trick at all for Americans to extend that mind-set to external colonials and thereby become full-fledged, tough-minded international imperialists. U.S. imperialism was a perfectly natural outgrowth of attitudes that Americans had developed for dealing with the savages in their midst. And right up to the turn of the century, Americans had continued to strengthen, polish, and perfect these attitudes as they dealt with those Hispanics in the Southwest whom they had liberated from Mexican sovereignty.

"Californios are a degraded race," wrote a San Francisco newspaper editorial writer in 1851; "a part of them are so black that one needs much work to distinguish them from Indians." In fact, "there is little difference between them and the Negro race."[90] Although a few well-to-do Hispanic landowners won acceptance in California's higher social circles, by and large the Anglo population in the Bear Flag State continued for many generations to concur in the judgment of the San Francisco newspaperman. Legislators moved to deny voting rights not only to Negroes but also to mulattoes and mestizos. Californians considered all Hispanics, except for "pure-blooded" Spanish dons, to fit into the category of "persons of African or Indian descent" for whom the legislature decreed separate schools in 1870. While court decisions of 1890 and 1921 officially ended the practice first for those of African and later for those of Indian descent, the tradition of segregated education lingered on de facto. In the latter part of the nineteenth century, writer Francis Bret Harte depicted a California scene in which Americans steadily rose to new levels of privilege and prosperity while Hispanics declined.[91] Concluding that the latter were basically uneducable, California Anglos did not try to provide them with quality education. Incapable of uplift, Hispanics must remain isolated in their degradation.

Texans demonstrated even stronger antigreaser prejudices than Californians, sometimes justifying their attitudes by pointing to the bloodthirsty Mexican bandits who infested the border area. They thought little of killing a Mexican, because Mexican cutthroats along the Rio Grande allegedly regarded "the killing of a Texan as something to be proud of."[92] In the Beadle dime novels that became best-sellers in the late nineteenth century, Texas cowboy heroes did not engage so much in cowpunching as in killing Mexicans and Indians, whom authors depicted as equally lacking in humanity. Meantime, Anglos living in Arizona and New Mexico, faced with a swelling tide of immigration from south of the border,[93] nurtured anti-Hispanic prejudices of their own—though in this regard they did not, by and large, match the Texans. Arizonans and New Mexicans, like Californians, did distinguish between mestizo rabble on one hand and reasonable, responsible, cooperative, well-born Hispanic landowners on the other. With the latter, Arizona's and New Mexico's Anglos often collaborated in exploiting poverty-stricken Hispanics and stripping impoverished agricultural communities of the common lands bequeathed them by the

Spanish crown and protected, theoretically, by the Treaty of Guadalupe Hidalgo.[94]

Meanwhile in Tucson and other cities of the Southwest, the Hispanic enclaves or barrios gained reputations as dens of iniquity, where prostitution and all other conceivable vices flourished.[95] U.S. congressional reluctance in the early years of the twentieth century to admit the Arizona and New Mexico territories as states of the Union reflected the same belief in the inferiority of Latins that led some Americans to oppose Caribbean imperialism. But the taste that Anglo mine owners and businessmen in the Southwest acquired for paying Hispanics niggardly wages, while relying on law-and-order mechanisms to discipline them, produced effects that would whet the imperialist appetite. The success of exploitative tactics in the Southwest suggested the ease with which overseas colonials might be exploited. Already in the Southwest, Americans had learned the advantages of colonized areas.[96] Already, too, they had learned another lesson about imperialism: it was easy to find sensible, cultured, "white" Hispanics anxious to collaborate with Anglos in disciplining inferior Hispanics. Even as in the Southwest, American colonialism overseas could not have been so easily accomplished and so profitable without the collaboration of the gente decente.

The real problem for imperialists operating in overseas beachheads once a part of the Hispanic empire was likely to come not from advantaged colonials but from the dispossessed, the subversive counterparts of Indians and immigrant anarchists who in America itself had fought the civilizers. In the Philippines, especially from 1899 to 1902, and in Cuba, especially in the so-called race war of 1912, it was the down and out, the elements that American troops referred to contemptuously as "Indians and niggers," who engaged the imperialists and their gente-decente collaborators in bloody combat. From this experience Americans learned that overseas subversive barbarians had to be kept in their place just as much as internal upstarts and troublemakers. Both at home and in imperial dominions, racist prejudice both demanded and justified the repression of groups allegedly refractory to civilization. And, around the turn of the century, Americans manifested some of the most virulent symptoms of racism that have ever afflicted them.

American Racism Intensifies Contempt for the Other

Insofar as the Civil War had originated in southern desire to keep Negroes, as an allegedly inferior race, "in their place," the South had by the 1890s won the war. The northern-imposed steps toward integration associated with Reconstruction had long been abandoned, and the Jim Crow system reigned supreme, providing separate but by no means equal facilities for the white master race on one hand and, on the other, for the black race of internal colonials. Historian George Fredrickson observes that "although the child of slavery," racial prejudice "not only survived its parent but grew stronger and more independent after slavery's demise."[97] In much the same way, prejudice against Hispanics in the Southwest as well as Cubans and Filipinos had intensified after they were liberated from, respectively, Mexican and Spanish control. In both instances, moreover, exacerbated racial prejudice found justification in late nineteenth- and early twentieth-century scientific theories.

Far more consistently than the optimistic rationale for uplift as previously described, what passed for Darwinian evolutionary theory had become a rationale for blatant racism. In the hands of its most prominent proponents, both in Britain and in the United States, the theory was twisted so as to proclaim that "the highest products of social evolution were large-brained white men, and [that] only large-brained white men, the highest products of organic evolution, were fully civilized." In "scientific" thinking, "savagery, dark skin, and a small brain and incoherent mind were, for many, all part of the single evolutionary picture of 'primitive man,' who even yet walked the earth."[98] Concepts of racial hierarchy were so widespread and deeply entrenched that virtually all biological theories, "including Lamarckism," were used to justify them.[99] Furthermore, according to some scientists, evolution was just as likely to result in degeneration as in progress; and primitive races rather than destined to advance were as apt to revert back to more animalistic levels of existence.[100] According to a University of Virginia professor of medicine writing in 1900, "the negro race is reverting to barbarism with the inordinate criminality and degradation of that state."[101]

A series of Supreme Court decisions between 1873 and 1898 "undergirded the legal segregation, disfranchisement, and radical degradation" of Negroes that characterized not only the South but the North and the middle and far West as well during the first half of the twentieth century. As the unofficial means of honoring the laws of "racial degradation," southern and occasionally northern and middlewestern whites resorted to lynching. In 1900, white mobs lynched 107 blacks; at least the figure was lower than in 1892, when lynchings of Negroes had soared to their all-time peak of 162.[102]

Springfield, Illinois, witnessed a particularly vicious race riot in 1908 when a white woman claimed to have been raped by a black man, George

Richardson. Hoping to save Richardson from the inevitable lynch mob, authorities spirited him to a nearby town. Enraged by this ploy, the local citizenry rampaged through Springfield, looting stores and seizing weapons, and vandalizing homes and businesses that belonged to blacks. After lynching a Negro barber the mob dragged his corpse through the streets. During a second night of violence the mobs lynched an eighty-four-year-old black man within a block of the state capitol. Apparently his crime consisted of being married, for thirty years, to a white woman. The "orgy of violence in the hometown of Abraham Lincoln" inspired several black leaders, among them W. E. B. Du Bois (the first "man of color" to earn a Harvard Ph.D.) "to launch what became the National Association for the Advancement of Colored People."[103] Two years later, in November 1910, Du Bois established *Crisis* as the association's journal. In an early editorial he contended that the twenty-five years between 1885 and 1910 had witnessed some twenty-five hundred lynchings of "colored men."[104]

In 1927 the African American poet Langston Hughes created what surely is one of the most haunting reminders of America's lynch-law traditions. In "Song for a Dark Girl," he uses crucifixion symbolism to depict the plight of blacks.

Way down South in Dixie
  (Break the heart of me)
They hung my black young lover
  To a cross roads tree.

Way down South in Dixie
  (Bruised body high in the air)
I asked the white lord Jesus
  What was the use of prayer.

Way down South in Dixie
  (Break the heart of me)
Love is a naked shadow
  On a gnarled and naked tree.[105]

According to the conventional wisdom of racism as expressed in the 1911 edition of *Encyclopaedia Britannica,* although the Negro was inferior to the white and stood on "a lower evolutionary plane," nevertheless black children at times showed a capacity for intellectual progress. Inevitably, however, as the child matured there occurred an "arrest or even deterioration in mental development." This was "no doubt very largely due to the fact that after puberty sexual matters take the first place in the negro's life and thoughts."[106] Even the ragtime music that blacks cultivated in the early twentieth century attested, allegedly, to their "sensual," "demonic," and sinfully sexual nature, to their inability to emerge out of the degeneracy of primitive stages.[107] Faced with an adversary stereotyped in this manner, white Americans decided that above all else they must defend "the white goddess of civilization against the sex-crazed barbarians at the gates." Fear of the sexually overcharged barbarians "provided the most explosive fuel" for interracial hatred and lynching. As a Georgia woman expressed the matter in 1898: "If it needs lynching to protect women's dearest possession from the ravening human beast—then I say lynch, a thousand times a week if necessary."[108] In Wilmington, North Carolina, previously a model integrated community of eleven thousand blacks and eight thousand whites, the latter carried out the kind of advice proffered by the Georgia woman. With the alleged rape of a white woman by a black man providing the justification, whites in 1898 went on a rampage of bloodshed and mayhem.

Wilmington provides in microcosm a stunning example of the way in which turn-of-the-twentieth-century white Americans took up the defense of civilization against barbarism. To understand the racial violence that whites directed against blacks, one must remember that the white woman, whose destruction the black man ostensibly plotted, was more than a woman: she was the emblem of, she stood as a metaphor for, refined, sensitive, and high-minded civilization; and this civilization, whether in America, where it had matured and flowered, or in the Caribbean and Philippines, where it had only recently been introduced by agents of U.S. imperialism, was vulnerable. One could not take for granted its continuing supremacy over savagery. That supremacy had to be won anew virtually every day by struggle and warfare (just as constant vigilance was required to keep wilderness from reclaiming newly tilled fields), whether by lynching in the United States or by punitive measures enacted by the armed forces of occupation dispatched to America's new empire.

Not only the Negro but also mulattoes and mixed-bloods in general, whether in America or foreign colonies, represented the enemies of civilization. Until the Civil War era, southerners and northerners alike had developed some degree of tolerance toward mulattoes, according them a degree of acceptance that actually led these mixed-bloods to identify with white rather than with Negro Americans. However, a critical change began in the decade before the Civil War and steadily gained momentum after the struggle. As a result of this change, Americans abandoned "a Latin-like tolerance of mulattoes."[109] For the first time they became inflexible in enforcing the "one-drop" rule: even a drop of colored blood rendered a person unfit and subject to the same treatment as accorded purest Africans. Disdained, rejected, and violently harassed by white Americans, mulattoes came to recognize that their destiny lay exclusively with "their darker brothers and sisters."[110]

Soaring racial prejudice among white Americans victimized not only blacks and mulattoes but also mestizos and all other varieties of mixed-bloods. Typically, Daniel Garrison Brinton, the first professor of anthropology in the United States, warned in the 1880s against the dire consequences of the mixing of the white and Indian races.[111] Even Franz Boas, later to emerge as the preeminent prophet in America of cultural pluralism, "was by no means certain" in 1894 of the overall quality of half-breed Indians. He "did not rule out the possibility that further studies would show 'a decided deterioration of race, due to mixture.'"[112] In Texas and throughout the South and in much of the North as well, the animus against miscegenation "seemed to reach a crescendo . . . around 1907."[113] At this time, American anthropologists prevailingly dismissed half-breeds as having nowhere produced a "high civilization." Their attitude held clear implications for American evaluations of Latin Americans. "The Latin Europeans of South America," according to conventional anthropological wisdom, "were paying for their racial liberality, and so would all Europeans who participated in the 'unhappy mixture of races' which was everywhere 'the curse of tropical states.'"[114]

In 1916 New York patrician Madison Grant, educated at Columbia and Yale, published the book that became the veritable Bible for those Americans who recognized the perils that race mixture posed to their nation. In *The Passing of the Great Race,* Grant warned that all the fruits of civilization produced by the white races could be destroyed through mixture with other races. "Whether we like to admit it or not," he proclaimed, "the result of the mixture of the two races [black and white], in the long run, gives us a race reverting to the more ancient, generalized and lower type." He continued: "The cross between a white man and an Indian is an Indian; the cross between a white man and a Negro is a Negro; the cross between a white man and a Hindu is a Hindu; and the cross between any of the three European races and a Jew is a Jew."[115]

To the Indian who remained an Indian, even when crossed with white blood, American attitudes hardened at the turn of the century. Various social experiments aimed at uplift seemed only to have proved that despite the white person's best efforts, Indians did not change. Instead, they went on "exactly as before, looking on imperturbably, eating, sleeping, idling, with no more thought of the future than a white man's child." President

Roosevelt's commissioner for Indian affairs, Francis Leupp, believed that Indians were of little use except as manual laborers.[116] Leupp, it seems, would have found no cause to disagree with the Washington official who argued in the 1890s that the skills needed for progress in the modern world simply lay beyond the Indians.[117]

With racial prejudice flourishing as never before in their own country, Americans picked an unfortunate time to extend an imperialist net over blacks, Indians, mulattoes, and mestizos in foreign lands. With more than ample justification Alexander Walters, a bishop in America's African Methodist Episcopal church, stated he did "not think that America is prepared to carry on expansion at this time [the beginning of the twentieth century], especially if it be among the dark races of the earth. The white man of America is impregnated with color phobia."[118] The times were indeed inauspicious for Americans to embark on imperialism. As that great historian of the American South C. Vann Woodward has shown, the reaction of American imperialists to their new colonials reflected the increasingly virulent racist attitudes that emerged from the Jim Crow era in the United States. In turn, the racist attitudes that Americans nourished in dealing with the eight million or so "inferior-race" inhabitants of the Caribbean and Philippines and other Pacific Ocean domains over whom they assumed tutelage at the turn of the century fed into and intensified the prejudices toward "inferior-race" residents of the United States.[119]

Given racism's domestic background, it was predictable that American occupying forces from the Philippines, Guam, and Hawaii in the Pacific to the Dominican Republic in the Caribbean would refer to the natives as "spicks," "niggers," and Indians,[120] and that military and political officials alike would deride the "mongrelization" of native populations in Puerto Rico, Cuba, and Central America.[121] Diplomat Sumner Welles did no more than reflect the spirit of the times in the 1920s when, with the Dominican Republic in mind, he declared that "responsibility could be borne only up to a certain point" by persons of color.[122] And Welles was one of the least prejudiced persons in the diplomatic service.

Racism, Imperialism, and American Fairs

In the late nineteenth and early twentieth centuries, Americans did not have to leave their country to encounter colonials from far-off lands who reinforced homegrown prejudices toward people of color and mixed blood. Americans could encounter alien beings from abroad conveniently displayed at the various fairs that became the entertainment rage beginning in

1876 with the Centennial Exhibition staged in Philadelphia. At these fairs, "backward primitives," gathered first from among Indian and African American internal colonials and later from foreign colonials, were glaringly juxtaposed to the latest products of the white man's science and technology: the awesome machines that symbolized modern civilization and provided it the means to humble nature. The juxtaposition, moreover, served to emphasize the distance that separated humanity's "natural state" from "the higher forms of cognition and social conduct."[123]

Dominating Chicago's 1893 Columbian Exposition and many subsequent American international fairs was a "white way," a cluster of gleaming buildings in which were displayed the newest wonders of American technology. Along with the white way, most turn-of-the-century fairs featured the "midway": a section that indulged voyeurism, provided sleazy entertainment, "cheap thrills and monkey houses."[124] In a way, the fairs provided the model for the later contrast that Broadway's "Great White Way" provided to Harlem's nearby jungle of blacks, where whites in search of titillation, of sex, booze, and drugs, could indulge their appetite for the primitive, confident always that the proximity of civilization's white way safeguarded them against losing their identity in the symbolical bush.

Originally, the midway presented "authentic" displays of American Indian villages and African American communities. Here the Other, often scantily attired so as to emphasize the primitive's notorious lack of modesty, was displayed to audiences dominated by thrill-seekers but sprinkled perhaps with those who sought a glimpse of alternatives to life-limiting civilization. By the end of the century, Cubans, Filipinos, Puerto Ricans, and Mexicans had been added to the specimens exhibited on the midway. One could view them along with bearded ladies, sword swallowers, and grotesquely fat men and ladies.[125] Especially at the Buffalo Pan American Exposition of 1901 (which, incidentally, witnessed the assassination of President McKinley by a deranged individual under the sway of alien, anarchistic delusions) and the St. Louis Louisiana Purchase Exposition of 1904 (later immortalized by the film *Meet Me in St. Louis,* starring Judy Garland), the juxtaposition of Native American villages and clusters of Filipinos and Caribbean peoples "made explicit the connection between America's imperial past and its imperial future." The moral was clear: just as the resplendent white way lorded it over the tacky midway, so must the white race dominate the darker ones. But the white man's destiny was not an easy one. An orator at the 1898 Omaha Trans-Mississippi International Exposition informed an audience that "Uncle Sam's wards in Cuba and the Philippines are liable to be as intractable as its wards on the Indian reservations."[126]

A taste for fairs and for imperialism was not unique to Americans. In popular late nineteenth-century fairs staged in the Austro-Hungarian empire, Africans—prominent among the beneficiaries of Europe's new imperialism—made popular display items. Africans, and especially the Ashanti, became "the sexual icons for the 'royal and imperial' monarchy," conveying the message that uninhibited sexuality was the badge of racial backwardness, and, paradoxically, at the same time arousing "secret envy among [white] males, and fear that [their] women would find the Africans tempting."[127] The British seem to have gone in for zoos more than fairs. The animals they captured in far-off lands and then displayed in their zoos furnished "impressive symbols of British domination both of vast tributary territories and of the natural world."[128] Americans evidently preferred gazing on human specimens collected from their old Indian frontier, from the black belt of their South, and from their new Latin American frontier.

The Atlanta and Nashville fairs of 1895 and 1897, respectively, left little doubt that the course of the new empire lay southward. The fairs' directors stressed the strategic location of the American South as the gateway to and from Mexico, Central America, and the West Indies, areas where U.S. business had unique opportunities for expansion. As if to remind viewers of where the new frontier lay, the directors saw to it that Mexicans and Cubans were displayed "in villages on the entertainment avenues."[129] Both fairs, moreover, along with the 1885 New Orleans World's Industrial and Cotton Exposition, stressed the economic potential of the "New South," to which "a docile and intelligently directed labor force," represented by the African American villages on the entertainment avenues, could make a telling contribution. Not only the dark races of the American South but those of Latin America could advance the prosperity of white Americans. Indeed, this might be the only contribution primitive peoples could make in the immediate future. Engaged for centuries in a struggle to survive on a low, superannuated level of existence, they had squandered the energies and vitality required to cope with the demands of progress in the modern age.

James Earle Fraser's bronze sculpture titled *End of the Trail* proved the most popular work of art displayed at the 1915 San Francisco Panama-Pacific Exposition. (See illustration 14.) It depicted an anonymous, exhausted Indian "slumped in the saddle of a worn-out pony. With remarkable candor, the artist later explained the message of his work: 'It was [the] idea of a weaker race being steadily pushed to the wall by a stronger that I wanted to convey.'" Significantly, Fraser's sculpture was positioned next to the statue of an American frontiersman that bore the title *Pioneer*. This was a symbolic figure who, according to a guidebook, had a "challenge in his face" as he gazed "into the early morning." *Pioneer* symbolized, so the

14. James Earle Fraser. *End of the Trail*. 1918. Bronze, height 33¾ in. Courtesy Buffalo Bill Historical Center, Cody, Wyoming, Clara Peck Purchase Fund.

The sculpture suggests one of imperialism's favorite myths, that of "progress." Hopefully through uplift by "advanced races," but one way or another, "primitive races" located within civilization's reach were fated to disappear.

guidebook instructed its readers, "the white man and the victorious march of civilization."[130] The Indian had reached the end of his trail, but the pioneer endured. And now he had to look southward, where other weaker races awaited his coming that promised them cultural death and, just possibly, rebirth.

Americans at Fairs: The Midway, the White Way, or Both Ways?

In the midway's displays of primitives, some Americans found not just sources of condescending amusement and titillation. Some found in the displays, as their organizers had intended, evidence of the skill, intelligence, and artistic ability that the people of different cultures and traditions possessed and that, if given a fair chance, they might contribute toward the enrichment of modern civilization. Furthermore, as they contemplated the white ways of international expositions, intended to fill them with pride, some American fairgoers felt misgivings. Did the white way really epitomize all that was finest in life? Rather than looking on the villages of Indians, blacks, Samoans, Cubans, Mexicans, Puerto Ricans, and Filipinos as showcases of nature's freaks, some Americans, I feel certain, wondered if the midway might symbolize the means for redressing the shortcomings of the sterile and materialistic existence epitomized by the too precisely structured, too sanitized white way. Obviously, some Americans had good feelings about the midway: Chicago professional football fans, after all, affectionately dubbed their heroes the "Monsters of the Midway."

In their fascination with the white way *and* the midway, with the sun realm of rationality, predictability, and order and also with the dark world of instinct, intuition, spontaneity, and yes, even chaos, Americans remained true to their quest to transcend the need for choice. Like Whitman, they felt themselves enormous enough to envelop opposites. Those who see only the manifestations of racism in America's new imperialism, and in the white way–midway juxtaposition, miss a part of the mythic essence of what it has meant to be American.

Not just the 1893 Columbian Exposition but Chicago's entire nineteenth-century history symbolized the myth of the fusing of opposites.[131] The city's remarkable rise rested on the integration of metropolis and hinterland, of urban capitalism on one hand and untapped resources on the other—in short, of civilization and nature. On the symbiosis of city and countryside, dramatically abetted by the railroad, rested the development both of metropolitan Chicago and the Great West, so recently a wilderness extending from the Appalachians to the Rockies. At the turn of the century, Americans were poised to build on this tradition of symbiosis—a venerable one long before its stunning reenactment in the nation's heartland in the decades immediately preceding and following the Civil War. Never mind that this tradition whenever and wherever enacted had inflicted grievous harm on undeveloped lands and their native inhabitants. Incredible material progress had also ensued, along with the dramatic betterment of countless lives, and always within a remarkably short span of time. There could be no turning back. Urbanizing and developing America, its breathtaking progress issuing out of a stunning symbiosis of opposites, now would penetrate backward Latin America and pursue its destiny in the Great South.

CHAPTER 6

From Arielism to Modernism: Hemispheric Visions in the Age of Roosevelt and Wilson

Arielism, North and South of the Border

Ernest Hemingway referred to excessive abstractness in speech, writing, and thinking, to the unrestrainedly theoretical and highfalutin, to what lacked grounding in practical common sense as "horseshit."[1] Americans have often been inclined to dismiss Latin American culture as so much horseshit. And this is the epithet that many Yankees would have attached to the book *Ariel* that began to take Latin America by storm soon after its publication in 1900.

The author of *Ariel,* Uruguay's José Enrique Rodó, soon gained celebrity status from Mexico City to Buenos Aires for having produced Latin America's declaration of cultural independence from, and superiority over, the United States. Latin America and her people, according to Rodó, "possessed a superiority of spirit and a sensitivity to enduring moral and aesthetic values" that placed them on an altogether higher cultural plane than the northerners, with their crude materialism, their bourgeois mediocrity, and their moral laxness typical of industrialized nations. Latins must safeguard the cultural distinctions that elevated them above the Calibans and Cyclopes of the North. By doing so, Latins would retain the capability someday to fulfill their mission, which was to tame the brute strength of the vulgar louts to the north and to harness their vitality and admirable sense of the useful and aptitude for mechanical invention in the service of more exalted cultural, aesthetic, and spiritual values. When this day came, the Greeks of the New World would fashion a fruitful union with its Romans. Thus, fusion of opposites was the ultimate destiny that Arielism proclaimed.[2]

Not only Latin America but Spain as well, so recently bested by the Colossus in war, jumped aboard the Arielist bandwagon. Indeed, Spain from this time forward intensified its efforts to establish close cultural ties with the former colonies so that, mutually reinforcing each other, they could stiffen their moral resistance to the North American clods with their materialistic concepts of modernization. Meantime, many Americans themselves sympathized with the Arielist credo.

Throughout the nineteenth century, Americans sensed and sometimes openly acknowledged their cultural inferiority to Europeans. In compensation, they proudly proclaimed their moral superiority, and inferred, or out-and-out asserted, the unimportance of culture—generally defined in that century as "the knowledge of the highest achievements of men of intellect and art through [all of] history."[3] But, as the Gilded Age moved toward its dreary conclusion at century's end, many of America's leading thinkers began to suspect that their country's materialism had undermined its morality, that morality and culture actually went hand in hand, and that in their disdain for culture their countrymen had set themselves on the road to moral bankruptcy. American thinkers of this persuasion had begun to toy with their own version of Arielism, casting themselves as the redeemers of a continent reduced to crass materialism.

American Arielists saw the majority of their countrymen as Rodó saw them: rather than aspiring to the realm where all was lofty and enlightened, the majority happily cavorted in the domain of coarseness and vulgarity, where the animal appetite for material satisfaction, and satiation, took precedence over everything else. Rather than the refined thinkers and artists, it was the American masses who wallowed in horseshit. If eventually refined and cultured Americans were to prevail over the barbarians who seemed to have gained control over national destiny through democratic processes that had reduced values to the lowest common denominator, perhaps they would have to join with enclaves of like-thinking elites to the south. In this elitist vision of hemispheric solidarity slowly beginning to emerge at the turn of the century, Americans recognized the need for Latin allies in waging the defense of culture.

British novelist E. M. Forster (1879–1970) never hesitated to proclaim his belief in aristocracy: not an aristocracy of wealth and material influence but rather one made up of considerate people with a sense of noblesse oblige whose members could be found in all nations and classes, and who experienced a secret understanding whenever they met. This international set of aristocrats, of select spirits, in short, recognized each other across class and national boundaries as comprising the better element of humanity, the element capable of rising above crass materialism and providing disinterested overlordship to less gifted souls. Undoubtedly, most Americans who felt themselves members of a select elite looked to England for soul mates with whom they might best strike a secret understanding. But some recognized the existence of kindred souls south of the border.

In his novel *Conversations in the Cathedral*, Peruvian writer Mario Vargas Llosa (who tried his hand at politics, finishing second in his country's 1990 presidential election) has one of his characters, the refined, aristocratic Don Fermín, render the following opinion of North Americans: "I'll never understand the gringos, don't they seem like little children to you? . . . Half-savage besides. They put their feet on the desk, take off their jackets, wherever they are. And the ones I'm talking about aren't nobodies." Don Fermín concludes that when around gringos he generally feels like giving them a book on etiquette.[4] If my own feelings are in any way typical, then I must conclude that many gringos have themselves felt a bit like bumpkins upon first entering the salons of cultivated Latin Americans. Certainly many nineteenth-century travel accounts hint at a certain awe that Yankees felt when exposed to the refinements of Latin American culture. Already toward the beginning of the century, upon encountering well-bred Latins in their native locales, Americans inclined to wonder if their own historical circumstances had somehow rendered them too materialistic and even too addicted to a democratic credo that reduced cultural values to a shockingly low level. Does this assessment of American attitudes toward Latin Americans tend to contradict what I have written earlier about gringo stereotypes of the south-of-the-border Other? Of course it does. But paradox often lies at the heart of stereotyping, indeed of all human judgment of other humans.

Although generally disdainful of Latins encountered in the travels that he described in his classic *Two Years before the Mast* (1840), Richard Henry Dana expressed a certain awed fascination with an elegant, graceful, refined hidalgo type he came upon in California. The contrast that Dana drew between his aristocrat and an American he encountered at the same time clearly inclines the reader to favor the "Spaniard"—and make no mistake about it, the aristocrat is a light-skinned Spaniard, unblemished by race mixture. The American, as described by Dana, was a "fat, coarse, vulgar, pretentious fellow of a Yankee trader."[5]

About the time Dana recorded his observations on the Californian personification of the better elements of Latin society, an American traveler to Brazil praised the cultural refinement typical of the country's upper classes, noting also the fine opera houses and theaters in Rio de Janeiro and other cities. A few years later another traveler, this time in Chile, commented on the high cultural level of the privileged sectors.[6] Moreover, in *Jack Tier*, the novel he wrote toward the end of the Mexican War, James Fenimore Cooper drew an empathetic sketch of the aristocratic "Spanish don,"

Señor Montefalderón—note that Montefalderón's aristocratic demeanor transforms him into a Spaniard. Cooper describes Montefalderón as "a man of polished manners, as we maintain is very apt to be the case with Mexican gentlemen, whatever may be the opinion of this good Republic on the subject just at this moment."[7] Cooper also believed that for all its shortcomings, Mexico had redeeming qualities, "not the least of which was that 'chivalrous courtesy' found among the descendants of Old Spain."[8]

A half century later George Grinnell, a New York aristocrat, an early conservationist, and a close friend to Theodore Roosevelt, described a Mexican he admired as a person of reserve, "with the polish and suavity of a real hidalgo." Again and again, in fact, Americans in the late nineteenth century wrote admiringly of the courtesy of wellborn Latin Americans. Melville's archetypal Latin American gentleman, Benito Cereno, is described as "courteous even to the point of religion." Theodore Roosevelt in 1914 summed up what was coming to be the conventional appraisal rendered by important Americans whose station gave them the opportunity to know important Latin Americans. The South Americans, Roosevelt observed, "often surpass us, not merely in pomp and ceremony but in what is of real importance, courtesy: in civility and courtesy we can well afford to take lessons from them." Some thirty years later, Sumner Welles singled out Gen. Horacio Vázquez of the Dominican Republic as representative of its better elements: "He possessed an old-time courtesy modeled on those previous Spanish traditions which unfortunately today are fast disappearing."[9]

In American ability to admire Latin American elites for their polish, gentility, manners, and concern with the life of the mind and spirit, two points merit emphasis. First, Americans had begun to do what Latin American elites had long chided them for not doing: they had developed some ability to distinguish between purportedly uncouth Latin American masses and highly refined elites. For well-educated and cultivated Americans at least, the Latin American masses might still represent crude and unrefined nature, but the upper classes stood for a culture toward which all too many Americans remained openly disdainful. If Latin American elites represented something of a negative identity for America's clods who set cultural norms in their own country, then for America's elites, Latin America's refined elements, along with those of Britain and Europe, exhibited positive characteristics. This leads into the second point which is that the turn-of-the-century spirit of American Arielism, which fostered admiration for Latin American culture, grew out of mounting dissatisfaction on the part of the guardians of refinement with the cultural shortcomings of an ever-more-prosperous middle class that set the tone of U.S. society. As an increasing number of discerning Americans saw the situation, something had gone terribly wrong with the ethos of national progress. Paying homage to a golden age in the past, before the contamination introduced by newly risen, crude captains of industry, American cultural elites "dreamed of an eventual return to power of a temporarily dispossessed natural aristocracy." [10]

As the nineteenth century came to an end, there surfaced a veritable host of American pursuers of nonmaterial, cultural, and elitist values. Some of America's Arielists harked back to the Transcendentalists and even to earlier champions of cultural over economic values, but many drew on unexpected sources as they took up the struggle against the Philistines. The distinguished architect Ralph Adams Cram, admirer of Europe's medieval culture as shaped by Catholicism, carried to extremes some of the ideas articulated by Henry Adams, [11] who happened to be the most distinguished American gentlemanly thinker of Arielist persuasions. Cram confessed in the 1880s: "I believe only in art . . . the ultimate expression of all that is spiritual, religious and divine in the soul of man. I hate material prosperity, I refuse to justify machinery. . . . I desire absolute individuality and the triumph of idealism." [12] In the same decade, novelist Edward Bellamy "formulated a powerful moral case against a pecuniary civilization." Those uncomfortable with the values of the Gilded Age tended to agree with Bellamy and also with some of the principal ideas expressed by Henry George. Famous for his single-tax prescription for social ills, as well as for garnering more votes than Theodore Roosevelt in the 1884 New York mayoral election, George maintained that the only true measure of a country's achievement was the "productiveness of a higher kind" that resulted in "the creation of culture." [13]

For a time after 1910 the most concerted counterrevolution against the onslaught of mass-culture materialism "came from a group of critics—largely Anglophile and academic—who called themselves the New Humanists." The leaders included Paul Elmer More at Princeton and Irving Babbit at Harvard, and several other academicians who had "undergone initiation into the anti-mass-culture tradition of Harvard's Charles Eliot Norton and some of his likeminded associates." [14] In the 1920s the crusade to turn back the tide of crass materialism, and also to restore in America the values of a preindustrial community in which people "lived closer to the land and the natural rhythms of life," [15] switched to the South, specifically Vanderbilt University from where the so-called Agrarians preached an elitist message against mass society. Among the Agrarians, John Crowe Ransom, Allen Tate, and Robert Penn Warren denounced the American

Everyman, lamented the spread of northern materialism into the New South, and extolled the village mores of the Old South, where persons prized communal, organic wholeness above economically inspired competition. Some of this spirit found its way into Franklin D. Roosevelt's New Deal in the 1930s, nourished no doubt in the years of the Great Depression by the indications that American free-enterprise capitalism had made a colossal mess of the country. As much as any one person, brain truster A. A. Berle, Jr., the son of a Congregationalist minister who had imbibed the ethic of social service and noblesse oblige, who had married into wealth, and who as a young man admired the integrated, organic life as led by Pueblo Indians, Puerto Ricans, and Dominicans, exemplified the New Deal's Arielist spirit. Berle insisted that "man must work for ideals and service rather than for money"; and he urged an economics tinged with mysticism. "The great desideratum," he told a colleague, is that life be "dominantly spiritual and not economic."[16]

Basically, what united American Arielists from the 1890s to the 1930s was the conviction that "men of education and ability and even of inherited traditions had some special responsibility for maintaining standards." America's better elements, with *better* defined according to cultural rather than economic achievements, must set the tone of society, blunt the greed of politicians and businessmen, and "temper the destructive fury of the masses."[17] In this frame of mind, America's discontented upholders of cultural values, worried about what they perceived to be the declining status of genuine gentlemen and natural aristocrats in an age of rampant, leveling materialism, stood ready to applaud what so many Americans had traditionally condemned about Latin America: its lack of modern progress. Backwardness signified that Latin America, and with it the Iberian motherland, lay closer to that golden age in the past to which alienated elites wished to return, a past in which elite status derived from letters, arts, and breeding rather than from money-making, and in which the better persons knew how to keep inferiors in their place, in part because of their willingness to shoulder the traditional obligations of paternalism that maintained a community's organic integrity.

For all the political turmoil that marked Latin America's political processes and inspired typical gringos to scornful and derisive stereotyping, some perceptive Americans nevertheless saw beneath these surface phenomena. They realized that below the surface—down at the level of what Spain's great philosopher Miguel de Unamuno termed "intrahistory" (in Castilian, *infrahistoria*), the vast sea of historical reality underlying the deceptive waves and ripples of the surface—lay surprising stability. In basic social patterns, Latin America, reflecting its Old World origins, its con-

tinuing ties to a medievalist, corporatist tradition, and its refusal to be re-
made by a frontier environment, maintained continuity. In large measure,
continuity derived from the willingness of dependent masses to acknowledge the right of paternalistic masters to dominate. Frightened by the
specter of rising social instability and the rebelliousness of the American
masses, many self-perceived patricians, highly suspicious of the social as
well as cultural implications of democracy, admired what they judged to be
the timeless continuity of Latin America's intrahistory. A ruling class that
had understood for over three centuries how to preserve this continuity
and stability had much to recommend it to American Arielists. Predictably, almost as much as their counterparts in Spain and Latin America,
American cultural elites joined in lionizing Spanish philosopher José Or-
tega y Gasset and seconding the message in behalf of tradition and elite
culture that he advanced in his most widely read book, *The Revolt of the
Masses* (1929).

Unfortunately, American patricians distrustful of the leveling effects of
democracy and fearful of social upheaval often looked at the world through
the blinders of race prejudice. Such a person was Madison Grant, whose
influential *Passing of the Great Race* (1916) I cited in the preceding chapter.
Also symptomatic of the racism of antidemocratic Americans was Lothrop
Stoddard, a Massachusetts attorney with a Ph.D. in history whose widely
read and influential publications included *The Rising Tide of Color* (1920)
and *The Revolt against Civilization: The Menace of the Under Man* (1922).
Both men, in line with Arielism as it existed north and south of the border,
urged that elites of culture and race accept beneficent stewardship not only
over the earth but also over inferior races and social classes.[18]

Americans of the Grant and Stoddard persuasions prevailingly admired
the large estate, or hacienda, tradition in Latin America that, even as in the
antebellum and, for that matter, the postbellum American South, ostensibly nurtured a class marked by "an aristocratic, antibourgeois spirit with
values and mores emphasizing family and status, a strong code of honor,
and aspirations to luxury, ease, and [cultural] accomplishment."[19] Here
was a tradition that seemed in line with the Hellenistic ideals of Arielism,
ideals that modern-day patricians hoped to achieve through an updated
version of the servitude of the masses. Latin America's patrician classes
seemed clearly to have hit upon such a version. In consequence, they knew
how to keep mestizos and Indians, mulattoes and blacks content and
happy in their servitude.

Both north and south of the border, Arielists perceived that the great
bourgeois fallacy lay in the attempt to buy off the masses through "econo-
mism," through material rewards alone. The Arielists believed that this at-

tempt led only to the constant escalation of wants and in the long run rendered underlings increasingly difficult to control. True social stability, they insisted, depended on the ability of cultured elites to provide underlings with nonmaterial rewards. Arielism, in both Anglo and Latin America, proclaimed the need to awaken in the masses some appreciation for the "higher things," for literature, art, and classical music. By learning to perceive, however dimly, and to appreciate, however imperfectly, the higher truths and beauties of life, the lower classes would gain liberation from exclusively material desires, from base passions and appetites, from selfish inclinations and resentment and rancor against those who ranked above them in the social order. Humans thus liberated would attain a more harmonious and fully developed character while at the same time finding the solace and joys necessary to make them content and resigned to their station in life. Above all, they would willingly, even happily, accept dependence on those whom they recognized as their cultural superiors, on those savants who supplied them with nonmaterial rewards. Intellectuals and cultural elites, banded together in various educational-extension programs that would introduce working classes to the higher things, would reclaim their proper hierarchical status; for their societies would come to realize that order and stability depended on them, the elites, not on businessmen who concerned themselves with the mere creation of material kingdoms and in the process threatened social stability.

Arielists sought in culture a substitute for the social pacification once associated with Christianity's call for the masses to substitute anticipation of otherworldly rewards for expectations of temporal riches. One need read no further than Sinclair Lewis's *Babbitt* (1922) or *Elmer Gantry* (1927) to understand that in the early twentieth century men of religion had anticipated the preaching style of a vulgar religious right in the 1980s with its assurance that true godliness guaranteed accumulation of hordes of this world's treasure. Religion, it seemed, could no longer be relied upon to shield the masses from corruption by materialism. So, patrician Americans saw the need for a secularly based defense of higher values. This brought them all the closer in outlook to Latin America's Arielists, most of whom professed indifference if not hostility to the Catholic religious establishment. Arielists, after all, wanted to become the new priests of higher values.

A bit of the Don Quixote myth pervades American and Latin American Arielism. The elegant, refined, and cultured but eminently impractical aristocrat would find wholeness when linked with the embodiment of bourgeois vulgarity and practicality, Sancho Panza. Dana caught this vision when, as already mentioned, he juxtaposed the figure of an elegant Spanish aristocrat in California with a "fat, coarse, vulgar, pretentious fellow of a Yankee trader."[20] California, Dana realized, needed both types. Many thinkers on both sides of the border sensed that the hemisphere as a whole required the Don *and* his modern-day, bourgeois Sancho if America was to achieve its potential. Let Yankee businessmen prosper in their native land and work their wonders through their knack for the practical; let them go to Latin America, also, and work their prodigies there as they complemented the talents of firmly entrenched elites. In both cases, though, in North and South America, let the gentlemanly classes, recognizing each other across national boundaries and united by an informal understanding, preserve their hierarchical precedence over the Sancho Panzas; but, above all, let the opposites, the Dons and the Sanchos, interact in harmony. All the more did the need for harmony gain recognition as the class-struggle message of Marxism-Leninism appeared on the horizon.

Theodore Roosevelt, Woodrow Wilson, and Hemispheric Visions

Teddy Roosevelt had his own fling at harmonizing opposites. Indeed, he seems to have dedicated his whole life to this quest, and on more than one occasion Latin America provided the backdrop for the quest. An East Coast aristocrat, Roosevelt in the 1880s took for a time to the pioneering cowboy life on his ranch in the Dakota Territory, feeling the need for renewal after confronting personal tragedy and political setbacks. For a while, he combined in himself the two opposites that Cooper had focused on in *The Pioneers* (1823), the first of the Leatherstocking Tales: Judge Temple, the aristocratic founder of a new community, and the down-to-earth frontiersman-hunter and precursor of the mountain man and cowboy, Natty Bumppo. In 1898, Roosevelt pursued the great American myth on Latin American terrain. In Cuba, he helped lead the colorful Rough Riders in the war against Spain. In their ranks, the Rough Riders melded East Coast, club-member, polo-playing bluebloods with rough-and-ready western cowboys, some of them down on their luck because of the end of the open-range days of the classic cattle drives. The successors of Judge Temple and of Leatherstocking mutually derived strength from contact with their opposite types as they united to bring civilization to a virtual extension of the American frontier.

In 1909, in search of new invigoration in nature, beyond what he derived from the hunting expeditions in America that his friend John Muir frowned on, Roosevelt went on an African safari. Then in 1913, after the failure of his Bull Moose candidacy in the previous year's presidential election, Roosevelt responded to the call of the wild as it sounded from Brazil, the country that he believed enveloped the greatest of the world's remaining frontiers.[21] Before plunging into Brazil's uncharted Amazonian jungle region, Roosevelt hobnobbed with the leading figures of science, politics, and culture in Rio de Janeiro and other cities. He got on well with them, verifying E. M. Forster's thesis that common interests and values quite overcome differences of national origin in uniting the "better" elements of society: those capable of rising above crass materialism because, in many instances at least, they had been born to affluence and influence.

Once out of the cities and engaged in the wilderness exploration for which he had come to Brazil (and which very nearly cost him his life as a result of a leg injury that became badly infected), Roosevelt established easy rapport with the less-refined elements of Brazil's frontier society, often praising their vigor and resourcefulness and foreseeing their ultimate success as tamers of the wild. Moreover, he recorded favorable impressions of Brazil's mulattoes and mestizos.[22] In all, he seemed fascinated by the country's melting-pot mestizaje, in stark contrast to so many of his contemporary countrymen who remained insensitive to myths of the dialectic, at least when applied to race.

Ever mindful of the need to combine culture and nature, Roosevelt dedicated himself almost every night, as did his son Kermit and Notre Dame University's biologist-priest John Zahm who accompanied him on most of the expedition, to reading the classics. Almost every evening, moreover, Roosevelt set himself to writing the notes from which he would shortly compose his account of the adventure, *Through the Brazilian Wilderness* (1914). One marvelous picture in the book shows Roosevelt at his notes, with not a pinhead of flesh exposed to the voracious insects: his hands are encumbered by gloves and his head and neck are covered by the mosquito netting attached to his jungle helmet. Seldom does one encounter photographic evidence of such devotion to the cause of culture while in the midst of a jungle. But then this was typical of Roosevelt: he insisted on having it all, on synthesizing civilization and nature. As he emerges from this photograph, even as in his earlier western dude-and-cowboy experience in Dakota, Teddy Roosevelt was the living embodiment both of Judge Temple and of Natty Bumppo. Moreover, even as in Dakota, Roosevelt in Brazil did not hold a region's state-of-nature wilderness against it. Instead he relished wilderness as providing a wonderful opportunity not so much to remake nature as to remake the civilized gentleman: to toughen him in his pursuit not of material profits but of excellence of character.

Roosevelt empathized with the Latin Americans he encountered in various walks of life in Brazil and in the countries he visited after his exploration there: Argentina, Uruguay, and Chile. Caribbean republics might not yet have moved very far toward civilization in Roosevelt's estimation; they might still require heavy-handed, paternalistic U.S. interventions, as he stated in so many words in his corollary to the Monroe Doctrine. But the leadership classes in Brazil and the southern-cone republics had not only attained cultural refinement while escaping the menace of "a purely materialistic industrial society"; they also had the glorious prospect of toughening and reinvigorating themselves as they faced up to the challenge of conquering their remaining frontiers. In the process Roosevelt hoped they might be more successful than the United States in avoiding abuse of the aboriginal population while guiding it toward assimilation.[23]

Although encouraged by the prospects he saw for the emergence of new, more vigorous and virile leadership classes, Roosevelt continued to have doubts about the Latin American riffraff, as evidenced by his response to Stephen Crane when the author sent him a copy of one of his masterful short stories. In this particular story ("A Man and Some Other") an Anglo old-timer in the American Southwest pits himself against some Mexican desperados and loses his life after a furious gun battle. TR acknowledged receipt of the story with a note in which he expressed the hope that Crane would someday write "another story of the frontiersman and the Mexican Greaser in which the frontiersman shall come out on top; it is more normal that way!"[24] (See illustration 15.)

In the southern-cone republics, many members of the leading classes appreciated Roosevelt's ability not to confuse them with the riffraff of Mexico and the tropical, turbulent Caribbean republics. At last, here was a prominent American capable of distinguishing among Latins.[25] Some of the southern-cone elites could even appreciate the way in which Roosevelt combined the traits of the childish, impetuous cowboy with those of the aristocratic Arielist. Here is how the leading Chilean newspaper, *El Mercurio,* assessed the president: He is "vigorous, impulsive, not heedful of the consequences of his actions, strongly susceptible to error, but at the same time possessed of the noblest of humanitarian sentiments."[26]

In the "New Nationalism" that he articulated between his African and Brazilian nature plunges as he headed a third-party bid for the presidency in 1912, Roosevelt seemed to urge a coming together of America's well-born, wealthy elements, endowed with a chivalrous sense of noblesse oblige, and its hard-driving, energetic working classes. Many of Latin America's ruling elites at the beginning of the century had a similar view of the ideal society, and so they could accept this American patrician, for all his cowboy bumptiousness, as one of them. Indeed, as Roosevelt once described the cowboy code of honor, it was not terribly far removed from old-line Iberian hidalgo concepts: "A cowboy will not submit tamely to an

15. Frederic Remington. Illustration for a book, the pertinent text of which reads:
". . . them three Mexicans is eliminated. . . ." Alfred Henry Lewis, *Wolfville* (New
York: Stokes, 1897), p. 268.

From Texas Rangers to east-coast friends Teddy Roosevelt and Frederic Remington,
prevailing stereotypes cast the "greaser" as a sneaky varmint who in a fair fight could
never match civilization's paragon: the Anglo American male.

insult, and is ever ready to avenge his own wrongs; nor has he an over-
wrought fear of shedding blood. He possesses, in fact, few of the emascu-
lated, milk-and-water moralities so much admired by the pseudo phi-
lanthropists; but he does possess, to a very high degree, the stern, manly
qualities that are invaluable to a nation."[27] Perhaps Roosevelt felt that
Latin America's ruling classes, as they faced up to the task of settling their
national frontiers, stood on the verge of producing their own cowboy-
aristocrat presidents.

As cowboy-aristocrats, Roosevelt hoped Latin American leaders could
avoid becoming mere exploitative destroyers of wilderness resources.
Manifesting the strong conservationist tendencies that he had developed
toward the end of the nineteenth century, Roosevelt in 1914 rendered a
judgment that would gain in timeliness as the years went by: "There is

every reason why the good people of South America should awaken, as we of North America, very late in the day, are beginning to waken . . . to the duty of preserving from impoverishment and extinction the wild life which is an asset of such interest and value in our several lands; but the case against civilized man in this matter is gruesomely heavy." [28]

Roosevelt had not always associated himself with the protection of natural resources. In his four-volume *Winning of the West,* published between 1889 and 1896, he asserted that it had been the nation's task "to wage war against man, to wage war against nature for the possession of the vast lonely spaces of the earth which we have now made the seat of a mighty civilization." [29] When Roosevelt began this impressive historical study, the nation's resources appeared endless, and promulgation of Turner's end-of-the-frontier thesis lay several years in the future. The older he became, the more seriously Roosevelt concerned himself with the need to retain a touch of the wild in the midst of American civilization, so that from it future generations might derive the inspiration and the spiritual strength, and that larger, cosmic vision, that would enable them to grasp that mere material gain must not become the primary objective in national life. [30] In no way did Roosevelt's Arielism manifest itself more clearly than in his desire to check the materialistic excesses of modern civilization by maintaining a healthy reverence for all that was numinous in nature. This desire mitigated, at times anyway, Roosevelt's imperialist excesses in regard to Latin America and helped him to see that area as one that required some degree of protection against the plundering instincts of American businessmen.

In all probability, though, had Roosevelt triumphed in the 1912 election, his New Nationalism would have proved no more effective than did Woodrow Wilson's New Freedom in curbing the excesses of dollar diplomacy. And Roosevelt's exuberant and childish militarism that continued unabated in his late years would have led him to concentrate so much on involving his country in the Great War in Europe that Latin America would have gotten lost in the shuffle. Nevertheless, Roosevelt possessed many positive instincts that, had circumstances permitted their maturing and their application to hemispheric policy making, could have produced beneficent results. Foremost among these instincts lay Roosevelt's positive response to nature, out of which came the conviction that nature deserved protection from the exploitation of rapacious capitalists.

Writing in 1977, a western rancher expressed sentiments typical for over a century of men of his calling. "I just don't agree that the United States can afford to lock up a huge scope of country and let it go back to wilderness. That's what this country all was originally, and it wasn't worth a damn until it was made into something productive. Made by enterprise, initiative, hard work and a lot of guts."[31] The ranching Roosevelt of the 1880s might have been partially sympathetic to this view, but not the president whose time in office approached its end in 1908. In that year Roosevelt was denouncing the "predatory wealth" that derived from oppressing wage earners. Almost as much as the muckrakers he derided (partly because they stole some of his thunder), the president railed against the "malefactors of great wealth" as downright un-American. And, since moving into the White House upon the assassination of William McKinley in 1901, Roosevelt had perceived that protectors of the environment and businessmen were natural enemies. Businessmen, the president believed, always took the short-range view, seeking the quickest route to the maximum profit. Statesmen, on the other hand, must look to the ages ahead as they exercised their stewardship over citizens and natural resources.[32]

With some justification, later generations of environmentalists have accused Roosevelt of being interested primarily in conservation—the wise utilization of nature so as to guarantee that it would yield optimal profits for future generations—rather than in preservation. Preservation implies the desire to protect nature not as a means to maximize future profits but as an end in itself somehow associated with spiritual enrichment. Still, politics is the art of the possible, and Roosevelt probably proceeded as far as the times permitted toward altering the rules of the contest between civilization and nature. And, beyond all doubt, Roosevelt was more kindly disposed toward nature and naturalness than the man who defeated him in the 1912 presidential election.

Before entering the White House in 1913, Woodrow Wilson had been the president of Princeton University. Before that this scion of a Virginia family, caught in a pattern of moderate downward mobility, had been a professor of jurisprudence, political economy, and history—though he always seemed less the historian than the political scientist. All his life Wilson tended to regard politics as a science, while his great adversary, Roosevelt, took to a visceral, intuitive approach. Predictably, the stern Wilson brought an entirely different perspective than the ebullient Roosevelt to the civilization-nature dichotomy. This difference reflected itself in their distinctive approaches to Latin America and to life in general.

During his time in the White House, Roosevelt presided over a process that increased the number of national parks by four, bringing the total to seven and thereby gladdening the heart of his old camping companion John Muir.[33] Wilson, who gave the impression of a man who would never want to dirty his hands or soil his clothes by roughing it, saw no useful purpose to be served by an extensive national park system. American character, in his view, had been shaped primarily by the cultural "germs" that early-arriving settlers from England brought with them. Because their exceptionalism was not owing to an ongoing encounter with the frontier, Americans had no need to preserve the natural setting or to seek nature experiences in those last remaining wilderness areas that lay south of the border. Early in his presidency Wilson supported the bill that resulted in the damming and flooding of the Hetch Hetchy canyon near Yosemite so as to provide San Francisco with a source of cheap water. Resolved that there was no need to protect the splendors of nature against commercial invasion (for it was economic competition rather than struggle against untamed lands that perfected character), Wilson facilitated the destruction of one of California's natural wonders, reduced the size of Yosemite National Park—breaking the heart of John Muir—and dealt a severe setback to the Sierra Club that had for years waged the fight to preserve Hetch Hetchy in its pristine splendor.[34]

Basically unable to perceive nature, whether internal or external, in terms of its mythic promise of redemption and rebirth, Wilson—whose rigid Presbyterianism had no room for the mystical, mythical elements that had attached themselves to America's civil religion—seemed driven by the compulsion to control and discipline the natural. To this man of order, nature was threatening, not fulfilling. If he did not strive constantly to control it, he might be overwhelmed by its tumultuousness and so suffer erosion of his human potential. So far as Wilson was concerned, the frontier experience tended to dissolve civilizing restraints and to produce ruffians and barbarians of the sort Cooper had derided in some of his Leatherstocking novels. Wilson went so far to the other extreme as to resemble at times Dr. Obed Tattius, whom Cooper portrayed in *The Prairie* (1827): a man whose knowledge was all bookish, rational, totally unrooted in nature, and therefore often irrelevant to real-life situations.

Distrustful of the effects of outward nature on character formation, Wilson also looked with apprehension on inward nature's seething passions. On one occasion he wrote: "If I were to interpret myself, I would say that my constant embarrassment is to restrain the emotions that are inside of me. You may not believe it, but I sometimes feel like a fire from a far . . . volcano, and if the lava does not seem to spill over it is because you are not high enough to see into the basin and see the cauldron boil."[35] What a contrast he presented to Roosevelt, who in his exuberance seemed to delight in letting his cauldron boil over.

Comfortable in informal clothing, in contrast to Wilson who gave the impression of being corseted, Roosevelt did not concern himself with masking the body's natural lines or with unduly repressing the natural passion of anger—especially when he believed some practical purpose might be served by a display of temper. But Wilson judged temper displays under any circumstances a setback to the civilized person's constant quest for self-control. Once Wilson lost his temper when a delegation of Negro spokesmen did not treat him with what he deemed proper deference. Angered by the delegation's spirited assertion of Negro rights, Wilson (who instituted far more rigorous segregation in Washington's Civil Service than had heretofore obtained) curtly terminated the meeting. Almost immediately afterward he regretted his display of temper, telling a colleague: "I was damn fool enough to lose my temper and to point them to the door. . . . I lost my temper and played the fool." [36] Wilson's abhorrence of showing temper could only have struck Roosevelt as unmanly.

According to a biographer, Wilson projected onto the United States "his own need to overcome 'a background of passion.'" [37] All Americans, if they were to be worthy citizens and live up to their potential, must curb their passions and dedicate themselves to the disciplined, rational, level-headed pursuit both of morality and of material success. To do otherwise was to play the fool. Wilson, it seems, also projected this need to control passion onto Latin Americans. Rather than empathizing with the uninhibited emotionalism that stereotyping attributed to Latins, as Roosevelt could do, Wilson felt that not until the Latins submitted their nature to restraint could they become worthy beings who deserved Yankee respect.

Some Latins Wilson saw as well on the way to acquiring the personal restraint that led to morality and material success. Argentines, Brazilians, and Chileans had scored notable progress in this regard. Mexicans, however, lagged behind the southernmost (and whiter) Latins, and trailing still farther back came the Central Americans and the residents of such Caribbean republics as Haiti and the Dominican Republic. Until they had acquired the self-control that made possible the intelligent exercise of liberty, these nearby neighbors must, like the North American Indians before them, be protected against the machinations of outside, extracontinental influences. Germans and Japanese might take advantage of the immaturity of Mexicans and residents of the circum-Caribbean area. Whether Occidental or Oriental, emissaries of Old World cultures, who had never been purified by American-style free competition, would find congenial the aristocratic privileges and state interventionist practices traditional to Latin Americans. These representatives of Old World cultures could, in fact, be relied upon to strengthen these traditional aberrations, as Wilson implied in his notorious October 27, 1913, Mobile address.[38] Because extracontinental powers would impede progress toward individual maturity and responsible nationhood, they must be excluded from the hemisphere.

As World War I cast its shadow over the New World, simple security requirements joined with sweeping visions of hemispheric uplift to stiffen Wilson's resolve to drop the Monroe Doctrine's protective mantle over Latin America, at least those parts of it where inhabitants remained too immature to recognize danger and to guard themselves against it.

The maturity of responsible manhood, in Wilson's opinion, resulted from the personal discipline that free humans acquired as they engaged in the open, uninhibited competition for professional success and from the personal security afforded by accumulation of the material resources needed to guarantee self-reliance. Wilson's outlook was that of upwardly aspiring middle-class Americans, while Roosevelt's was that of patrician America, resting on faith in the ability of "better elements" to impose moral restraints and standards from above. Wilson's New Freedom, with its insistence on the removal of artificial restraints on competition whether imposed by an interventionist government or by monopolies, struck Latin America's traditional ruling classes as a prescription for anarchy. They much preferred what they imputed to Roosevelt's New Nationalism: an Arielist acceptance of service to high ideals as the means of imparting a moral tone to society, an openness to state planning and governmental as well as private paternalism, and a partiality toward the organic or corporatist society.

To some degree, the New Nationalism model existed already in Latin America—or Latin elites at least claimed that it did; but Wilsonian New Freedom was altogether alien to the area's cultural ambience. If Wilson chose to push New Freedom–type reforms southward, if he opted to strike a blow in behalf of the sort of socioeconomic conditions that would encourage Latins to take up the pursuit of morally cleansing self-reliance, then he would have to resort to the most sweeping sort of intervention the United States had yet undertaken, for he would be proceeding against the Latin American grain. As it turned out, Wilson did choose to impel the New Freedom southward, at least as far as Mexico, Haiti, and the Dominican Republic, to begin with. Probably he had in mind the well-being not only of the Latins affected but also of American entrepreneurs who, having been purified by the New Freedom's stimulus to competitive self-reliance in their own country, would welcome fields afar where they could continue to perfect themselves—once the social and economic environment of those fields had been reformed so as to stimulate free competition.

Thomas Jefferson had associated American virtue and destiny with the yeoman farmer—a yeoman being defined as a freeholder of a class below the gentry who worked his own land.[39] Wilson saw American destiny as attached to the well-being of the yeoman entrepreneur: the person below the gentry who worked his own capital holdings. Like Jefferson, Wilson's ideal of American virtue and destiny reached out to envelop the entire hemisphere. If Wilson had his way, he would reshape life not only in the United States but also in much of Latin America and indeed—with the Fourteen Points as his blueprint—the world as a whole. Wherever the eye could see, the yeoman entrepreneur would be happily at work, improving himself and the world.

In 1914 the immediate challenge to the Presbyterian reformer lay in Mexico, then controlled by Victoriano Huerta, a heavy-drinking general who had seized power by overthrowing and then engineering the murder of the legal president and vice-president. Huerta had no intention of allowing the masses to learn about the wonders of political democracy and economic free competition. So, Huerta had to go; and to speed him on his way Wilson ordered the occupation of Veracruz by U.S. Marines so as to block delivery of foreign arms to the dictator. Wilson, who as noted generally tried to eradicate passion, confessed that "my passion is for the submerged eighty-five percent of the people of the Republic [of Mexico], who are now struggling for liberty." [40] The precision of the scientific scholar in measuring Mexican public opinion from the banks of the Potomac is astounding, but soon Wilson had to concede his calculations might have been off and that only the more enlightened elements of Mexican society wanted to import the New Freedom. In any event, to his consternation the Mexican people in their struggle for liberty did not on the whole appreciate help from U.S. Marines, and some of them gave up their lives resisting the Veracruz occupation. With the mediation of the ABC powers (Argentina, Brazil, and Chile) helping to provide a figleaf of multilateral statesmanship, Wilson called the occupation forces home.

Some Americans involved in taking Veracruz hated to see the seven-month occupation end, for they had taken pride in bringing civilization to benighted beings. The man in charge of cleaning up Veracruz, Frederick Funston, who had served with distinction in subduing turn-of-the-century Filipino insurgents, boasted of having imposed strict regulations on the operation of bordellos, thereby mitigating the ravages of venereal disease. He took pride also in the posting of signs that prohibited spitting in public places and dumping garbage in the streets. Given a bit more time, he believed, his cleanup would have yielded still more dramatic effects. Meanwhile, novelist Jack London, who arrived in the city not long after the troops had landed, saw Veracruz as "an unkempt mestizo hovel that the Americans were desperately trying to clean up. The occupiers ('white-skinned fighting men who knew how to rule as well as fight') brought democracy and order to the city. City streets were now 'quiet and seemly.'

The military government had weeded out the 'riff-raff' and the 'able-bodied loafers.'"[41] Like Funston, London hoped the occupation might be prolonged. For rather more down-to-earth reasons, some of the marines hated to go home. Life in Veracruz had its attractions. According to one serviceman, "We slept afternoons and fooled around with the Mexican girls when we were not on duty." With such friendly Mexicans at hand, the marines did not try to understand the motives of those natives who remained hostile. Mexicans who opposed their presence they contemptuously dismissed as "spicks." They echoed, of course, "the sentiments of their superiors, like General Hugh L. Scott who said he believed that 'firmness is essential in dealing with inferior races.'"[42]

During the course of the Veracruz occupation, Huerta had resigned the presidency and gone into exile. Wilson now had to decide which of several people contending by force of arms for the vacated presidential office deserved Washington's good wishes. Assured by the astute Mexican lobbyist Luis Cabrera that Venustiano Carranza and his Constitutionalist forces were consummately bourgeois in their aspirations and dedicated to democratic and economic freedom—in short, to a Mexican version of the New Freedom—the gullible Wilson extended the support that helped Carranza come to power in 1915. Wilson now saw immediate prospects for the success of his Mexican policy, "designed to educate and uplift the downtrodden."[43] Soon, though, he understood that he had been duped into supporting a group totally indifferent to the made-on-the-Potomac New Freedom. By then, though, Wilson's attention had turned mainly to Europe. After a brief interlude in which U.S. forces under Gen. John J. Pershing chased Pancho Villa, who in his anger over being edged out by Carranza in the contest for U.S. recognition had shot up an American border town or two, Wilson left Mexicans to their own devices.

At least toward the conclusion of his presidency, after suffering a partially paralyzing stroke, Wilson did manage to block a military invasion to protect U.S. business interests in Mexico. The chastened president, realizing he had not succeeded in reforming even the United States according to New Freedom standards, did not wish to turn unreconstructed capitalist predators loose on Mexico, with the backing of the U.S. armed forces. For this exit performance, Wilson merits the gratitude of Mexicans; but, understandably miffed by the president's early arrogance in believing that he could and must remake Mexico in a mold in which as it turned out he could not even recast his own countrymen, citizens of the Aztec republic have been loath to recognize that they owe Wilson even an iota of gratitude.

After the Veracruz fiasco, Wilson had indulged his Prometheus fantasies by ordering the occupation of Haiti in 1915 and the Dominican Republic in

1916. At the moment the marines landed in Haiti, the local populace did present some evidence of having reverted to a state of nature that cried out for the interposition of civilization. A mob rampaged through the streets of the capital, some of its members carrying pieces of the hacked-up body of the just-deposed president. There was also the security issue to justify U.S. intervention, for evidence suggested German interest in acquiring a naval base on Haiti's Mole St. Nicholas. The need to protect the Caribbean from the Hun had rather less plausibility as a justification for the Dominican intervention. But, when Dominicans resisted the endeavors of the occupation forces to civilize them and struck back against the troops in guerrilla warfare, American officers often detected German influence. One of the Marine Corps officers in charge of the occupation wrote to an associate: "Whoever is running this revolution is a wise man; he certainly is getting a lot out of the niggers. . . . It shows the handiwork of the Germans."[44] The attitude is, of course, remarkably similar to that displayed by early nineteenth-century American officers engaged in pacifying Indians. Whenever the natives proved particularly recalcitrant or especially effective in resisting the imposition of civilization, Americans invariably assumed that outside agitators from some relatively civilized country must be calling the shots.

Even when acting on their own, nineteenth-century Indians had contrived to thwart the spread of civilization by their incessant intertribal warfare. Haitians and Dominicans seemed just as bad in this regard. By their chronic regional and personalistic rivalries, both people, U.S. officers complained, frustrated the best-conceived plans for their uplift,[45] a situation exacerbated in Haiti by the bitter contests between mulattoes and Negroes of undiluted African blood. In striving to maintain order among Indians, American officials had hit upon one fairly effective expedient: the creation of Indian auxiliary forces, dating from 1877.[46] In these auxiliary forces one detects the precedent for native constabularies that U.S. occupation forces established in Haiti and the Dominican Republic, and also in Nicaragua, which became subject to prolonged intervention beginning in 1912 in line with the Taft administration's dollar-diplomacy tactics buttressed by uplift and "white-man's-burden" rationalizations. Fruitfully implemented among American Indians, the native constabulary idea proved monstrously ineffective when exported to Latin America. There, the native constabularies created a spawning ground for particularly unsavory tyrants.[47] The moral of the tale is this: if uplift expedients sometimes produce hoped-for results when imperialists surround and maintain a stranglehold on a small number of colonials, they prove counterproductive when applied sporadically at long range through the instrumentality of fleetingly present and sparsely manned beachheads of occupation. In the latter circumstances, natives develop a positive genius for co-opting the means of Americanization and using them to accomplish quite opposite ends. Thereby Latin Americans perhaps confirm Yankee stereotypes of them as sly, devious, and vicious little animals, most resembling foxes, weasels, and jackals—the animals that so often make fools of larger, more puissant, more forthright ones.

Racism, Once More, as an Issue in Internal and External Colonialism

The overt racism of American occupation forces served in its own way to defeat high-minded policies concocted in the White House out of a brew of arrogance and naivete. James Weldon Johnson, an African American whom Theodore Roosevelt had appointed an American consul to Nicaragua in 1909 (where he had written his soon-to-be-celebrated *Autobiography of an Ex-Colored Man*), devoted some of his time in 1917 to studying race riots and lynchings in East St. Louis and abuses perpetrated by America's occupation troops in Haiti. According to his study of the Haitian situation, three problems stood out: (1) the power of the National City Bank of New York that, in its Haitian operations, exhibited precious few of the enlightened approaches that Wilson hoped would result from his New Freedom reforms of business; (2) the fondness of American advisers for large retinues of servants, for jewelry and fancy automobiles and other emblems of success, all to be paid for out of the Haitian treasury; and (3) the "rough-and-tough" treatment that American officers believed essential to shape up the natives. In respect to the last point, Johnson, who in 1919 became the first Negro to head the National Association for the Advancement of Colored People, saw little to distinguish the disciplinary approach of white lynching posses in America from that of the occupation forces in Haiti.[48]

With their "rough-and-tough" methods, American officers at least succeeded in forcing upon Dominicans a reform similar to one that an earlier generation of Indian Affairs officials had imposed on Native Americans. Acting on principles inherent in the Dawes Act (1877) and also underlying New Freedom individualism, occupation officers moved to abolish the Dominican peasantry's traditional system of collective property ownership. Ostensibly high-minded American ethnocentrism as applied to Dominicans facilitated, in this instance, the long-held ambitions of the republic's large landowners to create a defenseless rural proletariat as a permanent labor source.[49]

Joseph Conrad, that supremely gifted novelist of imperialism, believed that in seeking wealth and power through control of overseas Others, "we [the Caucasian colonialists] engage in a slow process of self-destruction. . . . Imperialism is a massive dehumanization and desensitization of the West which will slowly erode Western morality."[50] Precisely this fear inspired many a thoughtful American to oppose imperialism at the turn of the century. Insofar as there may have been a connection between the actions of white Americans in Cuba, Haiti, the Dominican Republic, and Nicaragua, and in American cities where white vigilantes intimidated Negroes, the supposedly high-minded imperialism pursued by Woodrow Wilson vindicated the darkest forebodings of Joseph Conrad and America's anti-imperialists. But there is another side to this story, as would not surprise Conrad, who could be notoriously of two minds in assessing imperialism, ever inclined to withdraw with one hand what he had extended with the other. Sometimes marines who were engaged in bringing civilization to Caribbean republics developed ties of true affection for the natives, just as an earlier generation of Americans engaged in settling the West had sometimes become so fond of Indians as to begin to have doubts about the glories of Caucasian civilization. Wherever found, the frontier, and its people, always manage to seduce at least a few of those who entered it intent upon taming and improving or even obliterating it.

Upon leaving Haiti in 1917, one Marine Corps officer observed: "It is strange I should feel a very real regret at leaving this beautiful island and its black people."[51] Often officers accompanied their respect for the peasants with a mounting disdain for native elites, thereby reversing the Arielist precedent that led Americans to regard Latin America's gente decente as natural allies. Haitian peasants, according to a marine officer, were likeable because of their ability to find happy-go-lucky pleasure in their simple lives.[52] But the peasants' social betters, the beneficiaries of what struck some American observers as a degenerate form of civilization, thought only of how to live better at the expense of their unfortunate dependents. Some on-the-spot officers and enlisted men in their country's imperial outposts in Central America and the Caribbean had the opportunity to see through the myth of the enlightened, paternalistic Latin hidalgo that so appealed to Americans who had never had the chance to know the recipients of the hidalgo's reputed beneficence.

While few of the American soldiers felt the guilt that Quaker Marine Corps officer Smedley Butler acknowledged ("I helped in the rape of half a dozen Central American republics for the benefit of Wall Street," he confessed in 1931[53]), many veterans of the occupation forces did undergo at least a partial transformation of attitudes, returning home with an abiding respect for the downtrodden classes of colonials, whose plight they feared had only been exacerbated by an imperialism that made allies of rapacious Yankees and unconscionable native capitalists. In this, occupation-force veterans anticipated the reactions of Peace Corps volunteers, many of whom returned home—beginning in the mid-1960s—with sympathy for the overseas victims of oppression. This sympathy helped inspire returning volunteers to become more sensitive champions of oppressed people in America itself. The spirit of the returning Peace Corps volunteers contributed its grain of salt to the civil rights movement of the 1960s and 1970s. Just possibly, some veterans returning from Mexican, Central American, and Caribbean adventures made their contribution to the easing of American race relations that timidly, tentatively, teasingly, and abortively got under way in the 1920s. If so, then foreign imperialism did not invariably harden Americans in their attitudes toward the internal colonial. Conceivably, imperialism may have enhanced the moral stature of at least a few people who had set out to enhance the moral standing of the Other. In human relations, there's always the unexpected, often for worse but sometimes for better.

Modernism's Revolt against Modernity

Despite confusion occasioned by similarity of the words, modernism embodied a reaction against modernity, the latter characterized by an obsession with material progress, by empiricism, and by whatever at the moment happened to pass for rationality and scientific method. If Arielism embodied a challenge to the bourgeois order posed by old-line elites fretful over a perceived status decline, modernism represented a challenge issued by would-be elites set upon creating a new and better form of human existence, based on the cultural, aesthetic, subconscious, spiritual, and sometimes mystical values that they—the new elites—would intuit, guard, and mediate. This, at least, was one of the radical elements of modernism, an enormously complex, protean movement with many inherent contradictions, but with a shred of consistency provided by the desire to replace a society obsessed with producing and consuming goods with one that stressed production and consumption of culture. But that shred of consistency in turn gave rise to endless wrangling.

Frequently apologists for one of the currently fashionable varieties of socialism and/or anarchism, radical modernists proved notoriously unable to agree about what constituted an ideal political, social, or aesthetic culture. Their constant quarrels attested to their utter inability to forge com-

munity among themselves. Undeterred by internal divisiveness, they celebrated the idea of community between artists, intellectuals, and visionaries
on one hand and the people of the streets, factories, and fields on the
other.

Among those seeking community with the masses below were the artists who comprised the "Ash-Can School" of New York realists. This
loosely bound group of artists found inspiration in what others saw as
simply the seamy and best-ignored side of urban life. According to John
Sloan, perhaps the most vital member of this school, "The streets seem
pulsing with human life and warm blood and a feeling of animal love, honest animal affection."[54] Robert Henri, instrumental in drawing disparate
artists together into the Ash-Can School, found the all-important contact
with life-quickening masses not only in the streets of East Coast cities but
also in the classrooms of the anarchist Ferrer School in New York City,
directed by Russian émigré Emma Goldman,[55] whose advocacy of workers' and women's rights, of birth control, free love, and free speech would
soon earn her the epithet "Red Emma." In the Ferrer School, Henri and
other members of modernism's politically radical wing found revivifying
contact with the masses to whom they in turn imparted the new aesthetic
values that would, ostensibly, transform the lives of the underprivileged
and shortly bring about a restructuring of the social order. Artists and intellectuals who were charmed, fascinated, and perhaps sometimes titillated
by the masses recognized that good instincts inhered in the lower classes;
but these instincts had to be liberated from "the pecuniary morals of competitive business" with which conventional society sought to twist, distort,
and misdirect the natural inclinations of America's real and most authentic
people.[56]

Avant-garde elites also came together with social underlings and outcasts during the demonstrations in behalf of Frank Tannenbaum, an impecunious young member of the anarchist Industrial Workers of the World
(IWW) who would go on to become one of the best-known historians of
Latin America that the United States has produced. Tannenbaum's attempts to pressure New York City's municipal officials and church digni-
taries into providing nighttime shelter for the homeless led to his arrest
and to a trial attended by the wealthy Buffalo-born Mabel Dodge, a de-
votee of modern art who presided over a fashionable lower Fifth Avenue
salon. Dodge and other radical intellectuals of Greenwich Village rubbed
shoulders with IWW organizer William ("Big Bill") Haywood and Emma
Goldman in the parade that celebrated Tannenbaum's release from prison
at the end of the short term to which he was sentenced. The same explosive mixture of well-born and sometimes wealthy intellectuals turned
social radicals with defenders of the downtrodden who had risen from

their ranks yielded the 1913 Paterson Strike Pageant staged at Madison Square Garden. Mabel Dodge and her Oregon-born lover John Reed joined with Haywood and the rank and file of radical labor groups to stage this pageant in which some twelve hundred workers dramatized the struggle they were waging against the textile industry in Paterson, New Jersey.[57]

Radicals from above came together with radicals from below also in the offices of *Masses*, where editor Max Eastman worked with John Reed and other writers to spread the vision of a new America safe for free love, divorce, birth control, and homosexuality, a new America of social justice where workers could live in material security as they soaked up the new era's culture. Artists on the staff of *Masses*, especially the Ash-Can School's socialist John Sloan, created a golden period of social-consciousness art as they depicted "the Negro, the immigrant, the down-and-outer . . . [as] human beings, not as stock symbols."[58] The drawings published in *Masses* proved, as Mabel Dodge observed in a different connection, that art can be "subversive of civilization."[59]

Above all, the Fifth Avenue salon over which Mabel Dodge presided symbolized the symbiotic mingling of avant-garde culture with the vital spontaneity and natural forces welling up from the masses. Here, art and music critics, experimental writers, painters and sculptors, modern dancers, musicians, and journalists—with some members of the mixed crowd overt homosexuals and lesbians—mingled with tough labor organizers who had risen through the ranks, with blacks, and in general with people who were down and out by every measure save talent, verve, imagination, and a penchant for exalted visions of a better future.[60] Dodge's gatherings could be seen as transcendent rites, presided over by modernism's muse: they constituted the rites of passage whereby Americans would learn to combine in a new way the art and culture of the cognoscenti with the instinctual energies of the masses so as to forge a fresh consciousness, a unique way of being that would fortify and indeed reinvent American exceptionalism. In a way the concept might seem new, but in other ways it was very traditional, for it harked back to frontier mythology that glorified the fruitful coupling of civilized refinement with nature's raw vitality so as to guarantee Americans perpetual youth. Mabel Dodge's salon constituted a surrogate frontier, now that the real frontier, supposedly, was gone.

In the old days, the frontier had exemplified the raw, chaotic forces to which pioneers would bring order—to their own advantage as well as nature's. Now, in the early twentieth century, a new generation of artists and litterateurs would enter into the chaos of the masses and somehow fashion that chaos into a new harmony. In the process, they would be revitalized themselves. By and large the cultural pioneers intent upon immersing themselves in manifestations of the natural did not want for conceit. Like avant-garde composer Charles Ives, one of the most original and creative forces in the entire history of American classical music (though he may have fudged the dates of some of his compositions to mask his borrowing from European atonalists), modernism's intellectuals saw the need for the hand of supreme conductors—themselves—to arrange the chaos of disparate sounds and rhythms into a new music. At the same time, they appreciated their own dependence upon the chaotic vitality of the masses below for the chance to become supreme conductors of a new cultural-spiritual order. Just as Ives found inspiration in American musical primitivism, in the hymns and folk melodies that emerged from the masses, so the avant-garde of Greenwich Village and elsewhere recognized their dependence on the pulsating rhythms and primordial voices of the masses in creating the new symphony of American civilization. The masses were their new frontier, and modernism's elites needed them just as much as an earlier generation of pioneers had needed the physical, geographic frontier to forge an American civilization—fresh in its day, but now, purportedly, grown listless and decadent.

Near the end of 1913 (some few months before Wilson sent the marines to Veracruz), John Reed went off to Mexico in search of fulfilling masses, and also in quest of adventure in the violence of the revolution that had erupted three years earlier. His possessive mistress Mabel Dodge accompanied him most of the way, but discreetly proceeded no farther south than El Paso, Texas. In Mexico Reed sought out Pancho Villa, whom he described as "the most natural human being I ever saw—natural in the sense of being nearest to a wild animal."[61] Villa also struck Reed as "a hearty man," like Big Bill Haywood, to whom the journalist had been close back in Greenwich Village: "familiar with violence, a passionate gambler, and with an even more macho record [than Haywood's] with women."[62] Villa and the earthy, loosely disciplined followers (men, women, and children) who comprised his "army" represented the very antithesis to American bourgeois values that, especially when channeled into military undertakings, assumed the need for iron-fisted discipline. Indeed, for Americans shaped in the tradition extending from Puritanism to Victorianism, Villa and his hordes symbolized the very incarnation of the negative identity— although for a time secretary of state and fundamentalist Protestant William Jennings Bryan admired Villa, having learned that he neither smoked nor drank. Perhaps Reed understood that this quirky abstinence permitted Villa to devote undiminished energies to the pursuit of women. In any event, Reed and the new pioneers of radical modernism in general found in Villa and Mexican revolutionaries as a whole a life-enhancing positive identity. Nevertheless, before he left Mexico, Reed had come to see that Villa was too much the incorrigible savage, too much the unregenerate mountain-man and Indian-killer type of first-wave settlers of the American frontier, to lead Mexico into the future. Attainment of the future demanded the mediation of John Reed types, and their Mexican counterparts, who could fuse creatively with the masses.

Art might provide an avenue to the sort of fusion that fired Reed's imagination. So, at least, some of Europe's modernist artists imagined. With Picasso in the lead, these artists turned to African art for inspiration. Civilized men themselves, reared in the culture of machinery and scientific thought, they hoped to assimilate some of the mysterious, nonquantifiable, magical powers and telluric forces with which natives of the Dark Continent had remained in contact and to which they gave expression in some of their glorious pagan sculpture.[63] Primitivism also exerted an influence on America's modernist art world. Its leaders organized exhibits of African, Mexican folk, and pre-Columbian art, and even of the artwork of children.[64] Each of these varieties of primitive art grew out of the spontaneity of psyches not repressed by the basically antihuman restraints and inhibitions that allegedly stifled Western civilization. By drawing inspiration from wellsprings of unmitigated vitality, modern artists could remake the Western world.

Referring to certain "Futurist" artists who sought inspiration in the prehistoric art of French and Spanish caves, Theodore Roosevelt observed that they should really be called "past-ists."[65] TR hit the nail squarely; many of modernism's artists were past-ists. Their future utopia had its roots in an imagined golden age in the past when humans had been wise enough to recognize and revere their oneness with nature.

Modernists sought inspiration not only in the energy of supposedly natural persons, whether the teeming masses at home or exotic primitives. They sought it also in the untapped drives of the psyche, of the unconscious, the id. Challenging bourgeois positivism, they joined in an "introspective revolution."[66] Dismissing mere intellect, they hailed primal passion as the source of creativity and discovery; they sought virtually any means to reinforce intuition and spontaneity; they embraced cults of vitalist energy that promised the victory of mind over matter; they enthused over experiments in thought transference and other aspects of parapsychology; they turned to Oriental religions, to Theosophy, to Christian Science, and to spiritualists from abroad;[67] they hailed artists who spurned "conscious factors of . . . experience . . . in favor of the substitution of subconscious factors."[68] Sometimes they would even ingest that consciousness-expanding drug of American Indians, peyote, as they sought "recovery of the primal, irrational forces in the human psyche."[69] And, in order to overcome alienation, they went to alienists or psychiatrists who, ostensibly, would put them in touch with the unconscious.

Just as modernism's cult of the psyche had been nourished by the cult of outer-world primitives, so the introspective revolution in turn fed the desire to liberate from alleged suppression not only the domestic laboring classes but foreign colonials as well: in short, all the exemplars of naturalness not yet contaminated by civilization. If for no other reason than their physical location, America's avant-garde intellectuals concerned themselves primarily about Latin America's purported colonials, allegedly the victims of U.S. colonialism. And they sought to ally themselves with kindred revolutionary souls among Latin America's intellectuals bent upon toppling the materialist, capitalist order. American modernists and Latin American visionary revolutionaries were, so it seemed, soul mates who, across the border, could recognize each other—just as Arielists had recognized soul mates among Latin America's traditional elites.

Whether or not they found the soul mates they sought, America's modernist radicals cast a long shadow, one that fell on the new counterculture that emerged in the late 1950s. Clearly, modernist radicals are the spiritual parents of the New Left, whose representative figures enthused over the efforts of Fidel Castro and Ernesto "Che" Guevara (and also of Mao Zedong and prophets of "African socialism" too numerous and often too spurious to merit identification by name) to eliminate the preeminence of crass materialism and construct societies based on nonmaterial rewards. Almost as much as modernism's avant-garde, the Arielists had urged the importance of nonmaterial rewards as the preferred means to keep the masses content in their dependence. Modernists and Arielists alike, the one group seeking the good society through new elites and the other through traditional aristocrats, saw themselves as liberated already from materialism and therefore qualified to instruct the masses in how to cure their addiction while at the same time distancing the bourgeoisie from the levers of power.

To Woodrow Wilson, modernist radicals provided a mirror image. They and he, in diametrically opposed ways, wanted to remake first America, then the Western Hemisphere, and then the world. Wilson by 1920 had tried and utterly failed to realize his dreams of reforming American bourgeois society by making it more bourgeois (in ways conforming to his Presbyterian morality) and then exporting the product in all directions. In the coming decade his opposites would have their go at radical transformation based on undermining the bourgeois ethic. But before they did, they had to survive a post–World War I resurgence of unregenerate middle-class and robber-baron normalcy that for a time threatened to bury those radicals who modestly believed they had caught a vision of a better future toward the fulfillment of which they alone could lead the unenlightened.

CHAPTER 7

The Twenties: Normalcy, Counterculture, and Clashing Perceptions of Latin America

America Breaks in Two

Raging out of control since 1918, the great influenza pandemic had by the latter part of 1919 claimed more than five hundred thousand American lives. There was something positively un-American about this outburst of natural forces, of germs, that defied the best efforts of a scientific civilization to gain the upper hand; and the fact that rampaging, killing nature had a Hispanic connection, bearing the name "Spanish influenza," tied in with long-established American stereotypes. As Willa Cather has one of her characters in the novel *My Ántonia* (1918) express the matter, "You were likely to get diseases from foreigners."[1] Americans tended to forget that Indians, threatened by the white man's smallpox, had once felt the same way about the matter, as had Panamanians in the 1850s who blamed the outbreak of various epidemics on the scruffy Americans who crossed the isthmus on their way to or from the gold diggings in California. In viewing one another, stereotypers and stereotyped often behold the same image.

As the Great War came to an end, not only foreign germs but also the laboring classes, many of whom were immigrants, and therefore alien and barbaric, raged out of control. In 1919 four million workers, one out of every five and "a proportion never since equaled," went on strike.[2] Race riots occurred in twenty-five cities and towns in the summer of 1919. America's black internal barbarians, the leading classes assumed, must have been instigated by foreign agitators, for like germs, subversive ideas emanated from foreigners. So, the upheavals, perceived as deriving from Russian bolshevism, were dubbed the "Red Summer race riots."

It was now, in the period after the war, that Americans found themselves locked in combat with what seemed the worst un-American threat they had ever faced: international communism. British, French, and Spanish agitators among Indians had in a previous century sparked occasional challenges to the advance of civilization. But those foreigners had posed a minor menace in comparison to the wild-eyed Bolsheviks who agitated among the more threatening and still unsubdued savages of America: immigrants and Negroes.

Attorney General A. Mitchell Palmer in the late days of the Wilson administration initiated the defense of civilization against its subverters. "Assuming that radicalism was a foreign product, Palmer promised to deport radicals by the thousands." Among those he deported was "Red Emma" Goldman—shortly, John Reed would encounter her in Russia, whither he had gone, voluntarily, hoping to witness the birth of a new order that he had earlier sought in Mexico. Palmer vowed he would not stop the deportations until "the country was cleansed of the alien poison."[3] Many Americans assumed it was not enough to deport alien agitators. Beyond that, it behooved them to curtail the vast hordes of unassimilated and perhaps unassimilable alien workers who provided the raw troops that foreign organizers hoped to turn loose against the American system. Like Indians, immigrants had to become a vanishing race; otherwise, they would continue to pose a threat to civilization.

Right-thinking Americans, upon whose resourcefulness rested the defense of civilized values, had no time for romantic myths about the constant remaking of the nation through the melting-pot process. Americans now constituted a completed, a "done" race. The frontier was gone and its passing need not be regretted, for renewal no longer seemed necessary. Similarly, the rebirth once promised by immigration could henceforth be eschewed. America's mature race needed no new barbarian infusions.

An American eugenics movement, originating in the early part of the century, nourished itself on the supposed findings of IQ tests administered to World War I soldiers. Allegedly, the tests proved that native Caucasians and Americans of Nordic background were more intelligent than their fellow citizens of Latin and Slavic origins. Test results also purported to document low intelligence among Negroes. So, the tests bolstered the national tendency to lump together southern and eastern Europeans, Latins, and Negroes as inferior beings. American racism entered a new era, accompanied by a resurgence of anti-Semitism and anti-Catholicism.[4] Out of the new racism came the 1923 legislation that severely curtailed immigration from the supposedly retrograde parts of Europe. Immigrants from such areas would, according to the author of a 1922 *Saturday Evening Post* article, produce a "hybrid race of people as worthless and futile as the good-for-nothing mongrels of Central America."[5] Because the world's genetic refuse that had resettled in America seemed the most responsive to foreign agitators, right-thinking citizens must take steps to keep out additional refuse; they must close the golden door.

Meantime, the years just before and after the war had produced increasing American apprehension about good-for-nothing mongrels from Mexico. During the first decade of that country's revolution that exploded in 1910, various groups down on their luck in the infighting that the upheaval unleashed crossed the border into the United States. Once there, they plotted their eventual return to the homeland. While they awaited auspicious opportunities, they sought to spread their revolutionary ideologies, especially anarcho-syndicalism, in the United States. In particular, they gravitated toward the Industrial Workers of the World, the so-called Wobbly movement. American capitalists in Arizona, Texas, and California found these Mexican revolutionaries, or *revoltosos,* altogether insufferable, for they spread their disruptive ideas among the once relatively docile Mexican laborers on whom the mining, agricultural, and industrial corporations of the Southwest had come to depend. Allegedly, they posed the threat of fomenting social revolution in the United States. The animosity building against the revoltosos for well over a decade lent impetus to the massive repatriation of Mexicans that began in 1930. By then the Great Depression had intensified fear of a massive uprising from below.[6] Meantime, Cuban and Italian immigrants planted fear among the righteous capitalists of northern Florida. Especially in the area around Tampa, the Latin immigrants spread doctrines of anarchism and socialism of various stripes even as they produced the cigars that affluent Americans savored.[7]

The radical spirit epitomized for many Americans by Latin Americans was altogether anathema to the "gospel of Prosperity First" that mainstream citizens worshiped in the 1920s.[8] If businessmen were allowed without interference to control the American scene, and if they enlisted as helpmates scientists who understood the technological requirements of the coming utopia, then nothing could impede the country's progress. Such, at least, was the conviction that underlay American boosterism that thrived as never before in the 1920s. Even thoughtful, reform-minded Americans assumed the essential beneficence of capitalism. Occasionally they might acknowledge the system's shortcomings, especially the inequitable distribution of wealth and power, but they felt the system had self-correcting mechanisms and that radical change would threaten not only prosperity but also American freedom. Essentially, they tended to agree with Herbert Hoover, the high-minded master engineer and self-made man who succeeded Calvin Coolidge as president in 1929, that American exceptionalism arose out of individualistic competition and the ceaseless contest to impose order, on both inner and outer nature.

Americans still devoted to the old gospel of abstention, self-control, and sublimation could take pride in the fact that as the 1920s began, the country's respectable citizens had resolved to eschew drugs. Through self-discipline they had prevailed over the nation's first drug epidemic that began in the 1890s. Blacks and also Oriental and Latin American immigrants might continue to use cocaine, marijuana, and opium-derived drugs, but real Americans had kicked the habit.[9] Moreover, with enactment of the Eighteenth Amendment just after the end of World War I, America seemingly had completed the crusade begun about a century earlier when reformers had taken up the cause of temperance and resolved to correct the flaws of the alcoholic republic. As never before, Americans—at least some of them—resolved to reinvigorate the iron self-discipline that had made their country great. Even if they felt they had earned the right to tolerate a certain self-indulgence among themselves, they would surely impose order and discipline on minorities that had not yet learned the ways of civilization.

Prohibition did not deliver the results its champions had anticipated. Some Americans attributed Prohibition's failures to unscrupulous foreigners, often with Italian names, who waxed rich by undermining national morality, conveniently shifting blame from native consumers to foreign suppliers. Alien bootleggers, gnawing away at the nation's moral foundation, complemented radical agitators from abroad who by means of their anarchist and socialist doctrines threatened American political traditions. As might have been expected, given prevailing stereotypes, Latin Americans figured conspicuously among those subversives who tempted Americans to surrender to their natural cravings by flaunting the Eighteenth Amendment. In ever greater amounts alcohol, sometimes accompanied by marijuana, entered the United States from Mexico. In much of the Southwest those who sold spirits to Americans in speakeasies were not just Mexicans, but Mexican women.[10] Once again, the Latin temptress threatened American male virtue. And, from the Latin Caribbean, especially from Cuba, came endless supplies of rum. Cuba not only exported rum but also imported Yankee tourists to consume intoxicants and to gamble and go whoring about to a degree that revealed just how much well-heeled Americans felt the need to escape from the sort of moral restraints that, as some people told the story, had made their country great.

Some Americans, of course, understood that national character was not being destroyed by foreigners. If destruction there was, it was self-inflicted. F. Scott Fitzgerald in *The Great Gatsby* (1925) proved particularly effective in depicting America's internal rot. In this splendid novel the bootleggers were not "spicks" and "dagos" but respectable-appearing Americans out to fulfill the great national dream of acquiring the wealth that solved all problems and conferred all delights. Gatsby illustrated the degree to which "glittering swinishness" had become an inherent part of the pursuit of the American Dream.[11]

A prominent *New York Times* reporter filed many interesting stories in 1928 on the campaign that American marines had undertaken against Augusto César Sandino and his guerrilla followers in Nicaragua. He saw the struggle as one of civilization versus barbarism, of order against chaos.[12] But the members of a swelling counterculture, the most important one this country was to know prior to the 1960s, saw a hemispheric morality play unfolding in which the heroes and villains were reversed. They perceived a contest in Nicaragua, and in the United States itself, between Negroes, Indians, mixed-bloods, and the underprivileged in general, whom they romanticized unconscionably, and America's affluent classes with all their Caribbean lackeys, whom they blanketly villainized as exemplars of "glittering swinishness."

In an introductory note to a small collection of essays that she published in 1936, Willa Cather observed, "The world broke in two in 1922 or thereabouts."[13] Whether or not the world as a whole broke in two in 1922, America did seem to split into two camps in the course of the 1920s.[14] In one camp clustered those who claimed to defend traditional values, persons who professed to see control and repression as essential ingredients of a Protestant ethic that had made the nation uniquely great, and who liked to ignore the degree to which prosperous, respectable, godly American capitalists had come to rely on the uncontrolled spending habits of a majority of citizens. In the other camp stood the proponents of alternative values,[15] who promised personal and national transcendence through liberation from the old restraints that, allegedly, had served the purposes only of the basest type of American, the single-minded pursuer of economic gain.

Calvin Coolidge, who succeeded to the presidency in 1923 on the death of Warren G. Harding, epitomized the first of the two Americas at its shallow worst. He believed that the relentless self-control that he identified as the underlying principle of Calvinist morality guaranteed its practitioners the maximum economic rewards; and beyond that, one need not worry, for outer success per se guaranteed the presence of inner virtue. Succeeding Coolidge in 1929, engineer-statesman Herbert Hoover represented the first of the two Americas at its idealistic best. Like Coolidge, Hoover believed in the need for self-control in the pursuit of individual economic security; and he saw American capitalism as an awesomely beneficent mechanism containing all needed self-correcting devices. But the economic rewards of capitalism he saw not so much as an end in themselves as

useful means to be employed in developing nobility of character, in tran-
scending mere greed and selfishness.

For Coolidge and maybe even more for engineer Herbert Hoover, the
compulsion for control over inner nature accompanied, perhaps helped to
father, an obsession with imposing rational domination over outer nature.
Appropriately, Coolidge and, much later, Hoover gave their names to two
of the great prodigies of dam building in American history. Moreover, the
first of these great dams, constructed between 1927 and 1928, inundated old
Indian burial grounds. What an appropriate symbol of all that Coolidge
and Hoover and most of their partisans believed the United States was all
about: the triumph of scientific civilization over nature and primitive
superstition.

In the 1920s, defenders of what they regarded as true Americanism not
only had to contend with remnants of the pre–World War I avant-garde
and with the Lost Generation that surfaced after the war; they also had to
deal with a new manifestation of "primitive superstition," one that fascinated many adversary-culture Americans: Soviet communism. More tenacious than expected, communism had refused to yield to the initial
onslaught directed against it as Woodrow Wilson's term expired. Paradoxically, defenders of capitalist America, basing their actions ostensibly on
principles of individual freedom, became the champions of repression,
while those who showed an opening toward communism, which in its
Leninist guise embraced totalitarian dictatorship, rallied around the cause
of freedom. Apparently neither side was altogether honest in its protesta-
tions. But there could be no doubt that the two sides stood in fundamental
disagreement. At the heart of their disagreement lay an issue that had divided mainstream and adversary-culture Americans even while they were
still British colonials: the proper relationship of civilization to nature, of
progress to primitivism. For mainstream Americans, the menace posed by
communism was simply a reappearance of the primitivism against which
right-thinking, civilized, and civilizing Americans had always had to
struggle.

Communism as the New Primitivism Sparks American Divisiveness

As the 1920s began, the Pueblo Indians were engaged in a determined
struggle to defend their communal landholdings—and with those holdings, their culture. Doggedly, they resisted the endeavor of civilized persons to seize their property and transform it into fee-simple holdings that
would yield profits to modern, progressive, and Caucasian Americans. In

total disregard of truth, leaders of the fight to dispossess the natives charged that Communist money from Moscow financed the Indians in their attempts to perpetuate primitive communism.[16] At the same time in New Mexico, "modern artists" appeared on the scene, challenging the accepted canons of traditional art by attempting to portray the raw nature that underlay surface appearances. They flouted the commonsense perceptions and perspectives and the positivism on which capitalist civilization rested. An outraged critic in Santa Fe asserted the "new school" in art had its roots in bolshevism: it epitomized a subversive attempt to unleash the dark realms of the animalistic unconscious that the armies of civilization had struggled for generations to repress. A few years later Senator George Dondero of Michigan accepted this line of reasoning when he flatly asserted, "Modern art equals Communism."[17]

Yet another reason underlay the tendency to equate certain schools of modern art with communist principles. In its abstractness much of modern art seemed linked to a primitive and therefore communalist view of humanity. Every person, it has been said, is in some ways like every other person, like some other persons, like no other person. Modern men and women, and perhaps Americans above all others, emphasize what makes one human unique from every other one. This is a manifestation of the stress that modernity places on individualism. Individualism dictates, above all else, that each person be clearly distinguished from all others. Primitives, according to stereotyping that happens in this instance to be more often right than wrong, stress communalism and concern themselves with the features that make each human very much like every other one within a particular community. Like communists, therefore, primitives ignore individualism. In their art, they tend to portray men and women in a generic or abstract style. They provide enough details to let the viewer perceive that a woman, or a man, or a child is portrayed, in painting or sculpture. But they do not provide enough detail to allow viewers to identify the subject as a particular, specific, individual man, woman, or child. And many modern abstract artists appearing on the scene in the first third of the twentieth century adopted a similar approach. In their abstract depictions, they seemed to suggest it was not individuality but common or communal humanity that mattered. Like primitive artists, therefore, they eschewed the individualism that lay at the heart of what most Americans regarded as true civilization; they were content to stop with nonindividuated human nature. They were, in the eyes of outraged defenders of capitalist civilization, Bolsheviks at heart, even if not card-carrying Communists.

Whether they knew it or not, America's defenders in the 1920s of modern, capitalist, individualistic civilization were the intellectual heirs of John Locke; for the English political philosopher had taught that civilization had arisen out of the human endeavor to subject the state-of-nature terrain held communally by primitive beings to private ownership. In the purview of early twentieth-century Americans, the primitives who still remained in the world inveterately clung to communal property. Ideologically, culturally, they were relatives to the Bolsheviks who though claiming to be "futurists" actually were "past-ists," to use the words Theodore Roosevelt had employed in critiquing modern art.

Little wonder that Americans out to convert native property in the Southwest into the privately owned estates of civilized white persons harped on the communist leanings of the Indians; and little wonder that American statesmen who wanted to make Mexico, Nicaragua, and the rest of Central America as well as the Caribbean safe for the civilizing principles of private property saw the advocacy of communal landownership by many south-of-the-border intellectuals and revolutionaries as a sure indication of communism. Furthermore, attitudes deeply imbedded through decades of stereotyping fed the conviction bursting into American national consciousness in the 1920s that Latins to the south and primitives in general inclined inherently toward communism—or, perhaps, as Americans came to fear in the 1930s, toward fascism with its inherent minimizing of the individual.

So, then, primitives in the modern world were, like modern artists, communists at heart. And for Caucasian Americans who prided themselves on the capitalist spirit that defined modernity, the primitive Other invariably bore a dark skin. It followed, in the strained logic of some defenders of American values, that forebearance toward mestizaje indicated a softness toward communism. Certain California defenders of civilized standards forthrightly proclaimed that tolerance of miscegenation suggested "communist inclinations."[18] A century earlier, an openness to miscegenation was thought to reveal an alarming readiness to revert to nature. Now, in the 1920s—and still in the 1960s and the 1990s, at least in some quarters—it revealed a leaning toward communism, for reversion to nature had come to be linked to communist predisposition.

New Questers after New Frontiers:
The Reemergence of a Counterculture

In the 1920s many of the intellectual heirs of the pre–World War I bohemians tended to give up on the possibility of reforming America. Some became expatriates and retreated into the sort of alcoholic escapism that Ernest Hemingway depicts in *The Sun Also Rises* (1926). Other exemplars of the Lost Generation remained in America and entered into the hedonistic, nihilistic spirit of what music critic, journalist, and novelist Carl Van Vechten has dubbed the "splendidly drunken twenties."[19] But, for other Americans dismayed by the status quo, escapism did not provide the answer. Those who had not abandoned hope in reform sometimes toyed with ideas of "being reborn into a new life." As historian Richard Pells writes, the ultimate appeal of communism to American intellectuals "lay in what it stood for psychologically and culturally." This added up to nothing less than death and rebirth, "the old world decaying as the new emerged in all its youthful strength."[20]

In a way communism could seem to be, as one of its American officials in the 1930s claimed it was, as American as apple pie. As interpreted by some counterculture figures, communism offered the newest twist on frontier mythology. A group of people not adequately understood or appreciated or rewarded by conventional society would plunge into a new domain that provided scope for the exercise of their particular talents and for the realization of their aspirations. Early pioneers had sought this domain in the wilderness. Their successors, now that the land frontier had closed, would find their Wild West in "the stink and sweat and obscene noises" of the masses.[21] Thereby they, like their nonconforming pioneer ancestors, would be remade. Unlike twentieth-century communists, however, frontier renegades of the previous century had not dreamed of destroying the civilization that had vexed them.

Counterculture and the Cult of the Natural

Not surprisingly, the cult of the child flourished among America's new pursuers of old dreams. African American writer Jean Toomer caught this spirit when he wrote: "I am satisfied that it is entirely possible to eradicate the false veneer of civilization, with its unnatural inhibitions, its selfishness, petty meanness and unnatural behavior, under proper conditions. Adults can be reeducated to become as natural as little children before civilization stamps out their true subconscious instincts."[22]

The vogue of the child in America's counterculture of the 1920s was nourished by adulation for the "Bambino" (lovable child, or babe), that wonderful overgrown boy "Babe" Ruth who played the great American game as it had never been played before. Theodore Roosevelt had been the archetypal man with a stick for Americans at the turn of the century. But the stick that he wielded (while speaking softly as befitted the well-born gentleman) was the rod with which to discipline recalcitrant children in the Caribbean and elsewhere. The big stick that the Bambino wielded was more a phallic symbol, proclaiming the need for uninhibited pleasure on the part of the perpetually childlike American hero. "His interest in sex seemed limitless," according to a cultural historian, "and he frequented the better brothels even while in training or on tour with the ball club. His gluttony became legendary. . . . Americans enjoyed the Babe's excesses; they took comfort in the life of apparently enormous pleasure Ruth enjoyed." [23]

Babe Ruth became a symbol that proclaimed to Americans they could have it all: they could combine opposites, they could go through life with childlike exuberance and fecklessness and still command astronomical salaries; they could succeed in capitalism's game while thumbing their noses at the moral restraints it had characteristically, and so often hypocritically, preached. The sense of fulfillment that John Reed had found in Pancho Villa, Americans in general found in Babe Ruth.

"The Ruth is mighty and shall prevail," Heywood Broun wrote in 1923. [24] Broun's words captured a part of the spirit of the 1920s, the spirit of rebellious counterculture America that laughed at the efforts of moralizing middle-class citizens to cut off the supply of alcohol so as to help their countrymen better control their passions. At times baseball's national hero became the living embodiment of the "splendidly drunken twenties." The Babe would prevail. And this meant that passions and enthusiasms would prevail, that the natural man would triumph over all the prudes who sought to civilize him. Respectable, traditional Americans liked to glorify the national pastime because ostensibly it placed a premium on refining basic, natural skills through incessant, devoted practice, because it held up to the unruly masses the example of respect for the umpire's authority. Baseball, seen from this angle, was a "manly" game that frowned on "boisterous displays of uncontrolled enthusiasm"; it was played by "manly men . . . [who] were self-controlled." [25] But Babe Ruth furnished a different angle. Seen from this new angle, baseball provided an American counterculture with vindication of its preferred life-styles.

The Bambino was Peter Pan, the boy who refused to grow up—slightly older, though, than Peter, past puberty and therefore sexually active. The fact that Americans idolized him in the 1920s suggests that many had grown tired of the old moralizing on the merits of civilization and the defects of the natural. [26] They rejected Calvin Coolidge's pronouncement that the business of America was business. It was also monkey business, as indulged in by those Americans who had managed to stay natural.

Along with the Babe and children, women—proverbial symbol to the male imagination of the natural that ordinarily requires repression—had a day of their own in the 1920s. Not only did women begin to make their way into man's workaday world,[27] but men began to wonder if it did not behoove them to become more like women—more like women as males stereotyped them: emotional, irrational, intuitive, passive, communalist, noncompetitive, and sharing. The flappers of the 1920s bobbed their hair, while men let theirs grow long. Some Americans, men and women, believed the age of androgyny had arrived. The vision that James Oppenheim had proclaimed in his 1910 epic drama *The Pioneers* seemed on the verge of fulfillment a decade or so later. According to Oppenheim, a new woman was rising, manly in her freedom and strength yet imbued with the grace and beauty of the eternal feminine. Only a new man would be worthy of mating with the new woman—a man as heroic as the old, yet distinguished also by "tenderness and emotion."[28]

Establishment-type Americans might have misgivings about the Bambino's uninhibited ways; and certainly they worried about the cult of the child, about the new permissiveness called "progressive education," about feminism and the feminization of manhood. But counterculture Americans, whether sincerely or merely hoping to attract attention, exuded enthusiasm for whatever symbolized the natural. They even went so far as to profess their love for Negroes. Counterculturalists further manifested their love of the natural by romanticizing and taking up the cause of American Indians and also of Latin America's masses. Among alienated Americans, close-to-nature stereotypes that mainstream citizens intended as pejorative attested to virtue.

Exploring the African American Frontier in the 1920s

White Americans, as already noted in chapter 3, have tended to look at blacks "in essentially two ways. Blacks are either children and loved, or beasts and hated."[29] In the 1920s the second approach remained much in evidence. A new Ku Klux Klan found white support in much of the country, and in some sections violence against Negroes remained endemic.[30] At the same time, however, the Negro became almost a cult figure for various whites who wanted to flaunt their contempt for the establishment, its values and its prejudices. One cultural historian perceives in the 1920s, both in England and in the United States, a "first wave" of white self-hatred accompanied by glorification of Negroes; the second wave arrived in the 1960s.[31]

Southern novelist William Faulkner in his remarkable works of the late 1920s and the 1930s inclined to praise "the quiet, enduring stoicism and wisdom of the heart" that distinguished Negroes and other socially marginal types,[32] juxtaposing their virtues with the vices of whites gone mad in their pursuit of private profit. Also associated with the vogue of the Negro was a tendency among whites at odds with capitalist values to see in African Americans a great wellspring of spirituality. In fact, white counterculturalists seemed in accord with the thesis advanced by W. E. B. Du Bois and with assumptions underlying the negritude movement that appeared among black intellectuals of the Caribbean region and French Africa. According to Du Bois and to various proponents of negritude, persons of African descent possessed greater spiritual resources than whites, whose racial drives focused more on external, commercial accomplishments. The tendency to give a racial and not just an economic or class content to the spiritual-superiority-of-the-downtrodden thesis had appeared previously in a vast variety of social reform thought; American critics of the capitalist status quo periodically singled out not only blacks but also Latin Americans as exemplars of the moral superiority of the economically disadvantaged. Specifically, the spiritual-superiority-of-blacks thesis harked back to the "romantic racialism" of the mid–nineteenth century and also looked ahead to the "second wave" of Negro modishness of the 1960s. At the same time, the romantic racialism flourishing in the 1920s tied in with the decade's cult of the child. "Innocence without artifice" ostensibly characterized both Negroes and children.[33] Negroes, children, and also women were perceived as innocents capable of freshening a corrupt civilization.

English author Wyndham Lewis regarded himself as a defender of the traditional values of Anglo Saxon civilization. He detested the glorification of "feminine" values preached by rebels against civilization on both sides of the Atlantic. Above all, he excoriated the interrelated cults of the Negro and the child. In a particularly vicious moment in 1929, he overtly expressed what many self-styled defenders of the values of Western civilization (some of whom, like Lewis, acquired fascist sympathies) only hinted at.

> Ah, if the White Mommer and Pop could only understand! As the Nigger understands! The Child is a thing that requires understanding! He is a wild, Rousseauesque thing, a fragment of wild Nature. He hates discipline! He wants to run wild! The Nigger is nearer to Nature: he understands the Child. *Up the Nigger! Down the White Mamma!* And especially *Down the White Papa!* . . . The Nigger and the Children are kindred souls—both are giggling, emotional—laughing and crying—Children of Nature. . . . Only the adult

White is no sport, is *against* Nature! It is he that has invented discipline!
Down with the White! Let children and Niggers, moist-eyed and hand in
hand, run wild and free! [34]

Despite Lewis and the generally more circumspect American writers who
shared his views, the vogue of the Negro continued to grow, especially in
New York and its environs where the Harlem Renaissance flourished.

According to Nathan Irvin Huggins, perhaps the most successful historian of the Harlem Renaissance, the Negro, after a history of being an out-
cast, "of being viewed with contempt or pity . . . was now courted and
cultivated by cultured whites. How grand it was to be valued not for what
one might become—the benevolent view of uplift—but for what was
thought to be one's essential self, one's Negro-ness." [35] But, who was the
"real" Negro for whom so many whites professed admiration during the
heady days of the Harlem Renaissance? Was the real Negro a Harvard
Ph.D. like W. E. B. Du Bois, a superb poet or singer-actor like, respectively, Langston Hughes and Paul Robeson, a talented novelist like Claude
McKay or Jean Toomer, a deeply probing painter like Aaron Douglas, a
"primitivist" dancer like Josephine Baker, who first achieved fame in Paris
as a bare-breasted dark femme fatale of the jungle who brought a charged
sexuality to her performances, or a superb musical innovator like Duke
Ellington whose "jungle music" set whites to dancing in both uptown and
downtown New York? Or, was the real Negro a dope-taking sex-craved
sociopath? Perhaps no white man did more than Carl Van Vechten to encourage Negro writers and to find publishers for their books and articles,
or to integrate social gatherings in New York City. Yet in his celebrated
novel *Nigger Heaven* (1926), black sociopaths sometimes seem the most
unforgettable characters.

"White men pretend to be black men of their fantasy," Huggins
writes. [36] Even during the Harlem Renaissance when, as Langston Hughes
observed, the Negro was in vogue, the black man of the white person's
fantasy generally was not the intellectual, artist, or writer but instead a
primitive or renegade from civilization of the sort encountered on a geographical frontier or within the psychic frontier of the id. Not only whites
but blacks as well sometimes contributed to the notion of Negroes as a
frontier people, primitives rooted in the earth, whether the earth lay without or within.

"Paradise," according to a historian who has studied American frontier
imagery, "may be conceived as a Rousseauistic state of nature, a millennial
situation, or a utopian community, and be located in the Fortune Islands,

Kentucky, or Polynesia." Psychologically considered, though, "it is simply a projected haven from the harsh demands of the social order and . . . an existence which . . . satisfies desires of every fundamental kind."[37] For Americans in the 1920s, the frontier paradise sometimes lay in the black belts of the South. Here, ostensibly, close-to-nature people lived happily "by following only their feelings and impulses, especially sexual." Here lived "'noble savages,' challenging by their very existence the values and systems" associated with civilization. As they fantasized about a new frontier in the South's black belt, some white Americans conjured up visions of a carnival atmosphere as "children of the sun, lovers of light and heat" entered the cotton fields "with shout and song and wild, barbaric mirth."[38] Even Jean Toomer, a light-complected black man who could and sometimes did "pass," seemed occasionally to deal in stereotypes in his best-known novel *Cane* (1923)—publication of which was arranged by Waldo Frank, whom we meet in this chapter's next-to-last section. In the opening chapter of *Cane*, Toomer evokes the sexuality, the natural, instinctual way of life, and the uninhibited emotionalism of black Georgia sharecroppers; and he suggests the degree to which his black protagonists have been shaped by the powers and rhythms of the natural environment of which they have become a projection.

For many Americans the new frontier lay not in the rural South but, unlikely though it might seem, in the urban North: in the Chicago southside and in the slums of Kansas City but above all in Harlem, "a cultural enclave that had magically survived the psychic fetters of Puritanism." Here, white Americans might seek revitalization. Questing after primitives in a frontier setting, white Americans could actually believe they flattered Negroes by stressing the primitivism of those Harlem "creatures who characteristically gave free rein to all their passions." Harlem offered disaffected whites "the means of soft rebellion," the possibility "to redefine themselves in more human and vital terms."[39] Harlem fulfilled the most deeply felt needs of a white counterculture, offering all that was forbidden by civilization's conventional moralists: a junglelike source of vitality where restraints could be discarded and lust freely sated.

Having discarded restraints and having experienced in Harlem the vitality of the uninhibited, ostensibly natural existence, the white new frontiersmen could return, even as Owen Wister's Virginian had returned, to the humdrum world of capitalist competition, with all the instincts that contributed to success in that world recharged by the temporary return to nature. Uptown and downtown New York; southside and northside Chicago: here are some of the sets of opposites, the symbols of nature and civilization that questing Americans always believed would provide wholeness if only they could combine them in just the right way. The frontier spirit still lived in America. And the object of its desire had a Latin as well as Negro tinge. Not only Harlem but also Havana and Tijuana appealed to Americans longing for exotic yet reasonably accessible oases of the primordial. Even closer to hand, and in many ways far more wholesome, were oases of Hispanic and Indian naturalness in the American Southwest.

Exploring America's Indian and Hispanic Frontiers in the 1920s

As they entered the 1920s, a good many U.S. Caucasians inclined to tar Negroes and Indians with the same brush, a fact attested to by a two-pronged offensive against African Americans and Native Americans that the Ku Klux Klan undertook in Oklahoma. Nevertheless, as with blacks, Indians in the 1920s found more and more defenders, even admirers and adulators, among Anglo Americans. And what proved significant about Oklahoma in that decade was not so much the crude and largely ineffectual attempts of the Klan to fan anti-Negro and anti-Indian sentiments as the pride with which many of the state's native sons and daughters pointed to Indian ancestry. The beloved cowboy comedian and social satirist Will Rogers, with his Cherokee blood, provides one of the best-known examples of an Oklahoman for whom prestige was augmented by Indian background.[40]

"If the history of Indian-White relations has been one of unending attempts to assimilate the Indians," writes a historian well known for his sympathies for the Native American, "it has also been one of continued struggles by the Indians to preserve their religious and spiritual unity and strength."[41] The statement overlooks the degree to which non-Indian American counterculturalists have steadfastly acted to defend Native Americans against assimilationist goals consistently advocated by the establishment. Almost as much as Indian resolve, survival of aboriginal cultures has depended on the determination of non-Indian Americans to preserve a way of life that they find enormously appealing.

In the first third of the twentieth century French intellectuals and artists discovered in African primitivism the necessary antidote to their culture's prevailing materialism. Many of their American counterparts found the antidote in the "exotic primitivism" and communalism of Indian life. The Indian stood for what the white man had "so long tried to prune out of his own culture," to that culture's eternal loss: "worshipful reverence for nature, acceptance of the body and the sensual appetites, and a subjugation of the individual for the good of the group." Poet William Carlos Williams was by no means alone in judging the life of the solitary American inferior to that of the communal Indian.[42] Moreover, just as some whites praised the superior spirituality of blacks, others enthused over the mysticism of red men and women, over their religious insights and wisdom that derived from extrarational means of perception, from visions and states of consciousness enhanced by meditation or by peyote.

Just as Wyndham Lewis had derided the cults of the black and the child among Caucasians who should have known better, so various Americans scorned compatriots who spewed forth "the mystical nonsense of God, the Indian and the good dark earth."[43] Above all, Ernest Hemingway, though not without his own penchant for primitivism, used his 1926 novel *The Torrents of Spring* to ridicule the notion of the Indian as the source of redemption to a society mired in rationalism and mechanism. In a travesty of some aspects of Pocahontas mythology, Hemingway introduces an Indian maiden who will restore Yogi Johnson, a Yankee who has become impotent while wandering in the Europe that epitomizes enervating civilization, to the full gamut of human pleasure. In reality, as Hemingway tells it, the Indian maiden who symbolically shouldered the responsibility of revitalizing American life was a smelly, besotted, venereal disease–ridden little whore.

Hemingway proved no more successful in reversing the 1920s romanticization of the Indian than Wyndham Lewis in eradicating the Negro and child cults. Toward the end of the decade yet another novel appeared that exemplified much of the sentimentalization of the noble red man and woman that Hemingway had parodied: Oliver La Farge's *Laughing Boy*. A real tearjerker in its defense of Indian culture against the crassness of the white man's civilization, *Laughing Boy* sounded a theme that Frank Waters developed effectively, and also sentimentally, in his widely read novel *The Man Who Killed the Deer*. Published in 1942, Waters's novel was virtually the last gasp of the Indian cult that had soared during the 1920s, and that would reemerge with the new counterculture of the 1960s. Appropriately, Waters dedicated his novel to Mabel and Tony. As much as any two figures in America, Mabel and Tony symbolized the tide of romantic Indianism that began in the 1920s to challenge conventional appraisals of the native.

Mabel we last encountered as Mabel Dodge, the lover of John Reed who presided over a lower Fifth Avenue salon that came to epitomize pre–World War I bohemian radicalism. Tony Lujan was the Taos Indian she married in 1923, after living with him for several years following her 1917 arrival in New Mexico, where she had rejoined her third husband, the Russian Jewish artist Maurice Sterne. Sometimes Mabel honored the conventions that at other times she flaunted, and so she married a fair number of her lovers. To Tony she remained relatively faithfully married, even after encountering the sting of the natural when she contracted syphilis from him. After her marriage to Tony, Mabel anglicized the spelling of her name, and so it became Luhan. Tony retained the traditional Lujan orthography.

Thirty-eight years old when she arrived in New Mexico, Mabel had become rather dumpy of figure. Her dark gray, often brooding eyes dominated a large oval face, topped by dark, bobbed hair with a bang descending halfway down the forehead. Rather than pretty, it was an interesting and expressive face. With some frequency it informed viewers that Mabel was in one of her sulks. Artists liked to render its portrait, but perhaps that was because Mabel rewarded them amply for their efforts. The wealth of the Buffalo family into which she was born as an only child generally proved adequate to indulge her free-spending ways—although beginning in the 1930s Mabel adapted gracefully to rather more straitened circumstances.

From 1917 onward, so far as Mabel was concerned the frontier that would produce the new America no longer existed in Greenwich Village but rather in New Mexico, and its headquarters was located some sixty miles north of Santa Fe in Taos, where eighty years or so earlier mountain men had traded with Indians and dallied with Hispanic women, whom they sometimes married. Even in the 1830s and 1840s, Taos had seemed to present the promise of a new race and culture based on an amalgamation of Anglos, Indians, and Hispanics. The time had come, Mabel believed, to realize that promise.

With her background in Greenwich Village radicalism, Mabel Luhan remained alive to the need to incorporate the Negro into the pool of primitivism that must act as an antidote to the evils of America's White Anglo Saxon Protestant civilization. At times she returned to New York. Guided by Carl Van Vechten and accompanied by an entourage that generally included the homosexual poet Witter Bynner whom she had persuaded to take up permanent residence in Taos, she and Tony would explore Harlem's hot spots, where Tony would sit in on drums with jazz combos. Around five in the morning she and her group would return downtown to the elegant Plaza Hotel on the southeastern rim of Central Park.[44] In all of this one encounters rich symbolism of the New America that would join opposites of almost every conceivable type.

Above all other places, though, it was Taos that interested and fascinated Mabel after 1917. Here she found the sort of refuge that artist Thomas Cole about a century earlier had discovered along the Hudson River: a haven from a rising tide of utilitarianism where, as Cole had put it, mankind could "preserve the germs of a future and purer system."[45] In 1822, some dozen years before Cole had looked hopefully to the Hudson

River oasis of pristine nature, gringo adventurer Thomas James had pronounced the current inhabitants of New Mexico unfit to measure up to the demands of civilization. The region from Taos southward, he maintained, could be improved only by Americans, in whose hands "the country . . . would bloom like a garden." Left to its present Indian and Hispanic occupants, the land would continue to languish in, at best, "a state of half wilderness–half cultivation."[46] For Mabel and for many of those she induced to follow her to New Mexico, the hope that the area held for present and future generations of Americans lay precisely in its long-demonstrated ability to keep modern civilization at bay.

For much of her life, as her most successful biographer puts the matter, Mabel had responded to "a Dionysian drive to experience and devour all forms of life, in her frantic search to connect with something larger than her solitary ego." Always in her incompleteness, she was seeking something new, something more. Now, in the land of the Pueblos, she found her antithesis, she found a culture "of timeless and stable values." She found also, so she thought, a model of integrated opposites. In Pueblo culture, so she believed, the personal and the communal fused; father sun and mother earth, the two cosmic dualities, came together and surrendered their separate identities. "The fact that Mabel rarely differentiated between male and female when she talked about the Pueblos was at least partly due to the essentially androgynous psychology she associated with them."[47]

For Mabel, aboriginal cosmic wisdom was confined largely to the Pueblos. However, in the cult of the Native American that flourished in the 1920s, many a questing American ascribed to different Indian groups the same qualities that Mabel associated with the Pueblos. In considering the love affair of an American counterculture with Indians, I focus on Mabel because she just might be the best archetypal figure of her era to illustrate the felt need for completion and fulfillment in the primitive that led so many of her compatriots to seek salvation in the mystical, intuitive wisdom not only of Indians but also of blacks, children, and Hispanics: in all those who, purportedly, remained unalienated from nature.

In the primitive Taos setting Mabel sought not the sort of social revolution that had concerned her while living on the East Coast but rather a personal, mystical rebirth into a life that more closely approximated completeness. However, at the beginning of the 1920s she had to put aside temporarily the quest for personal regeneration in her frontier oasis. She had to call into play all of her this-worldly organizational skills and all of her contacts in the New York cultural world as she responded to the challenge of saving the Pueblos from the intensified assault that Anglo civilization had launched against them.

In 1922 Senator Holmes O. Bursum of New Mexico introduced a bill, backed by Secretary of the Interior Albert B. Fall and Commissioner of Indian Affairs Charles Burke, that would have resulted—to begin with—in the transfer to Anglo Americans of some sixty thousand acres of land along the Rio Grande rightfully claimed by Pueblo communities and in some cases by Hispanic descendants of Spanish land grantees. The Indians and Hispanics, it seemed, were not fit owners, in part because of their communalist approaches to land use that smacked of communism. The opening salvo in a broad-ranging campaign of enforced assimilation that would deprive Indians and Hispanics not only of their land but their culture as well while at the same time enriching Anglo American ranchers and land speculators, the Bursum Bill might well have made its way quietly through Congress during the Warren G. Harding administration had it not been for a massive lobbying effort unleashed against it: an effort that marked the coming of age of America's Indian rights movement. The effort mobilized the Campfire Girls and Boy Scouts, a broad assortment of women's organizations, various pro-Indian groups that ranged the country from the East to the West Coast, and the Catholic Bureau of Missions whose work among the Pueblos might have come virtually to a standstill had the Indians lost their land. Intellectuals and artists—with John Sloan, onetime illustrator for *Masses,* and his wife Dolly playing particularly conspicuous roles—also joined in the campaign. In organizing the massive opposition to the Bursum Bill, Mabel Dodge Sterne (and about to be Luhan) played a significant role, drawing on old East Coast connections and enlisting new recruits as she went along. By 1922, though, principal leadership for the nationwide mobilization against the Bursum Bill and all that it portended in Anglo relations with the Other came from John Collier.[48]

Born in 1884 into an Atlanta family of some social prominence but declining economic security, Collier had graduated from Columbia University, after which he traveled in Europe where he discovered the writings of various utopian socialists. Back in America, he had become active in New York social work. Relaxation as well as intellectual stimulation he often found at the Mabel Dodge salon. Disillusioned by the tide of reaction that set in just after World War I, Collier, like so many radicals of the era, complained of "the fading away of practically all that I, we, all of us, had put all our being into." Having lost faith in "the 'occidental ethos and genius' as the hope of the world,"[49] Collier headed to California where he hoped to find an ambience still supportive of millennialist visions. When the Red Scare had spread to California, Collier soon aroused Justice Department suspicions because of lectures he presented on the Russian Revolution and the need for a spirit of communalism to mitigate American individualism. Resigning his position in the California adult education program, Collier at age thirty-six started for Mexico, where he hoped to discover in that country's revolution, so excoriated by his country's incumbent administration, the birth of a new social order. En route to Mexico he received an invitation from Mabel—whose invitations were often more like summonses—to join her and the various friends with whom she had already surrounded herself in Taos.[50]

Arriving in northern New Mexico in 1920, Collier at once came to admire the tribal Indians as much as he detested the one-dimensional, individualistic products of civilized modernity. Virtually overnight he came to see "the Indian as the last remnant of natural perfection, a model that must be preserved for human rejuvenation."[51] The Pueblos, he believed, were onto a secret that all Americans must discover: how to be "both communists and individualists at the same time."[52]

Tending at once to judge all Native Americans by the Pueblos (a tendency he never fully overcame), Collier decided that Anglo Americans could save their society only by adopting the Indian value system. Had he stayed in New York, Collier might have joined in a resurgent counterculture that viewed the Negro as the blessed Other who could redeem a decadent, moribund civilization. But, because he had gone west, he found the redeeming Other in the Indian. Just barely, owing to Mabel's intervention, Collier had failed to find the redeemer in Mexico. Nevertheless, he would soon thrill to the Mexican revolution's purported attempt to forge a new society on a foundation of Indian communalism—even though he deemed Mexican Indians inferior to his own country's Native Americans.[53]

Animated by a "growing sense of what he later called 'cosmic consciousness,' the sense of being a part of a great plan for the betterment of mankind,"[54] Collier quickly eclipsed Mabel and her writer-artist friends in mobilizing public opinion against the Bursum Bill. Owing largely to his efforts, the numerous groups that opposed the bill coalesced in 1923 in the American Indian Defense Association.[55] Victory came in March of that year when the bill failed to garner sufficient congressional support for enactment, as did a quickly concocted substitute bill. Disarray overtook the assimilationists and would-be land grabbers later in the year when involvement in scandals forced Fall to resign as secretary of the interior and started him on the road to prison. Nevertheless, Collier's work was just beginning, for Indian Affairs Commissioner Burke and his allies pushed on with the assault against Indian culture.

Despite the skills, power, and unscrupulousness of his foes, Collier fought the assimilationists to a standstill through the remainder of the 1920s. At one point in the struggle Collier, destined to become commissioner of Indian affairs in 1933 at the start of Franklin D. Roosevelt's New Deal, received assistance from a young attorney named Adolf A. Berle, Jr.—one of the persons cited in the previous chapter as exemplifying some of the traits of American Arielism. In 1918 Berle had undertaken a Caribbean mission for the War Department. Deeply impressed by both the poverty and nobility of spirit of Puerto Ricans, Dominicans, and Haitians, Berle soon concluded that U.S. intervention in the attempt to alter the culture of these people had a doubly negative effect: it undermined the moral integrity of the Caribbean natives and contributed at the same time to a loss of honor and decency among Americans bent on uplift. His perceptions already sharpened by observations of U.S. interventionist policies in its external empire, Berle saw mutual moral weakening as the inevitable result of Anglo America's attempt to uplift its internal colonials, the Indians. So, he enthusiastically lent his legal skills to the antiassimilationist struggle commanded by Collier. And while living in New Mexico, he entered happily into Mabel and Tony's circle of friends.[56]

Like Collier, Berle would serve Franklin Roosevelt's New Deal, but almost as often in unofficial as in official capacity. One of the architects of the noninterventionist approach of the New Deal's Latin American policy, Berle came to his convictions because of what he had observed of the disastrous consequences of American attempts to remold the customs and values of Caribbean natives and Native Americans. At times as a New Dealer he might accept intervention if security considerations seemed to dictate it, but throughout the 1920s and 1930s, he rejected it as a means of cultural uplift. Even as in the case of Collier, Berle had sharpened his dislike of forced assimilation of any and all alien groups by his observations of not only the moral smugness but also the moral sleaziness that often characterized the assimilationists.[57] In the past an interventionist Latin American policy had often grown out of the same sort of mind-set that produced crusades to Americanize the American Indians. In the 1920s in New Mexico a new policy of self-determination for Indians came into being, and it would contribute a decade later to a noninterventionist stance vis-à-vis Latin America.

In a publication of the 1930s, historian Herbert Eugene Bolton described the Spanish borderlands in general as "the meeting place and fusing place of two streams of European civilization, one coming from the south, the other from the north."[58] Well before the time Bolton wrote these words, Californians had in general become too caught up in the commercial spirit to pay attention to romantic notions of the meeting and fusing of cultures; what is more, the Hispanic-Indian presence had become no more than a drop in an Anglo American sea. Meanwhile, Texans remained by and large too mired in racist prejudice to enthuse over any notion of fusion. In contrast, in various cultural enclaves in New Mexico, people exemplified by Mabel Luhan and her friend Mary Austin, a fellow seeker of cosmic consciousness and admirer of primitive wisdom who settled permanently in Santa Fe in 1924, envisaged "the rise of a new and fruitful culture in the Southwest" as a result of the cross-fertilization not just of the two but of the three main streams: Spanish, Indian, and Anglo.[59] At last a vision not just of cultural but even of racial mestizaje found adherents in America. If ever the vision spread out beyond the confines of small counterculturalist enclaves, it held the promise of a whole new set of attitudes toward Latin Americans.

Altogether striking is the degree to which recently arrived Anglo women in New Mexico disseminated the message of the moral superiority of previously disparaged racial and social elements. Mabel Luhan, Mary Austin, and Willa Cather (whom Mabel befriended and lodged in Taos while she was writing *Death Comes for the Archbishop*) are but three among a group of remarkable women whom New Mexico inspired to take up the banners of "romantic racialism" first raised by women abolitionists beginning almost a century earlier. Moreover, a broad coalition of women's groups had played a conspicuous role in the nationwide Indian rights movement that had defeated the Bursum Bill and other schemes of forced assimilation hatched by Bureau of Indian Affairs bureaucrats. It was as if women in the 1920s realized, like their abolitionist forebears, that men would not accept the other sex in equality until they had been goaded into accepting the racial and cultural Other. Unquestionably, the role that women played in the struggle for Indian and Hispanic rights helped create the climate of opinion that in the coming decade contributed to the more tolerant American attitudes toward Latin Americans that underlay the Good Neighbor policy.

Somehow Mabel Luhan, the catalyst in the whole movement that developed in New Mexico in behalf of Indian and Hispanic rights and in pursuit of cultural mestizaje tied to mystical visions of a new humanity endowed with cosmic consciousness, seems to have remained curiously diffident about the role she assigned women. Perhaps this was because Mabel saw herself primarily as a muse. As such, she hoped to inspire men whom she deemed more talented than herself to enlighten others as to how they could experience—as she had—a spiritual rebirth that derived from the land and the ancient peoples of New Mexico. Above all others, the man Mabel hoped to inspire to tell the world about the return to origins that Taos promised decadent civilization was the British visionary writer D. H. Lawrence.

By dint of persuasion exercised through indefatigable, voluminous correspondence, Mabel had persuaded Lawrence to come to Taos early in the

1920s. But she failed to seduce him either physically (Lawrence's formidable wife Frieda proved too attentive, too jealous and possessive to permit that) or spiritually.[60] Lawrence liked Taos, so much so that both his and Frieda's cremated remains are buried on the ranch he acquired just outside the small community. Somehow, though, Lawrence seemed to feel that Taos was just too small a point in the universe from which to begin the regeneration of the world. He proceeded to Mexico and was fascinated by the return-to-nature mythos that he thought he discovered in its unfolding revolution. In Mexico he wrote *The Plumed Serpent,* the novel that Mabel had hoped he would write about New Mexico—in a way, New Mexico is lucky to have eluded the Luhan design. Published in 1926, *The Plumed Serpent* depicts the death of white civilization occurring in Mexico. Out of that death comes "a new germ, a conception of human life, that will arise from the fusion of the old blood-and-vertebrate [aboriginal] consciousness with the white man's present mental-spiritual consciousness. The sinking of both beings, into a new being."[61] Lawrence modeled Kate, the novel's heroine, partly on Mabel. But this is not necessarily a compliment, for Kate is by no means an altogether empathetic character.

John Collier had started for Mexico in search of the new order and the new humanity, but summoned by Mabel, he had found what he sought in New Mexico. Lawrence had been called to New Mexico to spread the news about the cradle of a new and better humanity. Unpersuaded, he had gone to Mexico and discovered, so he thought, the origins of a new mode of consciousness. And Englishman Lawrence's path was taken by many Americans who firmly believed that humanity's future had begun to emerge not in New but in Old Mexico. To Mexico came a substantial number of Americans discontented with their own country's established culture. As expatriates, they fashioned a way of life they firmly believed their stay-at-home compatriots would soon be driven to emulate. To the expatriates, New Mexico had, in many instances, provided an essential gateway; it was there that many of those who moved to Mexico during the 1920s had first experienced the lure of Indian and Hispanic culture. Only after this initial experience had they gone on to Mexico in quest of the origins of what had fascinated them in their own country's kernel of alternative life-styles.

Latin America's Lure as an Alternative and Complement to American Civilization

From Pennsylvania Avenue to Main Street, official and unofficial America joined in the early and mid-1920s to condemn the bolshevism and/or anarchism into which revolutionary Mexico purportedly was slipping. Developments across the border posed a direct threat to all the established values of civilization that Americans held dear; so, at least, national officeholders and countless chamber-of-commerce spokesmen proclaimed. Furthermore, at least until the mid-1920s when the Mexican government began to lodge effective complaints, Hollywood moviemakers delighted in portraying Mexicans as the stereotyped greaser: thievish, underhanded, vengeful, lascivious, and carousing.[62] If Hollywood bowed at least a bit to diplomatic pressure and cleaned up its depiction of Mexicans, mainstream American public opinion continued to see Mexico, Cuba, and much of the rest of Latin America for that matter as lands inhabited by deviates from the norms of moral conduct. When George Marvin reported in an article of the early 1920s published in *World's Work* that the killing of Mexicans by official and unofficial U.S. law enforcers along the border had reached "almost incredible" proportions,[63] many Americans shrugged their shoulders and concluded that no other means existed whereby respectable people living close to savagery could protect their virtue. How, after all, in an earlier age had decent Americans managed to protect civilization except through occasional Indian massacres?

Americans repelled by normalcy and chamber-of-commerce moralizing took an altogether different view of the scene to the south. In segments of the counterculture the old millennialism that had flourished at various times in the previous century surfaced anew; only now the millennium would be achieved not in rural America, through the union of men and women with nature, but rather in Mexico, with Indian agrarian communities providing the basic building blocks for an ideal society.

In the eyes of their American admirers, the Mexican revolutionaries who had risen up to challenge the corrupt capitalism that Porfirio Díaz and his Yankee collaborators had imposed on the country seemed a "vivid, passionate, and spontaneous people, not acquisitive but endowed with a great capacity to enjoy the moment, communal in their use of land, responsive to arts, and devoted to gracious customs and impressive rituals which derive from ancient traditions." For counterculture writers of the 1920s, the noble Mexican had replaced the "backward, unmechanical, dirty, lazy, savage, and superstitious" semihumans depicted by the novelists and chroniclers who had created the stereotypes that nourished earlier generations of Americans.[64]

Not all Americans would settle for observing the birth of a new order from their side of the border. In considerable numbers, *norteamericanos* flocked to Mexico either as tourists or as long-term expatriates. Members of the Lost Generation who had abandoned hope for the human condition frequently led the expatriate life in Paris; those still fraught with hope often made their way to Mexico, either for brief journeys or to settle down for extended periods. Not only drifters but also writers, intellectuals, and artists figured prominently among those seeking in-depth exposure to Mexico.

Some of the newly arrived expatriates came upon a longtime settler in Mexico, the father of Langston Hughes. He had been living in the country well before it became fashionable to do so. Mexico he prized as affording an escape not only from a bad marriage but also from the color line that had defined the sphere permitted to him north of the border. Langston Hughes himself spent a winter in Mexico and formed friendships with many of the country's muralist artists as well as its writers and musicians. Providing a link between the Harlem Renaissance and what some Americans perceived as civilization's rebirth in Mexico, Hughes felt uplifted by his winter visit. He discovered an affinity for Latin Americans and for the Spanish language. The nearest he ever came to leading "*la vie de Boheme,*" he confided in his autobiography, was during his time in Mexico.[65]

U.S. ambassador to Mexico James R. Sheffield (1924–1927) feared that gushingly enthusiastic American visitors to Mexico, among them clergymen, intellectuals, and artists, some of them allegedly in the pay of the Mexican government, were spreading false impressions about the country and stiffening its resolve to resist Washington's efforts to make it deal reasonably with Yankee capitalists. Some of the visitors and expatriates spread not only anti-American but also procommunist ideas, he alleged.[66] Moreover, the State Department seemed especially perturbed by the alleged communist leanings of American Jewish intellectuals who came to Mexico in the mid-1920s and praised every aspect of the revolution. Actually, the real connection between American expatriate praise for the revolution and communist sympathies and even Communist party affiliation came about mainly in the 1930s, when "Shoals of refugees" from the depression flocked to Mexico as "the New Land of Promise."[67] By then many American intellectuals, convinced that the depression heralded capitalism's demise, had indeed taken up with communism; and into the ongoing Mexican revolution they hopefully read a communist essence.

Whether communist sympathizers or not, Americans in the 1920s and 1930s who traveled and lived in Mexico often praised that country's revolution in the same terms used by fellow citizens who visited Russia and fell under the spell of the real communist revolution. Some American travelers believed that in the USSR they had discovered people "untrammeled by convention," "childlike and wise," "frank, gay, hospitable"; people who had an "organic" relationship to nature, who occupied a "homogeneous world," all its parts "in organic rhythm"; people who revealed "elements of the Noble Savage" and embodied the qualities of the "Powerful Proletarian, the Earthy Peasant, the Happy Poor," and provided "a glimmer of the Renaissance Man of Utopia."[68] Apparently, defenders of American establishment values have not always misread the situation when they perceive a connection between those who lean toward primitivism of various sorts and those likely to be tempted by what they perceive as the communist vision.

One of the Americans who after residing for a time in Mexico bestowed the most lavish praise on the country was neither a Communist nor a consistent fellow traveler. Exceptionally naive, however, he was, and also thoroughly disillusioned in his own country's capitalism. The very embodiment of the fraught-with-hope mind-set of counterculturalists in the 1920s and especially the early 1930s, economist Stuart Chase published *Mexico: A Study of Two Countries* in mid-1931.[69] Based on a five-month stay in Mexico the previous year, Chase's book, a Literary Guild selection, enjoyed bestseller status for six months after its publication. Chase employed as his "major thematic device a comparison of Middletown [as depicted by sociologists Helen Lynd and Robert Lynd, and actually a description of Muncie, Indiana] with the village of Tepoztlán, which had recently been studied by anthropologist Robert Redfield and which Chase found to be 'still following the leisurely patterns of the handicraft age.'"[70] "Mexico," Chase enthused, "takes no back talk from clocks." Addressing the occupants of Middletown, U.S.A., he admonished, "It is an art which you too some day must learn; for it is the art of living." In Tepoztlán, the people "take their fun as they take their food, part and parcel of the organic life." In contrast to Middletowners, "they are not driven to play by boredom; they are not organized into recreation by strenuous young men and women with badges on their arms and community chests behind them." To the Mexicans, play comes naturally; it bubbles up out of lives that are unalienated. Unlike Middletown where the gospel is work, "the gospel of Tepoztlán is play," Chase enthused. Reversing the sanctimonious condemnations with which typical nineteenth-century Yankee travelers had responded to the fiesta system, Chase enthused: "One day in three, the year around, the southern community is celebrating a major or minor fiesta." Moreover, "flowers are more important to Mexicans than are motor cars, radios, and bathrooms combined, to Americans."[71] Chase's romanticism appealed to many Americans perhaps hoping themselves, in the throes of the depression, to learn how to derive satisfaction from flowers now that automobiles increasingly seemed beyond their reach.

Shaping his ideas against the backdrop of the Great Depression, Chase believed that mass industrialism was not inevitable for Mexico, and that it could be reversed even in the United States. "The future for industrialism in the sense of mass production is not rosy, for which we can thank whatever gods there be. As a result Mexico has an unparalleled opportunity to evolve a master plan whereby the machine is admitted only on good behavior." What a heady picture for Americans disillusioned by their country's civilization: the machine on good behavior, not threatening nature with oblivion. Predictably, given the nature of American millennialist thought through the decades, Chase urged a combination, a synthesis, a fusion of the ways of Tepoztlán and Middletown. Let the Mexican village preserve "all that is rich, beautiful and useful" in its Indian traditions but at the same time absorb "all that can be used of the new and modern in science" and medicine. Meantime, let Middletowners cling to modern inventions but learn to cherish their soil, nourish their group life and warm to the beauty of arts and crafts rather than coveting surfeits of mass-produced products.[72]

To the delight of America's counterculturalists, the revolutionary spark that promised hemispheric renewal seemed to be spreading beyond Mexico in the latter part of the 1920s and the early 1930s. In Nicaragua, Augusto César Sandino staged a revolution against an established order that the United States had propped up by one means or another since early in the century. As the ideological basis for the revolution he initiated in 1927, Sandino drew on influences that included theosophy, Freemasonry, and the "Magnetic-Spiritual School,"[73] though the State Department quite mistakenly saw a Bolshevik push behind his movement. Having first sought tomorrow's utopian order in Mexico, journalist Carleton Beals now went to Nicaragua, interviewed Sandino even as he was chased by the U.S. Marines, and—much in the manner of Herbert Matthews reporting some thirty years later in the *New York Times* to Americans on the heroic qualities of Cuba's Fidel Castro—depicted the guerrilla chieftain as the savior of his country.[74]

By the beginning of the 1930s, Beals and other American writers counting on a revolution that would revitalize America's "botched civilization"— "an old bitch gone in the teeth," as Ezra Pound described it—suspected that Peru might provide the spark of renewal.[75] There, so they believed, the Incas were awakening from the long sleep into which Spanish conquest had plunged them. Like Mexico's Aztecs and Nicaragua's mixed-bloods, they had begun to stir. From Peru the young Víctor Raúl Haya de la Torre, under the influence of various spiritualist theories that posited the imminent arrival of an age of Aquarius,[76] proclaimed a revolutionary movement that would liberate all the oppressed people of Latin America—

he preferred to call it Indo-America, because he saw its true identity as rooted in indigenous traditions, values, and character. Not surprisingly, given his faith in a dialectic that derived as much from Heracleitus as from Marx by way of Hegel, Haya de la Torre foresaw the emergence of an Indo-American civilization based on synthesis of Indian and Caucasian cultures. To him, the Indian was the archetypal Other with whom the New World's white populace must somehow fuse. To the select circle of Mexico's revolutionary prophets and to Nicaragua's Sandino, Beals and other American believers in an imminent re-creation of their hemisphere added Haya de la Torre (although Beals worried about his fascist leanings); they also added Peru's Marxist-inspired philosopher-journalist José Carlos Mariátegui, a formidable mystagogue in his own right, in some of whose theories Peru's fanatical *sendero luminoso* revolutionary guerrillas of the 1980s and 1990s claimed to find inspiration.

To Americans possessed of boundless capacity to believe in delusions, a capacity that at times seems a national trait, it appeared that from Harlem and Taos down through Mexico and Nicaragua and all the way to Cuzco and Lima a new hemisphere was in the making. In the Old World the West might be in decline, as Oswald Spengler had proclaimed in the mid-1920s. But in the New World, primitivism and modernity would join to produce humanity's finest moment. Such at least was the faith that inspired many counterculturalists. Preeminent among those who held to the new but really very old faith stood Waldo Frank. Through his adaptation of a civilization-nature mythology deeply embedded in America's dissident tradition, Frank issued a new challenge to what may well be the American establishment's preeminent myth: the rise of civilization through progressive assertion of mastery over nature.

Variations on Arielism Challenged by Waldo Frank's Variations on Modernism

Of the American establishment's preeminent myth purporting to define the proper relationship between civilization and nature, no higher-minded or more influential advocate existed than Henry L. Stimson, secretary of state for Republican Herbert Hoover and later secretary of war for Democrat Franklin D. Roosevelt.[77] Almost as avid a hunter as Theodore Roosevelt had been, Stimson turned his own Long Island estate into a virtual hunting club for himself and a few elite friends. In addition he made frequent excursions into untamed fields abroad, where he not only hunted but also came into contact with people he deemed wild and primitive. Typically racist in his reaction to such people, Stimson tended to look down on them and yet also to hope—like John Updike's previously cited "good-hearted imperialist racists"—that they, the primitives, could be uplifted by civilization's emissaries. So, then, at the same time Stimson asserted civilization's right to destroy nature, a deed that was ritualized and even sacralized in the hunting rite, he also recognized civilization's duty to improve nature by, among other things, befriending and elevating primitives. In this latter respect, Stimson harked back to the late nineteenth-century "Friends of the American Indian" and other affluent and "benevolent" assimilationists.

As an aristocratic hunter who felt bound in conscience to extend the tutelary hand to humans not yet fully bathed by the light of civilization, Stimson stood in the tradition of James Fenimore Cooper's fictional creation Judge Temple, mentioned in the preceding chapter in connection with Theodore Roosevelt's quest for regeneration in the Dakota Territory. Even more than Natty Bumppo or the noble Indian Chingachgook, Judge Temple is Cooper's hero. Engaged in transforming wild land into the settlement of Templeton, he recognized hunting as an act preparatory to the spread of civilization. To Stimson a century later, hunting remained symbolically associated with civilization's dissemination. Moreover, both to the well-to-do Judge Temple and to the affluent Stimson, it seemed axiomatic that the dedicated, devoted practice of capitalism brought with it not only material but—what was more important—individual moral development as well as the ongoing purification of political processes. On its acolytes capitalism also bestowed the wealth that facilitated the private pursuit of cultural refinement. By the time of Stimson, moreover, capitalism bestowed social blessings on a scope that Judge Temple could scarcely have foreseen. It rewarded its practitioners with the kind of resources that enabled them to support museums, libraries, schools, and universities as well as churches and charitable institutions that mitigated the hardships of the deserving poor. Truly, all good things came packaged together in the right kind of civilization.

Already the civilizing process that produced superior, beneficent beings in America was beginning to function, so Stimson believed, in Latin America. This process must be encouraged, from the north, so that soon there would be more elites to the south in whom America's better elements could recognize kindred souls. Thus Stimson aligned himself with a capitalist variation of Arielist mythology, the original form of which was described in the preceding chapter. On the other hand, Waldo Frank identified with the radical modernism embraced by America's counterculture in the pre–World War I era. In almost every respect, he challenged the establishment's vision of capitalist civilization's interrelated blessings.

For Frank and like-minded thinkers, capitalism, rather than offering the means whereby humanity might rise morally and materially above its primitive origins, was inherently corrupt and corrupting. Frank envisaged the good society as one based on a union of those who had remained pure and undefiled by functioning at levels both above and beneath capitalism: a union of economically disinterested intellectuals with the masses, supposedly not yet hopelessly polluted by material greed. Culture and nature would come together to create a new kind of civilization in which undefiled, natural, primitive elements remained a vital ingredient.

In the era of the Great Depression when capitalism lay in shambles and Americans could no longer assume the interconnectedness and interdependence of private morality, civic virtue, public culture, individual prosperity, and national well-being, the myth that drove Frank attracted a growing mass of Americans. But, his anticapitalist mythos was destined to wither with the eventual return of prosperity, even though elements of it resurfaced in the counterculture of the 1960s and found their way into that decade's new approach to Latin American policy, the Alliance for Progress. But this is to get ahead of the story.

The possessor of a portentous, overblown writing style well suited to his inflated vision of himself as the prophet of a new American civilization, Waldo Frank, after attracting considerable attention with his novel *Our America* (1919),[78] never quite made it into the literary big time, except in Latin America. Again, though, that is getting ahead of the story; for Frank did not seriously turn his attention southward until 1929. Prior to then, he had built his literary reputation in America on his ability to articulate many of the ideas loosely blowing in the countercultural breezes of the 1920s.[79]

Born in 1889 into a Jewish family with keen literary, artistic, and musical interests (his mother was a musician who helped oversee her son's training as a cellist), Frank graduated from Yale in 1911. After an extended European tour he began work as a journalist and free-lance writer. In 1916 he collaborated with Van Wyck Brooks and Randolph Bourne in founding the review *The Seven Arts* and married Margaret Naumburg who, like Frank, was deeply interested in Thoreau and Whitman, Oriental religion, and the new theories of psychoanalysis. Already in 1919 when he published *Our America,* Frank had turned to mysticism and a study of medieval cabalists as he sought to come to grips with his Jewish heritage. Intrigued by the possibility that his generation was on the threshold of attaining a "four-dimensional" consciousness that would free it from conventional space-time limitations (some of the language of Albert Einstein was in the air, even if its meaning escaped most who used it), Frank contended that he and his contemporaries had started in quest of a new America, and that "in seeking we create her."[80] A good number of counterculture intellectuals, many of them fascinated by aspects of esoteric thought and bits and snatches of quantum mechanics, shared Frank's millennialist optimism. As the 1920s advanced he acquired at least a fringe position among his country's best-known visionary writers, critics, and art-world figures.

Many of Frank's ideas grew out of an American cultural heritage of dissent, stretching back to colonial times, that questioned the connection between human fulfillment and economic success. In the second half of the nineteenth century, Walt Whitman had articulated better than anyone else certain aspects of that heritage. Whitman insisted that Americans, having accomplished the economic development of their continent, must transcend their material feats by fulfilling their spiritual and aesthetic potential. Influenced by the Orientalism common in his day, Whitman believed that only by returning to Western civilization's nest of origins in the East could Americans tap into the wellsprings of inward, spiritual, intuitive, extrarational resources that would enable them to fashion a rounded and whole mode of human existence. He also believed that in order to realize their full capacities, Americans had to synthesize into their lives some of the values of indigenous people and also of the Hispanic settlers of the Southwest. The legacy of these settlers he saw as a subterranean river that, "dipping invisibly for a hundred or two years, is now to emerge in broadest flow and permanent action." The reemerging river is, of course, a symbol of rebirth. And Whitman implied that American civilization would be reborn once cleansed of obsessive materialism by submerged cultural resources now beginning to resurface.[81]

To the Whitman influence on his vision of America's future, Frank added a perspective deriving from his Jewish origins. Throughout much of the Western world at the turn of the twentieth century, Jewish thinkers had emerged as defenders of virtually all pariahs, in part because in defending pariahs they defended themselves and, so they hoped, advanced the day of their full acceptance by the societies in which they lived. Frank had witnessed the degree to which many Jews had scored financial success in the United States but had nevertheless failed to gain social acceptance. They had played the game according to the rules of the capitalist setting in which they operated and they had triumphed; but still they faced social rejection. Like Indians before them who had assimilated the values of mainstream culture but still met rebuff, American Jewish thinkers in frustration disavowed that culture. While frustrated Indians had retreated back into their traditional values and withdrawn from Anglo American life, many Jews, drawing on their richer cultural heritage derived from both East and West, dreamed instead of remaking America's mainstream life. Like Whitman, they thought the time had come to transcend the values of materialism, now that Americans had built the economic foundations capable of supporting the rich cultural life that persons more nobly endowed than mere moneygrubbers stood ready to create.

In line with Whitman, with D. H. Lawrence and also Mabel Luhan and her coterie of intimates in Taos, and also with leaders both black and white of the Harlem Renaissance, Frank believed that authentic cultures must originate in people who had remained in contact with the telluric forces of the environment and also with inward psychic nature. Because Americans had for generations consciously sought to divorce themselves from nature, to dominate its forces and obliterate its vitality, they had cut themselves off from those very origins to which they must return in the quest for a fuller existence. In the coming quest, Americans might need to have recourse to Jewish mediation, for Jews, many of them still close to their rural roots in the Old World and also especially attuned to the inward realm of the psyche (having, after all, virtually just invented psychiatry and psychoanalysis), were ideal mediators between the spheres of civilization and nature. Just as such black musicians as Duke Ellington and Louis Armstrong seemed at first to require the services of Jewish agents to mediate between them and the capitalist world so that their revitalizing, primitive art might enrich mainstream culture, so Indians and Hispanics might require the mediation of Jews in order to fulfill their potential for recharging and respiritualizing a tired civilization.

In gaining mastery over nature Americans had at least developed to the fullest degree their masculine traits. They needed now to wed themselves, culturally, spiritually, and aesthetically, to "feminine" people closer to nature and therefore closer to divine wisdom. In this conviction, Frank may well have been influenced by strains of mysticism and spiritualism that harked back to the cabala, with its concept of the Shechinah as the feminine aspect of God. According to cabalist myth, the Shechinah had at one point been alienated from the godhead. Ultimately, through a *coniunctio,* or sacred marriage, God would be reunited with the feminine principle, embodied in or at least symbolized by the chosen people in exile, the Israelites.[82] However much Frank may or may not have been influenced by the cabala, he did feel a desire for union—for his fulfillment as well as theirs—with abused and suffering workers, ostensibly longing for spiritual succor as much as higher wages. This desire drove him—as it did many Jewish intellectuals of the era—toward communism, into which they read mystical concepts of wholeness and fulfillment that would no doubt have amused most party leaders in the USSR.

Waldo Frank's mystical vision had roots also in nineteenth-century American culture. A formula for some of that century's fiction derived from the vision of a materialistic, domineering, masculine Yankee culture fusing with the spiritual, innocent, feminine South.[83] At the time of the

Harlem Renaissance, the supposed traits of the South had been projected onto the Negro. Negro innocence ostensibly derived from rejection of the materialistic scramble that set the tone of capitalist civilization. Similarly, woman's "spiritual superiority," her tender, caring qualities, her mystical, intuitive powers had often been associated with the rejection of competitive and individualistic materialism. Waldo Frank's friend and collaborator Van Wyck Brooks figured among counterculturalists who in the 1920s hoped for a reconciliation between the basic antipodes of American life: "masculine" business and "feminine" culture.[84] Frank's contribution to the history of American culture was to provide a hemispheric perspective to long-established traditions of seeking wholeness in the merging of North and South, white and black, masculine and feminine opposites—in short, of civilization and nature. Perhaps he felt that he and other Jews, often stereotyped and perhaps sometimes perceiving themselves as androgynous beings, had a special mission to bring about the hemispheric coniunctio that would result in integrated persons of the sort that "third-sex," or homosexual, Walt Whitman had once described:

> I am old and young, of the foolish as much as the wise,
> Regardless of others, ever regardful of others,
> Maternal as well as paternal, a child as well as a man,
> Stuff'd with the stuff that is coarse and stuff'd with the stuff
> that is fine. . . .
> A Southerner soon as a Northerner . . . [85]

For Waldo Frank, North and white and masculine coalesced in the typical American, while South and black and feminine came together in the Latin American. His prophetic mission, he came to believe, was to unite the intellectuals and artists of North and South America so that they could provide the wisdom and leadership necessary to forge an integrated hemispheric culture, in the process establishing new, largely spiritual ties with the downtrodden. On their own, North America's cultural elites lacked the power to challenge the materialism of the business culture and to feminize the land. Buttressed by an alliance with Latin American cultural elites, however, the American intelligentsia could help their countrymen transcend the materialism of the business society and fulfill Whitman's vision of a cultural superstructure atop a solid economic base. Furthermore, with American intellectuals acting as a conduit to pass along to them, in controlled and attenuated doses, America's passion for material development, Latin Americans would learn how to build an adequate infrastructure to sustain an admirable spiritual culture that had grown out of an almost pagan regard for nature.[86] United from north to south, the New World's creative minorities could accomplish a deeper synthesis of humanity than the world had ever known.

It was in Taos that Waldo Frank first intuited the importance of Ibero to Anglo America. In northern New Mexico he came upon people he persuaded himself were not psychically alienated, because their conscious and subliminal selves fused into a whole. He found also—even as Mabel Luhan and many of those she attracted to the area thought they had found—a people who lived harmoniously rather than in an adversarial relationship with the physical environment, a people in tune with the cosmos. Like Whitman before him, Frank deduced that this mode of existence arose as much out of the Southwest's Hispanic as its Indian heritage. Seeking verification of this insight Frank went to Spain, and he fell in love with the mystical, traditional, unalienated life-style he convinced himself he had found there. Returning home in a state of spiritual excitement, he published *Virgin Spain* in 1926. Shortly translated into Spanish, this book helped make Frank's reputation in both Spain and Spanish America. Anxious to verify the presence of a mystical, intuitive, inward sensitivity resulting from its Hispanic and Indian legacies (and not averse to reaping some economic gain from his new fame in the Spanish-speaking world), Frank undertook a Latin American lecture tour in 1929.[87]

Speaking in Spanish before large and enthusiastic audiences in such centers as Mexico City, Buenos Aires, and Lima, Frank evoked an almost frenzied response from many Spanish American intellectuals—as he claimed also to have evoked from a beguiling daughter of nature he chanced upon in a Brazilian town during a later tour and whose coupling with him he saw as a deeply symbolical act.[88] Frank's success as an orator during the 1929 tour, certainly not facilitated by his high-pitched and rather unpleasant speaking voice,[89] resulted from telling audiences what they wanted to hear. Instead of chiding Spanish Americans for their economic backwardness and challenging them to uplift themselves by emulating their advanced northern neighbors, Frank praised the southern continent's intellectuals for their mystical sensitivity and spoke of their destiny to help redeem the spiritually starved United States and thereby initiate a process of "re-creation."[90] Only through a re-creation whose ultimate product would be "new men" could America become a New World "rather than 'the grave of Europe.'"[91] Realization of the American hemisphere's potential for re-creation depended upon the two "half-worlds" becoming "one mystical organic whole, existing in harmony and combining the best qualities of the materialistic North and the spiritual South."[92]

Here was a message that appealed to the leaders of what in the 1920s had emerged as Latin America's most striking intellectual phenomenon: the university reform movement that dedicated itself—among other objectives—to saving the southern continent's spirituality from the one-dimensional materialism allegedly spawned by Yankee cultural imperialism. Both Waldo Frank's ideology and that of the university reform movement emerged out of one aspect of radical modernism: the desire to place power in the hands of the best persons, with best being defined by spiritual, cultural, aesthetic gifts—not by marketplace skills. At the same time, Frank's ideology and that of the university reform movement shared in the Arielist credo, to which Henry L. Stimson in his own way subscribed. However, Frank and his Latin American counterparts rejected the Stimson variation on Arielism, introduced at the beginning of this section. According to that variation, which harked back to the Protestant ethic and to the aristocratic tradition that so appealed to Theodore Roosevelt, the best men and therefore those most fully entitled to govern were precisely those persons most likely to profit in the marketplace and, having profited, to proceed to the altruism that would bring to the noblesse oblige tradition its finest hour.

Waldo Frank's and the Latin American university reformers' cautious and inconsistent dalliance with Marxist mythology provided a fundamental point of disagreement with America's aristocratic tradition. In its vision of a new and perfect social order liberated from the individualistic pursuit of wealth, Marxism denies the compatibility of capitalist competitiveness with altruism, and with high-mindedness in general.

Even more than Marxism, frontier mythology provided an unbreachable wall between the hemispheric hopes and aspirations of Waldo Frank on one hand and Henry Stimson on the other. Harping on re-creation, Frank propounded a new version of frontier mythology. He envisioned Latin America as a permanent frontier, a place where pristine nature and the primitive virtues of disinterestedness and community would exist in perpetuity to refresh and renew, balance and complement America's individualistic and materialistic civilization. Stimson, on the other hand, as Judge Temple's latter-day incarnation, calmly accepted primitivism's inevitable disappearance in its encounter with civilization—even if civilized Americans in their frontier to the south had occasionally to allow primitives like Sandino to slow and interrupt the inevitable process.

Waldo Frank, Franz Boas, and the Background to the Good Neighbor Policy

In his native country Waldo Frank never fulfilled the expectations aroused by some of his early publications. Nevertheless, for some fifteen to twenty years beginning around 1930 he reigned as the best-known contemporary

American author in the Spanish-speaking world.[93] The opinions that many Latin American intellectuals formed of the United States in the years just prior to and continuing on to nearly the end of the Good Neighbor era in the mid-1940s derived to some considerable extent from Waldo Frank— from his books and his lecture tours, from what journalists reported about those books and tours, and from the wide circle of influential friends that he cultivated in Latin America.[94]

Toward the end of the nineteenth century ambitious Latin Americans intent on amassing greater wealth had welcomed Yankee capitalists and collaborated with them, hoping to utilize external connections in fulfilling their material aspirations. In the 1930s, Latin American intellectuals striving for the recognition and perhaps ultimately the political power they thought their due saw in Waldo Frank the promise of new connections with the north that would serve their quest for status. Mistaking their wishes for reality, they accepted Frank at his own evaluation: as the spokesman for an emerging United States that would collaborate not with Latin America's on-the-make lackeys of Yankee corporations but rather with those exalted beings who by dint of superior culture, virtue, and wisdom deserved to preside over their nations' destinies.

Because they misperceived Frank's message as a genuine indicator of the thrust of the Good Neighbor policy, various sectors of Latin America's intelligentsia at first waxed unduly optimistic about what that policy portended in the way of revised hemispheric relations. Ultimately, the intellectuals turned indignant when their false expectations were not fulfilled. Their indignation came about because the prophet they had relied upon to explain the new American mind-set turned out in the end to be, however unwittingly, little more than a confidence man. Ultimately, in their outraged reaction, Latin Americans would turn not so much against Frank himself as against the United States in general.

For a brief moment in the early 1930s, though, the influence that Waldo Frank exercised in Latin America contributed to the Good Neighbor policy's auspicious beginnings. So, too, did the abandonment of conventional, mainstream American efforts to uplift Latin Americans—the topic that leads off the following chapter. Also contributing to the Good Neighbor era's promising inception was the cultural pluralism credo through which Jewish immigrant Franz Boas and various colleagues began to challenge mainstream racist assumptions early in the twentieth century—the second topic in the next chapter. Even more than Frank, Boas leads one to the conclusion that the background to the Good Neighbor era owed a great deal to the rising importance of Jewish intellectuals in the United States and to the messianic mood that many of them revealed in the first third of the twentieth century. As their world and lives collapsed in Europe and as Zionist hopes for a homeland in the Middle East crumbled, they turned to the New World with millennialist expectations. However, as the next chapter makes clear, Jewish thinkers by no means could claim a monopoly on exaggerated hopes about the New World's coming utopia.

CHAPTER 8

The Quest for Equilibrium with Nature: The Good Neighbor Policy, 1933–1945

The Failure of Uplift

"To be good is noble, but to show others how to be good is nobler and no trouble."

—Mark Twain

Writing in a 1911 issue of *The Review of Reviews,* A. W. Dunn exuded confidence in the ability of Americans to uplift the people of Central America and the Caribbean, even though uplift would necessitate expensive armed intervention and occupations. The expense would represent money well spent. Soon the natives would see "that prosperity follows peace; that there is more profit in tranquility than revolution; that a government supported by the United States must be honestly conducted."[1]

Confidence in the feasibility of uplift remained strong among American statesmen as the 1920s began. Soon the forces that occupied the Dominican Republic and Haiti and sporadically took over parts of Nicaragua would transform those chronically disturbed areas, introducing order and stability of such enviable dimensions that neighbor countries would adopt on their own the methods whereby Americans had transformed trouble spots into showcase republics.

Many Americans had their doubts. They took to heart the warnings that Rudyard Kipling had sounded toward the end of his 1899 poem "The White Man's Burden." Kipling had predicted a long succession of "thankless years" and of wisdom purchased at a high price by those who took up the task of spreading civilization. In 1907 historian Albert Bushnell Hart published the final volume in The American Nation Series under the title *National Ideals Historically Traced.* The Puritan, Hart maintained, had provided "the little leaven that leavens the whole lump." But he wondered if the leaven could continue even to survive, let alone perform the tasks still expected of it, within the lump of expanding immigrant hordes.[2] If the leavening process faced perhaps insuperable obstacles within the United States proper, how could it succeed overseas?

As early as 1892 Capt. Richard H. Pratt, founder of the Carlisle Industrial-Training School for Indians, had observed: "What a farce it would be to attempt teaching American citizenship to the negroes in Africa. They could not understand it; and, if they did, in the midst of such contrary influences, they could never use it. Neither can the Indians understand or use American citizenship theoretically taught to them on Indian reservations. They must get into the swim of American citizenship. They must feel the touch of it day after day, until they become saturated with the spirit of it, and thus become equal to it."[3]

In effect, the United States in its Caribbean imperialism had embarked upon the task of Americanizing African, mulatto, and mestizo peoples in their native habitats, on distant reservations, as it were, that at best could be no more than barely touched by American culture. Before long the task began to appear dreary and unrewarding, perhaps even hopeless: and Americans have never been a people to endure a long succession of "thankless years" in assuming the white man's burden. If they could not expect quick victories, such as those of soldiers and cowboys over Indians in the twenty years or so after the Civil War, then they quickly lost interest in overt imperialism. Besides that, imperialist uplift required at the outset protracted periods of paternalistic protection in addition to the education of uncivilized beings. And Americans have always felt uneasy about extending paternalistic protection to anyone. That process runs contrary to the national grain. Prevailingly, they had hoped within a short time to dismantle Indian reservations and force the natives to sink or swim in the mainstream of American life. They had approached the post–Civil War problems of freed slaves in the same spirit, shortly abandoning Negroes to the whims of the old and unrepentant slaveocracy. Continued pursuit of Reconstruction goals would simply have resulted in too many thankless years. In the early twentieth century Americans continued to be colonialists on the cheap. If uplift of Caribbean and Central American semisavages required protracted paternalism and expenditures of money and manpower, they were not interested. What Twain had said, tongue in cheek, turned out to be untrue. Uplifting others might be noble, but it was a great deal of trouble.

In 1921, the marines had been in the Dominican Republic for five years. Yet in his January report for that year the military governor informed the secretary of the navy that the republic was on the brink of total breakdown. Courts of justice and schools were closed in many parts of the country, and public works had been discontinued. Moreover, from a wide variety of sources American statesmen learned that public opinion on the island, in the Caribbean in general, and indeed throughout Latin America had become inflamed against the occupation. So three years later the occupation came to an end. American officials tried to put the best face on things, contending that withdrawal resulted from the fact that they had accomplished their mission and initiated the Dominicans into the ways of civilization. Thus, Americans withdrew in honor. And they left behind the *Guardia Nacional,* that American-trained constabulary that would maintain order and back civilian officials as they completed the transition to democracy. But Rafael Leonidas Trujillo commanded the Guardia, and soon would use it as the means to impose his barbarous tyranny upon the island republic. As an astute American historian comments, "There is no better example than the Guardia Nacional Dominicana to illustrate the inability of the United States to impose reforms by fiat."[4]

By 1930 Henry L. Stimson, principal architect of the American intervention in Nicaragua that had aimed to rid the country of Sandino so that its "better" and right-thinking people would have the opportunity to demonstrate the efficacy of democracy and capitalism, was ready to end the quest for that country's uplift. Public opinion, he recognized, would no longer tolerate a situation in which each new American intervention seemed only to undermine the ability of the Nicaraguan government to maintain order.[5] By 1930, moreover, overwhelming evidence had accumulated as to the failure of the U.S. occupation forces in Haiti, present since 1915, to accomplish much more than to inflame sentiment and arouse indignation among not only Haitians but Latin Americans in general against the United States. Before 1934 came to an end, the United States had withdrawn its troops from both Haiti and Nicaragua. In the latter republic the story of the aftermath of Dominican withdrawal was quickly reenacted as Anastasio Somoza, commander of the Guardia Nacional, used his American-trained troops to arrange the assassination of his rival Sandino and to project himself into the presidency, to which he and his family clung tenaciously for decades to come despite occasional expressions of concern from Washington.

The United States had terminated its Dominican intervention under the pretense that it had accomplished its mission. It proved more difficult, but not impossible, for resourceful propagandists to maintain this pretense with Haiti and Nicaragua, and also with Cuba and Panama in 1933 and 1934, when the United States abandoned some of the Caribbean interventionist rights it had unilaterally assumed at the beginning of the century.

With Haiti and Nicaragua, Cuba and Panama, honor in withdrawal derived from the pretense that Washington had yielded to the intensifying demands from south of the border that the United States acquiesce in an emerging body of hemispheric international law, shaped largely by Latin American jurists, that prohibited intervention by one republic in the internal affairs of another. The real reason for America's temporary withdrawal from intervention as of 1934 had little to do with hemispheric international law as codified by Latin Americans. It had a great deal to do with the depression, which imposed the need to economize. Even more, temporary abandonment of intervention arose out of the recognized failure of agents of U.S. civilization to correct the ways of nature and those who still lived in its thrall.

American loss of confidence about uplifting Latin Americans seems to parallel, and may even have its roots in, discouragement over Indian assimilation. Reservations had been intended to accomplish acculturation as resident Indians underwent conversion to the white man's religion and culture. For most reservation Indians, however, "the changes were a shattering experience, demoralizing rather than uplifting. The self-reliance and self-support that underlay the hopes of the reformers for Indians were little in evidence" as the 1920s ended. Even as with Latin Americans, failure to educate the redskins "stemmed in part from the unwillingness of the educators to consider the Indians' cultural heritage and its persistence in spite of their efforts to eradicate it."[6] What a Marines Corps history of the occupation of Haiti noted about the natives applied to Caribbean and Central American republics in general and also to American Indian reservations. For the most part, the history noted, the natives "failed to respond enthusiastically to either training or rewards."[7]

Americans themselves had failed to respond to the endeavor of ostensibly more civilized citizens to uplift their countrymen and women. In droves they resisted the attempt of reformers to curb basic appetites. Throughout the country speakeasies flourished in the 1920s, often along with prostitution. Uncurbed consumption, whether of spirits or sex or commodities, had become the order of the day. Against this background, Prohibition's "noble experiment" proved a fiasco, except for criminals and the firms that sold Thompson submachine guns to them as well as to their would-be law-enforcer subduers. As Americans prepared to abandon Prohibition in 1933, they seemed little inclined to instruct Latin Americans or any other primitives on how to bend natural and instinctual ways to the laws of civilization. Indeed, the signs of change that were discernible in the hemisphere implied reverse cultural imperialism; they suggested that Americans were becoming more like Latin Americans and Indians. In the

1920s, more and more Americans expected to strike it rich not so much by hard work as by gambling—on the stock market.

Cultural Pluralism Abets the Rejection of Uplift

The distinguished diplomat Sumner Welles, whose sanity some of his colleagues doubted when he chose Latin America as his preferred field of operations, played a key role in shaping Franklin D. Roosevelt's Good Neighbor policy—until at the end driven from power by a scandal involving alleged homosexuality and alcoholism. In the 1920s Welles had realized that the end of Dominican Republic occupation represented not withdrawal in honor, with the mission accomplished, but withdrawal in failure. Dominicans, he observed, had steadfastly resisted the programs that the occupying forces sought to impose, for they realized the programs "conformed solely to the customs, habits and prejudices of the intervening power." He continued: "In the occupation of the Dominican Republic the American Military Government not only failed to consider local customs and prejudices, but was actually ignorant of what they were. Under such circumstances, how could an alien administration, operating under martial law, be productive of results of permanent benefit to the country occupied?"[8] In his critique of U.S. policy Welles implied that Dominican values, customs, and habits were worth understanding. Certainly he stopped short of moral equivalence, of placing the values and mores of the Other on as high a plane as those of the imperialists. But his assessment of U.S. intervention in the Dominican Republic suggests he had to some limited degree fallen under the influence of currently stylish theories of cultural pluralism: a term largely replaced in the late 1980s by *multiculturalism,* the latter used by conservative Americans to designate the cardinal sin of Americans deemed insufficiently reverential toward the Western tradition.

During the 1920s the theories of a Jewish immigrant from Germany who proclaimed the virtue of all cultures, including those once dismissed as backward, primitive, and savage, began to overwhelm the opposition in citadels of scientific thought and to seep down to the level of popular awareness. The immigrant was Franz Boas (1858–1942), who arrived in the United States in 1889 and ten years later became Columbia University's first professor of anthropology, a position he held for thirty-seven years. Boas's cultural pluralism theories challenged the assumptions of such champions of Anglo Saxonism as Madison Grant and Lothrop Stoddard that virtue inhered only in the culture, in the life-style and values, developed by Anglo Saxons, and that Anglo Saxon virtue arose out of superior racial endowments developed through a Darwinian process of natural selection. According to the new school of cultural anthropology as pioneered by Boas, cultures developed not in response to determinants of race but rather to those of environment. Anthropological relativism, more popularly known as cultural pluralism, proclaimed that the totality of the cultural influences that operated on human beings, far more than genetic factors, determined behavior. Cultural influences were transmitted from generation to generation by exogenetic or nongenetic influences: by the totality of influences that parents, peer groups, schooling mechanisms, churches, the media, and society in general brought to bear in the process of "socialization" through which new generations acquired the codes of conduct that their society had developed through all its preceding generations in response to the various circumstances of environment, both physical and social.

Cultural anthropologists challenged the concept of stages popularized by Lewis Henry Morgan. Morgan, it will be recalled, divided mankind into stages along a line of progression, designating the principal stages savagery, barbarism, and civilization. For cultural anthropologists there were no stages of culture, only multiplicities of culture. Furthermore, there were no absolute laws of progress; all one could point to were different concepts of and different approaches to what each culture in its own way had come to deem desirable.

Because different cultures were equally virtuous, it followed that enlightened people should develop tolerance toward other ways of life.[9] Indeed, people of one culture would be better off if they permitted themselves to enjoy some of the distinctive ways of different cultures. Boas himself, after spending time among Eskimos, noted: "The more I see of their customs, the more I realize that we have no right to look down on them. Where amongst our people would you find such true hospitality?"[10] Americans when among Latin Americans had often asked themselves the same question. But having been conditioned by the claims of their culture to a monopoly on virtue, they often felt guilty because of their positive response to the ways of the Other. Once persuaded by the teachings of cultural pluralism, they could happily discard guilt feelings.

Boas had published his best-known work, *The Mind of Primitive Man,* in 1911. In it he sought to demonstrate the unscientific basis of racial prejudice. Not until the 1920s, though, did the book begin to have a major impact on American science, its tenets advanced most enthusiastically by anthropologists though still combated sometimes by sociologists who tended to cling to evolutionary assumptions and responded warmly to new theories of eugenics. In the 1930s as Adolf Hitler helped make eugenics increasingly odious, more and more sociologists joined the revolution in social science. During the 1930s the new science filtered down to the level of informed layperson, making it possible for protagonists of racial equality "to quote science on their side."[11] For one of the few times in a century or more, science and social decency converged, even if it is not altogether clear to this day whether the new science was sound. Nor has it been clear whether by embracing the tenets of cultural pluralism Americans have so weakened the concepts of what their culture entails, what it is essentially all about, as to render increasingly difficult the socialization of new generations and newly arriving immigrants. There are always those damnable trade-offs that beset the mingling of old and new values.

While proclaiming neutrality in assessing cultures, sometimes cultural pluralists threw objectivity to the winds in registering preference for the ways of premoderns over moderns. Thus Edward Sapir, a Jewish immigrant prominent among the first generation of Boas's students (briefly he had wanted to marry another of those students, Margaret Mead), "openly avowed his preference for the 'genuine' culture of American Indians over the 'spurious' civilization of modern America." Praising the "inherently harmonious, 'balanced' culture of the American Indians, Sapir contrasted it with the spiritual hybrid of contradictory patches" that passed for a culture among modern Americans.[12]

Especially once the Great Depression had undermined their confidence that competitive capitalist hustle would position them permanently beneath an inexhaustible cornucopia, Americans in increasing number wondered if so-called primitives had, in their nonrational, intuitive way, stumbled onto more fulfilling and even more realistic approaches to life. With interest and often with approbation Americans turned to a book published in 1934 by another of Boas's students, and a later collaborator of his, Ruth Benedict.[13] In *Patterns of Culture,* one of the most widely read anthropological studies ever published in America, Benedict drew an enticing picture of the relaxed, noncompetitive communalism of Zuni culture. In a somewhat different way, she did for the Zuni of the Southwest what her friend and occasional lover Margaret Mead had done for Samoans in her 1928 book, *Coming of Age in Samoa.*

Benedict and Mead figured prominently among an impressive array of women anthropologists and sociologists, some of whom might have hoped— consciously or not—that as American men were stripped of their old rationales for oppressing people who were different, they would learn to tolerate the feminine Other as an equal. Considerations of a related nature, as suggested in the previous chapter, may have contributed to Jewish championing of underdogs. However that may be, neither Benedict nor Mead nor the other women who entered into fields of scientific inquiry once assumed the exclusive province of males could have struck a responsive chord among a mass audience if Americans had not already come to feel uneasy about some of the values and assumptions on which their culture had traditionally rested. By the 1930s, Hollywood's products began to reflect this unease. Many of that decade's movies stressed the theme that reconciliation in some degree of equality was possible between men and women, old and young, urbanites and ruralites, haves and have-nots (whether individuals, families, or classes).[14] Once again, the Jewish influence may have been at work as Hollywood moved to popularize, however subtly and even unwittingly, cultural anthropology's new faith.

When Friedrich Nietzsche proclaimed "God is dead," he meant, I suppose, that modern beings had lost faith in the traditional values of which God had been considered both guarantor and emblem. Americans, even some mainstream, Main Street Americans, caught up in the disruptions loosed by their country's Great Depression and by its revolution in scientific thought spearheaded by the cultural pluralists, had lost faith in many of their once-cherished "eternal" verities. Insofar as God had been found useful in justifying blanket condemnation of the Other, the supreme being as of the 1930s seemed in extremis, for the ethnocentric intolerance once allegedly sanctioned by divine intentions faced mounting repudiation. But for this repudiation, Americans would not have endorsed a new hemispheric policy that called on them to become good neighbors.

Meantime, cultural pluralism crossed the border. Burgeoning faith in its tenets among a new generation of Latin American thinkers, for whom Boas became "arguably the most important intellectual influence from the United States" in the first third of the century,[15] fostered a new sense of national self-confidence. In the past, Latin America's light-skinned gente decente had inclined to be every bit as racist as white Americans. They had denigrated the dark-hued masses, adopting pessimistic, defeatist attitudes about the racial potential of their countries, and prevailingly they had welcomed any sort of collaboration with their mighty northern neighbors through which they might buttress the power needed to keep the inferior masses in line. Once they began to pick up on concepts of cultural pluralism, however, a new generation of Latin Americans found comfort in Boas's conviction of equality among different cultures and his speculation that mestizaje actually might produce an end product in some ways elevated over the distinct components that went into the mix (a conclusion at odds with his early doubts about the consequences of mestizaje).

Intellectuals inspired by Boas's theories to embrace a new optimism about their continent's future included Brazil's Gilberto Freyre, who studied under the master at Columbia, Mexico's Manuel Gamio and José Vasconcelos, and also a robust contingent of Andean American thinkers who in the 1920s and 1930s trumpeted the worthiness of Indians and mestizos. Even in predominantly light-skinned Chile and Argentina, Indianist sentiments came into vogue. Furthermore, in some Chilean circles pride in mestizaje became as conspicuous as in Oklahoma.

Waldo Frank assured the Latin American intelligentsia of their spiritual grandeur, and Franz Boas helped awaken confidence in the racial worthiness of their people. Finding confirmation among thinkers to the north for some of the ideas they had been developing on their own, Latin America's intellectuals enthused over the inherent virtue of their national cultures and resolved to stiffen their resistance to colonialism in all its guises. Had U.S. leaders maintained their old colonialist mind-set, bitter clashes would have been inevitable. But it just so happened that many American intellectuals and statesmen, themselves under the influence of cultural pluralism, abandoned imperialist assumptions or at least, recognizing the way the winds were blowing, toned them down.

In one of the more widely quoted utterances to emerge from the Good Neighbor era, Franklin D. Roosevelt noted that Latin Americans "think they are just as good as we are and many of them are." In this bow toward cultural pluralism, Roosevelt indicated the enormous distance that separated his era from Theodore Roosevelt's. Even if TR could have harbored such a thought, he would hardly have found it politically expedient to flaunt publicly even so condescending a compliment to Latins.

Cultural pluralism in the United States complemented another of the developments that helped make possible the Good Neighbor era: the already-discussed abandonment of uplift expectations. Acceptance by the late 1920s that uplift, or cultural change, *could* not be imposed on others complemented the pluralist credo that change *should* not be imposed. Together, the two convictions made possible widespread American acceptance of nonintervention, a key element in the Good Neighbor approach to Latin America. In some ways, of course, nonintervention to the Good Neighbor meant simply a switch to more subtle, and hopefully more ultimately effective, means of intervention—recalling Talleyrand's dictum that nonintervention is simply another means of intervention. Without being able to prove it, I suspect that the new approach to issues of intervention reflected the changing approach to nature, to the natural environment, that evolved during the New Deal years. As it gradually emerged, the new environmental wisdom counseled that nature be controlled through subtler, gentler means than heretofore, means that took into account and worked with, rather than at cross purposes to, nature's own inclinations.

The New Deal and the Quest to Live More Respectfully with Nature

Like his cousin Theodore, Franklin Roosevelt when he came to the presidency had had his encounter with nature. Unlike Theodore, who fashioned his vaunted manliness by subduing nature in a wilderness setting, Franklin had ventured deep into his interior resources after having succumbed to the ravages of natural calamity. Eventually, by plumbing his inward depths Franklin discovered the intangible power of will needed to survive the scourge of poliomyelitis that had robbed his legs of the strength that once had been a source of pride. FDR's experience seemed to hold symbolic meaning for Americans in the depression era, suggesting that weakness and affliction were no disgrace.

Theodore Roosevelt had symbolized an America of virile self-confidence, its citizens always ready to rely on the physical power of which they were so proud. Franklin Roosevelt stood for a country weakened by the atrophying of its economic muscles, a country whose citizens were ready to reach out for a supporting hand, just as their president reached for braces and crutches as he struggled against his natural affliction. TR and the men of his era had contrived to overcome yellow fever and other forms of pestilence as they asserted their mastery over nature in building the Panama Canal. But FDR had fallen before the power of nature. TR and the leaders of his age had confidently dreamed about creating a new frontier for American farmers by means of reclamation projects. In FDR's era Americans contemplated the spectacle of the Dust Bowl as nature arose to reclaim a frontier that settlers had occupied only some forty years earlier.

Virtually overnight Alexandre Hogue became one of the country's best-known artists when *Life* magazine in the late 1930s published photographs of his Dust Bowl paintings that depicted massive erosion in the Southwest. Never before had an American artist painted such frightening indictments of the damage humans inflict on nature by seeking too insistently to bend her to their will.[16] Particularly in his painting *Mother Earth Laid Bare*, Hogue gives a symbolic interpretation to erosion induced by unwise use of the soil. (See illustration 16.) Windstorms have blown away the topsoil to reveal underneath a mass of earth shaped in the form of a naked woman. In the central foreground Hogue has placed a plough, a fitting symbol of technology's rape of the southern Great Plains.

The drought of the 1930s combined with the prolonged and heedless ploughing of vast fields, intended perhaps by nature to remain under the cover of grass that grew wild, to produce the Dust Bowl. The drought extended from the southern plains all the way up to Montana. Dust storms

16. Alexandre Hogue. *Erosion No. 2-Mother Earth Laid Bare.* 1938. Oil on canvas, 44 × 56". The Philbrook Museum of Art, Tulsa, Oklahoma.

Along with John Steinbeck's *The Grapes of Wrath* (1939), Alexandre Hogue's depictions of erosion helped lead Americans in the New Deal era toward awareness of the need to deal more restrainedly with nature.

in part of that state led settlers to talk about the "dirty thirties." One observer of the calamity placed the blame on nature herself: "Like a young bride with a sinister secret, the land revealed herself as she truly was: harsh, cruel, unrelenting."[17] In contrast, Alexandre Hogue blamed human recklessness and the intrusive forces of technology for the debacle.

In 1931, just before the Dust Bowl phenomenon came along to shatter the self-confidence of Americans in their ability to do as they wished with nature, midwestern artist Grant Wood completed a painting that he called *Fall Planting*. It is an idyllic depiction of a family-sized farm with fertile, productive, gardenlike small fields. In the central foreground, even as in Hogue's *Mother Earth Laid Bare*, stands a plough. For Wood, the plough is a beneficent phallic symbol. It conveys the promise of rendering fertile the eagerly awaiting earth. The painting glorifies what the noble yeoman farmer has accomplished. It was the sort of painting that regionalist artists had specialized in during the 1920s, and its image appealed alike to urbanites and to the one in four Americans who lived on farms. But Hogue saw the situation differently. For him, the plough symbolized the threatening rapist who assaults nature and blights her existence.[18]

John Steinbeck took this theme as his point of departure in his 1939 best-selling novel, *The Grapes of Wrath*. Here he offers a masterful account of the "Oakies" driven by drought to start anew in California. In a lukewarm review in *Newsweek*, Burston Rascoe wrote, "I can't quite see what the book is about, except that there are no frontiers left and places to go."[19] Given the whole history of America, could any book possibly have been about a more significant topic? If indeed national frontiers had forever closed, with the implications at last beginning to dawn on the general public, might not Americans have to abandon their traditional approach to nature and learn to live as her partner rather than her master? Speaking before a congressional committee in 1936, Secretary of Agriculture Henry A. Wallace suggested what facing up to the end of the frontier might mean to Americans. Natural disasters then afflicting the nation, he asserted, "bring home the fact that we have been thus far in our history a spendthrift people, squandering natural resources. It is time that we develop a sense of thrift in these vital matters, and a sense of shame."[20]

The meaning that Commissioner of Indian Affairs John Collier derived from the natural disasters of the 1930s was that his countrymen must begin to heed the wisdom of the Native Americans, who considered themselves part of rather than the masters of nature. Otherwise the inevitable depletion of soil resources and food-producing potential would take on "catastrophic speed."[21] Whether or not they chose to bow in awe before the wisdom of Indians, Americans in the 1930s did come, in growing number, to suspect "that nature could not be relied upon to produce and yield crops as assembly lines produced automobiles." Some even began to suspect that, as radical environmentalist Edward Abbey put the matter some years later, "original sin, the true original sin, is the blind destruction for the sake of greed of this natural paradise which lies all around us."[22]

If, contrary to long-cherished myths and stereotypes, freely acknowledged impotence to master nature conveyed no suggestion of moral inferiority, then not only Indians but Latin Americans and primitives in general did not deserve the disdain customarily accorded them by Americans because of their failures to tame, correct, and tyrannize nature. Perhaps the willingness of people once maligned as backward to recognize their insignificance before nature's forces testified to the sort of inner, spiritual superiority that counterculturalists had for decades and generations assigned to the primitive Other.

Although not going as far as radical environmentalists wished, Franklin Roosevelt proved as enthusiastic a conservationist as cousin Teddy had been. In helping him to realize his conservation goals, FDR was fortunate to have a person sometimes—but by no means universally—described as the best secretary of the interior ever to serve his country. Even if he was compulsively belligerent and given to bitter feuds as he sought to defend what he regarded as his bureaucratic turf, Harold Ickes left no doubt about his commitment to saving nature, and also nature's children, the Indians, from the greed of businessmen.[23] Thanks in large measure to Ickes's doggedness and a commitment to resource conservation that matched the president's and thanks also to a supportive national mood, America struck a new deal with nature in the 1930s. Perhaps the most conspicuous feature of that new deal was the Tennessee Valley Authority (TVA) in its early days.

TVA's first director, Arthur E. Morgan, exuded the visionary's zeal as he assumed his duties at the beginning of the New Deal. Under the spell of the utopian hopes that always seem to thrive in calamitous times, Morgan believed that the TVA would spark a back-to-the-land movement, while also stimulating small-scale, rural-based industry and handicrafts. Technology once wrested from the exclusive control of greedy private interests and taken over by social planners would provide the means to achieve a new commonwealth, in which freewheeling capitalism was balanced by a mutualism that embodied a new ethic of relations among humans and between them and the soil.[24] Morgan saw the town of Norris, built for the workers employed in constructing the dam that was the centerpiece of the TVA project, as the model for planned, small-scale "producerist" communities that would set the tone for the valley's vast social experiment and ultimately reach out to transform the rest of rural America. Thereby America would advance toward a society that was collectivist, democratic, humane, and free.

Through planning and the stimulus of a beneficent government, Americans could create a new frontier. On the partially humanmade new frontier, descendants of the pioneers would fuse symbiotically with nature, the old adversarial poles coming together in harmony. Similar utopian expectations about a new type of frontier experience helped inspire various projects in the West, including the Central Valley project in California and the Columbia River Basin development in Oregon and Washington.[25]

However, the New Deal's approach to the environment was not shaped exclusively by utopianists such as Secretary of Agriculture Wallace and TVA director Morgan. Indeed, FDR dismissed Morgan in 1938, partially on the grounds of his "contumacious nature." Whatever the reasons for the dismissal, it brought a check to the Morgan-inspired attempt to use "comprehensive regional planning to promote cooperative simplicity." This objective gave way to "power development, flood control efforts, and fertilizer production under the direction of David Lilienthal," the new head of TVA.[26] The change in orientation signified that nature would now be utilized in the long-range interests of a slightly modified capitalism, not to produce an alternative to capitalism.

The same sort of divisiveness over how to deal with nature that underlay the New Deal's approach to the environment also appeared among those who shaped the Good Neighbor approach to Latin America. In the dispute over the basic thrust of hemispheric policy, at one extreme stood those who, responsive to a radicalized counterculture's romanticism, perceived in the Latin American masses a primitive purity that could be preserved only by exorcizing Yankees of the whole capitalist ethic that drove them to become imperialists and exploit the natives to the south—and in their own country as well. Another and far more influential group in shaping hemispheric policy wanted simply to subject to some degree of bureaucratic restraint the individual Yankees who sought their fortunes south of the border. Just like nature herself, the stereotyped children of nature must be protected against the ruthless exploitation of American capitalists, not necessarily for the good of the children so much as for the long-term good of short-sighted capitalists. Once restrained by Uncle Sam's bureaucracy from actions that would end their welcome in Latin America, American capitalists could count on that area as a long-term frontier of opportunity. Both in environmental and in Latin American policy, Americans in the 1930s pursued what they had never yet been able to discover, however much they had dreamed about it: a frontier that could be prolonged indefinitely.

"After Franklin Roosevelt," writes a historian of the American conservation movement, "most conservationists were Democrats."[27] And, after FDR, most Americans who favored the exercise of some element of government control over the actions of their country's capitalists who operated in lands to the south were also Democrats. The environmental–Latin American connection is not accidental: it springs from deep-lying philosophical convictions about the American experience, what it has been and what it should be.

In his *History of the Peloponnesian War*, Thucydides has Athenians inform the hapless Melians that "the strong do what they can and the weak suffer what they must." In depression-era America, many a New Dealer wanted to curb what the powerful could do and place limitations on what the powerless, whether ostensibly inanimate nature or flesh-and-blood human underlings, need suffer. Accomplishment of this objective required, in

New Dealer eyes, a considerable shift of power away from the private sector to the public sector. The idea of control by the public sector, staffed as never before in New Deal days by intellectuals expected to devise programs to buffer the suffering of the powerless, seemed very much in line with Latin America's statist, corporatist traditions.[28] Happily surprised by the unexpected turn of events to the north, Latin American intellectuals began to anticipate better prospects for their future relations with the Colossus than they had previously thought possible. Buttressing this expectation was a sharp upswing in indicators of American goodwill toward Latin America.

Goodwill toward Latin America: Counterculture Values Enter the Establishment

Goodwill toward Latin Americans seemed especially evident in Yankee reassessments of their immediate neighbors in Mexico. Reviled since well before the day of Manifest Destiny as ignoble savages, Mexicans now began to impress many of their northern observers as the creators of a political economy and a culture from which Americans could learn a great deal. A cynical interpretation might suggest that American readiness to praise Mexicans stemmed from the need to keep in the good graces of a country on whose uninterrupted supply of temporary workers U.S. farmers had become increasingly dependent when the wartime draft dried up the sources of native-born laborers. Goodwill, however, antedated World War II.

Speaking in Mexico City in 1940, Commissioner of Indian Affairs John Collier rendered unstinting praise to retiring president Lázaro Cárdenas (1934–1940), perhaps the most radical chief executive ever to preside over his country's destiny. Obviously sympathetic to Cárdenas's nationalization of foreign oil and agricultural holdings, Collier found proof of the president's greatness in his concern for the Indian and his vision of a future society in which indigenous communalist values curbed the excesses of individualistic capitalism.[29] The elevation of Mexico's natural man and woman over the interests of foreign capitalists was not the customary basis on which a highly placed Washington official judged the virtues of a Latin American leader. Nor had it been commonplace in the past for American officials to laud Latin American visionaries who wished to place the values of "primitive" society on an equal footing with those of capitalist civilization. Yet here precisely were the grounds on which Collier formed his appraisal of Cárdenas. Similar considerations may have influenced the United

States ambassador to Mexico, Josephus Daniels (discussed below in some detail), when he hailed Cárdenas as "the best president Mexico has had since [Benito] Juárez." [30]

Then there was Henry Wallace, the New Deal's secretary of agriculture until 1940 when he became the vice-presidential candidate in Roosevelt's successful bid for a third term. In 1942 Vice-President Wallace phoned Waldo Frank on the eve of the latter's departure on a Latin American lecture tour under State Department auspices. The phone conversation convinced the Jewish seer that Wallace was another true believer in the vision of creating a new American hemisphere that fused its two "half-worlds." [31]

Already in 1939 Wallace had written: "We are challenged to build here in this hemisphere a new culture which is neither Latin American nor North American but genuinely inter-American. Undoubtedly it is possible to build an inter-American consciousness and an inter-American culture which will transcend both its Anglo-Saxon and its Iberian origins." [32] The words might easily have come from Waldo Frank, and to Latin American wishful thinkers they carried the imprimatur of official policy. So did the well-known Wallace thesis, advanced from 1941 onward, that once the struggle against fascism had been won, the United States should commit its surplus capital not so much to rebuilding the Old World as to fashioning viable economies in the underdeveloped world to America's south. Here was a message calculated to win approval from Latin America's upper classes. However, it was the downtrodden, especially the peasantry, that most aroused Wallace's interest and sympathy. And this sympathy rendered him popular primarily among Latin America's reformist and even revolutionary elements who, not without arrogance, claimed to represent the interests of the downtrodden.

The year after Frank embarked on his lecture tour, Henry Wallace visited Peru, where in effect he issued a call to all Americans, Latin and Anglo, to build a new civilization rooted in the values of the Incas. "At long last," he enthused to a Peruvian audience, "I have been able to see with my own eyes the original Andean agricultural terraces, upon which are based the most modern systems of irrigation and of conservation of soil." Even more important to the vice-president was the "law of solidarity" that constituted the spiritual foundation of Inca culture. "This law does not permit any citizen to lack minimum subsistence; this law guarantees the right to obtain help for all those who can no longer work; this law favors the harmonious development of all peoples as such and of the well-being of the individual." Wallace concluded that Americans regarded Peru as a "fountain of inspiration, especially in times like these in which we are struggling to establish democracy with equality of economic opportunities and equality for cultural opportunity for all the peoples of all nations the world over."[33] Wallace's remarks may have thrilled left-leaning Peruvian intellectuals aspiring to seize power from entrenched interests. But they must have evoked cynicism and disdain among the conservative elements then ruling the country who regarded with horror all kinds of socialism, whether originating with the Incas or with Marx and Lenin; who knew that their country had scrupulously avoided racial democracy and cultural pluralism; and who expected it to continue to do so.

Like Collier, Wallace had transferred to Latin America's indigenous people some of the admiration he had first felt for the Pueblo culture of the Southwest. For one thing, Wallace had admired the religious spirit and ceremonies that permeated the lives of these "primitive peoples" of North America. Because the Pueblos remained concerned with enlisting supernatural help "to make it rain or to cure sickness or to make the crops grow better," they performed ceremonies that they believed established an intimate relationship "with nature and the mysterious powers that reside in nature."[34] Given his own streak of mysticism that seemed to owe a great deal to nontraditional religions and that granted primacy to nonmaterial over material causation, Wallace was predisposed to admire the "pagan" or popular-religion elements that underlay much of Latin America's spiritual life and that religiously mainstream Americans had traditionally derided. No wonder Latin American reformist intellectuals, many of whom responded themselves to mystical visions of a new humanity emerging out of the ruins of the depression years and shaped according to the desires of philosophers and artists, hailed Wallace as a refreshingly different kind of gringo proponent of hemispheric unity. No more than Waldo Frank did Henry Wallace conform to Latin stereotypes of the North American.

Impressed like Waldo Frank with the supernatural, numinous qualities of telluric forces, Wallace perceived a spiritual superiority in "way-of-life" farmers precisely because they had "never lost touch with the soil, the mother of us all." Owing to their contact with the earth, way-of-life farmers had remained "human beings, at a time when capitalism was having such a de-humanizing effect on increasing numbers in labor, agriculture and business."[35] The hope of Latin America, and also of the Soviet Union where Wallace discovered a people who exemplified "the grandeur that comes when men wisely work with nature," purportedly lay in the development of the peasantry through creation of agricultural cooperatives, such as those established in Mexico under President Cárdenas that resuscitated ideals of ancient Europe and Indo-America. Moreover, programs of decentralized industrialization could bring small-scale manufacturing into the midst of rural settings, resulting—as Stuart Chase had foreseen—in factories in the field: a new form of the machine-in-the-garden myth so important in shaping one aspect of the American Dream. Above all, the future that Latin Americans had begun to shape, as they returned to a golden-age Indian past, would provide workers with an ongoing opportunity to find renewal through contact with nature.[36] Here Wallace sounded a theme that appealed to his country's chief executive, though Roosevelt himself certainly knew too much about Stalin's agricultural policies and the sordid underside of politics to the south to believe that Soviets and Latin Americans had begun to approximate mythical ideals. Dedicating the Shenandoah National Park in Virginia in 1936, FDR had extolled "the perspective that comes to men and women who every morning and every night can lift up their eyes to Mother Nature." He closed his remarks "by recalling a favorite figure in Greek mythology, the giant Antaeus, invincible on the ground but crushed by Hercules when he lost contact with the earth. 'There is merit for all of us in that ancient tale,' he said."[37]

Characteristically, FDR was thinking mythologically. The entire Good Neighbor policy and indeed the whole New Deal owed a great deal to the fact that his favorite myths, as exemplified by the tale of Antaeus united with his earth mother, were those of wholeness, community, and inclusion. Still, like Antaeus but altogether unlike Wallace, FDR kept his feet on the ground and generally did not pursue myths to the point of self-delusion.

Henry Wallace believed that revolutionary Mexico had already begun to carry out reforms inspired by the dream of safeguarding the privilege of its citizens to pursue ongoing rebirth in nature. It behooved North Americans to begin to catch up with the Mexicans. Understandably Wallace found a warm welcome in Mexico where all those associated with the government found it de rigueur to mask cynicism, to mouth Indianist shibboleths, and to locate in aboriginal peasants the virtue that—nourished by an avowedly idealistic government—would nullify the vices that ordinarily overwhelmed countries in the throes of modernization.

When Wallace visited Mexico in 1943, Ambassador Josephus Daniels reported enthusiastically that no other man could have been so effective in nullifying Nazi propaganda. "No man could have served so well as Henry Wallace as a symbol of democracy to Mexicans, whose whole revolutionary program centered around the efforts of Mexico to help the common man. Everywhere Mexicans—especially the campesinos—greeted him with spontaneous and ceremonial affection."[38]

Before assuming his duties in Mexico in 1933, Daniels had been briefed by Herschel Johnson, head of the State Department's Mexican desk. Johnson expressed to the newly appointed ambassador his warm enthusiasm for Mexican efforts to aid the Indian peasantry. "Despite all the grossness and selfishness of the leaders of the revolution, there is a germ of sincerity that you trace through all the movement, even with the worst of the leaders. They desire to uplift the illiterate Indian peasant."[39] During his lengthy stay as ambassador (1933–1942) Daniels revealed a concern for Mexico's Indians that matched, perhaps even exceeded, Johnson's. Perhaps incidentally, and perhaps not so incidentally, he also showed a concern for the status of women. When presenting his credentials to President Abelardo Rodríguez, Daniels insisted on violating protocol by having his wife and the wives of the embassy staff present at the ceremony.[40]

Enthusiastic about the Mexican revolution, especially under the presidential leadership of Indian-blooded and apparently incorruptible Lázaro Cárdenas, Daniels saw its primary purpose as the restoration of land to Indians. Noting that "today nearly all the population is pure Indian or mestizo," Daniels praised the Indians for having remained "rooted in the soil." During the Porfirio Díaz dictatorship (1876–1911), however, many Indians had been despoiled of property, frequently, Daniels observed, at the hands of North Americans in connivance with the dictator. Applauding Cárdenas's zeal for land reform, and showing scant sympathy for the agrarian claims of some U.S. citizens, Daniels noted: "My residence in Mexico has made me more interested than ever in the problems of putting tenants on the land and giving them a stake in old mother earth."[41]

"His Jeffersonian view of the importance of the small landholder in a democratic society naturally led Daniels to sympathize with the aims of the Mexican agrarian program," writes E. David Cronon in a masterful account of Daniels's diplomatic career in Mexico. However, both Thomas Jefferson and Woodrow Wilson, another of Daniels's heroes and one he had served as secretary of the navy, would have been dismayed by the communalist philosophy that guided the Cárdenas approach to land reform. Not so Daniels. In a genuine spirit of cultural pluralism, he accepted the applicability, in the light of Mexican traditions, of a semisocialist approach to landownership. Familiar with and favorably impressed by Eyler N. Simpson's 1937 study *The Ejido, Mexico's Way Out*,[42] Daniels embraced the concept of semicollectivized agricultural communities that, in Simpson's view, could become sites for factories in the field. By applying this formula, Daniels hoped Mexicans could proceed toward an era of social justice in which human rights took precedence over property rights.

As a mentor on Mexican history and destiny, Daniels also had Frank Tannenbaum, the onetime anarchist agitator in New York City befriended by Mabel Dodge, who in 1933 had published his influential *Peace by Revolution: An Interpretation of Mexico*. Tannenbaum hailed the revolution as a death-and-regeneration process whereby Mexico would undo the effects of Spanish conquest and liberate the energies of the true sons and daughters of the soil. "Mexico is returning to the children of the Indian mother, and will be colored largely by her blood and her patterns," Tannenbaum averred,[43] sounding a great deal like D. H. Lawrence in his novel *The Plumed Serpent*. Regarded suspiciously by the State Department in the 1920s as a member of an allegedly Jewish-Bolshevik clique of Americans in Mexico who plotted against U.S. national interests,[44] Tannenbaum less than a decade later was the close personal friend of President Cárdenas and a trusted adviser of the U.S. ambassador. Toward the end of the 1930s, moreover, the U.S. Embassy in Lima used Tannenbaum—as it would Waldo Frank in 1942—to strengthen its ties with Víctor Raúl Haya de la Torre, the Peruvian firebrand who preached Indian regeneration in Andean America and who in the 1920s had been under State Department surveillance as a dangerous radical.[45] In a certain way, then, official policy was keeping pace with and to some extent being guided by the reversal of stereotyping of "primitive people" and their revolutionary champions that had begun at the level of a counterculture. Meantime, counterculture values had spread from intellectual circles and certain fringes of the foreign-policy establishment to Main Street, a fact that Wall Street failed to reckon with in 1938.

In response to Cárdenas's nationalization of foreign oil holdings, U.S. big business unleashed a vicious propaganda assault against Mexicans, trading in traditional stereotypes to depict them as less than fully human, as lazy Indians, as naughty children, and as a people that had undergone "racial degeneration." The old epithets and stereotypes appeared in abundance in a July 1938 edition of *Atlantic Monthly* aimed at whipping up popular indignation against Mexicans and forcing the State Department into a heavy-handed response to the nationalization, depicted as criminal expropriation.[46] Rather than mobilizing Americans, the July *Atlantic Monthly* seemed to embarrass them and even to arouse their ire against the propagandists.

Meanwhile in Mexico City, Ambassador Daniels sided more with Cárdenas than the oil interests and prevented the State Department, headed by Cordell Hull who had been outraged by the nationalization, from adopting a hard-line defense of the foreign capitalists. Moreover, Adolf A. Berle, Jr., appointed assistant secretary of state in March 1938 precisely at the moment Cárdenas announced the expropriation, had little sympathy with his country's oil interests. In 1938 and also in 1945, when he served as ambassador to Brazil, Berle believed that the life of a U.S. diplomat was "incomplete without a scrimmage with the international oil people."[47]

Throughout his life, Berle professed admiration for the simple persons who lived close to the soil, and hostility toward profit-mad capitalists who exploited them. This had been apparent in his warm response to the peasant sectors of the Dominican Republic and Puerto Rico when he first observed them in 1918, and in his simultaneous disdain for the American firms operating there. And Berle became all the more set in his viewpoints through his encounter with the Pueblos, mentioned in the preceding chapter, as he participated in the successful movement to defeat the Bursum Bill, in the process becoming ever more convinced as to the pernicious effects that imperialist intervention in the name of uplift produced both on colonialists and colonials. Moreover, Berle, a man of vast ego, believed that many Americans had begun to undergo a spiritual rebirth that would awaken in them the capacity to share in his enlightened vision of the just society. In the new nation that would arise from the ashes of the depression, Americans would come to understand, as Berle believed he did, that people "must work for ideals and service rather than for money." Always attracted by persons who "retained a purely spiritual and mythical quality," Berle once wrote: "Not impossibly, the teacher, the artist, the poet and the philosopher will set the pace for the next era."[48] Latin American intellectuals, running the gamut from left to right, had been predicting this for years. Now they believed they had friends not only among America's writers and poets but also among its highly placed political figures.

In the past, Berle believed, the overconsumption of some Americans had led to the underconsumption of others—an idea that FDR shared and that found expression in his 1932 Commonwealth Club address in San Francisco that Berle wrote.[49] Amelioration-minded public servants, Berle averred, could correct the imbalance. Within the confines of a more harmonious social and economic culture, American capitalism would continue to grow, but it would grow at a more moderate rate, at a rate that would help assure the indefinite survival of natural resources over which government would have to establish a wise stewardship. Growth would come to American capitalism in part through expansion into foreign markets, and Berle had no doubt about the need to open up new markets in Latin America; but here, too, the operating principle must be one of beneficent stewardship. The wise and just utilization of markets to the south would require planning on both the American and Latin American ends. However, Berle doubted the short-term ability of the Latins to provide the sort of planning that he deemed essential. Until the Latins acquired the requisite organizational skills, Americans might have to furnish somewhat unilaterally the kind of leadership and foresight that would prove advantageous to U.S. capitalists, to their middle-class counterparts to the south, and also to the Latin American masses. To his credit, though, Berle was almost as dubious about American as about Latin American bureaucratic planners. It would be touch and go as to whether America could produce enough influential bureaucrats inspired by his own perceptions and understanding.

Berle's vision of a future hemispheric capitalism that harmonized diverse elements left room for a transition stage of enlightened Yankee imperialism and in some ways may not have been altogether removed from the Wilsonian vision. And yet, paradoxically, Berle remained enough the counterculturalist to admire nature that refused to be rationalized. Exhibiting a streak of biophilia shortly after he arrived as ambassador to Brazil in March 1945, Berle penned this romantic depiction of the Amazonian forest: "The forest is unmaliciously impregnable; never hurrying, never stopping, capable of absorbing into itself inside of two years any scar that man can make on it. What is inside of it no one yet knows. It defends itself economically; its riches, though vast, are so scattered that they cannot be organized as we like to organize things."[50] Had Berle lived into the 1990s, he would have had to revise his optimistic assessment of the Amazonian forest's recuperative powers.

Like many other Americans capable of empathizing sometimes with the negative identity, Berle could in some moments admire Latin Americans precisely because, like nature at its most irrepressible, they defied the organization that Yankees so liked to impose. Most of the time, though, Berle inclined toward being imperious, high-handed, and cantankerous as he sought to rationalize nature and people, for their own good. In him, some of the basic American paradoxes found their embodiment. Perhaps it was his readiness to live with paradox, with opposites interacting hopefully in harmony, that inclined Berle so favorably toward the people of Puerto Rico and various Caribbean and Central American republics. Among these people Berle admired cultural and racial mixture, the same mixture that Latin America's avant-garde champions of mestizaje and negritude had begun to hail as the basis of a new humanity.

In Puerto Rico's amalgam of Negro, Indian, and Spanish ingredients, an Anglo Saxon element, added after 1898, increased its presence and influence as New Dealers devised measures intended to turn the island dependency into a model of what enlightened social planning could accomplish. Berle himself observed the results in 1954 and pronounced himself pleased: "Here in Puerto Rico . . . the Anglo-Saxon civilization has met the Spanish-American civilization, mixed with Negro and some Indian, and the result is wholly successful. That ought to prove something to somebody."[51]

The man principally responsible for shaping the New Deal's Puerto Rican policy shared Berle's capacity to welcome paradox and also some of his mystical compulsion to harmonize opposites. First visiting Puerto Rico in 1934, Rexford G. Tugwell was appalled by the example it afforded of waste, inefficiency, and human suffering occasioned by the one-dimensional, individualistic capitalism that American imperialism had fostered. On this occasion and on a subsequent visit in 1937, Tugwell enthused over what enlightened leaders could accomplish in transforming the troubled island into a model of development and social justice. Relinquishing his role as one of FDR's so-called brain trusters in Washington, Tugwell came to Puerto Rico in 1941 as its governor. Influenced by some of America's utopian thinkers of the past, including novelist Edward Bellamy who had also cast a spell on TVA's first director Arthur E. Morgan, Tugwell envisioned a future for the island not unlike the one Lázaro Cárdenas dreamed of for Mexico.[52] A new style of managed, communitarian capitalism would combine socialist and individualistic drives. At the same time, urban and rural culture would fuse in a new socioeconomic structure that featured factories in the field. In the island utopia, the virtues of dusky primitivism would fuse with those of Caucasian civilization. Propounding largely the same vision, native Caribbean thinkers who championed negritude had been viewed from Washington, in the 1920s, as dangerous radicals who posed a threat to civilization in America's "back yard." Now, in the late years of the Good Neighbor era, Washington appointed as governor of Puerto Rico a man who shared in the vision of negritude.[53] What is more, at its outset the Roosevelt administration had appointed a like-minded intellectual the Government Secretary (the principal executive official) of the U.S. Virgin Islands. The man appointed, in spite of the fact he had voted for the Socialist party ticket in 1932, was Robert Herrick.

Like so many other persons who marched to a counterculturalist drummer, Herrick, originally a Chicago-based novelist, had formed his vision of the new social order while living under the spell of New Mexico's Pueblo and Hispanic peoples. Visiting Taos in 1923, Herrick found, so he believed, the ideal antithesis to the crass materialism that vitiated America's capitalist culture and seemed at its virulent worst in Chicago. "In sacrificing all the comforts and prestige of life," the Indians and Hispanics had "retained their civility and their inner selves." Leading lives that were "deeply unconscious" (here we encounter shades of D. H. Lawrence and Carl Jung), they remained in touch with their traditions or race memory. Comforted by the nature that surrounded them, they did not seek solace in the goods that "the white man had encumbered his life with." Even their houses, in whose adobe they had "mixed their blood," harmonized with nature.[54] In all, the Indians and Hispanics and mixed-bloods of New Mexico had a great lesson to teach their white exploiters.

Up to his death on St. Thomas Island in 1938, Herrick, who for much of his life had extolled racial and cultural mestizaje, proved enormously successful in establishing a warm relationship with the Negro and mulatto Virgin Islanders. Just as Josephus Daniels applauded the Mexican dream of a society that harmonized the distinctive cultures of Indians and Hispanics, Herrick endorsed the Caribbean vision of the simultaneously black and white new person. Neither man is necessarily discredited, any more than Tugwell in Puerto Rico, by the fact that their hopes for a new order resting on combining opposites, among them modernity and primitivism, capitalism and socialism, ended in shambles within twenty to thirty years.

Goodwill toward Latin America: American Music, Classical and Popular

Not only official diplomats encouraged the blending of North and South, white and dark, artifice and nature during the Good Neighbor era. Composers, exemplified by Aaron Copland and George Gershwin, showed an interest in the merging of disparate cultural influences as they experimented with compositions that wed the traditions of classical music to Latin American melody and rhythm.

Aaron Copland (1900–1990), whose compositions already had made and would continue to make use of American popular and folk music that bubbled up from the bottom of the socioeconomic ladder, turned in 1932 to Mexican sources for a shot of the primitivism that would keep his compositions vibrant and vital. Visiting Mexico for the first time late in that year, he was bowled over by the experience. "Mexico," Copland wrote to his composer–music critic friend Virgil Thomson, "has turned out even grander than I expected—and I expected pretty grand things. The best is the people—there's nothing remotely like them in Europe. They are really the 'people'—nothing in them striving to be bourgeois. In their overalls and bare feet they are not only poetic but positively '*émouvant*.'" To another friend Copland wrote at the beginning of 1933: "Europe now seems conventional to me by comparison. Mexico offers something fresh and pure and wholesome—a quality which is deeply unconventionalized. The source of it is the Indian blood which is so prevalent. I sense the influence of the Indian background everywhere—even in the landscape."[55]

Out of Copland's first visit to Mexico came the sometimes rollicking, sometimes hauntingly melancholy *El Salón México*, an inspired piece of music. The actual Salón México was a combination bar, dance hall, and probably also bordello that Copland along with countless tourists liked to visit at this time in Mexico City. In that "hot spot," Copland wrote, "one felt a close contact with the Mexican people. It wasn't the music I heard, but the spirit that I felt there, which attracted me. Something of that spirit is what I hope to have put into my music."[56] The native themes that Copland employed in the work came mainly from the *Cancionero Mexicano* (Mexican songbook) compiled by Frances Toor, a remarkable woman who figured among the American expatriates seeking life-renewing forces in Mexico.

For his 1942 composition "Danzón Cubano" and for the later work "Three Latin-American Sketches" (1959–1965), Copland turned once more to the Latin ambience for musical spice. Meantime, for such works as the ballets *Billy the Kid* (1938) and *Rodeo* (1942) he found inspiration in musical themes and legends out of the Wild West. The physical frontier had indeed ended, but its revitalizing spirit could be preserved in the music that it inspired. In Copland's musical new frontier listeners encountered the natural as it derived not only from the Wild West but also from Latin America. Here lay fitting testimony to the spirit of hemispheric unity that soared for a brief moment during the Good Neighbor era.

Vacationing in Cuba in February 1932, George Gershwin was as much taken by the earthy quality of Latin music as Copland had been in Mexico. Indeed, Gershwin's fascination with the Latin beat went back to his first public appearance, staged at his high school in 1914. On that occasion the fifteen-year-old Gershwin played a piano composition he called "Tango." During his two-week 1932 stay in Cuba, Gershwin came to realize as never before that the Latin beat was also an African beat. Fascinated by the intricate rhythms that, sometimes through an alcoholic haze, he heard small dance orchestras perform, Gershwin decided he must return to the island every winter. He succumbed to brain cancer in 1937 without having made it back. But, during the few years remaining to him he never forgot that 1932 vacation, about which he wrote, "I spent two hysterical weeks in Havana, where no sleep was had, but the quantity and quality of fun made up for that."[57] A notorious womanizer, in sharp contrast to the somewhat austere and homosexual Copland, Gershwin apparently found all that he could have hoped for in Cuba, musically and sexually. But, unlike the fruit of Copland's first visit to Mexico, the composition that emerged from Gershwin's Cuban experience, an approximately ten-minute piece called "Cuban Overture," is mediocre at best.

Could mediocrity in some way be owing to a condescension Gershwin may have felt toward Cuba, in contrast to Copland's genuine and deep response to Mexico? Through the years, it has been said, Americans regarded Cuba as symbolizing three aspects of the natural. They saw it "at various times as a greenhouse, an outhouse and a whorehouse."[58] Perhaps

Gershwin fits into this pattern. Cuba was a fun place to visit, but one would not want to spend too much time there lest one risk going native. Writing compositions derived from Cuba's melodies and rhythms was tantamount to taking listeners on a tour of the midway.

Gershwin's masterpiece, so it is said, is the folk opera *Porgy and Bess*. Here the "primitivism" to which the composer turns for inspiration is not that of the Latin masses but of American Negroes. Just possibly, though, Gershwin's empathy for put-upon social underlings had been sharpened by the excitement he had experienced in discovering the all-pervasive African influence on Cuban music. Liking what he observed of Cuban culture, Gershwin had understood that part of the culture was African.

This is the explanation that puts Gershwin in the most favorable light. To many listeners, though, something remains troubling about Gershwin's quest for inspiration in "primitivism"; and what troubles, though not nearly so much with the African as with the Latin influences, is the suspicion of condescension. On the other hand, the homage that America's black social underlings paid Latin culture comes across as unfeigned and unreserved. This element of sincerity helps impart genuine artistic stature to the fusion that black Americans achieved between their music and Latin America's music of the streets, saloons, dance halls, and whorehouses.

Down at the level of popular or folk culture, American Negroes added a Latin element to their own musical roots and, in the process, helped forge a new music that exceeded in importance what America's classical composers were creating. Only at this popular level was the melting-pot myth truly realized in music. From its New Orleans inception and in its gradual trek up the Delta and into the cities of the North, jazz managed to fuse "African sensibility" and "Latin musical traditions." Symbolic of the fusion were the many early jazz musicians and composers commonly designated creole (a term originally denoting black and white-French mixture) but actually of Mexican origin.[59] In another way, the legendary Jelly Roll Morton, who perhaps with a touch of hyperbole claimed to be the inventor of jazz, provides an example of jazz music's Latin connection. A creole born in Gulfport, Louisiana, in 1885, Jelly Roll (who was christened Joseph Le-Menthe) as a youth played piano in various "sporting houses" of the Gulf area and also in Mexico where he sojourned on several occasions. By the time he began recording in the 1920s, his music had absorbed influences not merely from Afro-American but also from Latin American sources.[60] Intellectuals might write about cultural and racial mestizaje, but it was mainly down at the lowest socioeconomic levels that Americans actually accomplished it.

In the 1920s the first dance craze from Latin America swept the United

States: the tango. It was followed by the rumba craze in the 1930s, with the cults of the conga, the samba, and then the mambo following in fairly rapid succession. The rhythms of the dances from below the border added a new tinge to American jazz: a tinge that was Latin by way of Africa.[61] Meantime, to cite just one example of the influence of Latin American–born jazzmen, Puerto Rican Juan Tizol had added a Latin tinge to the Duke Ellington orchestra, in which he played trombone for many years. Tizol wrote various songs that the group recorded in the 1930s and early 1940s, including "Moonlight Fiesta" (originally titled "Porto Rican Chaos"), "Moon over Cuba," and best known of all, "Perdido." Moreover, Ellington's 1943 tone poem "Black, Brown, and Beige," with its "vaguely Latin rhythms in the drums" in one movement, exulted in the Caribbean, specifically the West Indian, influence on America's black culture.[62] On a considerably lower level of artistic merit, the 1940 hit tune "Rhumboogie" pointed in its own way to the importance of the Latin tinge in American music. Harlem's new creation has a Cuban syncopation, the lyrics proclaim, a combination of boogie woogie and a little rumba rhythm. The result is "a killer"—jive talk for what is sensational and great. Whether appropriately or not, the song was featured in the movie "Argentine Nights,"[63] perhaps suggesting that even in the Good Neighbor years one part of Latin America was the same as another to most gringos.

In a way, when white "high culture" figures like Copland and Gershwin turned to Latin and Afro-Latin influences for musical inspiration they simply followed in the footsteps of mainly black musicians down at the grass-roots level of American culture. When Anglo Americans began to take this music seriously, they thought the "primitivism" that liberated them for a time from middle-class anxieties, that brought gooseflesh and made them tap their feet and dance and clap their hands derived from African American sources. So it did; but it derived also from Latin American and Afro–Latin American roots. Under the influence of counterculture values and the impetus of Good Neighbor–era feelings, middle- and upper-class Americans expanded their cultural horizons to hemispheric dimensions. Down at the lowest social levels, dark-skinned musicians for generations had, without even having to reflect on the matter, accepted the Latin tinge as a natural part of their lives.

By the 1930s, though, a good number of American intellectuals out to end alienation by reincorporating the primitive into their lives began to look elsewhere than Latin America and Afro-America for what seemed lacking. They placed their hope for renewal and regeneration in Spain, specifically in the Republican peasants locked in battle with the sort of fascist reactionaries that throughout the Western world, according to current

Marxist-Leninist gospel, had taken on the final and doomed defense of capitalist civilization. Traditionally, Americans had tended to regard Spain as of greater moment than the Iberian New World. Never was this fact more clearly in evidence than when America's utopian intellectuals in the mid-1930s turned their attention from Ibero-America, where despite earlier expectations the revolutionary spark had not spread beyond Mexico, to the Iberian motherland. At least in the transition under way, the "primitivism" that so appealed to many Americans did retain a Hispanic face. The Iberian identity of the face is significant. In light of prevailing American prejudices, as already alluded to in these pages, a Spanish face somehow suggested more grandeur and attracted more respect than a Latin American visage could claim. Even in the Good Neighbor era, this remained true.

Spanish Republicans Eclipse the Attraction of Latin American Revolutionaries

The admiration that some American travelers in the 1920s had felt for what they observed either in the Soviet Union or in Mexico carried the implication that something had gone terribly wrong with their own civilization. By the 1930s the conviction as to modernity's malaise had taken deeper root, and the Spanish Republic emerged as the new cause for intellectuals alienated in one way or another from capitalist civilization, which had entered into a deep economic depression. With the Russian and Mexican revolutions becoming old hat, Spain, with its recently overturned monarchy, became the preferred "image of death and rebirth, of the old world decaying as the new emerged in all its youthful strength."[64]

No single factor can come even close to explaining why American intellectuals unhappy with their country's traditional bourgeois values took the Spanish Republic to their hearts. However, two attitudes do surface with some degree of consistency among the majority of Americans who identified with the republic. One of these is an openness toward Marxism, however intellectuals chose to define that protean ideology. Whatever else it might mean, Marxism did stand for opposition to the sort of materialism and greed that depression-era intellectuals tended to excoriate. In the 1930s, moreover, Marxism to many American intellectuals meant human beings alive with a new intensity "to the beauty and rawness of self-creation,"[65] human beings caught up in a cause bigger than the individual ego, a cause that satisfied the longing for community—and, not so coincidentally, accorded scant recognition to the rights of the *individual*. Marxism, indeed, provided what Freud called the "oceanic feeling": a feeling that belittles the importance of the solitary human, a feeling that some Americans of the 1930s imagined their ancestors must have experienced in the now-vanished wilderness. And, whatever else it might mean, anti-individualistic Marxism promised an alternative to the paradox of capitalism that, as I. F. Stone expressed it in 1938, "puts want amid plenty, idle men beside idle factories, underfed children in a land of rotting crops."[66]

The second attitude that recurs consistently among intellectuals who fervently championed the republic is an openness toward primitivism. With its many facets, primitivism is as resistant to precise definition as Marxism, though one of its most constantly recurring motifs must surely be the desire of persons perplexed by and alienated from the present to start anew amidst people not yet crushed by the ills of civilization and all of the burdens and responsibilities and liberties it heaped on the individual.

So, then, Marxism and primitivism, however difficult to define, tended to distinguish the liberal and radical intellectuals of the 1930s who made the republic their sacred cause. And this fact confirmed conservatives in their old suspicions as to an insidious connection between those who were soft on communism and those who romanticized the primitive.

As well as any single American, Ernest Hemingway (notwithstanding his already-noted disdain for the vogue of the noble redskin) illustrates the cult of primitivism that underlay the attraction so many intellectuals felt toward the Spanish Republic. To them, the republic represented the old Spain, the Spain of peasants and of passions, threatened by the invasion of modernity in its latest, fascistic stage. The threatened, invaded Spain was a country of "authentic" people, in touch with basic humanity, a people of "animal strength" and "triumphant lust," at home with "twitching death" and "ruthless fate." This was how Hemingway described the people he wrote about in his deservedly acclaimed novel set in civil-war Spain, *For Whom the Bell Tolls* (1940).[67]

Before he arrived on the Spanish scene, Hemingway had extolled Ethiopians as they resisted the imperialist armies that Benito Mussolini had unleashed against them in the early 1930s. Depicting Ethiopians as living in a society of primitive virtue, Hemingway described the brutal intrusion among them of mechanized modern civilization, symbolized by that diabolical instrument of modern technology, the dive-bomber. His accounts of the struggle of men close to nature against machine-age brutality created a vivid impression among many Americans, especially perhaps among African Americans. Then, almost at the very inception of the Spanish civil war, Italian and German bombers put in their appearance on the side of the Nationalists—a fact of which Picasso reminded all who viewed his monumental painting *Guernica* that propagandized blatantly in behalf of Marxism and of primitivism. Whether perceived by Hemingway or Picasso, Spain's Loyalists became the embodiment of premodern innocence; they stood for the spontaneity and freedom of the organic community as opposed to the regimentation and tyranny of the twentieth century as it had, inexorably, come to be served by Fascist planes. Just twenty years earlier when peasants had made their revolution in Mexico, they had stood pretty much on an equal footing with the forces of repressive capitalist modernity clustered around Porfirio Díaz. But now modernity had new weaponry to unleash against those who resisted it and denounced its tendency to assign full-fledged human rights only to the wealthy and the powerful. Spain might be the last place where underlings could turn back the crushing tide of modernity.

But, it wasn't to be. With the fall of the Spanish Republic in 1939 much of the heart went out of America's adversary culture, and much of the esprit that had united black and white intellectuals disappeared. Leftist intellectuals looked on resignedly, and even with burgeoning approbation, as American participation in World War II resulted not in a crusade to create a new world and a new humanity but rather in a defense of traditional free-enterprise, individualistic, middle-class values. Obviously, there was not going to be a new world, called into being by intellectuals and the primitives they hoped to defend and perhaps ultimately to command. This being the case, American intellectuals tended to lose interest in "primitives," whether Spanish peasants or the blacks and immigrants in their midst or the lowly masses to their south. If intellectuals were not fated to overthrow the establishment, perhaps they had better position themselves to join it. By the beginning of the 1940s the Good Neighbor policy reflected the change in national mood. It had lost much of the utopian thrust provided by counterculturalists who had expected to transform the new hemispheric policy into a radical movement at odds with the intentions of most of the statesmen who devised it.

The Late Good Neighbor Policy: Normalcy Triumphs over Utopianism

Always, even from its very inception, the Good Neighbor policy had contained in its mix of disparate elements a sharp cutting edge of economic interest. To radical journalist Carleton Beals, the whole "Good-Will Racket" that purportedly underlay the policy was a carefully contrived sham, created simply to serve national economic interests. "The 'Good-Will Racket' and the Good Neighbor Policy seemed [to Beals] intended to wedge Latin America into the capitalist mold with its boom-bust cycles, unrealistic debt policies and unfair exchanges between industrial and non-industrial nations."[68]

Even if not necessarily as cold-bloodedly calculating as Beals thought, Washington officials devoutly hoped that reciprocity, one key element of the Good Neighbor policy, would produce definite economic benefits for American capitalists. The United States government would refrain from the sort of political intervention that the Latins so hated, and the Latins would reciprocate by facilitating the private economic penetration into their midst that the Yankees so coveted.[69]

As the war clouds gathered in Europe and the eventual involvement of the United States in global conflict became ever more likely, policymakers thought increasingly in terms of security, and reciprocity assumed new expectations: if the United States refrained from so much as the semblance of intervention by, for example, turning the other cheek when governments raised taxes on Yankee operations or mandated wage increases for the native laborers they employed, then the Latin Americans would reciprocate by rooting out the Fascist threat in the hemisphere and extending all-out support to the Allied cause,[70] by producing huge surpluses of raw materials and accepting in payment less than the going market rate.

In the interest of aligning Latin American nations solidly on its side in the event of war, the United States often found itself pressured into being a much better neighbor—that is, more tolerant of the way in which the southern republics dealt with American investors—than it had originally intended to become. But many Washington officials chafed at this and longed for the day when they could return to business as usual in dealing with the Latins. Included in this camp was the secretary of state, Cordell Hull. From 1941 on, he bided his time to redirect policy away from what he considered Sumner Welles's coddling approach and back to a resolute, consistent defense of American business interests. Hull's indignation over what he deemed Latin violation of the spirit of reciprocity on the economic front—and he had the Mexican oil expropriation especially in mind—soon gave way to even greater pique over failures to reciprocate in security matters. Some Latin American nations, with Argentina in the forefront, refused to acknowledge what Hull considered their reciprocal obligations by joining wholeheartedly in the war against international fascism.[71] Moreover, the officials of some countries balked at weeding out "fascist" elements in their midst. Actually, many foreigners whose attitudes and actions Washington officials branded fascistic indulged in no worse crime than competing with U.S. firms and investors. But in the era following the "loss" of Spain to so-called fascism, Americans responded with some of the same hysteria with which they later reacted to the threat of international communism following the "loss" of China to Mao Zedong's armies in 1949.

Indeed, the disillusionment and pique of American intellectuals over the inability of Spaniards to stem the fascistic tide translated into a certain dubiousness about the reliability of Spanish Americans in resisting the forces of evil. Portuguese Americans, or Brazilians, also incurred the suspiciousness of American intellectuals and politicians when Fascist-leaning Antonio de Oliveira Salazar became Portugal's dictatorial premier in 1932. Some of the dislike directed against him transferred onto Brazil's strong-man ruler in the 1930s and first half of the 1940s, Getulio Vargas. In him, many Americans, who had become overly suspicious on the issue as a result of their frustrated expectations for Spain, thought they perceived a closet Fascist. Meantime, though, many Americans with the strongest economic ties to Latin America remained indifferent to issues of crypto-fascism. For them, the 1930s and 1940s meant business as usual with Latin America.

Much of the time during the Good Neighbor era politicians and intellectuals in Washington proved less important in determining hemispheric relations than the long-established "informal empire" that linked American private investors together with their Latin American collaborators.[72] While visionaries like Waldo Frank and also a fair number of State Department romantics dreamed of an alliance between intellectuals north and south that would regulate the operation of hemispheric capitalism and assure the underprivileged their day in the sun, they had virtually no effect on the informal empire. Networks of Latin American capitalist-politicians locked into a symbiotic relationship with U.S. investors managed to retain effective control in most Latin American countries; they stemmed the revolutionary tide that many Yankee dreamers had expected would sweep down from Mexico all the way to Tierra del Fuego and, as they saw the situation, helped make the hemisphere a haven for civilization rather than a redoubt of primitivism. Like those American Indians who had themselves become successful capitalists and who branded the John Collier–inspired attempts to strengthen native communalism as some sort of communist scheme,[73] the Latin American capitalist-politicians locked into the informal empire resented the interference of Washington utopianists and confidently awaited the day when bureaucrats would return to their senses and mystical intellectuals to their ivory towers.

Even as World War II came to an end, Sumner Welles clung to the cultural pluralism, commented on toward the beginning of this chapter, that he had voiced in assessing U.S. occupation of the Dominican Republic in the 1920s. In a book published in 1946, three years after his fall from grace at the State Department, he urged that Juan D. Perón, recently elected president of Argentina, be given a chance to implement the reform programs he had proclaimed. According to Welles, Perón had "the inherent capacity and the chance to make of his promised 'social revolution' a New Deal for the Argentine people." For one thing, Perón would, Welles believed, abolish the prevailing agrarian system based on huge, privately owned estates and turn "laborers and tenants into proprietors."[74] On similar grounds, Josephus Daniels and dozens of American intellectuals had defended the Mexican revolution in the mid-1930s. But times had changed. With prosperity restored by the economic impetus issuing out of the war effort, Americans in droves abandoned their reform-minded mood. The traditional free-enterprise system, according to the new consensus, should not be tampered with. Leave it alone, and the good times would roll. Latin Americans must understand that the old economic wisdom was still the only wisdom; they must abandon statist intervention in the economy— unless, of course, that intervention served the purposes of the informal empire. In the purview of the new American consensus as the cold war commenced, social reform, whether in Latin America or the United States itself, smacked of communism.

During the course of World War II, cultural pluralism lost much of its attractiveness to Americans. How could they embrace concepts of the moral equivalence of disparate cultures and different peoples when locked in a mighty struggle with Hitler's Germany and Emperor Hirohito's Japan? Probably a majority of Americans agreed with Adm. William Halsey that the war with Japan involved nothing less than the struggle of an evil alien race against benevolent "white civilization."[75] Increasingly, those caught up in war-induced emotions placed the Japanese in the same category that frontiersmen had placed Indians and that turn-of-the-century imperialists had placed Filipinos.

John Collier's departure as commissioner of the Bureau of Indian Affairs in 1945 indicated the demise of cultural pluralism as an element in shaping U.S. policy with Native Americans. Once more, Indians would be pressured to conform to the ways of the country's one good culture, that of the enterprising, entrepreneurial white middle classes. Given the historical association between attitudes toward Indians and Latin Americans, Collier's departure provided a tip-off about the elimination of cultural pluralism as an element in American assessment of Latin Americans. And it may be significant that after returning in 1945 to Taos where he spent the remaining fifteen years of his life, Collier had virtually no contact with Indians.[76] Perhaps he had lost interest in them because he understood he could no longer use them as instruments in a crusade to change the United States in line with his own anticapitalist values. Perhaps American counterculturalist intellectuals lost interest in Latin Americans for similar reasons.

By the mid-1940s, familiar stereotypes of disparagement or at least belittlement had reestablished themselves in Hollywood's treatment of Latins. With their sexuality and lack of inhibitions, Latin Americans (as portrayed in such vehicles for "Brazilian Bombshell" Carmen Miranda as *Weekend in Havana* and *That Night in Rio*[77]), supplied a certain spice to the fantasy lives of Americans. But when it came to real-life usefulness, Latins had little to offer except as sex kittens for Yankee rovers and unskilled employees for American firms. This message came across in the Andrews Sisters' 1944 hit "Rum and Coca-Cola." According to the song's lyrics, Latins provided unexcelled all-night "tropic love"; beyond that, they had to be kept in their place, "working for the Yankee dollar."[78]

U.S. sailors going on a 1943 rampage in the Chavez Ravine area of Los Angeles provided a distressing glimpse of the attitude of some representative Americans toward Latin Americans. In the course of the "zoot-suit riots," Mexicans and Mexican Americans were attacked and sometimes badly beaten (miraculously, none were killed) mainly because of their inclination to flaunt cultural differences by wearing suits, originated by East Coast Negroes, out of line with conventional sartorial standards.[79] Some Los Angeles law-enforcement officers sympathized with the rampaging sailors and in order to justify them revived time-worn stereotypes of Mexicans as bloodthirsty criminals. Writing at the time of the riots, Capt. E. Durán Ayres, chief of the Foreign Relations Bureau of the Los Angeles Sheriff's Office, proclaimed that Mexicans were driven by the desire to kill, "or at least let blood." That is why it proved difficult for Anglo Saxons to understand the psychology of Mexicans and also, according to Ayres, of Indians. When one added to this "inborn characteristic" both of Mexicans and Native Americans the chronic use of liquor, then "crimes of violence" had to be expected.[80] In a way, then, the Anglo rioters acted only to forestall crimes of violence—even as had frontiersmen when they wrested the West from the aborigines.

A poll taken at the end of 1940 provided more or less scientific corroboration to the deductions that anyone could have drawn by watching movies, listening to popular songs, and reading newspapers. In this poll, conducted by the Office of Public Opinion, respondents were given a choice of nineteen adjectives with which to describe Central and South Americans. Between 40 and 50 percent of the respondents chose "quick tempered," "emotional," "superstitious," "backward," "lazy," "ignorant," and "suspicious." At the bottom, "selected by just 5 percent of those questioned, came 'efficient.' Above that, in order, were 'progressive,' 'generous,' 'brave,' 'honest,' 'intelligent,' and 'shrewd'—none of which were chosen by more than 16 percent." At the very top of the list came "dark-skinned," the designation chosen by 80 percent of respondents as applicable to Latin Americans.[81] By dint of dark skin, Latins were guilty of what for many Americans was an unforgivable breach of propriety, for as the war came to an end the Negro and all others of less than white complexion had definitely passed out of vogue. Just as much as the zoot-suit riots, race riots, with Negroes as their target, announced America's return to normalcy.

Throughout the New Deal era, departure from normalcy had not extended very far in some respects. True, Eleanor Roosevelt in 1939 arranged for an outdoor concert before the Lincoln Memorial, attended by an audience of seventy-five thousand, when the Daughters of the American Revolution prevented the great African American contralto Marian Anderson from appearing in Constitution Hall, which they owned and from which they excluded Negroes. But the Metropolitan Opera still maintained (until 1955) the whites-only tradition that had resulted in 1933 in assigning the role of the Negro Pullman porter turned Caribbean island king in Louis Gruenberg's opera *Emperor Jones* to white-skinned Lawrence Tibbet rather than to black-skinned Paul Robeson. Moreover, white audiences had been spared the spectacle of seeing Robeson portray Othello, Shakespeare's dark-skinned Moor who wooed and won the fair Desdemona—a role that had earned Robeson the plaudits of London audiences, even when it became known he was having an affair with the leading lady. Furthermore, so as not to offend white sensitivities, the miscegenation scene with its implied criticism of southern attitudes on race had to be played down in revivals and also in the 1936 movie version of the musical drama *Show Boat*, first staged in 1927 when racial prejudice had seemed a mite more odious to many Americans. Negro entertainers were all right when they performed in all-Negro casts (*Porgy and Bess* had such a cast, disappointing Al Jolson who had longed to play Porgy in blackface); but they had better not try to step out of their place and assume a presence among white performers, unless their roles were confined to buffoonery and dancing, activities in which whites could tolerate blacks without having their stereotypes upset.

The prizefight ring had also become an acceptable arena for Negroes, but Americans undoubtedly felt relief that Joe Louis was the "Brown Bomber" rather than a black bomber. Jackie Robinson was permitted to cross the color line when he joined the Brooklyn Dodgers in 1947, but he and the few blacks who entered major league baseball shortly thereafter clearly understood they had to "keep their place." For one thing, they must retain a polite and resigned demeanor in the face of questionable umpire calls. Only the white race could argue with white arbiters. Moreover, during the New Deal era, the South insisted more than ever on the "blacks for the land, whites for the factories" principle.[82]

If, in the South, factories were for whites, throughout the country they were the preserve of males—though not necessarily just white males in the North. Women, pressed into wartime service in man's world, were expected to return home at the war's end and resume their natural function of producing babies.

To confront their Fascist foes, symbolized as the greatest threat that barbarism had ever posed to civilization, Americans had had to raise industrial and scientific capacity and organizational skills to new levels. Thereby they acquired unprecedented power. Having used that power to defeat their fearsome enemies, they could now utilize it to establish previously undreamed of measures of control over nature—wherever it was found and in whatever manifestation.

By 1945, interest in ecology had died. Nature and all those persons who served as metaphors for nature resumed their customary status of dependence or subjection when confronting civilization. Nothing symbolized the trend so dramatically as an event that took place in New Mexico near the end of the war. Here, in the area that in the 1920s had spawned the cult of the natural, the first atomic bomb was detonated. Now, as never before, Americans could bask in hubris over their ability to do as they wished with nature. Radical critic Dwight Macdonald observed in 1945 that from President Harry Truman down, Americans "emphasized that the Bomb has been produced in the normal, orderly course of scientific experiment, that it is thus simply the latest step in man's long struggle to control the forces of nature, in a word that it is Progress."[83]

As World War II ended and then as the cold war began, Americans exulted in their ability not only to dominate nature but also to use its power to discipline savage peoples, such as the Japanese and now the Russians, the latter manifesting their primitivism by their predilection for communism. All the while the American government showed sophisticated ingenuity as it lied to its own citizens about the dangers of radiation attendant upon the manufacture and testing of nuclear weaponry. Ostensibly, the domination of nature produced no undesirable side effects. Science had progressed beyond that. Science, and business, could do no wrong. More clearly than ever, they epitomized civilization while serving as its cutting edge.

Might-Have-Beens in Hemispheric Relations Yield to Old, and New, Realities

It was during the 1920s and most of the 1930s that Americans had their last opportunity in the twentieth century—unless the 1990s should produce some cataclysmic transitions—to redefine themselves and their civilization. But for the war (and but for the rise of Hitler and Japanese militarism that made the war not only inevitable but also just and good), the depression's economic effects might have lingered on, even if in attenuated form, and the country might have had to adjust to an ethic of slow growth and of seeking compensation less in economic rewards and more in noneconomic satisfactions. But for the war, cultural pluralism might not have been so readily discarded, in which case discrimination against Others who did not show special aptitude for dramatic economic gain might have abated more quickly and more completely. But for the war, Americans might never have produced a middle-class population explosion, yielding baby boomers with constantly expanding expectations of material satisfaction and little inclined to scruple—until it was almost too late—over how safe it was, and how expedient in the long term, to torture nature into yielding the last measure of its bounty.

If America had managed to redefine itself along the lines foreseen by so many counterculture intellectuals, writers, artists, and also statesmen, in the 1920s and 1930s, would the country, and the world, have been better off in the long run? Probably it is foolish to raise a question that cannot possibly be answered; and certainly it is essential to remember that the prophets of a new order had more than their share of bitter divisiveness, of self-delusion and self-serving hubris. Even without the war, the dream of a new America might have been an impossible dream. And, even if realized, it might have turned into a nightmare.

For better or for worse, America by the end of the war was back on a familiar track, back to the pursuit of growth for growth's sake, back to blazing intolerance for all "primitive" people and cultures that did not deify the values of individualism and economic growth, back to running roughshod over nature. Between 1939, when John Steinbeck's *Grapes of Wrath* reflected the widespread suspicion that Americans had to begin to behave differently, and the end of the war only six years had elapsed. In those six years, a sea change had taken place. Americans had come home; or at least they had returned to *one* of their cultural-ideological homes. And the cold war, to which Communists in the USSR certainly contributed every bit as much as capitalists in America, strengthened their smug satisfaction about being at home once more amidst the values of civilization. The 1920s and 1930s had been, even as British historian George Trevelyan once described the year 1848 in Europe, a turning point in history that didn't turn.

Not only did the turning point fail to turn, but during the New Deal era, conditions had developed that actually would render a genuinely fruitful turn in hemispheric relations more, rather than less, difficult to achieve. Increasingly during this era, America's adversary-culture intellectuals had flirted with communism and in the process contrived to impart a Marxist-Leninist tinge to what had been a thoroughly indigenous tradition of social protest. Waldo Frank for a time joined the Communist party of the United States (CPUSA) but soon recognized its true nature, saw he could not alter that nature (as he had foolishly and pompously thought he could), and left the party. But a good number of other American intellectuals, whether actually having joined the party or served as fellow travelers, were slow to make the break. For this they paid a price in postwar America. To minimize that price and to atone for their own misjudgments and those of their peers, many intellectuals became blatantly anti-Communist. For some this represented the avenue to renewed self-respect, for others the best way back into the establishment.

Meantime, communism, sometimes the official variety as defined in Moscow but far more often indigenous adaptations of it, spread like wildfire among Latin American intellectuals. Survivors of the reform movement in America, intent upon weeding out the Marxist-Leninist influences that had seduced many of them in the 1930s, found it difficult to establish rapport with the increasingly Marxist-tinged antiestablishment intellectuals in Latin America, ever more blatant in proclaiming their Marxism and not at all abashed to maintain warm if unofficial ties with Soviet-directed communism.

So, then, the communist temptation withered among U.S. intellectuals but flowered among their Latin American counterparts. Basically, divergence came about because America's free-enterprise capitalism scored some of its most remarkable achievements after the war, achievements of such magnitude as to blind most people to continuing failures in areas of social justice. In Latin America, on the other hand, what masqueraded as capitalist engines of progress continued to sputter and misfire. The failures of statist capitalism south of the border seemed to justify Marxist demands for sweeping the prevailing system away, lock, stock, and barrel. The relative success of the traditional American system, and the relative failure of the methods that the Latins had used ever since independence to muddle through from crisis to crisis, served to fortify gringo convictions that in their hemisphere civilization extended no farther south than the Rio Grande.

Indeed, these convictions had taken on new life for many Americans during the war years as they contemplated Latin flirtations with fascist varieties of statism. Furthermore, some irate Americans complained about having to bribe Latin Americans into supporting the war against the Axis powers. Allegedly, bribery had entailed the showering of U.S. public funds on Latin governments in the form, among many others, of loans and commodity purchase agreements. Bribery had, purportedly, also taken the form of Washington's pusillanimous acceptance of measures, little better than those enforced in Germany, Italy, and Japan, that created a hostile environment for private investment—especially private foreign investment. As the day of victory over the Axis enemy approached, a considerable number of Americans who had never acquired much goodwill toward Latins during the Good Neighbor era eagerly awaited the time when they could steer their own country away from New Deal statist aberrations and then take up anew the hemispheric mission to whip their southern neighbors into conformity with the standards of civilization. Actually, one of the more remarkable features of the Good Neighbor era is the amount of ill will toward Latin America that accumulated in its late years.

CHAPTER 9

America's Postwar Generation: New Variations on Old Themes

Civilization Cleansed, Civilization Triumphant

As World War II ended, many Americans who had lost faith in capitalist civilization during the 1930s were reborn as true believers. The American-British alliance that rested on the values of political and economic freedom, material progress, and rationality had triumphed over an aberrant strain in Western civilization that encouraged people to escape from freedom into totalitarianism, finding consolation for freedom's loss in mystical leadership, in myth, and in the glory of an all-powerful and ostensibly paternalistic state. With the defeat of the Axis powers, Western civilization had been cleansed of this deviant strain.

True, the Allies' triumph had depended on collaboration with Joseph Stalin's Communist empire. The American-British alliance had rationalized this fact through wartime propaganda that depicted Communists as undergoing a cleansing process of their own that shortly would bring them into compliance with the standards of bona fide Western civilization. When the absurdity of this view became patent, defenders of the "Free World" entered resolutely into the cold war, confident that the clear superiority of their economic, political, and religious institutions would prevail in a competition that for all its military underpinning would stop short of all-out war. With a new enemy to face, with a new struggle against evil to wage, Americans were ill disposed toward any and all notions about the moral equivalence of basically different cultures. Moreover, they had ceased by and large to condone poverty, as they had inclined to do during the depression when even upright middle classes had been poor, suggesting that a moral stigma did not inevitably attach to impoverishment. With national prosperity restored as peace returned, Americans seemed little inclined to regard poverty in their own midst, in Latin America, or elsewhere in the world as anything save a moral blemish—but one that could be removed when and if the blemished person resolved upon its removal.

Successfully fought wars, necessitating sacrifice while the conflict rages, often give rise to succeeding eras of rampant materialism as people seek economic rewards for sacrifices incurred during the armed struggle. By no means all Americans had contributed to the war effort through personal sacrifice. Liberal economist John Kenneth Galbraith observed: "In the war years, consumption of consumer goods doubled. Never in the history of human conflict had there been so much talk of sacrificing and so little sacrificing."[1] Still, many Americans *had* sacrificed, and they now sought compensation: material compensation. And those who had not sacrificed, who had mainly profited from the war effort, wanted the profits to continue and to multiply. The profit-making process, they rationalized, had contributed to victory in war; it could contribute just as much to the ongoing triumphs of their godly, decent, and freedom-loving civilization in the ensuing era of peace cum cold war. Leading economists in the postwar era assured Americans that the vision of uninterrupted progress was no mirage. They led the public to believe "that perpetual economic growth was possible, desirable, and, in fact, essential." The expectation of unending plenty thus became "the reigning assumption of social thought in the two decades after 1945."[2] American liberalism embraced unquestioningly the faith that economic growth would solve all problems, eventually passing this faith along, in the 1980s, to conservatives and neoconservatives. In America's refurbished civil religion, virtue belonged to those most successful in the pursuit of economic gain.

No wonder Horatio Alger's novels enjoyed their greatest vogue in America not when Alger first wrote them in the latter part of the nineteenth century, but rather in the late 1940s and the 1950s.[3] These works cast in the role of hero or civil saint precisely those persons most spectacularly successful in augmenting personal wealth: those persons who had proved most responsive to the "need-to-achieve" stimulus.[4] No wonder, too, that the classic modern novel written to extol rugged individualism in the quest for personal economic achievement appeared just as the end of World War II came into sight: Ayn Rand's *Fountainhead*, published in 1943. The book proved a smash hit especially on college campuses in the immediate postwar years and regained some of its initial popularity after the counterculture of the 1960s and early 1970s subsided. Not only did *The Fountainhead* extol individualism, it exalted selfishness as the cardinal virtue of American identity. F. A. Hayek's *Road to Serfdom*, published in 1944, reinforced Rand's message and wove an economic-social theory that exalted individualism, and/or selfishness, as the essential ingredient of civilization.[5]

In 1947 the Andrews Sisters (whose "Rum and Coca-Cola" was cited in the preceding chapter) joined with Danny Kaye to record one of their greatest hits: "Civilization (Bongo, Bongo, Bongo)."[6] The song was a tongue-in-cheek reference to the primitivism in vogue during the halcyon counterculture days preceding World War II. "Bongo, Bongo, Bongo," the singers exclaim, they "don't want to leave the Congo." "Bingle, bangle, bongle," they're so happy in the jungle that they want to stay; as to civilization, "take it away!" As they drove the song to the top of the Hit Parade, Americans were, in effect, making fun of their temporary defection from civilization. They found it amusing that just a few years before many of them had seriously challenged civilization, proclaimed the superior values of the jungle, and held up communal, "laid-back," non-Western life-styles as providing desirable alternatives to American culture.

Among Americans feeling a mite sheepish about their recent defection from capitalist civilization were intellectuals. As the 1950s began, sociologist Daniel Bell noted that intellectuals had grown weary of their alienation from American life.[7] By then, they had begun "to enjoy the rewards and perquisites of power. . . . They discovered that their talents were useful to government, the corporations, the foundations, and the military." And they had begun to revel in their new function as specialists, "problem solvers, advisers to policy makers, managers of crises, technicians of postindustrial civilization."[8] Boasting of the powers of science, empiricism, and rationality to solve human problems, intellectuals scorned the mysticism and the cult of the extrarational that only a decade or so earlier had attracted them to non-Western peoples and cultures. English poet W. H. Auden caught the spirit of a host of American writers, artists, and intellectuals when, in 1948, he expressed astonishment at the degree to which his countrymen in the prewar years had succumbed to the mysticism and occultism proffered by Irish poet William Butler Yeats (1865–1939). How could persons laying claims to superior intelligence, Auden wondered, have taken "such nonsense seriously. . . . Mediums, spells, the Mysterious Orient—*how* embarrassing."[9]

As "technicians of postindustrial civilization," American engineers and scientists threw themselves with renewed faith into the mission to banish primitive superstitions about the divinity of nature and to accomplish fresh prodigies in asserting civilization's mastery over the environment. Federal protection of the environment, according to a Westerner who articulated what had become a widespread conviction, was tantamount to communism.[10] Just as weed killers and insecticides made possible the expansion of scientific agriculture and the painless extension of suburbia's big-lawn culture, so also American technological inventiveness would devise the means necessary to eradicate communism, that insidious pest that hampered the spread of civilization.

More clearly than any other development of the 1950s, the "atoms for peace" program that President Dwight D. Eisenhower announced in 1954 showed the interconnectedness of the will to prevail over nature and the determination to triumph over communism. Americans reacted with astonishment and dismay to the news that the Soviet Union had managed to detonate an atomic bomb far sooner than national experts had believed possible; and they chose to explain this puzzling event through the conviction that Julius and Ethel Rosenberg, recruited as spies, had passed the secrets of the bomb to the Soviets, assumed to be incapable on their own of mastering civilization's latest breakthrough in harnessing the powers of destructiveness. Against this background President Eisenhower sought to reestablish U.S. claims to technological supremacy by launching a program to generate power for civilian purposes that would complement the nuclear industry's military functions. The synergism of combined military- and civilian-inspired research would yield a power that neither communism nor nature could withstand. Work on the Shippingport reactor near Pittsburgh that inaugurated the country's entry into the peaceful use of the atom began in 1954. Three years later this first reactor dedicated to generating power for civilian use was ready to operate. One year later, in 1958, "Lewis Strauss, the second chairman of the Atomic Energy Commission, made his now-famous prediction that nuclear energy would soon be 'too cheap to meter.'"[11] The power of atoms inexpensively harnessed to tasks of peacetime development would force nature into unconditional surrender. Compared to atomic power, steam had been little more than a child's toy in civilization's battle with nature. Civilization had now attained manhood.

According to historian Roderick Nash, in spite of occasionally recurring romantic enthusiasm for the natural and the wild, Americans have never overcome the basic aversion to wilderness and the natural environment that generally ruled the pioneer mind. Enthusiasm and appreciation, when they appeared, "resulted from a momentary relaxation of the dominant antipathy."[12] Up to the late twentieth century, moreover, appreciation for people prevailingly stereotyped as uninhibited, childlike, and natural seems also to have resulted from momentary relaxation of the dominant antipathy. The depression-era adversary culture, challenging traditional antipathy, had ascribed virtue to nature and her ostensibly unspoiled people. But that adversary culture had disappeared with the return of prosperity. With prosperity's resurgence, nature and her people reverted to their customary status.

In the years just following the end of the war, singer Peggy Lee provided a hint that conventional evaluation of old stereotypes was back in vogue. In her song "Mañana (Is Soon Enough for Me)," written in collaboration with her guitarist-husband Dave Barbour, she dealt deftly and in "sizzlingly percussive" style with south-of-the-border types who dedicate themselves to taking it easy and avoiding responsibility: why repair the roof against today's rain when tomorrow will bring a sunny day? The song's popularity (it proved the greatest hit in Peggy Lee's long and highly successful career[13]), combined with dance crazes imported from the south, and also the enormous popularity of the TV series *I Love Lucy* that paired Lucille Ball with her laid-back bongo-playing Cuban husband Desi Arnaz, indicated that Americans welcomed Latin American light-heartedness and buffoonery. In serious matters, though, white middle-class Americans, who according to a 1945 *Saturday Evening Post* editorial writer, were "not as other men are,"[14] preferred to deal with people as much like themselves as possible. In this preference, they were by no means unique, but rather altogether like "other men are."

Even had cold-war considerations and hardheaded business and trade objectives not dictated the policy, Americans would have opted—wisely, no doubt—in favor of the Marshall Plan's project to rebuild England and Europe, rather than Henry Wallace's suggestion to use surplus economic resources to attempt to bolster living standards among the marginalized inhabitants of the underdeveloped world. Rather than lavish vast amounts on people who allegedly possessed endless capacity to squander the capital that civilized men produced, Americans preferred to help people who, like themselves, had demonstrated the ability to rise above the limitations of natural man and to create capitalist civilization. Continuing to be soft on nature, Henry Wallace grew increasingly soft on communism, as the connection that many Americans believed inevitable manifested itself anew. Praising the Soviet Union and wooing Communist support for the Progressive party for which he ran in the 1948 presidential election, Wallace went down to ignominious defeat, garnering barely more than a million votes. Much to the surprise of Thomas Dewey and his Republican supporters, underdog Harry Truman, who as vice-president had succeeded to the presidency on Roosevelt's death in 1945, was elected chief executive in his own right.[15]

Civilization Threatened

The year before his surprise endorsement by the electorate, Harry Truman had articulated what came to be known as the Truman Doctrine. Originally intended to protect independent central European countries against Moscow-inspired revolutions and coups, "the Truman Doctrine implied that Americans possessed the right and the obligation to intervene on behalf of pro-Western anticommunist regimes whenever their survival seemed endangered." If under Theodore Roosevelt the United States had assumed the role of Caribbean policeman, now, under Truman, the country "cast itself in the role of world policeman . . . , committing the nation's energies to a limitless defense of the international status quo."[16]

Thoroughly civilized people in the Old World, especially Englishmen, could be counted on to defend themselves against the Communist scourge. But the weaker peoples of central and eastern Europe, about whose immigrants in their own midst Americans had long been dubious, needed special help to firm up their resolve and, perhaps in the final analysis, energetic intervention by the world policeman in order to prevent them from succumbing to their natural weakness and yielding to the inward communist temptation and to the outward threat of force.

Through the years, Americans had also remained dubious about the virtue and reliability of Orientals. Some of them saw their doubts validated in 1949 by events in China. In that year, as the United States stood by and failed to intervene effectively, the Chinese Nationalists—irresolute and corrupt—fell to their Communist adversaries, and the so-called Bamboo Curtain descended on China. American conservatives, rallying behind Senator Joseph McCarthy of Wisconsin, blamed the United States for not having prevented the fall of an ineffectual people unable to recognize and protect their own best interests. The international policeman had failed to discharge his duties in behalf of bumbling primitives because his resolve had been undermined by Communists who had infiltrated the ranks of his advisers and bureaucrats. Such, at least, was the interpretation of the fall of China proffered by the demented McCarthy, and by his staunch ally, FBI Director J. Edgar Hoover.

The witch-hunt against Reds and radicals that Attorney General A. Mitchell Palmer had unleashed in the days immediately following World War I issued, in many ways, out of the desire of establishment Americans to wreak vengeance on the bohemians, the anarchists and socialists, the labor agitators, the Jews and feminists, and all the "subversives" who had challenged the status quo in the immediate prewar years. Palmer's crusade provided a foretaste of McCarthyism. To some considerable degree, McCarthyism represented the revenge of conservative, establishment, status-quo Americans against the counterculture intellectuals of the 1920s and 1930s who had preached moral equivalence and cultural pluralism, extolled the virtues of primitive communalism, and tarred the values of individualistic, free-enterprise capitalism—and occasionally joined the Communist party or become fellow travelers. All Americans who still harbored the delusions of the adversary culture of the Jazz Age and depression era must be hounded out of public service and, if possible, out of organized labor, the media, and the universities. Either soft on communism or else actively committed to the alien ideology, they were traitors to genuine Americanism. Furthermore, in the years immediately after both world wars, Americans fretted over the Bolshevik influences believed to be at work among Latin Americans, threatening the economic and military security of the hemisphere. After the second war, some grounds did indeed exist for suspecting Communist influence to the south, a point generally ignored by the remnants of the adversary culture whose representative thinkers ridiculed Washington's fear of hemispheric subversion.

With their triumph in World War II, Americans reacquired faith in their mission to uplift those who were alien. Not only could American Indians at last, once and for all, be Americanized, but so also could the Japanese. In their occupation of Japan, presided over initially by Gen. Douglas MacArthur, Americans set out to resocialize and Americanize an ostensibly savage people, and they entertained little doubt about their ability to do so. Once the cold war extended its reach to Latin America, the United States took up once more its temporarily abandoned quest to plant its values among the Latins. In pursuit of this goal, it would of course be necessary, before anything else, to stamp out all traces of Communist influence in Central and South America.

The post–World War II Communist specter first threatened the New World, or so American officials proclaimed, in Guatemala. There the Jacobo Arbenz administration in the early 1950s began to champion sweeping social and economic changes, the precise nature of which it never managed to define very clearly. Partly this was because Arbenz, by no means an intellectual giant, became the magnet for disparate reformers and selfseekers, including his radicalized Salvadoran wife, who hoped to use him for their own purposes. One thing did seem clear about the Arbenz administration: it threatened United Fruit Company interests, and in this oldline Boston firm some members of the Eisenhower administration, including John Foster Dulles and Allen Dulles, respectively the secretary of state and director of the Central Intelligence Agency, had a financial stake.[17] Covert action, masterminded by the CIA, took care of the Communist threat, real or invented, and returned Guatemala to the free world in 1954. The United States had saved Guatemalans from international communism and from their own purportedly deluded aspirations for social reform.[18]

Covert action to save Latin Americans from Communists and from themselves was a last resort. Conveniently forgetting past failures, U.S. statesmen by the late 1950s, as Eisenhower's second term neared its end, decided that uplift must take precedence in everyday hemispheric policy. Shortly President John F. Kennedy (1961–1963) introduced an all-out campaign of uplift. Economic, social, and political uplift, the parameters defined by U.S. experts, ostensibly would not only save Latin Americans from communism but ultimately rescue them from their natural ineptness as well. Largely by the carrot of economic assistance, Latin Americans could gently be enticed toward the ways of the free market and political democracy. Occasionally, though, ruthless dictators, natural products of a not-yet-civilized people, might provide the only effective means of combating communism, and the new team in Washington was ready to accept this possibility, albeit far more reluctantly than the preceding Eisenhower administration. A century and a half earlier, after all, Americans had turned a blind eye to the unsavory conduct of various Indian leaders counted as "friendlies." They demanded only that their redskin friends refrain from collaborating with foreign nations that might pose a threat to U.S. control of the frontier.

In some instances when communism's threat was so immediate that it could not be met by long-term civilizing processes, and when local anti-Communist dictators possessed of sufficient clout were not at hand, the only recourse might still be the stick of intervention, especially now that refinements in covert action had come to provide a fig leaf for that stick. In Cuba, intervention seemed indicated; and so Kennedy followed through, half-heartedly, on the combination covert and overt action planned in the late days of the Eisenhower administration after Fidel Castro, who came to power at the beginning of 1959 following a lengthy guerrilla struggle, aroused well-justified suspicions about his Marxist-Leninist leanings. Americans identifying in one way or another with a new adversary culture just beginning to surface found it difficult to forgive Kennedy for sanctioning the Bay of Pigs invasion of Cuba in 1961. At the same time, they censured Kennedy on the basis of rumors about his complicity in a failed CIA plot to assassinate Castro at the time of the invasion—rumors to which Michael R. Beschloss lends strong circumstantial support in his 1991 book *The Crisis Years: Kennedy and Khrushchev, 1960–1963.* On the other hand, many Americans of a conservative bent never forgave the president for abstaining from the sort of U.S. military support that would forever have banished Castro from Cuba, just as Arbenz had been banished from Guatemala in 1954. At least those Americans who supported military confrontation in meeting the menace of communism applauded when Kennedy stared down Soviet leader Nikita Khrushchev in 1962 and forced removal of Soviet missiles from Cuba. But they abhorred the rumored agreement—confirmed in later years—that the Soviets wrested from the Kennedy administration to refrain from further invasions of Cuba, even as adversary-culture citizens applauded the concessions that appeared to guarantee continued life to the revolution and to the hope that it might spread. As Kennedy discovered from the wildly divergent reactions to the most dramatic of his initial Latin American initiatives, the United States was getting harder to govern; for, once again, the country was splitting in two. Even on the level of musical tastes, the split had become apparent.

Classical and Popular Music and the Reemergence of an Adversary Culture

Control and discipline have long been cherished as supreme virtues by those intent upon exalting the civilized over the natural. As the postwar generation began, one segment of Americans set out to rededicate the country to these virtues. At that time, incongruous though it might seem, no one in America seemed to symbolize the drive for control and discipline quite so thoroughly as the diminutive, dapper, Italian-born maestro Arturo Toscanini, who finished out his eminently distinguished career as conductor of the NBC Symphony Orchestra between 1937 and 1954. From professional critics to casual aficionados of classical music, Americans hailed Toscanini, during his stint at the head of this orchestra, as the greatest conductor in the relatively short history of the art. Especially as the end of his career approached, Toscanini received the sort of media hype later reserved for rock-and-roll's superstars.

At least as exploited by the commercial interests that sponsored him and the NBC Symphony, Toscanini symbolized an America that had discarded cultural pluralism in favor of defending the one right standard that genuinely civilized beings must adhere to. His approach to conducting epitomized the entire spirit of the cold war: for, almost as much as the drumbeaters of his cult, Toscanini himself insisted that he strove to conduct music in the *one* right way, the way intended by the composers. Members of his cult and, only slightly less so the maestro himself, professed that Toscanini's was the *right* way, the only authentic way to re-create the music of the masters. To the cult's true believer, the thought of moral equivalence in musical interpretation was abhorrent.

In the immediate postwar years, David Sarnoff, head of the huge RCA conglomerate of which NBC was a part, unleashed an advertising blitz calculated to sell the notion that Arturo Toscanini, the world's greatest conductor, headed the world's greatest orchestra, the NBC Symphony, created by perhaps the greatest exemplar of American capitalism: the Radio Corporation of America. Backed by the might of corporate America, a culture-god had undertaken to bring classical music—the only authentically good, noble, uplifting, and civilizing music—to the masses. The whole venture reflected the uplift imagery that had begun anew to figure in America's approach to the underdeveloped world. Even in the United States there still lived culturally underdeveloped people, but corporate America was out to correct that situation, in part by bringing music—the only genuinely exalted music, played in the only correct way—to heretofore underprivileged people. Here was an example of the multifaceted civilizing mission that American classical economics, the unique product of the proper and scientific approach to economics, could fulfill. Undergoing uplift and enlightenment, Americans would come to appreciate that all parts of the good life, the only truly good life, were packaged together, that out of the right politics and the right economics emerged the right kind of music that elevated the soul and nourished people in those moments when they rested from nourishing their bank accounts.

In the 1920s, and also the 1930s, classical composers turned to folk and popular music, to African rhythms and Latin melodies for inspiration. Such stooping to natural taste was not to be countenanced in the immediate postwar era. Popular music, the music of the masses that sometimes derived from primitive, instinctual, and "backward" people, must be banished as Americans came culturally of age, as their taste rose to a level to match their political and economic standards. Having "more or less the devil in it,"[19] having in it primitivism and vulgarity and sensuousness, popular music must not be allowed to sully classical music, any more than primitive communalism, reappearing in the modern world in the guise of Marxism, could be allowed to debase classical economics. Both in music and in economics, people must be guided toward an understanding of the need to eradicate atavistic impulses. Joining with the greatest classical musician in the world, RCA, as emblematic of free-enterprise greatness, could help spread this understanding. In the process, RCA could quicken devotion to the sort of one-dimensional Americanism that had to triumph internationally in the cold war even as, domestically, it safeguarded the recently won victory over a subversive counterculture.

Toscanini became the highest-paid conductor in the history of classical music, up to that time, not only because of his artistic genius but also because he joined forces with a corporation that epitomized capitalist success. The Italian noted for his childish temper tantrums became dependent on American capitalism. Here in microcosm was a projection of the relationship that Americans hoped to establish with Latin America, subjecting on a hemispheric scale the passions to the interests.

Joseph Horowitz, whose controversial study of the Toscanini phenomenon rings true to this writer, observes: "Once the nerve center of a nation's performing arts, Toscanini became an appendage to a corporate cultural hegemony."[20] A great artist, Toscanini was a naive human being. He thought he was using the American system to help propagate the best of classical culture, but the system was using him to sanctify its profit-making. When Toscanini retired and within three years died (at age ninety in 1957), the NBC Symphony lost its superstar and with him its advertising clout. So, RCA promptly abandoned the orchestra. At least when rock-and-roll, not the classical music that Sarnoff had backed, became the dominant American musical idiom for virtually all classes, performers and their corporate sponsors clearly understood that each was using the other.

Meantime, Leonard Bernstein (1918–1990) had appeared on the classical music scene and had managed to impart an entirely new dimension to it. A living embodiment of the Dionysian spirit, Bernstein was oversexed and bisexual, though primarily homosexual; he chain-smoked and often drank to excess. Not for Bernstein the Freudian concept of sublimation, with its assumption that suppression of the sex drive and redirection of its energies can lead to prodigious artistic, intellectual, and economic accomplishments. If there were anything to the theory, Bernstein once remarked, "Wagner could not have fucked as many women as he did and put on paper all the notes that he did."[21]

The fact that Bernstein, appointed music director beginning with the 1958–1959 season of the New York Philharmonic (the post Toscanini had held prior to directing the NBC Symphony), was the first native-born American (and a Jew, at that) to head a major orchestra in the United States served notice in itself that something new was afoot. And Bernstein seldom disappointed those who sought new perspectives rather than old axioms from classical music. In his all-embracing cultural pluralism, he championed new music, especially new music by American composers. In his own compositions he found inspiration in the rhythms, harmonies, and dissonances of jazz. He reached down below, as it were, to find in African American spontaneity the means to revitalize the music of "high culture." Beholden to the "primitive" in musical matters, Bernstein consistently sided with the underprivileged on social issues. He became an emotional but articulate defender of virtually any black cause, however dubious, he could find; he even extolled the Black Panthers. Bernstein figured prominently among those in the 1950s and 1960s who made even the most mindless radicalism chic once again, thereby proclaiming the advent of a new counterculture.

In 1957, the year before he took up his conducting post at the head of the New York Philharmonic, the dazzlingly versatile Bernstein had the satisfaction of seeing his musical drama *West Side Story* emerge as a smash Broadway hit. While in some of his earlier music Bernstein had turned (as he also would in later compositions) to the idiom of African American jazz for important ingredients, this time he drew on Latin influences. Much of Bernstein's score for *West Side Story* (which boasted lyrics by Stephen Sondheim and was based on the book by Arthur Laurents), a reworking of the Romeo and Juliet tale with inner-city gangs substituting for the Capulets and the Montagues, has a marvelous Latin lilt to it. In dramatizing how prejudice gets in the way of and destroys the natural love match between the Anglo Tony and the Puerto Rican María, Bernstein in effect admonishes American society to take a critical look at itself, to become aware of, so it might combat, the prejudices that keep persons of one race and culture from merging with the racial and cultural Other. Bernstein's ability to look sympathetically on Latinos in America was symptomatic of the way in which a counterculture began to look empathetically on Latins to the south. It evidenced some of the attitudes that had helped make possible the Good Neighbor policy and that, in a fresh manifestation, would facilitate John F. Kennedy's attempt to forge a new hemispheric solidarity through the Alliance for Progress.

West Side Story can advance claims as valid as those of *Porgy and Bess* to being the great American music drama. Both present the listener with genuinely indigenous classical music, one drawing on the Latin and the other on the African American strains that mix down at the roots of national culture. Both deal, at least indirectly, with the effects of internal colonization and express yearning for a day when a racially and culturally fractured people can find wholeness by opting for inclusion and repudiating exclusion. While Gershwin's vision was confined to mainland America, Bernstein hinted at hemispheric dimensions.

Bernstein's later musical drama *Candide* can be seen as a great American counterculture proclamation. It is based on the eighteenth-century play of the same name in which Voltaire heaped scorn on those contemporaries who ignored all problems and abhorred change because they knew, as the protagonist Dr. Pangloss knew, that they lived in "the best of all possible worlds." In the hands of Bernstein and his collaborators, *Candide* in effect invites Americans to question if, in the midst of mounting social and racial and international hatreds, conventional, conservative free-enterprise capitalism has indeed provided the best of all possible worlds.

Arturo Toscanini retired in 1954, just before Leonard Bernstein began to help recast the spirit of classical music in America. An even greater cultural revolution, one from below and spearheaded by a new music, was just getting under way. In the very year Toscanini retired, Elvis Presley cut his first commercial recordings. In effect, the advent of Presley announced that high-culture music imported from the Old World would not, as Sarnoff had hoped, unite Americans in pursuit of the capitalist dream; nor would high-culture music incorporating "primitive" elements, such as Bernstein wrote, unite Americans in a march toward an inclusionary society and perhaps even a synthesized hemisphere. Instead, low-culture rock-and-roll would appropriate black and other primitive elements and create a new national—and international—musical idiom that cut across class lines and held out the promise of uniting people on the basis of visceral excitement and hedonism.

A fair amount of rock-and-roll music in the 1950s found its "primitivist" inspiration in Latin as well as Negro influences. The Coasters' 1956 hit "Down in Mexico" described a night's adventure in the city of Mexicali. It was one of the first rock-and-roll songs to feature a Latin rhythm and story line. According to the lyrics, an American could venture into Mexicali bars and find drinks that, like the loitering women, were hotter than chili sauce. Latin American influences also abound in the music of black piano player, singer, and songwriter Ray Charles, who liked to be called "the Genius." One of his most famous songs of the 1950s, "What'd I Say?" (1959), relies heavily on a rumba beat as it celebrates the life of uninhibited sexuality. The year before this the Charles song "You My Baby" incorporated the feel of Cha Cha Cha. The great African American rock-and-roll innovator Chuck Berry, moreover, openly acknowledged the Latin influences on his music in a 1972 interview.[22] Even more consistently than on Berry, the "Latin feel" had an influence on black guitarist Bo Diddley. A typical example is provided by his song "I'm a Man," which uses maracas to impart a Latin feel. In the lyrics, Diddley tells a group of "pretty women" to stand in line so he can make love to them in half an hour's time, for "I'm a man." Teddy Roosevelt's concept of what it meant to be manly had passed out of vogue, and the new counterculture turned for its models to macho types associated through the years both with blacks and with Latin Americans.

As rock-and-roll became the great American art form of the 1950s, 1960s, and 1970s, corporate America reached out to co-opt and commercialize it; and the rock musicians put up precious little resistance. In a way, the marriage was a natural one, far more so than the union of high culture and corporate America envisaged by David Sarnoff. For rock is fresh, driving, disrespectful of tradition, brash, raucous, innovative, rude, self-centered, vulgar, nonconventional, constantly reinventing itself. In all this it demonstrates the very features commonly associated with entrepreneurial success, just as did the sometimes brutish ways of frontier life, whose exemplars often traded on frontier-sharpened instincts to rise to the top in the business world—or so an American myth has had it.

Directors of America's large corporations soon saw they could make far more money from rock than from Arturo Toscanini and Leonard Bernstein and classical music in general. The partnership of business and rock resulted in what many Americans judged to be the debasement of culture and taste. But this is doubtful. What happened was that culture and taste remained consummately American, with a niche reserved for the primitive, the natural and instinctual, the uninhibited and the vulgar. Even as with an earlier physical frontier, exploration of a new musical frontier made Americans more themselves. An elitist might ask more of a country's popular music, but a civilized country needs a popular art that embodies the very features that rock does. Wholeness demands it.

The Counterculture, the Establishment, and John F. Kennedy's New Frontier

With each month that passed in the late 1950s, America's new adversary culture gained in numbers and volubility. When the first year of the next decade produced the razor-thin triumph of John F. Kennedy over Republican Richard M. Nixon, American radicals and even some liberals began to believe that the wildly disparate elements comprising the New Left could remake the country, maybe even the world. True, the specter of atomic annihilation sometimes routed optimism. It loomed large in 1962 when the Cuban missile crisis seemed to bring the United States and the Soviet Union to the brink of nuclear war. But optimism persisted and quickly resumed its growth curve. Americans learned how to live with the fear of world destruction and along with it developed an underlying faith in the emergence of a new and better world: better both in the quality and quantity of the nonmaterial and material rewards that it conferred.

The fondly envisioned better world seemed far more attainable for the New Left than ever it had been for the Old Left, and this is one of the most significant points of generational division between the two adversary cultures. In the depression years of the 1930s, radicals, making a virtue of necessity, had abandoned hope in the good life of material prosperity as they set their eyes on a new America that substituted nonmaterial rewards and a renewed sense of community for the obsessive pursuit of individual gain. But with the backdrop of affluence against which the New Left operated, there seemed no need to face up to alternatives. Apparently the American economic system had reached the stage that permitted it to be taken for granted. However much reviled, it could still be counted on to shower its bounty on those who attacked every value that had made the system possible. The vision of combining the affluence of capitalism with the realization of nonmaterial ideals that, so they said, motivated them vitalized the resurgent counterculture.

Some Americans had a different kind of dream for combining opposites, a dream that grew out of the hope of seeing the country's races mingle at last in equality. Building on the spirit set loose by the Supreme Court decision in *Brown v. Board of Education* (1954) that struck down the "separate but equal" doctrine that had undergirded racial discrimination since the end of the nineteenth century, Americans—both black and white—launched the civil rights movement, the finest product of the new adversary culture. The movement soared to what seemed new heights (although threatened beneath the surface by bitter dissension) when Martin Luther King, Jr., delivered his great "I Have a Dream" speech in Washington, D.C., in 1963. His inspired oratory gave a new meaning to the old American Dream, so often associated with the frontier, of joining opposites. With the physical frontier closed, the racial frontier still presented Americans the chance to chase the dream.

Sometimes counterculturalists turned to interracial sex as the means to personal enhancement and fulfillment on the new frontier. Interracial sex became "an affirmation of raw impulse against the overupholstered paleface mind."[23] One of the Beat Generation's many gurus, Jack Kerouac, felt interracial sex might help him become more like the Negro. With many remnants of redneck prejudice, Kerouac hated "Commies" and Jews, but he professed love for the Negro and the wish to assimilate the Negro's identity. In his book *On the Road* (1957), which became a beatnik bible, Kerouac wrote: "At lilac evening I walked with every muscle aching . . . in the Denver colored section, wishing I were a Negro, feeling that the best the white world had offered was not enough ecstasy for me. . . . I was only myself, . . . sad, strolling in this violet dark, this unbearably sweet night, wishing I could exchange worlds with the happy, true-hearted, ecstatic Negroes of America."[24] In his celebrated 1957 essay "The White Negro," Norman Mailer, another counterculture guru but one who proclaimed the virtue of the hipster rather than the hippie, joined Kerouac in expressing the conviction that it was not enough to be white. Salvation for the white man lay in becoming as the black, joining if not in interracial sex then at least in cultural coupling.[25]

Americans sometimes found their racial frontiers in far-off places. As volunteers in President Kennedy's Peace Corps many young persons, to their credit, began to worry about the mission with which they had been charged: to uplift and civilize the natives. Feeling it was not enough to be just themselves, as Americans, they wished that they could somehow become more like Africans, or like Latin Americans: people who knew how to deal with scarcity, how to share, how to be content (or at least resigned) even without a plethora of material goods. Returning home with broadened perspectives, many Peace Corps veterans added a loftier dimension to the New Left than that provided by the likes of Kerouac and Mailer.

Stay-at-home counterculturalists during the Kennedy years, and just before and after those years as well, extolled every close-at-hand exemplar of "primitivism." The Negro was in, and so was the Indian. For a time it seemed difficult to find new movies or books that did not glorify the noble red man and vilify those white Americans who had nearly snuffed out the native presence. Like blacks, Indians provided role models because they pursued, ostensibly, an extrarational approach to truth that quite surpassed those reasoning processes in which civilization trusted. Rather than being guided by science, with its underlying ambition to master nature, blacks and Indians arrived at truth by being one with nature. Nature spoke to them, through dreams and visions. It spoke to them when they entered into altered states of consciousness, whether induced by meditation, drumming, chanting, or gospel singing, by jazz improvization, or by ingesting drugs. Riding the wave of primitivism, of concern for the mystical, the intuitive, and the occult, and also of drug consumption, anthropologist Carlos Castañeda, who studied at the University of California at Los Angeles, became a cult figure for the New Left with his 1968 book *The Teachings of Don Juan: A Yaqui Way of Knowledge*. This best-seller launched a series of books in which Castañeda suggested that the traditional wisdom of a Yaqui shaman held the real key to knowledge and to spiritual power. Don Juan's wisdom, permitting those who possessed it to mediate between two worlds, those of spirit and matter, had nothing to do with the science in which Western civilization took such inordinate pride. Especially in the 1968 book, Castañeda also suggested that drugs smoothed and straightened the road to enlightenment.[26]

If the civil rights movement was its proudest legacy, the popularization of drug use stands as the counterculture's worst contribution to American life (followed closely by general boorishness and the hedonistic quest for self-gratification). And yet a handful of poets among the Beat Generation, with Allen Ginsberg offering perhaps the clearest example,[27] found in dope a conduit through which somehow they managed to connect the lowest, most depraved depths of the flesh in which they freely wallowed with the most exalted realms of the spirit. Orgies and visions: here were the opposites that Americans could unite in order to retain their exceptionalism.

Along with African Americans, Indians, and Yaqui shamans, the child enjoyed a new vogue in the counterculture years. "I'll find a different way of not growing up," former Beatle John Lennon declared in the lyrics of one of his songs,[28] promising to remain infantile forever—which in many ways he did, up to the tragic moment of his assassination by a demented onetime fan. On a different level Dr. Benjamin Spock contributed to the cult of the child. In his *Common Sense Book of Baby and Child Care,* published in 1946, Spock warned—perhaps in reaction to his beloved mother's overly stern discipline—against frustrating the child by excessive restraints. For the next twenty years or so Spock's book claimed best-seller status as some twenty-two million readers pored over its pages. Spock's message echoed the one that Ashley Montagu conveyed in his widely read books of pop anthropology. Both men warned against inhibiting the child's natural, beneficent inclinations; both men wanted "to save the child from the coercive and crippling repressions of past generations."[29] Picking up on this theme, the counterculture's "flower children" wanted to become not just as the Negro and the Indian but as the child; and as the child (that very epitome of self-centeredness), they wanted to remain free from crippling repression. While it must not coerce them, society was expected to care for them and meet their needs, emotional and economic. The flower children coveted the fruits of the civilized world that adults had made, along with the enjoyments of the newborn's kingdom of spontaneity and narcissism.

If counterculturalists wanted to become more like the child, the male species of the breed wanted to become more like that other symbol of nature, of instinct and passion rather than reason, of nurturing rather than competing, the woman. According to literary critic Leslie Fiedler, "To become new men, these children of the future seem to feel, they must become not only more black than white, but more female than male."[30] Men let their hair grow long, as an outward sign of their quest for feminization of the psyche. And women, liberated from old taboos and gender stereotyping as one of the most important feminist crusades the country has ever known went through its growing pains, claimed rights to the liberated behavior previously reserved to males.

Given the history of stereotypes and myths, it seems altogether predictable that the new counterculture's fascination with African Americans and

Indians, with the child and the woman, would extend also to Latin Americans. Taking advantage of this situation, whether consciously or not, John Kennedy—much like his Democratic predecessor who had launched the Good Neighbor policy against a background of growing goodwill toward the Other—unveiled at the outset of his administration a new policy for rapprochement with Latin America that he called the Alliance for Progress. The Alliance was part and parcel of the domestic program that Kennedy called not the New Deal but the New Frontier. In hemispheric policy, the Kennedy administration concerned itself with bringing progress to what many Americans had long regarded as their new frontier, the one in Latin America. Someday a new Frederick Jackson Turner will appear to explain the significance in American history of the closing of the Third World frontier, to delineate the dimensions of the transformation involved when Latin America and the rest of the underdeveloped world began shipping surplus population to the United States along with mounting tides of goods, both raw *and* finished.

As the 1960s began, however, the Latin American portion of the Third World frontier still seemed enticingly open. Cubans had, it is true, reclaimed a part of *our* frontier, a situation almost as galling as if the Sioux had reclaimed the Dakotas. All the more, then, must the remainder of the wide-open hemispheric frontier be resolutely Americanized.

But this was a nebulous goal, and so the Alliance for Progress could mean many different things, even apparently to the president himself. As the son of a largely self-made, swashbuckling, and prevailingly unscrupulous captain of industry, Kennedy could understand and even sympathize with the view that the Alliance should help create in Latin America a climate favorable to the private investor, native and North American. But as an Irishman well into the process of acquiring Ivy League intellectual credentials and East Coast gentility, and with aspirations to the aristocratic status of such White House predecessors as Theodore and Franklin Roosevelt, Kennedy could sympathize with the Arielist tradition, in both North and South America, that favored the intellectual's vision over the businessman's profit seeking. Kennedy's patrician instincts were balanced by the understanding of how Irish and other immigrants had had to struggle on their own in order to claim a stake in the American Dream. And so from the vantage point of classical American populism, he could sympathize with the need for the Latin American masses to participate in a bootstrap operation of upward mobility rather than counting on the helping hand of the solicitous aristocrat. Thus he could endorse community-development projects in Latin America, initiated by American "experts" and intended to empower the masses and turn them into effective agents of their own progress—political, social, and economic. And yet, the uplift-from-above model never lost its appeal; so, Kennedy sympathized with the "Democratic Left" spokesmen, highly placed in his administration, who wanted to collaborate with Latin American counterparts in inaugurating planned-by-experts programs to be implemented by expanding armies of bureaucrats.

Perhaps above all else, Kennedy's New Frontier–Alliance for Progress vision seems to have been shaped by faith that somehow this time—which might be the last time Americans had a readily available, close-at-hand Third World frontier—he and his countrymen would get it right. Yancey Cravat in Edna Ferber's novel *Cimarron* (quoted at some length toward the beginning of chapter 5) had hoped that out in Oklahoma in the 1890s America would finally get it right and achieve the ideal fusion of civilization and the natural. In Oklahoma, though, the dream once again had slipped away. This time, the New Frontiersman in the White House would escape the frustrations of the past and finally realize the mythic goal that, generation after generation, had enticed those of his countrymen susceptible to believing in dreams. Kennedy didn't know just how the dream could be fulfilled, but lack of specific knowledge often contributes to faith. And, after all, "Over the Rainbow" was one of Kennedy's favorite songs. He loved to have Judy Garland (who had immortalized it in the 1939 film classic *The Wizard of Oz*) sing it to him at night, over the telephone. Perhaps one *could* wish upon a star and wake up in a new and better world, where troubles melted like lemon drops.

Embracing numerous contradictions that reflected those in the president himself, the Alliance for Progress in its first three years never acquired consistency and coherence. It was born anew each day, according to the results of that day's bureaucratic infighting. Following Kennedy's assassination in November 1963, the succeeding Lyndon B. Johnson administration turned the Alliance into a rather more consistent vehicle, designed to suit the tastes of American and Latin American capitalists, ostensibly the only persons who understood how to move countries out of natural states of underdevelopment. This, however, was a long-range process. Given the needs of the moment, American military strategists and their Latin counterparts might have to play the key roles. In some countries at least, they would have to bear the brunt of combating the advance of communism. Succeeding Johnson as president in 1969, Richard Nixon preserved intact the capitalist and security thrusts of his predecessor's Latin American policy.

LBJ's critics in the mid-1960s accused him of betraying the spirit in which the Alliance was conceived. In truth, the Alliance had been conceived in many spirits, and the particular ones on which the Johnson administration chose to focus had been present from the creation. But if Johnson picked up on some of the Alliance's innate characteristics, he discarded the element of mystical-mythical utopianism that had surfaced in the Kennedy years. He appeared impervious to the "Over the Rainbow" mentality. Precisely this mentality had endeared Kennedy to many segments within the counterculture. The absence of this trait in the wheeler-dealer, the instinctual gunslinger from Texas, would contribute to the revulsion toward him that the counterculture quickly developed.

While he had lived, Kennedy seemed confident of his destiny to lead Americans into new frontiers where they could achieve the ideal symbiosis between the natural and the civilized. As president he had symbolized this mix, turning the White House into both a sex house and a culture house that staged glamorous and glittering fine-arts presentations. After his death, some Americans continued to believe that had Kennedy lived, he could have forged a hemispheric marriage of opposites. In a way Kennedy's uncanny ability to combine personally, in himself, an amazing array of apparently mutually exclusive characteristics suggested powers little short of those of the wizard. In the American Camelot, Kennedy was not just King Arthur but Merlin the sorcerer as well.

Because Kennedy was assassinated before he had an opportunity really to define himself, to clarify the mystery and contradictions of his fluid personality and policies, Americans never had an adequate opportunity to learn what kind of a person he was, or was capable of becoming. In a public opinion poll conducted in 1988, 30 percent of respondents judged Kennedy the "greatest" president ever to serve the United States—a higher rating than that garnered by any of the nation's other chief executives.[31] One reason for his standing may be the lack of distinction among the presidents who came after him, combined with the notorious American lack of knowledge about those who preceded him. Perhaps a more fundamental reason for the high Kennedy rating is that he continued up to the moment of his death to be a man of paradox. Americans at opposing ends of the national spectrum could read into the fallen leader what most pleased them.

No man could have fulfilled the mythic expectations that Kennedy, in life and death, had aroused—even though Johnson made a strong start by steering through Congress the civil rights legislation that had bogged down in the late days of Kennedy's administration, and by gaining congressional approval for a populist social-reform program that exceeded in scope anything envisioned by his predecessor. Still, adversary-culture Americans never trusted Johnson. His domestic civil rights stance might have been impeccable, but by the mid-1960s American leftists were well along toward shifting their primary concern from the dark-skinned Other in their midst to overseas "primitives," whether only ninety miles away in Cuba or across the Pacific in Vietnam. Johnson, his critics charged, intensified the pressure his predecessor had applied against Castro. Worse still, he dispatched marines to the Dominican Republic to stifle an alleged Communist threat that American radicals and many liberals perceived as the bid of underlings for social justice. Worst of all, Johnson backed South Vietnam's armed forces and used American troops to wage ever-escalating combat against North Vietnamese warriors fighting to absorb the southern republic. To Johnson, the North Vietnamese were imperialist, Communist aggressors; to the counterculture, they were liberators inspired by the aversion to capitalist civilization purportedly ingrained in the mentality and moral attitudes of genuine, uncorrupted peasants.

Cuba and Vietnam were key foreign-policy issues on which counterculturalists judged Kennedy. Ultimately, some of them at least found it possible to overlook the shades of capitalist imperialism that colored the fallen leader's policy toward Cuba, and then toward Vietnam. Unaware that Kennedy may have been involved in schemes to assassinate Castro after the Bay of Pigs fiasco, they rationalized that had he lived he would have achieved rapprochement with the revolutionaries in Cuba, and also with those in Southeast Asia against whom he initially committed American forces. The counterculture had a mixed appraisal of Kennedy because the president's policies had been mixed. On Johnson, their judgment was unequivocal. Vietnam was the key foreign-policy issue on which they judged Johnson, and they found him without redeeming feature. So, ultimately, did conservative Americans once a disheartened LBJ decided to abandon the all-out quest for armed victory.

Third Worldism and the Issues of Cuba, Vietnam, and Nicaragua

Throughout much of the developed world, Third World sentimentalism reached epidemic proportions as the 1960s began and as yesterday's colonialists watched their former colonials attain independence. The year 1960 saw seventeen newly independent "nations" admitted to the United Nations. In all, within less than twenty years, the UN would help oversee the creation of more than seventy independent countries. Old empires were falling apart, from their ruins new countries were emerging, and Americans, perhaps rather more than observers from elsewhere in the developed world, tended to applaud the process and to entertain wildly optimistic expectations about the consequences.

Americans, at least those who identified with the amorphous New Left, saw the crumbling of colonialism as the harbinger of a higher form of human existence. In the decolonizing world, a young, innocent, vigorous, idealistic, socialist leadership would capture the resources and energies once misappropriated by colonizers and channel them into the construction of prosperous national economies, free from the cruelties and contradictions of the capitalism that had vitiated the imperialist era.[32] Africans and other Third Worlders, once emancipated from Western colonialism, would create social relations that were "harmonious, honest, and 'natural.'" Endowed with an ancient wisdom and virtue, Third Worlders, purportedly, understood how to harmonize with nature rather than just to utilize it; they remained attuned to the "basic goodness" of physical nature, recognizing it as a "'gentle wilderness' to engage, instead of an antagonist to master technologically, or an array of neutral phenomena to analyze scientifically." Third Worlders understood the blessings of spontaneity; they remained free "to go with the flow."[33] Released at last from colonialism, they would point First Worlders, with all their tired blood, toward a rendezvous with a higher destiny than coldly calculating, empirical thinkers had been able to visualize.

In order to create new and more perfect societies, Third Worlders might have to inflict a violent death on unregenerate defenders of the old colonial order. Violence by the oppressed constituted a return to raw nature, a restoration of wholeness, and only by the baptismal plunge into violence could Third Worlders assure their rebirth. So, at least, said the black French Indian writer and psychiatrist Frantz Fanon in *The Wretched of the Earth,* his best-known book that focused on the bloody Algerian struggle for independence from France. Appearing in English translation in 1963, the book became a campus best-seller in the United States, proudly displayed by students who wanted to appear "in," and assigned by professors who wanted to be "with it." At the same time, U.S. counterculturalists lionized Latin America's "Third World Priests," some of whom advocated violence in pursuit of vaguely defined "liberation" and "justice" for the "people," a designation that did not include the well-to-do.

Justifiably cynical about Third World utopianism, V. S. Naipaul, born in Trinidad of Hindu parents, scorned its assumptions in several of his novels. In one of the best, *A Bend in the River* (1979), Naipaul has a gullible and sycophantic character describe the Big Man, actually a rhetoric-spewing, on-the-make, power-mad president of a newly liberated country, in these terms: "He is the modernizer and he is also the African who has rediscovered the African soul. He's conservative, revolutionary, everything. He's going back to the old ways, and he's also the man who's going ahead,

the man who's going to make the country a world power by the year
2000."[34] A composite of the delusions through which many American
counterculturalists viewed visionary and also demented Third World leaders, the Big Man knew, ostensibly, how to combine opposites, how to have
it all.

Unlike an earlier generation of American dreamers who had hoped to
perfect first the United States and only after that the rest of the world, the
new dreamers thought utopia might first have to be won in the Third
World before they could create it at home. And to many Americans who
thought along these lines, the millennium-bound Third World lay not only
in Algeria or sub-Saharan Africa but also in Latin America. It lay as close
as Castro's Cuba. Taking up the revolutionary torch that had blazed for a
tantalizing moment in Mexico a generation earlier, Fidel Castro had embarked on a hemispheric regeneration movement that, after sweeping
Latin America, would wash back to undermine the capitalist foundations
of America itself.

The surge of liberation in Africa helped unleash the Black Power movement in the United States. And the revolution in Cuba, where a liberation-
minded white Big Man purportedly had begun to free the black underclass
and to guide its members, together with properly disposed whites and
mulattoes, toward a bright future, inspired many white Americans. Perhaps they could play a similarly hegemonic role in awakening and leading
their own dark-skinned masses; perhaps they could help America catch up
with Third World pacesetters on the march toward an ideal world. In his
book *Listen, Yankee,* published at the beginning of the 1960s, radical sociologist C. Wright Mills gave the most forthright expression to these
expectations.

The motives that led the amorphous counterculture to endorse Castro
and his revolution are complex and varied. Some Americans saw the revolution much as an earlier counterculture had perceived the Harlem Renaissance, as a vast release of energy and exuberance. A huge fiesta was in the
making ninety miles from Key West, and Castro, coming across as a warm,
spontaneous, irrepressible overgrown boy (a new Bambino to fascinate
Americans grown petulant about the vexations of adult life), would show
his people how to enjoy life and live it to the hilt, even while engaged in
the serious business of building a new society. But others who approved
the revolution showed "the reformist seriousness of the very Puritans they
so despised."[35] They found, quite literally, deadly earnestness in the revolution, and this they applauded.

Probably many Americans supported the revolution in Cuba, and any
other that came along in the 1960s, because they wanted to cast off a self-

image of unassertiveness, over-refinement, and docility by identifying with guerrilla fighters. Paul Hollander may have a point when he writes that "the Jewish radicals' identification with the tough Third World guerrillas, rioting Negroes, Black Panthers, and other victimized yet assertive groups, had a strong contemporary flavor. Some groups like the Weathermen quite consciously cultivated toughness, and modelled (or imagined they had modelled) themselves on such groups."[36] In some ways the cause did not matter nearly as much as simply being a rebel—an attitude reflected in the enormous popularity enjoyed by a mediocre film, the James Dean vehicle *Rebel Without a Cause*. By identifying with rebels, Americans could prove they had not fallen into the conforming patterns of the organization men in gray flannel suits that various sociologists had expressed misgivings about in the 1950s.[37] Living vicariously through Third World rebels, the precise nature of whose cause might not even interest them, Americans could cultivate, inwardly, the primitive manhood in quest of which earlier generations of pioneers had ventured into the wilderness.

In still other ways reminiscent of frontier experiences in the distant past, Americans welcomed the opportunity that the revolution in Cuba offered them to take on new personalities, literally to be born anew. Visiting Cuba in 1960, Carleton Beals exulted in "a surge of long-absent enthusiasm." "I felt much younger," he wrote. "I feel rejuvenated. It seems that everything around me is filled with youthful energy."[38] Other Americans saw the revolution as affording an opportunity to recapture the days of childhood: days that were "fresh and vibrant and immediate," days in which people strolled along the streets seeking fun and relaxation, not "chasing after money."[39] Predictably, Waldo Frank, the perennial chaser after dreams of a return to Eden, found himself transported back to days of youthful rapture when he visited Cuba shortly after Castro took power. He enthused over the island's return to what was fresh, natural, innocent, and organic.[40]

In many cases, favorable attitudes toward Castro's movement and Third World revolutions in general tied in with the "back-to-nature movements" that "were truly characteristic of the estrangement of the 1960s."[41] Even as its 1910 predecessor in Mexico, the Cuban revolution aimed—so some of its American admirers believed—at breaking up the large, artificial, technologically oriented corporations that had turned agriculture into a heartless, impersonal, and mechanized business and returning the land to the people. This was seen as a decided plus, even if the people were organized into rigorously state-controlled cooperatives. Back-to-the-natural enthusiasts found many other laudable aspects of the revolution. Dress codes, for example, went out the window and slovenliness became incumbent upon the revolutionaries. American visitors to the island in the early months after the revolution took over saw Havana's once swanky hotels crowded with dusty, dirty, khaki-clad youths, sometimes with their booted feet resting on lobby or even dining-room tables. They presented symbols of natural men and women, liberated from arbitrary restraint, symbols that appealed to American beatniks and hippies who equated boorishness with naturalness.

Some serious observers who delved beneath surface appearances saw the revolution in terms of the liberation of people not from rules of social decorum but from the false consciousness of capitalist individualism and greed. Thus liberated, Cubans could return to humankind's natural, primordial estate of sharing, of communalism. Perhaps this would enable them to realize Marx's dream of a society in which, with the elimination of the massive profits that capitalists constantly drained from the economy, people could produce all that the good life required with no more than four hours or so of work three or four days a week. The rest of the time they could enjoy themselves, swimming, sunning, chatting in cafés, reading and studying, attending sports and cultural events, and making love. When they did go forth to work, perhaps in the sugar fields, they would do so happily, singing, dancing, frolicking. This vision appealed to romantic anarchist elements in America's New Left, and it attracted American adventurers to the island to share in the work of harvesting sugar crops. More dour types, captivated by Leninist concepts of rule by the vanguard of the proletariat, applauded the heavy-handed discipline that the revolutionary state established; and they found perfectly congenial the rigorous campaigns of thought control by which the ideologically pure few sought to root out the false consciousness of capitalist civilization among the many. Nor were they repelled by the new puritanism that resulted in the harassing of homosexuals, prostitutes, and other "deviate" types.

Then there were American counterculturalists who, even as their predecessors of the pre–World War I years, were caught up in visions of a new consciousness, of a "democratized shamanism"[42] that would permit properly initiated persons to commune between the worlds of material appearances and spiritual reality and, even more wonderful, to remake the material world through the powers of enhanced consciousness. American seekers after the age of higher consciousness found much to excite them in the early days of the Cuban revolution, as already suggested toward the end of chapter 6 with the allusion to the mind-over-matter Marxism not only of Cubans and African socialists but also of Mao Zedong. Castro's right-hand man, the Argentine-born medical doctor Ernesto "Che" Guevara, stressed the importance of consciousness, the power of emanations from the mind to shape outer economic and social realities. He even spoke, mystically, of a universal bank of Marxist higher consciousness on which Cubans, who had not yet had time in the new revolution fully to develop their own Marxist consciousness, could draw.[43] With his Marxism, Guevara mixed whiffs and puffs of hermetic mysticism, Masonic symbolism, Neoplatonic idealism, popular Catholicism, esoteric millennialism, and maybe even a trace of the cabala that, given the sizable Jewish community in his native country, had found its way into Argentina's nonconventional thought. Above all, Guevara demonstrated that communism's appeal could lie, as English novelist Graham Greene once observed, in its *mystique* rather than its *politique*.[44]

The college-student counterculture of the 1960s, writes historian R. Laurence Moore, "having discovered parapsychology, quickly decided that the people who possessed the most . . . knowledge of psi phenomena [a general term that covers psychokinesis, or the ability of the mind to move objects, and extrasensory perception phenomena, or ESP] lived in Asia."[45] But American believers in higher consciousness also found a guru in Cuba, one with good Marxist credentials to boot—even though like many Latin American fellow believers he tended to turn Marxism, as conventionally defined by its ideologists, on its head, stressing the primacy of the ideological superstructure over the economic base. But Guevara also appreciated what went on down at the base of material reality. Thus he bore arms bravely in the struggle that brought Castro to power, and later he plunged into the interior of South America to bring deliverance to Bolivian peasants. In the wilds of Bolivia he won a martyr's death, done in by the forces of reaction trained by the CIA. Guevara had everything required to qualify for the hero's role that the American counterculture assigned him.

Americans immersed in the counterculture's broad stream of occultism as well as in its somewhat narrower stream of violence and lust for power found what they sought in the Cuban revolution. So did those intellectuals and artists who longed for a hierarchically organized society in which businessmen, with their ability to bestow material rewards, would no longer exercise power. Instead, control would pass into the hands of the intellectuals and artists who produced what was needed to satisfy the craving of the masses for nonmaterial satisfactions. At least since the early nineteenth century, American intellectuals alienated from capitalist society had entertained hopes of this nature. All in all, the New Left's contingent of alienated intellectuals and artists found as much to their liking in Guevara's esoteric Marxism with its stress on nonmaterial rewards—to which Castro increasingly subscribed—as did counterculture occultists and seekers after Frantz Fanon's vision of releasing the inward capacities of the alienated being through violence. Just as much as when contemplating the infatuations of an interwar counterculture with the occultism of Yeats, Auden could have looked at the infatuation of American intellectuals with the Cuban revolution and proclaimed, "*how* embarrassing." And yet there was another aspect of the revolution, one that merited cautious approbation.

Undoubtedly the great majority of gullible Americans (this writer included) who supported Castro in the early stages of the Cuban revolution did so out of vague feelings of discontent with the status quo in their own country, out of the conviction that America's capitalist system had not, by and large, done well enough by the lower classes, especially its darker-skinned constituents. Perhaps our attitudes were shaped by the amorphous traditions of historical American populism. Americans in the populist tradition found themselves predisposed, probably for longer than was justifiable in view of the mounting evidence of Castro's tyranny, to give the benefit of the doubt to a revolution whose leaders, apparently endorsed by the spontaneous "democracy of the streets," could present at least some evidence of mitigating poverty, eliminating illiteracy, reducing infant mortality, and making adequate medical treatment and housing universally available, while converting old haunts of affluent and decadent Cubans and American tourists into vacation spas for the working classes.

After the 1960s and early 1970s, it would be at least another twenty years (and that time frame could be extended by smug national satisfaction nourished by the smashing 1991 victory in the Persian Gulf) before Americans in huge numbers would again assume that somehow it was both possible and morally incumbent on them to move resolutely to reduce the gulf between the privileged and the underprivileged, the participating and the marginalized, in their own country. Out of glowing expectations as to what social engineering could accomplish in America itself had sprung a readiness in the counterculture's golden age to sympathize with Third World leaders who, like Castro, could talk exultantly about reforming society, the economy, and ultimately—in the time-honored tradition of utopianist thought at its worst—human nature itself.

Also nourishing support for Castro in the 1960s and 1970s were resurgent Social Gospel strains out of the Protestant past, reinforced by Catholicism's new liberation theology. According at least to some of the gospel's and the theology's proponents, poverty seldom if ever indicated moral weakness; instead, it consistently pointed to moral superiority. With a theologically justified preferential option for the poor, religiously inspired counterculturalists brushed aside mundane objections to their quest for a system that rewarded those who retained, ostensibly, their natural, child-like virtue, while penalizing those who had discarded it in the scramble to get ahead. Castro, they liked to believe, had set out to construct such a system: one in which the vices of civilization would yield to the virtues of the natural.

Religiously activated counterculturalists, many of whom foresaw the imminent synthesis of Christianity and Marxism, envied Castro the ability to rid himself of the island's allegedly debased bourgeoisie, whose members emigrated en masse to Florida. With the capitalist virus or sin removed, perhaps Cuba would become the sort of tropical paradise that had excited America's utopianist imagination, religious and secular, for generations. Perhaps Cuba's transition to paradise status would point the way toward *The Greening of America,* which Charles Reich foresaw in his widely read book of that title published in 1970. Meantime, who cared if Cuba's machines were breaking down and its roads breaking up. As singer-composer Paul Simon put the matter in his 1975 song "If I Could" (set to an Andean folk tune), "I'd rather be a forest than a street."[46]

Higher regard for forests than streets also characterized the counterculture's response to the drama that began to unfold during the Kennedy years in Vietnam. There, the forest was threatened, along with peasant villages, by the juggernaut of America's military technology that spewed bombs, napalm, and Agent Orange. Symbolically, events in Vietnam amounted to a repeat of the drama enacted thirty years earlier in Spain, when the Old Left and the remnants of the Lost Generation had rallied to the Loyalist cause. The New Left set out to defend, to lionize, the communist forces of Vietnam and the way of life that, purportedly, Ho Chi Minh's Vietcong or National Liberation Front (NLF) represented: a way of life the adversary culture transformed into the moral equivalent of a highly romanticized vision of native American culture.

Mary McCarthy, considered by some the grand dame of American letters at the time of her death in 1990, visited North Vietnam and in 1968 published her findings in a book titled *Hanoi.* In the Communist Third World of Southeast Asia she found the living fulfillment of the pastoral ideal, the sort of natural paradise Americans had vainly pursued in their Old West. In the Vietnam War, moreover, she found "a cowboy-and-Indian story, in which the Indians, for once, are repelling the cowboys."[47] In the same year that McCarthy's book appeared, Susan Sontag published the impressions she had formed during a trip to North Vietnam's capital. Earlier, Sontag, whom many Americans on the left regarded hopefully as the new Mary McCarthy, had visited Cuba and rhapsodized over its revolution. Now, in Communist Vietnam, she found people whom she couldn't help regarding "as children—beautiful, patient, heroic, martyred, stubborn children." Among these people, she discovered, "the phenomena of existential agony, of alienation just don't appear." Much like Mabel Dodge Luhan in response to the Pueblo, Sontag described the Vietnamese as "whole" human beings, not "'split' as we are."[48]

Another book, and a worthier one, inspired by the Vietnam struggle is *The Tunnels of Cu Chi* (1985). In it, authors Tom Mangold and John Penycate relate how the Vietcong responded to American dynamite, chemicals, and bulldozers by burrowing into the soil. A superb military tactic, the burrowing of tunnels was also fraught with symbolism. As NLF peasant soldiers dug thousands of miles of tunnels, they reaffirmed their identity with nature, becoming a part of Mother Earth. Adversary-culture Americans verbalized about being an underground; the Vietnamese actually became one. Rooted in the soil, literally, the Vietnamese managed to defeat civilization's technology. Exulting along with the New Left, the Old Left found compensation for the loss sustained when Franco's "fascists" had crushed the people of natural virtue in Spain.

In Cuba and then in Vietnam, mainstream, establishment Americans perceived updated versions of the Indian wars in which a happy ending demanded that civilization triumph over primitivism. In both cases, adversary-culture Americans rooted for surrogate Indians, and in both cases the symbolical Indians triumphed. Counterculturalists took heart. Then, in the 1980s, President Ronald Reagan regrouped traditionalist forces and promised them victory. In the new morality play taking place out on a Third World frontier, Nicaragua's Marxist Sandinistas, who came to power in 1979 following several years of armed struggle, took on the role of Indians. Throughout Reagan's two terms, the Sandinistas withstood the schemes of Washington-based cowboys to humble them. Paradoxically, though, the American counterculture, originally convinced that radical triumphs in the Third World would lead to similar triumphs at home, had by now sustained crushing defeat.

As it turned out, primitivism's triumph over modern technology's war-waging capacity in the periphery had if anything proved counterproductive to the radical cause within the core country, for the underdog Davids who had stood up to the Yankee Goliath soon showed their total inability to fashion the utopian societies that their American cheerleaders had anticipated. The abuses against humanity perpetrated in Cuba and in South Vietnam once conquered by the Marxist-Leninists began to disillusion many of their supporters on the American left. It was as if the left had discovered Stalinism all over again and awakened to the possibility of evil in the natural man and in the children of nature. The effects of this rediscovery tarnished the image of Latin Americans in general, associated as they were in the realm of American stereotypes with what was natural.

Sandinistas proved far gentler with their foes than the Cubans and the Vietnamese. But, while successfully enriching themselves, they failed to advance the country appreciably toward realization of their professed ideals. When given the chance to act out their dreams, defenders of primitive purity proved if anything less able to benefit the masses than the hardened lords of capitalist civilization. Somehow the classical confrontation between civilization and nature that lay at the heart of so much American mythology had turned out to be far more complex than the partisans of either side had anticipated.

Meantime, African socialism had fared no better than its Caribbean and Central American counterparts, thus vindicating Naipaul's skepticism rather than the counterculture's credulity. African socialist leaders, with First World economic experts often concurring, had anticipated annual growth rates during the 1960s of 6 percent. As it turned out most of the African countries experienced negative growth rates, not only in the 1960s but in the 1970s and even in the 1980s as well; those that registered moderate growth turned out to be the countries that resorted to the market mechanisms of the developed world. No more than the frontier myth did Third World social-revolutionary mythology actually yield perfect societies by returning them to roots, to origins. Many of America's romantic myths lay shattered by the 1980s.

The Advent of a New Generation

The free-market system in whose behalf Americans proselytized Latin Americans during the Reagan years (1981–1989) smacked of the "free-market imperialism" through which Britain and other nineteenth-century European powers had hoped to establish economic hegemony over colonial markets. Free-market imperialists promised that if backward areas opened their markets and all of their resources to the advanced country's commerce and investment, then the wisdom and know-how possessed by the advanced country's capitalists would begin to percolate in the underdeveloped region. Ultimately, this wisdom and know-how would lift the backward area and its citizens to developed status. As a character in a mid-nineteenth-century British novel explained it, "these children of nature" in a far-off land were destined to become full-fledged men, economically well-off and Christian at the same time, by dint of "my bringing Commerce to their shores."[49]

However, the Reagan years abounded in paradox and in many ways resonated not just with conservative values enshrined in the nineteenth-century British and American community but also with the ideals of the 1960s counterculture. Here is one example of resonance with the 1960s. In their pursuit of pleasure without social responsibility, the hippies of the 1960s are morally equivalent to the yuppies of the 1980s who pursued profit without social responsibility—even though the one group professed its return to primitive authenticity while the other claimed to be responsive to civilization's highest calling.

Ironically, what is more, President Reagan's brand of conservatism in the 1980s gave to counterculturalists, once bent upon introducing into America the ostensibly undefiled, natural values of Third Worlders, a taste of the victory that had eluded them in the 1950s, the 1960s, and the 1970s. Out of Reagan's policies came changes in certain basic American practices that actually brought them into line with Third World precedents—the very goal that the adversary culture from flower children to Weathermen had proclaimed. Against the backdrop of an economic recession that extended from late 1981 into early 1983, President Reagan persuaded legislators and the electorate that old, tried-and-true methods of uninhibited, laissez-faire capitalism, combined with the new, for the United States, element of monumental deficit financing could guarantee prosperity, at least for accommodated Americans. Among those seduced by the overt reversion to classical Yankee capitalism, accompanied by more or less covert acceptance of undisciplined Third World fiscal traditions, were a good number of yesterday's counterculturalists. In quite unanticipated ways, they found the Latin Americanization of U.S. finances—discussed at some length in the following chapter—to their liking and christened its product supply-side economics.

President Reagan, as the embodiment of the mythic cowboy figure who synthesized nature and civilization, the exuberant, living-for-the-moment child and the grasping, self-interested adult, excelled at bringing off the illusion of reconciling opposites. Americans, in a large majority, believed in the affable and avuncular—to some even lovable—president. They believed in him because he made them feel that anything was possible, that they could, like Whitman, be one thing and its opposite.

At various times during his presidency (1977–1981) Jimmy Carter had warned Americans of the perils they faced from a no-longer-to-be-trifled-with nature, whose patience in the face of long-sustained plundering was not inexhaustible. He had warned them, too, that time might be running out on their ability to trifle, with impunity, with the rights of people traditionally disdained as passive and helpless. Like natural resources, the patience of such people could be exhausted. But then came the happy western hero, convinced even in the 1980s that the closing gate on the frontier that Remington had depicted in his 1895 painting *The Fall of the Cowboy* (described in chapter 5) was really an opening gate. There was no need to worry over boundless nature's resigned readiness to sustain civilization's endless assaults. Nor was there need to fret unduly over high-handed treatment of primitive peoples. Against Pangloss's perspective from Santa Barbara, California, Jeremiah's vision from Plains, Georgia, didn't stand a chance with the American electorate.

CHAPTER 10

Change and Permanence in Myths and Stereotypes: Civilization and Nature toward Century's End

The Balance Shifts in Civilization's War on Nature

A few nineteenth-century Americans, as suggested in an earlier chapter, attributed frontier problems not just to savage Indians but also to civilized capitalists who profited by selling arms to the natives. Britain's contemporary master of the spy novel, John le Carré, provides an update to this sort of assessment. Dismayed by the First World's brutish and amoral capitalism, epitomized by munitions merchants avid to deal with any customers no matter the threat they pose to international order, le Carré near the end of a 1991 novel has his protagonist conclude that with communism defeated, "we were going to have to set about defeating capitalism."[1] Through the words of the character he created, le Carré renders his own judgment that today's international order requires the imposition of some stiff regulations on free-enterprise capitalism—even though he has his mouthpiece concede that the system's flaws lie ultimately in human nature. Essentially, le Carré makes the point that modern civilization, for all its hubris, is really not so different from nature: both operate by the laws of the jungle. Nowadays, even the hubris, together with the myths and stereotypes it has spawned, may be crumbling. With the Reagan era at an end, civilization, as encapsulated in free-enterprise capitalism, begins to accommodate to mounting pressure to adopt restraints. At the same time, nature seems more and more to elude civilization's attempts to impose control. Here is a role reversal, a paradox that might have delighted Emerson and Whitman.

Nature showed signs of turning more unruly in the 1980s, as a historian reminded his readers when contrasting the AIDS crisis with the 1918 pandemic of Spanish influenza: "The pathogens, particularly the newly recognized ones, seem to the general public to have become nastier faster than scientists have become smarter."[2] The whole sexual revolution that penicillin helped make possible after World War II seemed in jeopardy. In other ways as well nature flaunted powers that far surpassed the capacity of human restraints. With the age of Reagan barely at an end, Americans encountered frightening reminders of their helplessness in the face of such natural disasters as hurricanes and earthquakes. In the fall of 1989, only days after Hurricane Hugo devastated Caribbean islands and the southeast coast of mainland North America, a mighty earthquake struck northern California, even disrupting a sacrosanct rite, the World Series. In light of the blows dealt by germs and the elements, Americans seemed ready to take to heart the appraisals conveyed by Edward Tenner in a 1987 article titled: "Warning: Nature May Be Hazardous to Your Health."

About the time Tenner's article appeared, more and more newspaper columns drew attention to the perils that radon, "a colorless and odorless product of the decay of the Uranium-238 that occurs naturally in the soil," posed to a large number of households. At the same time, more and more warnings made the point that the sun's ultraviolet light was a dangerous carcinogen; and the dairy cow, once "a national heroine," was blamed for producing prodigious quantities of methane gas that contributed to a suspected global warming trend. Even most of America's evergreen and deciduous trees, along with decaying leaves and drying hay, added to environmental problems by emitting terpene hydrocarbons.[3] As if this were not bad enough, studies appeared suggesting that nature actually produced more carcinogens than those that humans pumped into the environment in the form of pesticides, herbicides, and the like.

For many generations Americans laid claim to superior virtue in comparison to all other people precisely because of their vaunted ability to dominate nature. This, ostensibly, was what the good, the God-pleasing life was all about. During the 1980s, though, it had become dramatically evident to more and more scientists and even casual observers that things were not working as it had once been assumed they would. Windmills, augmented in the post–World War II era by diesel-driven centrifugal pumps, once had raised enough water from the Ogalalla aquifer to turn the Great Plains into the country's and even the world's breadbasket. Nature's inhospitality and unpleasant habits in the Great Plains seemed to have yielded to civilization's genius. By the mid-1970s, though, more and more environment watchers awakened to the fact that while in some places "farmers were withdrawing four to six feet of water a year" from the aquifer, "nature was putting back half an inch."[4] Some scientists who studied the situation began to speak of the plains as a "monument of American self-delusion"—the delusion being that humans could forever control nature and rectify her shortcomings and omissions.[5] The author of an influential 1986 study of the plains warned in an eloquent concluding chapter that mankind's victory over nature was still problematic.[6] Some thirty years earlier Walter Prescott Webb, historian nonpareil of the Great Plains, had sounded similar warnings: although "greening the desert" had become "a kind of Christian ideal," the ideal remained unattainable. The Great Plains, Webb concluded, was "a semidesert with a desert heart"; its soul was too dark to permit its genuine conversion.[7]

Virtually from coast to coast, and from Canada to the Gulf, nature in America had begun to show her dark soul and to challenge myths about her tractability. Long successful in their efforts to keep the Mississippi River confined to a southern bed and outlet into the Gulf that assured maximum economic advantage to the Baton Rouge to New Orleans area, the Army Corps of Engineers had to resort to ever more massive, ever more monumentally expensive feats of engineering to keep the awesome river from escaping its old confinements and establishing a new, more natural mouth some one hundred miles from its present one. At least a few among the army engineers began to do the unthinkable: to express lack of confidence in their continuing ability to control the nature of the river's flow.[8] Meantime came warnings that engineering projects along the American coasts designed to protect the shoreline, and not so incidentally the oceanfront homes and resorts of the affluent, were destined to prove expensive failures. The warnings represented a dramatic "retreat from American dreams of engineering conquest."[9] The New World's counterpart of the Faustian dream to benefit mankind by asserting human control over the sea had surrendered much of its credibility. All the while, mankind's crowning victory over nature, the mastery of nuclear energy, yielded fearsome side effects. Human beings and the environment faced poisoning by atomic wastes.

Atomic wastes were merely one among many of the products with which a prosperous society poisoned the atmosphere, with humans doing far more than cows to speed the process along. Pouring from car exhausts and countless other sources, carbon dioxide threatened to trap the warmth of the sun in the earth's atmosphere and create the "greenhouse effect" that could, according to which scientist one heeded, raise global temperatures anywhere from one to nine degrees by midway in the next century. Some scientists doubted the global-warming thesis, noting that in the 1970s doom mongers had prophesied a new ice age. Still, the majority of scientists throughout the 1980s and into the 1990s worried that global warming had commenced, though conceding it might be ten years before they could develop sufficient data and technology to be certain. They disagreed whether a delay of ten years before commencing earth-protecting measures could prove disastrous if the data ultimately confirmed worst-case predictions.[10]

The jeremiads preached by some environmentalist scientists and the uncertainty admitted to by others eroded confidence in cherished myths that lay at the heart of American culture—and modern culture in general. Could it be true, as mystics long had warned, that Americans "must live together with the rest of nature or . . . die altogether with the rest of nature"?[11] Serious recessions will delay facing up to the question, for during such periods people are not likely to think beyond economic expansion, regardless of consequences. Delay may also issue out of the 1991 Persian Gulf War. Successful wars, especially when based on the glittering performance of new technology unleashed against people pictured as primitives if not barbarians, build confidence in the ability of a technological civilization to do whatever it wishes with nature. Still, the jeremiads cannot be ignored forever. Nor can the havoc wrought by "smart" weaponry.

A "New History" Begins as a Century Ends

In the era that followed the end of the cold war in 1990, some Americans began to concern themselves with scaling back the longest and most pervasive of all wars: the war against nature that previously had helped to define civilization. They set out to devise the restrictions and centralized planning mechanisms needed to curb the freedom of humans to live by the old urge to wrest from nature the last measure of profit, regardless of long-term consequences. The Communist world indeed lay in tatters as the century neared its end, indicating that total systems of centralized planning by their very nature become dysfunctional, in part because of the corruption that inevitably undermines government processes. But worldwide pollution and a rapidly deteriorating biosphere, accompanied by heedless squandering of certain natural resources, suggested that systems of maximum liberty from centralized planning, as found among some of the developed free-world countries, contained basic shortcomings of their own. Far more than the collapse of communism, it was broad-based willingness to reconsider the rules of civilization's encounter with nature that heralded the possible dawn of a "new history."

The resolution of the cold war meant that "Adam Smith may indeed have vanquished Karl Marx in the semi-finals." But this only set the stage for the "final" that "pits Smith against [nineteenth-century German economist] Friedrich List"—and ever-so-many other proponents of a balance between free enterprise and state control—"and the result is far from a foregone conclusion."[12] This "final" will, I suspect, be the centerpiece of America's new history: a history that will record the attempt to limit economic policies according to the needs of embattled, vulnerable nature. Like all history, what I foresee in sporadic moments of optimism as a new history has many harbingers in the past.

To the extent that they begin to enter a new history, Americans will have to heed more consistently than ever they have in the past a small but never-silenced voice of the national conscience. Since colonial times this nagging voice has counseled a modus vivendi with nature. In line with this, it has urged restraints on the lust for affluence thought to result from the rapid exploitation of natural resources. The quest to achieve a harmonious relationship between civilization and nature has always been a part of the American tradition. Even more a part of that tradition, however, is the opposite custom of holding nature and "children of nature," wherever found, in disdain and denying them rights to respectful treatment by civilized men and women. So, as Americans begin to confront a threatened scarcity of natural resources, they may initially—and perhaps even ultimately—respond by intensifying their efforts to control and exploit what remains of diminishing supplies. They may also redouble their efforts to dominate Others, whether in Latin America or the Middle East or elsewhere, who currently own some of those supplies. Meanwhile Americans, having acquired some initial restraint in unleashing toxic, carcinogenic pesticides and herbicides against nature in their own country, still export the most noxious varieties to Latin America and other developing regions. There, the chemicals duly combat nature's annoyances and in the process poison primitive people deemed unworthy of the protection that civilized beings have come to demand. In this respect, the main thrust of the old history seems already to threaten the emergence of the new.

Old myths, moreover, still shed light on the way in which some Americans, and moderns in general, refuse to take action that might curtail prospects for immediate gain in the long-range interests of nature—and of themselves. Robert May, readers may recall from the first chapter, has posited an archetypal male myth, exemplified by the tales, among many others, of Icarus, Faust, and Don Juan. This myth pertains to choosing utmost immediate satisfaction even at the price of ultimate disaster.[13] Pick up almost any daily newspaper and you will find tales attesting to that myth's continuing appropriateness.

May, it will also be recalled, perceives not only a masculine but also a feminine archetypal myth. This latter depicts life in terms of lengthy periods of travail that give way at last to contentment and tranquility. In a bygone era, the presence of the frontier may have served to reinforce the feminine myth, both among American women *and* men. Within the context of frontier mythology, not just women but men as well could bring forth new lives after privation and hardship had well-nigh ruined their old lives.

Leonard Bernstein's considerable claim to being *the* quintessential American composer rests, I would argue, precisely on the grounds that in virtually all of his major musical compositions, he deals with "new beginnings emerging from confusion, disillusionment, and tragedy."[14] This, after all, is in line with America's great corpus of frontier mythology. But Bernstein came to his myth long after the frontier had ended. All his life, moreover, he was the urban man, through and through. Rather than a frontier context, Bernstein, in spite of his irreverence for so many conventions and beliefs, gave a religious sense to his vision of a new life. Not surprisingly, among all the great works by Gustav Mahler that Bernstein loved and performed so gloriously, he seems to have been most deeply devoted to that composer's second symphony: the *Resurrection* Symphony.

In the postfrontier age Americans can claim, according to innumerable studies, a far higher percentage of religious believers than the people of any other Christian nation, though how consistently they act on their beliefs is another matter altogether. Interestingly, the percentage of American nonbelievers in 1990 was highest—but still quite insignificant in comparison to European and also Latin American countries—in the Far West. As residents of the final frontier area, westerners may have been the last Americans to recognize the obsolescence of frontier mythology and to feel the need to replace it with Christian faith in a new life of spiritual dimensions.

Oregon is the state with the highest percentage of nonbelievers among all Americans—but even there nonbelievers make up considerably less than 20 percent of the inhabitants. Perhaps above all others, Oregon symbolizes the last frontier state: even Californians now desert their old paradise to seek a new life in Oregon. Logically enough, Bernard Malamud in his *A New Life* (1961), a takeoff on the classic western novel genre, sends New Yorker Seymour Levin to Oregon in 1950 in bumbling pursuit of the old American dream of rebirth. Levin was no more successful in seeking regeneration in nature than was Hemingway's Yogi Johnson, portrayed in the already-cited *Torrents of Spring* (1926), in looking to an Indian maiden for regeneration. Both of these less-than-memorable novels attest to what has become increasingly apparent to Americans: once-meaningful secular myths have lost their power. If surrogates for religion are no longer effective, perhaps religion itself must be tried.

What may be the effect of American religious beliefs in determining whether a new history emerges out of the old? To this observer, the prospects appear mixed. On one hand, many Christians figure among America's most dedicated environmentalists, and also among those Americans most sensitive to the rights of modern-day "primitives," wherever found. On the other hand, I have grave doubts about certain Protestant evangelicals and fundamentalists who believe the end of the world is nigh. Men and women of this persuasion are hardly likely to fret over the rate at which natural resources are depleted.[15] More than likely, though, they do concern themselves with converting as many persons as possible to the "true faith" before the world ends—to assure that vast legions of humanity will be saved. This latter attitude scarcely suggests to me much respect for humanity in its unsaved, unredeemed estate. In fact it smacks of the despair over the basic humanity of unbaptized Indians found among many Protestant clergymen dating back to colonial times in America and also among many Catholic priests in Latin America dating back to the time of the conquest. To the extent that such attitudes endure in coming years, I worry whether the new history will have a happy tale to tell about "civilized" attitudes toward people historically stereotyped as close to nature. Through the years, after all, people branded as close to nature have tended to be those outside the "true faith" as received from on high by purported emissaries of civilization.

Shaped in part by apocalyptic expectations, American Protestant proselytizing zeal has acquired a revitalized thrust, one directed not only at fellow citizens but also at Third Worlders and especially at those living south of the border, a development alluded to in more detail later in this chapter. In Latin America, the millenarian faith of Protestant fundamentalists and evangelicals resonates sympathetically with the beliefs of popular-religion offshoots of that region's Catholicism that have periodically since the age of conquest fostered apocalyptic visions and expectations. Hopeful about their ability to save souls through their proselytizing efforts before the world ends, some Protestant fundamentalists adamantly oppose effective population-control measures—coinciding here not with popular-religion offshoots but with the official, pontifical Catholic church, and providing reinvigorated religious backing for policies that can only intensify human pressure upon natural resources. This, too, is a topic important enough to merit a second mention later in this chapter. The pressure of unchecked population on fragile environments could, after all, doom the new history to being only a more somber repetition of the old.

Many Americans skeptical about archetypal myths, whether masculine or feminine, and also unconvinced and even appalled by religiously inspired apocalypse-now beliefs, have their own sense of what the hemisphere's future could be within the context of a new history. They can view the New Deal era, as depicted in chapter 8, as prologue to the main drama that they see beginning to unfold toward century's end. Principal protagonists in the prologue, that actually harked back to the days of Theodore Roosevelt, were two disparate groups of environmentalists. One group, the preservationists, hoped to parlay professed reverence for nature into an assault against the very essence of the capitalist system. Conservationists comprised the other camp. They sought through rational and beneficent control to save nature and her resources from short-sighted businessmen so that they, in spite of themselves, could rely on renewable resources capable of sustaining their profits, albeit somewhat circumscribed, for generations to come. The main drama began toward the end of the 1980s, the plot gaining in clarity because by then the Marxists of one stripe or another who once seemed seriously to threaten traditional American institutions no longer posed a real menace, although a major and prolonged recession in the capitalist world could breathe life into various mutations of their cause. For the moment, though, radical environmentalists stood virtually by themselves as the assault troops against classical capitalism. Occasionally business responded by branding all environmentalists the enemy, failing to distinguish adequately between extremists genuinely out to destroy the corporate structure and moderates anxious to save as much as possible of the structure as nature would permit.

The main confrontation as the new history's drama unfolds in the post-Communist era could assume hemispheric dimensions. Conceivably, environmentalism could become the cause that links radicals, north and south, in a new crusade against free-enterprise capitalism. Even if this scenario never is acted out in the New World, changing American perceptions of the environment will have an impact on hemispheric relations.

Latin America in the Context of Changing American Perceptions of the Natural World

Nowadays Americans do not automatically assume that decreasing natural abundance implies the necessity, together with the right, of ever-more ruthless exploitation of remaining resources, wherever found. Even outside the ranks of professed environmentalists, a fair number of Americans assume that mounting scarcity implies they can no longer reasonably hope to maintain their old claims to total mastery over nature. From this assumption, and building on an implicitly accepted relationship between na-

17. Alexandre Hogue. *Drouth Survivors.* 1936. Oil on canvas, 30 × 48″. Formerly owned by Musée National d'Art Moderne, Paris; destroyed by fire. Photograph and reproduction permission provided by the artist.

Hogue projects a vision of technology reduced to impotence by the nature it had briefly and heedlessly conquered. Some Americans suspect that in the encounter with "primitives," civilization faces similar defeat and must—even as in the contest with nature—settle for a modus vivendi.

ture and certain people of nature, some revisionist-minded Americans advance to the conclusion that it is no more possible to maintain domination over the people of nature than over nature itself. (See illustration 17.) Slowly, the American patriarchal establishment begins if not exactly to accept then at least to mull over the possibility that it can no longer discipline Latin Americans, any more than it can really shape and reshape such internal "natural" beings as women, teenagers, African Americans, and Hispanic immigrants. (Granted, political extremists who refuse to admit such possibilities could become more powerful in the years ahead.)

Here are some recent indications of loss of hegemony over Latin Americans that Americans have had to learn to live with—even as they grudgingly face up to the need to contemplate the escape of nature and its resources from relentlessly incremental control. In 1973 Chileans took matters largely into their own hands when it came to ridding their country of Salvador Allende and his Marxist administration, American plans to accomplish this objective having come to naught. And the general who succeeded Allende in power (Augusto Pinochet) refused to kowtow to Washington throughout the ensuing fifteen years. In the early 1980s, Argentines could not be deterred by Washington from waging war against Britain over the Falkland/Malvinas Islands. As of 1990, Fidel Castro had defied for over thirty years all American efforts to oust him; and if fated for an imminent fall as the new decade began, it would result more from the tide of history, from the general collapse of the communist world, than from specific U.S. pressures. Beginning in 1979, Nicaragua's Marxist Sandinistas managed for over ten years to stare down the United States in its efforts to oust them, and when defeat came it proceeded not so much from pressure applied by the American-trained *contra* guerrillas as from abandonment of the Sandinistas by a retrenching Soviet Union and from the electoral process conceived in San José by Costa Rican president Oscar Arias Sánchez that the Reagan administration made every effort to undercut. It proceeded, also, from the conciliatory attitudes toward the Sandinistas of Violeta de Chamorro, the presidential candidate who triumphed over them in the February 1990 elections and who resisted American pressures to toughen her stance, both before and after the elections.

Some Americans refuse to accept the thesis of their country's declining power in hemispheric affairs. They insist that generous aid to the military in El Salvador prevented victory by Marxist revolutionaries in that country's civil war that ground into its tenth year as 1991 began. And they refuse to accept blame for the human rights abuses perpetrated by the Washington-backed Salvadoran military in the course of fighting Marxist insurgents. To many American apologists for their government's policies, Central Americans whether with or without support from the United States are naturally, basically inclined to discard all pretense of decency in their treatment of foes. In this respect, they are no better than nineteenth-century Native Americans. Moreover, Americans who believe their country still exercises righteous hegemony over Central America and perhaps even republics much farther to the south, offer interpretations of recent Nicaraguan events that differ markedly from those that I advanced immediately above. Their interpretations are not to be lightly dismissed.

Those who cast the best light on recent American actions in Central America insist that, in the case of Nicaragua, a war conceived and directed from Washington, carried out by both economic means and a surrogate army of contras, saved the country from the sort of tyranny and economic collapse that Cuba endured under Castro. Then, there are Americans who assume continuing U.S. hegemony in hemispheric affairs but who cast recent American actions in the worst light. According to them, U.S. economic sanctions combined with a surrogate invasion aborted a promising revolution dedicated to replacing the abominations of the Somozas' protracted rule with a new era of social justice.

In the midst of debate over whether or not America still possesses the great-power capacity to mold events in Central America and whether it uses whatever power it may have for good or ill, one thing does seem certain. Recent American policy toward Central America has resulted in a breakdown of constitutional order within the United States itself, leading to the circumvention of domestic and international laws, to the formation of a rogue state, monolithic, clandestine, and more powerful than the official state of constitutional checks and balances—a rogue state that violated national laws, connived in and profited from drug trafficking, and contributed to the frauds perpetrated through the Bank of Credit and Commerce International (BCCI) that finally began to surface in 1991. Apparently the United States could no longer impose its will with impunity on recalcitrant Central American states. Instead, it could impose its will only by undermining the principles upon which western civilization presumably rests. Perhaps this is a symptom of the "Latin Americanization of America" discussed under a separate heading in this chapter.

Recent events in Panama have provided some symptoms of declining American hegemony in the hemisphere. Above all, though, they suggest that America can pursue successful interventionist policies only by violating the very principles of rule by law to which its government pays lip service. Panama, the very country that America under Theodore Roosevelt had called into being, wrested from the Jimmy Carter administration concessions that called for the United States to relinquish control at the end of the century over the canal that Yankee technological and medical know-how had created. As if this were not an adequate reminder of the loss of omnipotence, Gen. Manuel Antonio Noriega, a monstrous ruler originally created and nourished by the United States when his thuggery seemed to serve American purposes, refused to step down when Washington bade him do so. As with countless Indian collaborators in frontier days, Americans had trained Noriega and introduced him into the ways and wiles of civilization, but instead of responding to civilization's uplift, Noriega seemed only to have been corrupted by it.

For four years, between 1985 and December 1989, Noriega (who had come to power in 1981) defiantly resisted all American efforts to end his rule. Desperate, in the pre–Persian Gulf War days, for a dramatic act that would bolster confidence in the ability to control primitives *somewhere* in the world, President George Bush unleashed an army of some twenty-four thousand men and women against Panama that finally succeeded in top-

pling Noriega. Perhaps as a former director of the CIA, Bush was especially anxious to atone for the agency's earlier blunders and mistaken judgment in collaborating with Noriega. Be that as it may, the destruction
occasioned by the invasion, combined with the devastating effects of economic sanctions that the United States had imposed during the prior two
years in the vain attempt to topple Noriega peacefully, literally destroyed
much of Panama's economic base.

Nevertheless, Americans overwhelmingly supported their country's actions, demonstrating perhaps the survival of old frontier myths that assumed the need periodically to destroy the natural and the primitive so as
to serve the cause of civilization. Subsequently, the American public did
not appear, to this observer, to suffer second thoughts when news releases,
appearing a few months after the relatively speedy withdrawal of the invading troops, indicated that drug trafficking in Panama—which provided
some of the justification for the intervention—had returned to preinvasion
levels. Americans also seemed to remain indifferent to reliable accounts
that the "new" Panamanian armed forces consisted basically of the same
personnel whose insensitivity to human rights had provided further rationalization for the intervention. Nor, apparently, did Americans allow
their approval for the invasion to wane when reports filtering out of Panama indicated that in the liberated country respect for human rights was
not dramatically higher than under Noriega, even if the victims of abuse
were now less likely to be members of the upper class.

Meanwhile, events did not proceed smoothly in Nicaragua, after democratic elections ousted the Sandinistas from office early in 1990. By that
time Nicaragua lay in such devastation, resulting from its Marxist government's ineptness and from the actions Washington had pursued for a
decade to chastise that government, that one could only pity the demo-
cratically elected regime in its attempts to rescue the country from chaos.
What is more, Washington's power wielders soon grew impatient with the
unwillingness of Nicaragua's elected government to deal with either its political or economic problems in what was deemed an acceptable manner.
To signal its displeasure, the Bush administration held up the disburse-
ment of congressionally approved funds. The carrot of funds apparently
had proved as ineffective as the stick of armed intrusions in yielding desired consequences.

Back in 1954 it had seemed so easy to rescue a Central American country, in this instance Guatemala, from threats to civilization. But, in the ensuing three to four decades Third Worlders to the south had become as
difficult to manage as nature itself.

Still, as already indicated, U.S. intervention in Nicaragua and also in

Panama had initially produced results in those countries desired and intended by Washington, even if concomitantly damaging the legal and constitutional fabric in America itself; intervention rid the two Central American countries of governments anathema to the United States and to many Nicaraguan and Panamanian citizens. However, in contemplating this initial success, Americans should remember that the interventions arose out of the need to correct the unintended damage resulting from earlier meddling—even as a great deal of ongoing environmental engineering arises out of the need to correct the problems created by previous engineering projects. Just as much as it does environmental engineers, consistent and enduring victory eludes social engineers who intrude among "undeveloped" people. Meanwhile, the engineering grows more expensive.

Even assuming that, miraculously, recent Central American interventions produce few long-range deleterious side effects, the fact remains that Latin America as a whole seems increasingly to elude America's grand scheme for rationalizing the affairs of the hemisphere. By the 1970s and 1980s, U.S. administrations seemed resigned to the fact that European and Japanese firms were capturing markets once thought destined exclusively for Yankee control and exploiting natural resources once assumed to have been providentially set aside to provision American industries. World War II had been fought, in some small measure at least, precisely to prevent such developments. The fact that some of the foreign firms operating in Latin America are multinationals in which U.S. investors have a stake only partially offsets the setback to old American dreams of hemispheric economic hegemony. Responding to this situation, the Bush administration encouraged free-trade agreements among the Americas—even as it urged Japan to abandon free-market concepts and accord special treatment to U.S. imports. Increasingly discussed in Washington and throughout the hemisphere in the early 1990s, a pan-American free-trade zone might dramatically tilt Latin American commerce toward the United States. Still, the United States faced an uphill struggle just to reclaim the ground it had lost since the end of World War II in comparative indices of hemispheric trade.

In an earlier age, American counterculturalists might have applauded the fact that their country's leaders and official institutions seemed to have suffered relative loss of control over nature and primitives. Always, in whatever age they had appeared, counterculturalists had spoken up for the rights of nature and primitives. But when the remnants of counterculturalists gazed southward in the late twentieth century, they tended to be as disheartened as establishment figures grieving over the diminution of hegemony, for they beheld not so much a primitive as a bourgeois Latin

America. Cuba was the one exception, as Fidel Castro in late 1990, facing a cutoff of aid from the disintegrating Soviet Union, toyed with plans to replace gas-guzzling tractors with some four hundred thousand bulls and to move vast sectors of the urban population to the countryside, where they could hopefully survive by practicing communal agriculture. If Mexico had announced such a scheme in the 1920s or 1930s, a fair number of starry-eyed Americans would have applauded the move as providing a glimpse of the happy future that awaited the world as a whole. In the 1990s, however, only a tiny handful could pretend that events in Cuba portended anything except Latin America's last aberrant gesture of defiance against an inevitably rising tide of bourgeois values.

Embourgeoisement: The Counterculture's Loss of Illusions about Latin America

Perpetuation of myths and stereotypes about the Other demands that the Other remain essentially unchanged. But Latin Americans have changed. For one thing, they no longer ignore their frontiers, as Americans once accused them of doing. In quest of quick wealth they now ravage virgin land as heedlessly as nineteenth-century American expansionists, for which they are chided by twentieth-century Americans suddenly become environmentally conscious. Nor do Latin Americans cling still to the otherworldly Catholicism that progress-obsessed Yankees excoriated in the nineteenth and early twentieth centuries, but that a few American cultural elites praised as an antidote to crude materialism. For some time now, even as Catholicism advanced to become the most widely practiced faith in the United States, Protestantism has been making steady inroads into Latin America's religious life. Indeed, as the 1990s began evangelical Protestantism was said to be winning Latin American converts at a rate of four hundred per hour. Almost certainly it had "replaced Roman Catholicism as Brazil's most widely *practiced* faith."[16] In parts of Central America its progress has been equally dramatic; and even in Colombia and Peru, traditionally Catholic strongholds, the spread of evangelical Protestantism has picked up momentum. Oriented almost as much toward temporal achievement and bourgeois aspirations as toward salvation in the next world, Latin America's new faith seemed to fulfill the aspirations of nineteenth-century Americans who, like Merrill E. Gates (referred to in chapter 5), hoped to inculcate in American Indians as well as south-of-the-border primitives the sort of material wants that could best be satisfied through the dedicated practice of privatized, individualistic, muscular Christianity.

In many other scarcely less striking ways Latin Americans have changed. The old American notion that Latins suffer from the lack of a middle class is no longer tenable, and hasn't been since the mid–twentieth century.[17] And this in particular has dismayed adversary-culture Americans who used to look hopefully toward Latin America.

An American hippie of the 1960s gave this appraisal of what had gone wrong with his country: "The middle class [was] always trying to improve things, and that's why they keep getting worse. Because they keep getting more and more middle class."[18] In the late 1980s, this appraisal, at least for all Americans who still clung to counterculture values, seemed to explain not just the American malaise but that of Latin America as well.

No longer was it possible to look on Latin America as the land of mystical rather than material longings, of rapport with nature, of pursuit of Arielist goals, of processions and religious festivals revered precisely because of the links they supposedly forged with a world set apart from mere material reality. By the 1980s, and really well before that, Latin Americans, many of the most visible ones at least, had become a people whose most cherished shrines and citadels of culture were shopping malls. These had become the preferred destination for processions. Once arrived there, consumption-mad Latin Americans performed the rituals most meaningful to them. And the only soil that the new Latin bourgeoisie revered as connecting them to something transcendent was the earth that lay beneath the banks where they deposited their gains.

If, as suggested later in this chapter, the United States has undergone Latin Americanization, then just as clearly Latin America has moved toward Americanization: its old culture has largely disappeared beneath waves of the vulgar materialism that non-Americans, always seconded by American counterculturalists, have tended to equate with Yankee civilization—even though such stereotyped materialism has always been just one aspect of that civilization. In response to the Americanization of their culture, some Latin American survivors of the Arielist tradition who look for values that transcend those of conspicuous consumption voice the hope that in years to come the European Old World will spread its allegedly more benign influence in Latin America and help rescue the area from U.S. cultural hegemony.[19] But Latins of this persuasion place their hopes on a frail reed, one that has already bowed before the wind that seems to threaten, or promise, depending on one's taste, the Americanization of the world. In any event, Latin Americans cannot realistically hope to be saved by the Old World, or by any other deus ex machina, from the effects of indigenous cultural seeds that did not have to be imported from America, however much they have benefited from Yankee nourishment in attaining full development.

Counterculturalists are not the only Americans let down as they gaze southward, for the new, hustling, on-the-make Latin middle classes do not necessarily endear themselves to America's most zealous defenders of private initiative and free-enterprise capitalism. The wealthiest, most powerful of Latin America's capitalists seem tainted, in the eyes of many American observers, because they rely, allegedly, more on government favoritism than entrepreneurial skill and personal initiative to get ahead. They feel more at home in sprawling, inefficient parastatal enterprises than trimmed-down, efficient, and competitive private corporations. They practice a backward form of capitalism, somewhere between the highly evolved version that allegedly flourishes in the United States and the statism of Communist primitivism.

Some Americans in recent years have begun to look favorably, perhaps romantically, on a pure version of free-enterprise capitalism alleged to exist at the base of Latin American society—practiced by the resourceful lower classes in violation of the endless government restrictions that theoretically regulate every aspect of enterprise, regardless of how humble. More cynical Americans, however, see the so-called underground economy as a survival of practices dating back to colonial times in which sharp operators among the urban poor (the *pícaros* featured in picaresque literature originating in Spain) lived by their wits, altogether unscrupulously and sometimes even viciously. It may be significant that some of America's capitalist elites have come to identify with the pícaro.

Latin America: Still in a State of Nature?

In the early, heady days of the Kennedy administration, some Americans developed wildly optimistic expectations about what a briefcase brigade from Washington could accomplish in reforming and uplifting backward Latin American republics. Civilization's moment had come, and now its emissaries would spread its blessings southward. Against this optimism economist Simon G. Hanson often raised a cynical voice. One of the most trenchant American writers of his era on the Latin American scene, Hanson liked to quote Eugene Black, onetime head of the World Bank, who warned, "We are coming to the situation in which an optimist will be the man who thinks the present living standards [in Latin American and other Third World countries] can even be maintained." As with Black, Hanson's pessimism about Latin America's immediate future stemmed from the conviction that increases in employment opportunities, economic output, and social services, including health and education, could not keep pace with rapidly burgeoning populations. Because of rapid population growth, Latin Americans were, as Hanson put it, ending what once had been "symbiotic harmony with [the] environment."[20] In consequence of refusing to impede the natural results of the most natural of human acts, Latin Americans faced the prospect of remaining in the backwardness that Americans traditionally had stereotyped as a state of nature. As it turned out, Hanson's and Black's pessimism was more than justified, though obviously for many more reasons than Latin America's runaway population increases.

In its 1989 edition, a highly respected guidebook warned tourists about an increasing number of trouble spots in virtually every Latin American country, admonishing them to steer clear of these sites or to approach them with extreme caution.[21] Latin America seemed to have remained in a state of nature: a state that was threatening to life and limb, certainly not in any way life renewing.

Commenting also in 1989 on Latin America's ills, a Brazilian psychoanalyst noted that without ideas that give hope, "with no cultural referents to give direction to one's life or to protect one from existential anguish, the human being becomes like an animal." And hopeless despair abounds, he believes, throughout the region. Having lost confidence in their culture and faith in the future, all too many Latins have, he fears, fallen into a state of "narcissistic panic."[22] If Latin Americans have themselves begun to think this way, the pessimism that grips so many contemporary Americans when they look southward is understandable.

From the U.S. media in the late twentieth century came report after report, their factual veracity often above doubt, drawing attention to signs that Latin America had become—or remained—a chaotic jungle. Certainly chaos seemed the order of the day in Haiti. The U.S. ambassador to that country told a human rights delegation visiting the island republic in 1989: "I don't see any evidence of a [Haitian] policy against human rights, any more than they have a policy about anything. . . . It's been the law of the jungle out there."[23] At the time the ambassador made his comment, the then nearly ten-year-long civil war in El Salvador (which had resulted in half again as many casualties as American forces sustained in Vietnam and displaced about a million citizens) continued to produce chaos challenging Haiti's, though it showed signs of winding down. Indeed, on the last day of 1991 that struggle may have ended with the signing of a UN-mediated ceasefire. Having once encouraged Salvadoran rulers to push for total victory, at least Washington belatedly pressed them toward conciliation. It remains to be seen, however, how quickly the spigots of hatred can be closed down. All the while in neighboring Guatemala conditions remained explosive beneath a superficial calm. That country's military in league with the gente decente waged a low-intensity but nonetheless savage war against those segments of the population (whether Indians or college students or intellectuals or labor organizers) who wanted their land to become something more than the domain of the viciously exploitative privileged few.

Shifting their gaze from Central America to Colombia, observers encountered scenes that also suggested the chaos of the jungle, even though in much of the country the social fabric remained intact and people led decent, worthy, and productive lives. According to a knowledgeable letter writer to the *Wall Street Journal* in August 1988, some 140 death squads and paramilitary units operated in Colombia, totally beyond the government's control.[24] A few months earlier a reporter for the same newspaper described the country's "infrastructure of death," wherein hit men and private armies of various sorts operated almost at will. A student told the reporter: "People are beginning to solve all the problems of everyday life with violence." To a reporter representing the *New York Times,* a prominent Colombian newspaper editor lamented: "We have grown used to living by the law of the jungle. I have no confidence that in the end good shall triumph over evil."[25] Even as the Colombian made this observation, his government faced the prospect of losing effective sovereignty over more and more sections of the interior. The jungle was spreading in Colombia, and also in neighboring, depression-ridden Peru.

In 1990 terrorism claimed over three thousand Peruvian lives and inflicted some three billion dollars' worth of property damage—a figure equivalent to 15 percent of the gross domestic product. Along with enterprises of terrorism and coca-leaf production, companies offering security to beleaguered citizens figured among the few growth activities.[26] In 1991 civilization suffered a new setback as a cholera epidemic threatened to overwhelm Peru's medical resources and to spread to neighboring republics.

Moving on to Brazil, the American observer encountered a country described in his or her press as one falling ever further behind in the indices by which the developed world likes to measure civilization: indices including those on infant mortality and the number of years children spend in school. Moreover, with the eighth largest economy in the West, Brazil ranked forty-ninth in per capita income and found it increasingly difficult (like Argentina, Mexico, Venezuela, and Peru, among other sister republics) to service staggering foreign debts, or to control runaway inflation rates.[27] And, as in many other Latin American republics, clergymen who spoke out in defense of the dispossessed faced harassment and death, even as did some persons who raised a plea in defense of the natural environment.

Shifting the gaze to relatively prosperous Mexico, the late twentieth-century American observer might have fretted over the irony that the Aztec republic had made a bold move toward economic privatization just when this system's prototype was producing symptoms of dysfunction and malaise within the United States. Certainly the observer found no trace of the bucolic, racially fused utopia that Henry Wallace, Stuart Chase, and other dreamers had expected to result from the revolution. Instead of the tranquil communal farm, or *ejido,* Mexico City, with its teeming millions who had fled rural life, stood as the nation's microcosm. The only indication that the integration of elites and masses foreseen by American romantics in the 1930s had actually occurred is that the shacks of the poor, Indian-origin masses sometimes abut the walls of residences where the well-to-do of less obviously Indian heritage reside. Similar juxtapositions of poverty and wealth prevail in most major Latin American cities. At least well-to-do Americans have been rather more successful in keeping the indigent safely distanced from their homes, enabling them to feel more secure in their civilization.

Like the poor in general, Latin America's forty to fifty million discarded children, its homeless street urchins who must live by their wits and their bodies, are more numerous and more visible than the swelling ranks of their American counterparts—and also more likely to be murdered by law-and-order vigilantes anxious to "clean up" the streets. So, once more Americans take pride in their benign civilization while shaking their heads over the state of nature from which the Latins seem unable to escape. And they wonder how it is that "institutional disintegration" in Latin America seems to gather momentum "irrespective of the system of government."[28]

The tone of U.S. media coverage sometimes emerges out of, while simultaneously reinforcing, conventional American stereotypes of the Latin Other. Often enough, though, news coverage emerges out of reality. Furthermore, Americans do not have to rely on the national media for evidence of disintegration to the south. They can turn also to the sentiments of despair that abound in the refrains of many Latin American contemporary songs, some of which become popular north of the border,[29] and also in the mass-market English translations of Latin fiction. More likely than not, this fiction tells of societies red of tooth and claw; beset by wile, cunning, duplicity, treachery, and depravity of surrealistic proportions; and wracked by cultural, political, ethnic, and class warfare.[30] Colombian novelist Gabriel García Márquez maintains that Latin America's novels and also its best films tend to depict "human beings struggling to find their place in societies where any venture, from love to politics, is likely to end badly."[31]

Ignoring the provocation afforded by violence-prone revolutionaries,

American leftists still bewail the savagery of repressive military governments in Argentina, Uruguay, and Chile (the southern cone, predominantly white countries in which Americans once placed high hopes) that,
during the 1970s, tortured and "disappeared" countless thousands of citizens. Meanwhile conservative Americans bemoan the continuing cruelty
of Fidel and Raúl Castro and their henchmen in Cuba, as well as the
bloodthirstiness of the Marxist rebels who function in so many republics,
most notoriously in Peru where the *sendero luminoso* (shining path) movement has descended to new lows in Western Hemisphere barbarism.
Whether radical or conservative, Americans readily enough find ample indications of Latin barbarism.

Americans do not have to look south of the border to find signs that
make them wonder about the "civilizability" of Latins. They can read
about the high dropout rates and the gang violence of Hispanic immigrants living in American cities, overlooking all the worthwhile contributions of the law-abiding, upstanding Latino or Chicano majority to the
social and economic fabric of American life—just as they overlook the
abundance of positive factors in the republics to the south. Americans inclined to give up on "primitive" Others can also look to New Mexico,
where in the early twentieth century some of their forebears saw the cradle
of a new civilization, arising from an amalgam of Indian, Hispanic, and
Anglo sources. If today's American tourists visit Taos, they may initially be
overwhelmed by the sight of fast-food establishments, Wal-Marts and
shopping malls, glitzy motels, and sleazy novelty shops. The splendor of
the natural setting is certainly still there, and so is much of the traditional
charm of Taos; but to find that charm the tourist must dig beneath the
surface. A real stretch of the imagination is necessary in order to appreciate that this onetime frontier outpost still seemed in the early twentieth
century to promise something more than another abject surrender to
consumerism.

If today's Anglo Americans want a more authentic glimpse of New
Mexico's Hispanic past they might investigate the out-of-the-way northern town of Coyote. Hispanics living there have not yet been deluged by
tourists, and property values have not shot up in response to the quest of
affluent Anglos for chic, off-the-beaten-path places to live or vacation. But
Anglo civilization in many of its manifestations has invaded the old Hispanic community, and the resulting mix is not a happy one. Obviously a
profoundly disturbed people, the residents of Coyote have resorted to
bloodletting on a heroic scale. The homicide rate in this town and the surrounding Rio Arriba area is four times higher than the national average.
Along with murder, Coyote's statistics point to drunkenness and feuding

and general lawlessness of epidemic proportions. The town, "which has long been proud of its strong families, self-sufficient farms, independence from government assistance and strong Catholic faith is now a parody of those values," according to an American journalist.[32]

Coyote, at least as described in the popular U.S. press, abounds in the sort of negative, stereotyped views that Americans like to conjure up when thinking about the Hispanic Other. Always anxious to read material that fortifies their prejudices, they are little interested in the less-sensational, scholarly accounts that document the steady, calm, peaceful lives of most Hispanics living in northern New Mexico.[33]

Bolstered no doubt by the popular media's accounts of Latin Americans in a state of nature, whether the Latinos lived south or north of the border, old American stereotypes continued to flourish as robustly as in the past. One American woman described her basic reaction to Central Americans to a media interviewer this way: "I have this overwhelming feeling of just 'ooh.' Sort of like living here at the ghetto in New York or Chicago—all the bad things that happen." The same interviewer concluded that Americans prevailingly tended to dislike Central Americans for being, among other unpleasant things, dark-complected, uncultivated, Spanish-looking, scruffy, unshaven, dirty, trigger-happy, loud, uncompassionate, unfriendly. (Somehow the gracious hospitality that even the most prejudiced of nineteenth-century North American travelers had found among Central Americans from the best-born to the most humble seemed to have disappeared.) Owing largely to prevailing stereotypes, according to the interviewer in question, Americans did not want their government to squander resources on trying to assist the people of Central America.[34] Aid to savages simply did not make sense. Earlier generations of Americans had reached similar conclusions about extending aid to redskins.

In the late eighteenth and early nineteenth centuries Noah Webster, the schoolteacher from whose textbooks several generations of Americans learned their grammar and spelling, contended that "savage" Indians, "when uncorrupted by the vices of civilized men, are remarkable for their hospitality to strangers, and for their truth, fidelity and gratitude to their friends." But, let civilization begin to penetrate and the Indians became downright animalistic. Rather than being uplifted, they suffer corruption from this penetration, losing their old virtues and failing to acquire the new ones proffered by civilization.[35] In the late twentieth century Americans could draw once again on Indian analogies as they sought to understand what had gone wrong in Latin America. They could also turn to the moral Herman Melville had drawn from his contact with Polynesian primitives. In his 1846 book *Typee,* Melville concluded: "in every case where

Civilization has in any way been introduced among those whom we call savages, she has scattered her vices, and withheld her blessings." [36]

The State of Nature Spreads to America

Americans did not have to look to their past relations with Indians and other primitives to discover models through which they might get a grasp on contemporary Latin America's perceived inability to escape nature and its enslaving appetites. Americans had only to look to the degrading poverty in their own midst, a poverty often accompanied by drug use. When Americans did look at the degrading and imbruting poverty in their midst, they felt the need for a scapegoat, and Latin Americans furnished a convenient one: Latin Americans, through the drug trade, helped to account for the spread of the jungle in the United States itself. Sometimes there is a grain, just a grain, of truth to stereotyped images of the scapegoat. *Narcotraficantes* (narcotics traffickers) and cocaine cowboys from below the border *have* had a part in the reversion-to-wilderness saga that tells the story of many a present-day American city.

So, predictably, the war on drugs as waged in the 1980s became the struggle of civilized persons against "Latinate peoples." In this war, Latins assumed the role that blacks had played in the 1930s when respectable society battled the black purveyors of marijuana, and that Southeast Asians played when, in the 1960s, decent Americans moved to protect their society against golden-triangle heroin. In each instance, the enemy was the most readily available person with the image of savagery, the person who threatened civilization. Like the product they sold, which they came to symbolize, the dealers stood for the wildness of nature as it menaced the controlled, "tight, methodical world" of reason. [37]

Drugs and the Struggle of Civilization with Nature

As America's war on drugs, officially declared in September 1989, acquired an intensity that would prove short lived, many citizens wondered if the struggle could be won. Some of them counseled legalization of drugs, seemingly conditioned to concede defeat—before the ghost of Vietnam was temporarily banished by Operation Desert Storm—in yet another late twentieth-century war. A majority of policymakers and of the general public showed some resolve to wage the war, but an increasing number of Americans accepted the impossibility of total victory. They expected no more than the isolation of zones where the enemy had entrenched itself; they would settle for constructing the equivalent of containing walls around the perimeters of urban wilderness. The six-gun and the Winchester may have won the Wild West and eliminated Indian "savagery," but assault rifles enabled modern-day savages (acting out their version of the American myth of regeneration through violence) to preserve the autonomy of wild domains beyond the law. Colombia and Peru were not the only New World countries where the sphere of effectively exercised national sovereignty was shrinking as the wilderness spread.

"Wilderness," a correspondent to the *Saturday Evening Post* wrote in 1965, "is precisely what man has been fighting against since he began his painful, awkward climb to civilization. It is the dark, the formless, the terrible, the old chaos which our fathers pushed back. . . . It is held at bay by constant vigilance, and when the vigilance slackens it swoops down for a melodramatic revenge."[38] The correspondent had no doubt that civilized human beings in America could not only keep wilderness at bay but steadily diminish its dimensions. A quarter of a century later, Americans had begun to acknowledge their doubts. By then, civilization had sustained defeat after defeat as inner-city jungles reached out to ensnare well-to-do Americans, hooking them on drugs and making them, symbolically, captives of the wilderness.

Underlying the whole drama of drugs and the war against them there seems to lurk the symbolism of karma, of action and reaction. First came the action: Americans in quest of mercantile profits undermined Indian cultures by encouraging alcohol dependence among them. Moreover, in colonial times Americans inflicted on Africans the scourge of rum so as to facilitate their enslavement—not unlike the British who later imposed opium on the Chinese so as to swell the profits of colonial enterprise. At a later time, the sale of American-processed goods to Latin America (often manufactured from south-of-the-border raw materials, as in the typical and already-cited case of the Sparrows Point steel mill) introduced a world capitalist system that for better and for worse undermined native cultures. In the grand scheme of things, Latins were to be discouraged from processing their own raw products into finished goods. This was a task reserved to civilized countries. Then came reaction: especially in the post–World War II years, Latin Americans accomplished some industrialization of their own and began to cut into America's export surpluses. And in the 1980s, responding to the capitalist credo of progress, some Latin Americans found that the heftiest profits resulted from processing coca leaves and introducing the product into the United States. As they pursued their profits, they threatened to undermine Yankee civilization, as precious to Americans as native cultures and indigenous traditions had once been to Indians and Latin Americans. Thus they had to be confronted in righteous war.

By the end of 1990 it appeared that the menace to civilization was not so great as originally feared. By then, various studies pointed to a decline in drug use by "respectable" citizens. As this good news spread, accommodated Americans began to lose interest in the war on drugs. Inner-city blacks and the poor of all shades continued to be ravaged by the scourge. But to "decent" elements these people were irredeemable savages who might as well be abandoned to the equally savage and predominantly "Latinate" drug dealers. In dividing their own populace into gente decente and people of a mala raza, Americans attested to what might be diagnosed as their Latin Americanization—but what in reality was simply a new manifestation of deep-lying racial and social prejudice present from the creation of the Republic.

The Latin Americanization of America

In the 1950s sociologist Oscar Lewis came up with his controversial concept of a "culture of poverty." The concept pertained to an underclass that, allegedly, lived by a different set of values and expectations than their accommodated fellow citizens. Lewis applied his "culture-of-poverty" analysis, primarily, to Mexico, Puerto Rico, and other parts of Latin America. Forty years later, though, many Americans seemed hopelessly mired in their own culture of poverty, unable to respond to the success myth and the norms of conduct that allegedly guaranteed its fulfillment. This was an important reason why various students of the hemisphere began, already in the early 1980s, to speak and write about the Latin Americanization of the United States. The words bore a pejorative connotation, both in regard to Latin America and to the United States: they implied that the United States was on the way to becoming a huge banana republic, its power vitiated not only by mounting economic divisions between haves and have-nots but also by the graft, lawlessness, and general irresponsibility of the haves as well as the have-nots.

Latin Americanization implies basically that Americans (and not just those of the underclass) have themselves assumed the identity of the Latin Other—as traditionally stereotyped. *They* have not become as we are, but *we,* regardless of station in life, have become as they are. The old American dream of remaking the southern continent in the image of the northern sphere has given way to the reality of a northern continent to some extent remade in the stereotyped image of the southern one. This perhaps is one reason why thoughtful, perceptive Americans—not necessarily the person on the street interviewed about his or her gut reactions to Central Americans—have grown uncomfortable about applying hoary stereotypes. Motes once perceived only in their neighbors' eyes now afflict their own. In calling attention to the Other's affliction, they invite scrutiny of their own defects.

Irresponsible and dishonest politicians, Americans once believed, were predominantly confined in the New World to Latin America; they emerged out of the area's loose morality. Moreover, Americans expected the Catholic clergy to the south to manifest venality and corruption, among other vices. Nowadays, though, political scandals rock the United States, and outrage is gradually dulled by their frequency. Mounting evidence shows that some government agencies have been run as inefficiently and dishonestly as Latin America's parastatals; and prominent American clergymen, Protestant and Catholic, are disgraced by their sexual transgressions (both hetero- and homosexual and committed with children as well as adults) and their fiscal chicanery in such a way as to make Sinclair Lewis's exposé novel *Elmer Gantry* seem both understated and more timely than when it first appeared in 1927. In comparison to their American counterparts, the contemporary Latin American clergy often seems distinguished. The comparison affords a stunning rejoinder to one set of stereotypes that Americans broadcast in the nineteenth century. Many other types of cross-border stereotyping have also been set at naught by recent developments in the United States.

Nowadays in America (at least in nonrecessionary times), private bills are likely to be paid by consumer borrowing. Government bills are met similarly, by incurring more debt, both internal and external; in consequence of the latter expedient the country is drained of resources. We Americans now worry that the Japanese are doing to us what the Latins have traditionally accused us of doing to them. We never had much sympathy with Latin complaints about the draining effects of foreign investment and lending, but now the shoe is on the other foot, and it pinches. Once priding ourselves on our self-control, we Americans subsequently joined in a race to discard restraints. Now we try to convince ourselves that discipline and self-control as practiced by the Japanese produce distortions of character. We have come to see the Japanese, and to some extent the West Germans, as the Latins once saw us. And we have even had to learn to listen to the Japanese lecturing us, as we once lectured Latin Americans, on the need to adopt a work ethic, to take education more seriously, to learn to save and accommodate to delayed gratification.

In the nineteenth century, Americans looked down on Latins because of their alleged loose morality, their addiction to alcohol and tobacco, their uncurbed sexuality, their high rates of illegitimacy, the frequency of de facto relationships not sanctioned by formal marriage vows, the high incidence of murder and of crimes committed against property. No longer, though, can Americans concern themselves over the moral shortcomings of their southern neighbors. Although they can congratulate themselves on a sharp decrease in alcohol and tobacco consumption registered in the 1980s, they must puzzle over a plethora of social problems that include exploding teenage sexuality that helps to lift the country's illegitimacy rates toward Third World levels. Nor is it comforting that among the ethnic groups that make up the U.S. citizenry the highest rates of illegitimacy and welfare dependency occur among Puerto Ricans: a people who have been under America's imperial custody since the turn of the century and who seem to have been no more benefited by the opportunity to mingle traditional culture with Yankee civilization than reservation Indians.

In their major cities Americans now confront the sort of problems they once thought confined to backward and primitive parts of the world. A previously cited American traveler to Buenos Aires noted at the beginning of the 1830s that he went to sleep armed with musket, pistols, and sword, recognizing the need to rely on his good aim for survival among savage people. Today many Americans have followed suit. They sit in their houses and apartments equipped with sophisticated weaponry to protect themselves against marauders.

During the past century, when Americans sought to subject the passions to the control of the interests, they derided the gambling lust that afflicted Indians and Latins and various uncouth types out on the frontier who had contrived to flee civilizing constraints. Late in the twentieth century, though, Americans became more and more addicted to the win-the-lottery mentality. Capricious Dame Fortune, not the habits of rational planning, controlled destiny. "Some experts fear," the *New York Times* reported in 1989, "that America is turning into a nation of lottery addicts, the first step on the way to a nation of gambling addicts. These experts worry that the new legitimacy of once-illegal forms of betting is undermining traditional attitudes toward work and play, saving and investing, even right and wrong."[39]

Once Americans derided Latin American governments that taxed the poor to support the rich. Nowadays America's states rather than impose taxes that might impinge on the wealthy to pay for such services as education opt instead for legalized gambling: a form of revenue raising that drains the poor of proportionately more funds than the rich. Well-to-do

Americans have caught the Latin infirmity—they used to call it the "Italian disease"—and have decided that allergy to paying taxes is no disease at all. Their senators and congressmen do little to disabuse them of this attitude, even as the infrastructure deteriorates on all sides from lack of maintenance funds.

Whether a connection exists between tax minimalization at one end of the socioeconomic scale and increasing impoverishment at the other end remains uncertain; it may be true, as some students of the matter contend, that increased taxes would only impede development in one America without noticeably improving living standards for those trapped in the other America. This is an issue that American development experts used to debate as they formulated the policies that they pressured Latin Americans into adopting. Now the issue has to be faced at home.

As noted in the second chapter, Americans in their early days of nation building prided themselves on anger control—or at least the "better" elements among them did so. In that remote past, "anger was thought appropriate only to special minorities: grumpy primitives, for instance, who knew no manners because 'civilization' had failed to reach them . . . ; and adolescents, who have always been grudgingly allowed to behave abominably as a rite of passage." Anger was assumed also to be natural to Latin Americans: primitives all! By the 1990s, the basis of contrast—assuming there ever was a valid basis—had disappeared. Almost universally, according to various social observers, Americans seemed angry at other Americans, and they took it as good form not to mask that anger.[40] At one time, Americans saw Latin Americans as primitives made happy by doing what came naturally; subsequently, Americans let down the barriers and began to live this way too. But happiness eluded them, and so they grew angry not only at each other but also at alleged primitives to the south for having provided conduct models that didn't deliver anticipated rewards.

In some ways the most striking testimony to Latin Americanization emerges out of the recent corruptions of America's vaunted "free enterprise" system. Symbolizing these corruptions for all time is the savings and loan scandal, the magnitude of which began to become apparent at the beginning of the 1990s. Described as "the fruit of a decade of commercial lawlessness unmatched anywhere in our history," the savings and loan debacle will ultimately cost U.S. taxpayers a minimum of $500 billion.[41] The scope of this debacle and its long-range ramifications raise almost as many questions about the soundness of the American system as the collapse of the Soviet Union poses about Marxism-Leninism. Apparently the systems that civilizations adopt have little more effect on underlying human nature than clothes on the basic physiques of those who wear them.

Corruption is nothing new in American history, in part because the United States has never consistently operated by the rules of genuinely free enterprise—except at the bottom and middle of the socioeconomic structure. Always the closer one approaches the top, the more the system has smacked of official—if clandestine—protection and favoritism. Indeed, the free-enterprise myth may well be not only the cardinal but also the least tenable myth of American civilization.

As far back as one looks in history, the most dazzling individual success was as likely as not assured or abetted by political favors, whether originating with local and state or with national legislative, executive, and judicial branches of government. Perhaps, though, even more than was traditionally the case, the more dramatic triumphs of "free enterprise" during the Reagan years derived out of special ties to the institutions of government. More and more in the 1980s (with a Republican in the White House but with Democrats in control of Congress), the United States in the overlap of politics and economics seemed to conform to the sort of stereotypes that Americans through the years applied, in disparagement, to Latin America. More and more the American government took pains to reduce the risks faced by big-league capitalists. In the "private enterprise" system as practiced at the top, the profits indeed remained private, but risk and losses increasingly were socialized and made the responsibility of taxpayers.

Probably it was inevitable that American politicians—just like Latin politicos as customarily stereotyped by Yankees—would begin to demand institutionalized payoffs for the institutionalized favors they granted to select "private" capitalists. Toward this end, political action committees acted with spectacular success in the 1980s. Through the PACs, and other ingenious and devious campaign-financing arrangements, politicians extracted from business rewards for the favors they had lavished on business—or were expected to confer in the future. The ideological basis for this system did not have to be borrowed from Latin America. A genuine free-enterprise system had always been too basically natural to permit Americans, obsessed with control over nature, to tolerate its unregulated operation. As much in the United States as in Latin America, the assumption was that, as F. Scott Fitzgerald once put it, the rich were different. Because of this, they were not expected to suffer the natural economic buffeting to which the less fortunate were prey.

American capitalism has not produced the splendors foreseen by fictional Judge Temples and real-life Henry Stimsons. Rather than producing a civilization in which economic success and altruism fuse, in which all private and social desiderata are packaged together, it has in many ways only encouraged the morality, private and social, of the stereotyped banana republic.

If in its ingenious and disingenuous adaptation of a free-enterprise system the United States has not been able to fulfill the periodic predictions of some of that system's more intemperate enthusiasts as to the imminent eradication of business cycles, it has at least managed to remain on the whole a strikingly prosperous nation. In this, it has showed stunning success—so far—in avoiding much of the economic malaise that most Americans assumed to be natural to Latin American culture. In the long run, America's continuing prosperity may be the greatest boon it can offer to Latin America, especially if the hemisphere begins to move toward closer economic integration. But a prosperity based on the irresponsible financing condoned by both major political parties, on using funds supposedly earmarked for social security and highways and other long-term infrastructure objectives to mask the reality of current deficit obligations while hoping that massive waves of future immigration combined with internal population increments will produce enough taxpayers tomorrow to cover the debts incurred yesterday and today, offers little hope for the future: for our future or Latin America's. Staking future prosperity on such irresponsibility strikes some Americans as the clinching proof of their country's Latin Americanization.

In many ways, the rhetoric about the Latin Americanization of America that abounded in the 1980s is unconscionable. Failure to live up to norms of conduct sanctified by national mythology is nothing new in American history, though that failure may have become unusually widespread toward the end of the twentieth century. When Joan Didion writes perceptively in 1991 about the unraveling of New York into a Third World city, she points—among many other causes—to the collusion between the heads of vastly bloated public bureaucracies on one hand and private contractors on the other, to white-collar rather than to ghetto crime.[42] It would seem that a vastly enlarged Tweed Ring, and with it all kinds of other urban "rings" across the country, has reemerged out of some of the sorriest pages of nineteenth-century American—not Latin American—history.

The flaws associated with what some depict as the Latin Americanization of America spring from internal weaknesses present in national culture virtually from its inception. These flaws did not have to be imported from Latin America. In many ways, end-of-the-century American disdain for Latin Americans represented displacement: the transfer of inner guilt feelings onto the Other.

What the subterfuge of transference suggests is that Americans have been no more able to refine their inward nature than to control and perfect the natural environment. On both fronts the alchemist's dream of simultaneously converting base into precious elements has eluded them. On both fronts the myth of American exceptionalism should have collapsed. But American inability to part with the myth results in ongoing psychological and environmental distress and also poisons the environment of foreign relations with projects to refine and perfect Others—sometimes sincere and sometimes a fig leaf to cover naked self-interest.

Popular Music and New Life for the Cult of the Natural

Latin Americans, many of them immersed still in stereotyped, and real, chaos and revolutionary ferment, continue to fascinate at least a few Americans as symbols of the heroic, the natural, the well-nigh saintly Other. In the 1980s a counterculture still persisted in the United States, its relatively few numbers made up largely of youths (among whom one can always find a good number swimming against the tide) and old-line ideologists still convinced that socialism of one stripe or another held the solution to personal, national, and international imperfections and discontents. What Todd Gitlin wrote of the beatniks and hippies in the 1960s applies equally well to the few adversary-culture survivors in the 1980s and 1990s:

> A part of ourselves looked with respect, even awe, even love, on an ideal vision of ourselves who we thought existed—*had* to exist—out there in the hot climates. We needed to feel that someone, somewhere in the world, was fighting the good fight and winning . . . that out of the rubble, somehow, somewhere, might be constructing a good society, at least one that was decent to the impoverished and colonized. If the United States was no longer humanity's beacon [and no longer possessed its own frontier where that beacon might be rekindled] . . . the light had to be found outside.[43]

John Lennon's 1971 song "Imagine" captures perfectly the mood that Gitlin describes. And the mood was still alive twenty years later, however diminished the ranks of those who shared it. If they tried hard enough, some Americans, even in the 1980s and early 1990s, could still imagine reverting to, or advancing toward, the beautiful, the primitive, the natural way of life. Although it required a supreme effort, some Americans could still imagine Fidel Castro as the admirable primitive revolutionary. Commenting on Mikhail Gorbachev's 1989 visit to Cuba, conservative professor and statesperson Jeane Kirkpatrick drew attention to the contrast between the Soviet and Cuban leaders: "Fidel in fatigues and scraggly beard reminiscent of the radical students of the late 1960s in Berkeley, and Gorbachev standing beside him, the essence of modern man. Castro parochial, Gorbachev cosmopolitan. Castro the military, Gorbachev the civilian." She concluded, "It's as though communism in Latin America is sort of caught in a cultural lag and a time warp and remains 20 years behind."[44] To a very few Americans, though, Castro still represented the virtuous repudiation of corrupt modernity; he still held forth the promise of a return to a golden age in the past and through it entry into a future utopia. If, ultimately, Castro succumbed to the forces of reaction unleashed against him, then have a little faith and *imagine* what some future revolutionary could accomplish toward redeeming a world grown rotten.

The mere fact that the myth of perfection someday to be accomplished through civilized man's entry into the frontier never translated into reality did not prevent Americans from clinging to the myth. Nor has the failure of utopian Third World revolutions to bear fruit persuaded all persons to abandon hope in the myth that ultimately natural persons will revitalize and redeem civilizations that for all their initial virtue and promise had succumbed to fatigue, senescence, and corruption. Myths come into being in order to explain baffling reality; but once created, they have an existence of their own, altogether uninfluenced by observations of mere reality.

Despite all failures of the past, the old quest—in one form or another—for wholeness, inspired by the visions of the coming together of opposites, still endures. Paul McCartney and Stevie Wonder paid homage to this quest in their 1982 song "Ebony and Ivory." And Andrew Greeley, the Catholic priest-sociologist-novelist who delights in assaulting establishments of every kind, argued that rock superstar Bruce Springsteen, with his "appeal to the *whole* person, not just the head," delivered a message that many American Catholics found more appealing than the one-dimensional pronouncements of Pope John Paul II and his hierarchy.[45]

Whether Catholic or Protestant, agnostic or atheistic, America's surviving radicals agreed with Sting, another popular-music superstar, who titled a 1987 song "History Will Teach Us Nothing." It was the new world somewhere out there, the world in the making, that mattered, not the fouled-up world of the past. Myths must never be restrained by past, or present, reality.

An eighteenth-century Scottish philosopher observed he did not care to know who wrote the laws of a country; rather, he wanted to know those who wrote its songs, for they were the real opinion molders.[46] This eighteenth-century observation seems valid still. Through a thoroughly unscientific sampling of opinion among my undergraduate college students during the 1980s, it became clear to me that *some* pop-music lyrics (students proved highly selective as to *which* pop-culture bards they heeded and which they disdained) had more of an influence on young minds than what lawmakers, and certainly more than what professors, had to say, for the songwriters often are attuned to mythic reality. On balance, it just might be a good thing that youth responds during its brief moment more to mythic reality than to uninspiring outer-world reality.

Buttressing the Scottish philosopher's eighteenth-century thesis, journalist Etta Mooser has found that a surprising number of young people throughout the 1980s had their political philosophies formed by rock lyrics "whose roots lie in Dylan and the Beatles, not Plato or Montesquieu. Rock music's egalitarian message, its antiauthoritarian stand, its acknowledgement of the hollowness of much of [established] . . . society . . . makes up . . . a realm of knowledge and a world view that is at odds with much of the school curriculum."[47] Even in the Soviet Union, American- and British-origin rock helped to undermine the Marxism taught in the school system. Indeed, in penetrating behind the Iron Curtain with their exaltation of individual freedom, rock-and-rollers entered by wildest chance into an alliance with President Reagan as he sought to destroy the Soviet empire by means of rearming America.

Rock has also had its impact on the American hemisphere's Zeitgeist. By celebrating the primitive's world where restraints, allegedly, do not exist, rock has *reduced* the need that American seekers of the pristine once felt for Latin America's stereotyped primitivism. This paradoxical development constitutes an important new turn in the hemisphere's cultural history; and it represents a stunning departure from the attitudes that many pages in this book have highlighted.

Rock Music and the Displacement of the External by the Internal Primitive

In the 1980s more and more Americans seemed to discover what Rousseau had known long ago. Rousseau came to understand that the primitive, "the Wild Man," was internal, that "he lives in all of us, that when we strip ourselves of the . . . refinements of civilization, we find naked savages."[48] Like Rousseau, America's own Herman Melville insisted that "the primitive exists in the heart and minds of Western men. . . ."[49] Unwittingly heeding this wisdom of the past, Americans during the Reagan years awakened to the fact that they could drop out of the establishment and at the same time avoid the risks always incurred by actual pioneers and revolutionaries, by all persons in flight from or in revolt against civilization as they sought the primitive. To avoid the risks but still to have the satisfactions associated with defying civilization's prevailing norms, it was necessary only to retreat into the internalized realm of the primitive. In a way, every person's frontier, every person's revolution, was no farther away than the nearest hi-fi set or Walkman. Through the wonders of transistorized and computer-chip civilization, one could be transported by means of rock rhythms and lyrics into the realm of primitive, raw, revolutionary feelings; one could live for a time, inwardly, as a savage. Rock music facilitated rites of passage, available at the flick of a knob, that initiated its devotees into life-styles once thought virtually unattainable, the mere pursuit of them involving high-stakes risk. Middle-class Americans seeking union-of-opposites wholeness through immersion into what was wild or natural no longer had to venture into Harlem or Indian country, or cross the border into Latin America.

The more enterprising rock enthusiasts did not have to settle for transistorized experiences of tuning in and dropping out. They could attend one of rock's great revival meetings where rebirth experiences awaited many in the audience. In the auditoriums and stadiums, American exceptionalism was resuscitated. Here, periodically, Americans could become new Adams.

Rock performers served as shamans who led seekers on journeys, or flights of fancy, from one realm into another, from civilization into rebellious, sex-charged primitivism, from refinement and discernment back to the hunters and gatherers—a fair number of whose genes still do survive in modern men and women, available under propitious circumstances for rediscovery. But rock devotees did not have to remain long in rebelliousness and primitivism. They could flick off the hi-fi or exit the stadium and re-enter the workaday world, thus accomplishing the return that was always a part of the frontier myth. And the censure they received from the less daring, from the round-the-clock conventionally minded Americans who disapproved of rock was less severe than that accorded scruffy frontiersmen by "proper" nineteenth-century Americans.

Of course, rock is a hopelessly debased and trivialized surrogate for the frontier experience—or even for a good walk in nature. But at least it has democratized something of what that experience was all about, by making a minute and vulgarized facsimile of it readily available. No longer need the quest for revitalization or escape be confined to daring adventurers. Moreover, today's greenhorn does not have to hire a guide and outfit himself or herself expensively to enter the bush. Nor need the impecunious fret about engaging psychiatrists to lead them into the land of the id. Rock performers, abetted since the mid-1980s by "rappers," do it all. They put a high price on their services, but it's not generally prohibitive.

So, rock is "first, last and always a musical return to the primitive."[50] Like adventurers in the American past who sought the primitive, rock's gurus and aficionados occasionally find their ideal primitives in Indians and women. But these onetime exemplars of the natural have begun in such large numbers to gain access to the establishment that they no longer fulfill very well their old stereotypical function. More consistently than in them, rock has tended to find its primitivism and its vision of the eternal child in African Americans and, to a lesser extent, in Latin Americans, whose stereotyped cultural influences white, establishment rock aficionados have appropriated. To the extent that rock enables white Americans to internalize the African and the Latin, they tend to grow indifferent to incarnations of the Other in the outer world. Having internalized the traits conventionally attributed to the Other, and having then substituted narcissistic self-enjoyment for attempts to engage the Other in the outer world, white Americans in the 1980s seemed bored, by and large, by real-life African Americans and Latin Americans. Boredom with the external Other contributed to slackening white interest in the civil rights cause. Moreover, the indifference of a majority of Americans toward the Latin, far more than the pressure of a depleted leftist counterculture, accounted for the inability of President Reagan and his more ardent cold warrior advisers to implement, in their full scope, bellicose policies intended to cleanse Central America of Marxism.

In a Dark Time, the Eye Begins to See

As the twentieth century entered its final decade, Americans had grown accustomed to holing up in dark internal realms, feeding on their own "id-stuff."[51] Perhaps, though, American poet Theodore Roethke is justified in holding out a ray of hope; perhaps, as he contends, "in a dark time, the eye begins to see."[52] Maybe Americans will break out of the darkness and begin to see Latinos, whether in their midst or beyond the border, not—as their turn-of-the-century forebears saw them—as midway freaks, as deviates from the accepted norms of civilization. Maybe the people of paradox still have the capacity to mitigate their individualism, to concern themselves—as sometimes they did in the past—with community, not just with self-communing.

Admittedly, the basis for hope is slight. Up to now hemispheric relationships between the two half-worlds have not consistently resulted in dramatic mutual understanding and enhancement. And now the waves of Latin immigration that are browning what once was so preponderantly a Caucasian republic may initially heighten tension between whites and nonwhites, exacerbating some old stereotypes, fostering new ones, and generally contributing to bitter friction. Certainly many Americans express alarm over the fact that in the 1980s their country's Hispanic, or Latino, population increased by over one-third, five times as fast as the rest of the population. Confronting the fact that their nation had evolved into a multiethnic society, with the Hispanic Other no longer living south of the border but increasingly at arm's length, the native son and daughter is apt to feel uneasy, at best. Unease is heightened by the fact that the U.S. Hispanic population—according to a Census Bureau report released in June 1990—is much more likely to live in poverty than the national average, more apt to be employed in low-wage occupations and to lag behind educationally (60 percent of young Hispanic adults have completed high school, compared with 89 percent of non-Hispanics).[53]

Without realizing the connection to Arnold Toynbee (1889–1975) and his analysis of world history, many Americans seem to assume they are menaced by what the British historian-guru saw as a fundamental challenge to established civilizations throughout history: the combined onslaught of internal and external proletariats. The internal proletariat, as Toynbee saw the situation, comprised people who were in a given society but not of it, not genuine participants. The external proletariat was made up of foreign have-nots who because of population pressures and various other reasons abandoned traditional homelands and crowded into the nearest-to-hand advanced region.[54] As the 1990s began, many Americans prepared to harden civilization's defenses against both internal and external proletariats.

Undoubtedly a depression or even a stiff recession would sharpen the prejudice of native sons and daughters against immigrant Hispanics willing to work for wages, and under conditions, that the native-born have grown accustomed to spurn. Certainly the Great Depression that began in 1929 seriously heightened Anglo-Latino tensions in the American Southwest; and with the dramatic increase in Latin American and Caribbean immigration that has occurred since then, a new depression might well prove disastrous to relations between natives and immigrants and at the same time produce serious strains in hemispheric relations: and this is one reason why American prosperity remains so enormously important to Latin America. Even if depression is avoided, Americans will continue to disagree, sometimes passionately, over whether immigration constitutes an economic boon or the lamentable transfer of Third World conditions to the United States.

For now, the new immigration's effects on America's internal social fabric and on hemispheric relations remain in doubt.[55] One does not have to search very far to discover that the racist anti-immigration attitudes popularized early in the twentieth century by, among many others, Lothrop Stoddard and Madison Grant still persist toward the end of the century. Moreover, the ultimate effects on the environment of population growth, to which immigration now contributes a hefty percentage, justify legitimate concern with controlling the flow of new arrivals. To the degree that they act on this concern, native-born and already naturalized Americans will enrage would-be immigrants and Latin American countries anxious to avoid the consequences of population explosion by relying on the safety valve to the north. The basic problem is this: Americans remain reluctant to accept the fact that their country has become a frontier for Latin Americans. For generations, after all, Americans had assumed that Latin America was *their* frontier. Old myths, like hoary stereotypes, die hard.

According to William Dean Howells, Americans are most fascinated by literature that recounts "a tragedy with a happy ending."[56] The verdict is still out as to whether the tragedy-fraught encounter of American civilization with nature and with people stereotyped as children of nature will end happily.

For many Americans, the prospects of the 1990s for free trade with their neighbors to the south inspired hopes of a happy ending. Latin Americans, on the other hand, had reasons for apprehension. For the first time in the hemisphere's history, they did not have a clear and precise alternative force to play against American influence. The power of the British Empire to offset American hemispheric influence had long since disappeared, to be followed in due course by the collapse of fascism's and then communism's imperial thrust into the New World. In their rush at century's end to embrace—or to appear to embrace—free-market capitalism and electoral democracy, Latin Americans bowed to the new realities of power in the hemisphere, however uncongenial those realities might seem to many of them.

American might in the hemisphere could well be in decline, but Americans still retain a formidable power to define, even as in their earlier encounters with Indians, what constitutes acceptable civilized conduct on one hand and unacceptable primitive conduct on the other. With that power goes an equally formidable likelihood of abuse. And, together with likelihood for abuse goes the possibility that, as often as not, Americans will choose unwise policies for themselves and then try to force those policies on Latin Americans.

One should end a book on an upbeat note. But my eyes do not see well enough in dark times to perceive a clearly happy ending for the story of American hemispheric relations: a story that while by no means a tragedy in all respects has certainly had a full measure of down moments, a story that instead of consistently proving American exceptionalism symbolizes, much of the time, human existence in general.

Ordinary human existence with all its foibles prevails, of course, on both sides of the border. If we norteamericanos all too often have regarded our southern neighbors as unworthy New World partners, they have responded in kind. Faced with options conducive to an inclusionary hemisphere, Latin Americans have as often as not spurned these options. Very much like America's Indians and now increasingly like many African Americans, they have opted for exclusion and justified their choice by myths and stereotypes of self-identity no more flattering to us than ours to them.

As the old saying goes, it takes two to tango; and the North-South partners who grudgingly share a hemisphere seldom make it out together onto the dance floor. Occasionally, though, as in the Good Neighbor days, they do manage to dance. Even then their movements, as in the classic tango, demonstrate a love-hate relationship. But this is what brings spark and drama to their dance. It's a dance of love and hate, of death, and maybe rebirth, pitting civilization against nature, with both partners disagreeing as to who assumes which role. They have focused so long on disagreement that neither has noticed how much they have come to resemble each other and how well suited they both are to either role. Ignoring present-day reality, both partners turn to old myths as they seek self-understanding and comprehension of the Other. It's a fascinating spectacle and almost as good as a happy one with which to end this book.

Notes

Preface

1. See Lester D. Langley, *America and the Americas: The United States in the Western Hemisphere* (Athens, Ga., 1989), pp. xvi-xvii.

1. Nature and Its Enigmatic Images in American Lore

1. See Francis Paul Prucha, *American Indian Policy in the Formative Years: The Indian Trade and Intercourse Acts, 1790–1834* (Cambridge, Mass., 1962), pp. 240–241. For background see Jeremy Cohen, *"Be Fertile and Increase, Fill the Earth and Master It": The Ancient and Medieval Career of a Biblical Text* (Ithaca, 1989).

2. See Cecilia Tichi, *New World, New Earth: Environmental Reform in American Literature from the Puritans through Whitman* (New Haven, 1979), p. 18.

3. Ibid., pp. xii–ix.

4. Nathaniel Hawthorne, *The Scarlet Letter* (1850; New York, 1980), p. 193.

5. Roderick Nash, *Wilderness and the American Mind* (1967; New Haven, 1982), p. 43.

6. Both quotations appear in Hans Huth, *Nature and the American: Three Centuries of Changing Attitudes* (Lincoln, 1975), p. 5.

7. Roy Harvey Pearce, *Savages of America: A Study of the Indian and the Idea of Civilization,* rev. ed. (Baltimore, 1965), p. 3.

8. Albert J. Von Frank, *The Sacred Game: Provincialism and Frontier Consciousness in American Literature, 1630–1860* (Cambridge, Eng., 1985), p. 12.

9. Larzer Ziff, *Literary Democracy: The Declaration of Cultural Independence in America* (New York, 1981), pp. 51–52.

10. Von Frank, *The Sacred Game,* p. 50.

11. Max Scheler, quoted by Brian Easlea, *Witch Hunting, Magic, and the New Philosophy: An Introduction to Debates of the Scientific Revolution, 1450–1730* (Atlantic Highlands, N.J., 1980), p. vii.

12. Nash, *Wilderness and the American Mind,* p. 34.

13. William Gilpin, *Mission of the North American People, Geographical, Social, and Political, Illustrated by Six Charts Delineating the Physical Architecture and Thermal Laws of All the Continents* (Philadelphia, 1873), p. 99.

14. Patricia Nelson Limerick, *Desert Passages: Encounters with American Deserts* (Albuquerque, 1985), p. 84. To a greater degree than generally recognized, Puritans may actually have been interested almost as much in the pursuit of happiness as in the godly quest for progress. See Jack P. Green, *Pursuit of Happiness: The Social Development of Early Modern British Colonies and the Formation of American Culture* (Chapel Hill, 1989).

15. Anne M. Butler, *Daughters of Joy, Sisters of Misery: Prostitutes in the American West, 1865–1890* (Urbana, 1985), p. 1.

16. Quoted by Robert W. Rydell, *All the World's a Fair: Visions of Empire at American International Expositions, 1876–1916* (Chicago, 1985), p. 161.

17. Richard Slotkin, *The Fatal Environment: The Myth of the Frontier in the Age of Industrialization, 1800–1890* (New York, 1985), p. 53.

18. Quoted by William Cronon, *Changes in the Land: Indians, Colonists, and the Ecology of New England* (New York, 1983), p. xiii.

19. Nash, *Wilderness and the American Mind*, p. 188. The inner quotes are from Aldo Leopold, Papers (University of Wisconsin Archives), box 8.

20. Arthur K. Moore, *The Frontier Mind: A Cultural Analysis of the Kentucky Frontiersman* (Lexington, Ky., 1957), p. 95.

21. Frances Fitzgerald, *Fire in the Lake: The Vietnamese and the Americans in Vietnam* (New York, 1973), pp. 491–492.

22. James Axtell, *The European and the Indian: Essays in the Ethnohistory of Colonial North America* (New York, 1981), pp. 162–163.

23. John P. McWilliams, Jr., *Hawthorne, Melville, and the American Character: A Looking-Glass Business* (New York, 1984), p. 20.

24. On Cooper's perception of the regression that often accompanied frontier life, see the James Franklin Beard introduction to Cooper's *The Deerslayer* (1841; New York, 1960), p. xvi.

25. Mary Beth Norton, "The Evolution of White Women's Experience in Early America," *American Historical Review* 89 (1984): 593–619, shows that recent scholarship has challenged earlier beliefs that colonial women enjoyed something of a golden age of equality in the pioneering age.

26. Shelley B. Ortner, "Is Female to Male as Nature Is to Culture?" in *Women, Culture, and Society*, ed. Michelle Zimbalist Rosaldo (Stanford, 1974), p. 73. See also Camille Paglia, *Sexual Personae: Art and Decadence from Nefertiti to Emily Dickinson* (New Haven, 1990), p. 9.

27. Cooper, *The Deerslayer*, p. 170.

28. See Ellen L. Bassuk, "The Rest Cure: Repetition or Resolution of Victorian Women's Conflicts?" in *The Female Body in Western Culture*, ed. Susan Rubin Suleiman (Cambridge, Mass., 1986), pp. 143–144.

29. Limerick, *Desert Passages*, p. 68.

30. Arthur Brittan and Mary Maynard, *Sexism, Racism, and Oppression* (Oxford, Eng., 1984), p. 193.

31. Susan Griffin, *Women and Nature: The Roaring inside Her* (New York, 1978), p. 29.

32. Martin Green, *The Great American Adventure: Action Stories from Cooper to Mailer and What They Reveal about American Manhood* (Boston, 1984), p. 221.

33. Herman Melville, *Moby-Dick* (1851; New York, 1972), p. 484.

34. Quoted by Willie Lee Rose, "Reforming Women," *New York Review of Books,* Oct. 7, 1982, 45.

35. Robert E. Park, *Race and Culture: Essays in the Sociology of Contemporary Man* (Glencoe, Ill., 1950), p. 280.

36. Quoted by Pearce, *Savages of America,* p. 122.

37. Alexander Kinmont, *Twelve Lectures on the Natural History of Man and the Rise of Progress and Philosophy* (Cincinnati, 1839), pp. 289–290.

38. See Ernest Becker, *The Denial of Death* (New York, 1973), p. 33.

39. See George M. Fredrickson, "Piety and Paternalism," *Times Literary Supplement,* May 5–11, 1989, 478. See also *The Woman's West,* ed. Susan Armitage and Elizabeth Jameson (Norman, 1987), dealing—among many other topics—with images of the wanton Indian woman and the pure white woman.

40. Harvey Fergusson, *The Conquest of Don Pedro* (1954; Albuquerque, 1975), p. 221.

41. Quoted by Cecil Robinson, *Mexico and the Hispanic Southwest in American Literature* (Tucson, 1977), p. 93. For background to Anglo myths formed by contact with Mexicans in the Southwest, see David J. Weber, *Myth and History of the Hispanic Southwest* (Albuquerque, 1988).

42. Richard Chase, *The American Novel and Its Tradition* (Garden City, N.Y., 1957), p. 70. See also George L. Mosse, *Nationalism and Sexuality: Respectability and Abnormal Sexuality in Modern Europe* (New York, 1985), esp. pp. 16–17.

43. Helen Delpar, "Goodby to the 'Greaser': Mexico, the MPPDA, and Derogatory Films, 1922–26," *Journal of Popular Film and Television* 12 (1984): 40.

44. Robinson, *Mexico and the Hispanic Southwest,* p. 79, quoting from Harvey Fergusson, *Wolf Song* (1927).

45. For an example of the Anglo husband's perceived need to protect his Mexican, light-skinned wife against a mass of lecherous dark-skinned male rabble, see Juan R. García, "The Mexican in Popular Literature, 1875 to 1925," in *Down Mexico Way,* ed. Teresa L. Turner (Tucson, 1984), p. 11.

46. Butler, *Daughters of Joy,* pp. 11, 15.

47. *Cowboy Songs and Other Frontier Ballads,* collected and edited by John A. Lomax and Alan Lomax (1910; New York, 1986), p. 5.

48. Butler, *Daughters of Joy,* p. 1.

49. Quoted by David J. Weber, *The Taos Fur Trappers: The Fur Trade in the Far Southwest, 1540–1846* (Norman, 1971), pp. 7–8. On related themes see Sylvia Van Kirk, *Many Tender Ties: Women in the Fur-Trader Society, 1670–1870* (Norman, 1980).

50. Sander L. Gilman, *Difference and Pathology: Stereotypes of Sexuality, Race, and Madness* (Ithaca, 1985), p. 194.

51. George W. Stocking, Jr., *Race, Culture, and Evolution: Essays in the History of Anthropology* (New York, 1968), p. 25.

52. Quoted by Edward Baxter Billingsley, *In Defense of Neutral Rights: The United States Navy and the Wars of Independence in Chile and Peru* (Chapel Hill, 1967), pp. 83–84.

53. John Bartlow Martin, *Overtaken by Events: The Dominican Crisis from the Fall of Trujillo to the Civil War* (Garden City, N.Y., 1966), p. 115.

54. Karen J. Deming, "Miscegenation in Popular Western History and Fiction," in *Women and Western American Literature,* ed. Helen Winter Stauffer and Susan J. Rosowski (Troy, N.Y., 1982), p. 96. See also Polly Welts Kaufman, *Women Teachers on the Frontier* (New Haven, 1984).

55. See Alice Houston Luiggi, *Sixty-Five Valiants* (Gainesville, Fla., 1965), and "Some Letters of Sarmiento and Mary Mann, 1865–1876," *Hispanic American Historical Review* 32 (1952): 347–375.

56. See Bernard McGrane, *Beyond Anthropology: Society and the Other* (New York, 1989). McGrane traces the paradigm of the Other by focusing on attitudes of Western society toward non-Western peoples.

57. Annette Kolodny, *The Lay of the Land: Metaphor as Experience and History in American Life and Letters* (Chapel Hill, 1975), pp. 8–9.

58. Quoted by Moore, *The Frontier Mind,* p. 243.

59. Quoted by Henry Nash Smith, *Virgin Land: The American West as Symbol and Myth* (Cambridge, Mass., 1950), p. 254.

60. Quoted by Robert Glass Cleland, *The Reckless Breed of Men: The Trappers and Fur Traders of the Southwest* (New York, 1952), p. 101.

61. John D. Unruh, Jr., *The Plains Across: The Overland Emigrants and the Trans-Mississippi West, 1840–1860* (Urbana, 1979), p. 59.

62. Wallace Stegner, *The Sound of Mountain Water* (1946; Lincoln, 1985), p. 148. Writing elsewhere, Stegner describes Boone Caudill, the protagonist in A. B. Guthrie's *The Big Sky* (1952), as "an avatar of the oldest of all the American myths— the civilized man re-created in savagery, rebaptized into innocence on a wilderness continent." See Stegner's foreword to a later edition of *The Big Sky* (New York, 1982), p. ix.

63. Paul Horgan, *Great River: The Rio Grande in North American History* (New York, 1954), 2:638.

64. John P. Saylor, quoted by Nash, *Wilderness and the American Mind,* p. 248.

65. Theodore Dwight Bozeman, *To Live Ancient Lives: The Primitivist Dimension in Puritanism* (Chapel Hill, 1988), p. 10.

66. Quoted by David Dary, *Cowboy Culture: A Saga of Five Centuries* (New York, 1981), p. 280.

67. Helen Hunt Jackson, *Ramona* (1884; New York, 1970), p. 202.

68. Green, *The Great American Adventure,* p. 84, quotes Dana and adds his own observation.

69. Quoted by Moore, *The Frontier Mind,* p. 20.

70. Joseph M. Petulla, *An American Environmental History* (New York, 1977), quoted in *Wilson Quarterly* 11 (1987): 8.

71. *Selected Writings of Ralph Waldo Emerson,* ed. William H. Gilman (New York, 1965), p. 192.

72. Leo Marx, *The Machine in the Garden* (New York, 1964), pp. 69, 71–72. See also Bryan Jay Wolf, *Romantic Re-Vision: Culture and Consciousness in Nineteenth-Century American Painting and Literature* (Chicago, 1983), p. 25.

73. Quoted by Robert V. Hine, *The American West: An Interpretive History,* 2d ed. (Boston, 1984), p. 230.

74. Quoted by G. Edward White, *The Eastern Establishment and the Western Experience: The West of Frederic Remington, Theodore Roosevelt, and Owen Wister* (New Haven, 1968), p. 124.

75. Ibid., pp. 91, 110.

76. Robert F. Sayre, *Thoreau and the American Indians* (Princeton, 1977), p. 213.

77. See John J. Murphy, "The Virginian and Ántonia Shimerda: Different Sides of the Western Coin," in *Women and Western American Literature*, p. 167.

78. Wister and Roosevelt provide conspicuous examples of many late nineteenth-century American figures who may be seen as updated exemplars of captivity-tale mythology. On the symbolical, archetypal hero of this mythology, Richard VanDerBeets, *The Indian Captivity Narrative: An American Genre* (Lantham, Md., 1984), writes as follows: "This archetype is manifested in the captivity pattern of Separation (isolation from one's culture and symbolic death), Transformation (a series of excruciating ordeals in passing from ignorance to knowledge and maturity accompanied by ritualized adoption into a new culture), and Return (symbolic rebirth with a sense of moral or spiritual gain" (p. x).

79. Moore, *The Frontier Mind*, p. 204.

80. See Richard Slotkin, *Regeneration through Violence: The Mythology of the American Frontier, 1600–1860* (Middletown, Conn., 1973), pp. 278–279.

81. Green, *The Great American Adventure*, p. 80.

82. On Rory Wagner and his paintings of cowboys that attract buyers among successful eastern businessmen, see *Southwest Art*, Oct. 1981, 131–133.

83. See Lewis O. Saum, *The Fur Trader and the Indian* (Seattle, 1965), pp. 3–7 and following pages, and 26. Unruh, *The Plains Across*, writes that most of the 1840–1860 overlanders viewed Oregon and California as regions "of rebirth and hope, where upward mobility was not merely possible but virtually certain" (p. 91). Thus, mythological, mystical expectations went hand-in-hand with visions of economic gain.

84. John G. Cawalti argues convincingly that American cowboys and frontiersmen, as mythologically perceived, developed and maintained their virtue by keeping in check such symbolical exemplars of wild and untrammeled nature as Indians and outlaws. Yet, even as they did so there lurked inevitably in the wings the specter of civilization, about to rush in with its suffocating, routinized, and institutionalized order. Once this occurred, the cowboy and frontiersmen would become obsolete, for the very challenges that had awakened their unique talents, energies, and virtues would disappear. See Cawalti, "Savagery, Civilization, and the Western Hero," in *Focus on the Western*, ed. Jack Nachbar (Englewood Cliffs, N.J., 1974), p. 58.

85. Quoted by Frederick Merk, *Manifest Destiny and Mission in American History* (New York, 1963), p. 9.

86. William Walker, *The War in Nicaragua* (Mobile, New York, 1860), pp. 38, 39.

87. Ibid., p. 104.

88. See, for example, Lee Clark Mitchell, *Witness to a Vanishing America: The Nineteenth-Century Response* (Princeton, 1981), p. 103.

89. See *Florida Visionaries: 1870–1930* (Gainesville, 1989), a publication of the University Gallery, University of Florida, esp. pp. 10–17.

90. See Watt Stewart, *Henry Meiggs: Yankee Pizarro* (Durham, 1946).

91. Nash, *Wilderness and the American Mind,* p. 125. The inner quotations indicate John Muir's words.

92. Frederick Turner, *Rediscovering America: John Muir and His Times and Ours* (New York, 1985), quoted by John Tallmadge in his review of the book, *New York Times Book Review,* Nov. 3, 1985, 27.

93. For succinct, sympathetic treatment of Thomas Morton, see Cronon, *Changes in the Land,* p. 80; Richard Drinnon, *Facing West: The Metaphysics of Indian-Hating and Empire-Building* (Minneapolis, 1980), pp. 9–20; and William Carlos Williams, *In the American Grain* (1925; New York, 1956), pp. 75–80.

94. Green, *The Great American Adventure,* p. 41.

95. Quoted by Von Frank, *The Sacred Game,* p. 146.

96. Walt Whitman, *Complete Poetry and Collected Prose* (New York, 1982), pp. 470, 428, 300, 302. For other examples of Whitman on the regeneration-in-nature theme, see pp. 806–808, 925–926. All Whitman references throughout this book's notes derive from the cited volume, published as part of the outstanding Library of America series.

97. Thomas Wilkins, *Thomas Moran, Artist of the Mountains* (Norman, 1966), p. 22. See also Patricia Trenton and Peter H. Hassrick, *The Rocky Mountains: A Vision for Artists in the Nineteenth Century* (Norman, 1983), esp. ch. 7.

98. Saum, *The Fur Trader,* p. 96.

99. Henri Baudet, *Paradise on Earth: Some Thoughts on European Images of Non-European Man* (New Haven, 1965), pp. 10–11. For splendid studies that touch often on the American love affair with the natural, see Anne Farrar Hyde, *An American Vision: Far Western Landscape and National Culture, 1820–1920* (New York, 1990), and Peter J. Schmitt, *Back to Nature: The Arcadian Myth in Urban America* (Baltimore, 1990).

100. See Kolodny, *The Lay of the Land,* p. 61; and Moore, *The Frontier Mind,* esp. p. 31.

101. Quoted by David M. Kennedy, "We Enjoy Pushing Rivers Around," *New York Times Book Review,* Feb. 23, 1986, 7.

102. Quoted by Moore, *The Frontier Mind,* p. 27.

103. Hayden White, *Tropics of Discourse: Essays in Cultural Criticism* (Baltimore, 1978), p. 171.

104. Paul Hollander, *Political Pilgrims: Travels of Western Intellectuals to the Soviet Union, China, and Cuba* (New York, 1982), p. 9.

105. Hoxie N. Fairchild, *The Noble Savage: A Study in Romantic Naturalism* (New York, 1928), p. 2. On origins of "natural man" stereotypes, see Timothy Husband, *The Wild Man: Medieval Myths and Symbolism* (New York, 1980).

106. James H. Billington, *Fire in the Minds of Men: Origins of the Revolutionary Faith* (New York, 1980), p. 509.

107. See Ann Douglas, *The Feminization of American Culture* (New York, 1977).

108. See D. G. Charlton, *New Images of the Natural in France: A Study in European Cultural History, 1750–1800* (Cambridge, Eng., 1984), p. 162.

109. White, *The Eastern Establishment,* pp. 55, 56, 107.

110. See T. A. Shipley, "Getting and Spending," *Times Literary Supplement,* Feb. 1, 1988, 111.

111. David B. Davis, "Ten-Gallon Hero," *American Quarterly* 6 (1954): 119.

112. Deming, "Miscegenation in Popular Western History and Fiction," notes that the "domestication of the wilderness—the task of white women—" destroyed "the milieu in which white men" had enjoyed "guilt-free liaisons with Indian women" (p. 96).

113. Mary V. Dearborn, *Pocahontas's Daughters: Gender and Ethnicity in American Culture* (New York, 1986), observes, "Critics have long recognized . . . the pervasiveness of the 'dark lady' in American fiction, an exoticized and eroticized 'ethnic' heroine" (p. 190). On Pocahontas mythology see also Werner Sollors, "Literature and Ethnicity," *Harvard Encyclopedia of American Ethnic Groups,* ed. Stephan Thernstrom (Cambridge, 1980), esp. pp. 655–656.

114. Nash, *Wilderness and the American Mind,* p. 89. The inner quotes indicate Thoreau's own words.

115. See the David Cavitch review of Ross Parmenter, *Lawrence in Oaxaca: A Quest for the Novelist in Mexico* (Salt Lake City, 1985), in *New York Times Book Review,* Apr. 14, 1985, 30.

116. T. J. Jackson Lears, *No Place of Grace: Antimodernism and the Transformation of American Culture, 1800–1920* (New York, 1981), p. 20. On the American ethic as it involved the need to establish unremitting control over passions and instincts, see Ronald T. Takaki's outstanding study, *Iron Cages: Race and Culture in Nineteenth-Century America* (New York, 1979).

117. James Fenimore Cooper, *The Pioneers* (1823; New York, 1958), p. 469.

118. Quoted by David Rieff in "The Colonel and the Professor," *Times Literary Supplement,* Sept. 4, 1987, 960.

119. Nash, *Wilderness and the American Mind,* p. xi.

120. William J. McGrath (the author of *Freud's Discovery of Psychoanalysis* [1986]) letter, *Times Literary Supplement,* Nov. 21, 1986, 1311.

121. See Carl G. Jung, *Psychology and Alchemy,* trans. R. F. C. Hull (Princeton, 1968), passim.

122. See Erik H. Erikson, *Dimensions of a New Identity* (New York, 1974), pp. 70–74.

123. See Gilman, *Difference and Pathology,* passim.

124. Quoted by Elémire Zolla, *The Writer and the Shaman: A Morphology of the American Indians,* trans. Raymond Rosenthal (New York, 1973), p. 129. Michael Paul Rogin in his controversial *Fathers and Children: Andrew Jackson and the Subjugation of the American Indians* (New York, 1975), p. 8, notes: "Indians were perceived as connected to their past, their superstitions." On the other hand, American civilization "insisted upon work, instinctual repression, and acquisitive behavior; man had to conquer and separate himself from nature."

125. Michael Kammen, *People of Paradox: An Inquiry Concerning the Origins of American Civilization* (New York, 1972), p. 219.

126. See Herman Melville, *The Confidence Man* (New York, 1957), ch. 26, titled "Containing the Metaphysics of Indian-Hating. . . ."

127. Marx, *The Machine in the Garden,* pp. 86–87.

128. See White, *The Eastern Establishment,* p. 3.

129. See Pearce, *Savages of America,* p. 182.

130. See Robert May, *Sex and Fantasy: Patterns of Male and Female Development* (New York, 1980), ch. 1.

131. Emerson in his *Journal* (1842), quoted by Lewis, *The American Adam,* p. 24.

132. Quoted by Kenneth B. Murdock in his introduction to Perry Miller, *Nature's Nation* (Cambridge, Mass., 1967), p. xiv.

133. Simone de Beauvoir, *The Second Sex,* trans. H. M. Parshley (New York, 1968), p. 144.

134. Richard Chase, *The American Novel and Its Tradition* (1957; Baltimore, 1983), p. 63.

135. Nash, *Wilderness and the American Mind,* p. 81. For background see *Views of American Landscapes,* ed. Mick Gidley and Robert Lawson-Peebles (Cambridge, Eng., 1990), dealing with preconceptions and myths that shaped attitudes toward the North American continent. See also n. 99 above.

136. Richard A. Van Orman, *The Explorers: Nineteenth-Century Expeditions in Africa and the American West* (Albuquerque, 1984), p. 65.

137. Quoted by Huth, *Nature and the American,* p. 17. See also Edgar P. Richardson, Brooke Hindle, and Lillian B. Miller, *Charles Wilson Peale and His World* (New York, 1983), esp. Part 2.

138. Nash, *Wilderness and the American Mind,* p. 95. On Thoreau's admiration for the Indian not in his wild and original form but rather with the rough edges removed by civilization, see Sayre, *Thoreau and the American Indians,* esp. chs. 1, 5.

139. See Wilson O. Clough, *The Necessary Earth: Nature and Solitude in American Literature* (Austin, 1964), p. 111; and Smith, *Virgin Land,* p. 78.

140. Nathaniel Hawthorne, "The Maypole of Merry Mount," in *The Celestial Railroad and Other Stories* (New York, 1980), pp. 117, 120–121.

141. William J. Scheick, *The Half-Blood: A Cultural Symbol in Nineteenth-Century American Fiction* (Lexington, Ky., 1979), pp. 58–59.

142. Whitman, "Democratic Vistas," "Italian Music in Dakota," and "Proud Music in the Storm," in *Complete Poetry and Collected Prose,* pp. 984, 523, 526.

143. Edward S. Ellis and Edward L. Wheeler, *"Seth Jones" and "Deadeye Dick on Deck,"* ed. Philip Durham (New York, 1966), p. 147.

144. Saum, *The Fur Trader,* p. 220.

145. Quoted by Allan Carlson in his review of Robert Fishman, *Bourgeois Utopias: The Rise and Fall of Suburbia* (New York, 1987), *Wall Street Journal,* Oct. 30, 1987.

146. Ibid. On suburbia and its implications for American culture and values, see also Thomas Bender, *Toward an Urban Vision: Ideas and Institutions in Nineteenth-Century America* (Baltimore, 1982); James L. Machor, *Pastoral Cities: Urban Ideals and the Symbolic Landscape of America* (Madison, 1987); David Schuyler, *The New Urban Landscape: The Redefinition of City Form in Nineteenth-Century America* (Baltimore, 1988); and John R. Stilgoe, *Borderland: Origins of the American Suburb, 1820–1939* (New Haven, 1988).

147. See Stegner, *The Sound of Mountain Water,* p. 247.

148. Warren I. Susman, *Culture as History: The Transformation of American Society in the Twentieth Century* (1973; New York, 1984), pp. 136–137.

149. John R. Stilgoe, *Metropolitan Corridor: Railroads and the American Scene* (New Haven, 1983), pp. 139, 167.

150. See Peter Hassrick, *The Way West: Art of Frontier America* (New York, 1983), p. 85; Annette Kolodny, *The Land before Her: Fantasy and Experience of the American Frontiers, 1630–1860* (Chapel Hill, 1984), p. 5; and Smith, *Virgin Land,* esp. pp. 51–59.

151. Slotkin, *Regeneration through Violence,* p. 333.

152. Harry L. Watson, "Old Hickory's Democracy," *Wilson Quarterly* 9 (1985): 112.

153. Ibid., p. 133. Quotations indicate Jackson's words.

154. Evan S. Connell, *Son of the Morning Star: Custer and the Little Bighorn* (San Francisco, 1984), pp. 167–168.

155. Quoted by Slotkin, *The Fatal Environment,* pp. 471, 387.

156. Whitman, 1876 preface to 2-vol. ed. of *Leaves of Grass,* in *Complete Poetry and Collected Prose,* p. 1009.

157. David C. Huntington, *The Landscapes of Frederic Edwin Church: Vision of an American Era* (New York, 1966), pp. 114–125. See also Franklin Kelly, *Frederic Edwin Church and the National Landscape* (Washington, D.C., 1988); Katherine Emma Manthorne, *Tropical Renaissance: North American Artists Exploring Latin America, 1839–1879* (Washington, D.C., 1989); and Joe Sherman, "Frederic Church and his Great 'Great Pictures,'" *Smithsonian* 20 (Oct. 1989): 88–102.

158. See Gerald L. Carr, *Olana Landscapes* (New York, 1989).

159. On Church's Latin American paintings see, in addition to above-cited sources, William H. Goetzmann and William N. Goetzmann, *The West of the Imagination* (New York, 1986), pp. 31–35; and Stephen May, "Mountains: Spectacular Nineteenth-Century Visions," *Southwest Art,* Jan. 1985, 70–78.

160. See T. J. Jackson Lears, "William James," *Wilson Quarterly* 11 (1987): 88–89.

161. Arthur C. Danto, "Art: The Hudson River School," *Nation,* Nov. 7, 1988, 533.

162. Stanley T. Williams, *The Spanish Background of American Literature* (New Haven, 1955), 2:132.

2. Wild People in Wild Lands: Early American Views of Latin Americans

1. Europeans also depicted Arabs and Persians as decidedly undesirable people. Often the European image of Arabs seemed to coincide with pejorative views of Jews. See Edward W. Said's valuable study on stereotyping, *Orientalism* (New York, 1978), dealing with Western images of the Arab-Persian world. The stereotypes that Europeans attached to Arabs—and also to Jews—resemble in many instances those that Americans affixed to Latin Americans.

2. David K. Shipler, *Arab and Jew: Wounded Spirits in a Promised Land* (New York, 1986), pp. 47–48, 123, 182–183, 227, 290, 229, 128.

3. Arthur Brittan and Mary Maynard, *Sexism, Racism, and Oppression* (Oxford, Eng., 1984), p. 12.

4. British critic-historian Paul Johnson, quoted by K. L. Billingsley, "The Real

Reason Canadians May Vote against Free Trade," *Wall Street Journal,* Nov. 18, 1988.

5. Quoted by Sergio Sarmiento, "Mexico's Relations with the U.S.," ibid., Jan. 19, 1990. For helpful but less than comprehensive studies of Latin American stereotypes of the North American, see José A. Balseiro, *The Americas Look at Each Other: Essays on the Culture and Life of the Americas* (Coral Gables, 1969); Angel del Río, *The Clash and Attraction of Two Cultures: The Hispanic and Anglo-Saxon Worlds in America,* trans. and ed. James F. Shearer (Baton Rouge, 1965); and F. Toscano and James Hiester, *Anti-Yankee Feelings in Latin America: An Anthology of American Writings from Colonial to Modern Times in Their Historical Perspective* (Washington, D.C., 1982). To place hemispheric stereotypes in a comparative context, see David G. Gordon, *Images of the West: Third World Perspectives* (New York, 1989).

6. See Carey McWilliams, *North from Mexico: The Spanish-Speaking People of the United States* (Philadelphia, 1949), p. 36, and following pages; and Leonard Pitt, *The Decline of the Californios: A Social History of the Spanish-Speaking Californians, 1846–1890* (Berkeley, 1966), p. 58.

7. Albert Keiser, *The Indian in American Literature* (1933; New York, 1975), p. 154.

8. See Richard Drinnon, *Facing West: The Metaphysics of Indian-Hating and Empire-Building* (Minneapolis, 1980), p. 140.

9. Carl Sartorious, *Mexico about 1850* (New York, 1858), pp. 53–54.

10. William Gilpin, *The Cosmopolitan Railway: Compacting and Fusing Together All the World's Continents* (San Francisco, 1980), p. 293.

11. Quoted by Sacvan Bercovitch, *The American Jeremiad* (Madison, 1978), p. 184.

12. For the classic development of the controversial thesis that Americans were born free of aristocratic and feudal restrictions, see Louis Hart, *The Liberal Tradition in America* (New York, 1951).

13. John Bartlow Martin, *Overtaken by Events: The Dominican Crisis from the Fall of Trujillo to the Civil War* (Garden City, N.Y., 1966), p. 205.

14. Typical of nineteenth-century American observers of the Latin American scene, Richard Burleigh Kimball, *Cuba and the Cubans* (New York, 1850), p. 142, chastised Cuban mothers for spoiling their children. Owing to overindulgence, they allegedly raised children full of insolence and ingratitude.

15. Quoted by Wilson O. Clough, *The Necessary Earth: Nature and Solitude in American Literature* (Austin, 1964), p. 31.

16. Larzer Ziff, *Literary Democracy: The Declaration of Cultural Independence in America* (New York, 1981), pp. 72–73.

17. George Simpson, *Narrative of a Voyage to California Ports in 1841–42* (San Francisco, 1930), p. 29; Bayard Taylor, quoted by Neal Harlow, *California Conquered: The Annexation of a Mexican Province, 1846–1950* (Berkeley, 1982), pp. 25–26; Thomas Ewbank, *Life in Brazil* (New York, 1856), p. 145.

18. Quoted by Cecil Robinson, *Mexico and the Hispanic Southwest in American Literature* (Tucson, 1977), p. 71; quoted by David J. Weber, *The Taos Trappers: The Fur Trade in the Far Southwest, 1540–1846* (Norman, 1971), pp. 6–7; quoted by Reginald Horsman, *Race and Manifest Destiny: The Origins of American Racial Anglo-Saxonism* (Cambridge, Mass., 1981), p. 211.

19. Quoted by Paul Horgan, *Lamy of Santa Fe* (New York, 1975), p. 407.

20. Frederick Law Olmsted, *A Journey through Texas* (New York, 1857), p. 455.

21. Quoted by Pitt, *Decline of the Californios*, pp. 16, 75.

22. William H. Beezley, *Judas at the Jockey Club and Other Episodes of Porfirian Mexico* (Lincoln, 1987), p. 41.

23. Glenda Riley, *Women and Indians on the Frontier, 1825–1915* (Albuquerque, 1984), pp. 242, 244, 246.

24. Edward Baxter Billingsley, *In Defense of Neutral Rights: The United States Navy and the Wars of Independence in Chile and Peru* (Chapel Hill, 1967), p. 207, and following pages; Frederick Hassaurek, *Four Years among Spanish Americans* (New York, 1868), p. 163.

25. F. Scott Fitzgerald, "The Ice Palace," in his collection of short stories titled *Flappers and Philosophers* (1920; New York, 1959), p. 63.

26. George L. Mosse, *Nationalism and Sexuality: Respectability and Abnormal Sexuality in Modern Europe* (New York, 1985), p. 9. See also *Manliness and Morality: Middle-Class Masculinity in Britain and America, 1800–1940*, ed. J. A. Mangan and James Walvin (New York, 1987).

27. See Harold Beaver, "In the Land of Acquisition," *Times Literary Supplement*, Sept. 18–24, 1987, 1020.

28. Bercovitch, *The American Jeremiad*, pp. 159–160; Carroll Smith-Rosenberg, *Disorderly Conduct: Visions of Gender in Victorian America* (New York, 1985), p. 113.

29. Quoted by Peter Gabriel Filene, *Him/Her/Self: Sex Roles in America* (New York, 1974), p. 82.

30. Quoted by John Money, *The Destroying Angel: Sex, Fitness, and Food in the Legacy of Degeneracy Theory* (Buffalo, 1985), pp. 109–110, 84.

31. Quoted in ibid, pp. 66–67, 62.

32. Sexual abstemiousness definitely emerged as a middle-class value. And members of the middle class generally presumed the lower social elements to be incapable of controlling their sexuality. See Peter N. Stearns with Carol Z. Stearns, "Emotionology: Clarifying the History of Emotions and Emotional Standards," *American Historical Review* 90 (1985): 823.

33. V. G. Kiernan, *The Lords of Human Kind: Black Man, Yellow Man, and White Man in an Age of Empire* (New York, 1986), p. 135.

34. See Mosse, *Nationalism and Sexuality*, p. 85.

35. See Mary V. Dearborn, *Pocahontas's Daughters: Gender and Ethnicity in American Culture* (New York, 1986), p. 242, n. 46; and Ronald G. Walters, *The Antislavery Appeal: American Abolitionism after 1830* (Baltimore, 1976), pp. 70–87.

36. Ziff, *Literary Democracy*, p. 17.

37. Robert Pattison, *The Triumph of Vulgarity: Rock Music in the Mirror of Romanticism* (New York, 1987), p. 48; Robert M. Crunden, *Ministers of Reform: The Progressives' Achievement in American Civilization, 1889–1920* (New York, 1982), p. 170.

38. See George M. Fredrickson, *The Black Image in the White Mind: The Debate on Afro-American Character and Destiny, 1817–1914* (New York, 1971), p. 49; and Winthrop D. Jordan, *White over Black: American Attitudes toward the Negro, 1550–1812* (Baltimore, 1968), esp. pp. 150–151.

39. Arthur Silva White, "The Success of the Anglo-Saxons," *North American Review* 158 (1894): 354.

40. Anthony Ganihl, *Mexico versus Texas* (Philadelphia, 1838), pp. 205–206.

41. Josiah Gregg, *Commerce on the Prairies; or, The Journal of a Santa Fe Trader during Eight Expeditions across the Great Western Prairies and a Residence of Nearly Nine Years in Northern Mexico* (1844; Norman, 1954), p. 182; W. W. H. Davis, *El Gringo: or, New Mexico and Her People* (1857; Santa Fe, 1938), pp. 134, 89.

42. Robert V. Hine, *The American West: An Interpretive History*, 2d ed. (Boston, 1984), pp. 6–7,

43. Riley, *Women and Indians*, pp. 126–127.

44. John Steuart, *Bogotá* (New York, 1838), p. 22; Susan Shelby Magoffin, *Down the Santa Fe Trail and into Mexico: The Diary of Susan Shelby Magoffin 1846–1847,* ed. Stella M. Drum (New Haven, 1926), pp. 130, 95.

45. Robert W. Johannsen, *To the Halls of the Montezumas: The Mexican War in the American Imagination* (New York, 1985), p. 160.

46. Gilbert Haven, *Our Next-Door Neighbor: A Winter in Mexico* (New York, 1857), pp. 353–354.

47. Robert Hill, *Cuba and Porto Rico* (New York, 1898), p. 228.

48. Davis, *El Gringo,* pp. 88–89; Ray John de Aragón, *Padre Martínez and Bishop Lamy* (Las Vegas, N.M., 1978), p. 52.

49. Patricia R. Hill, *The World Their Household: The American Woman's Foreign Mission Movement and Cultural Transformation, 1870–1920* (Ann Arbor, 1985), p. 25; Henry F. May, *The End of American Innocence: The First Years of Our Own Time, 1912–1917* (Oxford, Eng., 1959), p. 343.

50. McWilliams, *North from Mexico,* p. 131; quoted by Money, *The Destroying Angel,* p. 95; Steuart, *Bogotá,* p. 184; Mrs. C. B. Merwin (pseud., "A Lady of Ohio"), *Three Years in Chile* (New York, 1863), p. 127.

51. Filene, *Him/Her/Self,* p. 135; Ben Bagdikian, "Tobacco Road: An American Cancer Society," *The Harmonist Magazine* 2 (1987): esp. 15, 17.

52. See the photographs in Malek Alloula, *The Colonial Harem,* trans. Myrna Godzich and Wlad Godzich (Minneapolis, 1986). The book is illustrated by some ninety postcards made from pictures taken by colonialist photographers between 1900 and 1930.

53. See Money, *The Destroying Angel,* pp. 17, 59, 70, 91–95.

54. Dr. David Ramsey, a leading light of nineteenth-century American medicine, quoted by W. J. Rorabaugh, *The Alcoholic Republic: An American Tradition* (New York, 1979), pp. 47–48.

55. Ibid., pp. 200, 202.

56. See, for example, McWilliams, *North from Mexico,* p. 131.

57. Thomas Wilkins, *Thomas Moran: Artist of the Mountains* (Norman, 1966), p. 171; Hassaurek, *Four Years among Spanish Americans,* pp. 266–267, 262–263; Frank Carpenter, *Carpenter's Geographical Reader: South America* (New York, 1899), p. 228; Francis H. Gregory, *Three Years in the Pacific* (Philadelphia, 1834), p. 177, and following pages.

58. Carol Zisowitz Stearns and Peter N. Stearns, *Anger: The Struggle for Emotional Control in America's History* (Chicago, 1986), pp. 3, 42, 194, 90, 20, 18, 25.

59. Hayden White, *Tropics of Discourse: Essays in Cultural Criticism* (Baltimore, 1978), pp. 165, 153, 178.

60. Quoted by Paul Horgan, *Great River: The Rio Grande in North American History* (New York, 1954), 2:470; Olmsted, *A Journey through Texas*, p. 456.

61. See John Lloyd Stephens, *Incidents of Travel in Central America, Chiapas, and Yucatan* (New York, London, 1841), p. 210. See also Franklin D. Parker, *Travels in Central America 1821–1840* (Gainesville, Fla., 1970), p. 226.

62. Witter Bynner, *Indian Earth* (New York, 1930), p. 19.

63. See George Gaylord Simpson, *Discovery of the Lost World: An Account of Some of Those Who Brought Back to Life South American Mammals Long Buried in the Abyss of Time* (New Haven, 1984), passim.

64. Quoted by Richard Rodriguez, "Lilies That Fester," *Wall Street Journal*, July 2, 1986.

65. Eugene F. Miller and Barry Schwartz, "The Icon of the American Republic: A Study in Political Symbolism," *Review of Politics* 47 (1985): 527–528. See also Paul K. Longmore, *The Invention of George Washington* (Berkeley, 1988), and Garry Wills, *Cincinnatus: George Washington and the Enlightenment* (New York, 1984).

66. See Richard Slotkin, *The Fatal Environment: The Myth of the Frontier in the Age of Industrialization, 1800–1890* (New York, 1985), p. 77.

67. Bercovitch, *The American Jeremiad*, p. 134.

68. Quoted in ibid., p. 144.

69. Quoted in ibid., p. 202.

70. See Arthur P. Whitaker, *The Western Hemisphere Idea: Its Rise and Decline* (Ithaca, 1954), esp. pp. 31–32, 38.

71. "Unpredictable" was the word Capt. James Biddle, commander of the USS *Ontario,* used to describe Chileans in 1818. See Billingsley, *In Defense of Neutral Rights*, p. 40.

72. Reginald Enock, *The Republics of Central and South America* (New York, 1913), p. 18.

73. Lester D. Langley, *America and the Americas: The United States in the Western Hemisphere* (Athens, Ga., 1989), p. 31.

74. Slotkin, *The Fatal Environment*, p. 193, quoting a *New York Herald* correspondent writing in June 1846.

75. Quoted by Victor Westphall, *Mercedes Reales: Hispanic Land Grants of the Upper Rio Grande Region* (Albuquerque, 1983), pp. 62–63.

76. William Gilpin, *Mission of the North American People, Geographical, Social, and Political, Illustrated by Six Charts Delineating the Physical Architecture and Thermal Laws of All the Continents* (Philadelphia, 1873), p. 126.

77. *Diplomatic Correspondence of the United States: Inter-American Affairs, 1831–1860*, ed. William R. Manning (Washington, D.C., 1932–1939), 3:382, 384; Parker, *Travels in Central America*, p. 131; Samuel Larned, quoted by Lawrence E. Clayton, "Private Matters: The Origins and Nature of United States–Peruvian Relations, 1820–1851," *Americas* 42 (1986): 377, 408; Richard Harding Davis, *Three Gringos in Venezuela and Central America* (New York, 1896), p. 143.

78. July 25, 1832, letter of Francis Baylies to Gen. John E. Wool, Inspector General, U.S. Army, reproduced in Samuel Rezneck, "Documents: An American Writes about Latin America in 1832," *Americas* 28 (1971): 210–211.

79. Ibid, p. 209.

80. Melville used this description in his short story "The Encantadas." See John P. McWilliams, Jr., *Hawthorne, Melville, and the American Character: A Looking-Glass Business* (New York, 1984), p. 177.

81. Quoted by Robinson, *Mexico and the Hispanic Southwest*, p. 139.

82. See Richard Magat's letter to the editor, *New York Times*, Jan. 19, 1985, 16.

83. Elaine Shannon, *Desperados: Latin American Drug Lords, U.S. Lawmen, and the War America Can't Win* (New York, 1988), p. 63.

84. Walt Whitman, "Democratic Vistas," in *Complete Poetry and Collected Prose* (New York, 1982), pp. 950–951.

85. See William Cronon, *Changes in the Land: Indians, Colonists, and the Ecology of New England* (New York, 1983), p. 33.

86. Slotkin, *The Fatal Environment*, p. 229. The inner quotations indicate Prescott's words.

87. Ray Allen Billington, *The Far Western Frontier, 1830–1860* (New York, 1856), p. 40.

88. Quoted by Aragón, *Padre Martínez and Bishop Lamy*, p. 51.

89. John Woodhouse Audubon, *Audubon's Western Journals: 1848–1850* (Cleveland, 1905), pp. 93, 101; Frederic Remington, *Pony Tracks* (1895; New York, 1961), p. 61.

90. Harry A. Franck, *Tramping through Mexico, Guatemala, and Honduras* (New York, 1917), p. 279.

91. Brantz Mayer, *Mexico: Aztec, Spanish, and Republican* (Hartford, 1851), 2:22, 348, 196.

92. Charles Dudley Warner, *On Horseback in Virginia, Etc.* (Boston, 1888), p. 198.

93. Isaac F. Holton, *New Granada: Twenty Months in the Andes* (New York, 1857), p. 540.

94. William L. Scruggs, *The Colombian and Venezuelan Republics* (1900; Boston, 1905), pp. 8, 76.

95. James Orton, *The Andes and the Amazon; or, Across the Continent of South America* (New York, 1870), pp. 37, 47, 68, 72–73.

96. The appraisal is that of a captain's mate aboard the USS *Macedonia*. See Billingsley, *In Defense of Neutral Rights*, p. 75. On alleged Latin American irresponsibility, see also Paul Horgan, *Josiah Gregg and His Vision of the Early West* (New York, 1979), p. 55.

97. Quoted by Cecil Robinson, "American Writers in Mexico, 1875–1925," in *Down Mexico Way*, ed. Teresa L. Turner (Tucson, 1984), p. 21.

98. See Frederick E. Hoxie, *A Final Promise: The Campaign to Assimilate the Indians, 1880–1920* (Lincoln, 1984), p. 240.

99. C. C. Andrews, *Brazil: Its Condition and Prospects* (New York, 1887), p. 267; David A. Wells, *Study of Mexico* (New York, 1887), p. 31.

100. Gregg, *Commerce on the Prairies*, p. 143. See also Davis, *El Gringo*, pp. 78, 80.

101. This is Margaret Mead's assessment of New Mexico's Hispanic population in her book *Cultural Patterns and Technical Change* (New York, 1955), p. 175.

102. Mayer, *Mexico* 1:170; Scruggs, *The Colombian and Venezuelan Republics*, p. 41.

103. Mayer, *Mexico* 2:23.

104. See David Landes, *A Revolution in Time* (Cambridge, Mass., 1983), esp. chs. 1–3, on the origins of clock-time and its spread, particularly in the Protestant areas of Europe where its contribution to an ethic of work, efficiency, and productivity was recognized and applauded. See also Anthony Aveni, *Empires of Time: Calendars, Clocks, and Cultures* (New York, 1989).

105. See "Chronometry: The Science That Rules Our Lives," an interview with David Landes in *Harvard Magazine* 95 (Jan.–Feb. 1984): 43.

106. Robinson, *Mexico and the Hispanic Southwest*, p. 81.

107. Thomas James, *Three Years among the Mexicans and Indians* (1846; Philadelphia, 1962), p. 88.

108. Davis, *El Gringo*, pp. 90, 56; Billington, *The Far Western Frontier*, p. 12; Edward Thornton Tayloe, *Mexico 1825–1828*, ed. G. Harvey Gardiner (Chapel Hill, 1959), p. 48; Benjamin Moore Norman, *Rambles in Yucatan; or, Travel through the Peninsula* (New York, 1842), pp. 32, 33; Steuart, *Bogotá*, p. 103; Orton, *The Andes and the Amazon*, p. 73.

109. See Edmund S. Morgan, *American Slavery, American Freedom: The Ordeal of Colonial Virginia* (New York, 1975), esp. ch. 3.

110. Stearns and Stearns, *Anger*, p. 34.

111. Quoted by Drinnon, *Facing West*, p. 30.

112. On this concept see Albert O. Hirschman's penetrating and fascinating study *The Passions and the Interests: Political Arguments for Capitalism before Its Triumph* (Princeton, 1977). Also useful is Joyce Appleby, *Capitalism and a New Social Order: The Republican Vision of the 1790s* (New York, 1984).

113. Jaime Rodríguez O., *Down from Colonialism: Mexico's Nineteenth-Century Crisis* (Irvine, Ca., 1980). The cited statistics appear toward the beginning of the unpaginated Rodríguez essay, presented originally as a Distinguished Faculty Lecture at the University of California, Irvine.

114. See Wilkins Kendall, *Narrative of the Texan Santa Fe Expedition* (London, New York, 1847), p. 326.

115. John D. Unruh, Jr., *The Plains Across: The Overland Emigrants and the Trans-Mississippi West, 1840–1860* (Urbana, 1979), p. 96.

116. William L. O'Neill, *Coming Apart: An Informal History of America in the 1960s* (Chicago, 1971), p. 128.

117. Quoted by McWilliams, *Hawthorne, Melville*, p. 34.

118. Quoted by Leo Marx, "Emerson and Socialism: An Exchange," *New York Review of Books*, May 28, 1987, 49. The quotation is from a relatively late essay by Emerson: "Wealth," published in his 1860 book *Conduct of Life*.

119. Stanley T. Williams, *The Spanish Background of American Literature* (New Haven, 1955), 2:131; D. G. Charlton, *New Images of the Natural in France: A Study in European Cultural History, 1750–1800* (Cambridge, Eng., 1984), p. 89.

120. See Nathan O. Hatch, *The Sacred Cause of Liberty: Republican Thought and the Millennium in Revolutionary New England* (New Haven, 1977).

121. See Lawrence J. McCaffrey, "Irish America," *Wilson Quarterly* 9 (1985): 78.

122. Ray Allen Billington, *The Protestant Crusade, 1800–1860: A Study of the Origins of American Nativism* (New York, 1938), pp. 345, 347.

123. See Juan R. García, "The Mexican in Popular Literature, 1875 to 1925," in *Down Mexico Way,* ed. Turner, p. 10.

124. In his book *The Conflict between the California Indians and White Civilization* (Berkeley, 1976), the distinguished scholar Sherbourne F. Cook writes that Roman Catholicism appeals to "primitive emotions" (p. 146). T. J. Jackson Lears, *No Place of Grace: Antimodernism and the Transformation of American Culture, 1800–1920* (New York, 1981), refers to the "liberal Protestant assumption that Catholic practices bred undisciplined emotion" (p. 160).

125. Lears, *No Place of Grace,* p. 249.

126. See F. S. C. Northrop, *The Meeting of East and West* (New York, 1946), pp. 46–47.

127. Marina Warner, "Making Up for Mother," *Times Literary Supplement,* June 12, 1987, 638.

128. See Hoxie, *A Final Promise,* pp. 134–137.

129. See Anita Brenner, *Idols behind Altars* (New York, 1929), and Billington, *The Protestant Crusade,* p. 351.

130. Marvin R. O'Connell, "The Roman Catholic Tradition," in *Caring and Curing: Health and Medicine in the Western Religious Tradition,* ed. Ronald L. Numbers and Darrell W. Amundsen (New York, 1986), pp. 116, 117.

131. Carlos Fuentes, *The Old Gringo,* trans. Margaret Sayers Peden and C. Fuentes (New York, 1985), pp. 130, 107.

132. See Max Weber, *The Protestant Ethic and the Spirit of Capitalism* (London, 1930), esp. pp. 105, 117; and Keith Thomas, *Religion and the Decline of Magic* (New York, 1971), esp. ch. 22.

133. Charles Anderson, *White Protestant Americans* (Englewood Cliffs, N.J., 1970), 105.

134. Warren Kiefer, *Outlaw* (New York, 1989), p. 10.

135. Quoted by Billington, *The Protestant Crusade,* p. 5.

136. See Fredrick B. Pike, "Christianity in Latin America since 1800," in *The Oxford Illustrated History of Christianity,* ed. John McManners (Oxford, Eng., 1990), pp. 426–430.

137. Gregg, *Commerce on the Prairies,* pp. 183–184.

138. Josiah Gregg, *Commerce on the Prairies* (Philadelphia, 1913), 1:263. This is a different edition of the work cited in notes 41, 100, and 137.

139. See Aragón, *Padre Martínez and Bishop Lamy,* pp. 47, 50–51; Horgan, *Lamy of Santa Fe,* p. 235; and McWilliams, *North from Mexico,* p. 70.

140. Willa Cather, *Death Comes for the Archbishop* (1927; New York, 1971), p. 146.

141. Billington, *The Protestant Crusade,* pp. 365, 366, 361–362.

142. Gregory, *Three Years in the Pacific,* p. 321; Steuart, *Bogotá,* pp. 162–164; Rev. D. P. Kidder, *Brazil and the Brazilians* (Boston, 1868), p. 141; John Reed, *Insurgent Mexico* (1914: New York, 1969), p. 61.

143. Franklin D. Roosevelt, "Annual Message to Congress" (Jan. 4, 1935), in *Papers and Speeches of . . .* (New York, 1938), pp. 17–23.

144. Wells, *Study of Mexico,* p. 98.

145. Ephraim George Squier, *Notes on Central America; Particularly the States of*

Honduras and San Salvador: Their Geography, Topography, Climate, Population, Resources, Productions, etc., etc., and the Proposed Honduras Inter-Oceanic Railway (New York, 1855), p. 324; John Lloyd Stephens quoted by Parker, *Travels in Central America*, p. 211; Billingsley, *In Defense of Neutral Rights*, p. 26

146. Ewbank, *Life in Brazil*, p. vii; Prof. and Mrs. Louis Agassiz, *A Journey in Brazil* (Boston, 1868), pp. 472, 496; Scruggs, *The Colombian and Venezuelan Republics*, p. 98; Louis Moreau Gottschalk, *Notes of a Pianist* (1870; New York, 1964), p. 395.

147. David Nasaw, "Fisticuffs," a review of Elliott Gorn, *The Manly Art: Bare-Knuckle Fighting in America* (Ithaca, 1987), in *Nation*, Feb. 28, 1987, 262.

148. Quoted by J. Alberich, *Bulletin of Hispanic Studies* 51 (1974): 185.

149. Quoted by Drinnon, *Facing West*, pp. 76–77.

150. Ewbank, *Life in Brazil*, p. xiii.

151. Williams, *Spanish Background of American Literature* 1:17.

152. See Francis Paul Prucha, *The Great Father: The United States Government and the American Indians,* abr. ed. (Lincoln, 1986), pp. 53, 54.

153. See Wilkins B. Winn, "The Efforts of the United States to Secure Religious Liberty in a Commercial Treaty with Mexico, 1825–1831," *Americas* 28 (1972): 311–332. See also William Gribbin, "A Matter of Faith: North Americans' Religion and South American Independence," ibid. 31 (1975): 470–487.

154. Bercovitch, *The American Jeremiad,* pp. 46–47.

155. Ibid., p. xiv.

156. T. J. Jackson Lears, "The Concept of Hegemony: Problems and Possibilities," *American Historical Review* 90 (1985): 575.

3. Latin Americans and Indians: Ambiguous Perceptions of an Alleged Connection

1. Stanley T. Williams, *The Spanish Background of American Literature* (New Haven, 1955), 2:189, 196.

2. Charles Howard Shinn, *Mining Camps: A Study of American Frontier Government* (New York, 1885), p. 6.

3. Walter Colton, *Three Years in California* (1850; Stanford, 1949), ed. Marguerita Wilbur, quoted by Leonard Pitt, *The Decline of the Californios: A Social History of the Spanish-Speaking Californians, 1846–1890* (Berkeley, 1966), p. 18.

4. Mary Elizabeth Blake and Margaret F. Sullivan, *Mexico Picturesque, Political, Progressive* (Boston, 1888), p. 96.

5. See Carey McWilliams, *North from Mexico: The Spanish-Speaking People of the United States* (Philadelphia, 1949), p. 10.

6. Pío Pico quoted by Gertrude Atherton, *The Splendid Idle Forties* (New York, 1902), p. 2.

7. Quoted by John L. Thomas, *Alternative America: Henry George, Edward Bellamy, Henry Demarest Lloyd, and the Adversary Tradition* (Cambridge, Mass., 1983), p. 90.

8. Bithia Mary Croker, *In Old Madras* (London, 1913), p. 11, quoted by V. G.

Kiernan, *The Lords of Human Kind: Black Man, Yellow Man, and White Man in an Age of Empire* (New York, 1986), p. 56.

9. Walt Whitman, "Leaves of Grass" (1855), in *Complete Poetry and Collected Prose* (New York, 1982), p. 145.

10. James Axtell, *The European and the Indian: Essays in the Ethnohistory of Colonial North America* (New York, 1981), p. 206.

11. William Cronon, *Changes in the Land: Indians, Colonists, and the Ecology of New England* (New York, 1983), p. 80.

12. The quotation, though stunningly applicable to many Americans in their attitude toward Indians, comes from Conrad Gorinsky, a Brazilian chemist working in London, and expresses the way many Brazilians in the latter part of the twentieth century feel about their vanishing natives. See Marlise Simons, "The Amazon's Savvy Indians," *New York Times Magazine,* Feb. 26, 1989.

13. See Elizabeth Atwood Lawrence, *Rodeo: An Anthropologist Looks at the Wild and the Tame* (Chicago, 1982).

14. Hugh Henry Brackenridge, writing in the Feb. 6, 1792, ed. of the *National Gazette,* quoted by Reginald Horsman, *Race and Manifest Destiny: The Origins of American Racial Anglo-Saxonism* (Cambridge, Mass., 1981), p. 98. Even in ancient times, "cultural primitivism," or the desire to return to an earlier, purer, uncorrupted time frequently manifested itself. See Arthur O. Lovejoy and George Boas, *Primitivism and Related Ideas in Antiquity* (Baltimore, 1935).

15. Ray Allen Billington, *Land of Savagery, Land of Promise: The European Image of the American Frontier in the Nineteenth Century* (New York, 1980), p. 323.

16. Peter Nabakov, "Return to the Native," *New York Review of Books,* Sept. 27, 1984, 44–45.

17. Frederick Turner, *Beyond Geography: The Western Spirit against Wilderness* (New Brunswick, N.J., 1980), pp. 215–216.

18. See Axtell, *The European and the Indian,* p. 136. The emphasis is in the original.

19. Quoted by Leo Marx, *The Machine in the Garden: Technology and the Pastoral Ideal in America* (London, 1964), p. 75.

20. See Billington, *Land of Savagery, Land of Promise,* p. 19.

21. Robert V. Hine, *The American West: An Interpretive History,* 2d ed. (Boston, 1984), p. 2.

22. Some of Morton's attitudes may have derived from Thomas More's *Utopia* (1516). See Elémire Zolla, *The Writer and the Shaman: A Morphology of the American Indian,* trans. Raymond Rosenthal (New York, 1973), p. 26.

23. Richard A. Van Orman, *The Explorers: Nineteenth-Century Expeditions in Africa and the American West* (Albuquerque, 1984), p. 67.

24. See Patricia Nelson Limerick, *The Legacy of Conquest: The Unbroken Past of the American West* (New York, 1987), p. 184; and Albert J. Von Frank, *The Sacred Game: Provincialism and Frontier Consciousness in American Literature, 1630–1860* (Cambridge, Eng., 1985), p. 77.

25. James Fenimore Cooper, *The Prairie: A Tale* (1827; New York, 1985), p. 211.

26. William Dean Howells, "Mrs. Johnson," extracted in *The Minority Presence in American Literature, 1600–1900,* ed. Philip Butcher (Washington, D.C., 1977), 2 : 160.

27. Joseph Bruchard, "Stealing Horses," *Parabola* 9 (1984): 59.

28. Nabakov, "Return to the Native," p. 144.

29. Chinua Achebe, *Anthills of the Savannah* (New York, 1987), p. 92.

30. See Rosemarie Zaggari and Jefferson Morely, "'Blending Instruction and Amusement': National Character in American Playing Cards, 1790–1865," *Journal of American Culture* 5 (1982): 57–58.

31. See Robert M. Utley, "The Frontier Army: John Ford or Arthur Penn?" in *Indian-White Relations: A Persistent Paradox*, ed. Jane F. Smith and Robert M. Kvasnicka (Washington, D.C., 1981), pp. 133–145. See also A. Carl Bredahl, Jr., *New Ground: Western American Narrative and the Literary Canon* (Chapel Hill, 1989), ch. 10; and *The Pretend Indians: Images of Native Americans in the Movies*, ed. Gretchen M. Bataille and Charles L. P. Silet (Ames, Iowa, 1980), passim.

32. On the externalist-internalist split in the analysis of foreign policy, see Gaddis Smith, *Reason and Power: American Diplomacy in the Carter Years* (New York, 1986), esp. p. 28.

33. See Francis Paul Prucha's introduction to *Indian-White Relations*, ed. Smith and Kvasnicka, p. 8.

34. Quoted by Wyndham Lewis, *Paleface: The Philosophy of the "Melting Pot"* (1929; New York, 1969), p. 174.

35. See Alden T. Vaughan, "From White Man to Redskin: Changing Anglo-American Perceptions of the American Indian," *American Historical Review* 87 (1982): 917–953.

36. James Adair quoted by Lewis O. Saum, *The Fur Trader and the Indian* (Seattle, 1965), p. 68.

37. Arthur K. Moore, *The Frontier Mind: A Cultural Analysis of the Kentucky Frontiersman* (Lexington, Ky., 1957), p. 95. See also Richard Drinnon, *Facing West: The Metaphysics of Indian-Hating and Empire-Building* (Minneapolis, 1980), pp. 68–69.

38. G. Edward White, *The Eastern Establishment and the Western Experience: The West of Frederic Remington, Theodore Roosevelt, and Owen Wister* (New Haven, 1968), p. 42; Robert Taft, *Artists and Illustrators of the Old West, 1850–1900* (1953; Princeton, 1982), p. 66.

39. Quoted by Francis Paul Prucha, *American Indian Policy in the Formative Years: The Indian Trade and Intercourse Acts, 1790–1834* (Cambridge, Mass., 1962), p. 233.

40. John Greenway, "Will the Indian Get Whitey?" *National Review*, Mar. 11, 1969, cited by Calvin Martin, *Keepers of the Game: Indian-Animal Relationships and the Fur Trade* (Berkeley, 1978), p. 161.

41. Quoted by Albert Keiser, *The Indian in American Literature* (1933; New York, 1975), p. 105.

42. Michael C. Coleman, *Presbyterian Missionary Attitudes toward American Indians, 1837–1839* (Jackson, Miss., 1985), pp. 86, 90, 126.

43. See Martin Green, *The Great American Adventure: Action Stories from Cooper to Mailer and What They Reveal about American Manhood* (Boston, 1984), p. 111; Hine, *The American West*, pp. 6–7; and Annette Kolodny, *The Lay of the Land: Metaphor as Experience and History in American Life and Letters* (Chapel Hill, 1975), p. 5.

44. John Russell, "A Popular Painter, a Poor Reputation," *New York Times,* Feb. 10, 1989.

45. Quoted by Roy Harvey Pearce, *Savages of America: A Study of the Indian and the Idea of Civilization,* rev. ed. (Baltimore, 1965), pp. 117–118.

46. Bill Richards, "Tribal Problems," *Wall Street Journal,* Jan. 31, 1984.

47. For indications of the massive American criticism of Indian gambling, see Coleman, *Presbyterian Missionary Attitudes,* esp. p. 129; and Michael Paul Rogin, *Fathers and Children: Andrew Jackson and the Subjugation of the American Indian* (New York, 1975), p. 115.

48. Forrest Fenn, *The Beat of the Drum and the Whoop of the Dance: A Biography of Joseph Henry Sharp* (Santa Fe, 1983), p. 149.

49. Robert F. Berkhofer, Jr., *The White Man's Indian: Images of the American Indian from Columbus to the Present* (New York, 1978), p. 173.

50. Martin, *Keepers of the Game,* pp. 151–152.

51. This was the conclusion of nineteenth-century Indian authority Henry Rowe Schoolcraft, quoted by Pearce, *The Savages of America,* p. 122.

52. Quoted by, among many others, Brian Easlea, *Witch Hunting, Magic, and the New Philosophy* (Atlantic Highlands, N.J., 1980), p. 140.

53. See *Americanizing the American Indian: Writings by the "Friends of the Indian" 1880–1900,* ed. Francis Paul Prucha (Cambridge, Mass., 1973), pp. 130–140.

54. Martin, *Keepers of the Game,* p. 34.

55. See, for example, Zolla, *The Writer and the Shaman,* esp. pp. 141–154, 182.

56. Michael T. Taussig, *The Devil and Commodity Fetishism in South America* (Chapel Hill, 1980), p. 7. See also Dennis Tedlock and Barbara Tedlock, *Teachings from the American Earth: Indian Religion and Philosophy* (New York, 1975).

57. See Arthur P. Whitaker, *The Western Hemisphere Idea: Its Rise and Decline* (Ithaca, 1954), p. 29.

58. Quoted by Drinnon, *Facing West,* p. 94.

59. See John Adams letter of 1812 to Thomas Jefferson, quoted by Zolla, *The Writer and the Shaman,* p. 81.

60. Vardis Fisher, *Mountain Man* (1957; New York, 1965), p. 112.

61. Quoted by Horsman, *Race and Manifest Destiny,* p. 202.

62. Thomas Jefferson Fernham, *Travels in California and Scenes in the Pacific Ocean* (New York, 1844), pp. 356–357.

63. Quoted by Horsman, *Race and Manifest Destiny,* p. 211.

64. McWilliams, *North from Mexico,* p. 80.

65. Capt. Lemuel Ford, quoted by Roxanne Dunbar Ortiz, *Roots of Resistance: Land Tenure in New Mexico, 1680–1980* (Los Angeles, 1980), p. 65. See also Charles Kenner, *A History of New Mexico–Plains Indian Relations* (Norman, 1969), p. 83.

66. Walter Prescott Webb, *The Texas Rangers: A Century of Frontier Defense,* 2d ed. (Austin, 1965), p. 24.

67. W. A. McClintock, "Journal of a Trip through Texas and Northern Mexico in 1846–47," *Southwestern Historical Quarterly* 34 (1930–31): 157.

68. Quoted by Limerick, *The Legacy of Conquest,* p. 247.

69. Arnoldo DeLeon, *They Called Them Greasers: Anglo Attitudes toward Mexicans in Texas, 1821–1900* (Austin, 1983), p. 16. See also the first section (dealing with

the 1836–1900 period) of David Montejano, *Anglos and Mexicans in the Making of Texas, 1836–1986* (Austin, 1987).

70. McWilliams, *North from Mexico*, p. 52.

71. On the concept of a racial frontier, see Harvey Fergusson's introduction to W. W. H. Davis, *El Gringo: Or, New Mexico and Her People* (Chicago, 1962).

72. On Manifest Destiny, see, in addition to the already-cited Reginald Horsman study, two older classics: Frederick Merk, *Manifest Destiny and Mission in American History: A Reinterpretation* (New York, 1963), and Albert K. Weinberg, *Manifest Destiny: A Study of Nationalist Expansion in American History* (Baltimore, 1935). For a more favorable view of Manifest Destiny than the one I present in the text, see Kenneth S. Lynn's thoughtful review of Horsman's *Race and Manifest Destiny* in *Times Literary Supplement,* Mar. 12, 1982: 272.

73. Cecil Robinson, *Mexico and the Hispanic Southwest in American Literature* (Tucson, 1977), p. 26.

74. On McKenney, see Herman J. Viola, *Thomas L. McKenney, Architect of America's Early Indian Policy: 1816–1830* (Chicago, 1974).

75. McWilliams, *North from Mexico*, p. 128.

76. Billington, *Land of Savagery, Land of Promise*, p. 287.

77. Webb, *The Texas Rangers*, p. 127.

78. Richard Slotkin, *The Fatal Environment: The Myth of the Frontier in the Age of Industrialization, 1800–1890* (Middletown, Conn., 1986), p. 178.

79. See Whitman, *Complete Poetry and Collected Prose*, pp. 66–67.

80. See Keiser, *The Indian in American Literature*, p. 233.

81. Slotkin, *The Fatal Environment*, pp. 180–181.

82. Dorothy Ross, "Historical Consciousness in Nineteenth-Century America," *American Historical Review* 89 (1984): 912–913. On the J. G. A. Pocock thesis, see his *The Machiavellian Moment: Florentine Political Thought and the Atlantic Republic Tradition* (Princeton, 1975), esp. ch. 15.

83. Ernest Hemingway, *Green Hills of Africa* (New York, 1935), p. 285.

84. Chilean anthropologist Alejandro Lipschütz coined the term "pigmentocracy." See his *El indoamericanismo y el problema racial en las Américas*, 2d ed. (Santiago, Chile, 1944), p. 75.

85. See Juan Montalvo, *Siete tratados* (Besançon, France, 1882), 1:121–123.

86. Luis Alberto Sánchez, *Un sudamericano en norteamérica: Ellos y nosotros* (1943; Lima, Peru, 1968), pp. 152–155. For a discussion of racial mixing in Venezuela, see Winthrop R. Wright, *Café con leche: Race, Class, and National Image in Venezuela* (Austin, 1990).

87. Horsman, *Race and Manifest Destiny*, p. 213.

88. See Robinson, *Mexico and the Hispanic Southwest*, p. 30.

89. Agustín Aragón, quoted by Frank Tannenbaum, *Peace by Revolution: Mexico after 1900* (New York, 1966), p. 32.

90. Quoted by Robinson, *Mexico and the Hispanic Southwest*, p. 31.

91. See Leslie Fiedler, *The Return of the Vanishing American* (New York, 1968), p. 77.

92. See Joyce Carol Oates, "So Young," *New York Times Book Review,* Sept. 30, 1990, 43

93. Quoted by Robert W. Johannsen, *To the Halls of the Montezumas: The Mexican War in the American Imagination* (New York, 1985), p. 173. See also p. 171.

94. Freeman Hunt quoted in ibid., p. 300.

95. Robinson, *Mexico and the Hispanic Southwest*, p. 116.

96. Johannsen, *To the Halls of the Montezumas*, p. 272.

97. Ibid., pp. 21, 34.

98. Letter to his wife of Feb. 11, 1883, in Thomas Moran, *Home—Thoughts from Afar: Letters of Thomas Moran to Mary Nimmo Moran*, ed. Amy O. Bassford (East Hampton, N.Y., 1967), p. 71.

99. See Johannsen, *To the Halls of the Montezumas*, pp. 92, 146, 161–164.

100. Cecilia Tichi, *New World, New Earth: Environmental Reform in American Literature from the Puritans through Whitman* (New Haven, 1979), p. 13.

101. Robert M. Adams, "Liberators," *New York Review of Books*, Oct. 11, 1990, 18.

4. Our Frontier and Theirs: American Perceptions of Latin American Backwardness

1. See Ramiro de Maeztu, "El espíritu de la economía iberoamericana," *Revista de las Españas* (Madrid), nos. 9–10 (May–June, 1927): 341.

2. Edmundo O'Gorman, *The Invention of America: An Inquiry into the Historical Nature of the New World and the Meaning of Its History* (Bloomington, 1961), pp. 142–143. The inner quotes indicate Acosta's words.

3. Ibid., pp. 128–129.

4. Luis Carranza, *Artículos publicados por . . . , segunda colección de artículos,* (Lima, 1888), 2 : 48, 51–53.

5. On limited-good concepts and how they shape traditional, premodern mindsets, see George Foster, "Peasant Society and the Image of the Limited Good," *American Anthropologist* 67 (1965): 293–315, and Fredrick B. Pike, *The United States and the Andean Republics: Peru, Bolivia, and Ecuador* (Cambridge, Mass., 1977), pp. 12–16.

6. See Richard Slotkin, *The Fatal Environment: The Myth of the Frontier in the Age of Industrialization, 1800–1890* (Middletown, Conn., 1986), p. 42.

7. These points are developed in the opening chapters of Allan MacFarlan's influential and controversial study, *The Culture of Capitalism* (London, 1987).

8. Alistair Hennessy, *The Frontier in Latin American History* (Albuquerque, 1978), p. 18.

9. Victor Westphall, *Mercedes Reales: Hispanic Land Grants of the Upper Rio Grande Region* (Albuquerque, 1983), p. 5.

10. Roxanne Dunbar Ortiz, *Roots of Resistance: Land Tenure in New Mexico, 1680–1980* (Los Angeles, 1980), pp. 5, 85–86; and Thomas E. Sheridan, *Los Tucsonenses: The Mexican Community in Tucson, 1854–1941* (Tucson, 1986), p. 14.

11. Robert V. Hine, *Community on the American Frontier: Separate but Not Alone* (Norman, 1980), p. 154.

12. See William Cronon, *Changes in the Land: Indians, Colonists, and the Ecology of New England* (New York, 1983), p. 78; and Frederick E. Hoxie, *A Final Promise: The Campaign to Assimilate the Indians, 1880–1920* (Lincoln, 1984), pp. 17–19.

13. Donald Worster, *Rivers of Empire: Water, Aridity, and the Growth of the American West* (New York, 1985), p. 120.

14. Scholarship in the second half of the twentieth century has produced evidence that the Latin American economy in the colonial period and the nineteenth century was less feudal and more capitalist than once assumed. For a comprehensive analysis of the literature on this topic, see Steve J. Stern, "Feudalism, Capitalism, and the World-System in the Perspective of Latin America and the Caribbean," *American Historical Review* 93 (1988): 829–872.

15. Arthur P. Whitaker, *The Spanish-American Frontier, 1783–1795* (1927; Lincoln, 1969), p. 47.

16. Slotkin, *The Fatal Environment*, p. 39.

17. Robert V. Hine, *The American West: An Interpretive History*, 2d ed. (Boston, 1984), p. 324.

18. Ray Allen Billington, *The Far Western Frontier, 1830–1860* (New York, 1956), p. 1.

19. Frederick Turner, *Beyond Geography: The Western Spirit against the Wilderness* (New Brunswick, N.J., 1980), pp. 259–260, 266–267.

20. Ibid., p. 268.

21. See "The Slaughter," in *The American West in Fiction*, ed. Jon Tuska (Lincoln, 1982), p. 348.

22. John D. Unruh, Jr., *The Plains Across: The Overland Emigrants and the Trans-Mississippi West, 1840–1860* (Urbana, 1979), p. 244.

23. See David Dary, *Entrepreneurs of the Old West* (New York, 1986), p. ix.

24. On the Jewish trader in the American West see *American Jewish Landmarks: A Travel Guide and History*, vol. 4, *The West*, by Bernard Postal and Lionel Koppman (New York, 1986).

25. Matthew F. Maury, quoted by Reginald Horsman, *Race and Manifest Destiny: The Origins of American Racial Anglo-Saxonism* (Cambridge, Mass., 1981), p. 281.

26. Quoted by Hennessy, *The Frontier*, p. 95.

27. On great awakenings and born-again experiences see, for succinct summaries, Arthur K. Moore, *The Frontier Mind: A Cultural Analysis of the Kentucky Frontiersman* (Lexington, Ky., 1957), esp. pp. 141, 229–230; and Hine, *The American West*, esp. pp. 242–245. See also William G. McLoughlin, *Revivals, Awakenings, and Reform: An Essay on Religion and Social Change in America, 1607–1977* (Chicago, 1977).

28. See Theodore Dwight Bozeman, *To Lead Primitive Lives: The Primitivist Dimension in Puritanism* (Chapel Hill, 1988), esp. pp. 358–359.

29. Walt Whitman, "Rise O Days from Your Fathomless Deeps," in *Complete Poetry and Collected Prose* (New York, 1982), p. 428.

30. Robert Frost, "The Gift Outright," quoted by Annette Kolodny, *The Lay of the Land: Metaphor as Experience and History in American Life and Letters* (Chapel Hill, 1975), p. 10.

31. See Patrick Brantlinger, *Rule of Darkness: British Literature and Imperialism, 1830–1914* (Ithaca, 1988), p. 125.

32. See Hennessy, *The Frontier*, p. 12. For a superb study that emphasizes the successive waves of settlers of American frontiers (or, as she prefers to call them,

"geographies") see J. Valerie Fifer, *American Progress: The Growth of the Transport, Tourist, and Information Industries in the Nineteenth-Century West Seen through the Life and Times of George A. Crofutt, Pioneer and Publicist of the Transcontinental Age* (Chester, Conn., 1988).

33. David R. Williams, *Wilderness Lost: The Religious Origins of the American Mind* (Cranbury, N.J., 1987), p. 23.

34. Quoted by Horsman, *Race and Manifest Destiny,* p. 184.

35. For a succinct description of Melanesian cargo-cult beliefs, see Mircea Eliade, "'Cargo Cults' and Cosmic Regeneration," in *Millennial Dreams in Action: Studies in Revolutionary Religious Movements,* ed. Sylvia A. Thrupp (New York, 1970), pp. 139–143.

36. Theodore Roosevelt, *Through the Brazilian Wilderness* (New York, 1914), pp. 324–325.

37. See Kristin Herzog, *Women, Ethnics, and Exotics: Images of Power in Mid-Nineteenth-Century American Fiction* (Knoxville, 1983), p. 180.

38. See *The Bandeirantes: The Historical Role of the Brazilian Pathfinders,* ed. Richard M. Morse (New York, 1965).

39. Quoted by Roy Harvey Pearce, *Savages of America: A Study of the Indian and the Idea of Civilization* (Baltimore, 1953), pp. 203–204.

40. See Cecelia Tichi, *New World, New Earth: Environmental Reform in American Literature from the Puritans through Whitman* (New Haven, 1979), p. 101. The inner quotes indicate Crèvecoeur's words.

41. Walter Prescott Webb, *The Great Plains* (1931; Lincoln, 1981), p. 87.

42. Ibid., pp. 245, 179.

43. Ibid., pp. 333–334.

44. David Humphrey, quoted by Tichi, *New World, New Earth,* p. 93.

45. Francis Paul Prucha, *The Great Father: The United States Government and the American Indians,* abr. ed. (Lincoln, 1986), p. 6.

46. Tom Lea, *The King Ranch* (Boston, 1957), 1:53.

47. These are the words that novelist A. B. Guthrie, Jr., gives to the Yankee Elisha Peabody, a richly drawn stock character of the American frontier, in *The Big Sky* (1952; New York, 1982), p. 264.

48. John R. Stilgoe, *The Metropolitan Corridor: Railroads and the American Scene* (New Haven, 1983), p. 173.

49. Quoted by Robert M. Utley, *Cavalier in Buckskin: George Armstrong Custer and the Western Military Frontier* (Norman, 1988), p. 126.

50. Quoted in Stilgoe, *The Metropolitan Corridor,* p. ix.

51. Slotkin, *The Fatal Environment,* p. 364.

52. Ronald T. Takaki, *Iron Cages: Race and Culture in Nineteenth-Century America* (New York, 1979), p. 150.

53. Billington, *The Far Western Frontier,* p. 292.

54. William W. Savage, Jr., *Cowboy Life: Reconstructing an American Myth* (Norman, 1975), p. 3, warns of the need to distinguish between an intelligent, aggressive, and successful cattleman and the cowboy, a rangeland dropout who worked for wages and died poor because he lacked the qualities needed to acquire and operate a ranch of his own.

55. See Hine, *Community on the American Frontier,* p. 154.

56. Alan Lomax, "Introduction," *Cowboy Songs and Other Frontier Ballads,* collected and edited by John A. Lomax and Alan Lomax (1910; New York, 1986), p. xxvii.

57. See P. Durham and E. L. Jones, *The Negro Cowboys* (New York, 1965), and K. W. Porter, *The Negro on the American Frontier* (New York, 1971).

58. See Jack Weston, *The Real American Cowboy* (New York, 1985), p. 30. Weston applies a Marxist interpretation to the subject.

59. *Cowboy Songs,* p. xxviii.

60. George A. Henty, *Red-skins and Cow-boys: A Tale of the Western Plains* (London, 1891), p. 186. Henty was one of the better English novelists who specialized in westerns.

61. Howard Lamar, *The Far Southwest, 1846–1912* (New Haven, 1966), pp. 30–31. See also Sheridan, *Los Tucsonenses,* p. 34.

62. For a well-written, perceptive account of cowboys in Canada, the United States, and Latin America—an account of cowboys as they existed in reality rather than myth—see Richard W. Slatta, *Cowboys of the Americas* (New Haven, 1990).

63. The standard source on the gaucho is Richard Slatta, *Gauchos and the Vanishing Frontier* (Lincoln, 1983).

64. Anonymous writer in the *Kentucky Gazette* of March 3, 1828, quoted by Moore, *The Frontier Mind,* p. 153.

65. See Werner W. Crane, *The Southern Frontier, 1670–1732* (Ann Arbor, 1964), pp. 31, 80, 112, and following pages; William C. MacLeod, *The American Indian Frontier* (New York, 1928), pp. 67–143; and M. Eugene Sirmans, *Colonial South Carolina: A Political History, 1663–1783* (Chapel Hill, 1966), pp. 17, 40–43, 53–54, 60.

66. George W. Stocking, Jr., *Race, Culture, and Evolution: Essays in the History of Anthropology* (New York, 1968), p. 116.

67. See Lewis Henry Morgan, *Ancient Society: Or, Researches in the Lines of Human Progress from Savagery, through Barbarism, to Civilization* (New York, 1877).

68. Quoted by Hoxie, *A Final Promise,* p. 23.

69. Roosevelt, *Through the Brazilian Wilderness,* p. 48.

70. John Lloyd Stephens, *Incidents of Travel in Central America, Chiapas, and Yucatan* (New York, 1841), quoted by Franklin D. Parker, *Travels in Central America, 1821–1840* (Gainesville, Fla., 1970), p. 211.

71. See Mark Derr, *Some Kind of Paradise: A Chronicle of Man and the Land in Florida* (New York, 1988), pp. 275–279; and Jane Landers, "Gracia Real de Santa Teresa de Mose: A Free Black Town in Spanish Colonial Florida," *American Historical Review* 95 (1990): 9–30. For succinct treatments of maroons, palenques, quilombos, and mocambos in general, see Hennessy, *The Frontier,* pp. 68–70; and David Brion Davis, "The End of Slavery," *New York Review of Books,* Mar. 30, 1989, 29. For a more detailed account see *Maroon Societies: Rebel Slave Communities in the Americas,* ed. Richard Price (Baltimore, 1979).

72. Michael T. Taussig, *The Devil and Commodity Fetishism in South America* (Chapel Hill, 1980), p. 43.

73. Ibid., pp. 57–58, 67.

74. Prof. and Mrs. Louis Agassiz, *A Journey in Brazil* (Boston, 1868), pp. 298, 139.

75. James Fenimore Cooper, *The Prairie* (1827; New York, 1985), p. 29.

76. On "Injun" Joe see Alan R. Velie, *Four American Indian Literary Masters* (Norman, 1982), p. 138.

77. See, for example, W. W. H. Davis, *El Gringo: Or, New Mexico and Her People* (1857; Chicago, 1962), pp. 83–86; Josiah Gregg, *Commerce on the Prairies* (1844; Norman, 1954), p. 154; and Frederick Law Olmsted, *A Journey through Texas; or, A Saddle-Trip on the Southwestern Frontier* (New York, 1857), p. 161.

78. Margaret Fuller Ossoli, *At Home and Abroad; or, Things and Thoughts in America and Europe* (Boston, 1856), p. 96.

79. Quoted by Robert H. Heizer and Alan J. Almquist, *The Other Californians: Prejudice and Discrimination under Spain, Mexico, and the United States to 1920* (Berkeley, 1971), p. 140.

80. Lewis D. Saum, *The Fur Trader and the Indian* (Seattle, 1965), pp. 206–207.

81. See Martin Green, *The Great American Adventure: Action Stories from Cooper to Mailer and What They Reveal about American Manhood* (Boston, 1984), p. 107.

82. Michael C. Coleman, *Presbyterian Missionary Attitudes toward American Indians, 1837–1839* (Jackson, Miss., 1985), pp. 123–124.

83. See Ray Allen Billington, *Land of Savagery, Land of Promise: The European Image of the American Frontier in the Nineteenth Century* (New York, 1981), p. 167.

84. Peter B. Kyne, quoted by John Higham, *Strangers in the Land: Patterns of American Nativism 1860–1925*, corrected ed. (New York, 1975), p. 131.

85. Erik W. Allstrom, quoted by Sheridan, *Los Tucsonenses*, pp. 228, 229.

86. Saum, *The Fur Trader*, p. 84. See also Hine, *Community on the American Frontier*, pp. 56–57.

87. Cecil Robinson, *Mexico and the Hispanic Southwest in American Literature* (Tucson, 1977), p. 75.

88. Hine, *The American West*, pp. 79–80.

89. Glenda Riley, *Women and Indians on the Frontier, 1825–1915* (Albuquerque, 1984), p. 132.

90. Quoted by Richard Drinnon, *Facing West: The Metaphysics of Indian-Hating and Empire-Building* (Minneapolis, 1980), pp. 309–310.

91. For the Northern Star–Southern Cross contrast, I am indebted to William Sammon who developed the concept in a seminar paper he wrote for me at the University of Notre Dame in May 1987.

92. Thomas Moran letter of Feb. 8, 1883, to his wife, in *Home—Thoughts from Afar: Letters of Thomas Moran to Mary Nimmo Moran*, ed. Amy O. Bassford (East Hampton, N.Y., 1967), p. 65.

93. Quoted by David J. Weber, "Turner, the Boltonians, and the Borderlands," *American Historical Review* 91 (1986): 70.

94. James Mooney, *Historical Sketch of the Cherokee* (Chicago, 1975), p. 80. An anthropologist, Mooney (1861–1921) worked for the Bureau of American Ethnology and developed genuine empathy for Indians. The cited work comprises some of his writings of the 1890s.

95. Stocking, *Race, Culture, and Evolution*, p. 179.

96. Ephraim George Squier, *Notes on Central America, Particularly the States of Honduras and San Salvador* (New York, 1855), pp. 57–58.

97. Ibid., pp. 234, 51–52.

98. William Walker, *The War in Nicaragua* (Mobile, New York, 1860), pp. 259, 261, 262–263.

99. Ibid., p. 349.

100. Quoted by Robert W. Johannsen, *To the Halls of the Montezumas: The Mexican War in the American Imagination* (New York, 1985), p. 22.

101. Isaac Strain, *Sketches of a Journey in Chile and the Argentine Provinces in 1848* (New York, 1853), pp. 267–269, 56–57.

102. C. B. Merwin (pseud. "A Lady of Ohio"), *Three Years in Chile* (New York, 1863), p. 31.

103. Henry Morris Myers and Philip Van Ness, *Life and Nature under the Tropics* (New York, 1871), p. 232.

104. Herbert H. Smith, *Brazil: The Amazon and the Coast* (New York, 1879), p. 468.

105. Hart Crane letter to his father, May 20, 1926, in *Letters of Hart Crane and His Family,* ed. Thomas S. W. Lewis (New York, 1974), p. 493.

106. Alexander Kinmont, *Twelve Lectures on the Natural History of Man and the Rise and Progress of Philosophy* (Cincinnati, 1839), pp. 153–154.

107. Quoted by Parker, *Travels in Central America,* p. 114.

108. Olmsted, *A Journey through Texas,* p. 163; Columbus Delano, quoted by Horsman, *Race and Manifest Destiny,* p. 240; C. S. Stewart, *Brazil and La Plata: The Personal Record of a Cruise* (New York, 1856), p. 72.

109. Quoted by Carey McWilliams, *North from Mexico: The Spanish-Speaking People of the United States* (Philadelphia, 1949), p. 121.

110. George M. Fredrickson, *The Black Image in the White Mind: The Debate on Afro-American Character and Destiny, 1817–1914* (New York, 1971), p. 17.

111. Ibid., pp. 148–149, 150, 49.

112. Robinson, *Mexico and the Hispanic Southwest,* p. 74.

113. "Cosmic race" ideology (or mythology) is associated with, among other Latin American thinkers, the Mexican José Vasconcelos who in 1925 published an influential book with the title *La raza cósmica.*

114. See Robert May, *Sex and Fantasy: Patterns of Male and Female Development* (New York, 1980), p. 164.

115. See David Leverenz, *Manhood and the American Renaissance* (Ithaca, 1989), passim.

116. See Harold Beaver, "On the Racial Frontier," *Times Literary Supplement,* May 30, 1980, 619. Beaver's perceptive essay is a review of William J. Scheick, *The Half-Blood: A Cultural Symbol in Nineteenth-Century American Fiction* (Chicago, 1979).

117. Turner, *Beyond Geography,* pp. 238–239, cautions against viewing the Pocahontas–John Rolfe match purely as a symbol of America's occasional openness to mestizaje. Rolfe in some ways reacted in horror to the thought of marrying the racial Other. Therefore, he desperately grasped for rationalizations, finding his principal one in expediency: the need to save the colony of new Israelites in America.

118. See Annette Kolodny, *The Land before Her: Fantasy and Experience of the American Frontiers, 1630–1860* (Chapel Hill, 1984), pp. 70–71.

119. See Lee Clark Mitchell, *Witness to a Vanishing America: The Nineteenth-*

Century Response (Princeton, 1981), p. 262; and Stanley T. Williams, *The Spanish Background of American Literature* (New Haven, 1955), 1 : 230–231.

120. See Robinson, *Mexico and the Hispanic Southwest,* p. 73.

121. See Harold Beaver's introduction to Poe's *Narrative of Arthur Gordon Pym* (New York, 1975), pp. 28–29. Southerner Poe may have believed that by merging with the savage Indian, American whites could acquire the strength needed to overcome the darkest threat of savagery in the New World, that posed by the African.

122. See Cecil Robinson, "American Writers in Mexico, 1875–1925," in *Down Mexico Way,* ed. Teresa A. Turner (Tucson, 1984), pp. 16–17.

123. Beaver, "On the Racial Frontier." See also Velie, *Four American Indian Literary Masters,* pp. 138–139.

124. Richard Chase, *The American Novel and Its Tradition* (New York, 1957), p. 9.

5. America in the Age of the New Imperialism

1. See Angie Debo, *And Still the Waters Run: The Betrayal of the Five Civilized Tribes* (Norman, 1980).

2. David Dary, *Entrepreneurs of the Old West* (New York, 1986), p. 292. For more complete coverage see Stan Hoig, *Land Rush of 1889* (Oklahoma City, 1984).

3. Edna Ferber, *Cimarron* (New York, 1929), p. 116.

4. Douglas C. McGill, "At the Met, a Hudson River Revival," *New York Times,* Oct. 8, 1987.

5. Michael Paul Rogin, *Fathers and Children: Andrew Jackson and the Subjugation of the American Indian* (New York, 1975), p. 107; Lee Clark Mitchell, *Witness to a Vanishing America: The Nineteenth-Century Response* (Princeton, 1981), p. 168.

6. Frederick Nash, *Wilderness and the American Mind,* 3d ed. (New Haven, 1982), p. 100.

7. Annette Kolodny, *The Land before Her: Fantasy and Experience of the American Frontiers, 1630–1860* (Chapel Hill, 1984), p. 7.

8. See Wilbur Zelinsky, *Nation into State: The Shifting Symbolic Foundations of American Nationalism* (Chapel Hill, 1988), pp. 232–233.

9. Frederick Jackson Turner, "The Significance of the Frontier in American History," a paper first presented in 1893, in Turner, *The Frontier in American History* (1920; New York, 1962), p. 37.

10. Louis Chapin, *Great Masterpieces by Frederic Remington* (New York, 1979), p. 58.

11. V. G. Kiernan, *Marxism and Imperialism* (New York, 1974), p. 111.

12. See Colleen Cook, "Nazism and the American West: The Literature of Karl May," *Red River Valley Historical Journal of World History* 5 (1981): 339–355.

13. Quoted by E. Berkeley Tompkins, *Anti-Imperialism in the United States: The Great Debate, 1890–1920* (Philadelphia, 1970), pp. 4–5.

14. Quoted by Michiko Kakutani, "Stanley's Expedition into Heart of Darkness," *New York Times,* Apr. 11, 1989.

15. Tony Smith, *The Pattern of Imperialism: The United States, Great Britain, and the Late-Industrializing World since 1815* (Cambridge, Eng., 1981), p. 4.

16. See Tompkins, *Anti-Imperialism,* p. 8.

17. See Mark T. Gilderhus, *Pan American Visions: Woodrow Wilson in the Western Hemisphere, 1913–1921* (Tucson, 1986), p. 133.

18. See Hugh Honour, *The New Golden Land: European Images of America from the Discovery to the Present Time* (New York, 1975), p. 189.

19. Ephraim George Squier, *Notes on Central America, Particularly the States of Honduras and San Salvador: Their Geography, Topography, Climate, Population, Resources, Productions, etc., etc., and the Proposed Honduras Inter-Oceanic Railway* (New York, 1855), p. 17.

20. See *Wilson Quarterly* 9 (1985): 154. For fuller details see Edward O. Wilson, *Biophilia* (Cambridge, Mass., 1984).

21. H. H. Powers quoted by Tompkins, *Anti-Imperialism,* p. 167.

22. See Noel Perrin, "'Forever Virgin': The American View of America," in *On Nature,* ed. Daniel Halperin (New York, 1986), pp. 13–22.

23. Letter of Aug. 4, 1820, to William Short, in Thomas Jefferson, *Writings,* ed. Merrill D. Peterson (New York, 1984), p. 1439.

24. See Arthur P. Whitaker, *The Western Hemisphere Idea: Its Rise and Decline* (Ithaca, 1954).

25. Ibid., pp. 29–31.

26. See *The Original Journals of the Lewis and Clark Expedition,* ed. Reuben Thwaites (New York, 1959), 7:248.

27. See Fredrick B. Pike, *The United States and the Andean Republics: Peru, Bolivia, and Ecuador* (Cambridge, Mass., 1977), p. 162.

28. T. J. Jackson Lears, *No Place of Grace: Antimodernism and the Transformation of American Culture, 1880–1920* (New York, 1981), p. 9.

29. Mark Derr, *Some Kind of Paradise: A Chronicle of Man and the Land in Florida* (New York, 1989), p. 102, refers to the efforts of superdevelopers and railroad builders Henry Flagler, Hamilton Disston, Henry Sanford, and Henry Plant to "revolutionize the face of nature." Like the mining magnates in Cuba, moreover, the Florida developers hoped to uplift the predominantly dark-skinned work force, about whose laziness and low morality they often complained.

30. See Mark Reutter, *Sparrows Point: Making Steel—the Rise and Ruin of American Industrial Might* (New York, 1988), pp. 73–74.

31. Ibid., p. 43.

32. Ibid., p. 80.

33. Ibid., pp. 83–84, 85–86.

34. On some of the symbolism of civilization's triumph over nature in Panama, see George Black, *The Good Neighbor: How the United States Wrote the History of Central America and the Caribbean* (New York, 1988), p. 21.

35. Paul Theroux, *The Old Patagonian Express: By Train through the Americas* (New York, 1979), p. 240.

36. Reutter, *Sparrows Point,* p. 52.

37. See John Anthony Caruso, "The Pan American Railway," *Hispanic American Historical Review* 31 (1951): 608–639.

38. William Gilpin, *Mission of the North American People, Geographical, Social, and Political* (Philadelphia, 1873), p. 110.

39. Thomas E. Sheridan, *Los Tucsonenses: The Mexican Community in Tucson, 1854–1941* (Tucson, 1986), pp. 53–54.

40. Taylorism derived its name from Frederick Winslow Taylor (1856–1915), an American efficiency engineer born in Germantown, Pennsylvania, who was widely celebrated for his 1911 book *The Principles of Scientific Management*. For a probing treatment of turn-of-the-century American ideology that equated the establishment of scientifically managed factories with the spread of Christian civilization, whether in the United States or, by implication, abroad, see Anthony F. C. Wallace, *Rockdale: The Growth of an American Village in the Early Industrial Revolution* (New York, 1978).

41. George A. Miller, writing in 1919, quoted by Black, *The Good Neighbor*, p. 34.

42. Quoted by Marvin R. O'Connell, *John Ireland and the American Catholic Church* (St. Paul, 1988), p. 455.

43. Frederick Godkin, quoted by Stanley Karnow, "America's Forgotten War in the Philippines," *New York Times*, Apr. 1, 1989.

44. See Samuel P. Hays, *Conservation and the Gospel of Efficiency: The Progressive Conservation Movement, 1890–1920* (Cambridge, Mass., 1959), pp. 110, 124.

45. See Francis Paul Prucha, *The Great Father: The United States Government and the American Indians*, abr. ed. (Lincoln, 1984), p. 102.

46. Sander L. Gilman, *Disease and Representation: Images of Illness from Madness to AIDS* (Ithaca, 1988), pp. 84–85.

47. See John J. Johnson, *Latin America in Caricature* (Austin, 1980), esp. pp. 116–156.

48. See Peter J. Bowler, *The Non-Darwinian Revolution: Reinterpreting a Historical Myth* (Baltimore, 1988), esp. pp. 71, 78, 97, 110, 157. See also George W. Stocking, Jr., *Race, Culture, and Evolution: Essays in the History of Anthropology* (1968; Chicago, 1982), esp. pp. 117–118, 241.

49. See Kenton L. Clymer, *Protestant Missionaries in the Philippines, 1898–1916: An Inquiry into the American Colonial Mentality* (Urbana, 1986), p. 153.

50. Lester D. Langley, *The Banana Wars: An Inner History of American Empire, 1900–1934* (Lexington, Ky., 1983), p. 222.

51. See Raymond Carr, *Puerto Rico: A Colonial Experiment* (New York, 1984), pp. 282–283.

52. See William Veeder, *Mary Shelley and Frankenstein: The Fate of Androgyny* (Chicago, 1966), pp. 111, 122.

53. Sinclair Lewis, *Main Street* (1920; New York, 1980), p. 194.

54. Sumner Welles, *Naboth's Vineyard: The Dominican Republic, 1844–1924* (New York, 1924), 2:917.

55. Letter of Feb. 18, 1803, to Benjamin Hawkins, in Jefferson, *Writings*, p. 501.

56. Francis Paul Prucha, *American Indian Policy in the Formative Years: The Indian Trade and Intercourse Acts, 1790–1834* (Cambridge, Mass., 1962), p. 266.

57. Quoted in *Americanizing the American Indians: Writings by the "Friends of the Indians" 1880–1900*, ed. Francis Paul Prucha (Cambridge, Mass., 1973), p. 15.

58. Quoted in *Americanizing the American Indians*, p. 194.

59. Prucha, *The Great Father*, p. 245; Robert F. Berkhofer, Jr., *The White Man's Indian: Images of the American Indian from Columbus to the Present* (New York, 1978), p. 150.

60. See Tompkins, *Anti-Imperialism*, p. 91. See also Stuart Creighton Miller, *"Benevolent Assimilation": The American Colonization of the Philippines, 1899–1903* (New Haven, 1982).

61. Quoted by Evan S. Connell, *Son of the Morning Star: Custer and the Little Bighorn* (San Francisco, 1984), p. 244.

62. Quoted in *Americanizing the American Indians*, pp. 102, 29. The emphasis is in the original. See also Robert H. Keller, Jr., *American Protestantism and United States Indian Policy, 1869–1882* (Lincoln, 1983), p. 153.

63. Quoted in *Americanizing the American Indians*, p. 137. Ultimately, of the 138,000,000 acres that Indians held upon enactment of the Dawes Act in 1887, only 48,000,000 remained in their possession by 1934. See ibid., p. 10.

64. Quoted by Federico Gil, *Latin American–United States Relations* (New York, 1971), p. 70. The emphasis is added. For background see Richard H. Collin, *Theodore Roosevelt's Caribbean: The Panama Canal, the Monroe Doctrine, and the Latin American Context* (Baton Rouge, 1990).

65. Quoted by Connell, *Son of the Morning Star*, p. 245.

66. Roy Harvey Pearce, *Savages of America: A Study of the Indian and the Idea of Civilization*, rev. ed. (Baltimore, 1965), p. 8.

67. Prucha, *The Great Father*, pp. 158–159.

68. Quoted in *Americanizing the American Indians*, pp. 334–335.

69. Ibid., p. 339.

70. Quoted by Tompkins, *Anti-Imperialism*, pp. 174–175.

71. Quoted by Ralph Edwin Minger, "William Howard Taft and United States Intervention in Cuba in 1906," *Hispanic American Historical Review* 41 (1961): 80.

72. *Americanizing the American Indians*, pp. 289–290.

73. William T. Hagan, "The Reservation Policy: Too Little and Too Late," in *Indian-White Relations: A Persistent Paradox*, ed. James F. Smith and Robert M. Kvasnicka (Washington, D.C., 1981), p. 162.

74. Late in the nineteenth century, some American officials charged with formulating Indian policy had begun to urge heavier-handed methods in forcing the Americanization of the natives. See *Americanizing the American Indians*, p. 252, and Frederick E. Hoxie, *A Final Promise: The Campaign to Assimilate the Indians, 1880–1920* (Lincoln, 1984), pp. 110-111.

75. Hoxie, *A Final Promise*, p. 187.

76. Michael C. Coleman, *Presbyterian Missionary Attitudes toward American Indians, 1837–1839* (Jackson, Miss., 1985), p. 9.

77. See John Patrick McDowell, *The Social Gospel in the South: The Woman's Home Mission Movement in the Methodist Episcopal Church, South, 1866–1939* (Baton Rouge, 1982), p. 67.

78. On "Americanization" as the "great school legend," see Collin Greer, *The Great School Legend: A Revisionist Interpretation of American Public Education* (New York, 1972).

79. Richard Slotkin, *The Fatal Environment: The Myth of the Frontier in the Age of Industrialization, 1800–1890* (Middletown, Conn., 1986), pp. 481, 352–353.

80. Nell Irvin Painter, *Standing at Armageddon: The United States 1877–1919* (New York, 1987), pp. 21–22. The best overall treatment of this period is Robert H. Wiebe, *The Search for Order, 1877–1920* (New York, 1967).

81. Lears, *No Place of Grace*, p. 31. On the building of armories so as to defend business interests and the established order in general against perceived threats of class warfare, see also Robert M. Fogelson, *America's Armories: Architecture, Society, and Public Order* (Cambridge, Mass., 1989).

82. See Richard Wade's review of Paul Avrich, *The Haymarket Tragedy* (New York, 1984), *New York Times Book Review*, Nov. 18, 1984, 43.

83. Quoted by Painter, *Standing at Armageddon*, p. 72.

84. Quoted by Robert V. Hine, *The American West: An Interpretive History* (Boston, 1984), pp. 313–314.

85. Lawrence J. McCaffrey, "Irish America," *Wilson Quarterly* 9 (1985): 78.

86. John Higham, *Strangers in the Land: Patterns of American Nativism 1860–1925*, corrected ed. (New York, 1975), p. 138.

87. Lears, *No Place of Grace*, p. 71.

88. Theodore Dreiser, *An American Tragedy* (1925; New York, 1981), p. 176.

89. Hoxie, *A Final Promise*, p. xiii.

90. Quoted by Leonard Pitt, *The Decline of the Californios: A Social History of the Spanish-Speaking Californians, 1846–1890* (Berkeley, 1966), pp. 204–205.

91. Robert F. Heizer and Alan J. Almquist, *The Other Californians: Prejudice and Discrimination under Spain, Mexico, and the United States to 1920* (Berkeley, 1971), p. 117; Stanley T. Williams, *The Spanish Background of American Literature* (New Haven, 1955), 2:233.

92. Carey McWilliams, *North from Mexico: The Spanish-Speaking People of the United States* (Philadelphia, 1949), p. 109. See also Paul Horgan, *Great River: The Rio Grande in North American History* (New York, 1954), 2:854; Tom Lea, *The King Ranch* (Boston, 1957), 1:264, 277–278; and David Montejano, *Anglos and Mexicans in the Making of Texas, 1836–1986* (Austin, 1987), passim.

93. Jack Weston, *The Real American Cowboy* (New York, 1985), p. 231; Sheridan, *Los Tucsonenses*, p. 78.

94. See Emlen Hall, *Four Leagues of the Pecos: A Legal History of the Pecos Grant, 1800–1939* (Albuquerque, 1984), passim; and Victor Westphall, *Mercedes Reales: Hispanic Land Grants of the Upper Rio Grande Region* (Albuquerque, 1983), esp. pp. 156, 201–211, 256.

95. Sheridan, *Los Tucsonenses*, pp. 80, 125. On this and related matters see also Mario Acuña, *Occupied America: A History of Chicanos* (New York, 1981); Mario Barrera, *Race and Class in the Southwest* (Notre Dame, Ind., 1979); Lawrence Cardoso, *Mexican Emigration in the United States, 1897–1931* (Tucson, 1980); Mario García, *Desert Immigrants: The Mexicans of El Paso, 1880–1920* (New Haven, 1981); and Robert Rosenbaum, *Mexicano Resistance in the Southwest: "The Sacred Right of Self-Preservation"* (Austin, 1981).

96. See Roxanne Dunbar Ortiz, *Roots of Resistance: Land Tenure in New Mexico, 1680–1980* (Los Angeles, 1980), p. 6.

97. Quoted by Richard S. Dunn in a review of George M. Fredrickson's *Arrogance of Race: Historical Perspectives on Slavery, Racism, and Social Inequality* (Middletown, Conn., 1987), *Times Literary Supplement,* June 17–23, 1988, 668.

98. Stocking, *Race, Culture, and Evolution,* pp. 121–123, 132. See also John S. Haller, *Outcasts from Evolution: Scientific Attitudes of Racial Inferiority, 1859–1900* (Urbana, 1971).

99. Bowler, *The Non-Darwinian Revolution,* p. 157.

100. Once prevailing assumptions about the reversion and decline of primitive races are examined in the essays that comprise *Degeneration: The Dark Side of Progress,* ed. J. Edward Chamberlain and Sander L. Gilman (New York, 1985), and in Daniel Pick's masterful study, *Faces of Degeneration: A European Disorder, c1848–c1918* (Cambridge, Eng., 1989). See also Joel Williamson's outstanding study *The Crucible of Race: Black-White Relations in the American South since Emancipation* (New York, 1984), esp. pp. 111–323.

101. Dr. Paul B. Barringer, quoted by George W. Fredrickson, *The Black Image in the White Mind: The Debate on Afro-American Character and Destiny, 1817–1914* (New York, 1971), pp. 252–253.

102. Painter, *Standing at Armageddon,* p. 8. On northern racism vis-à-vis African Americans, see Williamson, *The Crucible of Race,* pp. 327–395; Fredrickson, *The Black Image,* p. 273.

103. Benjamin Hooks, "Publisher's Foreword," *The Crisis Magazine, 80th Anniversary Issue,* Mar. 1989, 4.

104. Norman Riley, "W. E. B. Du Bois," ibid., p. 60.

105. Langston Hughes, *Fine Clothes to the Jew* (New York, 1927), p. 75.

106. Quoted by David Brion Davis, "Race of the Mind," *Times Literary Supplement,* Aug. 30, 1985, 940.

107. Neil Leonard, "The Reaction to Ragtime," in *Ragtime: Its History, Composers, and Music,* ed. John Edward Hasse (New York, 1985), pp. 103, 105, 108.

108. Paul Hoch, *White Hero, Black Beast* (London, 1979), p. 47; quoted by L. Leon Prather, Sr., *We Have Taken a City: The Wilmington Racial Massacre and the Coup of 1898* (Cranbury, N.J., 1984), p. 7.

109. Joel Williamson, *New People: Miscegenation and Mulattoes in the United States* (New York, 1984), p. 65. Williamson provides a memorable account of white America's rejection of the mulatto, 1850–1920.

110. Ibid., 3. See also Fredrickson, *The Black Image,* p. 277.

111. Hoxie, *A Final Promise,* p. 124.

112. Stocking, *Race, Culture, and Evolution,* p. 49. The inner quotation indicates the words of Boas.

113. Williamson, *New People,* p. 94.

114. Stocking, *Race, Culture, and Evolution,* p. 50. The inner quotation is from Nathaniel Shaler, "The Negro since the Civil War," *Popular Science Monthly* 57 (1900): 31.

115. Quoted by Williamson, *New People,* p. 45.

116. The quoted material is Ray Stannard Baker's opinion of Indians, expressed in 1903. See Hoxie, *A Final Promise,* p. 95. For Leupp's disparaging appraisal, see ibid., p. 202.

117. Ray Allen Billington, *Land of Savagery, Land of Promise: The European Image of the American Frontier in the Nineteenth Century* (New York, 1981), p. 140.

118. Quoted by Willard B. Gatewood, Jr., *Black Americans and the White Man's Burden, 1898–1903* (Urbana, 1975), p. 209.

119. C. Vann Woodward, *The Strange Career of Jim Crow,* 3d rev. ed. (New York, 1974), pp. 72–73.

120. On the extension of Indian stereotypes to Filipinos, see Ronald R. Takaki, *Iron Cages: Race and Culture in Nineteenth-Century America* (New York, 1979), esp. p. 279. For background on U.S. racist stereotyping in the Philippines, mixed with sincere humanitarian concern for "uplift," see Stanley Karnow, *In Our Image: America's Empire in the Philippines* (New York, 1989). On the Dominican Republic see Bruce J. Calder, *The Impact of Intervention: The Dominican Republic during the U.S. Occupation of 1916–1924* (Austin, 1984), esp. p. 124.

121. See, for example, Carr, *Puerto Rico,* pp. 52, 333. Carr also cites U.S. Gen. George W. Davis, who observed that Puerto Rico's vast horde of mixed-bloods were "no more fit to take part in self-government than our reservation Indians" (p. 323).

122. Calder, *The Impact of Intervention,* p. 249.

123. See Kim Blank, "Anthropologist of Himself," *Times Literary Supplement,* Dec. 15–21, 1989, 1380.

124. Robert W. Rydell, *All the World's a Fair: Visions of Empire at American International Expositions, 1876–1916* (Chicago, 1984), p. 94.

125. See Dinitia Smith, "Nature Playing," *Nation,* May 15, 1989, 674. For fuller treatment see Robert Bogdan, *Freak Show: Presenting Human Oddities for Amusement and Profit* (Chicago, 1988).

126. Rydell, *All the World's a Fair,* pp. 167, 143, 118.

127. Sander L. Gilman, *Difference and Pathology: Stereotypes of Sexuality, Race, and Madness* (Ithaca, 1985), p. 110.

128. James Serpell, "A Place with the Beasts," *Times Literary Supplement,* Mar. 11–17, 1988, 288.

129. Rydell, *All the World's a Fair,* pp. 93–94.

130. Hoxie, *A Final Promise,* pp. 93–94.

131. See William Cronon, *Nature's Metropolis: Chicago and the Great West* (New York, 1991), a highly original approach to frontier history that stresses the importance of ecological factors.

6. From Arielism to Modernism: Hemispheric Visions in the Age of Roosevelt and Wilson

1. Frederic Raphael, "Art in Action," *Times Literary Supplement,* Aug. 16, 1985, 894.

2. The quoted material comes from James D. Henderson, *Conservative Thought in Latin America: The Ideas of Laureano Gómez* (Athens, Ohio, 1988), p. 14. See also Fredrick B. Pike, *Hispanismo, 1898–1936: Spanish Conservatives and Liberals and Their Relations with Spanish America* (Notre Dame, Ind., 1971), esp. chs. 3, 6; and William

S. Stokes, "Democracy, Freedom, and Reform in Latin America," in *Freedom and Reform in Latin America*, ed. Fredrick B. Pike (Notre Dame, Ind., 1959), esp. pp. 120–125. On the use of Arielist symbolism by geographically dispersed Third World thinkers to express the ideal of societies wherein opposites would merge, see Garry Wills, "Goodby, Columbus," *New York Review of Books*, Nov. 22, 1990, 6–10. The blending-of-opposites ideal that so appealed to Arielists, wherever found, derived from the interpretations they attached to Shakespeare's play *The Tempest*.

3. Warren I. Susman, *Culture as History: The Transformation of American Society in the Twentieth Century* (1973; New York, 1985), p. 153. Susman notes that this definition of culture prevailed up to the 1930s in America. From that time on, culture tended to mean "all the things that a group of people inhabiting a common geographical area do, the ways they do things and the ways they think and feel about things, their material tools and their values and symbols." Susman's description coincides with the often cited T. S. Eliot definition of culture as all the characteristic activities and interests of a people, not merely the sum of several activities, but a way of life.

4. Mario Vargas Llosa, *Conversations in the Cathedral*, trans. Gregory Rabassa (New York, 1974), p. 259.

5. Quoted by Martin Green, *The Great American Adventure: Action Stories from Cooper to Mailer and What They Reveal About American Manhood* (Boston, 1984), p. 83.

6. Francis H. Gregory, *Three Years in the Pacific* (Philadelphia, 1834), p. 43; Isaac G. Strain, *Sketches of a Journey in Chili, and the Argentine Provinces in 1848* (New York, 1853), pp. 56–57.

7. Quoted by Cecil Robinson, *Mexico and the Hispanic Southwest in American Literature* (Tucson, 1977), pp. 25–26.

8. Robert W. Johannsen, *To the Halls of the Montezumas: The Mexican War in the American Imagination* (New York, 1985), p. 203. The inner quotation indicates Cooper's words.

9. John F. Reiger, *The Passing of the Great West: Selected Papers of George Bird Grinnell* (Norman, 1972), p. 435; Herman Melville, "Benito Cereno" (originally published in 1855), in *Great Short Works of Herman Melville*, ed. Warner Berthoff (New York, 1969), p. 313; Theodore Roosevelt, *Through the Brazilian Wilderness, with Illustrations from the Photographs of Kermit Roosevelt and Other Members of the Expedition* (New York, 1914), p. 46; Sumner Welles, *The Time for Decision* (New York, 1944), p. 188.

10. John L. Thomas, *Alternative America: Henry George, Edward Bellamy, Henry Demarest Lloyd, and the Adversary Tradition* (Cambridge, Mass., 1938), p. 302.

11. See T. J. Jackson Lears, "In Defense of Henry Adams," *Wilson Quarterly* 8 (1983): 89.

12. Quoted by Martin Green, *New York 1913: The Armory Show and the Paterson Strike Pageant* (New York, 1988), p. 6. Cram wrote the introduction to Henry Adams's influential *Mont-Saint Michel and Chartres* (Boston, 1905).

13. Thomas, *Alternative America*, pp. 258, 124.

14. See Ernest Earnest, *The Single Vision: The Alienation of American Intellec-*

tuals, 1910–1930 (New York, 1970), p. 56. See also David Hoeveler, Jr., *The New Humanism: A Critique of Modern America, 1900–1940* (Charlotte, N.C., 1970). For other indications of the questioning of democratic principles in the name of safeguarding culture, see Peter Conn, *The Divided Mind: Ideology and Imagination in America, 1898–1917* (New York, 1983), esp. p. 40; and Michael Kammen, *People of Paradox: An Inquiry Concerning the Origins of American Civilization* (New York, 1972), p. 129.

15. Stephen Fox, *The American Conservation Movement: John Muir and His Legacy* (Madison, 1985), p. 108.

16. Quoted by Jordan A. Schwarz, *Liberal: Adolf A. Berle and the Vision of an American Era* (New York, 1987), pp. 85, 89.

17. Henry F. May, *The End of American Innocence: The First Years of Our Own Time, 1912–1917* (Oxford, Eng., 1959), p. 7; Robert L. Beisner, *Twelve against Empire: Anti-Imperialists, 1898–1900* (Chicago, 1968), p. 38.

18. See Fox, *The American Conservation Movement*, pp. 346–347; and Susman, *Culture as History*, p. 117.

19. This is Eugene Genovese's description of the master class spawned by the plantation environment of the American South. See his *Political Economy of Slavery: Studies in the Economy and Society of the Slave South* (New York, 1965), p. 28.

20. Green, *The Great American Adventure*, p. 83.

21. Roosevelt, *Through the Brazilian Wilderness*, p. 324.

22. Ibid., p. 41.

23. Ibid., pp. 75, 152–153, 216, 225. Roosevelt, though, seems to have been of two minds in regard to Indian potential. On his pejorative assessment, see Frederick E. Hoxie, *A Final Promise: The Campaign to Assimilate the Indians, 1880–1920* (Lincoln, 1984), pp. 106–107.

24. See *The American West in Fiction*, ed. Jon Tuska (Lincoln, 1982), pp. 68–69.

25. Roosevelt once wrote of his father that he was "the only man of whom I was ever really afraid." And yet, he added, "we children adored him." See Robert M. Crunden, *Ministers of Reform: The Progressives' Achievement in American Civilization, 1889–1920* (New York, 1982), p. 3.

26. *El Mercurio* (Santiago de Chile), Nov. 20, 1913.

27. Theodore Roosevelt, *Ranch Life and the Hunting Trail* (New York, 1888), pp. 55–56.

28. Roosevelt, *Through the Brazilian Wilderness*, p. 70.

29. Roosevelt, quoted by Hoxie, *A Final Promise*, p. 105.

30. See Samuel P. Hays, *Conservation and the Gospel of Efficiency: The Progressive Conservation Movement, 1890–1920* (Cambridge, Mass., 1959), p. 145.

31. Dean Krakel quoted by Elizabeth Atwood Lawrence, *Rodeo: An Anthropologist Looks at the Wild and the Tame* (Chicago, 1982), p. 223.

32. See Fox, *The American Conservation Movement*, p. 126.

33. See Robert V. Hine, *The American West: An Interpretive History*, 2d ed. (Boston, 1984), pp. 202–205.

34. See Douglas Scott, "Conservation and the Sierra Club," *The Sierra Club: A Guide*, ed. Patrick Carr (n.p., 1989), pp. 21–22.

35. Quoted by John Milton Cooper, Jr., *The Warrior and the Priest: Woodrow Wilson and Theodore Roosevelt* (Cambridge, Mass., 1983), p. 246.

36. Quoted in ibid., p. 274.

37. Ibid.

38. See Arthur Link, *Woodrow Wilson and the Progressive Era* (New York, 1954), p. 79; and *Foreign Relations of the United States: The Lansing Papers, 1914–1920* (Washington, D.C., 1940), 2:469.

39. *Webster's New World Dictionary of the American Language,* College edition (Cleveland, New York, 1968), p. 1694.

40. Quoted by Lester D. Langley, *The Banana Wars: An Inner History of American Empire, 1900–1934* (Lexington, Ky., 1983), p. 101.

41. Ibid., pp. 107, 106–117.

42. Paul J. Vanderwood, "The Picture Postcard as Historical Evidence: Vera-cruz, 1914," *Americas* 45 (1988): 205. For fuller coverage see Vanderwood with Frank N. Samponaro, *Border Fury: A Picture Postcard Record of the Mexican Revolution and U.S. War Preparedness along the Border, 1910–1917* (Albuquerque, 1988).

43. May, *The End of American Innocence,* p. 358.

44. George Thorpe, quoted by Langley, *The Banana Wars,* p. 153.

45. Bruce J. Calder, *The Impact of Intervention: The Dominican Republic during the U.S. Occupation of 1916–1924* (Austin, 1984), p. xxxi.

46. Francis Paul Prucha, *The Great Father: The United States Government and the American Indians,* abr. ed. (Lincoln, 1986), pp. 196–197.

47. Had Theodore Roosevelt lived into the 1920s and 1930s, to say nothing of later decades, one hopes he would have revised an opinion expressed in *Through the Brazilian Wilderness,* pp. 46–47. "It is worthwhile for anti-militarists to ponder the fact that in every South American country where a really efficient army is developed, the increase in military efficiency goes hand in hand with a decrease in lawlessness and disorder, and a growing reluctance to settle internal disagreements by violence."

48. See Dondra Kathryn Wilson, "James Weldon Johnson Remembered on the Fiftieth Anniversary of His Death," *The Crisis Magazine, Eightieth Anniversary Issue,* Mar. 1989, 50–51.

49. Calder, *The Impact of Intervention,* pp. xxviii, 101, 107.

50. See Norman F. Cantor, *Twentieth-Century Culture: Modernism to Deconstruction* (New York, 1988), p. 7.

51. Quoted by Langley, *The Banana Wars,* p. 159.

52. Ibid., p. 174.

53. Quoted in ibid., p. 216.

54. Quoted by Green, *New York 1913,* p. 139.

55. See Crunden, *Ministers of Reform,* p. 108.

56. See May, *The End of American Innocence,* pp. 180–181.

57. For a detailed account see Green, *New York 1913,* ch. 7. For a much better analysis of the bridge that modernist intellectuals forged with the masses, see Steve Golin, *The Fragile Bridge: Paterson Silk Strike 1913* (Philadelphia, 1989).

58. May, *The End of American Innocence,* p. 317.

59. Quoted by Green, *New York 1913,* p. 95. See also *Echoes of Revolt: "The Masses" 1911–1917,* ed. William O'Neill (1966; Chicago, 1989).

60. See Leslie Fishbein, *Rebels in Bohemia: The Radicals of "The Masses," 1911–*

1917 (Chapel Hill, 1982), and Robert E. Humphrey, *Children of Fantasy: The First Rebels of Greenwich Village* (New York, 1978).

61. Quoted by Robert A. Rosenstone, *Romantic Revolutionary: A Biography of John Reed* (New York, 1975), p. 151.

62. Green, *New York 1913*, p. 220.

63. Important for providing background and perspective on primitivism are two insightful works: William Roseberry, *Anthropologists and Histories: Essays in Culture, History, and Political Economy* (New Brunswick, N.J., 1990), and (in a more impressionistic mode) Mariana Torgovnick, *Gone Primitive: Savage Intellects, Modern Lives* (Chicago, 1990). For good background insights on the the topic, see Bernard Sheehan, *Savagism and Civility: Indians and Englishmen in Colonial Virginia* (Cambridge, Eng., 1980).

64. See Edward Abrahams, *The Lyrical Left: Randolph Bourne, Alfred Stieglitz, and the Origins of Cultural Radicalism in America* (Charlottesville, Va., 1986), pp. 151, 162–164.

65. Crunden, *Ministers of Reform*, p. 114.

66. On the "introspective revolution," see Fred Weinstein and Gerald M. Platt, *The Wish to Be Free: Society, Psyche, and Value Change* (Berkeley, 1969), esp. pp. 136–137.

67. See Robert S. Ellwood, Jr., *Alternative Altars: Unconventional and Eastern Spirituality in America* (Chicago, 1979), p. 53. See also R. Lawrence Moore, *In Search of White Crows: Spiritualism, Parapsychology, and American Culture* (New York, 1977), p. 175; and James Webb, *The Harmonious Circle: The Lives and Work of G. I. Gurdjieff, P. D. Ouspensky, and Their Followers* (New York, 1980), pp. 301–392.

68. See Sharyn Rohlfsen Udall, *Modernist Painting in New Mexico, 1913–1935* (Albuquerque, 1984), p. xviii.

69. T. J. Jackson Lears, *No Place of Grace: Antimodernism and the Transformation of American Culture 1880–1940* (New York, 1981), p. 57.

7. The Twenties: Normalcy, Counterculture, and Clashing Perceptions of Latin America

1. Jake delivers this opinion in Willa Cather's *My Ántonia* (1918; Boston, 1949), p. 5.

2. Nell Irvin Painter, *Standing at Armageddon: The United States 1877–1919* (New York, 1987), p. 379.

3. Ibid., p. 377.

4. See John Higham, *Strangers in the Land: Patterns of American Nativism 1860–1925*, corrected ed. (New York, 1975), esp. pp. 173, 27; and George W. Stocking, Jr., *Race, Culture, and Evolution: Essays in the History of Anthropology* (New York, 1968), p. 289.

5. Kenneth Roberts, quoted by Higham, *Strangers in the Land*, p. 273.

6. See Edward J. Escobar, "The Los Angeles Police Department and the Mexican Workers: The Case of the 1913 Christmas Riot," in *Times of Challenge: Chicanos and Chicanas in American Society,* ed. Juan R. García, Julia Curry Rodríguez, and

Clara Lomas (Houston, 1988), pp. 101–114; W. Dirk Raat, *Revoltosos: Mexico's Rebels in the United States* (College Station, Tex., 1981), esp. pp. 22–24, 29–30, 54–57, 65–91, 217, 258–263, 275; Thomas E. Sheridan, *Los Tucsonenses: The Mexican Community in Tucson, 1854–1941* (Tucson, 1986), esp. pp. 208–310; and Frank H. Tucker, *The Frontier Spirit and Progress* (Chicago, 1980), p. 64. See also Sarah Deutsch's fine study *No Separate Refuge: Culture, Class, and Gender in an Anglo-Hispanic Frontier in the American Southwest, 1880–1940* (New York, 1987).

7. See Gary R. Mormino and George E. Pozzeta, *The Immigrant World of Ybor City: Italians and Their Latin Neighbors in Tampa, 1885–1985* (Urbana, 1987).

8. Henry F. May, *The End of American Innocence: The First Years of Our Own Time, 1912–1917* (Oxford, Eng., 1959), p. 394.

9. See David F. Musto, "Lessons of the First Cocaine Epidemic," *Wall Street Journal*, June 11, 1986.

10. Sheridan, *Los Tucsonenses*, p. 211.

11. See Anthony Lewis, "The Great Gatsby," *New York Times*, Aug. 6, 1987.

12. See George Black, *The Good Neighbor: How the United States Wrote the History of Central America and the Caribbean* (New York, 1988), p. 45; and "Our Man in Managua," *Nation*, Dec. 19, 1987, 759.

13. Quoted by Warren I. Susman, *Culture as History: The Transformation of American Society in the Twentieth Century* (New York, 1973), p. 105.

14. For the best overview see Geoffrey Perret, *America in the Twenties: A History* (New York, 1982).

15. See Edward Abrahams, *The Lyrical Left: Randolph Bourne, Alfred Stieglitz, and the Origins of Cultural Radicalism in America* (Charlottesville, Va., 1986), p. 6.

16. Alvin M. Josephy, *Now that the Buffalo's Gone* (New York, 1982), p. 119; and Emily Hahn, *Mabel: A Biography of Mabel Dodge Luhan* (Boston, 1977), pp. 160–161.

17. See Sharyn Rohlfsen Udall, *Modernist Painting in New Mexico, 1913–1935* (Albuquerque, 1984), p. 175; and Serge Guilbaut, *How New York Stole the Idea of Modern Art: Abstract Expressionism, Freedom, and the Cold War*, trans. Arthur Goldhammer (Chicago, 1983), p. 4.

18. See Carey McWilliams, *North from Mexico: The Spanish-Speaking People of the United States* (1949; New York, 1968), p. 233; and Elizabeth Broun, "Thomas Hart Benton: A Politician in Art," *Smithsonian Studies in American Art*, Spring 1987, 14.

19. See Bruce Kellner, *Carl Van Vechten and the Irreverent Decades* (Norman, 1968), esp. chs. 6, 9.

20. Richard Pells, *Radical Visions and American Dreams: Culture and Social Thought in the Depression Years* (New York, 1973), p. 65.

21. See Malcolm Cowley, *The Dream of the Golden Mountains: Remembering the 1930s* (1964; New York, 1981), p. 43.

22. Quoted by James Webb, *The Harmonious Circle: The Lives of G. I. Gurdjieff, P. D. Ouspensky, and Their Followers* (New York, 1980), p. 416. T. J. Jackson Lears, *No Place of Grace: Antimodernism and the Transformation of American Culture, 1800–1920* (New York, 1981), p. 146, notes that as early as the late nineteenth century "a link between childhood and the unconscious emerged."

23. Susman, *Culture as History*, p. 146.

24. Quoted in ibid., p. 143.

25. See David Nasaw, "Those Were the Days?" *Nation,* Jan. 22, 1990, 95, a review of Warren Goldstein, *Playing for Keeps: A History of Early Baseball* (Ithaca, 1988).

26. Psychiatrist Erik Erikson contends that people periodically go through cycles of exalting childhood, in part because childhood symbolizes the absence of a sense of separateness from other forms of humanity. Childhood equates with a sense of wholeness especially coveted in times when concern over alienation peaks. See Margaret Brennan-Gibson, "Erik Erikson and the 'Ethics of Survival,'" *Harvard Magazine* 87 (Nov.–Dec. 1984): 64.

27. See, for example, Alice Kessler-Harris, *Out to Work: A History of Wage-Earning Women in the United States* (New York, 1982). Kessler sees the 1920s as a turning point for women. More and more of them found employment in business, social services, and the professions, and more of them aspired to combine marriage and wage work.

28. See Leslie Fishbein, *Rebels in Bohemia: The Radicals of "The Masses," 1911–1917* (Chapel Hill, 1982), p. 137.

29. Joel Williamson, *The Crucible of Race: Black-White Relations in the American South since Emancipation* (New York, 1984), p. 498.

30. See Nathan Irvin Huggins, *Harlem Renaissance* (New York, 1971), p. 57.

31. Leslie Fiedler, *The Return of the Vanishing American* (New York, 1968), pp. 84–85.

32. Richard Chase, *The American Novel and Its Tradition* (Garden City, N.Y., 1957), p. 213.

33. Kristin Herzog, *Women, Ethnics, and Exotics: Images of Power in Mid-Nineteenth-Century American Fiction* (Knoxville, 1983), pp. 102, 115–116; Huggins, *Harlem Renaissance,* pp. 85–86.

34. Wyndham Lewis, *Paleface: The Philosophy of the "Melting Pot"* (1929; New York, 1969), pp. 225–226. The emphasis is in the original.

35. Huggins, *Harlem Renaissance,* p. 118.

36. Ibid., p. 274.

37. Arthur K. Moore, *The Primitive Mind: A Cultural Analysis of the Kentucky Frontiersman* (Lexington, Ky., 1957), p. 131.

38. D. G. Charlton, *New Images of the Natural in France: A Study in European Cultural History 1750–1800* (Cambridge, Eng., 1984), p. 113; Dorothy Scarborough, *In the Land of Cotton* (New York, 1923), p. ix.

39. Huggins, *Harlem Renaissance,* pp. 89, 91; George M. Fredrickson, *The Black Image in the White Mind: The Debate on Afro-American Character and Destiny, 1817–1914* (New York, 1971), p. 328.

40. Weston La Barre, *The Peyote Cult* (New York, 1975), p. 167; Alan R. Velie, *Four American Indian Literary Masters* (Norman, 1982), p. 148.

41. Josephy, *Now That the Buffalo's Gone,* p. 91.

42. Udall, *Modernist Painting in New Mexico,* p. xviii; Robert V. Hine, *The American West: An Interpretive History,* 2d ed. (Boston, 1984), p. 2; Susman, *Culture as History,* p. 307, n. 81.

43. Udall, *Modernist Painting in New Mexico,* p. 172.

44. Kellner, *Carl Van Vechten,* p. 199. Mabel's close friend—most of the time—

and confidant Hutchins Hapgood, an important literary figure of the period, also accompanied the revelers on many occasions.

45. Quoted by Douglas C. McGill, "At the Met, a Hudson River Revival," *New York Times,* Oct. 8, 1987.

46. Thomas James, *Three Years among the Mexicans and Indians* (1822: Philadelphia, 1962), p. 104.

47. Lois P. Rudnick, *Mabel Dodge Luhan: New Woman, New Worlds* (Albuquerque, 1984), pp. 149, 150–159. While Rudnick's is the better documented biography, Emily Hahn's *Mabel* often offers penetrating insights.

48. See Donald T. Critchlow, *The Brookings Institution, 1916–1952: Expertise and the Public Interest in a Democratic Society* (DeKalb, Ill., 1985), p. 89; Lawrence C. Kelly, *The Assault on Assimilation: John Collier and the Origins of Indian Policy Reform* (Albuquerque, 1983), p. 375; and Kelly, "John Collier and the Indian New Deal: An Assessment," in *Indian-White Relations: A Persistent Paradox,* ed. Jane F. Smith and Robert M. Kvasnicka (Washington, D.C., 1981), pp. 229–230.

49. Kelly, *The Assault on Assimilation,* p. 16; John Collier, *From Every Zenith: A Memoir* (Denver, 1962), p. 116.

50. On Mabel Dodge Luhan's altogether favorable assessment of Collier, formed originally when the two became friends in New York City, see her *Movers and Shakers* (1935; Albuquerque, 1985): "As he could not seem to love his own kind of people, and as he was full of a reformer's enthusiasm for humanity, he turned to other races and worked for them. . . . Simply, he tried to stem the ponderous tide of Americanization" (p. 276). Mabel's assessment is in some ways equally applicable to herself.

51. John Collier, Jr., foreword to Kelly, *The Assault on Assimilation,* pp. xii–xiii.

52. John Collier, "The Red Atlantis," *Survey* 48 (Oct. 1922): 16. See also Kenneth R. Philp, *John Collier's Crusade for Indian Reform, 1920–1954* (Tucson, 1977), p. 172.

53. In a Sept. 1, 1931, letter to Lewis Meriam, Collier wrote: "We have Indian groups richer in their heritage than any in Mexico, and (this is a mere impression of course) more virile than any" (John Collier Papers, Yale University Library, New Haven). I am grateful to Donald T. Critchlow for providing me a copy of Collier's letter.

54. Kelly, *The Assault on Assimilation,* p. 11. On Collier's mystical visions of Indian culture and the Native American's cosmic consciousness, see his *On the Gleaming Way* (1949; Chicago, 1962).

55. See Critchlow, *The Brookings Institution,* pp. 88–89.

56. See *Navigating the Rapids, 1918–1971: From the Papers of Adolf A. Berle, Jr.,* ed. Beatrice Bishop Berle and Travis Beal Jacobs (New York, 1973), p. 15. See also the Max Ascoli introduction to this work, pp. xvii–xviii.

57. See Jordan A. Schwarz, *Liberal: Adolf A. Berle and the Vision of an American Era* (New York, 1987), p. 41.

58. Herbert Eugene Bolton, *Wider Horizons of American History* (New York, 1939), p. 98.

59. See Cecil Robinson, *Mexico and the Hispanic Southwest in American Literature* (Tucson, 1977), p. 337. During her ten years in Santa Fe until her death in 1934,

Austin wrote eight books, including *American Rhythm: Studies and Reexpressions of Amerindian Songs* (Boston, 1930) and her autobiography *Earth Horizon* (New York, 1932). She is best known for her *Land of Little Rain* (Boston, 1903).

60. For her version of the relationship, see Mabel Dodge Luhan, *Lorenzo in Taos* (New York, 1935).

61. D. H. Lawrence, *The Plumed Serpent* (London, 1926), p. 444. Out of Lawrence's visit to Mexico also came *Mornings in Mexico* (London, 1927), a short work in which the author reveals some of his reactions first to Mexico and then to New Mexico.

62. Helen Delpar, "Goodby to the 'Greaser': Mexico, the MPPDA, and Derogatory Films, 1922–1926," *The Journal of Popular Film and Television* 12 (Spring 1984): 35.

63. See McWilliams, *North from Mexico*, pp. 112–113.

64. Robinson, *Mexico and the Hispanic Southwest*, p. 211.

65. Langston Hughes, *I Wonder as I Wander* (New York, 1956), p. 291.

66. Helen Delpar, "North American Travelers and the 'Vogue of Things Mexican,' 1920–1932," pp. 10–11. Professor Delpar kindly provided a copy of this valuable unpublished paper.

67. See John A. Britton, "In Defense of Revolution: American Journalists in Mexico, 1920–29," *Journalism History* 5 (1978–79): 124–136; and William Spratling, *File on Spratling: An Autobiography* (Boston, 1967), p. 58.

68. Quotations of American travelers to Russia are taken from Paul Hollander, *Political Pilgrims: Travels of Western Intellectuals to the Soviet Union, China, and Cuba* (New York, 1981), pp. 131, 134–135.

69. Written in collaboration with Marian Tyler, Stuart Chase's *Mexico: A Study of the Two Americas* (New York, 1931) has, as its strongest feature, illustrations drawn by Diego Rivera.

70. Delpar, "North American Travelers," p. 14.

71. Chase, *Mexico*, pp. 327, 199, 16, 9.

72. Ibid., pp. 314–315, 311, 323, 327.

73. See Donald C. Hodges, *Intellectual Foundations of the Nicaraguan Revolution* (Austin, 1986), esp. chs. 2, 3.

74. See John A. Britton, *Carleton Beals: A Radical Journalist in Latin America* (Albuquerque, 1987).

75. See Carleton Beals, *Fire on the Andes* (Philadelphia, 1934).

76. See Fredrick B. Pike, *The Politics of the Miraculous in Peru: Haya de la Torre and the Spiritualist Tradition* (Lincoln, 1986), esp. chs. 4–7.

77. For an outstanding essay reviewing the most important literature on and by Stimson, see Alan Brinkley, "The Good Old Days," *New York Review of Books*, Jan. 17, 1991, 24–30. Not likely to be surpassed as a biography is Godfrey Hodgson, *The Colonel: The Life and Wars of Henry Stimson, 1867–1950* (New York, 1990).

78. On Frank's fiction see William Bittner, *The Novels of Waldo Frank* (Philadelphia, 1958).

79. On Frank see Michael Ogorzaly, "Waldo Frank: Prophet of Hispanic Regeneration," Ph.D. diss., University of Notre Dame (1982); and Pike, *Politics of the Miraculous in Peru*, ch. 9.

80. See Webb, *The Harmonious Circle*, pp. 271–272.

81. See "The Spanish Element in Our Nationality," written in 1883, in Walt Whitman, *Complete Poetry and Collected Prose* (New York, 1982), pp. 1146–1147. In earlier writings, Whitman had, like most Americans, assumed that the Indians would ultimately vanish, leaving scarcely a trace of their existence. By 1883, though, he had changed his mind.

82. See Gershom Scholem, *On the Kabbalah and Its Symbolism*, trans. Ralph Manheim (New York, 1969), pp. 108, 130. Note that several spellings are acceptable for *cabala*. On Jewish millennialism as it flowered in early twentieth-century America, see Werner Sollors, "Literature and Ethnicity," *Harvard Encyclopedia of American Ethnic Groups*, ed. Stephan Thernstrom (Cambridge, Mass., 1980), pp. 650–653.

83. See Williamson, *The Crucible of Race*, p. 336.

84. Van Wyck Brooks makes this point in what is arguably his best book, *America's Coming of Age* (New York, 1915). See Lears, *No Place of Grace*, p. 225.

85. Whitman, "Song of Myself," in *Complete Poetry and Collected Prose*, p. 203.

86. Frank's regard for Latin American literature was confined almost exclusively to works that stressed the molding influence of the natural environment on humans. As a result, he ignored the modernist, European influences that had, by the 1920s and 1930s, begun to shape the work of many Latin American writers. See Irene Rostagno, "Waldo Frank's Crusade for Latin American Literature," *Americas* 46 (1989): 53–69. Frank's obsession with the influence of telluric forces on character also drew him to Jean Toomer's novel *Cane*. Instrumental in arranging the 1923 publication of this work, Frank provided an introduction. Not long afterward his wife had an affair with Toomer. See Joel Williamson, *New People: Miscegenation and Mulattoes in the United States* (New York, 1980), p. 150. About this time Toomer also seems to have had an affair with Mabel Dodge Luhan in New Mexico. Mabel had encouraged him to come to Taos to spread the spiritualist message of G. I. Gurdjieff and P. D. Ouspensky in which she was for a while vitally interested.

87. See *Waldo Frank in America Hispana*, ed. J. J. Bernardete (New York, 1930).

88. See Waldo Frank, *South American Journey* (New York, 1943), pp. 47–57.

89. See Cowley, *Dream of the Golden Mountains*, p. 273.

90. Waldo Frank, *America Hispana: A Portrait and a Prospect* (New York, 1932), p. 370.

91. *Memoirs of Waldo Frank*, ed. Alan Trachtenberg (Amherst, 1973), p. 134.

92. This was Frank's message to Argentines, as described by Doris Meyer in *Victoria Ocampo: Against the Wind and the Tide* (New York, 1979), p. 105.

93. See Robert Spiller et al., *The Literary History of the United States* (New York, 1948), p. 1387.

94. See Rostagno, "Waldo Frank's Crusade," p. 41.

8. The Quest for Equilibrium with Nature: The Good Neighbor Policy, 1933–1945

1. A. W. Dunn, "Uncle Sam on Police Duty," *The Review of Reviews* 53 (Apr. 1911): 465.

2. See Henry F. May, *The End of American Innocence: The First Years of Our Own Time, 1912–1917* (Oxford, Eng., 1959), pp. 42–43.

3. Quoted in *Americanizing the American Indians: Writings of the "Friends of the Indians" 1890–1900*, ed. Francis Paul Prucha (Cambridge, Mass., 1973), p. 270.

4. Bruce J. Calder, *The Impact of Intervention: The Dominican Republic during the U.S. Occupation of 1916–1924* (Austin, 1984), p. 62.

5. See Henry L. Stimson, *The United States and the Other American Republics: A Discussion of Recent Events* (Washington, D.C., 1931), p. 154.

6. Francis Paul Prucha, *The Great Father: The United States Government and the American Indians,* abr. ed. (Lincoln, 1986), pp. 222, 228.

7. Quoted by Lester D. Langley, *The Banana Wars: An Inner History of American Empire 1900–1934* (Lexington, Ky., 1983), p. 175.

8. Sumner Welles, *Naboth's Vineyard: The Dominican Republic 1844–1924* (New York, 1928), 2:927–928.

9. See George W. Stocking, Jr., *Race, Culture, and Evolution: Essays in the History of Anthropology* (1968; Chicago, 1982), p. 227; and Frederick E. Hoxie, *A Final Promise: The Campaign to Assimilate the Indians, 1880–1920* (Lincoln, 1984), p. 137.

10. Quoted by Stocking, *Race, Culture, and Evolution,* p. 148.

11. Ibid., p. 194.

12. See Philip Gleason, "Americans All: World War II and the Shaping of American Identity," *Review of Politics* 43 (1981): 491, 514.

13. Strong biographies that illuminate the entire period by studying the lives of two of its most important anthropologists are Margaret M. Caffrey, *Ruth Benedict: Strangers in the Land* (Austin, 1989), and Regna Darnell, *Edward Sapir: Linguist, Anthropologist, Humanist* (Berkeley, 1990).

14. See Elizabeth Kendall, *The Runaway Bride: Hollywood Romantic Comedy in the 1930s* (New York, 1990), passim.

15. Alistair Hennessy, "Reshaping the Brazilian Past," *Times Literary Supplement,* July 14–20, 1989, 764.

16. See Hans Huth, *Nature and the American: Three Centuries of Changing Attitudes* (Lincoln, 1957), p. 193.

17. John L. Moore, "Bad Days at 'Big Dry,'" *New York Times Magazine,* Aug. 14, 1988, 26.

18. See Lee Rosson DeLong, *Nature's Forms/Nature's Forces: The Art of Alexandre Hogue* (Norman, 1984), p. 24.

19. Quoted by William Kennedy, "'My Work is No Good,'" a review of John Steinbeck's *Working Days: The Journal of "The Grapes of Wrath," 1938–1941*, ed. Robert DeMott (New York, 1989), in *New York Times Book Review,* Apr. 9, 1989, 45.

20. Henry A. Wallace, *Democracy Reborn,* selected from the Public Papers and edited with an introduction by Russell Lord (New York, 1944), p. 116.

21. John Collier, *On the Gleaming Way* (1949; Chicago, 1962), p. 64.

22. Huth, *Nature and the American,* p. 193; Edward Abbey, *Desert Solitaire: A Season in the Wilderness* (New York, 1968), p. 190.

23. For excellent biographies see T. H. Watkins, *Righteous Pilgrim: The Life and Times of Harold L. Ickes* (New York, 1990), and Graham White and John Maze, *Harold Ickes of the New Deal: His Private Life and Public Career* (Cambridge, Mass., 1985).

24. See David E. Shi, *The Simple Life: Plain Living and High Thinking in American Culture* (New York, 1985), p. 235.

25. See Richard Lowitt, *The New Deal and the West* (Bloomington, 1984), passim.

26. Shi, *The Simple Life*, p. 238.

27. Stephen Fox, *The American Conservation Movement: John Muir and His Legacy* (Madison, 1985), p. 217.

28. See Fredrick B. Pike, "Corporatism and Latin American–United States Relations," in *The New Corporatism: Social-Political Structures in the Iberian World*, ed. Pike and Thomas Stritch (Notre Dame, Ind., 1974), pp. 144–149.

29. See Josephus Daniels, *Shirt-Sleeve Diplomat* (Chapel Hill, 1947), p. 309.

30. See E. David Cronon, *Josephus Daniels in Mexico* (Madison, 1960), p. 113.

31. See Waldo Frank, *Ustedes y nosotros: Nuevo mensaje a Ibero América*, trans., from a manuscript written in English, by Frieda Weber (Buenos Aires, 1942), pp. 165–167.

32. Wallace, *Democracy Reborn*, p. 159.

33. Ibid., pp. 230–231.

34. Henry A. Wallace, *The Price of Freedom* (Washington, D.C., 1940), p. 49.

35. Wallace, *Democracy Reborn*, p. 138; and *The Price of Freedom*, p. 9.

36. Henry A. Wallace, *Soviet Asia Mission*, with the collaboration of Andrew J. Steiger (New York, 1946), p. 20; and *Democracy Reborn*, p. 44.

37. Fox, *The American Conservation Movement*, p. 199.

38. Daniels, *Shirt-Sleeve Diplomat*, p. 347.

39. Quoted by Cronon, *Josephus Daniels in Mexico*, p. 85.

40. Daniels, *Shirt-Sleeve Diplomat*, p. 25.

41. Ibid., p. 308; Daniels, quoted by Cronon, *Josephus Daniels in Mexico*, p. 130.

42. Cronon, *Josephus Daniels in Mexico*, p. 130; Daniels, *Shirt-Sleeve Diplomat*, p. 199.

43. Frank Tannenbaum, *Peace by Revolution: An Interpretation of Mexico* (New York, 1933), p. 6.

44. See John A. Britton, "In Defense of Revolution: American Journalists in Mexico, 1920–29," *Journalism History* 7 (1978–79): 124–136.

45. On Tannenbaum's meeting with Haya de la Torre, see *Secretos electorales del APRA: Correspondencia y documentos de 1931*, ed. Thomas M. Davies, Jr., and Víctor Villanueva (Lima, Peru, 1982), pp. 17–19. On Frank's 1942 meeting with Haya, see Waldo Frank, *South American Journey* (New York, 1943), p. 383.

46. See Daniels, *Shirt-Sleeve Diplomat*, p. 258.

47. Berle, *Navigating the Rapids, 1918–1971: From the Papers of Adolf A. Berle, Jr.*, ed. Beatrice Bishop Berle and Travis Beal Jacobs (New York, 1973), pp. 212, 561.

48. Jordan A. Schwarz, *Liberal: Adolf A. Berle and the Vision of an American Era* (New York, 1987), pp. 85–89, 104; Berle, *Navigating the Rapids*, p. 28.

49. Schwarz, *Liberal*, p. 79.

50. Berle, *Navigating the Rapids*, p. 524.

51. Ibid., p. 629.

52. John L. Thomas, *Alternative America: Henry George, Edward Bellamy, Henry Demarest Lloyd, and the Adversary Tradition* (Cambridge, Mass., 1983), p. 260; Raymond Carr, *Puerto Rico: A Colonial Experiment* (New York, 1984), esp. pp. 64–68.

See also Arturo Morales Carrión, *Puerto Rico: A Political and Cultural History* (New York, 1983), esp. ch. 13.

53. See the concluding chapter of Robert Herrick's autobiographical novel *Waste* (New York, 1924), esp. pp. 405–406, 418–420. Cynthia Lane, one of the novel's central characters, is modeled partially on Mabel Dodge Luhan.

54. See Daniel Aaron's introduction to Robert Herrick's novel *Memoirs of an American Citizen* (1900; New York, 1970), pp. v–xxvi. A helpful biography is Blake Nevius, *Robert Herrick: The Development of a Novelist* (Berkeley, 1970).

55. Copland letters of Dec. 5, 1932, to Virgil Thomson and of Jan. 13, 1933, to Mary Lescaze, in Aaron Copland and Vivian Perlis, *Copland, 1900 through 1942* (New York, 1984), pp. 214, 216.

56. Quoted in Philip Ramey's program notes for the CBS Masterworks compact disc MK 42429, "Copland Conducts Copland."

57. Edward Jablonski, *Gershwin, A Biography* (New York, 1987), pp. 13, 66, 227.

58. George Black, "The Long Goodbye," *Nation*, Feb. 11, 1991, 166.

59. See Jason Berry, Jonathan Foose, and Tad Jones, *Up from the Cradle of Jazz: New Orleans Music since World War II* (Athens, Ga., 1986), pp. 10–11.

60. See Robert Parker's notes to BBC compact disc 604, "Jelly Roll Morton: Great Original Performances, 1926–1934."

61. On this subject see John Storm Roberts, *The Latin Tinge: The Impact of Latin Music on the United States* (New York, 1979).

62. James Lincoln Collier, *Duke Ellington* (New York, 1987), pp. 163, 220.

63. "Rhumboogie" is by Dan Raye and Hugh Prince and was copyrighted by MCA Music Publishing, a division of MCA, Inc. (ASCAP).

64. See Richard Pells, *Radical Visions and American Dreams: Culture and Social Thought in the Depression Years* (New York, 1973), p. 65. For the overall setting see Fredrick B. Pike, "The Background to the Civil War in Spain and the U.S. Response to the War," in *The Spanish Civil War 1936–39: American Hemispheric Perspectives*, ed. Mark Falcoff and Pike (Lincoln, 1982), pp. 10–37.

65. See Paul Hollander, *The Survival of the Adversary Culture: Social Criticism and Political Escapism in American Society* (New Brunswick, N.J., 1988), p. 103, critiquing Vivian Gornick's explanation for the Marxist vogue among some American intellectuals in the 1930s in her book *The Romance of Communism* (New York, 1977).

66. Quoted in *Voices against Tyranny: Writings of the Spanish Civil War*, ed. John Miller (New York, 1986), p. 146.

67. See Stanley T. Williams, *The Spanish Background to American Literature* (New Haven, 1955), 1 : 239–240.

68. John A. Britton, *Carleton Beals: A Radical Journalist in Latin America* (Albuquerque, 1987), p. 159.

69. For classic descriptions of the economic priorities present even from the outset in the Good Neighbor era, see Lloyd Gardner, *Economic Aspects of New Deal Diplomacy* (Madison, 1964), and David Green, *The Containment of Latin America* (New York, 1971).

70. On the military aspects of reciprocity, among other topics, see Bryce Wood's fine study *The Making of the Good Neighbor Policy* (New York, 1961). Specifically on security, see David G. Haglund, *Latin America and the Transformation of*

U.S. Strategic Thought, 1936–1940 (Albuquerque, 1984). Robert Dallek judiciously blends economic and security factors in his *Franklin D. Roosevelt and American Foreign Policy 1932–1945* (New York, 1979). Dallek's study boasts a strong section on the Good Neighbor policy. Irwin F. Gellman also does justice both to economic and security considerations in his *Good Neighbor Diplomacy: United States Policies in Latin America, 1933–1945* (Baltimore, 1979). Interspersed throughout Warren F. Kimball's *The Juggler: Franklin Roosevelt as Wartime Statesman* (Princeton, 1991) are penetrating assessments of FDR's Latin American policy.

71. Bryce Wood in *The Dismantling of the Good Neighbor Policy* (Austin, 1985) concentrates on Argentina, Bolivia, and Chile as he explains the end of a unique period in hemispheric relations. For an overall assessment, there may be no more valuable single volume than Irwin Gellman's *Good Neighbor Diplomacy: United States Policy in Latin America, 1933–1945* (Baltimore, 1979).

72. What I call "informal empire," Whitney T. Perkins designates "real empire." In *Constraints of Empire: The United States and the Caribbean Interventions* (Westport, Conn., 1981), Perkins argues that America's real empire in the Caribbean was created by U.S. banana barons and entrepreneurs in collaboration with native capitalists. By World War II, the informal, or real, empire operated, I believe, throughout Latin America.

73. On Indian opposition to Collier's reforms, see W. David Baird, "Commentary," in *Indian-White Relations: A Persistent Paradox*, ed. Jane F. Smith and Robert M. Kvasnicka (Washington, D.C., 1981), pp. 217–220; Lawrence C. Kelly, "John Collier and the Indian New Deal: An Assessment," ibid., p. 239; and Kenneth R. Philp, *John Collier's Crusade for Indian Reform, 1920–1945* (Tucson, 1977), pp. 177–194.

74. Sumner Welles, *Where Are We Heading?* (New York, 1946), pp. 236–237.

75. Quoted by Ian Buruma, "Us and the Others," a review of John W. Dower, *War without Mercy: Race and Power in the Pacific War* (New York, 1986), in *New York Review of Books*, Aug. 14, 1986, 23. Dower's book describes in detail the torrents of racism that World War II released.

76. See John Collier, Jr., foreword to Lawrence C. Kelly, *The Assault on Assimilation: John Collier and the Origins of Indian Policy Reform* (Albuquerque, 1983), pp. xx–xxii.

77. See George Black, *The Good Neighbor: How the United States Wrote the History of Central America and the Caribbean* (New York, 1988), p. 170; and Jennifer Dunning, "Singers and Dancers Shake, Swing, and Sway to a Brazilian Beat," *New York Times*, Mar. 1, 1988, 15.

78. The song "Rum and Coca Cola," copyright by SBK Feist, Catalogue, Inc. (ASCAP), is by Jerry Sullivan, Paul Baron, and Morey Amsterdam. On background and ramifications of the rum-and-Coca-Cola iconography, see Cynthia Enloe, *Bananas, Beaches, and Bases: Making Feminist Sense of International Politics* (Berkeley, 1990).

79. For the best succinct account of the "zoot-suit riots," see Carey McWilliams, *North from Mexico: The Spanish-Speaking People of the United States* (Philadelphia, 1949), pp. 244–258. For a more extensive treatment, see Mauricio Mazón, *The Zoot-Suit Riots: The Psychology of Symbolic Annihilation* (Austin, 1984).

80. Captain Ayres is quoted by Mario T. García, *Mexican Americans: Leadership, Ideology, and Identity, 1930–1960* (New Haven, 1989), p. 172.

81. Black, *The Good Neighbor,* p. 61.

82. Joel Williamson, *The Crucible of Race: Black-White Relations in the American South since Emancipation* (New York, 1984), p. 440.

83. Quoted by Serge Guilbaut, *How New York Stole the Idea of Modern Art: Abstract Expressionism, Freedom, and the Cold War,* trans. Arthur Goldhammer (Chicago, 1983), p. 107.

9. America's Postwar Generation: New Variations on Old Themes

1. Quoted by Max Hastings, "Questionable Truths," *Times Literary Supplement,* Mar. 29, 1985, 313.

2. David E. Shi, *The Simple Life: Plain Living and High Thinking in American Culture* (New York, 1985), p. 248. See also William L. O'Neill, *American High: The Years of Confidence, 1945–1960* (New York, 1989).

3. On the post–World War II Horatio Alger cult, see Gary Scharnhorst with Jack Bales, *The Lost Life of Horatio Alger, Jr.* (Bloomington, 1985).

4. For the classic study of the "need to achieve" as an essential ingredient of American culture, see David McClellan, *The Achieving Society* (New York, 1961).

5. See Warren I. Susman, *Culture as History: The Transformation of American Society in the Twentieth Century* (New York, 1973), p. 209.

6. "Civilization" was written by Bob Hilliard and Carl Sigman, and published by Edward H. Morris and Co., a division of MPL Communications, Inc. (ASCAP). Copyright was held by Danny Kaye and ASCAP.

7. See James Atlas, "The Changing World of New York Intellectuals," *New York Times Magazine,* Aug. 25, 1985, 52.

8. Richard H. Pells, *The Liberal Mind in a Conservative Age: American Intellectuals in the 1940s and 1950s* (New York, 1985), pp. 120–121.

9. Quoted by Peter Redgrove, "Tapping the Great Mind," *Times Literary Supplement,* Nov. 30, 1984, 1366.

10. Stephen Fox, *The American Conservation Movement: John Muir and His Legacy* (Madison, 1985), p. 225.

11. See Seth Shulman, "Nuclear Power: The Dilemma of Decommissioning," *Smithsonian* 20 (Oct. 1989): 57, 61.

12. Roderick Nash, *Wilderness and the American Mind,* 3d ed. (New Haven, 1982), p. 65.

13. See Stephen Holden, "Peggy Lee at 67," *New York Times,* Jan. 31, 1988.

14. See Stephen Thorne, "Fighting for the Status Quo," *Times Literary Supplement,* Apr. 7–13, 1989, 436.

15. See Richard J. Walton, *Henry Wallace, Harry Truman, and the Cold War* (New York, 1976).

16. Pells, *The Liberal Mind,* p. 66.

17. John Patrick Diggins, *The Proud Decades: America in War and Peace, 1941–1960* (New York, 1988), p. 142.

18. On the U.S. role in ousting Arbenz, and some of the mainly unanticipated long-term consequences, see Richard H. Immerman, *The CIA in Guatemala: The Foreign Policy of Intervention* (Austin, 1982), and Stephen Schlesinger and Stephen Kinzer, *Bitter Fruit: The Untold Story of the American Coup in Guatemala* (New York, 1982). For context see Stephen R. Rabe, *Eisenhower and Latin America: The Foreign Policy of Anticommunism* (Chapel Hill, 1988).

19. Theodore Thomas, quoted in Joseph Horowitz, *Understanding Toscanini: How He Became an American Culture-God and Helped Create a New Audience for Old Music* (New York, 1987), p. 377.

20. Ibid., p. 315.

21. Quoted by Joan Peyser, *Bernstein: A Biography* (New York, 1987), p. 337.

22. *Rolling Stone Illustrated History of Rock and Roll* (New York, 1980), pp. 125–126, 58.

23. Todd Gitlin, *The Sixties: Years of Hope, Days of Rage* (New York, 1987), p. 47.

24. Quoted in ibid., p. 47.

25. See Philip H. Bufithis, *Norman Mailer* (New York, 1978), esp. pp. 58–62; and Stanley T. Gutman, *Mankind in Barbary: The Individual and Society in the Novels of Norman Mailer* (Hanover, N.J., 1975), esp. pp. 68–79, 85–87, 92, 110.

26. For brief, level-headed references to Castañeda, see Cecil Robinson, *Mexico and the Hispanic Southwest in American Literature* (Tucson, 1977), p. 292; and Ronald Sukenick, *Down and In: Life in the Underground* (New York, 1987), esp. p. 225.

27. Allen Ginsberg insisted on distinguishing between the Beat Generation, "with its philosophy of love and tenderness, and the beatniks, who were mostly weekend bohemians out for a good time." See Barry Miles, *Ginsberg: A Biography* (New York, 1989), p. 348. The book provides exceedingly valuable insights into many aspects of the counterculture.

28. See John Lahr, "King of Hiposie," a review of Albert Goldman, *The Lives of John Lennon* (New York, 1988), in *New York Times Book Review*, Sept. 25, 1988, 7.

29. This description of Dr. Spock's objective, provided by Diggins, *The Proud Decades*, pp. 201–202, applies just as accurately to Ashley Montagu.

30. Quoted by Godfrey Hodgson, *America in Our Time* (New York, 1976), p. 312.

31. See Jefferson Morley, "Camelot and Dallas: The Entangling Kennedy Myths," *Nation*, Dec. 12, 1988, 646.

32. See Crawford Young, "Patterns of Social Conflict," *Daedalus*, Spring 1982, 71.

33. See Steven M. Tipton, *Getting Saved from the Sixties: Moral Meaning in Conversion and Cultural Change* (Berkeley, 1982), pp. 15, 16–17, 20.

34. See V. S. Naipaul, *A Bend in the River* (New York, 1979), p. 138.

35. This description by Carleton Beals of the 1920s counterculture is applicable to that of the 1960s as well. Beals is quoted by John A. Britton, *Carleton Beals: A Radical Journalist in Latin America* (Albuquerque, 1987), p. 186.

36. Paul Hollander, *The Survival of the Adversary Culture: Social Criticism and Political Escapism in American Society* (New Brunswick, N.J., 1988), p. 112.

37. See William H. Whyte, Jr., *The Organization Man* (New York, 1956), and Sloan Wilson, *The Man in the Gray Flannel Suit* (New York, 1955).

38. Quoted by Britton, *Carleton Beals*, p. 219.

39. Ernesto Cardenal, quoted by Paul Hollander, *Political Pilgrims: Travels of Western Intellectuals to the Soviet Union, China, and Cuba* (New York, 1981), p. 209.

40. See Waldo Frank, *Cuba: Prophetic Island* (New York, 1961), passim.

41. Hollander, *Political Pilgrims*, p. 209.

42. The term "democratized shamanism" comes from Ake Hultkrantz, *Belief and Worship in Native North America*, ed. Christopher Vecsey (Syracuse, 1981), p. 75.

43. See R. M. Bernardo, *The Theory of Moral Incentives in Cuba* (Tuscaloosa, Ala., 1971), and *Man and Socialism in Cuba: The Great Debate*, ed. Bernard Silverman (New York, 1972).

44. See the concluding page of Graham Greene's novel *The Comedians* (New York, 1966), wherein the Haitian character Dr. Magiot presents an apologia for communism that purports to transcend mere rationality.

45. R. Laurence Moore, *In Search of White Crows: Spiritualism, Parapsychology, and American Culture* (New York, 1977), p. 220.

46. For indications of the wildly disparate elements that went into the New Left and the counterculture, often causing different Americans to see different virtues in the Cuban revolution, two of the best books to consult (in addition to those already cited) are Maurice Isserman, *If I Had a Hammer: The Death of the Old Left and the Birth of the New Left* (New York, 1987), and Allen J. Matusow, *The Unraveling of America: A History of Liberalism in the 1960s* (New York, 1984). For an excellent review essay dealing with some of the more important sources, see Maurice Isserman, "The Not-So-Dark and Bloody Ground: New Works on the 1960s," *American Historical Review* 94 (1989): 990–1010.

47. See John Hellman, *American Myth and the Legacy of Vietnam* (New York, 1986), pp. 84–86.

48. Susan Sontag, *Trip to Hanoi* (New York, 1968), pp. 15, 69, 77.

49. Harriet Martineau, *Dawn Island* (London, 1845), p. 9, quoted by Patrick Brantlinger, *Rule of Darkness: British Literature and Imperialism, 1830–1914* (Ithaca, 1988), p. 32.

10. Change and Permanence in Myths and Stereotypes: Civilization and Nature toward Century's End

1. John le Carré, *The Secret Pilgrim* (New York, 1991), p. 334.

2. Alfred Crosby, *America's Forgotten Pandemic: The Influenza of 1918* (1976; Cambridge, Eng., 1989), p. xi.

3. See Edward Tenner, "Warning: Nature May Be Hazardous to Your Health," *Harvard Magazine*, Sept.–Oct., 1987, 34–38. See also David Vogel, "The Politics of the Environment, 1970–1987," *Wilson Quarterly* 11 (Autumn 1987): 65.

4. Marc Reisner, *Cadillac Desert: The American West and Its Disappearing Water* (New York, 1986), pp. 453–455.

5. See Dennis Farney, "Abiding Frontier: On the Great Plains Life Becomes a Fight for Water and Survival," *Wall Street Journal*, Aug. 16, 1989.

6. See Craig Miner, *West of Wichita: Settling the High Plains of Kansas, 1865–1890* (Lawrence, Kan., 1986).

7. Webb sounded his warning in the article "The American West: Perpetual Mirage," published in the May 1957 *Harper's* magazine.

8. See John McPhee, *The Control of Nature* (New York, 1989), pp. 3–93.

9. Barnard L. Collier, "Crusader on the Beach," *New York Times Magazine,* Dec. 4, 1988, 77.

10. See James Trefil, "Global Warming and a Scientific Free-for-All," *Smithsonian* 21 (Dec. 1991): 28–37.

11. Edward Hoagland, "In Pursuit of John Muir," in *On Nature: Nature, Landscape, and Natural History,* ed. Daniel Halpern (San Francisco, 1987), pp. 55–56.

12. Aidan Foster-Carter letter, *Economist,* Aug. 3–9, 1991: 6.

13. On archetypal masculine and feminine mythology (cited first in ch. 1, n.130), see Robert May, *Sex and Fantasy: Patterns of Male and Female Development* (New York, 1980), ch. 1.

14. Edward Seckerson, "Music I Heard with You," *Gramophone,* Aug. 1991: 39.

15. On the belief that the Apocalypse is close at hand and that consequently there is little need to conserve natural resources, see Michael Dolan, "Conservation, Consumerism, and Other Things," *Harmonist Magazine* 1 (1986): 37; and Timothy Weber, *Living in the Shadow of the Second Coming: American Premillennialism, 1875–1982* (Chicago, 1987). On a contrasting environmental ethic that can be derived from Christianity and other religions, see Lewis G. Regenstein, *Replenish the Earth: A History of Organized Religion's Treatment of Animals and Nature—Including the Bible's Message of Conservation and Kindness to Animals* (London, 1991).

16. John Marcoom, Jr., "The Fire Down South," *Forbes,* Oct. 15, 1990, 56. The emphasis is added. The number of *baptized* Catholics still exceeds, far and away, the number of Protestants. For fuller coverage see David Martin, *Tongues of Fire: The Explosion of Protestantism in Latin America* (Oxford, Eng., 1980), and David Stoll, *Is Latin America Turning Protestant? The Politics of Evangelical Growth* (Berkeley, 1989).

17. See John J. Johnson, *Political Change in Latin America: The Emergence of the Middle Sectors,* 2d ed. (Stanford, 1965).

18. Quoted by Ronald Sukenick, *Down and In: Life in the Underground* (New York, 1987), p. 71.

19. See Carlos Fuentes, "Europe's Other Face," trans. John Butt, *Liber: A European Review of Books,* no. 2 (Dec. 1989): 20. *Liber* appears as an occasional supplement to the *Times Literary Supplement* and several European newspapers.

20. The Eugene Black quotation and the Simon G. Hanson appraisal are found in Hanson's essay "The Economic Difficulties of Social Reform in Latin America," in *Religion, Revolution, and Reform: New Forces for Change in Latin America,* ed. William V. D'Antonio and Fredrick B. Pike (New York, 1964), p. 189.

21. See the 1989 *South American Handbook,* ed. John Brooks (New York, 1989), passim.

22. Jurandir Freire Costa, quoted by Alex Shoumatoff, "Rio: Is the Carnival Over?" *New York Times,* Mar. 19, 1989.

23. Amb. Brunson McKinley, quoted by Amy Wilentz, "Haiti Goes Back," *Nation,* Dec. 4, 1989, 670.

24. Gary Emmons letter to the editor, *Wall Street Journal,* Aug. 12, 1988.

25. Mary Williams Walsh, "In Colombia, Killings Just Go On and On," ibid.,

Nov. 17, 1987; a Colombian, who requested anonymity, quoted by Alan Riding, "Cocaine Billionaires: The Men Who Hold Colombia Hostage," *New York Times Magazine,* Mar. 8, 1987. See also Tova María Solo, "The Privatization of Justice in Colombia," *Wall Street Journal,* Jan. 9, 1988; and Alan Weisman, "Dangerous Days in Macarena," *New York Times Magazine,* Apr. 23, 1989, 42.

26. Thomas Kamm, "Executives in Peru Are Getting a Bang Out of This Course," *Wall Street Journal,* Apr. 10, 1991.

27. Alan Riding, "Improving Brazilian Social Welfare Proves Far Easier Said than Done," *New York Times,* Aug. 9, 1988.

28. David Lehman, "States of Collapse," *Times Literary Supplement,* Mar. 10–16, 1989, 244.

29. See Larry Rohter, "Brazilian Pop, Uneasy in the Spotlight," *New York Times,* Apr. 23, 1989.

30. See Frederick M. Nunn, "'Mendacious Inventions,' Veracious Perceptions: The Peruvian Reality in Vargas Llosa's *La ciudad y los perros,*" *Americas* 43 (1987): 456.

31. See Larry Rohter, "García Márquez: Words into Film," *New York Times,* Aug. 18, 1989.

32. Tuss Callanan, "Coyote: A Town without Pity," *Sunday Chicago Magazine* of the *Chicago Tribune,* Apr. 12, 1987, 16, 19.

33. For an empathetic account of the Hispanos of northern New Mexico, see William DeBuys and Alex Harris, *River of Traps: A Village Life* (Albuquerque, 1990). In his important study *The Spanish-American Homeland: Four Centuries in New Mexico's Río Arriba* (Baltimore, 1990), Alvar W. Carlson attributes the present-day plight of Hispanics more to internal cultural traits than to an intrusive Anglo American culture.

34. See Stanley E. Greenberg, "Contras and U.S. Attitude toward Region," *Wall Street Journal,* Sept. 22, 1987.

35. See Robert H. Sayre, *Thoreau and the American Indians* (Princeton, 1977), p. 3.

36. Herman Melville, *Typee: A Peep at Polynesian Life* (1846; Evanston and Chicago, 1968), p. 198.

37. See Laurence Gonzales, "Caribbean Crusade," *Notre Dame Magazine* 19 (Summer 1990): 40, 46.

38. Robert Wernick, "Speaking Out: Let's Spoil the Wilderness," *Saturday Evening Post,* Nov. 6, 1965, 18.

39. James Baron, "States Sell Chances for Gold as Rush Turns to Stampede," *New York Times,* May 28, 1989.

40. See Melvin Maddocks, "The New Angries," *World Monitor,* June 1990, 79.

41. See Michael M. Thomas, "The Greatest American Shambles," *New York Review of Books,* Jan. 31, 1991, 30–35. See also Martin Mayer, *The Greatest-Ever Bank Robbery: The Collapse of the Savings and Loan Industry* (New York, 1991), in which a longtime champion of the free-enterprise system confesses to disillusionment. For additional insights on the financial scandals of the 1980s, see James B. Stewart, *Den of Thieves* (New York, 1991).

42. See Joan Dideon, "New York: Sentimental Journeys," *New York Review of Books,* Jan. 17, 1991, 45–56.

43. Todd Gitlin, *The Sixties: Years of Hope, Days of Rage* (New York, 1987), p. 262.

44. Quoted by Storer H. Rowley, "The More the World Changes, the More Castro Stays the Same," *Chicago Tribune,* July 27, 1989.

45. Andrew M. Greeley, "The Catholic Imagination of Bruce Springsteen," *America,* Feb. 6, 1988, 110–115.

46. Fletcher of Saltoun, quoted by Gordon K. Lewis, "The Laws and the Songs," *Times Literary Supplement,* Feb. 3–9, 1989, 104.

47. Etta Mooser, "What They Do Know," *Nation,* Jan. 9, 1987, 27.

48. Peter Thorslev, Jr., "The Wild Man's Revenge," in *Wild Man Within: An Image from the Renaissance to Romanticism,* ed. Edward Dudley and Maximilian E. Novak (Pittsburgh, 1972), pp. 298–299.

49. Kristin Herzog, *Women, Ethnics, and Exotics: Images of Power in Mid-Nineteenth-Century America* (Knoxville, 1983), p. 85.

50. Robert Pattison, *The Triumph of Vulgarity: Rock Music in the Mirror of Romanticism* (New York, 1987), p. 36.

51. See Gitlin, *The Sixties,* p. 40.

52. "In a Dark Time," *The Collected Poems of Theodore Roethke* (New York, 1966), p. 239.

53. See Alfredo Corchado, "Losing Battles: Schools Fail Hispanics, Whose Dropout Rates Exceed Other Groups," *Wall Street Journal,* Dec. 17, 1990; and Robert Pear, "Hispanic Population Growing 5 Times as Fast as Rest of U.S.," *New York Times,* Sept. 11, 1987.

54. Treatment of the external and internal proletariats emerges in clearest focus in various sections of the three-volume abridgement (titled *A Study of History,* comp. D. C. Somervelle [New York, 1947]) of the first six volumes of Arnold Toynbee's *Study of History* (London, 1934–1939).

55. Lester D. Langley presents a basically optimistic assessment of the likely effects of Mexican immigration to the United States in his *MexAmerica: Two Countries, One Future* (New York, 1988). Alejandro Portes and Ruben C. Rumbaut, *Immigrant America: A Portrait* (Berkeley, 1990), provide an excellent synthesis and foresee mainly positive results from the new immigration, with its Asian and Latino preponderance. On immigration see also David H. Bennett, *The Party of Fear: From Nativist Movements to the New Right in American History* (Chapel Hill, 1988), David E. Hayes-Bautista, Werner O. Schink, and Jorge Chapa, *The Burden of Support: Young Latinos in an Aging Society* (Stanford, 1988), L. H. Gann and Peter J. Duignan, *The Hispanics in the United States: A History* (Boulder, 1986), and David M. Reimers, *Still the Golden Door: The Third World Comes to America* (New York, 1985).

56. Quoted by James Wilcox, "Her Whole Life Passes before Our Eyes," *New York Times Book Review,* Aug. 13, 1989, 1.

Index